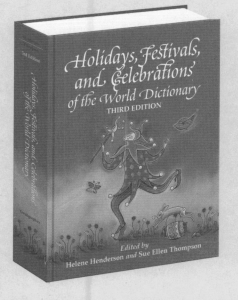

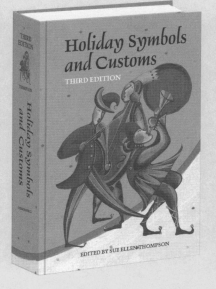

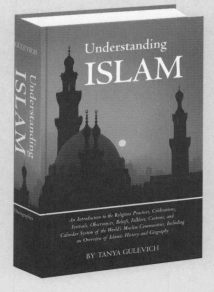

Holidays, Festivals & Celebrations of the World Dictionary

NEW EDITION! *3rd Edition. Edited by Helene Henderson and Sue Ellen Thompson. Library binding. 8½ x 11. 1,000 pages. Appendices. Indexes. 2004. 0-7808-0422-8. $98.*

Revised and expanded, this now-classic compendium describes some 2,500 holidays, festivals, commemorations, holy days, feasts and fasts, and other observances from all parts of the world. Entries cover popular, ethnic, religious, and historic events of international, national, regional, and local significance. Teachers and students will use this work to implement research projects and reports on different cultures, countries, and ethnic groups.

The first new edition in seven years offers:

- Nearly 500 brand-new entries
- Expanded section on calendar systems
- More web sites, e-mail addresses, and other contact information
- Perpetual calendar
- Updated facts about the U.S. Presidents, States, and Territories
- Revised General Index combines four indexes for easier use

A sampling of new entries includes East Timor Independence Day and national days of other new countries as well as more American festivals, such as the Bridge Walking Jubilee, Conch Republic Independence Day, Burning of the Socks, and additional Native American observances.

"The most comprehensive compilation available on the subject."
— *Booklist, American Library Association, Oct '03*

Holiday Symbols & Customs

A Guide to the Legend and Lore Behind the Symbols, Customs, and Traditions Associated with Holidays and Holy Days, Feasts and Fasts, Major Sporting Events, and Other Celebrations

NEW EDITION! *3rd Edition. By Sue Ellen Thompson. Library binding. 6 x 9. 895 pages. Index. 2003. 0-7808-0501-1. $68.*

Fully revised and updated, this guide uncovers the legend and lore behind the symbols, customs, and traditions associated with a wide range of holidays, including holy days, feasts and fasts, major sporting events, and other celebrations. The book explores the origins of more than 1,000 well-known symbols and the customs and traditions associated with 274 popular celebrations in the United States and around the world.

Expanded Areas of Coverage

- African and Native American holidays
- More international holidays from India, Tibet, Nepal, and the countries of Southeast Asia
- More major sporting events

"*Holiday Symbols* will be a working reference source for years."
— *American Reference Books Annual*

Understanding Islam

An Introduction to the Religious Practices, Celebrations, Festivals, Observances, Beliefs, Folklore, Customs, and Calendar System of the World's Muslim Communities, including an Overview of Islamic History and Geography

By Tanya Gulevich. Introduction by Professor Frederick Colby. Library binding. 6 x 9. 300 pages. Photographs and Illustrations. Appendices. Index. 2004. 0-7808-0704-9. $54.

This new guide addresses the widespread need for more information about Islamic religious practices and observances, holidays, and customs. Written for students, teachers, and general readers, this work explains specific religious observances and customs while introducing basic Islamic beliefs. Muslim holidays and festivals are described in considerable detail. Entries also include historical and geographical information to provide a context for further understanding.

Organized in Three Sections

- **A Brief Introduction to Islam** – covers the teachings of Islam, the history of Islam, and Muslims today
- **Religious Customs and Folklore** – provides detailed information about a wide range of customs and beliefs
- **Calendar System, Holidays, and Other Days of Observance** – explains the Muslim calendar and describes principal holidays and other days of observance

Additional features include a bibliography, list of useful web sites, glossary, and index.

Religious Holidays and Calendars

An Encyclopedic Handbook

3RD EDITION

Religious Holidays and Calendars
An Encyclopedic Handbook

3RD EDITION

Edited by
Karen Bellenir

Foreword by **Martin E. Marty**

Omnigraphics

615 Griswold Street • Detroit, MI 48226

Bibliographic Note

The information in this publication was compiled from the sources cited in the bibliography with guidance from the advisors listed in the Preface and from other sources considered reliable. While every possible effort has been made to ensure reliability, the publisher will not assume liability for damages caused by inaccuracies in the data, and makes no warranty, express or implied, on the accuracy of the information contained herein.

Karen Bellenir, *Managing Editor*

Bruce N. G. Cromwell, Ph.D., *Contributing Editor*

Wendy Heller, *Contributing Editor*

Patricia Lin, Ph.D., *Contributing Editor*

Laura Pleva Nielsen, *Index Editor*

EdIndex, Services for Publishers, *Indexers*

* * *

Omnigraphics, Inc.

Matthew P. Barbour, *Senior Vice President*

Kay Gill, *Vice President—Directories*

Kevin Hayes, *Operations Manager*

Leif Gruenberg, *Development Manager*

David P. Bianco, *Marketing Consultant*

* * *

Peter E. Ruffner, *Publisher*

Frederick G. Ruffner, Jr., *Chairman*

Copyright © 2004 Omnigraphics, Inc.

ISBN 0-7808-0665-4

Library of Congress Cataloging-in-Publication Data

Religious holidays and calendars : an encyclopedic handbook / edited by Karen Bellenir.--
3rd ed.
        p. cm.
Includes bibliographical references and indexes.
ISBN 0-7808-0665-4
 1. Calendars -- History. 2. Fasts and Feasts. I. Bellenir, Karen.
CE6.K45 2004
529'.3--dc22

2004041500

Table of Contents

Part Two: Calendars and Holidays for Religious Groups

Part Three: Appendices and Indexes

Foreword

Religious Holidays and Calendars is a friendly book about events that often inspire people to be unfriendly and hostile—even militant. For that reason, among many others, this book can be vital in our culture today, and I am confident it will be widely used for reference, to satisfy curiosity, and for enjoyment.

Enjoyment is the word one ought to associate with most holidays and observances marked on calendars. The majority of readers can recall happy scenes from childhood when families gathered to celebrate festivals that are part of their religion. As children they may have squirmed through some of the ceremonies in places of worship. But the "pay-off" came when everyone gathered at Grandpa and Grandma's house, savored the special odors that came from food associated with the event, sometimes exchanged gifts, and almost always expressed good will.

Enjoyment is still what ought to accompany holidays. This is the case not only of the joyful occasions but also of the many days in which people are called to be serious, sober, introspective, or contrite. Those somber occasions play their part in clearing and cleansing the minds and lives of individuals and communities so that they can again rejoice.

But what of the times when *enjoyment* is replaced by division and strife? All through history celebrations have also stimulated conflict within religious communities and among people across their boundaries. Not many years ago a book titled *The December Wars: Religious Symbols and Ceremonies in the Public Sector* (by Albert J. Menendez, Prometheus Books, 1993) appeared. Within its covers were accounts of the ways citizens in the United States fought over Christmas and Hanukkah and the symbols that led people to collide in anger.

Why? Because people of different faiths share the same public space. Few complain; indeed, they may even be happy, if a Christian crèche or a Jewish menorah is on someone's lawn or in someone's window. But when the different groups jostle with each other to place their particular symbols on the court house lawn or the public school walls, the religious meanings behind those symbols get obscured.

Wherever two or more faith communities are gathered, conflicts ensue over the location of sanctuaries or the days and styles of observance. People get maimed and killed in the name of zeal.

Much of the belligerence results from misunderstandings. One set of people feels that they "belong" and everyone else is a "stranger." And, truthfully, strangers can be unsettling. Immigrants and other newcomers may not be able to bring everything along from the countries they leave behind, but holidays and their trappings are very portable. Old-timers and newcomers meet when festivals come along on the calendar.

As a result, civic life experiences tremors and religious groups argue over which holidays, whose holidays, warrant a day off from work. Public school choruses are wary about their repertoires. Will this song from my tradition offend you in yours?

If I have painted a bleak picture of the misuse of holidays, it is only because religion is at the heart of so much conflict, and events on the calendars of the different religions are among the most visible expressions of opposing belief systems.

Holidays, though—both one's own and those of others—can also serve to bring people together. This may begin superficially, as when we observe parades and processions that belong to other faith communities. It can deepen when schools, libraries, cities, towns and ecumenical groups promote education about the meaning of holidays. (*Religious Holidays and Calendars* is an ideal text for such education.)

The next stage involves inviting the individual stranger or the member of the other community to look in on places of worship or to be invited to homes where celebrating goes on. Some may feel that inviting and visiting are risky propositions: the guest may find the holidays of others more attractive than those of their own, and convert. Still, I doubt whether there is very often much crossing of boundaries into conversion just because someone gets to taste the food, drink the drink, dance the dance, and overhear the prayers that go with someone else's holiday.

Instead, those who learn about the holidays begin to understand the stories behind them, the events that get marked on calendars. They will learn two things: first, that the days and doings that other faiths observe are truly different from their own. Page through this book and randomly put a finger on one entry and then on one dealing with another faith, and try to find out how much the two have in common. They both deal with time and eternity, life and death, joy and sorrow, hate and love, but they do so in their own particular ways. We do well to learn about the differences.

The second thing that becomes obvious is this: the holidays of diverse faiths *do* have much in common. Their observances mark universal dimensions of human life. Overall, they celebrate human dignity, give meaning to life, and often say in a sorrowing world "adherents and guests, *enjoy.*" God, or the gods, or the unseen powers want us to do so.

After figuratively visiting various other faiths, one of the great boons to a reader who is drawn to and defined by one of the faith communities is to have the chance to learn more about what is "at home." The Bantu people have a saying that "he who never visits thinks mother is the only cook." But the wanderer, the traveler, the experimenter, *comes back* to appreciate the home cooking, which is here the metaphor for the habits and customs we inherit or cook up to make life in our own kitchens—and prayer rooms—more meaningful.

I have been in the religious studies field for a half-century and have been a Christian for three quarters of a century, one would think that I would know most everything about Christian holidays. Yet in almost every entry dealing with Christian traditions, I learned something new. No doubt that will be the experience of every other reader who is religiously observant.

I hope that all readers, those who are religiously observant and those who are not, will use *Religious Holidays and Calendars* to start or continue a journey of understanding—to learn something new about themselves, their neighbors, their friends, and even their enemies—so that our lives can be enhanced and enriched by the enjoyment of the holidays.

Martin E. Marty
The University of Chicago

Martin E. Marty is the Fairfax M. Cone Distinguished Service Professor Emeritus at the University of Chicago where the Martin Marty Center was founded to promote public religion endeavors. Among his many other accomplishments, Marty served as past president of the American Academy of Religion, the American Society of Church History, and the American Catholic Historical Association, and served on two U.S. Presidential Commissions. Marty has authored more than 50 books including the three-volume *Modern American Religion* (University of Chicago Press), *The One and the Many: America's Search for the Common Good; Education, Religion and the Common Good; Politics, Religion and the Common Good,* and *Martin Luther.* His *Righteous Empire* won the National Book Award. Other honors include the National Humanities Medal, the Medal of the American Academy of Arts and Sciences, the University of Chicago Alumni Medal, the Distinguished Service Medal of the Association of Theological Schools, and the Order of Lincoln Medallion (Illinois' top honor).

Preface

Why Religious Holidays *and* Calendars?

In the broadest sense, a calendar consists of the set of rules a society uses to determine which days are ordinary and which are holy, or set apart. Religion and the calendar have been linked since antiquity. From the time of the ancient Egyptian, Babylonian, and Mesoamerican civilizations, members of the religious community determined how time was to be divided, established the beginning of a day, defined a week, described a month, and announced the new year. Holy day observances were—and still are—important for reasons as varied as the holidays themselves.

Religious Holidays and Calendars: An Encyclopedic Handbook offers the researcher—whether student, scholar, or seeker—an overview of the time-keeping and holiday traditions of the world's religions. Although other reference works in the field focus on the traditions of a single religion, no other existing source covers the unique relationship between religious calendars and religious holidays as does this volume.

Special Features of *Religious Holidays and Calendars, Third Edition*

This edition owes a special debt of gratitude to many people, including religious authorities and members of various religious communities, who participated in a review process that served as its foundation. The following people read portions of the previous edition and helped identify areas in which information needed to be clarified or expanded. Some of them continued with the project and helped write new material while others served as resources and guides during the revision process.

Vivek S. Adesh is an educational representative from the Antaraashtreeya Hindu Samaaj (Ahinsaa) in Georgia.

Ron Andrade heads the Los Angeles City/County Native American Commission.

Shahin Bekhradnia, Religious Affairs Director of The World Zoroastrian Organisation in London, is a lecturer and writer on the Zoroastrian faith. She is also active in interfaith movements concerned with religious toleration.

Omer Bin Abdullah is the editor of *Islamic Horizon,* a publication of the Islamic Society of North America.

Tony Brown serves as chancellor of the North Carolina Piedmont Church of Wicca. Other clergy members from the church also assisted in the review process.

Bruce N. G. Cromwell, Ph.D, serves as pastor of the Centralia Free Methodist Church and adjunct professor of Religion and Philosophy at Greenville College, Greenville, Illinois. He also writes about church history for *Light and Life* magazine. His Ph.D., from St. Louis University, is in Historical Theology.

Rabbi Jerome M. Epstein is Executive Vice President of the United Synagogue of Conservative Judaism, the association of Conservative congregations in North America, and the author of numerous articles related to various aspects of Jewish life.

Lynn R. Farny serves as a public relations representative for the Church of Scientology International, which is headquartered in Los Angeles, California.

The Very Reverend Nabil L. Hanna serves as chairman of the Department of Communications and Information with the Antiochian Orthodox Christian Archdiocese of North America.

Elaine Gounaris Hanna holds a Master of Divinity degree from Holy Cross Greek Orthodox School of Theology and has represented the Orthodox Church at the National Council of Churches and in many other ecumenical settings.

Wendy Heller is the editor of *The Journal of Bahá'í Studies*, a publication of the Centre for Bahá'í Studies in Ottawa, Ontario, and co-author of *Basic Bahá'í Dictionary*.

Shaikh Kabir Helminski was assisted in the review process by members of the Threshold Society, an organization offering training and study based on the principles of Sufism.

Navtej S. Khalsa serves as executive director of Sikh Mediawatch and Resource Task Force (SMART), an organization founded in 1996 to promote the fair and accurate portrayal of Sikh Americans and the Sikh religion in American media and society.

Robert Keller is the Director of the Cultural Research Program of the Soboba Band of Luiseño Indians in Southern California.

Richard L. Lewis is the editor of *Unification News*, a publication of The Unification Church (HSA-UWC: Holy Spirit Association for the Unification of World Christianity).

Patricia Lin, Ph.D is a professor in the Ethnic and Women's Studies Department at California State Polytechnic University in Pomona. She writes and teaches about Asian religions and cultures.

Yashwant K. Malaiya, Ph.D. is a professor at Colorado State University and a prolific writer on the Jain calendar and festival cycle.

Sarah McKechnie is a spokesperson for the Lucis Trust, an organization dedicated to preserving the teachings of the Arcane School.

Firdosh Mehta is president of the Federation of Zoroastrian Associations of North America (FEZANA), a participant in the Canadian Interfaith Calendar, and a Board member of the Edmonton Interfaith Centre. Mr. Mehta was assisted in the review process by the Chair, Ervad. Jehan Bagli and members of FEZANA's Religious Heritage and Preservation Committee.

Coke Newell is the author of *Latter Days: An Insider's Guide to Mormonism* (St. Martin's Press, 2001). He also serves as media relations manager for The Church of Jesus Christ of Latter-day Saints.

Beverly Peake works in the Committee on Publication of The First Church of Christ, Scientist and is also a Christian Science practitioner.

Ernesto Pichardo is Oba of the Church of the Lukumi Babalu Aye, Santeria-Orisha-Cuba, in Hialeah, Florida.

Lyn Quayle serves as a media relations liaison with *The Golden Thread Magazine*, a publication of JZK, Inc. which is affiliated with Ramtha's School of Enlightenment.

Dr. Krishna Sijapati is president of the American Hindu Association. Established in 1998, the organization works to meet the needs of Hindu people from various ethnic origins.

Rabbi Margot Stein is Director of Communications and Marketing for the Jewish Reconstructionist Federation (JRF). Her work includes developing program resources within the JRF and facilitating the exchange of information with the media and general public.

Lisa LaRue Stopp serves as Literature Review Coordinator for the Cultural Resource Center of the Cherokee Nation. The Cultural Resource Center is located in Tahlequah, Oklahoma.

Michael J. Torley is the founder of the Western Reform Taoist Congregation, an organization dedicated to promoting the growth of a Taoist religious community in North America.

Cora Tula Watters is Principal Chief of the Shawnee Nation Ohio Blue Creek Band and visiting lecturer of American Indian Studies at Antioch University. She is also a contributor to the *Encyclopedia of Appalachia* (University of Tennessee Press).

The comments and suggestions provided by these reviewers guided this book's development and led to many changes, including:

- More than 100 new entries have been added to describe holidays not previously covered.

- The addition of original artwork now helps illustrate important symbols, concepts, and places.

- To better accommodate the diversity of practices, the varying use of liturgical calendars, and the observance of different holidays, information about the Christian family of faith communities is now presented in three separate chapters:

  Christianity: Roman Catholic and Protestant Expressions

  Christianity: Orthodox Expressions

  Christianity: Non-Trinitarian and Non-Traditional Expressions

- Several chapters have received significant updates. For example, the chapter on Sikhism now includes information about the Nanakshai Calendar which was adopted in 1999. Several other chapters, including Chapter 18—Native American Religions, Chapter 20—Western African Religions and Their New World Expressions, and Chapter 21—Ancient Wisdom, Metaphysical, Other Faith Communities have been expanded.

This third edition also features more information about the history of time-keeping methods, more facts about the development of calendars, and sections on important calendar reform movements of the 20th and 21st centuries.

The book's end section has been updated. It features an expanded list of resources and a five-year chronological list of all the holidays in this book. As with the second edition, a bibliography, alphabetical list of holidays, calendar index, and master index are also provided.

Notes Regarding Content

Scope and Limitations

The notion that religion can be separated from secular society is primarily a Western concept that is often not paralleled in other cultures. In a sense, many celebrations including historic, social, political, promotional, and even sports-related, can be interpreted as being religious in nature. The holidays included in this book, however, are only those with a sacred component that celebrate, commemorate, or honor people, places, events, and concepts important to a specific religious community.

The descriptions of the holidays, especially concerning significance and meaning, are general representations that focus on the most common interpretations. Often different schools of thought within a religious community define events in different ways. For example, some people may view something as the anniversary of an event that happened in the historical past while others may interpret the event as legendary and honor the concept it embodies. In many ways the precise understanding of a holiday's significance, with all its psychological nuances and symbolic meanings, is unique to each individual who honors it.

Selection of Religions Included

The religions included in this book represent the world's major faiths and other smaller faith communities. These were chosen based on their historical and current cultural impact in the United States, where presumably this book will find most of its readers.

Names of Holidays and Spelling

Many of the holidays included in this book are known by more than one name. For example, the Pagan observance of Imbolc is also known as Imbolg, Oimelc, Oimelg, Brigid, Brigantia, and Gwyl Fair. Some of these alternates are variant spellings and others are different names used by various Pagan groups.

The holiday entries in this book list a primary name first followed by alternate names and variant spellings in parentheses. As much as possible spellings and forms for primary entries, calendar and month names, personal and place names, and concepts were standardized following suggestions made by the people who reviewed the text and other guidelines appropriate for each religion. When such guidance was unavailable, or when various schools or sects within a religious family disagreed, primary forms and spellings were chosen to reflect those that appeared most often in the sources consulted. Diacriticals unfamiliar to the non-specialist have been omitted except where they held special significance. To ensure easy access to all the holiday entries irrespective of the form known by the reader, the alternate forms are included in the index.

Dates

The task of explaining the year in which something occurred so that it can be compared to other events in history is complex because years are often counted from different beginning points. The individual chapters in this book describe many different methods used for dating. For example the Islamic dating system counts years with the designation A.H. (*anno hegirae*) which means "in the year of the hijrah." It begins in the year Muhammad and his followers left Mecca for Medina. Jains count years with the designation V.N.S. (Vira Nirvana Samvat) beginning with the year of Mahavira's death (achievement of Nirvana). Many Western readers will be most familiar with Christian dating methods using the designations B.C. (Before Christ) and A.D. (*Anno Domini*, a Latin term meaning "in the year of our Lord").

Although the diverse systems of many religions are explained, to avoid giving preference to any one religion's time-keeping system historical dates in this volume are given using the designations Common Era and Before Common Era (C.E./B.C.E.). This method is often used in academic writing and research to avoid giving preference to any one particular religion. In recognition of the fact that the year numbers associated with Christian dating are currently used in many countries and are arguably the most commonly understood, the C.E./B.C.E. system adopts these numbers, but makes no reference to their religious connotation. This means that the year 2004 A.D. is the same year as 2004 C.E.

Navigating the Chapters

Part One: The History of Calendars

The four chapters in this part provide general information about the development of calendars and other methods of time keeping. Chapter 1 discusses the earliest attempts to answer questions like: When does a day start and end? What other time periods are important to measure? Are the days in a month counted according to the moon's phases or by other celestial events? Is a year a cycle of moons or is it a cycle of seasons?

The varying way these questions were answered led to the development of different types of calendars: lunar calendars, which were based on the moon's movement around the earth; solar calendars, which were based on the earth's movement around the sun; and lunisolar calendars, which attempted to reconcile elements of both cycles. Chapter 2 focuses on cultures that adopted lunar and lunisolar time keeping methods. Chapter 3 presents information about the development of solar calendars.

Beginning in the eighteenth century and continuing through the present day, many diverse cultures have come into closer contact as a result of global exploration, political conquest, and the growing role of economic interdependence in the worldwide marketplace. These events resulted in attempts to revise calendars along nonsectarian lines and to create time reckoning systems that were globally understood. At the same time, others displaced by political turmoil or liberated from previous societal constraints sought to reconnect with their own cultural legacy by honoring or recreating timekeeping systems of the past. These types of calendar reform movements are summarized in Chapter 4.

Part Two: Calendars and Holidays for Religious Groups

The chapters presented in this part are listed in a sequence chosen to reflect a logical pattern to the Western reader. Their order is not intended to imply any preference or supremacy.

The religion chapters begin in the Middle East, the birth place of many religions with which the Western reader will be most familiar. These are listed in order of the historical appearance of their founders: Abraham (Judaism), Zoroaster (Zoroastrianism), Jesus (Christianity), Muhammad (Islam), and Baha'u'llah (Bahá'í).

Moving eastward, the next group of religions are those with origins in the Indian subcontinent. Hinduism as the oldest is listed first, followed by Jainism, Sikhism, and Buddhism, which serves as a bridge to the religions of the Far East: Confucianism, Taoism, Chinese folk religions, and Shinto.

Continuing around the globe in an easterly direction, the next group of religions are those of the Native Americans. These are followed by faiths that link the American continents with Europe and Africa.

Within each chapter, an introductory essay for each major religion or religious group provides background information to assist the reader in understanding the importance of the holidays. An essay describing the specific issues related to the religion and its sacred calendar provides insight into the interrelationship between a religious group and its timekeeping systems and philosophies. The festivals, feasts, fasts, and holy days are presented according to the most appropriate calendar. This emphasis retains the significance of the each holiday cycle within its own context rather than aligning it with the Gregorian calendar.

Part Three: Appendices and Indexes

Three appendices and three indexes help the reader locate precise information within this book or find additional facts from other resources.

Appendix A: Sources for More Information provides an annotated listing of organizational resources and websites. The resources selected were chosen to present a broad spectrum of calendar, holiday, and religious information. The listing is intended to serve as a starting point for people interested in further research; it is not an exhaustive list. Inclusion is not an endorsement and omission is not a criticism.

Appendix B: Bibliography and Additional Reading presents a topical list of all the sources used in compiling this text. It also incorporates suggested reading for further research.

Appendix C: Five-Year Chronological List of Holidays is a calendar of all the holidays included in this book for the years 2004 through 2008 (beginning and ending with leap years according to the Gregorian calendar). This compilation helps illustrate the interaction of movable and fixed holidays within religions and the changes that occur from year to year.

Indexes serve to provide quick access to the information in this book. The Holiday Index presents all the primary and alternate holiday names along with variant spellings, religion, and page numbers. The Calendar Index consists of two parts. The first part provides an alphabetical list of all the various calendars discussed in the text; the second part provides an alphabetical list of all the month names that appear on those calendars along with page ranges for holidays within them. The Master Index includes personal names, concepts, key terms, holidays, organizations, events, and other significant terms.

Acknowledgements

The production of this book would not have been possible without the support, encouragement, and assistance of many people. First, thanks go to Aidan Kelly, Peter Dresser, and Linda M. Ross who worked on the original edition of *Religious Holidays and Calendars*. They established the foundation upon which the subsequent editions have been built.

Although the people who reviewed the second edition and guided the development of this volume have already been mentioned, special thanks go to each of them. Their efforts helped make this book a more reliable tool for those who will use it. Some of them deserve special recognition for additional work on this project:

Bruce N. G. Cromwell, Ph.D., Contributing Editor

Wendy Heller, Contributing Editor

Patricia Lin, Ph.D, Contributing Editor

Ernesto Pichardo, Contributor

Cora Tula Watters, Ph.D., Contributor

In addition, several other writers worked on presenting new information and editing existing text in accordance with suggestions received. The vision for this volume was fulfilled by their hard work. They are:

Roger Foster, an ordained minister and author of internationally published works such as *What Is Your Destiny?* and *The Church Jesus Built*. He is employed by the United Church of God as a senior writer for *The Good News* magazine.

J. Gordon Melton, the director of the Institute for the Study of American religion, a religious studies research center located in Santa Barbara, California. Dr. Menton is also a research specialist with the Department of Religious Studies of the University of California at Santa Barbara. He is the author of more than 30 books on religion in America.

Clarissa Ross, a writer and editor in southeast Michigan. Clarissa's main areas of interest include Bible study materials, computer information, and fiction. In addition, she is a home schooling mother and a domestic engineer.

Amy Sutton, a writer and editor who contributes to magazines and websites and collaborates with businesses, publishers, and book packagers. Amy graduated from the University of Hawaii with a B.A. in history and currently resides in Lancaster County, Pennsylvania.

In addition, special thanks go illustrators Alison DeKleine, Melanie Manos, and Mary Ann Stavros-Lanning for their wonderful artwork and to editorial assistants Michael Bellenir and Sandra Judd for their help in keeping things on track and on schedule.

And a Personal Apology

In creating a book that discusses deeply personal and often emotional issues like faith, it is not possible to avoid giving occasional offense to one point of view or another. Sometimes a matter as seemingly simple as choosing how to spell a name has profound implications. Sometimes authorities have strong, irreconcilable opinions. Sometimes one person's insight is heresy to another.

The text in this book incorporates decisions made about a myriad of details, some of which I lacked the wisdom to understand. Although I have tried to treat each faith with respect, to arbitrate each controversy with fairness, and to ensure that the information presented is accurate and reliable, if I have failed, I am sorry. I ask for your forgiveness.

Karen Bellenir, Managing Editor
Religious Holidays and Calendars, Third Edition

If you wish to make comments on this text or suggest amendments for subsequent editions, please write to:

Editor, *Religious Holidays and Calendars*
Omnigraphics, Inc.
615 Griswold St.
Detroit, MI 48226
editorial@omnigraphics.com

PART ONE

The History of Calendars

CHAPTER 1

Basic Questions All Calendars Must Answer

Calendars throughout History

The calendar is so ordinary, and yet so important, that one can hardly imagine a time when it did not exist. It is a fundamental commodity of life. Its significance is so great that in many cultures the institution and maintenance of dating systems have sacred status, and they fall under the jurisdiction of religious authorities.

Around the globe, through centuries of human history, a wide range of different calendars have been used to order time in a systematic manner—a need which all human civilizations share. Today, the Western civil calendar serves as an international standard for business and diplomatic purposes. On the world's stage, this is a recent development, and people of various religions, nations, and societies, still employ many other calendars to mark the passing of time. The characteristics of these calendars are as diverse as the societies that developed them. All calendars, however, serve the common purpose of enabling people to work together to accomplish specific goals.

Origins of the Calendar

In the broadest sense, a calendar consists of the set of rules that a society uses to determine which days are ordinary and which are holy, or holidays.

The Earliest Calendars Were Informal

Thousands of years ago, before the written historical record begins, people lived in small tribal societies based on hunting and gathering. Activities were likely coordinated by word of mouth, and time-keeping methods were fairly uncomplicated. People probably used days as indications of time, and perhaps they even recognized periods similar to months. They would have observed seasonal and annual patterns, but without a formal system of reckoning them. Almost certainly, their needs did not demand anything as complex as a decade or century.

Over the course of time, people began living in agricultural communities with larger populations and diversified work forces. This shift required that people become more interdependent. For example, if farmers and city dwellers were going to conduct business efficiently, they must come to the marketplace at the same time. As a result, the need for a tool to arrange societal events became apparent.

Ancient Egyptians and Babylonians Systematize Their Calendars

The first two cultures to formally address the need to plan societal activities were the Babylonians and Egyptians. Both shared similar characteristics—an agricultural base, a large population spread over a significant expanse of land, and a need to gather together at regular intervals to observe religious festivals. The responsibility for forming a central time-reckoning system so that people would know when to arrive at these festivals was placed in the hands of the respective religious communities.

To develop their calendars, both groups followed similar approaches. They divided time into three major divisions—what we now recognize as days, months, and years—and then went about calculating the exact duration of each category. The questions faced by the ancient Babylonians and Egyptians were the same questions all subsequent calendar makers have had to address:

- How long is a day?
- How long is a month?
- How long is a year?

Table 1.1. What Year Is It?

Different calendar systems count years from different events. This table shows differences among some historic and currently used measures.

Designation	Means	Comparison
A.H.	*anno hegirae* (after Hijrah, or more literally, "in the year of the hijrah")	Based on Muhammad's movement from Mecca to Medina and the establishment of the Islamic community, 1 A.H. is equivalent to 622 C.E.
A.D.	*anno Domini* (in the year of the Lord)	Although modern scholarship places the event earlier, tradition established in the sixth century C.E. identified 1 A.D. as the year in which Jesus was born; A.D. and C.E. years are equivalent
A.M.	*anno mundi* (in the year of the world)	The Jewish calendar counts years from date of the world's creation as calculated by ancient Hebrew scholars; 1 A.M. is the equivalent of 3761 B.C.E.
A.U.C.	*anno urbis conditæ* (since the founding of Rome)	Although the precise date is uncertain, 1 C.E. is probably the equivalent of 753, 754, or 755 A.U.C.
B.C.	Before Christ (years before the birth of Jesus)	B.C. and B.C.E. years are equivalent
B.C.E.	Before Common Era	B.C.E. and B.C. years are equivalent
B.E.	Bahá'í Era	Beginning in the year of the Báb's declaration, 1 B.E. is equivalent to 1844 C.E. or 1260 A.H.
C.E.	Common Era	C.E. and A.D. years are equivalent
NANAKSHAI	According to the Nanakshai Calendar	The Sikh Nanakshai calendar counts years from the birth of *Guru* Nanak. 1 NANAKSHAI is equivalent to 1469 C.E.
S.E.	Saka Era	Measured from King Salivahana's accession to the throne in India, 1 S.E. is equivalent to 79 C.E.
R.E.	Runic Era	Measured from the time Odin received the Runes, 1 R.E is equivalent to 250 B.C.E.
V.N.S.	*Vira nirvana samvat* (Mahavira's achievement of Nirvana)	Jains count years from Mahavira's death; 1 V.N.S. is equivalent to 527 B.C.E.

Note: The starting points of the years measured by the above calendar systems vary. The year equivalents listed indicate only the overlapping portion of the compared years.

These values may seem obvious to a modern observer, but it took centuries of ongoing observations, measurements, and calculations to set them.

How Long Is a Day?

The basic building block of all calendars is the day. The length of the day is set by the amount of time in which the earth completes one rotation on its axis. During the fifth century B.C.E. (Before Common Era, which is equivalent to the term BC), the Babylonians, divided this duration of time into twenty-four segments which we now know as hours. However, because accurate measurement of seconds and even minutes was not possible until the sixteenth century C.E. (Common Era, equivalent to A.D.), the length of those hours has not always been fixed.

Using the Sun to Measure the Day

Early observers must have noted a pattern in the cycle of light and darkness. Although the length of light and darkness varied, they were always balanced with each other. When light grew shorter, dark grew longer and vice versa. In any case, the custom of counting one period of light and one period of darkness as a unit for the purpose of time-keeping seems natural.

Originally, the position of the sun was used to record the passing of time during the day. The problem with this was three-fold. First, because of the nature of the earth's revolution of the sun, the point at which the sun passes any given mark from one day to the next varies slightly. Second, the devices used to measure the movement of the sun, such as sundials, were not precise relative to the sun from season to season. For instance, according to a sundial, an hour in northern latitudes would have been longer in the summer than it would have been in the winter. Third, the devices used to measure the sun's movement were dependent on reasonably fair weather; an overcast day would obscure the sun's shadow on a sundial. While this was not a significant problem in the fair weather regions of Egypt and Babylon, it would be a factor in the development of time-keeping devices in other parts of the world.

A Starting Point Is Established

A question developed, however, about when to mark the beginning of the time-keeping unit known as the day. Two points seemed to make the most sense: sunrise and sunset. These two points are easy to define and can be observed without complex instrumentation or calculation. Hebrew culture chose to designate sunset as the beginning of a day. As a result, their Sabbaths and holy days begin at sunset on the evening before the daytime of the festival. In some instances, this tradition carried over into Western observances, giving rise to the celebration of such "eves" as Christmas Eve, New Year's Eve, and Halloween (All Hallow's Eve). Other groups chose sunrise as the beginning of the day.

Yet, because the balance of light and dark was always shifting, societies still faced inconsistencies when using the rising or setting sun to mark the beginning of the day. Large empires were particularly troubled. Because of the earth's rotation, significant differences existed between eastern and western regions; other more complex differences existed between northern and southern regions. To solve these problems, societies began searching for a more constant point of origin for the day.

Astronomers in ancient Rome observed that no matter what time the sun rose or set, the interval between when the sun reached its highest point overhead from one day to the next was always the same. The Romans established the point at which the sun was directly overhead as the beginning of the day. As history progressed, people realized that if there was a fixed time for midday, there would also be a fixed time exactly opposite in the middle of the night, midnight. Once this was recognized, the advantages of naming midnight as the beginning of the day became clear. Rather than changing a day in the middle of the business day, the change could be made at night when most people were sleeping or at least most business was not being conducted. A date change at that time would create the least interference with business and societal activities. Therefore, midnight became the most commonly accepted starting point of the day.

Subdividing the Day

Once a society had determined the starting point of its day, many searched for ways to subdivide it, tracking smaller intervals of time more precisely. These smaller intervals of time required the invention of a series of time-keeping devices to measure them. Probably the most common was the sundial, or at least a form of it.

Around the world, different societies observed that the sun changed its position in the sky throughout the day. They undoubtedly also observed the changing length of shadows as a result of the sun's apparent movement. These observations led to the development of shadow-casting devices that measured the sun's relative changes in position during the day. Although several different types of these devices were developed in different areas of the world, the means by which they function is generally the same. The sun shines on a pointer, called a gnomon, which casts a shadow across a dial marked in some fashion to indicate the approximate time of day. Examples of these devices range in complexity from simple sticks planted in the ground to highly detailed dials on angled planes.

In addition to shadow-casting devices, sighting devices were developed to measure the sun's altitude in the sky. An observer would hold the device and rotate pointers to measure the angle of the sun above the horizon. Others made devices to measure constant intervals of time. The sandglass or, as it is commonly known in present times, the hourglass, is one example.

Countries of the Far East were the first to use burning incense to measure time. Sticks of incense, which were used in religious practices, were marked to measure equal periods of time while they burned. This method was used to time watches at sea and other important activities. Burning incense to measure time became a common practice among philosophers, scholars, and government officials. The Chinese also developed an incense clock. Fine strings with a metal ball attached to each end were draped at even intervals over a stick of incense. As the incense burned, it would burn through the string. As a result, the balls would drop at regular intervals, making a clang when they fell onto a metal plate.

Classical Water-Clocks Increase Accuracy

Around 150 B.C.E., the water-clock, or clepsydra, came into use by the Greeks and Romans. These water-clocks measured time by allowing a steady flow of water to drip through a small opening into a collection chamber which was marked to indicate the passage of hours as the chamber filled. As the technical sophistication of clepsydras increased, a float attached to a rod was added to the collection chamber. As the water level rose, the rod moved, turning a gear with a pointer on one side. This pointer moved around a numbered dial which indicated the passage of hours.

During the middle-ages, an improvement in the design of the clock was made by replacing water with slowly descending weights to turn the gear. This change allowed the clocks to be mounted in the towers of churches which established a central time source for entire towns. Even with all these advances, however, the measurement of time was still not reliable.

Pendulums Swing into Action

In 1581, Galileo's discovery that a pendulum moved at a constant rate of speed provided a basis for more accurate time-keeping. Building on this notion, the Dutch astronomer Christian Huygens invented a clock around 1657 in which a pendulum was kept moving by descending weights; the regular swinging of the pendulum moved the gears of the clock. Huygens's method proved to be quite precise, eventually allowing for the division of the hour into minutes and minutes into seconds.

Uniform and Precise Time-Keeping Standards

In subsequent centuries, societal changes brought further need for uniform standards and increased accuracy in timekeeping. Proper scheduling of rail transportation, for example, could only be accomplished when clocks along a route were coordinated. One step in this process was the adoption of time zones. In the United States, four time zones were established in 1883. The following year, the International Meridian Conference divided the globe into 24 time zones.

The demands of industry and scientific study also led to the development of clocks with increased precision. In the first half of the twentieth century, technology using quartz crystal vibration instead of pendulum action enabled clock makers to produce time-keeping devices that varied by a mere .002 seconds (two one thousandths of a second) per day. By the middle of the century, an atomic clock, which was regulated by the movement of particles in a cesium atom, kept time with a variation of less than a nanosecond (one billionth of a second) per day.

The extreme precision of cesium clocks enabled scientists to measure tiny variations in the earth's rotational spin. As a result, the previous definition of a second based on a fractional portion of the earth's rotation (one sixtieth of a minute, which was one sixtieth of an hour; which was one 24th of a rotation) was no longer adequate. In 1967 a new definition of a second based on the resonant frequency of a cesium atom (9,192,631,770 oscillations) was adopted.

Currently a measure called Coordinated Universal Time (UTC) is used to track time. UTC uses an average of approximately 200 measures of atomic time from around the world. This average is then adjusted so that it remains constant with the earth's rotation. The adjustments are accomplished by adding or subtracting leap seconds. The International Earth Rotation and Reference Systems Services serves as the governing authority regarding leap seconds.

How Long Is a Month?

Although dividing the day into hours and seconds was important, a method of ordering a succession of days into larger units of time was also necessary for long-term planning. The development of what we now call a month, which is based on the orbit of the moon around the earth, grew out of such an attempt to organize days. We do not know when people first began to use a cycle of moon phases to define a month, but evidence from ancient civilizations suggests that it was done early in human history.

The Phases of the Moon

The moon's position relative to the sun and earth determines how much reflected sunlight will be visible from earth. Its phases are defined by how much of the moon's surface appears illuminated. The phases cycle through a predictable pattern of change.

Beginning with the appearance of a thin crescent moon in the western sky just after sunset, the size of the illuminated portion increases nightly. In about seven days, the moon appears as a half-circle, shaped like a capital letter "D" which is rounded on the western side and flat on the eastern side. This phase of the moon is called the first quarter. As subsequent nights pass the illuminated portion of the moon continues to increase in size, and the previously flattened eastern side takes on a rounded, or hump-like, shape. The hump continues to grow nightly until a full, round disc rises in the east almost exactly as the sun sets in the west.

The full moon lasts only one night; then the moon begins to diminish as its western side becomes flatter than the eastern side. About a week after the full moon, its disc will again resemble a half-circle. This time, however, the half circle faces the opposite direction, more like the letter "C." This phase of the moon is called the last (or third) quarter. The moon continues to diminish in size until only a thin crescent appears in the east before sunrise.

On the day after the appearance of this last thin crescent in the east, and the day before the reappearance of a thin crescent in the west, the moon will not be visible at all. The stage where no moon appears is called the new moon.

Specific terms are used to describe the changing phases of the moon. As the illuminated portion of the moon increases, from the appearance of the first crescent until it is full, the moon is said to be "waxing." As it diminishes from full, the moon is said to be "waning." When either the waxing or waning moon is less than full, but more rounded than the half circle of the first or last quarter, the moon is said to be "gibbous" (from a Latin word meaning "hump").

A time period called the synodical month is measured by the interval between one new moon and the next. A synodical month is about 29.5 days.

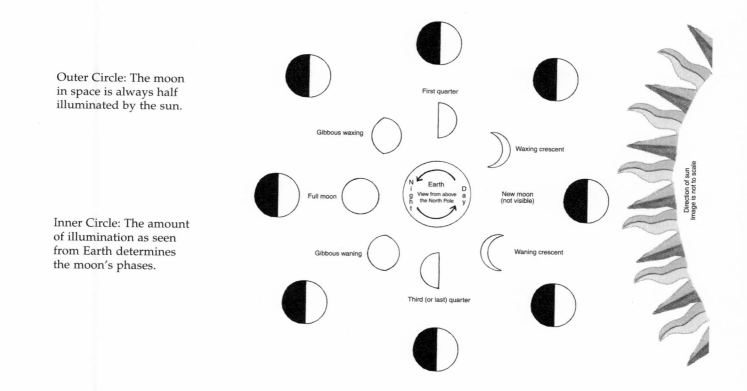

Outer Circle: The moon in space is always half illuminated by the sun.

Inner Circle: The amount of illumination as seen from Earth determines the moon's phases.

Figure 1.1. Half of the moon is always illuminated by the sun. The phases of the moon are determined by the illuminated portion that is visible from the earth.

The Priest Declares a New Month

When people were first beginning to use the phases of the moon as a basis for their month, the solemn duty of watching for the moon's first crescent was administered by the religious leaders of the community. This tradition lasted long after astronomers had developed methods by which the appearance of the thin crescent following the new moon could be predicted. In fact, it is from such an ancient Roman tradition that the word calendar comes. Each month, the high priest would watch for the new crescent; when it occurred, he would *calare* (the Latin word for "declare") a new month. The first day of the month was called *calends* from which we derive our word calendar—a chart which records all of the *calends*.

What Is the Sidereal Month?

Ancient astronomers watching the skies discovered that the moon changed its place nightly in relation to the stars behind it. By observing the change in position night after night, they determined that it took about 27 days for the moon to come back to the first position in which it had been observed. This cycle is called the sidereal month. It is slightly shorter than the synodical month because the earth itself is in motion against the background stars as it orbits the sun. As time measurement became more precise, the length of the sidereal month was discovered to be 27 days, 7 hours, 43 minutes, and 11.5 seconds.

Although the modern Western civil calendar developed from calendars based on the synodical month, other calendars such as the Hindu calendar (which is based on the constellations of the zodiac), use the sidereal month.

How Long Is a Year?

Perhaps the most difficult issue faced by calendar makers was establishing the length of the year. Although measuring a complete cycle of seasons may not seem complicated, it created significant problems for many calendar systems.

Each season in a cycle was marked by weather changes. Some seasons were warm, others cold; some had high levels of precipitation, others low. This cycling of the seasons originally defined the year—a period of time important to agrarian cultures that depended heavily on the ability to predict optimal planting and harvesting times.

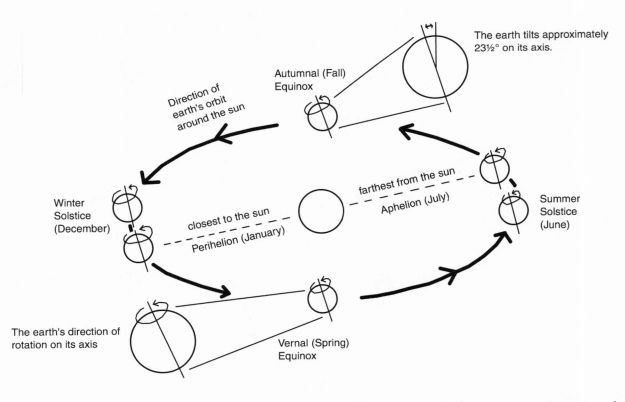

Figure 1.2. The earth's rotation around the sun marks the solar year. The angle of the earth's tilt on its axis determines the seasons. The earth is actually closer to the sun when it is winter in the northern hemisphere.

Each season contained several new moons or months. The cycling of the moon and the cycling of weather patterns were not synchronized. This led to different systems for measuring a year's length.

Babylonians and Egyptians Disagree

In the fifth century B.C.E., the Babylonians and Egyptians both arrived at a specific number of days in the year, but their conclusions were different. The Babylonians claimed that the year was 360 days long while the Egyptians more accurately estimated the year at 365 days. The discrepancy between the two lengths of the year is puzzling.

One possibility for the difference is that the Babylonians simply miscalculated. This is unlikely, however, in light of their sophisticated astronomical and mathematical systems. Another explanation is that they rounded their figure from 365 to 360 to facilitate the interaction of the year with their base-twelve numerical system.

The problem with the Babylonian's five-day omission was that the months would not stay in line with the seasons of the year. Each year the beginning of each month would occur at least five days earlier in relation to the position of the sun. Eventually, the months would be completely dissociated with the seasons in which they originally occurred. To correct this problem, the Babylonians periodically added months to the calendar, a process termed intercalation, which can also be used to add "leap" days or weeks.

The Babylonians were not the only people to face the problem of keeping the months coordinated with the seasons. Even though the Egyptians calculated the length of the year more accurately, they too realized that their determination was not exactly perfect.

The Solar System Affects the Length of the Year

Precise division of a year into months or days is impossible because the seasons, the phases of the moon, and the ever-cycling periods of daylight and nighttime are determined by the earth's relationship to the sun and the moon. The movements of these heavenly bodies do not neatly coincide with the mathematical systems of any human civilization.

The quest to discover the secrets of how the universe fits together has motivated astronomers throughout history. In the second century C.E., Ptolemy, a Greek astronomer formulated the theory that the earth was the center of the universe and that the sun, stars, moon, and other planets revolved around it. In the fifteenth century C.E., the Polish astronomer Copernicus advocated the notion that the earth rotated on an axis and, along with the other heavenly bodies in the solar system, revolved around the sun. Shortly after the Copernican assertion, Galileo presented supporting evidence based on observations he had made using his invention, the telescope.

The Gap between the Lunar and Solar Cycles

We now understand that an 11.25-day difference exists between the 354-day lunar cycle on which the months are based and the 365.25-day solar cycle which determines the seasons. Calendar systems have applied three main strategies in their search for a solution to this discrepancy.

The first, called a lunar calendar, ignores the seasons and allows the lunar (moon) cycle to be the basis of the year, as the Islamic calendar does. A second is called a lunisolar calendar. It involves an elaborate system of calculations to add days or months to the lunar year until it coincides with the solar year. The Hebrew calendar is one example. The third system, which originated with the Egyptians, is the pure solar calendar. It allows the sun to determine not only the seasons but the length of the months as well.

Chapter 2 explains lunar and lunisolar calendars. Solar calendars are addressed in Chapter 3.

The History of Lunar and Lunisolar Calendars

The Chinese Calendar

The Chinese calendar, with its origin believed to be 2953 B.C.E., is based on the longest unbroken chain of time measurement in mankind's memory. Hindu and Muslim influences have been introduced at various times, but none succeeded in changing the Chinese calendar. In 1912 the Chinese government adopted the Gregorian calendar for public use, but the traditional calendar still maintains wide popularity throughout Asia and among Asian people around the world.

Part of the reason that the Chinese calendar has survived intact for nearly five millennium is that, until the twentieth century, the document was considered sacred. Any changes to the calendar were tightly controlled by imperial authorities, and the penalty for illegally tampering with the time keeping system was death. Therefore, although minor adjustments in the astronomical calculations have been made to the calendar, its essential structure today is the same as it was nearly five thousand years ago. Until the rise of communism in China during the twentieth century, the official calendar was presented to the emperor, governors, and other dignitaries in an elaborate ceremony each year on the first day of the tenth month.

The Celestial "Roads"

The Chinese calendar, like most ancient time reckoning systems, is lunisolar. It is organized according to three paths, or roads, which map the movements of celestial bodies. The three celestial roads are called the Red Road, the Yellow Road, and the White Road. The Red Road helps define the solar month and year by tracing the constellations in a line roughly corresponding with the equator. Each of the 28 constellations along the Red Road

fall into one of 28 lunar mansions which vary in size from 1 to 34 degrees of the 360 degree circle in the sky around the earth. The earth's movement around the sun (or, according to a geocentric view of the universe, the sun's movement against the stars) is charted on the Yellow Road which also gives definition to the length of the solar year. The White Road follows the phases of the moon and is the basis for the lunar aspects of the Chinese calendar. Additional information about the Chinese calendar can be found in Chapter 16.

Table 2.1. The Chinese Zodiac and Celestial Signs		
Celestial Signs	**Zodiac Symbol**	**English Animal**
Kiah	Tse	Rat
Yih	Chau	Ox
Ping	Yin	Tiger
Ting	May	Hare
Wu	Shin	Dragon
Ki	Se	Snake
Kang	Wu	Horse
Sin	Wi	Sheep
Jin	Shin	Monkey
Kwei	Yu	Rooster
	Siuh	Dog
	Hai	Pig

The Chinese Zodiac

The Chinese zodiac is not comparable to other systems. The "twelve branches" are derived from the twelve positions in the sky to which the seven stars of the Big Dipper point during the year. The Chinese use the zodiac in two different cycles to name their years. The first system matches ten celestial signs with each animal of the zodiac (see Table 2.1). For example, the first zodiac sign is combined with the first celestial sign to form the year Klah-tse. The second year is Yih-chau, a combination of the second sign in each series. When all ten celestial signs have been paired, the eleventh zodiacal sign is matched with the first celestial sign. Thus the cycle continues through sixty years.

The Chinese use this system not only for counting years, but also for counting days. When it is used to enumerate days, it is known as the kah-chih system. The pattern of repeating the ten celestial signs probably led to the development of the hsun—the Chinese ten-day equivalent of the week.

Table 2.2. Partial Cycle of the Chinese Zodiac and Elements of the Earth

Zodiac Symbol	English Animal	Element
Tzu	Rat	Wood
Chou	Ox	Wood
Yin	Tiger	Fire
Mao	Hare	Fire
Shin	Dragon	Earth
Ssu	Snake	Earth
Wu	Horse	Metal
We	Sheep	Metal
Shin	Monkey	Water
Yu	Rooster	Water
Hsu	Dog	Wood
Hai	Pig	Wood
Tzu	Rat	Fire
Chou	Ox	Fire
Yin	Tiger	Earth
Mao	Hare	Earth

The second cycle for naming the years is used less frequently and never in conjunction with the other. Like the first system, it is a sixty year cycle, but instead of using celestial signs as counterparts to the zodiac, it uses the elements of the earth: wood, fire, earth, metal, and water (see Table 2.2).

Subdivisions within the Chinese Year

The Chinese year is divided into twenty-four parts. The Chinese New Year takes place on the new moon nearest to the point which is defined in the west as the fifteenth degree of Aquarius, roughly February 4 or 5 according to the Western civil calendar.

Each of the twelve months in the Chinese year is twenty-nine or thirty days long and is divided into two parts defined as the period of time covering 15 degrees of the sky—about two weeks. The Chinese calendar, like all lunisolar systems, requires periodic adjustment to keep the lunar and solar cycles integrated. Intercalation in the Chinese calendar takes place each time a month contains the beginning and end of only one of the 15 degree divisions.

Beginning with the New Year the names for the 24 divisions are:

1. Spring Begins
2. Rain Water
3. Excited Insects
4. Vernal Equinox
5. Clear and Bright
6. Grain Rains
7. Summer Begins
8. Grain Fills
9. Grain in Ear
10. Summer Solstice
11. Slight Heat
12. Great Heat
13. Autumn Begins
14. Limit of Heat
15. White Dew
16. Autumnal Equinox
17. Cold Dew
18. Hoar Frost Descends
19. Winter Begins
20. Little Snow
21. Heavy Snow
22. Winter Solstice
23. Little Cold
24. Great Cold

The Calendars of India

Throughout its history, India has used a plethora of calendars and dating systems of which there have been two basic types: a civil calendar which changed with each new regime (the current civil holidays are listed in Table 2.3) and a religious calendar maintained by the Hindus. Although each geographical region had its own Hindu calendar, most of the calendars shared some elements that they gleaned from a common heritage.

India's Original Calendar

India's first time reckoning system emerged before 1000 B.C.E. It was based on astronomical observations and consisted of a solar year of 360 days comprising 12 lunar months. The discrepancy between the length of the solar and lunar years was corrected by intercalating a month every 60 months.

In 1200 C.E., the Muslims brought the use of their calendar to India for administrative purposes, and the British introduced the Gregorian calendar in 1757. Despite these

occurrences, however, each separate state maintained a calendar which its citizens used in their daily interactions. Throughout India's colonial days, the entrenchment of these local calendars created havoc for the central government because any given date would have up to six different interpretations throughout the country. The difficulties continued as an indigenous government took control in 1947.

The Saka Era Calendar

When India became a unified and independent nation, the differences among regional calendars included more than thirty methods for determining the beginning of the era, the year, and the month. These variations in the Hindu calendar were the culmination of nearly 5,000 years of history.

In 1952 the Calendar Reform Committee was established and charged with task of devising a unified system that would adhere to modern astronomical calculations and accommodate the calculation of dates for religious festivals. As a result of the committee's work, the National Calendar of India was adopted in 1957.

The National Calendar of India is a twelve-month lunisolar calendar with traditional Hindu month names. Some months are 30 days in length; others are 31 days. The year is 365 days long, with an extra day added to the end of the first month every four years (coinciding with leap years in the Gregorian calendar).

The National Calendar of India counts years from the inception of the Saka Era—the spring equinox in 79 C.E. In the year in which it was adopted, the first day of the first month (Caitra) was Caitra 1, 1879 S.E., which corresponded to March 22, 1957 C.E. Using the Gregorian calendar for comparison, the year 1926 in the Saka Era, begins on March 22, 2004 C.E.

Dates for religious festivals, which depend on lunar and solar movements, are calculated annually by the India Meteorological Department, although regional variations still exist. (The calendar section in Chapter 12 provides a more detailed discussion of the Hindu calendar.) For administrative purposes, the Indian government currently follows the Gregorian calendar.

The Babylonian Calendar

The earliest Western system for constructing calendars was developed by Babylonian, Sumerian, and Assyrian astronomers living in the Mesopotamian Valley hundreds of years B.C.E. These calendars were based on the phases of the moon and were closely related to the religious life of the cultures that developed them. The influence of the Mesopotamian civilizations on the global art of

Table 2.3. Civil Holidays in India

Western date	National Calendar of India date	Holiday
March 22	Caitra 1	New Year's Day
April 13	Caitra 23	Vaisakhi (Old New Year's Day)
August 15	Sravana 24	Independence Day
October 2	Asvina 10	Mahatma Gandhi's Birthday
November 14	Kartika 23	Children's Day
January 26	Magha 6	Republic Day
January 30	Magha 10	Mahatma Gandhi's Martyrdom
February 22	Phalguna 3	Mother's Day

calendar making was far reaching because many of the techniques they developed were adopted by future societies.

Of the various cultures that thrived in the Mesopotamian valley, the Babylonians seem to have had the most significant influence on calendar making. Many details of the evolution of the Babylonian calendar have been lost over the centuries, but it is known that the calendar was lunar in nature, had a system of intercalation, had months divided into seven-day units, and had days with twenty-four hours.

Intercalation Reconciles Nature's Incongruous Cycles

Because these early calendar makers were pioneers in the field, they were among the first to be confronted with the discrepancy between the lunar and solar cycles—a problem that had the potential to render any calendar system ineffective. To reconcile the two natural courses, the Babylonians worked out a schedule whereby an extra month was periodically intercalated. The process of intercalation, termed *iti dirig*, seems to have been rather arbitrary at first, but by 380 B.C.E. a formal system was adopted adding an extra month in the third, sixth, eighth, eleventh, seventeenth, and nineteenth years. Many other cultures, including the Greeks, developed similar intercalation schemes which may have been based on the Babylonian model.

The Babylonians Introduce the Seven Day Week

Although the origin of the week has been a subject of much research and debate among scholars since the time of Plutarch (46-119 C.E.), most agree that the Babylonians are the primary source for the week in the Western civil calendar. Many researchers also conclude that the Babylonians devised the week as a part of their religious practices. They have observed that years, months, and days are all based on natural cycles, but the week is not. This observation has led to some questions: Why does the week have seven days? Why are the days named after celestial bodies? Why are the days not arranged according to the order of the planets in the solar system? Many proposed solutions to these quandaries have surfaced over the course of time.

The Babylonian View of the Universe

A different view of the universe may account for the structure of the week. Lawrence Wright articulates a theory on the origin of the week in his *Clockwork Man*, which may help a modern audience understand the ancient mind-set. Using available historical and archeological information, Wright has attempted to reconstruct the Babylonian view of the universe.

Wright proposes that the seven-day week was not based on any naturally occurring pattern, but was the result of other influences within Babylonian society. He suggests that the week may have been based on 168 hours rather than seven days.

Moreover, he suggests that the order of days maybe explained by the Babylonian belief in the earth as the center of the astronomical cycles they observed. Thus, if one lines up the sun, moon, and plants according to the Babylonian estimation of their distance from the earth (Saturn, Jupiter, Mars, Sun, Venus, Mercury, and Moon) rather than their order in the solar system, an interesting pattern arises. If each hour of the day is assigned a planet, by the time all of the hours have been assigned, and each planet has been given the first of our one day, a seven-day sequence has been completed. For example, beginning with the first hour of one day, a seven-day sequence has been completed. For example, beginning with the first day, assign the first hour to the farthest planet form the earth, Saturn. That day would be known as Saturn's day or Saturday. Assign each hour of the day to another planet so that the second hour would be assigned to Jupiter, the third to Mars, and soon, repeating the sequence of planets until each hour of the day has been assigned to a planet. A twenty-four hour period requires that each planet be assigned three times and three planets four times. The first hour of the second day is named for the next planet in the sequence, or the Sun (hence, Sunday). Although the Babylonians had different planet and day names, they occurred in the same pattern as that employed by the current Western calendar.

Another Theory Based on an Astrological System

Another explanation suggests that the week and the ordering of the days may have been important to Babylonian religious practices. According to archeological evidence, Babylonian religion involved worship of the "visible gods." These were the seven lights in the sky that appeared to wander against the background of fixed stars (these seven can be identified as the sun, the moon, and the five planets that can be seen without the aid of a telescope). This understanding formed a type of astrological system similar to the Greek zodiac. Each day of the Babylonian month was sacred to one of these seven gods. Thus a seven-day pattern of gods' days would have emerged. Although the names of the days of the week in English bear the influence of the Anglo-Saxons, the days in Latin and the Romance languages correspond to the ancient Babylonian "visible gods."

The Sabbath May Have Its Beginning in Babylon

The Sabbath, a day of rest, is a common occurrence in many cultures. Historians suggest that the Babylonians may have been the first to develop this idea. In fact, the modern word "Sabbath" can be traced to the Babylonian "shabattu" which means seventh. The Babylonians considered the four days that generally correspond with the moon's four quarters, numbered 7, 14, 21, and 28, along with a fifth day numbered 19, to be "evil days" because the god of the underworld was the deity governing those days. Proscriptions against certain activities were observed to help the evil day be favorable.

Some scholars have proposed that this seven-day week scheme was adopted by the ancient Hebrews when they were subject to Babylonian rule. They further suggest that the week was subsequently introduced to other cultures as the Hebrews were dispersed to other regions around the globe.

Details of the Babylonian Calendar

Details of the Babylonian calendar are few, but some are known. It appears that the major festival was the New Year celebration which took place in the spring of the year during the Babylonian month of Nisanu. On the first day of the festival, a ritual marriage was performed between the king and the high priestess, who symbolized the sovereignty of the land. On this day, the Babylonian creation myth (called *Enuma elish* from its opening words, "When on high") was read aloud. On the fifth day, Rites of Atonement were observed. During the Rites the king, as a representative of the people, endured a ritual of abasement to atone for the sins of the people against the gods. On the seventh day, the Festival of the Sun, or spring equinox, took place.

The Jewish Calendar

Jewish history can be traced with reasonable accuracy to the rule of King Solomon, approximately 1,000 B.C.E. However, it is difficult to assign accurate dates to events preceding the rule of King Solomon. It is not known exactly when the Jewish calendar was developed, and biblical references to a calendar system prior to the Babylonian captivity are rare. The Old Testament mentions four Jewish months by name: Abib, the first month; Ziv, the second month; Ethanum, the seventh month; and Bul, the eighth month. Other months in the ancient Jewish calendar are not referenced in the Old Testament, but have been recorded in Phoenician inscriptions; these include the months of Marpeh, Phauloth, Mizah, Mapha, Hir, and Zebah-shishim.

The Jewish day began at sunset, and Jewish holidays still begin at the setting of the sun. The day is 24 hours long, subdivided into 1,080 chalaks. The month likely began with the appearance of the new moon and its length probably varied with the lunar cycle, between 29 and 30 days. It appears that the calendar was lunisolar and directly related to the seasons. The year probably began during the harvest season in the fall. Months were intercalated occasionally to ensure that the harvest would be ripe in time for the Passover (the 16th day of the first month), where it was required that a portion of the harvest be sacrificed to God.

When Jerusalem fell to Babylon in approximately 600 B.C.E., the Jews adopted the Babylonian calendar and, according to some scholars, the seven-day week. Instead of using the Babylonian names, the Jews used numbers to identify the days of the week, except for the seventh, which was called the Sabbath.

The modern Jewish calendar is based on a theoretical moon, meaning the months are calculated based on the average period of a lunation rather than actual observation of the phases of the moon. Therefore, the month lasts exactly 29 days, 12 hours and 793 chalakim (29.5305 days). The theoretical moon will remain synchronized with the actual moon for more than 16,000 years. To keep the lunar cycle synchronized with the solar cycle, the Jews used the Metonic cycle (described below under "Greek Calendars") of intercalating seven months over a nineteen year period. The Jewish calendar is described in more detail in Chapter 5.

Greek Calendars

The ancient Greeks possessed calendar systems with common elements and variations among the city-states. The political powers of each city-state retained the right to intercalate months and days to reconcile the lunar and solar cycles. These intercalations were arbitrary and seem to have been more closely associated with political whimsy rather than natural cycles. The most influential calendar system was the Athenian.

The Athenian Calendar

Although there is some uncertainty about specific details concerning the Athenian calendar, in general many researchers believe it consisted of twelve lunar months that alternated between 29 and 30 days in length, plus an intercalary month of 30 days. This extra month, Poseidon Deuteros (second Poseidon), was inserted it the calendar after Poseidon, the sixth month. Also, an extra day could be added to the twelfth month, Skirophorion, to keep the months in phase with the moon. Days in the Athenian calendar began at sunset.

Table 2.4. Athenian Lunisolar Calendar

Hekatombion, "sacrifice of a hundred" (30 days)

1	Consecrated to the deities Selene and Apollo. This day always coincides with the appearance of the first visible crescent moon after the summer solstice.
4	Consecrated to the deities Aphrodite and Hermes, and the hero Herakles.
6	Consecrated to the deity Artemis.
7	Consecrated to Apollo. The *Hekatombaia* festival held, honoring Apollo. *Hyakinthia* begins.
8	Consecrated to the god Poseidon and to the Hero of Athens, Theseus.
9	*Hyakinthia* ends.
11–15	Nemean Games held in years two and four of each four-year cycle.
12	Consecrated to the Titan deity Kronos, the father of Zeus.
15	Consecrated to the moon goddess Selene.
16	"Federation Day." Consecrated to the goddess Aphrodite Pandemos, Peitho, and to the Horae, or season, Eirene, the personification of Peace.
21–28	*Panathenaea*, the "All-Greek Festival of Athena."
30	Consecrated to the fertility goddess Hekate.

Metageitnion (29 days)

1	Consecrated to Selene and Apollo.
4	Consecrated to Aphrodite, Hermes and Herakles.
6	The deities Artemis and Kronos honored with the sacrifice of a scapegoat.
6–14	Pythian games held at Delphi in year three of each four-year cycle.
7	Consecrated to Apollo; *Metageitnia* held in honor of Apollo. The people of Salamis sacrificed a pig to each of the deities Apollo Patroos, Leto, Artemis, and Athena Agelaa.
7–15	*Karneia*, a festival honoring Apollo Karneus; festivities included feasts, foot races, and musical contests.
8	Consecrated to the god Poseidon and to Theseus (Athenian Hero).
10	Athletic contests held at Olympus in honor of the goddess Hera in year one of each four-year cycle.
11–15	Olympic Games, held in year one of each four-year cycle.
15	Consecrated to the goddess Selene.
29	Consecrated to the goddess Hekate.

Boedromion, "month of helpers" (30 days)

1	Consecrated to the deities Selene and Apollo.
4	Consecrated to the deities Aphrodite and Hermes, and to the hero Herakles.
5	Genesia = Nekusia = Nemesia, the clans' feast of the dead.
6	Consecrated to the goddess Artemis.
6-7	*Boedromia* held, honoring the deities Artemis and Apollo.
7	Consecrated to the god Apollo.
8	Consecrated to the god Poseidon and to the Hero of Athens, Theseus.
13	Commencement of preparations for celebration of the *Eleusinian Mysteries*.
15	Consecrated to the goddess Selene. The advent of the *Mysteries* announced from the Painted Porch.
16	*Synoekia*, the sacrifice of two oxen to the god Zeus (in the form Zeus Phratrios) and the goddess Athena (in the form Athena Phratria), "of the clans."
19–23	The *Great Mysteries of Eleusis*.
30	Consecrated to the goddess Hekate.

Table 2.4. Athenian Lunisolar Calendar, continued

Pyanepsion, "month of boiling beans" (29 days)

1 .... Consecrated to the deities Selene and Apollo.
4 .... Consecrated to the deities Aphrodite and Hermes, and to the Hero Herakles.
6 .... Consecrated to Artemis. *Proerosia* held at Eleusis, a pig sacrificed to Theseus.
7 .... Consecrated to Apollo. *Pyanopsia* festival held with the expulsion of a scapegoat.
7–9 .... The *Stepterion, Herois*, and *Charilla* festivals held in honor of Apollo, once every eight years, at Delphi. A boy, representing Apollo, was placed in a hut called the palace of Python. The hut was set afire, and the boy removed from it and ritualistically "sent into exile." Then all the celebrants were purified at Tempe, and returned to Delphi in procession along the Pythian Way.
8 .... The *Oschophoria*, a celebration honoring the god Poseidon, held with foot races, feasting on beans, and carrying of grapes. Also, the Great Festival of Theseus.
9–13 .... The *Thesmophoria*, "bringing of treasures," honoring the deities Demeter and Kore; a fertility festival celebrated by women.
9 .... *Sthenia* held, honoring Demeter and Kore.
10 .... *Anodos*, "ascent," procession to the Thesmophorion, a temple of Demeter.
11 .... *Nesteia*, "fasting," observed.
12 .... The women built bowers, squatted on the ground, and ate roast pork.
13 .... *Kalligeneia*, "bearer of beautiful children," in which the rotting remains of the pigs sacrificed at the previous Skira were brought up and mixed with the seed corn to improve the crop.
11–13 .... *Apaturia* or *Koureotis*, festival observed by adolescent boys.
13 .... *Apaturia*, day three—children, young men who had just reached the age of maturity, and newly married women were enrolled in the phratries (clans) of Athens, with appropriate sacrifices.
14 .... *Anarhusis*, marked by the sacrifice of oxen to the god Zeus Phratrios and the goddess Athena.
15 .... Consecrated to the goddess Selene. The festival of Hera held at Olympia every four years.
16 .... Birthday of Homer, death of Demosthenes.
28 .... *Chalkeia* and *Hephaestia*: torch race for the goddess Athena and the god Hephaestus.
29 .... Consecrated to the goddess Hekate.

Maimakterion, sacred to the god Zeus Maimaktes, "stormy" (30 days)

1 .... Consecrated to the goddess Selene and the god Apollo.
4 .... Consecrated to the goddess Aphrodite, the god Hermes, and the hero Herakles.
6 .... Consecrated to the goddess Artemis.
7 .... Consecrated to Apollo.
8 .... Consecrated to the god Poseidon and the Hero of Athens, Theseus.
14 .... *Maimakteria* held, marked by the sacrifice of sheep to Zeus Maimaktes.
15 .... Consecrated to Selene.
30 .... Consecrated to the goddess Hekate.

Posideon, sacred to the god Poseidon (29 days)

1 .... Consecrated to the goddess Selene and the god Apollo.
4 .... Consecrated to the goddess Aphrodite, the god Hermes, and the hero Herakles.
6 .... Consecrated to the goddess Artemis.
7 .... Consecrated to Apollo.
8 .... The festival of *Poseidea* held, honoring the god Poseidon and the Hero of Athens, Theseus.
11–13 .... The Rural Festival of Dionysus.
12 .... The *Haloa*, honoring the "Green Demeter" (fertility goddess) and an agricultural Poseidon/Dionysus figure.
15 .... Consecrated to the goddess Selene.
29 .... Consecrated to the goddess Hekate.

Table 2.4. Athenian Lunisolar Calendar, continued

Posideon Deuteros, "second month sacred to Poseidon" (30 days)
This was the intercalary month in the Athenian system.

1 .... Consecrated to the goddess Selene and the god Apollo.
4 .... Consecrated to the goddess Aphrodite, the god Hermes, and the hero Herakles.
6 .... Consecrated to the goddess Artemis.
7 .... Consecrated to Apollo.
8 .... Consecrated to the god Poseidon and the Hero of Athens, Theseus.
15 .... Consecrated to Selene.
30 .... Consecrated to the goddess Hekate.

Gamelion, sacred to the goddess Hera Gamelia, "of marriage" (30 days)

1 .... Consecrated to the goddess Selene and the god Apollo.
4 .... Consecrated to the goddess Aphrodite, the god Hermes, and the hero Herakles.
6 .... Consecrated to the goddess Artemis.
7 .... Consecrated to Apollo.
8 .... Consecrated to the god Poseidon, and the Hero of Athens, Theseus.
10 .... *Lenaion* held on the island Mykonos, marked by sacrifices to the goddess Demeter and Kore.
12–14 .... The festival of *Lenaia* held, honoring the god Dionysus.
14 .... The *Gamelia* held, honoring the goddess Hera.
15 .... Consecrated to Selene.
30 .... Consecrated to the goddess Hekate.

Anthesterion, sacred to the god Poseidon (29 days)

1 .... Consecrated to the goddess Selene and the god Apollo.
4 .... Consecrated to the goddess Aphrodite, the god Hermes, and the hero Herakles.
6 .... Consecrated to the goddess Artemis.
7 .... Consecrated to Apollo. Celebration of Apollo's birthday, at Delphi, and commemoration of his return to Delphi following a three-month absence in winter.
8 .... Consecrated to the god Poseidon and to the Hero of Athens, Theseus.
11 .... The *Anthesteria*, "feast of flowers," a three-day festival of the god Dionysus and the dead which began with the *Pithoigia*, "opening of wine jars."
12 .... *Anthesteria*, day two, and *Choes*, "cups" or "jugs." Celebration included the blessing of new wine before the god Dionysus, the use of libations (a sacrifice performed by pouring a liquid onto the ground), and drinking contests. A ship-shaped wagon containing a statue of Dionysus was drawn in procession from the seashore to the Boukolion, the temple of Dionysus as Bull God, where the Basilinna (the wife of the Archon Basileus, or King Archon) underwent a ritual marriage to Dionysus. Dionysus's sanctuary in Limnae was opened.
13 .... *Anthesteria*, day three, and *Chytroi*, "pots". Pots of cooked fruit sacrificed to chthonian Hermes and the spirits of the dead.
15 .... Consecrated to the goddess Selene.
20–23 .... *Lesser Mysteries of Eleusis.*
23 .... The *Diasia* held, marked by a burnt offering of pigs made to Zeus Meilichios.
29 .... Consecrated to Hekate.

Elaphebolion, "month of shooting stags," sacred to the goddess Artemis (30 days)

1 .... Consecrated to the goddess Selene and the god Apollo.
4 .... Consecrated to the goddess Aphrodite, the god Hermes, and the hero Herakles.
6 .... The festival of *Elaphebolia* held, honoring the goddess Artemis.
7 .... Consecrated to Apollo.

Table 2.4. Athenian Lunisolar Calendar, continued

Elaphebolion, continued

8 .... Consecrated to the god Poseidon and the Hero of Athens, Theseus.
9-13 .... The "Greater"—or "City Festival"—of Dionysus, when the dramatic contests were held.
14 .... The *Pandia* held, honoring Zeus.
15 .... Consecrated to Selene.
30 .... Consecrated to the goddess Hekate.

Munychion, sacred to the goddess Artemis (29 days)

1 .... Consecrated to Selene and Apollo.
4 .... Consecrated to Aphrodite, Hermes, and Herakles. The people of Salamis performed sacrifices to Herakles, Kourotrophos ("nourisher of youths"), Alkmene, and Maia.
6 .... Consecrated to Artemis. The *Brauronia* held at Brauron, and the *Tauropolia* at Halai, for Artemis.
7 .... Consecrated to Apollo.
8 .... Consecrated to Poseidon and Theseus.
11–15 .... Isthmian Games in years two and four of each four-year cycle.
15 .... Consecrated to Selene.
16 .... The *Munychia* held, honoring Artemis as Moon Goddess.
29 .... Consecrated to Hekate.

Thargelion, sacred to Apollo (30 days)

1 .... Consecrated to Selene and Apollo.
4 .... Consecrated to Aphrodite, Hermes, and Herakles.
6 .... Birthday of Artemis.
7 .... The *Thargelia*, birthday of Apollo, celebrated with the carrying of the eiresione; condemned criminals were dedicated as pharmakoi, "scapegoats," hung with figs, and driven out of Athens.
8 .... Consecrated to Poseidon and Theseus.
11–13 .... The *Agrionia*, a festival honoring the god Dionysus, associated with the myth of the daughters of Minyas, or of Proetus, in Boeotia, Rhodes, Sparta, Kos, and Byzantium.
15 .... Consecrated to Selene.
24 .... The *Kallynteria* held, sweeping out Athena's temple. Torch race for Bendis, the moon goddess of Thrace.
25 .... The *Plynteria* held, washing Athena's robe and statue in the sea.
30 .... Consecrated to Hekate.

Skirophorion, sacred to the goddess Athena (29 or 30 days)

1 .... Consecrated to Selene and Apollo.
4 .... Consecrated to Aphrodite, Hermes, and Herakles.
6 .... Consecrated to Artemis.
7 .... Consecrated to Apollo.
8 .... Consecrated to Poseidon and Theseus.
12 .... The *Skirophoria* or *Skira* held. Pigs sacrificed to Demeter by being thrown down into rocky chasms, where the scavenger birds could not get at them.
13 .... The *Arrhephoria*, "carrying secret objects," honoring Athena and Aphrodite. Two young girls of noble birth were given unidentified, wrapped objects which they then carried at night, through a secret tunnel, from the Acropolis to the Sanctuary of Aphrodite in the Gardens.
14 .... The festival of *Diipolia*, or *Buphonia*, held, and an ox sacrificed to Zeus.
15 .... Consecrated to Selene.
29/30 .... Consecrated to the goddess Hekate. *Diisoteria* held, honoring Zeus and Athena.

Please note when using this and other calendars in this volume that ancient sources are often incomplete or misleading so dates contained herein are approximate.

The Athenians Divide Months into Three "Decades"

The Athenian calendar began in midsummer and comprised twelve months:

1. Hekatombion
2. Metageitnion
3. Boedromion
4. Pyanepsion
5. Maimakterion
6. Poseidon
7. Gamelion
8. Anthesterion
9. Elaphebolion
10. Munychion
11. Thargelion
12. Skirophorion

These months were divided into three "decades" of ten days each. The first ten days were called the "waxing moon"; the middle ten days were called "full moon"; and the last nine or ten days were called the "waning moon." Dates were assigned according to these decades, and days within the last decade were numbered from the end of the decade. For example, the first day of the month was called the "first day of the waxing moon" of whatever month. The eleventh day would be "the first day of the full moon." The twentieth day was called the "the tenth day of the full moon," but the twenty-first day was called the "the tenth day of the waning moon" (or the ninth day, if the month had only 29 days).

Religious Holidays and the Greek Liturgical Calendar

The celebration of religious holidays in the Athenian months followed some consistent patterns. For example, the first and seventh day of each month was sacred to Apollo, and the first and fifteenth days were sacred to Selene. Festivals of their gods fell into consistent patterns as well. Dionysus tended to be celebrated on days 11 to 13; sacrifices to Zeus on day 14; the cycle of games fell on days 11–15. Therefore, by knowing the Greek pattern of religious celebration, scholars can surmise the specific dates on which the festival of a deity was observed and reconstruct the Athenian calendar (see Table 2.4). Since the Renaissance, the religious practices of the Greeks have been studied with interest, and have been revived by various Neoclassic and Neo-pagan groups.

The Eleusinian Mysteries

The most important Athenian festival was that of the Eleusinian Mysteries. Because the contents of the Mysteries were an Athenian state secret, the many details of the festival are not known. The Mysteries were observed during two different time periods of the year. One, termed the Lesser Mysteries, occurred during the month of Anthesterion. The Lesser Mysteries probably involved a ritual or drama about the life, death, and resurrection of Dionysus. The other, called the Greater Mysteries, were observed in the month Boedromion. The Greater Mysteries centered on the myth of the Rape of Persephone, as told in the Greek poem called the *Homeric Hymn to Demeter*. Some have surmised that initiation into the Lesser Mysteries was a prerequisite to participation in the Greater Mysteries. This may not be accurate, however, especially as the Romans began to influence the Greeks. Many Romans and other inhabitants of the Roman empire came to Athens in Boedromion to be initiated at the Greater Mysteries.

Preparation for the mysteries began formally on Boedromion 15. The Hierokeryx (sacred herald) would stand on the Painted Porch in Athens and, in the presence of the Hierophant ("high priest" of Eleusis), announce the assembly for the Mysteries. After several days of sacrifices and preparations, the Procession of the Mysteries would leave Athens on the morning of Boedromion 19, reaching Eleusis after sunset, which was then Boedromion 20 (because the Athenian day began at sunset). Based on what is known of the rituals, the celebration of the Mysteries probably lasted three nights. The festivities included a torch lit search for Kore and an initiation of the candidates who were sworn to secrecy as the key of the Hierophant was laid upon their lips. The agenda may have also included a ritual drama about the reunion of Demeter and Kore. Finally, there was probably a ritual in the Telesterion (a great hall). It is possible that the entire festival lasted nine days or longer based on the tradition of a nine-day fast which was clearly a part of the observation of this event. Therefore, the ending date of the festival can be placed on or after Boedromion 23, nine days after the Proclamation of the Mysteries on Boedromion 15.

Cycle Attempts to Reconcile the Lunar and Solar Patterns

When the Atheans became rulers of the Delian League in the sixth century B.C.E., they realized the need to have an official calendar that could be used by all the League's members. In 582 B.C.E. they regulated the intercalation of months by using an eight-year (octennial) cycle in which a month was added to the third, fifth, and eighth years.

The Grecian concept of an eight-year cycle was devised by Cleostratus of Tenedos (circa 500 B.C.E.) and advanced by Eudoxus of Cnidus (390 to c. 340 B.C.E.). Called the octaëteris, the Greek cycle was based on a solar year of

365 days; thus the eight-year cycle was composed of 2,920 days. The octennial cycle closely matched the length of 99 lunations (a total of 2920.5 days), which made it a promising link between lunar and solar calendars.

The actual length of a solar year is 365.24 days, and eight solar years have a length of 2921.93 days. Therefore, the calendar based on the octaëteris accumulated an error of 1.5 days every eight years. After about a century of use, the discrepancy had accrued to nearly 30 days. When the Greek scholars realized the problems with their calendar, some of them began to search for a more effective system to reconcile the lunar and solar calendars.

The Metonic Cycle Is Developed

The most significant of all the early attempts to relate to the lunar calendar to the solar year was the Metonic cycle. The system, devised circa 430 B.C.E. by the Athenian astronomers Meton and Euctemon, is based on a nineteen-year cycle which intercalates months in seven of the nineteen years.

To determine the length for the solar year, Meton and Euctemon made a series of observations of the solstices—the point at which the sun's noonday shadow cast by a vertical pillar (called a gnomon) reaches its annual maximum or minimum. Assuming the value of the synodic lunar month to be 29.5 days, the two astronomers computed a difference of 11 days between 12 lunations and the solar year. To create a rule that would be accurate on a long-term basis, Meton and Euctemon constructed a nineteen-year cycle consisting of twelve years of twelve months and seven years of thirteen months for a total of 235 lunar months. The cycle contained 110 "hollow" months (of 29 days) and 125 "full" months (of 30 days), which totaled of 6940 days. The difference between this lunar calendar and a solar calendar of 365 days amounted to only five days in nineteen years and, in addition, gave an average length for the solar year of 365.25 days.

In practice, Meton's cycle is even more precise than he realized. The five-day difference that arose over the course of the cycle was based on a slightly inaccurate day count. Astronomers who came after Meton discovered the actual length of 235 lunar months to be 6939.69 days, and the number of days in nineteen solar years to be 6939.602. Thus, the actual difference between the two cycles accrues to less than one day in nineteen years—a discrepancy easily corrected by occasionally adding days to or subtracting them from the year.

The Metonic cycle succeeded in two primary areas: It established a lunar calendar with a rule for intercalating months to keep it in step with the solar year; and it gave a more accurate average number of days for the solar year. Although none of the Greek calendars appear to have adopted the system, the Persians did around 380 B.C.E. The Metonic system then passed into the Hebrew liturgical calendar, which is still based on the cycle as are the formulas used by the Christian churches to calculate the date of Easter.

Callippus Enhances Meton's System

The Metonic cycle was improved by Callippus of Cyzicus (c. 370–300 B.C.E.). He developed the Callippic cycle which is a variation on the Metonic cycle. Consisting of four nineteen-year cycles, the Callippic system takes into account that 365.25 days is a more precise value for the solar year than 365 days. The Callippic period encompasses 940 lunar months, but its distribution of hollow and full months differs from Meton's 440 hollow and 500 full months. Callippus adopted 441 hollow and 499 full months, reducing the length of four Metonic cycles by one day. The total number of days in the Callippic cycle, therefore, is 27,759. When his total is divided by 76 (the number of years in the cycle), the result is 365.25 days exactly. Thus, the Callippic cycle fits 940 lunar months precisely to 76 solar years of 365.25 days.

Hipparchus's Discovery of the Precision of the Equinoxes

Hipparchus, who flourished in Rhodes about 150 B.C.E., was probably the greatest observational astronomer of antiquity. He discovered that the equinoxes—where the ecliptic (the sun's apparent path) crosses the celestial equator (the celestial equivalent of the terrestrial equator)—were not fixed in space but moved slowly in a westerly direction. The movement, now known as the precession of the equinoxes, is small—no more than two degrees of arc in 150 years—yet it was important to the development of the calendar because of the methods used to calculate the length of the solar year. The solar year, the length of time it takes the earth to complete an orbit around the sun, can be measured in several different fashions, but the most accurate for keeping the seasons in alignment is the tropical year which is measured from one vernal (spring) equinox to the next.

Hipparchus calculated the tropical year to have a length of 365.242 days, which was very close to the presently calculated value of 365.242199 days. He also computed the precise length of a lunation, using a "great year" of four Callippic cycles. He arrived at the value of 29.53058 days for a lunation, which, again, is comparable with the present-day figure, 29.53059 days. Hipparchus's adjustments made the Metonic cycle the most accurate long-range time keeping system available to scientists until well into the modern age.

Although Meton's innovative cycle was not recognized by the political establishment of Greece during his lifetime, Greek religious leaders and classical astronomers did use Meton's cycle to calculate their calendars. The cycle has been passed down through the course of history as subsequent calendar makers, including the Julian and Gregorian reformers, have adapted its basic formula to fit their systems.

The Islamic Calendar

The Islamic day officially began at sunset. Muslims, like the Jewish people and the Babylonians, used a seven-day week. They numbered rather than named the days of the week except for the Day of Assembly (Friday), which was a day devoted to prayer.

The official Islamic Calendar is based strictly on the lunar cycle. The calendar consisted of twelve months, each of which contained either 29 or 30 days. As a result, the common year contained only 354 or 355 days. The basis of a calendar on the lunar cycle without intercalations to keep the calendar in step with the solar year lead to each year beginning earlier and earlier in the seasonal year. This caused the calendar to rotate through all of the seasons with a complete rotation through all four seasons every 32 Islamic years. The Islamic calendar is described in more detail in Chapter 10.

Separate Calendars for Religious and Business Purposes

Because of the differences between the solar year and the lunar year, the Islamic calendar was inconvenient for use in international trade. As a result, a different calendar known as the Marti calendar was used for business purposes from 1676 to 1927. In 1927, it was replaced with the Gregorian calendar.

British Traditions

Time-Reckoning Begins with Stonehenge

The first evidence of a time reckoning system in Britain is the monument of Stonehenge. Historians suppose that the construction was originally used to mark solstices and equinoxes, and that it was built over a fifteen hundred year period beginning around 3000 B.C.E. Little is known about the builders of Stonehenge.

Druid Priests and New Religious Traditions in Britain

Originally hailing from northern Europe, the Celtic tribes migrated to Britain in the sixth century B.C.E., bringing with them their religious holidays and customs.

The Druids, who were priests of the Celtic tribes, governed the rites observed in the celebration of festivals on the first day of February, May, August, and November. These holidays were based on the weather patterns in northern Europe, rather than the solar cycle that the earlier Britons formed their religion around. These two sets of holidays became a point of division between the Celts and Britons and have remained such throughout the history of the island until the present.

Traditionally, the days observed by the Britons were called quarter days and fell on the solstices and equinoxes (around March 22, June 22, September 22, and December 22); they also marked the date on which quarterly rent was due. The Celts' holidays became knows as cross-quarter days and celebrated the changes in season. Almost all of these days have several different names, reflecting their long and complex history.

The Celtic Worldview

The Celts' worldview divides everything into equal and opposite halves. Aylwin and Brinsley Rees point out in their *Celtic Heritage* that the Celtic worldview saw everything that exists as divided into two joined but opposing halves and that the seam between the two halves represented danger or evil.

This helps explain some of the festivals and holidays of the Celtic people. For example, their year began on November 1 with a festival, Samhain, marking the end of good weather. The Celts believed that ghosts and fairies could slip into this world from the netherworld on the eve of this festival because it was the meeting place between the good half and bad half of the year.

Similarly, the Celts believed twilight and dawn were perilous because fairies were most likely to steal into this realm and carry people off at these times. The two halves of the year were divided by Candlemas and Lammas; the night and the day were divided in half by midnight and noon.

The practice of beginning a celebration on the evening before a holiday, such as All Hallows Eve, is derived from the structure of the Celtic calendar. Like many other ancient societies, the Celts began their days at sunset. Therefore, like the Hebrews and others, their observation of festivals and holidays began at sunset.

Religious Conflict Influences the Calendar

In the second century C.E., Diocletian's persecution of Christians caused many believers to flee from the Roman Empire. Some of these people settled in Ireland and there established Christian communities and monasteries among the Celts.

Over the next four centuries, the Irish Church developed apart from the Roman Church which dominated the rest of the British Isles. In the sixth century, Irish missionaries began proselytizing in England and came into conflict with the previously established Roman Church. The two branches of Christianity competed with one another for official recognition and converts during the next hundred years, often engaging in heated debate over doctrinal issues. In 664 C.E., the council of Whitby was called by Oswy, King of Northumbria, to settle some of the differences most significantly, the method of determining the date of Easter.

The conflict over the date of Easter centered on the method used to calculate the phases of the moon. By the seventh century, the Roman Church had adopted the 532-year Victorian cycle to regulate the calendar. The Celts, on the other hand, still used the eight-year cycle developed in Rome before Diocletian's persecutions; the Celts also used the Eastern method for determining the night of the full moon. Therefore, the two methods arrived at significantly different dates for the celebration of the most sacred of Christian holidays. Eventually, the Roman Church prevailed and was declared to be the official Church in England.

Table 2.5. The Saxon Calendar

Name of Month Month	Alternative name	Western Civil
Afteryule	Wolfmonth	January
Sproutkale	Solmonth	February
Hlydamonth		March
Eostremonth		April
Threemilks		May
Forelitha	Shearmonth	June
(Threelitha)	(Intercalated month)	
Afterlitha	Meadmonth	July
Weedmonth		August
Harvestmonth	Holymonth	September
Winterfull	Holymonth	October
Bloodmonth		November
Foreyule		December

The Christian Era Is Developed

In 532 C.E. Dionysius Exiguus, Abbot of Rome, calculated that Christ had been born about 753 years after the foundation of Rome (753 A.U.C.—Anno Urbis Conditæ— which means in the year from the building of the city), and made that year the beginning of a new chronology. According to one theory, this date was determined by taking the average of the dates 747 A.U.C. (according to events in the Gospel of Matthew) and 759 A.U.C. (as indicated by events recorded in the Gospel of Luke) as the date of Jesus's birth. Although the accuracy of this date is no longer accepted, the Western civil calendar as well as several other systems still use the Christian era for dating because of the complications involved in changing to any other method.

Saxon Influence Changes the Calendar

During the Roman domination of the southern British Isles, the Roman calendar was adopted. The influence of the Roman system faded, however, under subsequent barbarian rule. The most significant of the barbarian groups to affect the calendar was the Saxons. They brought a lunisolar system of time reckoning with them when they came to power in England in the seventh century C.E.

The calendar was composed of twelve lunar months with a thirteenth month intercalated once every three years. The day began at sunset and was subdivided into segments beginning at noon and midnight. Yule, or the winter solstice, was the major festival of the year, and scholars have surmised that the summer solstice, Litha, was also an occasion of grand celebration.

Some variables affecting the months are uncertain and have been tentatively reconstructed as follows: The placement of the fall, or autumnal, equinox determined the order of the months, and fall equinox occurred during a month called Holymonth. If the fall equinox occurred in the month after Weedmonth, the order of months went Weedmonth, Holymonth, Winterfull. In years in which the equinox would not occur in the month after Weedmonth, the month order was Weedmonth, Harvest month, Holymonth, and Winterfull. The designation of the month containing the fall equinox was pagan in origin because there were no significant Christian festivals observed near the fall equinox during the seventh century.

The two months called Hlydamonth and Eostremonth were named after the goddesses Hlyda and Eostre. Although details about the goddess Eostre are few, historians suggest that it is from her name the English-speaking people derive the name "Easter" for the Feast of the Resurrection, which other languages call "Pasch," or something similar, derived from the Hebrew word for Passover. The notion of the Easter Rabbit is also derived from Eostre, for the rabbit was one of her sacred animals. Furthermore, this rabbit lays Easter eggs because in some of the Mystery religions of the Roman period, an egg dyed scarlet was the symbol of the reincarnation and immortality promised to the initiate. The mixture of Christian and pagan traditions is the result of Pope Gregory's policy of temperance and toleration which was articulated in a letter to Augustine of Canterbury early in the seventh century C.E.

Bede Popularizes the Use of the Christian Era in Dating

Information about both the Celtic and Saxon calendars as well as the Church controversies is found in Bede's *Ecclesiastical History of the English People*. The work was extremely poplar among those who could read in the eighth and ninth centuries, and used the dating system of Dionysius Exiguus (B.C./A.D.) for the first time. It is because of Bede's work that this method of dating was spread throughout the Christian world.

Under Dionysius's system, March 25 was New Year's Day. The English adopted this for the ecclesiastical years in the twelfth century and the legal and civil year in the fourteenth century. The only exception was if March 25 fell during Holy Week, especially on Good Friday. If this occurred, New Year's Day was moved to April 1. This move may be behind the origin of April Fool's Day.

Quarter and Cross-Quarter Days Become an Outlet for Protest

An interesting pattern related to the observance of quarter and cross-quarter days became evident in England during the early middle ages. Quarter days, marked by the solstices and equinoxes, divided the year into four

segments. The four cross-quarter days fell at the midpoints of the quarters. The major Christian festivals were close to the quarter days—Christmas to the winter solstice, Easter and the Annunciation to the spring equinox, St. John's Eve and Whitsuntide to the summer solstice, and Michaelmas to the fall equinox. Therefore, pagan protesters of the Christian establishment embraced the cross-quarter days as occasions for rebellion and celebration of traditions associated with their own belief systems. This may be the reason May Eve and Halloween are associated with witches; but, in fact, both the quarter days and the cross-quarter days are equally pagan in origin. For more information about the pagan calendar, see Chapter 19.

Pagan and Christian Traditions Melded Together

Through the course of time, the pagan agricultural and weather festivals have become so meshed with Christian movable feasts that depend on Easter that it is difficult to distinguish the pagan traditions form those of the Christians.

Of the cross-quarter holidays, Halloween is the only one still observed in the United States; the British have switched the festivities to Guy Fawkes's Day. May Day has become laden with political connotations which have removed any religious meaning from the day. Candlemas is still a minor church festival, but is otherwise remembered only as Groundhog Day. Lammas is completely forgotten in America, although it is still the reason for the British bank holiday on the first Monday in August, and is kept as a harvest festival in rural Ireland.

The Teutonic Calendars

The German speaking settlers of northern Germany and Scandinavia were known as the Teutons. They included Angles, Saxons, and the Vikings. Their twelve-month

---

Table 2.6. Cross-Quarter Holidays

Date	Christian Name	Gaelic Name
February 2	Candlemas	Oimbelg
May 1	May Day	Beltane
August 2	Lammas	Lughnasad
November 1	Hallowe'en	Samhain

Table 2.7. Teutonic Month Names

1.	Giuli	7.	Lida
2.	Solmonath	8.	Woedmonath
3.	Rhedmonath	9.	Halegmonath
4.	Eostromonath	10.	Winterfylleth
5.	Thrimilci	11.	Blotmonath
6.	Lida	12.	Giuli

calendar was based on lunar cycles. It began at the winter solstice. The first and last months of the year had the same name, Giuli, which was derived from the term "Yule-tide." The names of the sixth and seventh months were duplicated. On occasion a month called Thrilidi was added to the summer as an intercalation. Month names honored various gods. (See Table 2.7).

The Icelandic Calendar

The Vikings settled in Iceland in approximately 870 C.E. The original settlers observed a seven-day week and followed a lunar calendar, despite conditions that frequently made lunar observations difficult. The Icelandic year contained only two seasons, winter and summer.

Because of their northern location, Icelanders have nearly constant daylight in the summer and nearly constant darkness in the winter. This caused some difficulties in basing a calendar system on either the sun or moon alone, as neither was visible for the entire year. As a result, the summer season was measured using weeks of seven days and the winter was counted in months of thirty days each.

This system made calculation difficult, however; and it was reformed several times, finally resulting in a calendar year containing 52 seven-day weeks, for a total of 364 days. The summer season was 26 weeks and 2 days long. The winter season was the remaining 180 days. Every seven years, a week was intercalated into the summer season to give the average year a length of 365 days.

CHAPTER 3

The History of Solar Calendars

The previous chapter discussed lunar and lunisolar calendars. Addressed here is the third system of reckoning time, the solar calendar, which disregards the phases of the moon and stays in step with the seasons. Most modern Western nations use this system, as did the citizens of ancient Egypt and Rome. In addition, the Mesoamerican Mayan and Aztec civilizations used a complex calendar that included a solar component.

The Mayan and Aztec Calendars

Olmec Origins

The calendars developed by the Mayans and Aztecs shared many characteristics that may have derived from an earlier calendar developed by their predecessors, the Olmec people. The Olmec civilization flourished in Middle America between 1300 B.C.E. and 400 B.C.E. Their calendar system was based on astronomical observances and contained different cycles that interacted to monitor the timing of both ritual and social events. Because the Olmec people did not develop a written language, little is known about the precise workings of their calendar.

Mayan Calendar

Mayan civilization rose up after the Olmec society had declined. The Classical Mayan era is typically dated between 200 and 900 C.E. The Mayan people lived in the areas of Central America presently occupied by parts of Mexico, Guatemala, Belize, and Honduras.

The Mayan calendar system employed a complex correlation of two cycles. One cycle, called the haab (which means "cycle of rains"), had a solar basis and was used for agricultural purposes. In some areas the New Year began in the summer, but at various times during the Mayan era and in different parts of the Mayan domain, other times of the year were recognized as the beginning. The length of the year, however, was constant. Similar

to the modern measure of a solar year, it consisted of 365 days. The year was subdivided into smaller components, but unlike many other early calendars, these subdivisions were not based on lunations. The 365-day year was made up of eighteen named months, each of which had 20 named days, plus a five-day period, called Uayeb, at the end of the cycle.

In addition to the components of the solar year the Mayans also recognized smaller periods of time (analogous to weeks) that consisted of 13 numbered days. There were 28 such periods in the course of a solar year. The counting of months and weeks was done independently, but every 260 days (20 times 13) the cycle of months and weeks would begin anew.

This 260-day cycle formed the basis of the Mayan ritual calendar, often referred to as the tzolkin. Other names include Count of Days, Divinatory Calendar, Sacred Calendar, Sacred Almanac, and Earth Calendar. Scholars have puzzled over the origin and significance of the number 260. Some speculate it was important because it marked the approximate time between the planet Venus's emergence as evening star and its emergence as morning star; others consider it a factor that could be used in calculating many astronomical events; some note that it corresponds with the length of human gestation; and others see an association with planting and harvesting cycles.

The name day on which the tzolkin cycle began was called the Year Bearer. It was used to describe characteristics of the coming year. Because of the mathematics of the interlocking haab and tzolkin cycles, only four of the name days served as Year Bearers.

The ritual tzolkin cycle operated in conjunction with the solar haab cycle to form a complex and far reaching timekeeping system built on progressions of repetitive cycles. One of the most basic of these cycles is called the Calendar Round.

The Calendar Round covers a time period equal to 52 solar years or 73 ritual years. The time is significant because in every Calendar Round all the possible combinations of haab and tzolkin cycles will have been experienced and they will re-synchronize at the same starting point. This is because 52 solar years covers a time period of 18,980 days, and 73 ritual years also covers a time period of 18,980 days.

Although the Calendar Round covered a number of years, it was not long enough to cover the full extent of time envisioned by its users. Consequently, Mayans also developed a system known as the Long Count. The Long Count measured time from a mythical beginning of the current age until a distant point in the future when it was believed that the age would come to a close. The beginning of the age, according to Mayan calculations and transposed to the current Gregorian calendar, occurred in 3114 or 3113 B.C.E., and it will end in 2011 or 2012 C.E. (The year discrepancy seems to be related to a question regarding compensation for a presumed year 0 between the years 1 B.C.E. and 1 C.E.)

Mayans used a system of pictorial inscriptions (called glyphs) along with dots and bars to record Long Count dates. The Long Count method of recording dates worked on the basis of recording the time that had elapsed from the theoretical beginning point. It tracked cycles of time by marking periods known as days, unials, tuns, katuns, and baktuns. These time cycles are expressed using a five-decimal numeric notation with the shorter periods to the right and longer periods to the left. For example a date such as 11.3.2.9.6 would mean that 11 baktuns, 3 katuns, 2 tuns, 9 unial, and 6 days had passed since the beginning. When a cycle of shorter periods equaled the next larger period, the number re-set to zero and the number for the next period increased by one. The complete cycle within the Mayan Long Count calendar covered a time period of 13 baktuns.

Table 3.1. Mayan Month and Day Names

18 Month Names	20 Day Names
Pop	Imix
Uo	Ik
Zip	Akbal
Zotz	Kan
Zec	Chicchan
Xul	Cimi
Yaxkin	Manik
Mol	Lamat
Chen	Muluc
Yax	Oc
Zac	Chuen
Ceh	Eb
Mac	Ben
Kankin	Ix
Muan	Men
Pax	Cib
Kayab	Caban
Cumku	Ezznab
	Cauac
	Ahau

5-day period:
Uayeb

Table 3.2. Number of Days in Long Count Periods

Period	Consists of	Number of Days
unial	20 days	20 days
tun	18 unials	360 days
katun	20 tuns	7,200 days
baktun	20 katuns	144,000 days
complete cycle	13 baktuns	1,872,000 days

Table 3.3. Named Days of the Aztec Month

1.	Crocodile	11.	Monkey
2.	Wind	12.	Grass
3.	House	13.	Reed
4.	Lizard	14.	Jaguar
5.	Snake	15.	Eagle
6.	Death	16.	Vulture
7.	Deer	17.	Movement
8.	Rabbit	18.	Knife
9.	Water	19.	Rain
10.	Dog	20.	Flower

The Aztec Calendar

Between the 14th and 16th centuries C.E., Aztec civilization predominated in the area currently occupied by central and southern Mexico. There is no evidence that the Aztecs employed a Long Count calendar system, but the agricultural and ritual calendars they followed had many similarities with the Mayan Calendar Round.

The Aztecs recognized a solar year that was divided into eighteen months of twenty named days. At the end of the year, a 5-day period of bad-luck days brought the total number of days in the year to 365. The ritual calendar, which also served as a tool for divination, consisted of twenty months of thirteen days, for a total of 260 days. The passing of each of these months was marked by a festival, but the completion of a 52-year cycle, when the solar and ritual calendars would re-mesh at their staring points, was a momentous occasion.

One of the chief concerns addressed in Aztec religion was the ability of the cosmos to continue. At the end of every 52-year cycle people feared that the world would be destroyed. To commemorate the end of a cycle and help usher in a new one, the New Fire Ceremony (also called Binding of the Years) was held. Old fires were extinguished before dusk and people waited for a cosmic sign indicating that the sun would be reborn. To strengthen the power of the sun on its course, human sacrifices were offered. The passing of the constellation Pleiades through the zenith at midnight was the awaited sign. When it occurred, it signified the promise of another 52-year period, and the fires would be relit.

The Aztec Calendar Stone (or Sun Stone) was discovered in the late 18th century during excavations in Mexico City and is currently housed in Mexico's Museum of Archaeology and History. It conveys both mythological and astronomical information. Thought to have been carved during the late 15th century, the stone is dedicated to the sun, the primary Aztec deity. The Calendar Stone is circular with a diameter of 3.7 meters (just under 12 feet). It weighs 25 tons. The carvings on its face include depictions related to the creation and re-creation of the universe and the twenty named days of the Aztec months.

The Egyptian Calendar

The Egyptians Developed Multiple Calendar Systems

The earliest Egyptian calendar was regulated by the cyclical (helical) rising of the star Sirius or Sothis, which coincided with the annual flooding of the Nile. This calendar was only twelve minutes shorter than the true solar year, a much more accurate system than most of its contemporaries.

In time, the inherent discrepancies between the lunar and solar cycles caused problems for the Egyptians. Although details of the difficulties are not known and while the lunar calendar was preserved for agricultural use, a second calendar was developed for civic purposes. In this civil calendar, the year was composed of twelve 30-day months and five days added to the end of the year for a total of 365 days. Its days, unlike those of other ancient calendars, began at sunrise. There was no intercalation to compensate for the one-quarter day difference between this year and the true solar year of 365.25 days; consequently, the Egyptian civil year gained one day on the true solar year every four years. Therefore, over the course of 1,460 solar years, or 1,461 Egyptian years, the months of the Egyptian calendar would move completely through the seasons. This 1,461 year period is known as the Sothic Cycle.

Egyptian Legend Explains the Calendar

Egyptian religious myths sought to explain the origin of the civil calendar. The legends of the Osiris-Isis cycle indicate that the Egyptian calendar originally incorporated a year of 360 days. To this calendar of twelve 30-day months, the god Thoth added five days, the birthdays of the gods Osiris, Isis, Horus, Nephthys, and Set. When this civil calendar was introduced, its first day the first of the month Thoth coincided with the helical rising of Sirius.

Three Seasons

The importance of the Nile River to the survival of civilization near its delta was reflected in the Egyptian calendar. The months of the year were divided into three seasons of four months each, and these seasons were based on the flood stages of the Nile. The season of Inundation occurred when the river flooded its banks; Going Forth was the time of planting crops after the river had receded; and Deficiency was when the river was at its lowest point, but ironically, it was harvest time for the crops. Individual months within the seasons were indicated only by numbers: the third month of Inundation, the second month of Deficiency, and so on.

A Second Lunar Calendar

Over the course of time, the Egyptians realized that the discrepancies between their two calendar systems caused problems as they tried to set the days of holidays. They were accustomed to using the original lunar calendar, but this became confusing when the new civil calendar came into use. The best solution, they decided, was to create a third calendar, a second lunar one, for use in planning religious activities. This calendar, however, was related to the civil year and not, as the agricultural one was, to the helical rising of Sirius. It was kept in sequence with the civil year by the addition of an intercalary month each time the beginning of the lunar year preceded the beginning of the civil year. Eventually, a twenty-five year intercalation schedule was adopted.

Augustus Caesar Stabilized Egyptian Sothic Calendar

The Egyptian Sothic-cycle calendar remained in use and unchanged until Roman times. After Alexander the Great conquered Egypt in the forth century B.C.E., his successor Ptolemy III declared a change to the calendar which added a day every four years beginning in 238 B.C.E. Egyptian priests, however, unwilling to give control of their sacred practices over to a foreign ruler, ignored the decree. Finally, in 30 B.C.E., Augustus Caesar enforced Ptolemy's order, stabilizing the calendar so that the first day of Thoth always fell on August 29.

The Roman Calendar and Julian Reform

Legendary Beginnings

According to writers during the Augustan period, the first Roman calendar was developed either by King Romulus, to whom the founding of Rome is attributed, or by King Numa, the supposed founder of the Roman religious system. Although there is no concrete evidence to support either of these theories, their existence attests to the importance the Romans assigned to their calendar. To have given it the honor of being developed by the leading figures in their history reflects the great need the Romans saw for the ordering of time.

Civil Unrest over Access to the Calendar

The first Roman calendar for which there is historical evidence dates to 450 B.C.E. It was a list of "named days" (holidays on which the legal system shut down) that was published by the Decemvirate. Access to this information was limited to the aristocracy of priests and magistrates which meant that the average citizen did not officially know when he could attend to his legal matters. This caused such tension that in 304 B.C.E., Flavius was forced by plebeian outcry to post a calendar in the Roman forum that designated the legal days for conducting business. This calendar has become known as the pre-Julian calendar.

One interesting result of the popularization of the calendar in this manner was that many Romans began using the calendar as a decoration in their homes. Ornate renditions of Roman calendars (both pre-Julian and Julian versions) appear on the walls of Roman ruins which date as recently as the fourth century C.E. These pieces of artwork provide a great deal of the information about the Roman time reckoning system.

The Pre-Julian Calendar

According to the pre-Julian calendar, the year was 355 days long. It was divided into ten months which varied in length. Four months had 31 days: Marius, Maius, Quinctilis, and October. Seven months had 29 days: Januarius, Aprilis, Junis Sextilis, September, November and December. One month, Februarius, had 28 days.

Each month was divided into three sections by special days: the Kalends was the first day of the month; the Nones was the fifth day of a short month or the seventh day of a long month; the Ides was the thirteenth day of a short month of the fifteenth day of a long one. All of the other days were designated in relation to one of these special days. For example, Martius (March) 10 would be called the sixth day before the Ides. (The Romans counted inclusively. While March 15 was the Ides, it was also counted as the first day of the set before the Ides. Thus, March 14 would be the second day before the Ides, and so on.) Apart from these dividing days, there were forty-five named days in the Roman calendar, most of which were significant for religious reasons

Roman Beliefs

The Romans seemed to be a highly superstitious people. One of the Roman superstitions, a mistrust of even numbers, affected the calendar in several ways. First, it may have been the reason for the alternation of the length of month between 29 and 31 days rather than using twelve 30-day months. Also, the one month that did have an even number of days, February, was considered unlucky. The second way in which the Roman aversion to even numbers affected the calendar was that festivals which were noted as three-day festivals would actually take place over five days because the Romans did not count the even days in between.

The Roman System of Intercalation

To keep the months and years of the calendar in line with the seasons and solar year, an extra month was intercalated every other year. The Roman method of intercalation was quite unusual compared with other methods. They reduced the month of February to 23 or 24 days and intercalated a 27-day month after the shortened February. Holidays that were normally observed on the 24th and 27th of February were moved to the 23rd and 26th days of the intercalated month.

The problem with the Roman system of intercalation was that, over a four year period, a three to four day discrepancy built up between the calendar and the solar year. Instead of adjusting the length of the intercalary month, the Romans chose to omit it all together every time the man-made calendar resulted in a year at least twenty-seven days longer than the solar cycle.

The unusual nature for the intercalary schedule has long been a question among scholars. One highly plausible reason for the placement of the intercalation is that two holidays that fell at the end of February, the Regifugium and the Equirria, were significantly related to holidays in March and needed to fall in close proximity to them.

Celebrations of the Kalends, Nones, and Ides

According to the Roman writer Varro, who was a contemporary of Julius Caesar, the Kalends, Nones, and Ides were each celebrated in specific ways. On the Kalends, the pontifex maximus stood in the Curia Calabra on the Capitoline Hill and announced when the Nones would fall (thus indicating whether a month was long or short). The Nones was the day on which the festivals for the month were announced (all festivals took place between the Nones and the Kalends of the next month). The customs surrounding the Ides are less clear; it was apparently a day of ritual sacrifice (which adds to the poignancy of Julius Caesar's assassination on that day in 44 B.C.E.).

The origin of the customs surrounding the Kalends, Nones, and Ides dates to the time before the public had access to the calendar. According to Macrobius, a fifth century C.E. historian, the customs were developed while a lunar calendar was in place. A pontifex minor was assigned the task of watching for the crescent of the moon to be visible at night. When this occurred, he would inform he pontifex maximus (the most powerful religious leader of Rome) who would declare the Kalends the next day. The ceremony of declaration involved several sacrifices and a declaration of the day of the Nones. Word of when the Nones would occur was spread throughout the countryside and people traveled to Capitoline Hill for the announcement of which festivals would be celebrated during that month. The Nones occurred when the moon was at the first quarter. The sacrifice on the Ides coincided with the full moon.

These ceremonies, which served as a type of calendar for the people, would have become superfluous by the first century B.C.E. when the calendar was published openly. However, the traditions were maintained as part of the religious structure of Rome over which the pontifex maximus presided. There was also a strong political reason for the pontifex maximus to retain the official power of declaring months. Apparently even after the publication of the calendar, the pontifex maximus, as the most

powerful religious leader, had a high degree of influence on its structure. This became significant because the pontifex maximus was an elected official and could manipulate the calendar to hasten or stall elections according to his popularity (or lack thereof). Julius Caesar was able to reform the Roman calendar, not because he had become the supreme military and political leader, but because he had been elected pontifex maximus in 63 B.C.E. when he was a relatively young man.

Julian Reforms to the Republican Calendar Impact History

In 46 B.C.E., this plan was put into action: First, to reconcile the Roman year with the tropical year, 46 B.C.E. became, by decree, 445 days long. This was accomplished by lengthening most of the months and adding two extra months. Caesar declared that his year was the "last year of confusion," but his constituents preferred to call it simply the "year of confusion."

Second, 45 B.C.E. marked the first year of the new system. The date for the beginning of the New Year was moved from March 25 to January 1. January had 31 days and in regular year February had 29 days. Beginning with March, the rest of the months alternated regularly between 31 and 30 days. Every four years a second February 24 was added between the regular February 24 and February 25 as a leap day. Julius Caesar thus produced the sequence familiar to the Western civil calendar of three common years of 365 days and a leap year of 366 days. More importantly, he produced a calendar that required no intercalations, and that was therefore immune to political tampering. To commemorate this achievement, he had the month of Quinctilis renamed Julius.

Augustus Added Changes

Several years after the assassination of Julius Caesar, a misunderstanding of his leap-year rule emerged. Because of the Roman habit of counting inclusively, they began to count the fourth year of each leap-year cycle as the first year of the next one. This meant that they were adding the extra day every three years. Augustus Caesar corrected this problem between 8 B.C.E. and 8 C.E. by declaring that the leap years would be left out during this time. The Western civil calendar traces its cycle of leap-year dates to this occurrence.

Augustus also made other changes to the calendar which seem to have resulted more from pride than practicality. The month Sextilis was renamed Augustus to honor his own reform of the calendar, and he took a day from February and added it to his own month. Then, to avoid having three 31-day months in a row, he switched the lengths of September, October, November, and December. Although the switch disrupted the pattern established by Julius, it produced the sequence the Western civil calendar still maintains.

Augustus also revived many of the old Roman religious festivals. These events, however, had little meaning to the majority of Roman citizens who had not practiced them for generations. A great deal is known about how these festivals were celebrated from Ovid's *Fasti*, which gives an account of the monthly practices of the Roman people. Unfortunately, only a portion of the manuscript exists.

The Gregorian Reform

The changes Julius instituted were a vast improvement over any previous system, but they had one significant fault. The Julian calendar was based on a year of 365.25 days long, but the true solar year is 365.2422 days long. This error of 11 minutes 14 seconds per year amounted to three days every 400 years. In 45 B.C.E., when Julius Caesar established his calendar, the spring equinox fell on March 25. By 325 C.E., when the Council of Nicaea met to fix the Easter rule, the spring equinox was falling about March 21. This discrepancy had a greater impact on the dates of the Christian Movable Feasts than on agricultural or civil events.

Although the problem was noticed and considered by Church councils for 1200 years, the first action on the matter was not taken until 1545 C.E. when the Council of Trent authorized pope Paul III to investigate the problem and find a solution. After nearly forty years of investigation, a proposal was submitted to Pope Gregory XIII by a Jesuit astronomer, Christopher Clavius. In 1582, the Pope issued a papal bull (a type of official edict) instituting an adjustment based on Clavius's plan.

The Gregorian reform (named for Pope Gregory) instituted several significant changes: First, it subtracted ten days from the month of October 1582. The act of making the day following the feast of St. Francis (October 5) become October 15, affected the date of following the spring equinox, which was brought back to March 21.

Second, to bring the year closer to the true tropical year, a value of 365.2422 days was accepted. This value, which differed by 0.0078 days per year from the Julian calendar reckoning, amounted to 3.12 days every 400 years. It was therefore decided that three out of every four centennial years should be common years, and only one be a leap year. This resulted in the rule that a centennial year is a leap year only if it is divisible by 400. Therefore 1700, 1800, and 1900 do not count as leap years, but the year 2000 does.

Third, the Gregorian reform set January 1 as the beginning of the New Year, which in Britain was different from the old system where December 25 was commonly recognized as the beginning of the new year. The Gregorian calendar, therefore, gained the title "New Style" as opposed to the Julian "Old Style."

Gregorian Reform and Determining the Date of Easter

Prior to the Gregorian reforms, a medieval system known as golden numbers was used to determine dates for full moons and provide a date for the Christian celebration of Easter. At the time of the Gregorian reforms, however, the golden numbers system was rejected because it was astronomically inaccurate. The actual full moon could appear up to two days before or after the golden numbers indicated. (For a more complete discussion of golden numbers see the calendar section in Chapter 7). Once again, the Church looked to Clavius and Lilius, whose calculations lay behind the Gregorian reform, for a more accurate system to calculate the date of Easter.

Lilius used a method, termed the epact, that was already being used informally under the Julian calendar. The epact, which is derived from the Greek work meaning "to intercalate," is a system of numbers used to determine the age of the stage of the moon on the first day of the year.

The informal epact system was not completely accurate though, because it was based on the Metonic cycle, like the golden number system. This cycle occupied a period of 6,939.75 days, whereas to be accurate for the Moon, it should have lasted for 6,939.9 days. Although the difference is small—it amounts to one day in about 307 years—the New Moon would occur one day earlier than the epact table indicated after this time period.

Lunar and Solar Corrections Are Made

When the Gregorian calendar was adopted, the discrepancies in the epact system were taken into account. A correction (known as the lunar correction) was introduced which adjusted the age of the Moon, making it one day later on specific centennial years in a 2,500-year cycle. Seven of these adjustments were made, one every 300 years and an eighth time after a subsequent 400 years.

To keep the system of epacts in step with the other changes instituted by the Gregorian reforms, Clavius proposed another correction—a solar correction. The Gregorian calendar omitted most centennial leap years to accommodate the more accurate length of the year. Clavius's plan maintained that in ordinary centennial years, the number of the epact should be reduced by one. These two corrections kept the lunar and solar cycles in harmony with one another in relation to the date of Easter.

The epact system facilitated long-range planning more effectively than the previous system of golden numbers. It simplified the method of determining the dates of new and full moons throughout the year. Also, since the dates of full and new moons could be determined into infinity, the date of Easter could also be calculated to the same extent.

Religious Differences Slow the Spread of the Gregorian Calendar

Adoption of the Gregorian reforms seems to have been greatly based on religious similarities and differences. Roman Catholic countries carried out the reform promptly, but the Orthodox Christian countries did not. The disagreement is not over the facts of astronomy, but over community identity: the Eastern Orthodox Church seems to prefer to celebrate Easter on a date different from that chosen by Roman Catholics, in order to emphasize its independence from Rome. There was also resistance to the changes in Protestant countries since the calendar revision was proposed in the wake of the Reformation.

France, Italy, Luxembourg, Portugal, and Spain adopted the New Style calendar in 1582, and most of the German Roman Catholic states, as well as Belgium and part of the Netherlands, adopted it by 1584. In Switzerland, the change took place over 229 years, between 1583 and 1812. In 1587, Hungary was the last country to adopt the New Style before a break of more than one hundred years after which Protestant nations began to accept the system. The first of these to adopt the New Style were Denmark and the Dutch and German Protestant states in 1699–1700. The Germans, however, maintained their tradition of determining Easter through the use of the Tabulae Rudolphinae (Rudolphine Tables), astronomical tables based on the 16th century observations of Tycho Brahe. They adopted the Gregorian calendar rules for Easter in 1776.

From the mid-eighteenth century on, a steady stream of countries embraced the New Style. In 1752, Britain and the colonies adopted the New Style, with Sweden following in 1753. In 1740, however, the Swedes had taken on the German Protestant astronomical methods for calculating Easter; they did not accept the Gregorian calendar rules for this practice until 1844. When Alaska became part of the United States in 1867, it adopted the New Style. Japan converted in 1873 and Egypt in 1875. Between 1912 and 1917, there was a flurry of activity which resulted in its acceptance by Albania, Bulgaria, China, Estonia, Latvia, Lithuania, Romania, Turkey, and the former Yugoslavia. Russia embraced the New Style in 1918 immediately after the Revolution. Greece was the last major country to accept the calendar, doing so in 1923.

Confusion in Britain

When the switch to the New Style was made in Britain, the discrepancy between the Old and New Styles had accrued to 11 days. The difference was corrected in 1752 by a declaration that the day following September 2 of that year would be September 14. The legislators were faced with an unexpected response as many British citizens took to the streets demanding, "give us back our 11 days." The protest was not easily quelled even thought the declaration had been passed with careful consideration given to make sure no one would suffer financial or other penalties.

Many British people continued to celebrate their holidays Old Style well into the nineteenth century a practice revealing the deep emotional resistance to calendar reform. Even today, in western Ireland, the Celtic harvest festival of Lughnasad is celebrated more or less Old Style on the Sunday nearest August 13. George Washington, who was born on February 11, continued to celebrate his birthday Old Style after the calendar reform by moving it to February 22.

CHAPTER 4

Calendar Reform Since the Mid-Eighteenth Century

Moving toward a Secular Calendar

Beginning with European Enlightenment in the seventeenth century, cries were made to separate the calendar from the Catholic Church, a complicated proposition because, in most cases, the church was the authority with jurisdiction over the calendar. Early reform movements involved simply changing the names of elements already on the calendar with the goal of bringing it more into the secular realm. For example, the Catholic Church dedicated several days of the year to various saints. A proposal made in 1772 suggested that the names of these days be changed so that war heroes would be remembered instead. A 1788 a calendar was published giving honor to many different people who had benefited society.

The French Republican Calendar

Shortly before the French Revolution, calls for the secularization of the calendar also began to be heard in France. The first rumblings for reform came in 1785 and 1788. The storming of the Bastille in July 1789 intensified the demands, and support swelled for the notion of a new calendar which would start from "the first year of liberty."

In 1793 the National Convention took notice of the demands and appointed Charles-Gilbert Romme, president of the committee of public instruction, to develop a new system. He delegated the technical matters to two eminent mathematicians, Joseph-Louis Lagrange and Gaspard Monge, and gave Fabre d'Eglantine the responsibility of renaming the months. Their proposal was submitted to the convention in September 1793. The delegates immediately ratified the new calendar which became the official system on October 5, 1793.

The new calendar, known as the French Republican Calendar, was retroactive to September 22, 1792, the day the Republic was proclaimed. (September 22 also happened to coincide with the autumnal equinox in 1792.) September 22 was declared the New Year of the Republican calendar which had, in total, 365 days. The months were divided into twelve 30-day periods with five extra days added to the end of the year (September 17 through 22 in the Gregorian calendar). The extra days were to be used for vacations and festivals in celebration and honor of virtue, genius, labor, opinion, and rewards. In a leap year the additional day was to be added to this period and was celebrated as the festival of the Revolution. Leap years continued to be inserted every four years, but the first leap year was inserted one year early so the Republican and Gregorian cycles would not coincide. Each four-year period was known as a Franciade.

The seven-day week was replaced with a ten day period called a decade. Each month, therefore, contained three decades, the tenth day of which was the rest day. The day was reorganized into portions divisible by ten, but this was too great a change for the whole society to adopt and was abandoned because of popular disapproval.

Fabre d'Eglantine renamed the months according to the meteorological characteristics of the periods. Table 4.1 lists the names and approximate Gregorian calendar dates.

The appeal of the French Republican Calendar was limited to France. By September 1805, because of international standards, the Republican calendar had fallen into almost complete disuse. On January 1, 1806, the Gregorian calendar replaced the French Republican system as the official calendar of France.

The Positivist Calendar

The Positivist Calendar (*"Calendrier positiviste"*) was published by Auguste Comte in 1849. It featured a year of 13 months, each of which was named after a person—some religious and others secular—who had been a positive influence in human history. Each month contained 28 days. These were ordered in four seven-day weeks. Because the months contained only full weeks, each date within the month always occurred on the same day of the week. For example, the 1st, 8th, 15th, and 22nd were always on Mondays, and the 4th, 11th, 18th, and 25th were always on Thursdays.

The resulting year contained 52 weeks for a total of 364 days. In a manner similar to the month names, each day and each week was dedicated to a person of positive influence, or in some cases, more than one person.

In order to match his calendar to the 365 day solar cycle, Comte simply added one extra day to the year that was not a part of any week or month. The extra day was dedicated to women and the remembrance of the dead. During a leap year, two such days were added.

Comte's calendar as never widely adopted, but it helped generate ideas that were used by later calendar reformers.

Twentieth-Century Reform Proposals

In the 1930s, the former Soviet Union made a brief attempt at calendar reform. By shortening the week to five days and giving workers a random day off within the week, the factories could operate continually which would, in theory, increase production. This experiment failed, however, because the social structure could not bear the stress of this change.

The two other prominent twentieth-century proposals for calendar reform have been the International Fixed Calendar and the World Calendar. Both of these calendars recognize that the current Western civil calendar is sufficient astronomically, however, they offer slightly modified designs which would make its arrangement more convenient.

The International Fixed Calendar

The International Fixed Calendar is divided into thirteen 28-day months, with one day added to the end of the year. All of the present month names remain the same with the thirteenth month, named Sol, added between June and July. The extra day follows December 28, and is not included in any month or in any week. Leap day is treated in the same way and intercalated every four

Table 4.1. French Republican Calendar

French Month	English Translation	Approximate Gregorian Dates
Vendémiaire	Vintage	September 22–October 21
Brumaire	Mist	October 22–November 20
Frimaire	Frost	November 21–December 20
Nivôse	Snow	December 21–January 19
Pluviôse	Rain	January 20–February 18
Ventôse	Wind	February 19–March 20
Germinal	Seed–time	March 21–April 19
Floréal	Blossom	April 20–May 19
Prairial	Meadow	May 20–June 18
Messidor	Harvest	June 19–July 18
Thermidor	Heat	July 19–August 17
Fructidor	Fruits	August 18–September 16

years after June 28. In this calendar, every month contains exactly four weeks, beginning on Sunday and ending on Saturday. (The Tree Calendar currently used by some Pagans follows a similar pattern.) The main criticism of the International Fixed Calendar is that it does not divide into four equal quarters and is therefore inconvenient for business purposes.

World Calendar

To answer the major criticism of the International Fixed Calendar, the World Calendar was devised. Its four quarters are composed of 91 days each, with an additional day at the end of the year. Each quarter is divided into three months: the first month has 31 days and the second and third have 30 days each. The extra day and leap day are treated in the same manner as in the International Fixed Calendar, following December 30 and June 30, respectively.

Critics of this system argue that it is no better than the current Gregorian system because each month extends over part of a fifth week, and each month within a given quarter begins on a different day. Each of the four quarters is identical to the others, however, so a three-month calendar could represent the entire year.

Calendars in a New Millenium

At the beginning of the twenty-first century, dozens of calendar reform proposals were being advocated by various individuals and groups. Many of them incorporated features intended to make the accounting of days more standard from month to month. The following three proposals illustrate some of the concerns reformers sought to address.

The Global Calendar

The Global Calendar, advocated by Miklos Lente of Toronto, Canada, incorporates 13 identical months of 28 days (similar to Comte's Positivist Calendar and the International Fixed Calendar). The 12 month names currently used in the Gregorian calendar would be retained and the thirteenth month, to be called Midi, would be added in the middle of the year. Because this scheme accounts for only 364 days, an extra day that is not counted in any month or week—New Year's Day, which would be called January 0—is added. During leap years, which would occur every four years, two extra days would be added at the end of the year.

The Long-Sabbath Calendar

The Long-Sabbath Calendar was developed by Richard McCarty of North Carolina's East Carolina University. McCarty noted that proposals to maintain a correlation between the date and the day of the week, required the use of a day, or days, outside the normal counting scheme. This practice was inconsistent with the needs of religious groups who observed a holy day on every seventh day. The Long-Sabbath Calendar incorporated plans for extending the length of the Jewish Sabbath at the end of the year—on a Saturday—and the length of the next day (Sunday) to 36 hours each so that the two days would cover a time span of 72 hours. To accommodate leap years, every four years an additional Saturday and Sunday at the end of February would be similarly stretched.

The 60-Week Calendar

The 60-Week Calendar, developed by Ricardo Arturo Espinoza Reyes, a student in Mexico, divides the year into 12 months of 30 days. Each month consists of five six-day weeks, so the individual days of the month always fall on the same day of the week. To keep the calendar calibrated to the solar year, five out-of-calendar days are added: one at the beginning of the year, and one in each of the four seasons. A sixth out-of-calendar day is added in the summer during leap years.

Other Proposals

Many other proposals incorporate similar ideas in different ways. For example, a calendar with twelve 30-day months and a five-day out-of-calendar period at the end of the year; calendars that accrue days until leap months are added; calendars with months of differing lengths that repeat in predictable patterns, and calendars based on 5-day or 10-day weeks. Other proposals incorporate different ideas, such as defining months based on the zodiac, eliminating the concept of weeks, and even redefining how time itself is measured.

Although many of these systems seem to be more convenient that the Gregorian calendar because of their streamlined detail, none has gained wide-spread support. The problem with introducing reforms to the world community lies in the fact that the calendar has traditionally carried and continues to carry deep religious and cultural significance. Thus, the success of any calendar reform will depend on its adaptability to the many different traditions and religious expressions of the modern world.

PART TWO

Calendars and Holidays for Religious Groups

CHAPTER 5

Judaism

Overview of Judaism

What Is Judaism?

Judaism is one of the oldest, continuously observed religions in the world. Its history extends back beyond the advent of the written word. Its people trace their roots to a common ancestor, Abraham, and then back even farther to the very moment of creation.

Throughout history Jewish beliefs and practices have changed and varying expressions of faith within the Jewish community have arisen, but its core belief—the belief that separates Jewish faith from the faiths of other religions—has remained unchanged. This belief is characterized by faith in a specific creator God and by an individual and community attempt to live a life of holiness.

According to Jewish belief, the law given to the Jewish people by God contained everything they needed to live a holy life, including the ability to be reinterpreted in new historical situations. Judaism, therefore, is the expression of the Jewish people, attempting to live holy (set apart) lives in accordance with the instructions given by God.

The Relationship between God and the Jewish People

The Jewish people believe in one God, the creator of the world. The Shema, an expression of Jewish belief, states: "Hear, O Israel, the Lord is our God, the Lord is One."

The Jewish people believe they have a unique, distinct relationship with this God, but not an exclusive one. Other people can have the same type of relationship if they accept the teachings, practice the rituals, and adhere to certain ethical requirements. Communication with God is accomplished through prayer and meditation.

The Jews await the coming of a Messiah who will usher in God's kingdom.

Authorities and Sacred Writings

Although obedience to the Law is central to Judaism, there is no one central authority. Sources of divine authority are God, the Torah, interpretations of the Torah by respected teachers, and tradition. Religious observances and the study of Jewish Law are conducted under the supervision of a teacher called a Rabbi.

The Torah

The Hebrew Bible contains 24 books—a collection of writings that were compiled over a time period of about 1,000 years. They provide revelation from God to the Jewish people. It is the main source for all other teachings. The first five books are attributed to Moses, who received the Law from God. These five books are called the Pentateuch and the scrolls upon which they are written are called the Torah. The word Torah is also sometimes used to refer to the entire body of Jewish scared writings and tradition.

The Torah and its interpretations provide explanations of how to live a life that will bring the follower near to God. Its edicts are binding. All aspects of life are governed by the Torah; rules not specifically stated in the writing are inferred and interpreted by sages.

The Mishnah and Talmud

The Mishnah is a collection of rabbinic teachings covering a wide range of human endeavor including: agriculture, giving, holy day observances, rituals, family law, civil and criminal law, and moral teachings. The writings were compiled during the first and second centuries C.E. The Mishnah, in its final form, was adopted around the year 200 C.E.

The Mishnah is the first part of the Talmud. The Talmud contains further reflections on the Mishnah. Although there are two Talmuds, the Jerusalem Talmud and the Babylonian Talmud, the Babylonian Talmud is the one with the greater status. It was prepared during the fourth and fifth centuries C.E.

History of Judaism

In the Beginning

Jewish history begins at the beginning: with the creation of the world by a sovereign Creator God, and the Jewish people claim an unbroken heritage from that time through the succeeding ages. According to their beliefs, the unfolding of history is not merely a chain of episodes, but the playing out of a relationship between the Creator and his Creation.

The relationship between God and Creation became fractured when people, using the free will they had been given, disobeyed God's instructions. This disobedience opened the way for death and pain to enter the human experience. The eventual salvation and reunification between the world and God will come when people once again realize that they must accept the teachings about the God of the Jews.

A Chosen People

According to Jewish thought, God's way was originally open to all the people of the earth. Only after they had rejected him, did he turn to a specific group—the Jews. God entered into a covenant with the Jews for the purpose of demonstrating himself to the world. For this reason, the Jews are known as a "chosen people." They were chosen by God to be an example to the world. If the Jewish nation disobeyed God they would be punished; if the nation repented and obeyed God, they would be rewarded with grace and hope. The first people identified specifically with the faith that is now known as Judaism were Abraham, Isaac, and Jacob. These ancients are called the Patriarchs.

Abraham, known to the Jews as the father of their faith, entered the land of Canaan, later called Palestine, sometime around 1800 B.C.E. According to the Biblical account, Abraham left Mesopotamia, the land of his father, in response to God's call. God promised Abraham that he would become the father of a special, chosen nation. Circumcision was established as a sign of the covenant between the people and God.

Moses

Later, Abraham's descendants, called the Hebrew people, moved to Egypt during a time of famine. Although originally welcomed into the land, they subsequently became slaves. This period in Jewish history—when they were "strangers" in a foreign land—gave rise to the custom of practicing hospitality. It also set the stage for one of the central themes in Jewish thought—deliverance.

Escape from Egypt was accomplished under the leadership of Moses. The Exodus, or leaving, occurred around 1250 B.C.E. Following the Hebrew people's departure, Moses received the Law from God in an encounter on Mount Sinai. This receiving of the Law by Moses is the most significant event in Jewish history because it represents the receiving of divine revelation and the reestablishment of the covenant between God and his chosen people.

Although the Ten Commandments are perhaps the best known part of the Jewish Law, the total Law consisted of much more than these edicts. It included 613 commandments (248 things to do and 365 things to not do). In their totality and as they are interpreted, the Jews believe that the laws express God's will. They believe they have a duty to God and a duty to their fellow humans to obey them. Obedience results in peace. Disobedience brings strife and exile.

After receiving the Law, the Jewish people began settling in the land of Canaan. They initially developed a tribal governing structure which evolved as their population grew, culminating in nationhood under a monarch.

Rise and Fall of the Kingdom

The first King was Saul. He was succeeded by David (1013 to 973 B.C.E.), who was in turn succeeded by his son, Solomon. Under Solomon's leadership, the First Temple in Jerusalem was constructed.

The Temple became the central focal point of the Jewish religious experience. It was a place for the communal expression of faith, for ritual sacrifices, and for the presentation of offerings. The Temple was a destination for pilgrims and the seat of religious authority.

Following Solomon's reign, however, the people strayed from their obedience to God with tragic consequences. In 722-721 B.C.E., the ten northern tribes were conquered by the Assyrians and sent into exile.

Ancient Manuscripts Led to Reforms

According to the Biblical account in II Kings 22, apparently even the most rudimentary knowledge of the rituals surrounding the festivals had been lost until, during renovations of the Temple in Jerusalem, the High Priest, Hilkiah, discovered what he claimed were ancient manuscripts of the Law of Moses. These documents reportedly detailed the ceremonies necessary for observing the ancient Hebrew holidays. Hilkiah presented the discovery to King Josiah who required that all Hebrews observe its provisions. Participation in the religious feasts and festivals of Israel was mandated by King Josiah around 621 B.C.E.

Sweeping changes were made to the religious practices of the Hebrews as a result of the reforms. These included the establishment of Passover as a national festival and the designation of Jerusalem as the only acceptable site for observing the three Hebrew pilgrimage feasts: Passover, Pentecost, and Sukkot. Also, attendance at these feasts was made mandatory for all able-bodied men in Israel; they were required to bring their tithes, or religious taxes, to the Temple on these occasions.

Babylonian Conquest

Religious reforms did not last and the Judeans (the southern Tribe descended from Judah, from whom the name "Judaism" is derived) were then conquered by Nebuchadnezzar, the King of Babylon. The Babylonians destroyed the Temple in 587–86 B.C.E., took the ruling class of Israelites captive, and deported them to Babylon where they lived in exile for fifty years.

The Jewish people, in exile and without their Temple, began to focus on seeking God's favor by returning their obedience to him. Other faith expressions, such as communal prayer and the study and interpretation of the Torah, began to rise in prominence. Some researchers have suggested that many elements of modern Judaism, such as monotheism, were formalized at this time.

Return from Exile

The restoration of Jerusalem, the temple, and the Jewish community began when the Jewish people returned to their homeland in 539 B.C.E. They were permitted to return from exile after Cyrus, King of Persia, conquered the Babylonians. The temple was rebuilt in 515 B.C.E., and under the leadership of the priest Ezra, temple rituals were re-established.

According to some historians, the time spent in exile had a significant impact on Jewish theology. Persian influences, especially those of Zoroastrianism, blended with traditional Jewish thought helping to shape ideas about good and evil and develop the role of angels.

Greeks Rise in Influence

Jewish self-rule was short-lived. The Greeks rose to power in 331 B.C.E. Antiochus IV outlawed Judaism and captured the Temple.

The Temple's importance to the Jewish nation cannot be overstated. It provided access to God. The priests in the temple performed the functions necessary for the atonement of sin and for reconciliation with God. Pilgrims came to the temple to celebrate mandated festivals. Without the Temple, it was impossible to perform many of the sacred requirements of the faith.

The Temple was recaptured in a military victory led by Judah Maccabee. It was miraculously purified and rededicated in 165 B.C.E., an historical event remembered annually during the celebration of Hanukkah.

Greek influences, however, made a lasting impact on the practice of Judaism. The Greek focus on education led to increased interest in studying the Torah and resulted in a blending of traditional law with sophisticated intellectual discourse.

This trend led to the development of a group called the Pharisees, who held a dual focus on study and piety. Pharisees were a new type of leader—not priests nor traditional holy men—but teachers who rose to positions of eminence through the study of the Torah, Jewish oral traditions, and interpretations of the Torah. Their authority increased during the first century C.E.

The Second Temple Falls

The Romans were the next rulers in Jerusalem. Under their dominion, in 70 C.E., the second Temple was destroyed. One wall remained standing. Termed the Wailing Wall, it remains—two thousand years later—a place where pilgrims converge and serves as a symbol of Jewish exile and hope.

During previous times in Hebrew history when the Jews had been deprived of their Temple and its central role in communal rites, alternate methods of practicing the faith had emerged. Following 70 C.E., Jewish practices once again refocused on different avenues of religious expression. Houses of Prayer (beit tefillah) and Houses of Study (beit midrash) emerged. A House of Prayer was a location where prayer services were conducted three times a day: morning, afternoon, and evening, coinciding with the times when sacrifices had been offered at the Temple. Houses of Study developed when masters rose up and students gathered around them. The act of studying the Torah became an act of worship.

During the latter years of the first century C.E., Rabbinic Judaism became more firmly established and rabbinical academies gained in popular acceptance. An effort to gather together the oral interpretations and teachings from rabbinic houses of study was made. The result was the production of the Mishnah which was first canonized as biblical literature in 90 C.E. The Mishnah was later also studied, interpreted, and elaborated upon.

During the fifth and sixth centuries C.E., rabbinic commentaries were consolidated to produce the Palestinian and Babylonian Talmuds. The Babylonian Talmud, which emerged as the preeminent Talmud, was edited in the fifth century but contained writings dating back to the third century B.C.E. The traditional text of the Jewish scriptures was established during the eighth and ninth centuries C.E.

Persecutions

Beginning in the fifth century C.E. the changing political situation in Israel and in Babylonian areas led to persecutions of Jews. Jewish people once again faced exile from their traditional homeland. Two centers of Jewish life emerged: The Ashkenazi Jews settled in central and eastern Europe; and the Sephardi Jews settled in Spain and the Near East. The two groups developed different traditions and languages. The Yiddish language, a mixture of Hebrew and German along with other Slavic characteristics, emerged among Ashkenazi populations. Ladino, with Hebrew, Spanish, and Provencal characteristics, developed among Shephardi groups. Despite their differences, however, both groups remained as autonomous, distinctively Jewish communities.

The Jews were often a minority group within their larger culture, and they held firmly to their unique identity. Because they were easily identified and different from the majority classes, they were also frequently subject to periodic uprisings against them. These resulted in oppression, persecutions, and executions. As political sentiments shifted, Jews were expelled from places such as England, France, Spain, and Portugal. Throughout centuries of oppression, the Jews held to their hope of being reestablished in their homeland, and the coming of the Messiah who would rule over the land in perfect peace.

A Common Identity

During the time of the exile, the Jewish calendar helped the dispersed Jewish communities celebrate their common heritage. The calendar, along with shared rituals and sacred objects, served to unite Jewish communities and provided a means for Jews to assimilate into new Jewish communities when forced to move from one place to another. The first Jewish community in the New World was founded in 1654 at New Amsterdam, New York.

During the 18th century, new social patterns brought about by the European Enlightenment affected Judaism in two ways: Non-Jewish populations influenced by liberal thinking became more tolerant, helping bring an end to oppression and persecution; and, modern thought and reform brought new ideas and new expressions into the Jewish community, transforming old theological ideas. Modern reforms led to the development of sects of Judaism resisting traditional Orthodoxy.

Returning to the Promised Land

Throughout their history, the Jewish people have been subject to exiles from their homeland. They lived in Egypt, Persia, Babylonia, and around the globe. A Jewish nationalistic movement, called Zionism, emerged during the late 19th and early 20th centuries. Its goals were to re-establish Hebrew as the Jewish language and to resettle the Jewish people in Israel.

Zionistic sentiments were heightened by renewed persecutions in Europe at the hands of the German Nazis. During the war years, an estimated six million Jews were killed. Jews began returning to Palestine in large numbers. The state of Israel was founded in 1948.

Judaism Today

A Dispersed People

An estimated 13 million Jewish people live in nearly 100 different countries around the world. The two largest Jewish communities are in the United States (more than 5 million) and Israel (4.8 million). Cities around the world with significant Jewish populations include New York, Miami, and Los Angeles in the United States; Paris, France; London, England; Moscow and St. Petersburg, Russia; Buenos Aires, Argentina; Toronto and Montreal, Canada, and Kiev, Ukraine.

The Synagogue

Jews today worship the same God honored by their forefathers. Services are held in homes and in synagogues (the word synagogue means assembly). A synagogue can be created where ten or more Jewish men live close enough to meet together for worship and study. The synagogue typically serves as the center of the Jewish community. It is a place for worship, a place for learning, and a location for social functions. The leader in a synagogue is called a rabbi. Rabbis are not priests; they are teachers or lawyers. Chazzan are people who read from the scriptures and recite prayers. Cochen are priests who are descendants from the ancient temple priests.

Architecturally, a synagogue is a square or rectangular building. It contains the Arc which is situated so that it faces Jerusalem. The Arc contains the scrolls of the Law (the Torah). A reading-desk called the bema is where the Law is read and where prayers are said.

Sects within Judaism

Orthodox

Orthodox Judaism is characterized by an affirmation of the traditional Jewish faith, strict adherence to customs such as keeping the Sabbath, participating in ceremonies and rituals, and the observance of dietary regulations.

Reform or Progressive

Reform Judaism began in Germany during the European Age of Enlightenment (18th century). As some groups of Jews sought to reconcile their traditional beliefs with modern thought and learning, they abandoned many ancient ceremonial traditions. Reform Judaism stresses modern biblical criticism and emphasizes ethical teachings more than ritualistic observance.

Rabbi Isaac Wise was a leader who brought the reforms to the United States. One of the first issues addressed on this continent was the use of English in the synagogue. Reform Jews also place a diminished emphasis on nationalistic themes.

Conservative

Conservative Judaism sought to build a middle ground between Orthodox and Reform. Conservative Jewish congregations seek to retain many ancient traditions but without the accompanying demand for strict observance. Conservative synagogues typically use both English and Hebrew and men and women sit together, however, the tradition of wearing a head covering is maintained.

Hasidism

Hasidism is a mystical sect of Judaism that teaches enthusiastic prayer as a means of communion with God. It includes an emphasis on personal experience rather than abstract study and contains components such as miracles and shamanism.

Hasidism, with roots in the Middle Ages, was revived during the 18th century in Europe under Rabbi Israel Baal Shem. The movement was organized into schools headed by a local leader called a Rebbe. Leadership passed from the Rebbe to his heir, either a son or a follower.

As a result of the persecution of Jews during World War II, many Hasidic Jews emigrated to the United States. Many are located in Brooklyn, New York.

Zionism

Zionism refers to the nationalistic movement to return the Jewish people to the land of Israel. It was begun in Europe during the late 19th century and reached its pinnacle during the years surrounding World War II and culminated in the establishment of the state of Israel in 1948. Zionistic efforts continue, typically through fund raising campaigns to support the growth of Israel. Although many Jewish people are Zionistic to some degree, there are also anti-Zionistic groups.

Reconstructionist

The Reconstructionist movement began early in the twentieth century in an effort to "reconstruct" Judaism with the community rather than the synagogue as its center. Its organizers sought to recognize the diversity within Judaism and bring all factions together into a unified religious society.

Rabbi Mordecai M. Kaplan (1881–1983) founded the movement based upon his vision of a progressive, contemporary approach to Jewish life which integrates a deep respect for traditional Judaism with the insights and ideas of contemporary social, intellectual, and spiritual life.

The Shema, an expression of Jewish belief, states: "Hear, O Israel, the Lord is our God, the Lord is One."

Figure 5.1. A shofar (ram's horn) is sounded to commemorate Abraham's willingness to obey God's command that he sacrifice his son Isaac.

◼ ◼ ◼

The Jewish Calendar

A Lunar Calendar

The Jewish calendar is based on a lunar model. This means that the phases of the moon determine when a month begins and ends. A new month begins with a new moon; the full moon occurs on the fifteenth day.

History of the Hebrew Calendar

Structural details of the ancient Hebrew calendar are fragmentary. The first written evidence of a Hebrew calendar is the Gezer Calendar, a stone carving which lists the tasks associated with the agricultural duties for each of a series of 12 yereah (from a Hebrew word indicating a lunation). Historians believe this early calendar was derived from the Canaanite cycle sometime before the establishment of the Jewish monarchy around 1050 B.C.E. References in the Old Testament to the Hebrews using Canaanite month names help to support this theory. The months that are recorded in the Hebrew scriptures (Aviv, Ziv, Etanim, and Bul) correspond to the modern Jewish months of Nisan, Iyyar, Tishri, and Heshvan.

While many technical aspects of the Hebrew calendar remain a mystery, it is known that the lunar and solar cycles were reconciled in some manner because the Passover month always occurred in a specific season. This would be impossible unless the calendar also took the solar cycle into account.

Differences between Judean and Samaritan Calendars

Conflict arose over religious reforms in the seventh century B.C.E. under King Josiah. The mandates required all able-bodied men to attend three pilgrimage feasts at the Temple in Jerusalem and there present their offerings. These decrees angered many Hebrews who lived outside the region of Judea because they had been practicing their religious ceremonies in local houses of worship for hundreds of years. The distance and inconvenience of traveling to Jerusalem caused many of these people to break away from the reform movement and worship at their traditional sites.

The splinter group, located in northern Israel, became known as the Samaritans. As a result of the break in religious practices and the ensuing conflicts that arose, the Samaritans and Israelites developed slightly different practices regarding their calendars. The custom of the Samaritans was to figure the start of the month according to the absence of a moon while the Israelites defined the "new moon" as the evening on which the crescent of the waxing moon is first visible locally. A difference of one to three days is possible between these two systems. Both groups sought to impose their method over the other; each sect felt if they embraced the other method, they would break the law and offend God. This conflict was a source of division among Jews for centuries, but the Israelite method was the one which prevailed.

Exile in Babylon Influences the Hebrew Calendar

The Babylonians conquered Jerusalem around 586 B.C.E. The Babylonian influence on the Hebrew calendar is clearly evidenced by many similar elements within both systems. Scholars surmise that the Hebrews adopted many elements of the Babylonian calendar because the Babylonian system was clearly established by the sixth century B.C.E., and there is no evidence to suggest that the Hebrew system was explicitly defined at that time.

Structurally the influence of the Babylonians on the Hebrew calendar was manifested in the adoption of the Babylonian month names, the establishment of Nisan 1 as the point from which regnal years of the king were reckoned, and the incorporation of the seven-day week. As a result of these structural changes, the Hebrew calendar became a distinct entity with well-defined rules for calculating the passage of time.

Aside from technical elements, the Babylonian and Hebrew systems have other similarities. For example, both groups employ the wedding motif in various celebrations. One of the most important Hebrew celebrations, Passover, falls at the same time as the Babylonian new year, and both occasions incorporated some similar ceremonial rites. The Hebrews adopted some Babylonian rites into their own new year which occurs in the fall. Sir James Frazer argues in his *Golden Bough* that the account of Esther and Mordecai, the story at the center of the Purim celebration, is drawn from the Babylonian legend of Ishtar and Marduk.

In any case, the Babylonian-inspired calendar was used by the Hebrews until 70 C.E. except for the period during which Alexander the Great and the Ptolemies imposed the use of the Macedonian system (322–200 B.C.E.).

Complications Resulting from the Diaspora

The Babylonian and Israelite calendars both based the beginning of the month on the sighting of the new moon. In Hebrew society, the High Priest appointed watchmen to look for the new moon. When it appeared, the watchmen would report back to the High Priest who would proclaim the beginning of a new month. The Priests took

Table 5.1. The Hebrew Lunisolar Calendar

Name of Month	Number of Days
Nisan; liturgical new year	30
Iyyar	29
Sivan	30
Tammuz	29
Av	30 (29 if both Heshvan and Kislev are full)
Elul	29
Tishri; civil new year	30
Heshvan	29 or 30
Kislev	29 or 30
Tevet	29
Shevat	30
Adar	29 (30 when Adar-Bet is added)
Adar-Bet	29 (added in leap year)

Notes:

Nisan is traditionally designated as the first month because it is when Moses led the Israelites out of Egypt.

In order to accommodate laws that forbid food preparation on the Sabbath, even in conjunction with required feasts and fasts, the first day of the seventh month, Tishri, cannot fall on a Sunday, Wednesday or Friday.

The month of Heshvan is also sometimes called Marheshvan, maning "bitter Heshvan" because it has no holidays in it.

The "leap month" Adar-Bet may also be called We-Adar or Adar Sheni meaning "second Adar."

Leap months are added in the third, sixth, eighth, eleventh, fourteenth, seventeenth, and nineteenth years of every 19-year cycle of years.

great care to confirm the accurate proclamation of a new month because Hebrew religious practices prohibit the celebration of certain holidays on particular days of the week and require a specific number of days between festivals. The first day of Rosh Hashanah (New Year), for example, cannot fall on a Sunday, Wednesday, or Friday, but must fall 163 days after Passover.

The system of observing the new moon became impractical after the destruction of the Temple in 70 C.E. and the subsequent Diaspora of the Jews (the scattering of the community into distant geographic areas). The central system for proclaiming a new month could not adequately meet the needs of a dispersed population. As an attempt to solve this problem, a messenger system was instituted whereby a series of "runners" would travel from town to town bringing official word of the new month once it had been declared in Jerusalem.

In order to circumvent the difficulties involved in notifying outlying communities of the precise sighting of a new moon, a tradition arose in which some holidays were observed for two days. This practice ensured that the holiday was celebrated on its specified day. The tradition of celebrating holidays for two days is still observed by some Jewish groups.

An Equation Determines the New Month

By 200 C.E., Hebrew priests had developed an equation to replace the sighting method of determining the beginning of months. This formula was known only by a select group of priests in Jerusalem who continued to be the official voice to proclaim the new month. At the same time, many Hebrew communities were taking the matter into their own hands by appointing their own watchmen rather than waiting for the official word. This situation caused great strife and division among the Hebrews because, once again, the start of the new month varied from region to region. This division became especially crucial on the point of the celebration of Passover.

In 358 C.E., the High Priest Hillel II recognized the potentially destructive nature of the problem and, to maintain the unity of the Hebrew people, he made the secret equation public. Hillel's decision has been hailed as one which helped preserve the Hebrew faith through ensuing periods of dire crisis. Even though individual enclaves of Jews were often completely isolated from one another, they were able to maintain a sense of unity and identity partly because of their common religious calendar and observances.

From the time of Hillel II until the present, the Hebrew calendar has evolved into one of the most intricate systems of time reckoning in existence. The calendar includes such elements as varying year lengths, varying month lengths, and leap years—all of which are designed to meet the requirements of Judaic law regarding the celebration of feasts, festivals, and holidays.

Thus, beginning with the equation made public by Hillel II, the Hebrew calendar became schematic and independent of the true New Moon. In fact, if the dates of the Hebrew calendar are compared with the dates for astronomical full and new moons, they will often differ by several days. The "new moon" is defined as the evening on which the crescent of the waxing moon is first visible locally, not as the astronomical new moon, which will always be one to three days earlier. The "full moon" is defined as the fourteenth evening after the "new moon" (first crescent), not as the astronomical full moon, which may occur up to three days earlier.

Days, Weeks, Months, and Years

The structure of the modern Jewish calendar is lunisolar with the months based on the moon and the years on the sun. The day is 24 hours long but each hour is divided into 1,080 parts each of which are approximately 3.3 seconds long. The day officially begins at 6:00 p.m., but for religious purposes, sunset is considered the beginning of a new day.

The 12 months of the Hebrew calendar alternate between 29 and 30 days. Two months, Heshvan and Kislev, have variable lengths. Months containing 30 days are known as "full" and the 29-day months are called "defective." The calendar includes an intercalary month, Adar-Bet (also sometimes called We-Adar), which is 30 days in length.

To meet the requirements of the Jewish religious law and reconcile the lunar cycle with the solar cycle, the Hebrew calendar has years ranging in length from 353 to 385 days. First, to bring the 19-year lunar cycle into harmony with the 28-year solar cycle, the intercalary month, Adar-Bet, is added in years 3, 6, 8, 11, 14, 17, and 19 of the lunar cycle. Second, to ensure that their religious regulations are fulfilled, the months of Heshvan and Kislev vacillate between 29 and 30 days. Years in which both months are full are called "complete" years (shelema). If it is a regular year, it will contain 355 days; a complete leap year (in which Adar-Bet is added) will contain 385 days. A "normal" (sedura) year is one in which Heshvan is full and Kislev is defective and will contain either 354 or 384 days. "Defective" (hasera) years, totaling 353 or 383 days, occur when both Heshvan and Kislev contain only 29 days.

There are similarities between the Hebrew calendar and the Greek Metonic cycle. The Hebrew calendar picks up a common thread with the Greek Metonic cycle for reconciling the solar and lunar cycles. Although Adar-Bet is intercalated in seven out of every 19 years like the Metonic cycle, the specific years to which the month is added is different from the most prominent of the Greek methods, the Athenian calendar. The reason for the difference in the patterns is that Adar-Bet is added whenever it is needed to push the 15th ("full moon") of Nisan after the spring, or vernal, equinox because the Passover cannot be held before the equinox.

Naming Years

The basis for naming years in the Hebrew calendar is a code indicating the characteristics of the year. The character of a year (qevi'a, literally "fixing") indicates the important technical details of the coming year. It is signified by three Hebrew letters: the first and third give the days of the weeks on which the New Year occurs and Passover begins, the second is the initial of the Hebrew word for defective, normal, or complete. There are 14 types of qevi'a, seven in common and seven in leap years. According to Hebrew scholars, the era used to number the years of the Jewish calendar (designated anno mundi or A.M.) had its epoch in the year of Creation which they believe was 3761 B.C.E.

Figure 5.2. A menorah is one of the most widely recognized traditions associated with Hanukkah. It has eight candles. The shamash is a special candle in the middle of the menorah that is used to light the others.

Table 5.2. Jewish Holiday Cycle

Nisan

10	Miriam's Yahrtzeit
14	Fast of the First Born
15–21	Passover (Pesach)
22	Maimona
16–Sivan 5	Sefira (Counting of the Omer)
27	Yom ha-Shoah

Iyyar

4	Yom ha-Zikkaron
5	Yom ha-Atzma'ut
18	Lag b-Omer (33rd Day of the Omer)
26	Yom Yerushalayim

Sivan

6	Shavuot

Tammuz

17	Seventeenth of Tammuz
17–Av 9	Three Weeks of Mourning

Av

9	Tisha be-Av

Elul

1–29	Time of Preparation

Tishri

1–2	Rosh Hashanah
1–10	10 days of Teshuva (Ten Days of Repentance)
3	Fast of Gedaliah
10	Yom Kippur
15–21	Sukkot
21	Hoshana Rabbah
22	Shemini Atzeret
23	Simhat Torah

Kislev

25–Tevet 2	Hanukkah

Tevet

10	Asarah be-Tevet

Shevat

15	Tu Bishvat

Adar (or Adar-Bet in Leap Years)

13	Ta'anit Esther
14	Purim

Jewish Holidays

Weekly Observances

Sabbath
Friday/Saturday

The word sabbath means rest.

According to Jewish tradition, when God created the world, he rested on the seventh day. The Jewish Sabbath commemorates this rest. It is observed as a day of respite from work and is often accompanied with special rituals and meals.

The Sabbath begins at sunset on Friday evening and ends on Saturday evening. Although Sabbath observances vary greatly among members of the different streams of Judaism, synagogues typically offer both evening and morning services. Conservative and Reform congregational evening services and morning services are typically attended by men and women. Orthodox evening Sabbath services are typically attended by men while the morning services are more likely to be family oriented. In the Reform movement Friday night services are often the centerpiece of Sabbath observance for the whole family. Traditional evening synagogue services are called Kabbalat Shabbat (Welcoming the Sabbath) and they are followed by a festive observance called an Oneg Shabbat (Joy of the Sabbath). The services may include prayer called Kiddush (sanctification) in which a cup of wine is symbolically raised to sanctify (set apart) the sacred day.

In many Jewish homes before the Sabbath begins money is often put aside to give to the poor. The Sabbath celebration itself begins just before sunset when the woman lights the Sabbath candles and recites prayers for God's blessing on her and her family. Although tradition assigns this duty of lighting the candles to the woman of the house, candles must be lit by men when no women are present. Candles are lit before sunset because Jewish law forbids the kindling of fire on the Sabbath. Some observant families extend the prohibition against kindling fire to include the turning on of electric lights or the operation of electric appliances during the Sabbath. Traditional Jewish families light the Sabbath candles 18 minutes prior to sunset. Jewish calendars and many newspapers publish exact times for every Sabbath of the year. Although there is no maximum number of candles, there must be a minimum of two. In Sephardic Jewish communities, candles are frequently lit in honor of deceased family members.

The Sabbath dinner is an evening meal eaten in the home with all family members present. Families may also invite others to partake of the Sabbath dinner with them in honor of the Jewish tradition of hospitality. The meal is accompanied by many symbolic items including a white table cloth, two loaves of challah (traditional braided bread), and a cup of wine. As the meal begins, the man of the house chants praises and recites a blessing (Kiddush) over the cup of wine and the bread and then serves his family. The evening may also include the singing of traditional songs.

Saturday morning synagogue services typically begin with blessings, hymns, and psalms and the barchu (call to worship). The Shema, a traditional formulaic prayer affirming the oneness of God, is recited and a specific portion of the Torah is read. In some U.S. Jewish synagogues the Torah is read entirely in Hebrew, in others Hebrew and English are mixed. A commentary or discussion may follow the reading.

Saturday lunch is also special, beginning with blessings over wine and bread and foods not cooked on the Sabbath. The afternoon of rest is adhered to with varying strictness among the different streams of Jews.

The Sabbath ends after sunset, which is officially declared when three stars are visible. If it is cloudy, the Sabbath ends when it is no longer possible to tell the difference between a blue thread and a white thread held at arm's length. The ceremony marking the end of the Sabbath is called Havdalah (or Habdalah) which means "Separation," and it signifies the separation between the Sabbath and the rest of the week. Havdalah may be observed in the synagogue or home. The ceremony includes the lighting of a special taper and benedictions recited over wine, sweet spices, and the flame.

Annually

Nisan (March/April)

Preparation for Passover
Nisan 10

Nisan is the first month of the Jewish calendar. Months are counted beginning in the spring despite the fact that the Jewish New Year begins in Tishri, the seventh month. This peculiarity is thought to have occurred due to the adoption of the Babylonian calendar system during the time of the exiles. In addition, the Bible describes "Aviv" (or Abib), the Biblical name for Nisan and the modern Hebrew term for Spring, as the first month. Official preparations for Passover (see Nisan 15) begin on Nisan 10.

Miriam's Yahrzeit
Nisan 10

Miriam was the sister of Moses. Shortly after her brother's birth, Miriam courageously helped to keep him alive against Pharaoh orders. Following the basket where Moses was hidden, Miriam was near-by when the pharaoh's daughter found him. Boldly stepping forward Miriam arranged for his care.

As a prophetess, Miriam aided Moses in leading the Hebrews into freedom. After God delivered them from the Egyptians at the Red Sea, she led a victory dance.

On Nisan 10, she is honored in an observance called Miriam's Yahrzeit. A special candle lit in remembrance of a loved one is called a Yahrzeit.

Fast of the First-born
Nisan 14

The Fast of the First-born is practiced symbolically by firstborn males on the day before Passover. The fast appears to serve as a reminder of how the firstborn sons of the ancient Hebrews were miraculously spared while the Egyptians lost their firstborn sons to the Angel of Death. The obligation to fast may be avoided by participating in a síyyum—the study of a particular passage of the Talmud.

Passover (Pesach)
Nisan 15-21 (or 22)

Passover, or Pesach, is the Hebrew celebration of spring and of the deliverance from slavery in Egypt. It is also known as the Feast of Unleavened Bread.

According to the account in the book of Exodus, when Pharaoh refused to let Moses lead the Hebrews from Egypt to the Promised Land, God sent ten plagues on the Egyptians, including locusts, cattle disease, and hailstones. Pharaoh, however, refused to yield. The tenth plague was the visitation of the Angel of Death who was sent to kill the first-born sons of the Egyptians (see Fast of the First-born, Nisan 14). Hebrew families were instructed to sacrifice a lamb and place its blood on the doorposts of their homes as a signal to the Angel to "pass over" their sons. When the Egyptians discovered what had happened, they ordered the Israelites to leave the country immediately.

The observance of Passover was one of three pilgrimage festivals established by the Deuteronomic reform in 621 B.C.E (the other two are Shavuot and Sukkot). Before the reform, Passover had been celebrated by families in their homes. The Deuteronomic laws, however, required that the lamb for the Passover meal be sacrificed only at the temple in Jerusalem. This provision mandated that all Hebrew people had to come to Jerusalem for these festivals.

In Hebrew the three pilgrimage feasts are called the shalosh regalim or "three (foot) pilgrimages" because all adult males over the age of thirteen traditionally made a pilgrimage to Jerusalem for the celebration of those festivals. After the destruction of the Temple in Jerusalem in 70 C.E., the law requiring a central celebration of the festivals became impossible to fulfill. The holidays continued to be celebrated with local observances.

The rabbis restored the Passover to its former status as a family festival celebrated at home. Uncertainties of the ancient calendar, however, led to the custom of celebrating the Passover for eight days outside of Jerusalem during the period of the Second Temple. Orthodox and Conservative Jews living outside of Israel have retained this custom. In contrast, Reform and many Reconstructionist Jews have reverted to the original seven-day dating.

With the reestablishment of Israel as a nation, the pilgrimage aspect of the festivals has experienced a revival. For many, the culmination of a trip to Israel is to pray at the wall. It is often a joyous experience providing an opporunity to connect deeply and positively to the Jewish historial experience.

The heart of the Passover celebration, however, remains a family-oriented traditional liturgy known as the Seder, which indicates the order of services. The Seder is among the most universally observed elements of Judaism, even among those who do not practice most traditional Jewish concepts. The Seder includes a customary meal which consists of symbolic foods such as a "pascal lamb," bitter herbs, and wine. Matza, a flat, unleavened bread, represents the hurry in which the Israelites left Egypt—they did not have time to let their bread rise.

The Seder dinner is traditionally conducted on Passover eve with the entire family. (For Conservative and Orthodox Jews in the Diaspora it is observed on the second evening as well.) It is both a meal and a worship ceremony. The Haggadah is a worship book used during the Seder. The word Haggadah means "retelling" and it recounts partly in question and answer form the story of the Jewish emancipation from slavery in Egypt.

The symbolic foods present at the Seder meal are: a roasted shank bone (symbolizing the passover lamb); a roasted egg (representing the festival sacrifice); bitter herbs (typically horseradish, to recall the bitterness of slavery); haroset (an apple-nut mixture that symbolizes making bricks without straw); parsley dipped into salt water (symbolizing renewal); matza (representing the unleavened bread prepared when the Jews left Egypt in a hurry); and, four cups of wine (representing the fourfold promise of redemption). The cup of Elijah, placed in the middle of the table symbolizes hospitality and the hoped-for arrival of the messianic age of peace and harmony. A pillow or cushion on the leader's chair represents freedom.

The matza plays a role in a traditional Passover game. During the meal one piece of the three matzas is broken in half, and one half is set aside until the end of the meal. This half is called the Afikomen. The children take the Afikomen, hide it, and do not give it back until the leader gives a gift or promises to give a gift.

Although Passover is celebrated primarily in the home, it is also observed in the synagogue. During Passover services, additional psalms and prayers are usually read. Also, in some congregations, Passover marks the time when a traditional prayer for rain recited during the fall and winter months is replaced with a prayer for dew.

Sefirah (Counting of the Omer)
Nisan 16–Sivan 5

Sefirah is the season between Passover and Shavuot. It is a period lasting 50 days. In the home and in the traditional synagogue liturgy, a custom of announcing the "counting of the omer" is observed by counting the number of days. An omer is a sheaf of wheat, and the festival has its origins in practice of bringing offerings to the Temple (see Shavuot).

Although the season is not observed by all modern Jews, Sefirah was held in greater esteem during the Middle Ages. It was kept as a period of abstinence and repentance during which the Jewish people remembered historical massacres of their ancestors, particularly those that occurred in 134–35 C.E. under the reign of the Roman Emperor Hadrian and during the Crusades between 1095 and 1270 C.E. By tradition, weddings and other celebrations were not held during parts of Sefirah.

Maimona (Maimuna)
Day after Passover (Nisan 22)

Jews in North Africa commemorate the philosopher and rabbi, Moses Maimonides, on the evening of the last day of Passover and the day that follows. Since the news of Maimonides's death in 1204 reached many Jews during Passover, they were not able to mourn his passing, as custom would normally dictate, by eating bread and an egg. So they postponed it until the following day.

Yom ha-Shoah
Nisan 27

This solemn occasion is observed by Jews as the "Day of the Holocaust." It commemorates the mass killing of six million Jews by the Nazis during World War II. People of many faiths also mourn on this day in remembrance of Jewish victims along with the other six million people who were exterminated in Nazi death camps during the same period.

Observance of Yom ha-Shoah focuses on the fact that this catastrophe shocked and impoverished all mankind. It is dedicated to the hope that human beings will never forget the horror of the Holocaust and that they will assure that it never happens again.

In Israel on Yom ha-Shoah public entertainment is closed and a three-minute siren blast is sounded. In the United States, observances often include civic ceremonies and the teaching of history. Synagogue services may include special readings from Lamentations or Psalms. Typically such services are solemn with a quiet, somber atmosphere. Memorial candles are frequently lit as part of the service.

Iyyar

Yom ha-Zikkaron (Remembrance Day)
Iyyar 4

Yom ha-Zikkaron is primarily observed by Jews living in the state of Israel. It is a day set aside to honor the memory of those who died fighting for Israel's independence and continued existence.

Yom ha-Atzma'ut (Day of Independence)
Iyyar 5

Yom ha-Atzma'ut, the day on which Israel became a sovereign nation (May 15, 1948), is celebrated primarily in secular fashion with public gatherings, parades, singing of traditional music, and dancing. Frequently collections are also taken to support the state of Israel.

Lag ba-Omer (33rd Day of the Omer)
Iyyar 18

On the thirty-third day of Sefirah, restrictions relating to abstinence and repentance were relaxed for one day. Some authorities believe that this exception was created to accommodate rejoicing over the cessation of a plague among the Jews in the second century C.E. It is also possible that this celebration combines Hebrew traditions with an ancient pagan festival day, featuring customs much like those of May Day.

Yom Yerushalayim (Jerusalem Day)
Iyyar 26

Yom Yerushalayim commemorates the capture of Jerusalem during the Six Day War in 1967. The Six Day War was an important part of the struggle between Israel and the nation's Arab neighbors.

Sivan

Shavuot (Shabuoth; Pentecost; Feast of Weeks)
Sivan 6

Shavuot, or the Feast of Weeks, occurs fifty days after Passover and is the second of the three pilgrimage festivals (the other two are Passover and Sukkot.) This festival, which is also called Pentecost from the Greek word for "fiftieth," marks the end of the barley harvest and the beginning of the wheat harvest.

Historically, all adult Hebrew males were required to bring their first omer (or sheaf) of barley to the Temple in Jerusalem on this day as an offering of thanksgiving for the harvest.

When Moses led the nation of Israel out of slavery in Egypt, Shavuot gained a new name: the Festival of the Giving of the Law. It is on this day that Jews celebrate Moses's descent from Mt. Sinai with the Ten Commandments given to him by God. In the homes of Orthodox and Conservative Jews, Shavuot is celebrated for two days, but Reform Jews celebrate only one day.

During Shavuot it is customary to read from the book of Ruth in the synagogue. Other customs include decorating with plants and flowers. For some, Shavuot is also a time when young people who have come of age are accepted into the synagogue as full members.

Tammuz

Fast of the Seventeenth of Tammuz (Shivah Asar be-Tammuz)
Tammuz 17

The seventeenth day of Tammuz is one of the traditional days of fasting in the Jewish calendar. The purpose of the fast is to mourn over Jerusalem.

The fast is observed by from daybreak to sunset. It begins a three-week season of mourning in which restrictions, such as abstaining from pleasure, are observed until after the fast of Tisha be-Av.

Three Weeks of Mourning
Tammuz 17–Av 9

The three-week period between the Fast of the Seventeenth of Tammuz and the Ninth of Av is a time of mourning for the Jewish people because it is associated with the destruction of the Temple in Jerusalem. As the days draw closer to the ninth of Av, the signs of mourning increase in severity. Although there are differences between Ashkenazi (Jews with Northern and Eastern

European ancestory) and Sephardic (Jews from the Iberian peninsula) customs, the restrictions include not shaving or cutting one's hair, not wearing new clothes, and not eating fruit for the first time in season. Beginning with the first day of Av, the Ashkenazi custom is not to eat any meat nor drink any wine until after Tisha be-Av, while Sephardim refrain from meat and wine beginning with the Sunday preceding the Ninth of Av. On Tisha be-Av itself, it is not permitted to eat or drink, to wear leather shoes, to anoint with oil, to wash (except where required), or to engage in sexual relations.

Av

Tisha be-Av
Av 9

Tisha be-Av is one of four traditional days of fasting in the Jewish calendar associated with the destructions of Jerusalem (see also Fast of Gedaliah—Tishri 3, Asarah be-Tevet—Tevet 10, and Seventeenth of Tammuz—Tammuz 17).

The ninth day of the month Av marks the date on which both the First and the Second Temples were destroyed, in 586 B.C.E. and 70 C.E. It also commemorates the fall of Judea to the Romans after the Bar Kochba rebellion in 135 C.E. and marks the Jewish expulsion from Spain in 1492.

Traditionally the three week period prior to the Tisha be-Av is a time when weddings and celebrations are not held.

The fast of Tisha be-Av is observed with fasting and mourning from evening to evening. When Tisha be-Av falls on the day after the Sabbath, the Havdalah ceremony concluding the Sabbath observance is modified to include only one blessing over light. Other traditional Sabbath blessings are omitted or said at the conclusion of the fast of Tisha be-Av. In the synagogue, services are somber and the Torah may be draped in black. Readings are customarily taken from the book of Lamentations.

Although the fast is observed by some groups of Jews, it is less popular among others. One reason suggested to explain the lessening of interest in this commemoration is that grief over the destruction of the Temple is waning among modern Jews in favor of grief over the Holocaust. Others suggest that because Tisha be-Av focused on grief in exile, the day should be re-focused toward hope that the Messiah will come now that the nation of Israel has been established. According to legendary belief, the Messiah will be born on Tisha be-Av.

Elul

Elul
Elul 1–29

The month of Elul is observed as a time of preparation; preparing for the High Holy Days beginning with Rosh Hashanah on Tishri 1. The season is observed with prayers called Selichoth (asking for forgiveness of sin) and with the blowing of a Shofar (Ram's horn).

Tishri

Rosh Hashanah (Feast of Trumpets)
Tishri 1–2

Although Tishri is the seventh month in the Jewish calendar, Tishri 1 marks the beginning of the Jewish New Year. Rosh Hashanah starts a ten-day period of introspection, prayer, and penitence which culminates with the observance of Yom Kippur, or the Day of Atonement.

During the liturgy on Rosh Hashanah, the story of Abraham is read in the synagogue and the ram's horn or shofar is sounded to commemorate Abraham's willingness to obey God's command that he sacrifice his son Isaac. God honored Abraham's obedience by providing a ram for the sacrifice instead. The shofar also serves to symbolize the individual's need to experience spiritual awakening and renewal.

Special food is prepared for the New Year celebration, including round loaves of challah bread to symbolize the continuity of life and apples dipped in honey representing sweetness and health. Another tradition associated with Rosh Hashanah is the buying of new clothes, symbolizing new beginnings.

Ten Days of Teshuva (Ten Days of Repentance)
The ten days between Rosh Hashanah and Yom Kippur

The Hebrew word for this time period, "teshuva," means returning. It is a season set apart as a time for reflection, introspection and repentance. Custom dictates that people apologize to one another for wrongs they have committed. The Sabbath that falls during Teshuva is called Shabbat Shuvah.

Fast of Gedaliah (Tsom Gedalyah; Tzom Gedaliahu)
Tishri 3 (the first day following Rosh Hashanah)

In 586 B.C.E., the Babylonian King Nebuchadnezzar destroyed Jerusalem and its first Temple. He enslaved most of the city's Hebrew inhabitants, but allowed a number of farmers and their families to remain in Jerusalem

Table 5.3. Alphabetical List of Jewish Holidays

Holiday	Date(s)
Asarah be-Tevet	Tevet 10
Bi-Shevat *see* Tu Bishvat	
Chanukah *see* Hanukkah	
Counting of the Omer *see* Sefirah	
Day of Atonement *see* Yom Kippur	
Day of Independence *see* Yom ha-Atzma'ut	
Elul	Elul 1–29
Fast of Esther *see* Ta'anit Esther	
Fast of Gedaliah	Tishri 3
Fast of the First-born	Nisan 14
Fast of the Seventeenth of Tammuz	Tammuz 17
Feast of Dedication *see* Hanukkah	
Feast of Lots *see* Purim	
Feast of Rejoicing over the Law *see* Simhat Torah	
Feast of Tabernacles *see* Sukkot	
Feast of the Asmoneans *see* Hanukkah	
Feast of the Assembly (or Solemn Assembly) *see* Shemini Atzeret	
Feast of Trumpets *see* Rosh Hashanah	
Feast of Weeks *see* Shavuot	
Festival of Lights *see* Hanukkah	
Hamishah Asar Bishvat *see* Tu Bishvat	
Hanukkah	Kislev 25–Tevet 2
Hoshana Rabbah	Tishri 21
Jerusalem Day	*see* Yom Yerushalayim
Lag ba-Omer	Iyyar 18
Maimona	Day after Passover (Nisan 22)
Maimuna *see* Maimona	
Miriam's Yahrzeit	Nisan 10
New Year for Trees *see* Tu Bishvat	

Holiday	Date(s)
Passover	Nisan 15–21 (or 22)
Pentecost *see* Shavuot	
Pesach *see* Passover	
Preparation for Passover	Nisan 10
Purim	Adar 14 (or Adar-Bet 14 in leap years)
Remembrance Day *see* Yom ha-Zikkaron	
Rosh Hashanah	Tishri 1–2
Sabbath of Rabbi Isaac Mayer Wise	Last Sabbath in the month of March
Sefirah	Nisan 16–Sivan 5
Shabuoth *see* Shavuot	
Shavuot	Sivan 6
Shemini Atzeret	Tishri 22
Shivah Asar be-Tammuz *see* Fast of the Seventeenth of Tammuz	
Simhat Torah	Tishri 23
Sukkot	Tishri 15-21
Ta'anit Esther	Adar 13 (or Adar-Bet 13 in leap years)
Ten Days of Repentance *see* Ten Days of Teshuva	
Ten Days of Teshuva	The ten days between Rosh Hashanah and Yom Kippur
Tenth of Tevet *see* Asarah be-Tevet	
Thirty-third Day of the Omer *see* Lag ba-Omer	
Three Weeks of Mourning	Tammuz 17–Av 9
Tisha be-Av	Av 9
Tsom Gedalyah *see* Fast of Gedaliah	
Tu Bishvat	Shevat 15
Tzom Gedaliahu *see* Fast of Gedaliah	
Yom ha-Atzma'ut	Iyyar 5
Yom ha-Shoah	Nisan 27
Yom ha-Zikkaron	Iyyar 4
Yom Kippur	Tishri 10
Yom Yerushalayim	Iyyar 26

under the supervision of a Hebrew governor named Gedaliah ben Ahikam. Eventually those people who had fled to the hills during Nebuchadnezzar's attack returned to Jerusalem, and joined the farmers who had been left behind.

Distrustful of Gedaliah, some members of the community accused him of traitorous collaboration and assassinated him, along with the small garrison of soldiers Nebuchadnezzar had left stationed in Jerusalem. Subsequently, many of the farmers fled with their families to Egypt; those who remained behind were either killed or taken to Babylon.

These events triggered Judah's final collapse. The Jewish Fast of Gedaliah commemorates the tragic consequences of Gedaliah's assassination. This fast is observed from sunrise to sunset and is marked with additions in the synagogue liturgy.

Yom Kippur (Day of Atonement)
Tishri 10

Yom Kippur, the Jewish "Day of Atonement" is the holiest day of the Jewish year. Also known as Yom Tov (Day of Goodness), it is observed by strict fasting and ceremonial repentance.

The meal eaten prior to the beginning of the fast does not include the traditional blessings. Special candles may be lit in memory of close family members who have died.

The synagogue services on the eve of Yom Kippur are traditionally called the Kol Nidre services. The term Kol Nidre refers to a specific prayer which begins with the Hebrew words for "all vows." In the prayer, the people renounce all thoughtless vows they may have made during the preceding year and forgive all wrongs done to them. According to Jewish belief, only then will God forgive them for their violations of his laws. In the Middle Ages, it was understood that the Kol Nidre prayer was a renunciation of any vows a Jew had been forced to make under threats of violence or death. This prayer, therefore, allowed Jews to renounce forced conversions to Christianity and to continue to be accepted as Jews by the Jewish community. The tone of the Kol Nidre service is somber, penitential, and confessional.

The fast of Yom Kippur is observed with varying degrees of strictness among American Jews. Some may abstain from all food and water until after sunset; others may observe modified fasts. Children, pregnant and nursing mothers, and people in ill-health do not fast. Some families cover their table with a white cloth until the day is over.

Other traditions associated with Yom Kippur include wearing prayer shawls or other distinctive dress, attending all-day prayer services, and sharing a break-the-fast

meal with family and friends. One special garment sometimes worn by men is a white robe called a kittel. In some traditions, the kittel is typically received by men on their wedding day, and it is worn on Yom Kippur, during the Passover meal, and at the time of death it is worn as a shroud.

Sukkot (Feast of Tabernacles)
Tishri 15-21

Sukkot (also known as Sukkoth and Succoth) was one of three pilgrimage feasts established by the Deuteronomic reform in 621 B.C.E. It is also called the Feast of Tabernacles, Booths, or the Ingathering. Like the other pilgrimages, Sukkot was a celebration of the harvest. In later times it came to be a commemoration of the wandering of the Israelites in the wilderness where they lived in tent-like booths.

One traditional way Jewish families observe Sukkot is to build small booths or tabernacles and eat in them during the week-long festival. A booth is called a sukkah. Some families begin the preparation for Sukkot by driving the first nail of their sukkah as soon as Yom Kippur ends and before the fast is broken. Many congregations build a sukkah outside the synagogue. Reform Jews may construct centerpieces for their tables that represent the huts used by their ancestors during the years of nomadic wandering.

The booths are built of materials that are not intended to be permanent. This impermanence symbolizes the shortness of human life and man's dependence on God. According to rabbinic laws, the roof must be constructed in a way that permits rain to penetrate and so that those inside can see the starlight. These things serve to remind the people that God is over all. During the festival, the booths are decorated with produce. Jews are invited to visit a sukkah and have a meal in it.

Synagogue services are typically held on the first or first and second days of Sukkot. During the ceremony it is traditional to wave a LuLav, which is a palm branch bound together with a specified number of willow and myrtle branches. It is typically used with an Etrog (citron) and waved in six directions (the four compass points and up and down) at special times during the service as an act of rejoicing. This action symbolizes the belief that God is everywhere. By tradition, the Sukkot service also includes prayers for rain.

Hoshana Rabbah
Tishri 21

The seventh day of Sukkot, Hoshana Rabbah, has a special significance. As an extension of the Day of Atonement, it is the last possible day for people to seek and attain forgiveness for the sins of the previous year. On this day, the ceremony in the synagogue differs from that of the other six days of the Sukkot festival. The service reflects a blending of the harvest celebration with the religious significance of the day. Mankind's dependence on rain is emphasized through symbolic rituals, and a solemn liturgy for repentance from the sins of the previous year is conducted.

Shemini Atzeret (Feast of the Assembly or Solemn Assembly)
Tishri 22

Shemini Atzeret, the eighth day of assembly, comes at the end of Sukkot. It is celebrated in some synagogues with a special service during which the scroll of Ecclesiastes is read. Occasionally Shemini Atzeret and Simhat Torah celebrations are combined and called Atzeret HaTorah (Assembly of the Torah).

Simhat Torah (Feast of Rejoicing over the Law)
Tishri 23

The ninth day of the Sukkot festival cycle, Simhat Torah, has been celebrated since the Middle Ages. It was established as a day to celebrate the reading of the Law.

Simhat Torah celebrations may include synagogue services in which the Torah scrolls are removed from the ark and carried in a procession marked by wedding imagery, candles, and flags. Readings include the last portion of Deuteronomy and the first portion of Genesis. Celebrants consider it a special privilege to read one of the passages. The person who reads the last section is called Chazan Torah, or Bridegroom of the Law; the person who reads the first section of Genesis is termed, Chazan Bereshit or Bridegroom of Genesis. In Conservative synagogues in which women are called to the Torah, the special honor of concluding the Torah may be either Chazan or Kallah Torah (Bride of the Torah) and the one who begins the Torah may be either Chazan or Kallah Bereshit – Bride of Genesis. Special blessings on the children in the congregation may also be part of the service.

Kislev

Hanukkah (Chanukah; Festival of Lights; Feast of Dedication; Feast of the Asmoneans)
Kislev 25 to Tevet 2

Hanukkah is the Jewish Festival of Lights, celebrated for eight days, starting on the twenty-fifth day of Kislev. It commemorates the Maccabean recapture and rededication of the temple in Jerusalem in 165 B.C.E.

The story comes from the First and Second Books of the Maccabees. Antiochus IV, king of Syria, had forbidden Jews to practice their religion, and the temple was desecrated. Faithful Jews fled to the mountains. Under the leadership of Judah Maccabee they retook the town and temple. After military victory was achieved, they wanted to rededicate and purify the temple. The rededication ceremony required light for eight days, but only enough oil remained to kindle the necessary light for one day. The miracle of Hanukkah is that oil burned for the required eight days.

The celebration of Hanukkah is not commanded in Hebrew scriptures, as is the observance of many other Jewish holidays. It is, however, observed in synagogues with special readings and praise songs. Central themes of the service are liberty and freedom.

The best-known custom associated with Hanukkah is the lighting of the eight-candle menorah. The shamash is a special candle in the middle of the menorah that is used to light the others. One new candle is lit each night from right to left so that the light grows throughout the festival. As the candles are lit, family members praise God and say a prayer. The menorah is traditionally placed in a window so that passersby can see it.

Other Hanukkah traditions include eating latkes (potato pancakes), parties, games, and dances. In one popular game, the dredl game, children spin a dredl (a top-like toy) in a contest to win coins or candies.

Many Jewish families in the United States have adopted the practice of gift-giving during the eight-days of Hanukkah. It is supposed that this is a practice borrowed from the Christian celebration of Christmas.

Tevet

Asarah be-Tevet (Tenth of Tevet)
Tevet 10

One of four traditional days of fasting for Jerusalem is observed on the Asarah be-Tevet (the other three are the Fast of Gedaliah, Tishri 3; the Seventeenth of Tammuz, Tammuz 17; and Tisha be-Av, Av 9). The fast on the tenth day of the month Tevet remembers the beginning of the siege of Jerusalem by the Army of Nebuchadnezzar.

Shevat

Tu Bishvat (Bi-Shevat; Hamishah Asar Bishvat; the New Year for Trees)
Fifteenth day of Shevat

The New Year for Trees is a minor Hebrew festival which is somewhat analogous to Arbor Day in the United

States. The earliest reference to this holiday appeared late in the Second Temple period, at which time it was the final date for levying the tithe on the produce of fruit trees.

The practice of honoring trees is important because according to tradition, in ancient Palestine fathers planted trees when children were born; cedar for boys and cypress for girls. A child's tree grew during his or her childhood and was then cut down to make posts for the wedding canopy.

The observance of Tu Bishvat was given renewed emphasis in the 1940s with the return of Jewish colonists to Israel, the former Palestine. A massive reforestation program was undertaken by the settlers to reclaim barren land. It became customary to plant a tree for each newborn child—a cedar for a boy and a cypress or pine for a girl.

Today, Israeli children celebrate Tu Bishvat by planting trees and participating in traditional outdoor games. In other countries, the festival features the consumption of fruits from trees that grow in the Jewish homeland, such as oranges, figs, dates, pomegranates, and especially almonds—the first tree to bloom in Israel's spring.

Adar/Adar-Bet

Ta'anit Esther (Fast of Esther)
Adar 13 (or Adar-Bet 13 in leap years)

This fast is observed in commemoration of Queen Esther's fast during the plot to slaughter the Persian Jews during the reign of Ahasuerus (Xerxes I). See Purim.

Purim (Feast of Lots)
Adar 14 (or Adar-Bet 14 in leap years)

Purim is a joyful occasion to celebrate the deliverance of the Hebrews from an evil plot to exterminate them, which was put forward by an advisor to the Persian King, Ahasuerus (Xerxes I). Haman, who hated the Jews but had a particular bile toward a man named Mordecai, selected the execution day by means of purim, or casting lots. Unbeknownst to King Ahasuerus or Haman, Ahasuerus's wife Queen Esther was Jewish, and Mordecai was her cousin. Esther prayed and fasted, and then she appealed to her husband to stop Haman's plans. Ahasuerus responded to his wife's plea and had Haman executed instead.

The Book of Esther is read in the synagogue on Purim, and it is a tradition to give the children noisemakers with which they try to drown out the name of Haman whenever it is read. During Purim celebrations, Esther is not read from the typical holy scrolls but from a special parchment scroll called the Megillah. Other customs associated with Purim include carnivals, parties, costumes, dances and a special three-cornered pastry called hamantash.

From this holiday, other Purim have followed. Many Jewish communities observe their own festivals commemorating their deliverance from harrowing circumstances. For example, the Padua Purim celebrated on Sivan 11 honors the Jews' deliverance from a terrible fire in 1795. The Hitler Purim observed in Casablanca on Kislev 2 remembers the escape of the city from German domination in World War II.

Sabbath of Rabbi Isaac Mayer Wise
Last Sabbath in the month of March

Each year, on a date that varies in the Jewish calendar, adherents to Reform Judaism honor both the birth and death of Rabbi Isaac Mayer Wise (1819-1900). In 1873, Rabbi Wise organized a few scattered liberal congregations into what has become the Union of American Hebrew Congregations. In 1875, he founded the Hebrew Union Seminary, and in 1879 he founded the Central Conference of American Rabbis.

CHAPTER 6

Zoroastrianism

Overview of Zoroastrianism

What Is Zoroastrianism?

Zoroastrianism is a monotheistic religion named after the prophet, Zarathushtra, who is also sometimes called Zoroaster (the Greek version of the name). It is based on a belief in one god, known in the Avesta language as Ahura Mazda (or in the Pahlavi language as Ohrmazd). The names mean "Wise Lord". The religion is also known by the term Mazdayasna, which refers to the worship of Mazda.

Zoroastrians believe that entire universe, was created and is controlled by Ahura Mazda through the immutable law of Asha. This law refers to the principles of truth, justice, and righteousness that govern existence. It is understood in the same manner as descriptive physical laws (such as the law of gravity) rather than as an edict or decree. Asha embodies scientific laws, the functioning of reality, and natural consequences.

The teachings of Zarathushtra emphasizes that there are two mental aspects. These are described as Twins called Spenta Mainyu and Angra Mainyu. They mutually revealed themselves in thoughts, words, and deeds. The choosing of Spenta Mainyu—the Progressive or Holy Mentality—leads to a life of Righteousness. The other mentality—Angra Mainyu—is the choice of the deceit and it leads to a worthless way of life. Zoroastrians are confident that the choice of Spenta Mainyu will eventually prevail.

The values that humans should follow in life emanate from Ahura Mazda. They are known as Amesha Spentas (Bounteous Immortals). Some Zarathushtis understand the Amesha Spentas in an anthropomorphized role, somewhat similar to that of archangels. Others see them as more like attributes of Ahura Mazda that humans should emulate.

The battle between good and evil that forms the framework for human history in Zoroastrian understanding can either be understood as a struggle that takes place within the human mind or as a struggle that takes place in the physical world.

According to later (younger) Avestan literature, earthly history exists within a 12,000 year period which is subdivided into four sections of three thousand years each. The first period begins with spiritual creation of Menog. It is the perfect creation, absolute in purity, in righteousness, in unconditional love and compassion totally undefilable. The second period marks the creation of the perfect physical state of Getig, that is then afflicted with evil. The third period is the mix of struggle between the good and the evil. The final period begins when the prophet experiences revelation, and it culminates in the arrival of the three saviors, one in each millennium of the final three-thousand year period.

Fire in Zoroastrianism is a central icon and the focal point of acts of worship. Fire signifies the incarnation of Ahura Mazda in the physical world. Worship in front of the fire is worship to the Wise Lord, Ahura Mazda and not the worship of fire. Fire is, therefore, the presence of the God in all acts of worship.

The Relationship between God and the Zoroastrian People

Zoroastrians believe that Ahura Mazda created people with bodies and souls. They further believe that he gave them freedom of choice to think and express their thoughts in words and actions. To emulate Ahura Mazda, is to transform evil to good. The three cardinal virtues are: good thoughts, good words, and good deeds.

Zoroastrianism teaches that each person lives one life, a concept that differs sharply from the reincarnation beliefs of their neighbors in India. During a person's life, the outcome of his or her moral struggle will determine his or her destiny. Judgment occurs upon death. Righteous people pass over the Chinwad (also spelled Chinvat) Bridge, enter into the "best existence," to be one with Ahura Mazda. The deceitful will fall into the "worst existence" where they will endure suffering. Both good and evil people, however, will be resurrected and purified at the end of time.

The Zoroastrian faith is propagated by marriage and childbirth. Traditional Zoroastrians eschew intermarriage with people of different faiths and do not practice a policy of attempting to convert people to their faith. Zoroastrians believe that moral teachings of all religions are the same; therefore, converting from one faith to another is folly.

Sacred Writings

Avesta

Zoroastrian scriptures originated in the language known as Avesta. The words of the prophet are enshrined the 17 poetic hymns called the *Gathas*. They were orally transmitted for centuries, until they were committed to writing in third century C.E. Avesta, the ancient Persian language, is closely related to Sanskrit. The Avestan texts are made up of various books written at different times in the history of the religion, and recorded oral traditions that were centuries old when they were compiled. The canon of 21 volumes (called nasks) as it exists today was established between the fourth and sixth centuries C.E. during the ancient Persia's Sasanian era. The collection is called the Avesta (using the word for the language).

Three of the most important parts of the Avesta are the Yasna, the Yashts, and the Vendidad. The Yasna (which means "Act of Worship") has as its central core a set of seventeen hymns known as the Gathas which are ascribed to Zoroaster. The Yashts, meaning "Hymns of Praise", consists of litanies written in praise lesser divinities (Yazatas). The Vendidad (which means "Law against Demons") contains myths and laws to assist people in their struggle against evil and maintain purity of mind and body.

The most ancient parts of the Avesta are considered Old Avesta. Others form a body of writing that is referred to as the Late or Young Avesta.

Commentaries

The Pahlavi texts are another important source of Zoroastrian writings. They were compiled during the ninth century C.E. and include commentaries, translations, glossaries, and explanations of doctrines. Individual books include: *Dinkerd* (The acts of the religion),

Bundahishn (Book of Primordial Creation), *Dadestan-e-Dinig* (Opinions of the religion) and others that cover topics such as wisdom, cosmology, and eschatology.

History

The founder of the Zoroastrian religion was the prophet Zoroaster, as he is commonly called in Western countries. Zoroaster is the Greek form of the Persian name Zarathustra. (The Parsi form of his name is Zarthosht.)

Historical details of Zoroaster's life are few. According to tradition, he lived in northeastern Iran in the vicinity of Aral sea around 1700–1500 B.C.E. Some accounts place him much earlier between 8000 and 9000 B.C.E.

According to Younger Avestan mythology, the world was created by the god Ahura Mazda and that the first

---

Table 6.1. The Seven Amesha Spentas

Vohuman (variants: Vohu Mano or Vohu Manah)
  attribute or virtue: Good Mind; Good Thought
  presides over: animals

Ardwahist (variants: Asha or Asha Vahishta)
  attribute or virtue: Righteousness; Best Truth
  presides over: fire and energy

Shahrewar (variants: Kshathra or Khshathra Vairya)
  attribute or virtue: Sovereignty; Desirable Dominion
  presides over: metals and minerals

Spandarmard (variants: Armaiti or Spenta Armaiti)
  attribute or virtue: Beneficent Devotion
  presides over: earth and land

Hordad (variants: Hauvatat or Haurvatat)
  attribute or virtue: Welfare; Wholeness
  presides over: the waters

Amurdad (variants: Ameretat or Amerdad)
  attribute or virtue: Immortality
  presides over: plants

Spenamino (variant: Spenta Mainyu)
  attribute or virtue: Creative Energy
  presides over: mankind

man Gayomard (or Gayo Maretan) lived in an era unblemished by evil. Death, disease, hunger, and other types of corruption were caused by the hostile actions of Angra Mainyu, a spiritual being who killed Gayomard. From Gayomard's body, the first human couple sprang into existence. Mankind lived for a while during a Golden Age in a homeland that was lost due to climatic changes. These changes forced its inhabitants, the Aryans, to migrate. After the migration and under the influence of Angra Mainyu, polytheistic beliefs evolved. It was Zoroaster's radically innovative message that established the world's primal monotheistic religion.

At the age of 30 and through his spiritual consciousness, Zoroaster realized Divine revelations. He admonished people to accept Ahura Mazda as the One True God and to renounce other gods and spirits that promoted evil thinking. In addition, Zoroaster advocated a settled, agrarian life over nomadic existence, and he opposed the practice of offering blood sacrifices.

At first Zoroaster did not win many converts. After an 11-year period of without success, he moved eastward and reached the kingdom of Kay Vishtasp. With the king's support and help of the sages of the court Zoroaster's message began to spread.

Zoroastrianism flourished and waned in concert with the success of the Persian Empire. Its two peaks occurred during the Achaemenid dynasty (559 B.C.E. to 330 B.C.E.) and the Sasanian dynasty (226 C.E. to 651 C.E.).

During the early Achaemenid period, Cyrus (Avestan, Kurush), expanded the Persian Kingdom. In 539 B.C.E. he conquered Babylon. Jews who had previously been held captive by the Babylonians, were permitted to return to their homeland in Jerusalem under Cyrus's decree. Some scholars theorize that the contact between the Jews and the Zoroastrians at this time introduced many Zoroastrian notions, into Judaism and subsequently into Christianity and Islam. Among the doctrines with a basis in Zoroastrianism are: the notion of a struggle between forces of good and evil; the expectant waiting for a savior to be born of a virgin; the ultimate victory of good; the destruction of evil, and a final resurrection with complete renovation of the world.

By the time of Darius I (c. 522–486 B.C.E.), Zoroaster's teachings and influence had extended throughout the entire Persian empire, and Ahura Mazda was proclaimed to be the god of the Persians. Darius I was succeeded by Xerxes who ruled during the mid-fifth century B.C.E. and was later followed by Artaxerxes II (c. 402–359 B.C.E.). Militarily, the tide turned and the Persian Empire began to decline until it fell to the Greeks under Alexander the Great in 331 B.C.E.

Zoroastrianism experienced a revival during the Persian Sasanian dynasty (226–651 C.E.). In the formative years of the new Persian era, the high priests Tansar and Kerder were influential in reviving Zoroastrianism and promoting it. The faith was made the official religion of the empire. The resurgence of the faith lasted until the middle of the seventh century when Persian lands fell to Muslim rule. Although Zoroastrians were initially tolerated, the combined pressures of political and economic factors led many Zoroastrians to either convert to Islam or flee. Many of those who left their traditional homeland moved to India and settled in the area around the modern city of Bombay. Those who remained behind lived in small communities in the rural districts of Yazd and Kerman in Iran.

Figure 6.1. Fire is the central image in Zoroastrian worship. It represents Ahura Mazda. Zoroastrian worship is conducted in a fire temple. An Atash Behram contains the highest grade of consecrated fire. An Atash Adaran is a temple containing a middle grade of consecrated fire. It may be built where ten or more Zoroastrian families live and come together for worship.

Zoroastrianism Today

Today the two main population centers of Zoroastrianism continue to be in the vicinity of Bombay, India and in Yazd, Iran. Smaller communities, however, exist all over the world including Canada, the United States, England and other parts of Europe, Australia, and Sri Lanka. The total number of Zoroastrians is uncertain, but many estimates indicate that there are between 150,000–180,000 followers of the faith worldwide.

Worship

Zoroastrian worship is conducted in a fire temple. There are three grades of fire temples: An Atash Behram contains the highest grade of consecrated fire. There are eight of these in India. They were built between the 11th and 19th centuries. The oldest Atash Behram contains a fire that has been burning continuously for more than 700 years. An Atash Adaran is a temple containing a middle grade of consecrated fire. It may be built where ten or more Zoroastrian families live and come together for worship. The lowest grade of consecrated fire is called an Atash Dadgah. It is the hearth fire of a Zoroastrian household.

Zoroastrian rituals include actions, words, and objects that are intended to symbolically represent spiritual realities. The three important Zoroastrian prayers are called Ahuna Vairya, Ashem Vohu, and Yenhe Hatam. These are in the ancient Avestan language and have come down from the time of the prophet.

Important rites in the lives of Zoroastrians, include initiation rites, marriage rituals, purification rites, and funeral rites. In addition to personal observances, the Zoroastrian year includes a number of regular holidays. These include a set of six seasonal High festivals, called Gahambars, that are celebrated to honor the six Creations: sky, water, earth, plants, animals, and man.

Several different types of rituals serve different purposes and can be performed in different settings. The Yasna is a high inner liturgy, that can be performed only in a fire temple by priests who have been ritually prepared. The name for the ceremony is taken from the name of the sacred book from which the text for the service is recited. The ceremony serves as a symbolic sacrifice of Haoma, a plant believed to bestow long life to the one in whose name it is performed. In the ritual, the plant is pounded and its juice is extracted. The resulting liquid is sipped by the performer.

Another type of Zoroastrian ritual is the Jashan. A Jashan ceremony can be performed in a fire temple, meetinghouse, hall, or private home. Typically it is conducted by two priests, but it can be done by one or by a lay person. The Jashan requires the use of symbolic elements and specific prayers or manthras. A manthra is a text from the sacred writings that is recited in the Avestan language to invoke upon the divinity.

The seven Amesha Spentas are represented in the ceremony:

- Vohuman, who presides over animals, is represented by milk.

- Ardwahist, who presides over fire and energy, is represented by the ceremonial fire.

- Shahrewar, who presides over metals and minerals, is represented by the consecrated implements used to tend the fire.

- Spandarmad, who presides over earth and land, is represented by the place in which the ceremony is held.

- Hordad, who presides over the waters, is represented by a container of water.

- Amurdad, who presides over plants, is represented by fruit and flowers.

- Ahura Mazda, who presides over mankind, is represented by the people conducting the ceremony.

During the Jashan ceremony the specific portions of the sacred writings that are recited will vary depending on the time of day, the ceremony, and the occasion.

At specific points during the prescribed prayers, the priests conducting the ceremony perform a ritual of placing and exchanging flowers. The ceremony also includes prayers of praise for the particular divinity, that is propitiated. A Jashan ceremony concludes with a benediction and the sharing of foods, such as the fruits and nuts used in the ceremony.

Sects

Although there are no "denominations" in Zoroastrianism, there are differences in how the faith is practiced. These differences fall along a wide spectrum of beliefs between traditional and reform interpretations. Some of the doctrines under dispute include: the practice of disposing of dead bodies by Dakhma-nashini (corpse destruction by flesh eating birds); segregating women during their menstrual cycles; prohibiting non-Zoroastrians from entering Fire Temples; wearing the Sudreah/Kushti (a sacred garment given to an individual at their initiation into the Zoroastrian faith); and reciting prayers in the original language (vs. reciting them in translation). Zoroastrian ritual practices also differ based on which version of the Zoroastrian calendar they follow.

⊠ ⊠ ⊠

The Zoroastrian Calendars

The ancient Zoroastrian calendar was lunisolar, based on the Babylonian calendar. It was adopted during the early Achaemenid dynasty (559 B.C.E. to 330 B.C.E.). The calendar consisted of 12 months, each comprising 30 days. A 13th month was intercalated every six years to keep the calendar aligned with the solar year. Each of the 12 months was dedicated to a lesser divinity (Yazatas) and each day in the cycle of 30 days was likewise dedicated. Days on which the month name and day name coincided were held in special honor.

During the later Achaemenian period the calendar was revised. Instead of adding a 13th month every six years, five days were added to the end of the year, making for a total of 365 days. Each of the last five days were dedicated to a Gatha (prophetic utterances of Zoroaster). Because a year of 365 days did not coincide exactly with the solar year of 365.24 days, a plan to intercalate a 13th month every 120 years was adopted. The year the last Sasanian King, Yazdegard III ascended to the throne, 631 C.E., serves as the epoch (year 1) of the calendar.

During the tenth century C.E., some Zoroastrians from Islamic Iran fled to India and some remained in Iran. The two communities lost contact with each other. In subsequent years the practice of intercalating a 13th month every 120 years was inconsistently applied in the separate communities; however, both groups ultimately abandoned the practice. Without the intercalation, the days for specific observances progressed through the seasons, moving back 30 days every 120 years.

During the early eighteenth century, contact between the Parsi community in India and the Iranian Zoroastrians was reestablished and a discrepancy between their calendars was discovered: the Parsi calendar was one month behind the Iranian calendar. Some people, under the assumption that the Iranian calendar was more accurate, adopted it and called it the Qadimi (ancient ones) calendar. Others, holding firm to their own tradition, called their calendar the Shahanshahi calendar.

Under both the Qadimi (an alternate Parsi spelling is "Kadmi") and Shahanshahi (an alternate Parsi spelling is "Shenshai") calendars, the ceremonial days continued to recede through the seasons of the year. Early in the twentieth century, a reform was proposed to re-align the calendars with the seasons, and to fix the new year on the spring equinox. Proponents of the new calendar

Figure 6.2. The Farohar is a common Zoroastrian symbol. The meanings ascribed its components are interpreted differently among various groups.

hoped it would unite the Zoroastrians and establish a single time-keeping system. The proposed calendar was called the Fasli (seasonal) calendar.

The Fasli calendar, following the Gregorian model, adds one day every four years. This practice kept it aligned with the solar year and maintained the seasonal ties between the natural year and Zoroastrian feasts and festivals. It met with mixed success. Some Zoroastrians embraced it as a way to ensure that holidays were observed on the "right" day; others could not adjust to it. Rather than unite the Zoroastrians under one common calendar, the Fasli calendar became a third time-keeping system.

The three Zoroastrian calendars, Shahanshahi, Qadimi, and Fasli are all made up of the same twelve 30-day months with five Gatha days at the end of the twelfth month. The differences lie in the fact that the first two have no intercalation, while the Fasli is intercalated to be in consonance with the natural solar year. As a result, a single date on a Zoroastrian calendar has three equivalent days on the Gregorian calendar. For example, in 2003 C.E. the first day of the first month (Frawardin 1) fell on March 21 according to the Fasli calendar; it fell on July 21 according to the Qadimi calendar; and on August 21 according to the Shahanshahi calendar.

Table 6.2. The Zoroastrian Calendars

Number of Month	Month Names*	Alternate Spelling*	Approximate English Meaning
1st	Frawardin	Fravardin	Humanity
2nd	Ardwahisht	Ardibehest	Truth and Righteousness
3rd	Hordad	Khordad	Perfection
4th	Tir	Tir	Sirius (Dog Star)
5th	Amurdad	Amardad	Immortality
6th	Shahrewar	Shehrevar	Benevolent Dominion
7th	Mihr	Meher	Fair-dealing
8th	Aban	Avan	Water (Purity)
9th	Adar	Adar	Fire
10th	Dae	Dae	Creator
11th	Vohuman	Bahman	Good Mind
12th	Spendarmard	Aspandarmard	Holy Devotion

Days of the Month	Day Names*	Alternate Spelling	Approximate English Meaning
(the first section focuses on the divine attributes of Ahura Mazda)			
1st	Ohrmazd	Hormazd	Wisdom
2nd	Vohuman	Bahman	Good Mind
3rd	Ardwahist	Ardibehest	Truth and Righteousness
4th	Shahrewar	Shehrevar	Benevolent Dominion
5th	Spandarmard	Asfandarmard	Holy Devotion
6th	Hordad	Khordad	Perfection
7th	Amurdad	Amardad	Immortality

Table 6.2. The Zoroastrian Calendars, continued

Days of the Month	Day Names*	Alternate Spelling*	Approximate English Meaning
(the second section focuses on qualities of light)			
8th	Dae-pa-Adar	Daepadar	God's Day before Adar
9th	Adar		Fire
10th	Aban	Avan	Water (Purity)
11th	Khwarshed	Khorshed	Sun
12th	Mah	Mohor	Moon
13th	Tir	Tishtar	Sirius (Dog Star)
14th	Goshorun	Gosh	Cow (sentient life)
(the third section focuses on moral qualities)			
15th	Dae-pa-Mihr	Daepmeher	God's Day before Mihr
16th	Mihr	Meher	Fair-dealing
17th	Srosh		Harkening
18th	Rashn	Rashne	Justice
19th	Frawardin	Fravardin	Humanity
20th	Warharan	Behram	Victory
21st	Ram		Joy
22nd	Wad	Govad	Healthy Atmosphere
(the fourth section focuses on religious ideas)			
23rd	Dae-pa-Den	Daepdin	God's Day before Den
24th	Den	Din	Inner Consciousness
25th	Ard	Ashishvangh	Blessings
26th	Ashtad		Virtue of Truth
27th	Asman		Sky and Shinning Universe
28th	Zam	Zamyad	Earth or Height
29th	Mahraspand	Mahrespand	Holy Word
30th	Anagran	Aneran	Endless Light

Five intercalary days at the end of the year are named for the five Gathas (Songs of Zoroaster):

1st	Ahunawad	Ahunavad	
2nd	Ushtawad	Ushtavad	
3rd	Spentomad	Spentomad	
4th	Vohukhshathra	Vohukhshathra	
5th	Vahishtoist	Vahishtoist	

*Month and day name spellings are based on transliterations from the Pahlavi language; alternate spellings are based on Persian forms.

⊞ ⊞ ⊞

Zoroastrian Holidays

Daily

Private daily prayers include purification of the body, reciting specified prayers, observing physical gestures, and the ritual tying on of Kushti on a ceremonial garment called a Sudreh—a garment that is invested on, during the initiation ceremony. Tradition mandates that this prayer cycle be done five times a day during different Gahs (day-time watches) but many modern Zoroastrians perform them only twice a day or select to perform the rituals on specified days. Among more liberal Zoroastrians, the custom of wearing the Sudreh-kushti has been abandoned.

Table 6.3. The Five Gahs (day-time watches)

First Watch: Ushahin (midnight to sunrise)

Second Watch: Hawan (sunrise to noon)

Third Watch from Frawardin 3 (Ardwahist) until Mihr 30 (Anagran): Rapithwin (noon to 3:00 p.m.)

Third Watch from Aban 1 (Ohrmazd) until Frawardin 2 (Vohuman): Second Hawan— (noon to 3:00 p.m.)

Fourth Watch: Uzerin (3:00 p.m. to sunset)

Fifth Watch: Aiwisruthrem (sunset to midnight)

Annually
Frawardin

Nawruz (NoRuz; Nu Roz; Jamshedi Navroz, Pateti)
Frawardin 1 (Ohrmazd)

Gregorian Equivalents for dates between March 21, 2004 and February 2008: Fasli—March 21; Shahanshahi—August 20; Qadimi—July 20

Nawruz, or the Zoroastrian New Year festival, is known by several names including Jamshedi Navroz. It is also observed as Pateti, the Day of Atonement, according to the Younger Avesta. Zoroastrians who follow the Fasli calendar claim that the vernal equinox is the rightful day for beginning the new year. For other groups who observe the Shahanshahi and Qadimi calendars, the first day of the year recedes through the seasons, moving back 1 day every 4 years (or 30 days every 120 years).

For all Zoroastrians, this festival serves as a bridge between the old and new year and the day emphasizes the themes of renewal, hope, and joy. A festive atmosphere prevails as adherents visit fire temples and offer prayers and sandalwood, seeking atonement for any misdeeds committed knowingly or unknowingly. They exchange greetings, good wishes, visits, and presents. It is also a day of charity, so Zoroastrians give food, money, and clothes to the sick, needy, and poor.

Hordad Sal (Khordad Sal)
Frawardin 6 (Hordad)

Gregorian calendar equivalents for dates between March 21, 2004 and February 2008: Fasli—March 26; Shahanshahi—August 25; Qadimi—July 25

Hordad Sal is a celebration of the Prophet Zoroaster's birthday. It is typically observed with a Jashan ceremony.

Feast of Frawardignan
Frawardin 19 (Frawardin)

Gregorian equivalents for dates between March 21, 2004 and February 2008: Fasli—April 8; Shahanshahi—September 7; Qadimi—August 8

The Feast of Frawardignan is the day on which the month name coincides with that of the day. Although most other month and day names refer to spiritual beings, Frawardin honors the spirits of people who are living, dead, and not yet born. On Frawardignan a special Jashan ceremony is performed in memory of people from the community who have died.

Ardwahist

Feast of Ardwahist
Ardwahist 3 (Ardwahist)

Gregorian equivalents for dates between March 21, 2004 and February 2008: Fasli—April 22; Shahanshahi—September 21; Qadimi—August 22

The Feast of Ardwahist is a sacred day because the same spiritual being rules over both the month and the day. Ardwahist is the spiritual being who is Truth and Righteousness; Ardwahist also presides over Fire.

Maidyozarem (Maidhyoizaremaya; Mid-Spring Feast)
Ardwahist 11–15 (Khwarshed—Dae-pa-Mihr)

Gregorian Equivalents for dates between March 21, 2004 and February 2008: Fasli—April 30–May 4; Shahanshahi—September 29–October 3; Qadimi—August 30–September 3

Maidyozarem is the first of six great feasts, called Gahambars. The other five that are celebrated during the course of the year are Maidyoshahem (Tir 11–15), Paitishahem

(Shahrewar 26–30), Ayathrem (Mihr 26–30), Maidyarem (Dae 16–20), and Hamaspathmaidya (Spendarmard 26–30 plus five Gatha days). The Gahambar of Maidyozarem is linked to the creation of the sky. The spiritual being associated with it is Shahrewar, whose name means Desirable (or Benevolent) Dominion. Shahrewar presides over metals which are associated with the sky.

Traditionally the Gahambars were joyous festivals that lasted five days and included intricate rituals, specific prayers, and the sharing of food. The type of Jashan ceremony performed during this and the other Gahambars is called a Zinday-rawan. Part of the Jashan ceremony includes the recitation of a specific set of prayers called an afrinagan; a special Gahambar afrinagan is used for the Gahambar festivals. The term afrinagan is also used to refer to the container that holds the sacred fire during the ritual.

Hordad

Feast of Hordad
Hordad 6 (Hordad)

Gregorian Equivalents for dates between March 21, 2004 and February 2008: Fasli—May 25; Shahanshahi—October 24; Qadimi—September 24

The Feast of Hordad is a sacred day because the same divinity rules over both the month and the day. Hordad is the attribute of Perfection (or Health) and wholeness.

Tir

Maidyoshahem (Maidhyoishema; Mid-Summer Feast)
Tir 11–15 (Khwarshed—Dae-pa-Mihr)

Gregorian Equivalents for dates between March 21, 2004 and February 2008: Fasli—June 29–July 3; Shahanshahi—November 28–December 2; Qadimi—October 29–November 2

Maidyoshahem is the second of six great feasts, called Gahambars. The Gahambar of Maidyoshahem is linked to the creation of the waters. The divinity associated with it is Hordad whose name means Perfection or Health. Hordad presides over the waters. (*See:* Maidyozarem, Ardwahist 11–15, for additional information about Gahambar festivals.)

Tiragan
Tir 13 (Tir)

Gregorian Equivalents for dates between March 21, 2004 and February 2008: Fasli—July 1; Shahanshahi—November 30; Qadimi—October 31

The observance of Tiragan, a celebration in honor of Tishtar, the Dog Star (Sirius), occurs during the Gahambar of Maidyoshahem. It is a sacred name day on which the month and day names coincide. Zoroastrians believe that dogs serve as helpers of humankind. The festival's activities include sprinkling people with rose water bestowing blessings.

Amurdad

Feast of Amurdad
Amurdad 7 (Amurdad)

Gregorian equivalents for dates between March 21, 2004 and February 2008: Fasli—July 25; Shahanshahi—December 24; Qadimi—November 24

The Feast of Amurdad occurs on the day on which the Amurdad rules over both the month and the day. Amurdad is interpreted as Immortality. Amurdad presides over the earth.

Shahrewar

Feast of Shahrewar
Shahrewar 4 (Shahrewar)

Gregorian equivalents for dates between March 21, 2004 and February 2008: Fasli—August 21; Shahanshahi—January 21; Qadimi—December 21

The Feast of Shahrewar occurs on the day when the spiritual being Shahrewar rules over both the month and the day. Shahrewar is the divinity of Desirable (or Benevolent) Dominion. Shahrewar presides over metals.

Paitishahem (Patishahya; Feast of Bringing in the Harvest)
Shahrewar 26–30 (Ashtad-Anagran)

Gregorian Equivalents for dates between March 21, 2004 and February 2008: Fasli—September 12–16; Shahanshahi—February 11–15; Qadimi—January 12–16

Paitishahem is the third of six great feasts, called Gahambars. The Gahambar of Paitishahem is linked to the creation of the earth. The spiritual being associated with it is Spandarmad whose name means Holy Devotion. Spandarmad presides over the earth.

(*See:* Maidyozarem, Ardwahist 11–15, for additional information about Gahambar festivals.)

Mihr

Feast of Mithra (Mithrakana)
Mihr 1 (Ohrmazd)

Gregorian equivalents for dates between March 21, 2004 and February 2008: Fasli—September 17; Shahanshahi—February 16; Qadimi—January 17

The Feast of Mithra is a lesser feast celebrated on the first day of the seventh month which coincides with the autumnal equinox in the Fasli calendar. Mithra is an alternate name for the divinity Mihr, who is charged with overseeing contracts and fair dealing. Mithra also had responsibility to set right people who do not honor contracts or who dealt unfair with others. According to some scholars, the Zoroastrian concept of Mithra served as the basis for the Roman God Mithra.

Mihragan
Mihr 16 (Mihr)

Gregorian equivalents for dates between March 21, 2004 and February 2008: Fasli—October 2; Shahanshahi—March 3; Qadimi—February 1

Mihragan is a sacred day because the month and day names coincide. The festival is associated with Mihr, the spiritual being presiding over justice. The celebration includes symbolic imagery of the ripening world before the expected resurrection at the end of time.

Ayathrem (Ayathrima; Bringing Home the Herds)
Mihr 26-30 (Ashtad-Anagran)

Gregorian Equivalents for dates between March 21, 2004 and February 2008: Fasli—October 12–16; Shahanshahi—March 13–17; Qadimi—February 11–15

Ayathrem is the fourth of six great feasts, called Gahambars. The Gahambar of Maidyozarem is linked to the creation of the plants. The spiritual being associated with it is Amurdad, whose name means Immortality. Amurdad presides over the earth. (*See:* Maidyozarem, Ardwahist 11–15, for additional information about Gahambar festivals.)

Aban

Aban Parab
Aban 10 (Aban)

Gregorian equivalents for dates between March 21, 2004 and February 2008: Fasli—October 26; Shahanshahi—March 27; Qadimi—February 25

Aban Parab is a sacred name day on which the month and day names coincide. The celebration associated with it observes the creation of the waters. The spiritual being Aban, whose name means Water (or Purity), is the focus of ceremonies, prayers, and food offerings. Trips to the water are also often included.

Adar

Adar Parab
Adar 9 (Adar)

Gregorian equivalents for dates between March 21, 2004 and February 2008: Fasli—November 24; Shahanshahi—April 25; Qadimi—March 26

Table 6.4. Zoroastrian Holiday Cycle

Frawardin

1	Nawruz
6	Hordad Sal
19	Feast of Frawardignan

Ardwahist

3	Feast of Ardwahist
11–15	Maidyozarem

Hordad

6	Feast of Hordad

Tir

11–15	Maidyoshahem
13	Tiragan

Amurdad

7	Feast of Amurdad

Shahrewar

4	Feast of Shahrewar
26–30	Paitishahem

Mihr

1	Feast of Mithra
16	Mihragan
26–30	Ayathrem

Aban

10	Aban Parab

Adar

9	Adar Parab

Dae

1	Feast of Dae
8	Feast of Dae
11	Zarthastno Diso
15	Feast of Dae
16–20	Maidyarem
23	Feast of Dae

Vohuman

2	Feast of Vohuman

Spendarmard

5	Feast of Spendarmard
26–30	Muktad

Gatha Days

1–5	Five intercalary days extend the celebration of Muktad to 10 days. The Gatha Days are: Ahunawad; Ushtawad; Spentomad; Wohukhshathra; and Wahistotoisht

Adar Parab is a sacred name day on which the month and day names coincide. The celebration associated with it observes the creation of fire. People give thanks to Adar, the divinity that presides over fire, for supplying light and warmth. Traditionally prayers are offered in front of the hearth fires in the house. A portion of the Avesta (the Zoroastrian sacred writings) including the "Atash Niyayesh," the Hymn of the Divine Enlightenment, is recited.

Dae

Feasts of Dae

Dae 1, 8, 15, and 23, (Ohrmazd, Dae-pa-Adar, Dae-pa-Mihr, and Dae-pa-Den)

Gregorian equivalents for dates between March 21, 2004 and February 2008: Fasli—December 16, December 23, December 30, and January 7; Shahanshahi—May 17, May 24, May 31, June 8; Qadimi—April 17, April 24, May 1, and May 9

The Feasts of Dae, meaning God, occur during the this month on the days presided over by the creator, Ahura Mazda. Each month contains four days dedicated to the Creator: the 1st, 8th, 15th and 23rd days. As a result, there are four name day feasts in the month of Dae on which this Supreme Divinity is presiding over both the day and the month.

Zarthastno Diso (Zardosht-No-Diso)

Dae 11 (Khwarshed)

Gregorian equivalents for dates between March 21, 2004 and February 2008: Fasli—December 26; Shahanshahi—May 27; Qadimi—April 27

The observance of Zardosht-No-Diso commemorates the death anniversary of the Prophet Zoroaster. Traditionally, people make a special trip to a fire temple. Currently there are eight high fire temples in India. Outside of India, a special Jashan ceremony reserved for commemorating sad historical events is observed. The afrinagan (a specific set of prayers to be recited during the Jashan) associated with such commemorative prayers, is that of Ardafravash.

Maidyarem (Maidhyairya; Mid-Year Feast; Winter Feast)

Dae 16-20 (Mihr-Warharan)

Gregorian equivalent for dates between March 21, 2004 and February 2008: Fasli—December 31–January 4; Shahanshahi—June 1–5; Qadimi—May 2–6

Maidyarem is the fifth of six great feasts, called Gahambars. The Gahambar of Maidyarem is linked to the creation of the animal kingdom. The spiritual being associated with it is Vohuman, meaning Good Mind. (*See:* Maidyozarem, Ardwahist 11–15, for additional information about Gahambar festivals.)

Vohuman

Feast of Vohuman

Vohuman 2 (Vohuman)

Gregorian equivalents for dates between March 21, 2004 and February 2008: Fasli—January 16; Shahanshahi—June 17; Qadimi—May 18

The Feast of Vohuman is a sacred day because the same spiritual being rules over both the month and the day. Vohuman is the spiritual being who is Good Mind.

Spendarmad

Feast of Spendarmad

Spendarmad 5 (Spendarmad)

Gregorian equivalents for dates between March 21, 2004 and February 2008: Fasli—February 18; Shahanshahi—July 20; Qadimi—June 20

The Feast of Spendarmard is a sacred day because the same spiritual being rules over both the month and the day. Spendarmard is the spiritual being who is Holy Devotion. Spendarmard presides over the earth.

Muktad (Hamaspathmaidym; Equal Days and Nights; Coming of the Whole Group Farohars; Farvardegan Days; Festival of All Souls; Parsi Remembrance of the Departed)

Spendarmard 26–30 (Ashtad-Aneran) plus five Gatha Days—Ahunawad; Ushtawad; Spentomad; Vohukhshathra; and Vahishtoisht

Gregorian equivalents for dates between March 21, 2004 and February 2008: Fasli—March 11-20; Shahanshahi—August 10-19; Qadimi—July 11-20

Muktad, are the days for commemoration of the departed souls. The celebration includes the High festival of Hamaspathmaidym. This is the last of the six great feasts, called Gahambars. The other five that are celebrated during the course of the year are Maidyozarem (Ardwahist 11–15), Maidyoshahem (Tir 11–15), Paitishahem (Shahrewar 26–30), Ayathrem (Mihr 26–30), and Maidyarem (Dae 16–20). The celebration of Muktad, is linked to the creation of mankind. The other five Gahambars are each associated with a spiritual being created by Ahura Mazda, but Muktad is linked to the God himself. (*See:* Maidyozarem, Ardwahist 11–15, for additional information about Gahambar festivals.)

According to tradition, all the farohars (spirits) return to earth at the end of the year and before the beginning of the new year. Zoroastrian homes are kept clean in order to receive the spirits as guests. People offer prayers to the spirits for protection and blessings. During the last Gah (day-time watch) of the last day of Muktad, a special fire ceremony is performed to bid a final farewell to the spirits and prepare the way for the new year.

Originally, Muktad was a five-day festival during the last days of Spendarmard. When the calendar was changed during the Sasanian period (226 C.E. to 651 C.E.), five days were added to make it a ten-day celebration to avoid the problem of separating the Muktad festival from the beginning of the new year.

Table 6.5. Alphabetical List of Zoroastrian Holidays

Holiday	Date(s)
Aban Parab	Aban 10
Adar Parab	Adar 9
Ayathrem	Mihr 26-30
Ayathrima *see* Ayathrem	
Bringing Home the Herds *see* Ayathrem	
Coming of the Whole Group Farohars *see* Muktad	
Equal Days and Nights *see* Muktad	
Farvardegan Days *see* Muktad	
Feast of Amurdad	Amurdad 7
Feast of Ardwahist	Ardwahist 3
Feast of Bringing in the Harvest *see* Paitishahem	
Feast of Frawardignan	Frawardin 19
Feast of Hordad	Hordad 6
Feast of Mithra	Mihr 1
Feast of Shahrewar	Shahrewar 4
Feast of Spendarmad	Spendarmad 5
Feast of Vohuman	Vohuman 2
Festival of All Souls *see* Muktad	
First Feast of Dae	Dae 1
Fourth Feast of Dae	Dae 23
Hamaspathmaidym *see* Muktad	
Hordad Sal	Frawardin 6
Jamshedi Navroz *see* Nawruz	
Khordad Sal *see* Hordad Sal	
Maidhyairya *see* Maidyarem	

Holiday	Date(s)
Maidhyoishema *see* Maidyoshahem	
Maidhyoizaremaya *see* Maidyozarem	
Maidyarem	Dae 16-20
Maidyoshahem	Tir 11–15
Maidyozarem	Ardwahist 11–15
Mid-Spring Feast *see* Maidyozarem	
Mid-Summer Feast *see* Maidyoshahem	
Mid-Year Feast *see* Maidyarem	
Mihragan	Mihr 16
Mithrakana *see* Feast of Mithra	
Muktad	Spendarmard 26–30 plus five Gatha Days
Nawruz	Frawardin 1
NoRuz *see* Nawruz	
Nu Roz *see* Nawruz	
Paitishahem	Shahrewar 26–30
Parsi Remembrance of the Departed *see* Muktad	
Pateti *see* Nawruz	
Patishahya *see* Paitishahem	
Second Feast of Dae	Dae 8
Third Feast of Dae	Dae 15
Tiragan	Tir 13
Winter Feast *see* Maidyarem	
Zardosht-No-Diso *see* Zarthastno Diso	
Zarthastno Diso	Dae 11

CHAPTER 7

Christianity: Roman Catholic and Protestant Expressions

Overview of Roman Catholicism and the Protestant Reformation

What Is Christianity?

Christianity, with believers in countries around the globe, is the largest of the world's religions. The reported number of followers varies depending on how the term "Christian" is defined and the method used for counting, but many estimates place the number between 1.7 and 1.9 billion people.

The word Christian refers to a follower of Christ. Christ is a title derived from the Greek word meaning Messiah or Anointed One. The Christ of Christianity is Jesus of Nazareth, a man born two thousand years ago in the region of Palestine. The precise explanation and understanding of who Jesus was and what it means to be a follower differ among the many Christian groups; however, the three main branches of Christianity (Roman Catholicism, Orthodoxy, and Protestantism) share several core beliefs and practices concerning the nature of Jesus and the actions required of his followers.

Christians believe that Jesus was both divine and human. A doctrinal concept called the Trinity is used by the largest branches of Christianity to provide an explanation of how one God exists in three distinct persons—Father, Son, and Spirit. The Father is equated with the Creator, the Son with Jesus, and the Spirit with the Holy Spirit (also called the Holy Ghost). The Spirit is described as a gift given to believers to provide guidance and strength for life on earth.

According to Christian teaching, Jesus was killed by Roman authorities using a form of execution called crucifixion (a term meaning he was nailed to a cross and hung from it until he died). After his death, he rose back to life. His death and resurrection provide a way by which people can be reconciled with God. In remembrance of Jesus's death and resurrection, the cross serves as a fundamental symbol in Christianity.

Christians view the world as God's creation and acknowledge his sovereignty. His work is opposed, however, by a resistant spiritual being called Satan, or the Devil. God has spiritual beings, called angels, who work in accordance with his wishes. Satan also has a cohort of spiritual beings called demons. The struggle between good and evil is defined as a spiritual battle that has consequences in the material world. Christians await the Second Coming of Jesus at which time the final judgement will occur and God's perfect kingdom will be instituted.

The Relationship between God and the Christian People

The Christian God is the same creator as the Jewish God. The basic difference between Judaism and Christianity is that Jews await the coming of a Messiah; Christians proclaim that the Messiah has already come in the person of Jesus Christ.

According to traditional Christian belief, people are created by God and given one life during which the consequences of their free choices determine their eternal destiny. Those who embrace the teachings of the Christian Church will be reconciled with God in heaven and rewarded after death; those who deny God will be punished in hell. The precise understanding of heaven and hell and a third alternate, an interim place called purgatory, are understood differently among the several branches of Christians.

People possess the freedom to obey or disobey God, but perfect obedience in all things is impossible because the first man, Adam, disobeyed God. This original sin was passed along to Adam's descendants—all of mankind. The impossibility of obeying God in all things is resolved by receiving supernatural help in the form of forgiveness, a doctrinal concept described as "salvation by grace." This salvation is accessed by placing one's faith in Jesus Christ, believing in his resurrection, and receiving assurance from the Spirit.

Authorities and Sacred Writings

There is no one central authority for all of Christianity. The Pope (the bishop of Rome) is the authority for the Roman Catholic Church, but other sects look to other authorities. Orthodox communities look to Patriarchs and emphasize doctrinal agreement and traditional practice. Protestant communities focus on individual conscience.

All three main branches of Christianity acknowledge the authority of Christian scriptures, a compilation of writings assembled into a document called the Bible. Methods of Biblical interpretation vary among the different Christian sects.

The Bible comprises two major segments called the Old and New Testaments. The Old Testament contains the 39 books of Jewish scriptures. These include the five Books of Moses (Pentateuch), books of history, poetry, wisdom, and prophecy. The New Testament includes an additional 27 books written by (or ascribed to) disciples of the first and second centuries. The oldest of these writings are letters ascribed to the Apostle Paul dating from about 65 C.E. Jesus did not write any of the New Testament. Details of his teachings and life are known from being recorded by his disciples.

The complete canon of New Testament writings was established in 367 C.E. and it includes:

- **Four gospels.** The word "gospel" means "good news." The Gospels tell about events of the life of Jesus with the most significant attention paid to the last week of his life. The first of the four (in their traditional order) is attributed to Matthew, an original disciple. The second, the Gospel According to Mark, is attributed to a follower known as John Mark who may have been a second-generation believer. Mark's Gospel is judged by many to be the oldest of the four, thought to have been written around 70 C.E. The third Gospel, Luke, was written by an associate of the apostle Paul. The last of the Gospels, John, is attributed to an original disciple.

- **A book of history.** Acts of the Apostles is attributed to Luke, the author of the third Gospel.

- **Twenty-one Epistles (letters).** The Epistles include thirteen letters attributed to the apostle Paul, one Epistle written to the Hebrews and traditionally associated with Paul although its authorship is unknown, and seven other letters ascribed to Peter, James, John and Jude.

- **An apocalyptic book.** Revelation was probably written about 96 C.E. It is ascribed to the apostle John.

Some Christians recognize an additional set of books, called the Apocrypha, which is a collection of Jewish writings found in the Greek version of Jewish scriptures, but not included in the Hebrew version. Other books exist which were written during the first and second centuries of the Christian era but were not included in the official canon either due to their limited circulation, lateness of composition, or questionable apostolic authority.

History of Christianity

The founder of Christianity was a Jewish man, Jesus, called the Christ (a term derived from the Greek word for Messiah). Jesus was born in the first decade B.C.E. in Bethlehem. He grew up in Nazareth, and died in approximately 29–30 C.E. after being arrested by Roman rulers and put to death by crucifixion, a common means of execution.

The birth of Jesus is recorded in two of the Gospels: Matthew and Luke. According to the Gospels, Jesus was born to a Jewish couple, Joseph and Mary, during the reign of the Roman Emperor Augustus and before the death of Herod the Great (approximately 4 B.C.E.). According to biblical accounts, after Jesus's birth the governor of Palestine, attempted to kill him by ordering a massacre of all Hebrew children under the age of two. Jesus's family escaped by fleeing to Egypt until the threat had passed. The slaughtered children, called the Holy Innocents, are remembered on a special day in the Christian calendar.

Very little is known about Jesus's childhood. His public ministry began when he was an adult. His work was preceded by a prophet known as John the Baptist. In approximately 28 C.E., John began proclaiming a message concerning the coming of the kingdom of God. He exhorted people to turn back to God and undergo a ritual of baptism, signifying repentance. According to Christian tradition, Jesus underwent baptism by John and afterward endured a time of temptation and testing in the wilderness. Shortly after these events John the Baptist was arrested, and Jesus himself began to carry the message proclaiming God's coming kingdom.

The precise duration of Jesus's ministry is unknown, but many estimates suggest that his public work lasted between one and three years. During his time, Jesus was a wandering teacher in the Palestine area. He taught in parables and spoke out against some practices of the Jewish authorities. Several different kinds of miraculous events were attributed to him including command over nature, physical healing, and the casting out of demons. Many people followed him, but twelve specially selected disciples were closest to him. These twelve were called apostles.

Jesus's earthly life ended when he was executed by Roman officials. The events surrounding Jesus's death occurred during the time of the Jewish celebration of Passover. The last meal he shared with his disciples was a Passover meal. The celebration and remembrance of this meal, in which Jesus identified his body and blood with the bread and wine, forms a focal point for most Christian worship.

According to Christian teaching, after Jesus's execution and death, his dead body was placed in a tomb. Three days later, or more precisely on the third day (Romans counted days inclusively), he rose from the dead. Following his resurrection, Jesus appeared to his disciples during a 40-day period after which he ascended into heaven.

According to the book of Acts, after Jesus ascended into heaven, the disciples gathered in Jerusalem for the Jewish feast of Shavuot (also called the Feast of Weeks because it occurred seven weeks after Passover). Among Greek-speaking Jews the feast was called Pentecost because it fell 50 days after Passover. While they were gathered together, the disciples received the gift of the Holy Spirit. Many Christian denominations view the events at Pentecost as the birth of the Christian Church.

Following the giving of the Spirit, Jesus's disciples, who had been disheartened after his death, were revitalized. They began to proclaim Jesus's resurrection and to boldly preach his message despite being persecuted and even martyred.

Early practices of the first century Christians included fellowship, prayers, and the sharing of bread and wine. These three basic elements have remained a central part of practicing the Christian faith.

The first Christians were Jews who acknowledged Jesus as Messiah. They continued to follow the precepts of Judaism, read Jewish scriptures, follow Jewish laws, and meet at Jewish synagogues. In addition, however, they also met together to share bread and wine and celebrate Jesus's resurrection. These additional meetings were held on Sunday, the first day of the week, to coincide with the day of the resurrection.

One prominent Jew who converted to Christianity following the death of Jesus was the apostle Paul. According to Christian teaching, Paul (previously known as Saul of Tarsus) originally persecuted believers. He was confronted by a vision of Jesus in which he was blinded. Three days later he was healed and given instruction in the Christian faith. Following a period of discipleship, Paul was sent out as a missionary, and under his ministry churches were founded in Asia Minor and Greece. One of the main themes in Paul's teachings was that a person did not have to become a Jew to be a Christian.

The Christian movement initially spread in urban centers throughout the Roman empire. It was introduced to areas outside the region of Palestine as Jews moved to avoid oppression. Jewish synagogues were often the first focal points of missionary efforts. Missionary activities were also made among non-Jewish people (called Gentiles). As a result the Christian community began to grow, first as a sect within Judaism and then as a separate religion.

Under Roman law, Jews held an exemption from the requirement of worshiping the Roman Emperor, but Christians, as followers of a new religion, did not enjoy this privilege. Because they refused to worship the Roman Emperor or recognize his divinity, they faced persecution. The apostles Peter and Paul were executed under orders from Emperor Nero between 54 and 68 C.E.

In 70 C.E. the Romans destroyed the Jewish temple in Jerusalem. After the temple's destruction, Judaism became more focused on Rabbinic traditions and Christianity continued to evolve as an increasingly independent religion.

By the end of the first century, many Christian groups had grown from small gatherings to large assemblies. New forms of leadership structures emerged to give guidance to new converts and serve the needs of the rapidly expanding community. These positions included teachers, deacons, and bishops.

The persecution of Christians continued during the second century C.E. and intensified during the third as the Roman Empire faced ever-growing threats from invaders. Worship of traditional Roman gods was mandated and strictly enforced by Roman Emperors Decius (in the mid-third century C.E.), Diocletian (during the late third century C.E.), and Galerius (in the early forth century C.E.). Christians who refused to sacrifice to the Roman gods were imprisoned and often executed.

Many who suffered martyrdom are remembered on saint days in the calendars of several orthodox, catholic, and protestant sects. The basis of saint day remembrances is found in ancient Roman tradition. On the anniversary of a death, families would share a ritual meal at the grave site of an ancestor. This practice was adopted by Christians who began observing a ritual meal on the death anniversary of ancestors in the faith, especially martyrs. As a result, most Christian saint days are associated with the death of the saint. There are three important exceptions. John the Baptist, the Virgin Mary, and Jesus are honored on their nativities (birthdays).

Despite persecution, new converts continued to join the Christian ranks. By the end of the third century C.E., four cities had become important centers of Christianity: Rome, Antioch (in Syria), Alexandria (in Egypt), and Jerusalem. Bishops of these cities were charged with the responsibility of caring for the needs of the churches in the surrounding areas.

As the Roman Empire continued to decline, economic and social conditions deteriorated. Churches became more firmly established and provided necessary support to the poor, widows, orphans, and the sick. Some historians theorize that the attraction of social stability contributed to the spread of Christianity during an unstable time in history.

Following the death of the Roman Emperor Galerius in 311 C.E. a new Emperor, Constantine, came to power. Constantine won a decisive military victory and attributed his success in battle to a god he called the "Unconquerable Son." Christian apologists convinced Constantine that the god responsible for his victory was the Christian God.

Although Constantine was not baptized until the end of his life, he became an advocate for Christianity. His Edict of Milan, issued in 313 C.E., ended the age of persecution by mandating tolerance of Christianity. As a consequence of Constantine's advocacy, Christianity became the predominant religion of those in political power.

Constantine also presided over the Council of Nicaea in 325 C.E. The council was a meeting of Christian leaders who defined Christianity and attempted to separate it from heresies. The Council of Nicaea produced a creed, known as the Nicene Creed, which is recognized by all major branches of Christianity as a foundational statement of doctrine.

Under continued pressure from invaders, Constantine moved the political capital of the empire from Rome to Byzantium (which was later renamed Constantinople). The church in each of these two major cities was presided over by a bishop. Because the political seat had been moved to Byzantium, the bishop in Rome (called the pope) became more powerful in both church and secular affairs. This shift aided the process by which the Papacy amassed its vast power.

The move ultimately led to the creation of a geographic division between the Eastern and Western branches of Christianity. The western branch of Christianity focused its efforts on attracting new converts in northern Europe and sought to establish political alliances to aid in guarding security. The first Frankish lord, Clovis, converted to Christianity in the fifth century. (The Franks ruled over an area currently occupied by Germany, France, and Italy.) A later Frankish ruler, Charlemagne was made Emperor in 800 C.E. by the Roman Pope Leo III.

The Eastern practice of combining ecclesiastical and political power ultimately led to conflict. Nobles affiliated with the church in Rome had authority over unaffiliated nobles and the influence wielded by religious leaders brought more power to the pope in Rome.

Differences in the expression of Christianity also arose between the East and West. Western Christianity focused on the awesome holiness of God and developed precise rituals and a priestly class. In the east, practices focused on Christianity as a mystical experience and lay people retained more power. The mystical focus of the Eastern Church found its expression in a form of worship that used icons (images to be venerated as representations of the divine nature).

The Great Schism

As differences between Eastern and Western Christianity increased, tension also increased. Political power structures were challenged. Pope Leo IX (1048–54 C.E.) insisted that the Eastern people, who claimed to be representatives of Orthodox (correct) Christianity, shift their allegiance to him and the Catholic (Universal) Church. The Patriarch in Constantinople, Michael Cerularius (Greek spelling is Keroularios), refused. In 1054 C.E., the Pope and Patriarch mutually excommunicated each other, an event called The Great Schism.

During the next century, Muslims rose in power in the East and Western Churches sent military aid. The campaigns were called the Crusades. The Crusaders of 1204 C.E. attacked Constantinople itself, ending efforts aimed at achieving reconciliation between the Eastern and Western branches of Christianity.

The Crusades, however, caused a renewed interest in religious expression in the West. As universities were developed and discussion of spiritual matters escalated, church officials became zealous in attacking heresy. The Inquisition was established and the power of the pope reached its zenith. Many important doctrines unique to Roman Catholicism arose during the thirteenth century. These included the concept of transubstantiation (a doctrine meaning that the bread and wine used during the Eucharist actually became the body and blood of Christ) and the veneration of the Virgin Mary (Jesus's mother).

By the fourteenth century, however, authoritarian abuses and divisions within the Church hierarchy diminished the power of the pope. Between 1309 to 1377 the Roman popes moved from Rome to Avignon. At one time as many as three different men laid claim to the title Pope. The papacy was not reunified until the early fifteenth century.

The Reformation

Abuse of power and disunity within the Church helped plant the seeds for the coming reformation as some people sought a more personal, mystical experience. In the fourteenth century John Wycliffe, an English writer, advocated reforms including the translation of the Bible from Latin into the common languages of the people.

By the fifteenth century, the reunified Papacy had amassed tremendous political power. All priests in Europe received their authority from the Roman Pope. Only authorized priests were able to administer Church sacraments (which were baptism, confirmation, Eucharist, penance, holy orders, matrimony, and extreme unction). A person cut off from sacraments could not be assured of salvation and life after death. If a national ruler disobeyed the pope, an entire country would be placed under papal ban meaning that none of its priests could administer the sacraments. An individual who denied the authority of the Church could be excommunicated and refused the sacraments. These types of pressures over people led to protests which culminated in the Protestant Reformation.

Martin Luther (1483–1545 C.E.), a German priest and professor at the University of Wittenberg, is often credited with beginning the Reformation. Luther opposed the Roman practice of selling indulgences (selling the remission of punishment from sin in order to raise money to build a cathedral). He believed that people received salvation as a result of their faith. Luther denied the authority of the Pope and church tradition, believing instead that the Bible was the only source of true doctrine and that it alone served as a guide for proper Christian conduct. Luther also asserted that priests did not have the power to save or condemn people but that such power belonged exclusively to God and that each person was individually responsible to God.

Other protestant leaders followed and the movement swept through Europe. The main thrust of Protestantism was the belief that Christianity needed to return to its original, Biblical state. The protestant legacy, however, endowed the Church with an heritage of questioning authority and protesting abuses perpetrated by leaders. This willingness created conditions ripe for further splintering and the subsequent creation of progressively smaller and more numerous groups. As a result, by the late twentieth century there were more than 25,000 different Christian denominations.

Christianity Today

Christian Worship and Practices

Different groups of Christians worship in different ways. Some use elaborate rituals with prescribed prayers, others prefer informal gatherings. Some use music and dance; some worship in silence. Some meet in ornate cathedrals; some meet in private homes. Some use icons to focus their worship; some decry the use of icons as idolatry.

Most Christian worship, however, takes place within the context of a church. A "church" can refer either to a special building or to a faith community of Christians or to both. The purpose of the Church is to continue Jesus's mission until he returns at his anticipated second coming. Because Jesus's resurrection occurred on a Sunday, Sunday is the day on which many Christians meet for communal worship. Some sects, however, observe the Jewish Sabbath instead.

One of the central practices of Christianity, baptism, is a symbolic act that signifies dying with Christ and being raised to new life. Some Christians perform baptism by sprinkling or pouring water on candidates. Some groups practice baptism by total immersion, and others view baptism as a spiritual event rather than as a ritual performed with water. Some Christian groups baptize infants and children while others baptize only those old enough to make an informed decision.

Another practice common to most Christian groups is a ritual in which celebrants partake in a remembrance or reenactment of Jesus's last meal with his disciples. The celebration is known by different names, including the Eucharist, Holy Communion, and the Lord's Supper. It involves the sharing of bread and wine. Specific means and frequency of the celebration vary among Christian sects.

Sects within Christianity

From its beginning as a sect within Judaism, Christianity spread throughout the world. Three aspects of the Christian faith made it especially suitable for global growth: Its message was available to everyone irrespective of their place of birth, race, or gender; it had a strong historic basis; and, it possessed the ability to adapt to new situations in diverse cultures.

There are three major divisions within Christianity: Catholicism, Orthodoxy, and Protestantism. Historically each group has believed that it held the exclusive representation of true Christianity. More modernly, many representatives from various segments of the global Christian community have expressed an opinion that none is exclusive and others may be viable, although the degree of the acceptance and the roster of accepted denominations varies considerably.

A fourth division also exists within modern Christianity. It comprises movements that were founded on Christian beliefs, practices, and traditions but that also incorporate non-traditional doctrines. Frequently these new doctrines result from revelations received by individual leaders outside the framework of Biblical knowledge. Among many traditional Christians, these extra-revelational sects may be called "cults."

Roman Catholicism

The word "catholic" is derived from the Greek word meaning universal. In some contexts, such as in ancient creeds, it refers to the universal Christian Church and encompasses all Christian believers. In the modern sense, however, "catholic" is often used as a synonym for Roman Catholicism.

Roman Catholicism is the largest branch of Christianity. An estimated 17 percent of the world's population is Roman Catholic—more than 950 million people. The Church claims an unbroken link to the apostolic days and specifically to the apostle Peter. The tradition of assuming that Christians in Rome held responsibility and authority over others dates back to the second and third centuries C.E.

The ultimate authority in Roman Catholicism is the Pope. His office is derived from his election as Bishop of Rome. Other leaders within the Roman Catholic Church are called Cardinals. They are appointed by the Pope and serve as the Church's Supreme Council. In 2003, the number of cardinals serving the Roman Catholic Church world wide was increased to 194.

The Roman Catholic Church tends to place greater emphasis on doctrinal issues, traditions, the authority of the pope, veneration of saints, and the adoration of Mary than do churches within other Christian branches. The main worship service is called a Mass, which is a formal service comprising several parts that include chants, readings from the Bible, the recitation of specific prayers, an offertory, Holy Communion (Eucharist), and a benediction. The word mass comes from a Latin word meaning "sent"—a term used at the service's conclusion. There are two types of mass: High Mass and Low Mass. At High Mass most of the service is sung; at Low Mass, a simpler form of the service is used and its parts are read.

Protestantism

Protestant churches form the second largest major division within Christianity. Worldwide, Protestants number nearly 500 million people and represent about 25 percent of all Christians. Within Protestantism, however, there are thousands of denominations of varying sizes. Denominations tend to split into subsects over details such as the form of baptism, methods of government, and style of worship.

Many modern Protestant denominations have their roots in the fifteenth century European struggle to achieve freedom from the Roman Pope's authority. Four branches of Protestantism developed during the Reformation era: Lutheran; Calvinist (Reformed), Anabaptist, and Anglican. The label "Protestant" was derived from a protest signed by six German princes criticizing the Roman Catholic Church's withdrawal of tolerance toward Lutherans.

Lutherans trace their beginnings to Martin Luther, an Augustinian monk and theology professor. In the early 1500s Luther spoke out against abuses within the Roman Catholic Church, in particular against the practice of selling "indulgences" to help raise money to construct Saint Peter's Basilica in Rome (by purchasing indulgences, a person could escape punishments that resulted from his or her sins). Luther believed that a person's salvation was given by divine grace alone. In 1517 C.E. he published the Ninety-Five Theses with which he intended to help reform the errors he saw in the Roman Catholic Church. The Church, however, was not receptive to his views and Luther was excommunicated. Luther's ideas were published widely, and the Lutheran Church spread throughout northern Europe.

Calvinist churches (a group that includes Presbyterian, Congregational, and Reformed Churches) trace their beginnings to John Calvin, a sixteenth century French theologian who became established in Geneva, Switzerland. Calvin's writings helped further spread the Protestant movement.

Anglican Churches also joined the Protestant reformation in the sixteenth century. In 1534 C.E., King Henry VIII of England denied the Pope in Rome and assumed authority over the English Church himself. Some groups were dissatisfied, however, with the many Roman forms retained by the Anglicans (the official Church of England) and pressed for further reforms. Following the religious strife that ensued, some groups, such as the Puritans, left Europe to seek religious freedom in the New World.

Anabaptist groups were a more extreme form of Protestantism than the Anglicans, Lutherans, or Calvinists.

They denounced all relationships between the Church and state and emphasized doctrinal reforms. The Anabaptist reforms ultimately led to the development of denominations such as the Mennonites, the Amish, and the Society of Friends (Quakers).

Other Christian Expressions

The third main branch within Christianity is the Orthodox Church. The word orthodox comes from a Greek term meaning "right-believing." Orthodox Churches are headed by patriarchs, who hold administrative jurisdiction in a territory. Unlike the Roman Catholic Pope, patriarchs make no claim to infallibility. Orthodox Churches separated from Roman Churches in 1054 C.E. when the Patriarch in Constantinople and the Pope in Rome excommunicated each other. Differences between Orthodox and Roman Catholic Churches persist into the modern era. See Chapter 8 for additional information about the Orthodox Church.

A fourth type of Christian expression is found in other groups claiming to possess special understanding. Examples have existed throughout the course of Christian history. As early as the second century, some groups claimed to possess little-known knowledge. These people were called Gnostics (a word derived from the Greek word for knowledge). Marcion (in the second century) and Mani (who founded the Manichees in the third century) are both examples of founders of movements claiming to have received special knowledge apart from the writings and traditions recognized by the main body of Christian believers.

In the modern era, groups holding to non-traditional doctrines or recognizing the authority of extra-revelational writings include a vast array of organizations with memberships ranging from a few individuals to millions. A few well-known examples are the Church of Jesus Christ of Latter Day Saints (Mormons), Church of Christ, Scientist (Christian Science), and the Holy Spirit Association for the Unification of World Christianity (Unification Church). See Chapter 9 for additional information about non-traditional expressions of Christian-based faith.

———— " ————

A basic statement of Christian belief can be found in the New Testament of the *Bible*: "For God so loved the world, that he gave his only begotten Son, that whosoever believeth in him should not perish, but have everlasting life." (John 3:16; King James Version)

———— " ————

Christian Calendars

Hebrew Influences

Clearly visible within the Christian liturgical calendar are elements of both the Hebrew and Greek time-keeping systems. Most immediately recognizable, however, are the influences of the Hebrew calendar. The movable feasts within Christianity, such as Easter and Pentecost, have connections to Hebrew celebrations.

The Establishment of Sunday as a Meeting Day

The evolution of Christianity as a separate religion from Judaism is often misunderstood. The division between the two belief systems was not initially over the deity of Jesus of Nazareth and his position as the Messiah, as many people suppose; in fact, for the first fifty years that Christianity existed, it remained a movement within Judaism. Most Christians were Jews who believed that Jesus was the Messiah, and although many other Jews did not share the Christians' belief, the two groups continued to worship in the synagogues together.

Christians were only one of many sects within Judaism; others included the Sadducees, Pharisees, Essenes, Zealots, gnostics, the "God-Fearers" (a group composed of Romans who lived a Jewish lifestyle without formal conversion—perhaps up to 20 percent of the Roman population), and other groups. This diverse Jewish culture was fragmented in 70 C.E. following the Roman war.

After the Roman destruction of the Temple at Jerusalem, the surviving Hebrew rabbis argued that the disaster had been caused by "factionalism" and decided that unity was more important than individual expression. Thus, they merged the sects, drawing mainly from the Pharisaic tradition to create what is now known as normative or Orthodox Judaism. Christian Jews were invited to join this new, unified group, but the Christians decided not to merge because they could not accept the conditions and constraints of Orthodox Judaism. Jews and Christians continued to meet together in the synagogue on the Sabbath evening until about 80–85 C.E., when Christians began to form their own synagogues. At that point, they were no longer recognized as Jews under the Jewish and Roman law, and Christianity became illegal. More than two centuries passed before Christianity was legalized again.

While Christians continued to meet with other Jews in the synagogue for the Sabbath, they also observed their own special meetings on Sunday at sunrise to commemorate the resurrection of Jesus. Once they began to separate from the Jews, they slowly switched to Sunday mornings as their primary meeting time. The reasons for this change in meeting time were two-fold: First to remember the resurrection of Christ; second, to separate themselves more clearly from the Jews. This period marks the distinct point at which the two systems of belief moved in opposite directions, and it was here that the roots of longstanding resentments between the two groups began to grow.

Establishing Dates for the Easter Celebration

Initially, Christians celebrated the Jewish Passover as the anniversary of the Last Supper, and the Feast of the Resurrection (Easter) was observed on the first Sunday after the beginning of Passover. The Jewish Pentecost (Shavuot or Feast of Weeks) was maintained as the anniversary of the New Covenant, when the Holy Spirit descended on the disciples.

By the second century C.E., the relationship between Judaism and Christianity had deteriorated so greatly that it became impossible for Christians to find out when Passover would be celebrated. The date for Passover was movable and the equation for its determination had not yet been made public. As a result, Christians began to determine the date of the Easter celebration according to the rules of their individual communities.

The Christian Churches east of Greece celebrated Easter on the fourteenth of Nisan (in the Jewish calendar) whether or not it was a Sunday. The Western Church, however, developed a more complex system to determine Easter's date and ensure that it was celebrated on a Sunday in the Passover week. To claim authority for the date established for Easter, both groups appealed to the Gospels. The Gospel of John, however, gives a different date for the crucifixion than the date given by the other Gospels. This inconsistency, coupled with the controversy over how the evening of the fourteenth day of the month should be calculated, produced a schism between the Eastern and Western Churches.

According to the Jewish religious definition, the full moon was the fourteenth day after the new moon irrespective of astronomical calculations. Defining the evening of the fourteenth day would, therefore, determine the date on which the Passover was celebrated. A group called the Quintodecimans counted the evening of the fourteenth as the one after the fourteenth day. The Quartodecimans claimed that it meant the evening following the thirteenth day, since sunset was the beginning of a new day. Supporters of the two points of view tended to fall along geographical lines: the Eastern Church supported the Quartodecimans, while the Western Church supported the Quintodecimans.

Date of Easter Established by the Council of Nicaea

In 325 C.E., Constantine summoned all the bishops to the first Ecumenical Council, in Nicaea, to settle the numerous differences that were cropping up and threatening the unity of the Church. It was also around this time that the seven-day week became common in the Roman Empire, and schoolchildren had to begin memorizing the names of the weekdays in order to know which day was Sunday—indicating how strong the influence of Christianity had become in a short period of time.

The Council of Nicaea passed policies on many issues facing the Christian Church; among the most pertinent of these was a system for determining the date of Easter. Even though disagreement has arisen over the interpretation of the rule, it has been used by Christians ever since.

Because Judaism and Christianity had become mutually exclusive religions, the Christian authorities wanted to ensure that Easter would never coincide with Passover. The rule for the date of Easter as declared by the Council of Nicaea was in agreement with the Quintodecimans. The Feast of the Resurrection should be celebrated on the first Sunday after (not on) the first full moon after March 21 (which was the date of the vernal equinox the year the council met). This full moon became known as the Paschal moon. In addition, the Council ruled that if the designated Sunday coincided with either Passover or the Easter Day of the Quartodecimans, the festival should be held seven days later.

The decision of the Council delighted the Western Church. The Eastern Church, on the other hand, decided to retain the Quartodeciman position, as did the Church in England. During the sixth century, however, Roman missionaries to England introduced the Western system which was adopted and is still followed.

The effort of the Church Fathers to avoid the coincidence of Easter with the Passover feast underscores how far Judaism and Christianity had diverged. The notion that the Last Supper was an extension of the Passover Feast seemed to have been forgotten. The Church Fathers also fixed Pentecost as the seventh Sunday (fiftieth day according to the Roman inclusive counting method) after Easter, just as the Jewish Pentecost is the fiftieth day after Passover.

Determining the Date of Easter

The general rule of establishing Easter as the Sunday following the first full moon after the vernal equinox is more complex than simply applying raw astronimcal data. Using the criteria established by the Council of Nicaea, the Church later devised tables for establishing the date of Easter using the ecclestically recognized date of the vernal equinox (March 21) and the officially determined date of the Paschal moon (based on the age of the moon counted in days from the new moon; the Paschal moon always occurrs between March 21 and April 18, inclusive). These calculations sometimes yield results slightly different from astronomical observations.

To determine the date of Easter, two pieces of information are needed: the age of the moon and knowledge of which dates are Sundays. The method devised for determining the age of the moon relied on a chart of "Golden Numbers." Golden numbers are based on a 19-year cycle, much like the Metonic cycle. (For more information about the Metonic cycle, see Chapter 2.) Although the golden numbers were introduced in 530 C.E., the chart was constructed as if they had been accepted in the fourth century at the Council of Nicaea.

Table 7.1. Golden Numbers for the years 1900 C.E. through 2099 C.E.

Golden Number	Date of Pascal Moon
1	April 14
2	April 3
3	March 23
4	April 11
5	March 31
6	April 18
7	April 8
8	March 28
9	April 16
10	April 5
11	March 25
12	April 13
13	April 2
14	March 22
15	April 10
16	March 30
17	April 17
18	April 7
19	March 27

Source: Adapted from *The Book of Common Prayer* according to the use of the Episcopal Church, The Church Hymnal Corporation and The Seabury Press, 1978.

The origin of the name "golden numbers" dates to medieval times, but its exact derivation is uncertain. Some have suggested that they were named for the Greek name of the numbers within the Metonic cycle while others have conjectured that they were named after the gold color used for them in manuscript calendars.

The phases of the moon do not fall on the same dates every year because of differences between the lunar and solar cycles, but they do repeat every nineteen years. Using this information, a nineteen-year chart was constructed that predicted the phases of the moon for each year in the period. Once a person knew which one of the nineteen possibilities represented the current year, a chart indicated the date of the Paschal moon (*see* Table 7.1 for a chart based on modern dates).

A mathematical formula can be used to calculate the golden number for any year. To determine a year's golden number, take the year and divide by 19; then add 1 to the quotient's remainder. Using the year 2004 as an example: 2004 divided by 19 is 105 with a remainder of 9. Adding 1 to this remainder yields a golden number of 10. (An alternate formula sometimes used adds 1 to the year and not to the remainder. An additional rule under this formula further states that if the result is zero, then the golden number for the year is 19. Either formula produces the same results.)

The next step in determining the date of Easter is to find out which days after the Paschal moon are Sundays. In order to identify what dates would be Sundays in any given year, the Church adopted a system similar to the one that had been used by the Romans to determine market days. The code used for ecclesiastical use was known as the dominical letter.

The system of dominical letters assigned the first seven letters of the alphabet, A through G, to consecutive days beginning with the first day of the year. January 1st appears as A, January 2nd as B, and so on through January 7th as G, and then repeating the letters with January 8th as A, January 9th as B, et cetera. Using this system, every day of the week retains the same letter throughout the year. The letter given to the first Sunday in the year identifies all the Sundays for that year. For example, in the year 2002 January 6th was the first Sunday; the dominical letter for the year was the sixth letter, F.

Because a year of 365 days includes 52 weeks and one day, each subsequent year will be represented with the preceding letter. In 2003, the first Sunday was January 5th and the year's dominical letter was the fifth letter, E.

The series of dominical letters is adjusted during leap years. No dominical letter is assigned to the date February 29, but because it appears on the calendar like any other weekday, the series of letters changes by one after the intercalation. So if a leap year begins with the dominical letter E, it will change to the dominical letter D on March 1. In charts of dominical letters, leap years are designated with a double-letter notation such as ED. In 2004, a leap year, the first Sunday occurred on January 4th, identifying the year by the dominical letter D. On March 1, the letter moved back to C.

To determine the date for the Easter observance, one would look at the dates between which Easter must be celebrated (March 22–April 25), identify the corresponding Sundays by using the system of dominical letters, and determine which of these Sundays fell after the Paschal moon. The first Sunday to meet all the requirements established by the Council of Nicaea was officially declared to be Easter.

Christian Movable Feasts

When the Council of Nicaea undertook the task of establishing a date for Easter, the Feast of the Resurrection had already been a movable feast for so long that it could not easily have been established as a fixed feast on the actual anniversary of the event. Some researchers theorize that the Church authorities may have made the holiday movable as a compromise to avoid controversy. Questions persisted about the actual date of the resurrection. Although the official teaching of the Roman Catholic Church was that the crucifixion occurred on April 7, 30 c.e., modern scholars and medieval tradition agree that the actual date was probably March 25, 29 c.e. (In fact, medieval Christians established March 25 as the feast day of St. Dismas, the "good thief" who died on the cross next to Jesus.)

Another possibility for the establishment of a movable date for Easter may have been that the Church leaders wanted to avoid having the Annunciation, a day commemorating Gabriel's announcement to the Virgin Mary that she would be the mother of the Messiah which is celebrated on March 25, and the crucifixion fall on the same date. If March 25 falls during Easter Week, the Feast of the Annunciation is celebrated a week or two later.

Based on the date of Easter, a series of "movable Feasts" developed. These begin with Shrove Tuesday and end with Corpus Christi. They also include Ash Wednesday, Palm Sunday, Maundy Thursday, Good Friday, Ascension Day, and Whitsunday (also known as Pentecost).

There are three movable feasts that do not depend on the date of Easter. The Sunday after January 6 is the Feast of the Baptism of the Lord. The last Sunday of the Roman Catholic liturgical year (it falls on the third or fourth Sunday in November) is the Solemnity of Christ the King. The Sunday within the eight day celebration period following Christmas (or December 30, if Christmas is on a Sunday) is the Feast of the Holy Family.

Table 7.2. Dominical Letters Identify Sundays

A year's dominical letter will identify which dates are Sundays. In a year with a "G" dominical letter for example, March 25, April 1, April 8, April 15, and April 22 will be Sundays.

Dominical letter	Sunday dates
D	March 22
E	March 23
F	March 24
G	March 25
A	March 26
B	March 27
C	March 28
D	March 29
E	March 30
F	March 31
G	April 1
A	April 2
B	April 3
C	April 4
D	April 5
E	April 6
F	April 7
G	April 8
A	April 9
B	April 10
C	April 11
D	April 12
E	April 13
F	April 14
G	April 15
A	April 16
B	April 17
C	April 18
D	April 19
E	April 20
F	April 21
G	April 22
A	April 23
B	April 24
C	April 25

Source: Adapted from *The Book of Common Prayer* according to the use of the Episcopal Church, The Church Hymnal Corporation and The Seabury Press, 1978,

The Origins of Other Christian Holidays

Sunday, Passover, and Pentecost are the only Christian feast days mentioned by the prominent Church father, Origen, in the early third century. Other holiday traditions were quick to develop.

By the fourth century, Christians had become so numerous that the acts of persecution initiated by the Roman Emperor Diocletian a century before could no longer seriously endanger the movement. With the conversion of Constantine the Great in 312 C.E., Christianity became the official religion of the waning Roman Empire. This formal sanction spurred a massive evangelistic effort by Christians which resulted in the conversion of most inhabitants of the Empire and many barbarian groups on its outskirts.

To facilitate the acceptance of Christianity by pagans, the leaders of the Church instructed its missionaries to allow new converts to continue observing the festivals to which they were accustomed. Pope Gregory specifically instructed Augustine of Canterbury in the early seventh century that the only stipulation on the rule of acceptance was that a new meaning had to be assigned to the symbolism of the event which would bring it into line with Christian teachings.

One new festival the Church established about this time was Epiphany. The Alexandrian Church of Isis had long celebrated the day which became Epiphany as the day of Osiris's birth from the Virgin. The Mysteries of Isis originated under the Ptolemies as an Egyptian form of the Eleusinian Mysteries of Greece and had been imported into Rome by the first century B.C.E. For several centuries, the Alexandrian Church of Isis presented serious competition to the Christian Church in the Roman world. It was from the tradition of the Alexandrian Church that Christianity garnered the practice of having daily liturgical services in large ornate temples.

The worshippers of Mithras, a Persian god extremely popular among the Roman soldiers, had historically celebrated December 25 as the "Birthday of the Invincible Sun." In 273 C.E., the Christian Church established December 25 as the date of the Virgin Birth of their Invincible Son, and apparently about this time began emphasizing Christ as the Sacrificial Lamb as a substitute for the sacrificial bull of Mithraism.

Since December 25 had been established as the birthday of the Christ, the Council of Nicaea established March 25, nine months before, as the date of his conception or as the Feast of the Annunciation, the day when the angel Gabriel told Mary she had been chosen to be the mother of the Messiah. Similarly, the traditional date for the birth of Mary, September 8, determined the placing of the feast of Mary's Immaculate Conception on December 8. Each of these dates was originally a celebration of a Roman, Greek, or Egyptian deity.

Numbering Years from the Birth of Christ

In 463 C.E., Victorius of Aquitaine, who had been appointed by Pope Hilarius to undertake calendar revision, devised the Great Paschal period, which is also sometimes referred to as the Victorian Period.

The Great Paschal period, which covered 532 years, was a combination of the solar cycle of 28 years and the Metonic 19-year cycle. The lunar-based Metonic cycle indicated how long it would take for a particular phase of the moon to fall on a specific day of the month. For example, if a full moon fell on January 1, it would be 19 years before the full moon again fell on January 1. The solar cycle indicated how many years it would take a calendar date to make a complete, repeatable cycle (including leap year patterns) through all the days of the week. Combining these two cycles, a time period of 532 years elapses before the moon's phases repeat their progression through cycle of dates that fall on specific days of the week. Using this information Victorius calculated the dates of Easter for a complete Great Paschal period.

In the sixth century, the use of Easter calculations based on the Great Paschal period was extended by Dionysius Exiguus (and for this reason, the period is sometimes called the Dionysian period). Dionysius is credited with defining a new era, the Christian era. Tradition during Dionysius lifetime was to date years according to their relationship to events in the Roman Empire. Dionysius prefered measure years according to their relationship to Christ and placed the epoch (beginning) of the Christian era in the calculated year of Christ's birth. Several theories exist to explain how Dionysius determined the year in which to start counting. According to one, Dionysius used the number of years in the Great Paschal cycle and simply extended it using the year now called 532 C.E. as the beginning of a new cycle. Others suggest that he compared biblical accounts with Roman history. Whatever his method, the year now designated 1 C.E. was identified as the year of Christ's birth. Although some disputed Dionysius's calculations (and modern interpretations place the year of Christ's birth several years earlier), the dating practice began to find limited acceptance. It did not gain widespread popularity, however, until it was used by the Venerable Bede of Jarrow (c. 673–735 C.E.) in his *The Ecclesiastical History of the English People*.

Additional Calendar Reform

Through its early years and subsequent centuries the Christian church followed the Julian calendar. When compared with astronomical data and seasonal changes, however, the Julian calendar accrued a difference of approximately three days every 400 years. Calendar reforms undertaken by Pope Gregory in the middle of the sixteenth century allowed for a one-time adjustment of ten days to realign the seasons and instituted a system of adding leap days. These changes defined the Gregorian calendar, which has gained widespread acceptance in the modern era. (Additional information about the Gregorian calendar can be found in Chapter 3.)

The Current Christian Liturgical Calendars

Many branches of Christianity follow similar calendars to mark the holy days of the year. The calendar focuses attention on special incidents in Jesus's life and also provides for the remembrance of many saints and historical events. It includes two types of dates: movable feasts, which are typically established based on their relationship to the Feast of the Resurrection (Easter), and fixed holidays.

The Christian liturgical year begins in late November with a season called Advent. Advent is four weeks long and it provides a time during which Christians focus on preparing for Jesus birth. Advent is followed by Christmas and the Christmas season during which Jesus's birth is celebrated. Epiphany, in early January commemorates the manifestation of Jesus to the Gentiles (non-Jews). Lent is a season of introspection and penance in preparation for Easter. It concludes with Holy Week, a time during which events in the last week of Jesus's life are highlighted. The Easter season begins on Resurrection Sunday and lasts until Ascension Day, commemorating Jesus's ascension into heaven. The season of Pentecost begins with the celebration of the coming of the Holy Spirit. The longest season of the year, Trinity, completes the cycle.

The Roman Catholic calendar was revised in 1969, changing some of the days on which certain saints were honored and changing others from being noted as universally honored to locally honored. According to Catholic law, followers are obligated to participate in Mass weekly on either a Saturday evening or Sunday morning and on six other days identified as holy days of obligation: Christmas, Solemnity of Mary, Ascension, Assumption of the Blessed Virgin, All Saints Day, and Immaculate Conception.

Table 7.3. Common* Seasons and Movable Feasts in the Western Christian Liturgical Calendar

Advent Season
The First through Fourth Sunday of Advent

Christmas Season
The Nativity of Our Lord (Christmas)
The First Sunday after Christmas Day
The Second Sunday after Christmas Day

Epiphany Season
The Epiphany
The First Sunday after the Epiphany: The Baptism
    of Our Lord
The Second Sunday through the Eighth Sunday
    after the Epiphany
The Last Sunday after the Epiphany

Lenten Season
Ash Wednesday
The First through Fourth (or Fifth) Sunday in Lent

Holy Week
Palm Sunday
Monday in Holy Week
Tuesday in Holy Week
Wednesday in Holy Week
Maundy Thursday
Good Friday
Holy Saturday

Easter Season
Easter Eve
The Sunday of the Resurrection, or Easter Day
The Second through Sixth Sunday of Easter
Ascension Day
The Seventh Sunday of Easter: The Sunday after
    Ascension Day
The Day of Pentecost: Whitsunday

The Season After Pentecost
The First Sunday after Pentecost: Trinity Sunday
The Second through the Twenty-seventh Sunday
    after Pentecost
The Last Sunday after Pentecost

---

*Compiled from Roman Catholic, Lutheran, and Anglican sources.

▦ ▦ ▦

Christian Holidays

Weekly

Sunday

Many Christian groups observe Sunday as a day for communal worship. The practice of gathering on Sundays originated with the first generation of Christians, who were predominantly Jewish. In addition to meeting on the Jewish Sabath, they began meeting on Sunday in remembrance of Jesus's resurrection.

Many Christian ritual practices are drawn from Jewish sources. For example, the Jewish Passover Seder forms the basis of a Christian ritual meal of bread and wine. Called by various names (such as Eucharist, Communion, Agape Lovefeast, and the Lord's Supper), the meal is often the focal point of Sunday services. It is observed in memory of Jesus's last meal with his disciples. Some sects observe this ritual on a weekly basis, others less frequently. To support and surround this ritual, Christians developed a host of other practices including singing hymns, offering prayers, reading portions of the sacred writings, and listening to teachings.

Quarterly

Ember Days
Four times a year

Ember Days are solemn observations occurring at the beginning of each of the natural seasons. Traditionally marked by three days of fasting, Ember Days are the Wednesday, Friday, and Saturday following the first Sunday in Lent, Whitsunday (Pentecost), Holyrood Day (September 14) and St. Lucy's Day (December 13). The weeks in which these days occur are called Ember Weeks, and the Friday in each of these weeks is known as Golden Friday.

The word "ember" derives from an old English word referring to the revolution of time. Some historians have suggested that the Ember Days originated with pagan purification rituals that occurred at the seasons of planting, harvest, and vintage. The notion of fasting on these days was instituted by Pope Calixtus I in the third century, but the dates of the fast varied until 1095 when they were fixed at their current times.

In 1969, the Roman Catholic Church replaced these days with days of prayer for various needs. The Anglican Communion dedicates these days to prayer for those in formal ministry and for contemplation of one's own role in lay ministry.

Annually

November

Advent
Beginning on the Sunday closest to November 30 and continuing through December 24

The Christian liturgical year begins with Advent, the season of preparation for Christmas. In Roman Catholic and liturgically based Protestant churches, it begins on the Sunday nearest St. Andrew's Day and ends on Christmas Eve. Because of the movable beginning date, the season can last from 22 to 28 days. The third Sunday of Advent is designated Gaudete Sunday by the Roman Catholic Church and the Anglican Communion. On this Sunday, the altar may be adorned with flowers and the purple vestments of the priests may be replaced by rose-colored garb.

The most common Advent customs in the United States have been imported from Germany. The Advent calendar and the Advent wreath are perhaps the best known. To help count the days before Christmas, parents often give children an Advent calendar that contains twenty-four flaps, one of which is opened each day between December 1 and December 24. The Advent wreath may be used as part of family devotional meditations during the season. It contains four or five candles which are lit in a special ceremony each Sunday of Advent and on Christmas day. Another Advent tradition is the German "Star of Seven," a special candle with seven braches which are lit in increasing numbers throughout the season. A European advent tradition includes placing a branch from a cherry tree in water on the first Sunday of Advent so it will bloom on the last Sunday of Advent.

St. Andrew's Day
November 30

St. Andrew, the brother of St. Peter, was the first apostle called by Jesus, but he is primarily known today as the patron saint of Scotland (though he was also chosen to be patron saint of Russia). According to tradition, St. Andrew went to Greece where he influenced the proconsul's wife to convert to Christianity. He was condemned to be crucified. Fastened to an X-shaped cross by cords rather than nails, he eventually died of thirst and starvation.

St. Andrew's association with Scotland began four centuries after his death when some of his relics were brought there. Some Scots continue the custom of wearing a "St. Andrew's cross" on November 30. The St. Andrew's cross consists of blue and white ribbons shaped like the letter X. The tradition for this form of a cross began no earlier than the 13th century.

St. Andrew's Day is also a major feast in Lapland and a time for weddings and meeting new people.

December

Mother Seton Day
December 1

Observed by the Sisters of Charity of St. Vincent De Paul as the anniversary of their founding by St. Elizabeth Ann Bayley Seton, a Staten Island native and the first American-born saint canonized by the Roman Catholic Church.

St. Nicholas's Day
December 6

Very little is known about St. Nicholas, except that in the fourth century he was the bishop of Myra in what is now Turkey. One of the legends surrounding him is that he saved three sisters from being forced into prostitution by their poverty-stricken father. This was accomplished by throwing three bags of gold into their room, thus providing each of them with a dowry. This may be the source of St. Nicholas's association with gift-giving.

On December 6 in the Netherlands, St. Nicholas, or Sinterklass, still rides into town on a white horse, dressed in his red bishop's robes. He is preceded by "Black Peter," a Satanic figure in Moorish costume who

---

Table 7.4. Fixed Holidays in the Western Christian Liturgical Calendar

Compiled from Roman Catholic, Lutheran, and Anglican Sources, including Holy Days of Obligation, Red Letter Days, and Lesser Festivals; omitting Optional Feasts, Black Letter Days, and Commemorations

November
30 ....St. Andrew the Apostle

December
21 ....St. Thomas the Apostle
25 ....The Nativity of Our Lord Jesus Christ
26 ....St. Stephen, Deacon and Martyr
27 ....St. John, Apostle and Evangelist
28 ....The Holy Innocents

January
1 ....The Holy Name of Our Lord Jesus Christ
6 ....The Epiphany
18 ....The Confession of St. Peter the Apostle
25 ....The Conversion of St. Paul the Apostle

February
2 ....The Presentation of Our Lord Jesus Christ in the Temple
24 ....St. Matthias the Apostle

March
19 ....St. Joseph
25 ....The Annunciation

April
25 ....St. Mark the Evangelist

May
1 ....St. Philip and St. James, Apostles
31 ....The Visitation of the Blessed Virgin Mary

June
11 ....St. Barnabas the Apostle
24 ....The Nativity of St. John the Baptist
29 ....St. Peter and St. Paul, Apostles

July
22 ....St. Mary Magdalene
25 ....St. James the Apostle

August
6 ....The Transfiguration of Our Lord Jesus Christ
15 ....St. Mary the Virgin, Mother of Our Lord Jesus Christ
24 ....St. Bartholomew the Apostle

September
14 ....Holy Cross Day
21 ....St. Matthew, Apostle and Evangelist
29 ....St. Michael and All Angels

October
18 ....St. Luke the Evangelist
23 ....St. James of Jerusalem, Brother of Our Lord Jesus Christ, and Martyr
28 ....St. Simon and St. Jude, Apostles
31 ....Reformation Day (Lutheran)

November
1 ....All Saints

switches the bad children while the good are rewarded with candy and gifts. St. Nicholas is the patron saint of sailors, and churches dedicated to him are often built so they can be seen off the coast as landmarks.

The American Santa Claus, a corruption of "St. Nicholas," is a cross between the original St. Nicholas and the British "Father Christmas." The political cartoonist Thomas Nast created a Santa Claus dressed in furs and looking more like King Cole—an image that grew fatter and merrier over the years, until he became the uniquely American figure that adorns thousands of cards, decorations, and homes throughout the Christmas season. Although Americans open their gifts on Christmas or Christmas Eve, in the Netherlands, Switzerland, Germany, and some other European countries, gifts are still exchanged on St. Nicholas's Eve (December 5) or St. Nicholas's Day (December 6).

Feast of the Immaculate Conception of Mary
December 8

This Roman Catholic observance is a holy day of obligation on which church attendance is required. It is classed as a solemnity. It honors Mary in view of her calling to be the Mother of Christ and in virtue of his merits. The day celebrates the belief that Mary was preserved from original sin beginning with the moment of her conception and that she was filled with grace from the very beginning of her life. She was the only person, aside from Jesus, believed to be so preserved from original sin.

The present form of the Feast of the Immaculate Conception of Mary dates from December 8, 1854, when Pope Pius IX defined the dogma of the Immaculate Conception. An earlier feast of the Conception was observed in the East by the eighth century; in Ireland the feast dates to the ninth century. Centuries-old links also exist in other European countries. In 1846, Mary was proclaimed patroness of the United States under this title.

Saint Lucy's Day (Lucia Day; Luciadagen)
December 13

Lucia Day is a festival with Swedish origins which fell on the day of the winter solstice before the Gregorian reform. It is observed by Swedish-American communities in honor of Lucia, the Queen of Lights. Traditionally, the youngest daughter in the family dons a crown with lighted candles and wakes her parents to a breakfast of Lucia buns served in bed while the other children sing a hymn to Lucia.

Posadas
December 16–25

This feast of "The Lodgings" is celebrated in Hispanic communities to commemorate the journey of St. Mary and St. Joseph to Bethlehem. Folk plays in which children perform the roles of Mary and Joseph take place in the town. The children knock on doors and are turned away repeatedly until they finally find shelter in the parish church, at which point the community party begins. Another highlight of the celebration for the children is the breaking of the piñata which scatters gifts to those standing nearby.

St. Thomas's Day
December 21

St. Thomas the Apostle was dubbed "Doubting Thomas" because, after the resurrection, when the other apostles told him that they had seen Jesus, he wouldn't believe them until he had touched Jesus's wounds for himself. When the apostles left Jerusalem to preach to the people of other nations, as Jesus had instructed them to do, tradition says Thomas traveled eastward toward India. In Kerala, the smallest state in India, the Malabar Christians (or Christians of St. Thomas) claim St. Thomas as the founder of their church. For them his feast day is a major celebration. Thomas is the patron saint of India and Pakistan.

The Roman Catholic Church celebrates St. Thomas's Day on July 3.

Christmas Eve
December 24

The day before Christmas is a full or partial holiday in 29 countries, and in most of the United States. In central and northern Europe, Christmas Eve, rather than Christmas Day, is the occasion of the major family celebration, and some American families observe this custom as well.

A long-standing liturgical tradition of Christmas Eve has been the "Midnight Mass." Many parish churches, however, hold the service earlier than midnight so that entire families, including young children, can attend.

Another Christmas Eve custom, that of being especially kind to animals, was instituted by St. Francis of Assisi, who also introduced his Franciscan monks to the concept of a joyful Christmas carol (as distinguished from the solemn Christmas hymns). St. Francis is also credited with beginning the custom of setting up a manger scene (crèche) with statues or other representations of the holy family, the angels, the Magi, the shepherds, and the animals. Some families place the Magi with their camels far away from the manger scene. Each day of Advent, the children in the home move the figures closer to the manger scene until, on Christmas Eve, they reach the manger. The manger itself is left empty until Christmas morning, when the statue of the Christ child is put in place to complete the story.

Although Christmas is observed by the majority of Christians, there are a few sects that make a point of not observing Christmas or most other common Christian holidays. Instead these groups, including Adventist churches, Jehovah's Witnesses, and various British Israelite communities, often look to Hebrew sources for identifying holidays. Because these groups usually use the Christian calendar, however, the dates of the holidays they celebrate are often different from the Jewish celebration of the same events.

Moravian Love Feast
December 24

The Moravian Love Feast began on a Christmas Eve during the eighteenth century. Count von Zinzendorf, who was visiting in Pennsylvania, noticed the parallel between the shelter they were in and the shelter where Jesus was born in Bethelehem. As a result, the location where they established their settlement was named Bethlehem.

The Love Feast is still celebrated by Moravians. It begins during the afternoon of Christmas Eve. Churches are decorated with evergreens and sweet buns and cookies are served to all the children in the congregation. The service closes with a candle ceremony using specially made beeswax candles. Other Moravian Christmas customs include a trombone choir, a musical Christmas Eve vigil, and the making of two types of special cookies which are cut into traditional shapes and used as tree decorations.

Christmas Day (Nativity of Our Lord)
December 25

Christmas is the day on which Christians celebrate the birth of Jesus Christ. The Roman Catholic Church designates it as a day of holy obligation on which members must attend services.

As with many traditions surrounding Christmas, the selection of December 25 as a commemoration of Jesus's birthday may be an example of the blending of Christian ideas and the pagan traditions they replaced. December 25 was the date of the Mithric observance of the "Birthday of the Invincible Sun." This also coincided with Saturnalia and the winter solstice during the period when Mithraism was practiced in Rome. Since the day was already being kept as a holiday, Christians may have adjusted the symbolism of the day, declaring it the birthday of their "Invincible Son." According to events in the Gospel of Matthew, the date of Jesus's birth may actually have been much earlier in the year.

The word "Christmas" means "the mass of Christ." The term originated in the 11th century as a name for this feast. It was one of the most popular and universally celebrated holidays in Europe during the Middle Ages. During the Reformation, however, the celebration of Christmas began to decline in importance. Reformers engaged in complex doctrinal arguments in an attempt to prove the celebration of Christmas was unscriptural.

In some countries, the Protestant reforms brought about a ban of Christmas celebrations. By the time of the Restoration in 1660, however, the celebration of Christmas as a much more secular holiday was revived in these countries. In New England, Christmas remained outlawed until the mid-nineteenth century, and in Boston classes were held in the public schools on Christmas Day until 1870, with pupils who missed school that day being punished or dismissed. The mass immigration of Irish Catholics to New England brought about the reinstitution of Christmas celebrations.

In the calendar of the Roman Catholic, Lutheran, and Anglican confessions, Christmastide begins on Christmas Eve and continues until the Sunday after Epiphany. Christians generally attend services on Christmas Eve, and often on Christmas Day as well.

A vast number of non-religious customs are associated with Christmas in the United States. A traditional day of family gatherings, Christmas is often celebrated with a feast which typically includes such foods as turkey, goose, or ham, yams, mince pies, and plum pudding.

The Christmas tree has become a standard symbol of the season in the United States. Each year, families decorate fresh cut or artificial evergreen trees in their homes. The tradition may have its roots in the sixteenth-century custom of decorating a "paradise tree" with apples in remembrance of Adam and Eve. Another theory about the origins of the Christmas tree date back to ancient pagan veneration of evergreen trees.

Other legends surrounding the origin of the Christmas tree abound. In one story, an eighteenth century saint, St. Boniface, convinced people to abandon the practice of sacrificing children around an oak tree. Instead, he urged that a fir tree be cut down for celebrations. Another legend involves St. Winfred, a missionary in Scandinavia during the eighth century. St. Winfred cut down an oak tree and miraculously a fir tree grew. As a result, the fir was declared holy, symbolic of endless life.

The Germans brought the idea of Christmas lights or candles to the United States (although they were not placed on trees until perhaps the eighteenth century). This practice, combined with the Irish custom of putting lights in the windows, led to the lighting of houses and Christmas trees. At first, candles were used but they were a fire hazard. In the twentieth century, electric lights came into use and proved to be much safer.

Other plants are used in traditional Christmas decorations as well. Mistletoe, for example, was used by Druids for healing and as a symbol of peace and reconciliation (hence the kiss under the mistletoe). Holly's green leaves and red berries in the midst of winter make it another evergreen symbol. Ivy is associated with midwinter carousing. Laurel wreaths, worn as a victory symbol by the Romans, are hung on front doors as a symbol of Christ's victory over the forces of darkness and death. Poinsettia was introduced from Mexico in the nineteenth century and is especially appealing because of its red and green coloring.

Figure 7.1. Agnus Dei (Lamb of God) is a representation of Jesus Christ as the Lamb of God, an allusion to the sacrificial lamb offered at Passover. According to the Gospel of St. John, upon seeing Jesus, John the Baptist said: "Behold the Lamb of God, which taketh away the sin of the world." (John 1:29, King James Version). In this illustration, characteristic of depictions found in the Catacombs, the Agnus Dei stands on a mount and the four rivers of Paradise represent the four Evangelists and their gospels: The Gihon for St. Matthew; the Tigris for St. Mark; the Euphrates for St. Luke; and the Pison for St. John.

Another popular custom surrounding Christmas is the singing of carols. "Carols" were originally dance songs played on flutes. In current usage, carols are joyful songs of the Christmas season, typically focused on topics such as Christ's nativity, stars, or shepherds.

In many American homes, Christmas presents are wrapped and placed under the tree to be opened on Christmas Eve or Day. The Christian practice of gift giving is associated with the gifts brought to Jesus by the three Magi and may have originally taken place during Epiphany. In Europe, Epiphany is still the usual day for gift-giving. In Italy, presents are said to be brought by La Befana, a Fairy Queen or "Mother Witch" figure whose name appears to be a worn-down form of "epiphany."

Gifts are traditionally delivered to American children by Santa Claus. The name "Santa Claus" is derived from the Dutch name, Sinter Klaas, for Saint Nicholas. The popular concept of Santa is based on the immensely popular verse, "The Night Before Christmas," by Clement Moore, first published in the mid-nineteenth century.

Very sophisticated theological arguments are possible over the question of whether Santa Claus is still really a Christian saint because he has absorbed major characteristics of Hermes, Wotan, Thor, and various other pagan divinities. Another name for Santa Claus, Kris Kringle, was apparently derived from the German Christkindel, "Christ child," who is said to bring presents on Christmas Eve. Similar figures are Father Christmas (in England) and Knecht Rupprecht (Knight Rupert) in northern Germany.

Twelve Days of Christmas
December 25 through January 5

The twelve days of Christmas are counted from Christmas to Epiphany. Epiphany was the traditional date for the visit of the Three Magi, and is still the customary date for gift-giving in many parts of Europe, Mexico, and Latin America. Twelfth Night, the eve of the last day, marked the end of the Christmas season, usually by means of one last exuberant party. Because of Shakespeare's play *Twelfth Night*, the Twelfth Day of Christmas is generally observed as a festive occasion by actors. In many American homes, New Year's Day (rather than the Twelfth Day of Christmas) is considered the end of the holiday season.

St. Stephen's Day
December 26

On this day in about the year 35, St. Stephen became the first Christian martyr. The New Testament book of Acts records that Stephen was chosen by the apostles as one of the first seven deacons of the church in Jerusalem. He was later denounced as a blasphemer by the Sanhedrin (the Jewish council in ancient Palestine) and stoned to death. St. Stephen is the patron saint of brick-layers.

In many countries, St. Stephen's Day is celebrated as an extra Christmas holiday. In England, it is known as Boxing Day. In Austria, priests bless the horses. In Poland tossing rice symbolizes blessings and recalls Stephen's stoning. In Ireland, boys with blackened faces carrying a paper wren, go about begging and "hunting the wren." The hunting of the wren is most likely a carryover from an old belief that the robin, symbolizing the New Year, killed the wren, symbolizing the Old, at the turning of the year.

December 26, 27, and 28, otherwise known as St. Stephen's Day, St. John the Evangelist's Day, and Holy Innocents' Day, are considered examples of the three different degrees of martyrdom. St. Stephen's death is an example of the highest class of martyrdom, that is martyrdom in both will and deed. St. John the Evangelist, who showed that he was ready to die for Christ but was prevented from actually doing so, exemplifies martyrdom in will, but not in deed. And the children who lost their lives in the slaughter of the Innocents provide an example of the martyrdom in deed but not in will.

St. John the Evangelist's Day
December 27

St. John the Evangelist, also called St. John the Divine, was thought to be not only the youngest of the apostles but the longest-lived, dying peacefully of natural causes at an advanced age. Although he escaped actual martyrdom, St. John endured considerable persecution and suffering for his beliefs. He is said to have drunk poison to prove his faith (so he is the patron saint of protection against poison), been cast into a cauldron of boiling oil, and at one point banished to the lonely Greek island of Patmos, where he worked among the criminals in the mines. He remained healthy, vigorous, and miraculously unharmed throughout these trials and returned to Ephesus where it is believed he wrote the Gospel According to John. He is also believed to be the author of the New Testament book of Revelation, though some scholars disagree.

Holy Innocents' Day (Innocents' Day; Childermas)
December 28

This day is dedicated to the memory of the male children in Bethlehem who were slaughtered by King Herod in his attempt to kill the infant Jesus. The day has come to be considered unlucky; therefore, among those who observe it, few marriages or important ventures are consummated on this day.

January

Feast of the Circumcision (Solemnity of Mary; Holy Name Day)
January 1

This holiday is known by several different names throughout the Christian Church. Roman Catholics, who previously called it the Octave of the Birth of Our Lord, or the Circumcision of Jesus, now refer to the day as the Solemnity of Mary, the Mother of God. Episcopalians know the holiday as the Feast of the Holy Name of Our Lord Jesus Christ because it was on this day, according to Hebrew custom, that Jesus was given his name. Lutherans call it the Feast of the Circumcision and the Name of Jesus.

In the Roman Catholic Church, The Feast of the Solemnity supplants the former feast of the Maternity of Mary observed on October 11.

Universal Week of Prayer
The first Sunday through the second Sunday in January

This custom, begun by the World Evangelical Alliance of London, England, in 1846, has been adopted and sponsored by the National Council of Churches. It is marked by interdenominational services in many American communities; these are held in the evenings, and move from denomination to denomination during the week.

Epiphany Eve
January 5 in Anglican, Protestant, and many Roman Catholic Churches; the Saturday between January 1 and January 7 in the Roman Catholic Church in the United States

Epiphany Eve is also known as Twelfth Night or Old Christmas Eve. One myth associated with this day is that of the Glastonbury Thorn. According to the Grail cycle of Arthurian legend, there is a blackthorn tree in Glastonbury, England, that grew from the staff of Joseph of Arimathea (the man who owned the burial site of Jesus). Each year on January 5, the Glastonbury Thorn is said to bloom.

This legend gave rise to an annual pilgrimage to Glastonbury and lent an illusion of credence to England's claim as the cradle of Christianity. King Henry II of England used the legends of the Grail cycle to assert the authenticity of England's apostolic succession as independent of Rome.

Epiphany (Feast of Kings; Twelfth Day; Twelfthtide; Three Kings' Day; Day of the Three Wise Men)

January 6 in Anglican, Protestant, and many Roman Catholic Churches; the Sunday between January 2 and January 8 in the Roman Catholic Church in the United States

Epiphany commemorates the manifestations Christ's divinity: in his birth, in the homage of the Magi, and at his baptism by John the Baptist. It is one of the oldest Christian feasts, originating in the Eastern Church in the second century and antedating the Western feast of Christmas.

The Epiphany was adopted by the Western Church during the same period in which the Eastern Church accepted Christmas. In the Roman Catholic service, commemoration is made in the Mass of the homage of the Magi, or astronomers, from the East, and of Jesus's first public "miracle" or "sign," the changing of water into wine at the wedding in Cana.

Old Christmas Day

January 6

When the switch from the Julian to the Gregorian calendar was made in England, many people resisted the change because of emotional attachment to the previous system. One way in which people registered their dissatisfaction was to continue observing holidays according to the Julian calendar, placing them thirteen days later than their Gregorian counterparts. Old Christmas Day is one of these holdovers from the Julian system.

Feast of the Holy Family

The Sunday after Epiphany

The Roman Catholic Church commemorates the holy family of Jesus, the Virgin Mary, and St. Joseph on this day each year. As the model of the perfect family, they represent perfect holiness and virtue. The roots of the feast can be traced to the 17th century, and in 1921, Pope Benedict XV extended the Divine Office and Mass of the feast to the whole Church.

Feast of the Baptism of the Lord

The Sunday following Epiphany

This feast was originally combined with Epiphany commemorating the manifestation of the divinity of Jesus at his baptism and the beginning of his public ministry. In 1961 the Roman Catholic Church set aside a separate holy day to recognize this event. The baptism of Jesus is observed by almost all Christian Churches on some date in January.

At first, the date for the Feast of the Baptism of the Lord was January 13, but in 1969, the date was fixed on the Sunday following Epiphany. Since many countries have moved the celebration of Epiphany from the traditional date of January 6 to the Sunday between January 2 and 8, the two holidays sometimes coincide. In this case, the celebration of Epiphany takes precedence and the Feast of the Baptism is omitted.

Plough Monday

The first Monday after Epiphany

The origins of Plough Monday are thought to date back to the medieval custom of British farmers, or ploughmen, who would leave candles known as plough-lights burning in homage to the saints. Each year, the farmers would gather in town to collect money from the residents to buy the plough-lights. Although the adulation of the saints was quelled by the sixteenth-century Reformation, the festivities of the day continued.

By the nineteenth century, the day was filled with music, dancing, processions, and trick-or-treating by the local ploughmen. The trick-or-treat tradition included "The Bessy," a man dressed up as a buffoon in women's clothing, and "The Fool," a man wearing animal skins or a fur cap and tail, parading from door to door demanding money to fund their revelry. Another tradition was for the ploughmen to drag a beribboned plough from house to house, ploughing up the front yard of any homeowner who failed to financially sponsor the carousing.

These rural practices died out early in the twentieth century. The Church, however, continued to bless ploughs on Plough Sunday.

Death of George Fox

January 13

The death on January 13, 1691, of George Fox, founder of the Society of Friends, is observed worldwide by all Quaker Churches and Meetings.

Blessing of Animals

The Sunday nearest to January 17

The blessing of animals takes place in Catholic countries near the feast day of St. Anthony of Egypt, also known as Anthony the Abbot, the founder of monasticism and the patron saint of all four-footed beasts. (There are also some local blessings of animals on the feast of St. Francis of Assisi, whose love for animals is more well known.) Originally a day on which farm animals were blessed, the custom now extends to household pets, who are usually blessed at the church doors, but sometimes before the altar.

Birthday of Martin Luther King, Jr.
The third Monday in January

The birth of Martin Luther King, Jr., is observed as a holiday in most of the United States, usually on the third Monday in January. It is a political, rather than a religious, holiday; yet, its religious aspects cannot be ignored. King was a man of deep faith, and is regarded by millions as a modern-day saint much like Mahatma Gandhi. His accomplishments, and especially their foundation in King's Christian faith, are common topics for homilies in many Christian Churches in the United States on the Sunday of the holiday weekend.

Conversion of St. Paul
January 25

Saul of Tarsus, a highly educated, devout Jew, was converted to Christianity on the road to Damascus not long after the death of Jesus Christ. Later he was known as Paul. Through his life, his teachings, and his writings, he became the most influential leader in the history of the Church. The Church believes he was beheaded during Nero's persecution of Christians about the year 67.

At one time the weather on this day was linked to predictions about the coming year. Fair weather on St. Paul's day was said to presage a prosperous year; snow or rain an unproductive one. Clouds meant that many cattle would die, and a windy day was said to be the forerunner of war.

February

Presentation of Jesus (Purification of the Blessed Virgin Mary; Candlemas)
February 2

This day commemorates Jesus's presentation in the Temple which was in accord with the prescriptions of Mosaic Law and Mary's forty-day purification following the birth of her child. This presentation was also the occasion on which, according to the Gospel of Luke, Jesus was first publicly proclaimed as the Messiah by the prophets Anna and Simeon in the temple courtyard.

Also called the Feast of the Purification of the Blessed Virgin Mary, the holiday stemmed from a Jewish religious law that required a woman to abstain from sexual intercourse for forty days after the birth of a child and undergo a ritual purification bath at the end of that time.

The date set for this holiday was February 2, forty days after the celebration of Christmas which was fixed on December 25 in the fourth century. The feast was adopted earlier in the East than in the West and was celebrated by the Orthodox Church as a feast of Jesus rather than of Mary. The Roman Catholic Church, however, observed the holiday in honor of Mary until 1969. At that time, the feast became known as the Presentation of Jesus in the Roman Catholic Church as well as in the Orthodox Church.

The secondary name for this holiday is Candlemas, which is derived from the day's tradition of blessing candles to be used for healing and other sacred practices during the year. The blessing of candles, which became popular in the eleventh century, emerged from Simeon's proclaimation of the baby Jesus as "a light for revelation to the Gentiles."

Arrival of Roger Williams in the New World
February 5

American Baptists celebrate the coming of Roger Williams to North America on February 5, 1631, when he arrived in the Massachusetts colony from his native Wales. Williams and four other men were later expelled from the colony for refusing to recognize the government's authority to prosecute religious offenses. The men and their families then established the colony of Rhode Island based on the principle of absolute religious liberty. The first Baptist congregation on the continent was established on Rhode Island.

Vartanantz Day
The Thursday preceding Ash Wednesday

This day marks the Armenian commemoration of the death of their patron saint, along with 1,036 other martyrs, during the war with Persia in 451 C.E.

Race Relations Sunday
The Sunday nearest February 12

This day is observed on the Sunday nearest Abraham Lincoln's birthday because of the role he played in freeing the slaves during the Civil War. Up until 1965 it was sponsored by the National Council of Churches, but since that time, sponsorship has been undertaken by individual denominations. A number of Roman Catholic groups observe Race Relations Sunday as well, and some Jewish organizations observe it on the preceding Sabbath. Although it was originally conceived in 1924 as an opportunity to focus on improving relations among all races, the longstanding racial conflict between whites and blacks in the United States has made this the focal point in recent decades.

There are a number of other observances dealing with race relations at this same time in February. The NAACP (National Association for the Advancement of Colored People) was established on Lincoln's Birthday in 1909. Members of this organization combine the observance of Race Relations Sunday with their organization's founding and with the birthday of Frederick Douglass, the black abolitionist and early human rights activist, on February 7, 1817.

Carnival
Ending with Shrove Tuesday.

In general, the carnival period is just before Ash Wednesday, the beginning of Lent. Its name is said to be derived from the Latin carne vale, "farewell to meat." Carnival is a time of revelry prior to the season of fasting during Lent.

Observed as a holiday in thirteen countries, Carnival varies in length from one to three days—usually the days just prior to Ash Wednesday. Some regions, however, begin the festivities soon after Epiphany, engaging in weekly or even daily parties, dances, and festivities, as in the German Fasching customs. The celebration in Haiti is the biggest holiday of the year. A particular characteristic of the Haitian Carnival is the construction of "lamayotes" or wooden boxes decorated with paint and tissue paper. Boys in Haiti place a surprise inside the boxes—usually a mouse, lizard, or bug. Dressed in masks and costumes during Carnival, the boys roam the streets, trying to coax people to pay a penny for a peek inside the box. Brazil's Carnival is a major holiday as well, lasting five days and drawing participants from all over the world to Rio de Janeiro. Massive parades, dance competitions, and other merrymaking fill the days with joyous activity.

The most renown Carnival in the United States is the Mardi Gras festival held each year in New Orleans.

Fasching
The three days preceding Ash Wednesday

This Shrovetide festival is celebrated in Austria and Germany (especially in Bavaria) with costumed balls and parades on Fasching Sunday, Rose Monday, and Shrove Tuesday, the three days before Ash Wednesday, and is usually preceded by several weeks of parties. It is similar to the Mardi Gras celebrations around the world.

Rose Monday
The Monday before Lent

Rose Monday, or Rosenmontag, occurs before Ash Wednesday and is celebrated in Germany and German-American communities as part of the Fasching or Carnival season. The German name Rosenmontag ("Roses Monday") takes its name from a mispronunciation of Rasen Montag ("Rushing Monday") or "live-it-up Monday"—an appropriate characterization of this day of celebration.

Birthday of Richard Allen
February 11

Richard Allen, founder of the African Methodist Episcopal Church (AME), is commemorated by members of that denomination on February 11, the date of his birth. Allen was born in 1760 and started the AME Church in 1816. He also served as its first bishop.

Mardi Gras
The Tuesday before Ash Wednesday

Mardi Gras is French for "fat Tuesday," which is the day before Ash Wednesday. More broadly, Mardi Gras refers to the pre-Lenten gala in New Orleans. The carnival is celebrated with a myriad of parades, costume balls, and pageantry beginning right after Twelfth Night, and concluding with the famous parade on Shrove Tuesday. Major Mardi Gras festivals also take place in other U.S. cities particularly in Louisiana, Florida, and Alabama.

Lent
Forty days before Easter (exclusive of Sundays)

Lent is a period of introspection and penitence observed by Christians in preparation for the celebration of Easter. The tradition of prayer, fasting, and self-denial was initially practiced only for three days before Easter, beginning with Good Friday. In the late sixth century, however, the Lenten season was established at forty weekdays by Gregory the Great (590–604 C.E.). The significance of the length of days may reflect the importance of the number forty in the Bible: Moses fasted for forty days on Mt. Sinai, the Israelites had wandered for forty years with few provisions, Elijah's fast lasted forty days, and Jesus went forty days without food after his baptism and prior to the onset of his public ministry.

Because of the tradition of abstinence during the Lenten season, festivals such as Carnival and Mardi Gras became popular as the last opportunity Christians had to engage in restricted activities and consume forbidden foods.

Ash Wednesday
A movable observance, six and one-half weeks before Easter

Ash Wednesday marks the beginning of Lent, a season of introspection and penitence for Christians as they prepare for Easter. Ashes, symbolic of penance, are blessed and distributed among the faithful. They are used to mark the forehead with the Sign of the Cross. The reminder, "Remember, man, that you are dust, and unto dust you shall return," or "Repent, and believe the Good News," is recited as the cross is drawn. The ashes used are typically made from burning palms used on the Palm Sunday of the previous year or from burning brushwood.

World Day of Prayer
The first Friday in Lent

World Day of Prayer was first suggested in 1887 by the Presbyterian Church in the United States. As its observance has spread to other demominations, the number of participants has grown. The United Church Women of the National Council of Churches assumes responsibility for organizing prayers and selecting a theme upon which women around the world focus as they join together in prayer. Prayer starts as the sun crosses the International Date line and travels westward around the globe.

Quadragesima
The first Sunday of Lent

This holiday is named for the Latin word "fortieth" because it falls forty days before Easter. There are three other numbered Sundays in the pre-Lent season: Quinquagesima ("fiftieth"), Sexagesima ("sixtieth"), and Septagesima ("seventieth"). Septagesima, therefore would be the first Sunday after Epiphany, and so forth until Ash Wednesday, when Lent begins. These three are no longer in general use; the days are now reckoned in relation to Epiphany.

St. Matthias's Day
February 24

St. Matthias was an apostle and martyr. The story of his selection to replace Judas Iscariot is found in the book of Acts (Acts 1:15–26). There is no historical record of his deeds or death, and some Christian historians believe he was martyred shortly after his election as an apostle.

March

Mothering Sunday (Carling Sunday; Laetare Sunday; Rose Sunday; Mid-Lent Sunday; Refreshment Sunday)
The fourth Sunday of Lent

During the seventeenth century, a custom of visiting the "Mother Church," the church in which a person had been baptized, developed among English Christians. On the same day, many people would visit their parents with a small gift for the mother of the family. In England, the gift was often a simnel or fruit cake with an almond paste topping. In Scotland, however, a carling (a pancake made of soaked peas fried in butter) was the traditional gift. Hence, this Sunday is also known as Carling Sunday.

There are many other names for this day. It is called Laetare Sunday because the Introit of the Roman Catholic Mass begins with the word "Rejoice" which is *laetare* in Latin; Rose Sunday because of the color of the vestments worn by the priests and the blessing of the Golden Rose symbol; and Mid-Lent or Refreshment Sunday because of the brief intermission it offers in the Lenten season.

St. Patrick's Day
March 17

St. Patrick was born around 390 C.E. in Roman Britain. He was raised in the Christian faith but was kidnapped by pagan Irish raiders and sold into slavery when he was 16. During his time in Ireland, St. Patrick strengthened his Christian beliefs despite the Irish opposition, and when he gained his freedom, he returned to his home to train for the priesthood. Eventually he returned to the Irish people to share his faith with them, and he was highly successful in converting many to Christianity. The shamrock that has become a symbol of St. Patrick supposedly comes from his use of its three-part leaf to describe the Holy Trinity. St. Patrick later became the patron saint of Ireland.

The Feast of St. Patrick is celebrated by Roman Catholics, the Anglican Communion, and Lutherans on March 17. The city of Boston holds a St. Patrick's Day parade which dates back to 1737. New York City's parade is a major event for Irish-Americans and was started in 1762. Up to 125,000 participants march on the route which takes them past St. Patrick's Cathedral on Fifth Avenue in Manhattan.

Annunciation of the Lord (Feast of Annunciation of the Blessed Virgin Mary)
March 25 (or, if March 25 falls during Holy Week, April 1)

This holiday commemorates the manifestation of the Archangel Gabriel to the Virgin Mary, announcing that she was chosen to be the mother of Jesus. Celebrated by the Roman Catholic, Anglican, and Lutheran Churches, the Annunciation usually falls during Lent, but moves to April 1 if March 25 falls during Holy Week. Christians in the middle ages believed the coincidence of the Annunciation and Easter on the same date was a bad omen.

The feast was instituted about 430 C.E. in the East. The Roman observance dates from the seventh century, when the celebration was said to be universal. It was traditionally called Lady Day in England and Ireland, where it was a quarter day (one of four days that were observed in conjunction with the solstices and equinoxes), and a date for paying rent.

March 25 is also observed as St. Dismas Day in honor of the "good thief" who was crucified with Jesus. It was to St. Dismas that Jesus said, "Today thou shalt be with me in Paradise." Some scholars have asserted that the date for commemorating St. Dismas may be the true date on which Jesus was crucified.

Palm Sunday
The Sunday preceding Easter

Palm Sunday commemorates the day on which Jesus rode into Jerusalem greeted by a cheering crowd that had heard of his miracles. The people of Jerusalem saw Jesus as a leader who could free them from Roman rule, so they honored him by waving palm branches—a traditional symbol of victory—which they then spread in the street for him to ride over. Commemoration of this day began early in the history of the Church and was adopted by Rome in the ninth century when the blessing of palms was introduced. The use of palm leaves in a procession still marks the celebration of Palm Sunday; after the leaves are used for the procession, they are dried and burned to make the ashes for the next year's Ash Wednesday.

Figure 7.2. Palm Sunday commemorates the day on which Jesus rode into Jerusalem and was greeted by a cheering crowd.

————— " —————

"When they heard that Jesus was coming to Jerusalem, [they] took branches of palm trees, and went forth to meet him, and cried, Hosanna: Blessed is the King of Israel that cometh in the name of the Lord." John 12:12–13.

————— " —————

In the Roman Catholic Church, full liturgical observance includes the blessing of palms and a procession before the principal Mass of the day. The Passion, by Matthew, Mark, or Luke, is read during the Mass.

Maundy Thursday (Green Thursday; Shere [Sheer] Thursday; Paschal Thursday; Passion Thursday; Holy Thursday)
The Thursday before Easter

Maundy Thursday precedes Good Friday. It is also known as Green Thursday in Germany (from the practice of giving a green branch to penitents as a sign that their penance was completed), Shere or Sheer Thursday (meaning "free from guilt"), Paschal Thursday, Passion Thursday, or Holy Thursday. It commemorates Jesus's institution of the Eucharist during the Last Supper and has been celebrated by Christians since the middle of the fourth century.

The customary practice of ceremonial foot-washing in imitation of Jesus, who washed his disciples' feet before the Last Supper as a sign and example of humility and love, has been largely discontinued in Protestant Churches. The Roman Catholic Church and the Anglican Communion, however, still celebrate the rites of Maundy Thursday, but many modern customs may include handing out special coins known as "Maundy money" to the aged and the poor instead of foot washing. Also on this day, the sacramental holy oils, or chrism, are blessed.

The name "Maundy" probably comes from the Latin mandatum, or "commandment," referring to Christ's words after he washed the feet of his disciples: "A new commandment I give unto you, that you love one another as I have loved you." (John 13:34)

Good Friday
The Friday before Easter

The Friday before Easter is a major observance for all Christians. Liturgical elements of the Roman Catholic ritual observance commemorate the Passion and Death of Christ by a reading of the Passion (according to the Gospel of John), special prayers for the Church and people of all ranks, the veneration of the Cross, and a communion service. The Solemn Liturgical Action takes place between noon and 3 p.m. This is the only day in the year on which the Eucharistic Liturgy is not celebrated in the Roman Rite.

In Catholic Churches and in some Anglican Churches, ceremonies on Good Friday often include the Stations of the Cross (or the Way of the Cross). The tradition of observing the stations of the cross began in the 15th century with the erection of memorial stations in devotion to the sights associated with Jesus's crucifixion. The Stations of the Cross are observed as groups of people pray and sing at each of the stations.

Although Protestant denominations allowed observance of this day to wane, a recent emphasis on the holy day has brought back its nearly universal acceptance. Many churches hold special services called "Tre Ore" from the Italian for "Three Hours" between noon and three p.m. During the service, the seven last words of Christ are meditated upon, and Jesus's procession to the cross may be acted out.

Greek Catholics observe the Ceremony of Platsenitis (the Winding Sheet) on Good Friday. During the ceremony, church elders carry a cloth depicting Jesus's dead body in a procession to a shrine where the priest places it in a symbolic tomb.

Holy Saturday (The Easter Vigil)
The Eve of Easter

In Catholic and Anglican Churches, a Saturday night service is observed the night before Easter. Rituals associated with Holy Saturday include the Easter Fire and the lighting of the Paschal candle. The Vigil often begins with the church plunged into total darkness, the congregation listening to solemn, sometimes mournful music. Suddenly the rear doors are flung open, and the celebrant (the bishop, at a cathedral) enters, bearing the lit Paschal candle, and singing "Christ, our Light, the light of the world." The candles of those next to the aisle are lit from the Paschal candle, and the light is passed from one candle to the next, until the church is filled with light. The Paschal candle is a special candle that symbolizes the body of Jesus. Following the lighting of the Paschal candle, "Alleluia" is sung for the first time since it was discontinued on the third Sunday before Lent.

In Roman Catholic parishes, the Easter Vigil mass on Saturday night has become the liturgical focus of the Easter Triduum (which begins on Manudy Thursday). It is on this night that new adult converts are received into the Church, baptized, and receive their first communion.

Easter (Resurrection Sunday)
The first Sunday after the Paschal moon; between March 22 and April 25

Easter, the most important holiday of the Christian faith and one of the earliest observances of the Church, celebrates the resurrection of Christ from the dead (Mark 16:1–7). The ceremonies, customs, and rituals surrounding this mystery extend from Easter Sunday until the feast of Pentecost fifty days later. Easter ends the forty-day fast of the Lenten season.

The week preceding Easter is called Holy Week, and it is the culmination of Lent, the period of introspection and penance. Holy Week begins with Palm Sunday, commemorating Christ's triumphal entry into Jerusalem one week before his crucifixion. Maundy Thursday is the traditional date of the Last Supper and Jesus's arrest. On Good Friday, Christians mourn the crucifixion and death of Jesus; and on Holy Saturday, his resurrection is anticipated. Easter Sunday itself concludes the observances of Holy Week and specifically completes the liturgical observances of the Easter Triduum, which begins on Holy or Maundy Thursday.

The determination of Easter's date has been a subject of continual debate and revision for most of the history of the Church. Since the date of Easter determines the dates of most movable feasts throughout the Christian year, variances in the celebration of these feasts occurring between different branches of the Church are often due to disagreements in the way Easter is designated.

In many churches, Easter services are held at sunrise. The Moravian Church observes a special Easter ceremony in which worshipers gather in the pre-dawn hours to stand among grave markers and sing songs of faith and hope.

Many traditions have grown up around the celebration of Easter. One of these is the Easter egg. Long a symbol of new life, resurrection, and immortality in much of Europe, the egg was easily adopted by Christians as a part of the Easter iconography. The origin of coloring eggs is unclear because the practice is present in many traditions.

Another Easter tradition is the Easter Bunny. Each year, the Easter Bunny visits the homes of children, bringing colored eggs, candy, and gifts. The first record of a rabbit being associated with Easter dates to sixteenth-century Germany, although the custom may be even older. It is possible that both the Easter egg and Easter Bunny may have come from the ancient Teutonic goddess of spring and fertility, Eostre, from whom the English holiday derives its name. Another possibility is that the ancient Germanic goddess Ostara who was always accompanied by a hare inspired the tradition of the Easter Bunny.

Quasimodo Sunday (Low Sunday; Close Sunday; Low Easterday)
The Sunday after Easter

Quasimodo Sunday is named for the Introit of the Latin Mass recited on this day. It begins *Quasi modo geniti infantes*—"As newborn babes...." Quasimodo, the famous character in Victor Hugo's The Hunchback of Notre Dame, was named in honor of this day.

April

Salvation Army Founder's Day
April 10

Salvation Army posts and chapters worldwide commemorate the birthday of their founder, William Booth, on April 10, 1829, which is celebrated as the organization's birthday as well. The Salvation Army was established as a movement within Protestant Christianity, and it currently operates in over 80 countries. Organized in military fashion, the Salvation Army focuses on caring for people in need, working against poverty, and combating societal evils such as alcohol and drugs.

St. Mark's Day
April 25

Although he is often assumed to be one of the apostles, Mark was too young at the time to be more than a follower of Jesus. He is known primarily as the author of one of the four Gospels, which biblical scholars believe is based on what he learned from his close friend and traveling companion, St. Peter. St. Mark the Evangelist is also associated with Venice, Italy, where the church bearing his name was built over the place where his relics were taken in 815 C.E.

In England, it was believed that if you kept a vigil on the church porch from 11 o'clock on St. Mark's Eve until one o'clock in the morning, you would see the ghosts of all those who would die in the coming year as they walked up the path and entered the church. Young girls believed that if they left a flower on the church porch during the day and returned for it at midnight, they would see a wedding procession, including an apparition of their future husband, as they walked home. Because it involved an all-night vigil, St. Mark's Day eventually came to be associated with various forms of licentious behavior, which is why the parochial clergy in the Middle Ages decided that the day should be one of abstinence.

May

Saint Philip and Saint James's Day
May 1

St. Philip and St. James were both apostles and martyrs of the first century.

Family Week (Festival of the Christian Home)
Begins on the first Sunday in May

Protestantism, Roman Catholicism, and Judaism all observe Family Week. Although each faith celebrates this holiday in a manner unique to its own expression, the focal point for all three is the importance of religion in fostering strong familial bonds. Each congregation's members are encouraged to examine the manner in which they contribute to their family's religious life. Group discussions focus on social conditions having adverse effects on family life.

Family Week begins on the first Sunday in May and ends on Mother's Day. Some Christian families observe the Festival of the Christian Home.

A Family Day is also observed in many countries, particularly in some African nations. In Angola, the holiday falls on December 25; and in Nambia, December 26. South African families observe Easter Monday as Family Day.

Rogation Days (Rogation Sunday; Rural Life Sunday; Soil Stewardship Sunday)
Monday, Tuesday, and Wednesday preceding Ascension Day or fifth Sunday after Easter

These three days of prayer and fasting for the harvest have been observed in Europe since the Middle Ages. The tradition of praying for the crops was also intruduced to the United States and is observed by many churches on Rogation Sunday, the fifth Sunday after Easter. Since 1929, this day has also been known as Rural Life Sunday or Soil Stewardship Sunday.

In England, Rogation Days were a time when a procession of priests, prelates, and select parishioners walked the bounds of the parish. From these days, a tradition particular to rural England developed. The priests would drive young boys around the bounds of the parish by beating them with willow switches. The practice, known as "beating the bounds," served to both teach the boys the limits of the parish as well as purify their souls.

Ascension Day
Forty days after Easter

This holiday commemorates the ascension of Jesus back to heaven after his resurrection from the dead. It is celebrated forty days after Easter Sunday because the biblical account in the Acts of the Apostles indicates that Jesus spent forty days with his disciples after his resurrection. During the forty days, he instructed them on how to carry out his teachings. Then, on the fortieth day, he took them to the Mount of Olives near Jerusalem and ascended to heaven as they watched.

According to oral tradition, the observance of this day is one of the oldest celebrations of the Christian Church, dating to 68 C.E. The first specific documentary evidence of the feast dates from early in the fifth century. Many churches traditionally observe the following Sunday as

Ascension Sunday and structure their worship services around the Biblical account of Jesus's ascension.

Pentecost (Whitsunday)
Seventh Sunday (50 days counting inclusively) after Easter

Pentecost is a moveable celebration held on the seventh Sunday after Easter. According to St. Luke's account in the Acts of the Apostles, it was the day on which the Holy Spirit descended on the Apostles in a form likened to tongues of fire and accompanied by a sound like a rushing wind. According to Christian teaching, the Holy Spirit empowered St. Peter and the other believers with him to witness to Jews in Jerusalem. Three thousand conversions were reported in one day.

The name Pentecost comes from the word for fifty used by Greek-speaking Jews. It was the name of the celebration held fifty days after Passover. In England, Pentecost was called Whitsunday (Whit—"white"—Sunday) or Whitsuntide. As a traditional day for the baptism of new Christians, the name possibly derives from a reference to the white robes worn by converts. Pentecost remains a traditional day for baptisms and confirmations in some Anglican and Protestant Churches. In Roman Catholic Churches, Pentecost is marked by the wearing of red vestments.

Trinity Sunday
The first Sunday after Pentecost

Unlike other Christian observances, Trinity Sunday is not associated with any specific saint or historical event. Instead, it honors the Christian belief in one God with a triune nature. According to many traditional branches of Christianity, there are three manifestations of God—Father, Son, and Holy Spirit. In Roman Catholic tradition, a votive Mass of the Most Holy Trinity dates from the seventh century, an Office was composed in the 10th century, and in 1334, Pope John XXII extended the feast to the entire Church.

Aldersgate Experience
The Sunday nearest to May 24

On May 24, 1783, John Wesley experienced a conversion while reading Martin Luther's preface to St. Paul's Epistle to the Romans. The incident occurred while he was with some friends in a house on Aldersgate Street in London. This event is commemorated by the Methodist Church on the Sunday nearest to May 24.

Corpus Christi (Feast of the Most Holy Body of Christ)
The Thursday after Trinity Sunday

In the Roman Catholic Church, this is a movable observance held in the United States on the Sunday following Trinity Sunday; elsewhere it is celebrated on the Thursday after Trinity Sunday. This holy day, celebrated in honor of the Eucharist, has been observed since the thirteenth century C.E. Originating at Liege, France in 1246, Corpus Christi festivities spread throughout the Church in the West under the guidance of Pope Urban IV in 1264. The Office for the feast was composed by St. Thomas Aquinas.

According to tradition, the celebration began after a young nun saw a vision of the moon with a part of it broken away. The interpretation of the vision maintained that the moon stood for the Church and that the break stood for the Eucharist, which was not being held in proper honor. An early Corpus Christi tradition involved carrying consecrated bread in a procession through the town. This later evolved into elaborate parades which are still conducted in many parts of Europe. Although the exuberant public veneration of the Eucharist has waned in the United States since the Second Vatican Council, many other nations still observe Corpus Christi day with public processions and liturgies in honor of the "Blessed Sacrament."

Feast of the Sacred Heart of Jesus
The Friday after Corpus Christi

The Feast of the Sacred Heart of Jesus is recognized by the Roman Catholic Church as a solemnity of the greatest importance. On this day, homage is paid to Christ's all encompassing love for humanity. Devotion to the Sacred Heart was introduced into the liturgy in the 17th century through the efforts of St. John Eudes, who composed an Office and Mass for the feast. It was furthered as the result of the revelations of St. Margaret Mary Alacoque after 1675 and by the work of Claude de la Colombiere, S.J. In 1765, Pope Clement XIII approved a Mass and Office for the feast, and in 1856 Pope Pius IX extended the observance to the entire Roman Catholic Church.

Feast of the Visitation (Visitation of the Virgin Mary to Elizabeth)
May 31 in the Roman Catholic and Protestant Churches

July 2 in the Anglican Church

This feast commemorates Mary's visit to her cousin Elizabeth, the mother of John the Baptist. After the Annunciation, Mary spent several months with her cousin Elizabeth in the mountains of Judea. Elizabeth reported that the baby in her womb (who would become John the Baptist, the precursor of Christ) literally leapt with joy when Mary approached. According to the doctrine of the Roman Catholic Church, this was the moment at which John the Baptist was cleansed from original sin and filled with heavenly grace.

The Feast of the Visitation is a feast of the incarnation and is notable for its recall of the Magnificat, a canticle which acknowledges the unique gifts of God to Mary because of her role in the redemptive work of Christ. The canticle is recited at Vespers in the Liturgy of the Hours.

June

Feast of the Immaculate Heart of Mary
The Saturday following the second Sunday after Pentecost

This Roman Catholic memorial is observed as a day to honor Mary and obtain her intercession for "peace among the nations, freedom for the Church, the conversion of sinners, the love of purity, and the practice of virtue," according to Pope Pius XII's 1944 decree. Two years earlier, he consecrated the entire human race to Mary under this title. Devotion to Mary under the title of her Most Pure Heart originated during the Middle Ages, but was given great impetus in the 17th century by the preaching of St. John Eudes. A feast, celebrated in various places and on different dates, was authorized in 1799.

Children's Day
The second Sunday in June

Children's Day began as an observance in June 1856 at the Universalist Church of the Redeemer in Chelsea, Massachusetts. In 1868, it was formally adopted as the second Sunday in June by the Methodist Church. Currently it is still recognized on that date according to the calendar of the National Council of Churches.

In some Protestant Churches in the United States, Children's Day is marked as one in which children participate in special events during the service. Many other countries recognize a day on which children are allowed to participate in services, in government, and in various cultural and recreational activities. Children's Day is celebrated in Iceland (on April 24), Indonesia (June 17), Korea (May 5), Nigeria (May 27), and Turkey (April 23).

St. Barnabas's Day (Barnaby Day; Long Barnaby; Barnaby Bright)
June 11

St. Barnabas was a Christian in the first century. According to the Biblical account in St. Luke's Acts of the Apostles, he was one of the first to encourage and promote St. Paul.

Before England adopted the Gregorian calendar in 1752, St. Barnabas's Day (June 11) was the day of the Summer Solstice, the longest day of the year. This association gave rise to the old English jingle, "Barnaby bright, Barnaby bright, the longest day and the shortest night." It was a customary day for priests and clerks in the Church of England to wear garlands of roses and to decorate the church with them.

Magna Carta Day
June 15

Although Magna Carta Day is not cited in any official church calendar, it is nonetheless a day of great significance for the notion of religious freedom. The day commemorates the signing of England's "great charter" on June 15, 1215 by King John. The document ensured certain rights to his noble subjects including the freedom of the Church of England from royal domination.

Footwashing Day
On a Sunday in early summer

The practice of footwashing has its origins in the account of Jesus's Last Supper. According to the Gospel of John, Jesus washed his disciples' feet before their last meal together. Through his actions, Jesus entreated his disciples to show a similar love and humility to one another. Although originally performed during Maundy Thursday services, many American Protestant denominations practice the footwashing ceremony more frequently.

In some modern churches, footwashing has become a significant feature of the Eucharist. Congregations in the mountainous regions of Kentucky are particularly noted for this practice. Footwashing Day takes place only once a year, but is preceded by several weeks of preparation. When the day arrives, an elaborate ritual is practiced in which men and women are segregated and wash the feet of the members of the same sex. Children enjoy refreshments during the ceremony and, at its conclusion, all are invited to partake of a traditional meal.

Nativity of St. John the Baptist
June 24

It is unusual for a saint's day to commemorate his or her birth rather than death, but John the Baptist (who died in approximately 29 C.E.) and the Virgin Mary are two exceptions. Roman Catholics, Anglicans, and Lutherans honor St. John on the anniversary of his birth; the Roman Catholic Church commemorates his death as well, on August 29.

St. John the Baptist was Jesus's cousin, born to Zachariah and Elizabeth (a kinswoman of the Virgin Mary) in their old age. John was the one chosen to prepare the way for the Messiah. Roman Catholics believe that John was freed from original sin in his mother's womb when she was visited by Mary.

Until beginning his public ministry, John lived as a hermit in the wilderness where his diet consisted of honey and locusts. He preached repentance of sins and baptized many people, including Jesus. Because he denounced King Herod and Herod's second wife, Herodias, Herodias vowed revenge. Under her influence, Herodias's daughter, Salome, demanded the Baptist's head on a platter. The details of John's execution are recorded by the gospel writers.

Many St. John's Day customs date from pre-Christian times, when June 24 was celebrated as Midsummer Day. Celebrations in some areas still bear the hallmarks of the old pagan Summer Solstice rites, such as bonfires, dancing, and decorating with flowers. For the French in Canada, the Feast of the Nativity of St. John the Baptist is one of the biggest celebrations of the year, especially in Quebec. The San Juan Fiesta in New York City takes place on the Sunday nearest June 24 and is the year's most important festival for Hispanic-Americans.

St. John's Day (el Dia de San Juan) is a major holiday throughout Mexico. As the patron saint of waters, St. John is honored by decorating fountains and wells and by bathing in local streams and rivers. The bathing begins at midnight—often to the accompaniment of village bands—and it is customary for spectators to throw flowers among the bathers. In Mexico City and other urban centers, the celebration takes place in fashionable bathhouses rather than rivers, where there are diving and swimming contests as well. Street vendors sell small mules made out of cornhusks, decorated with flowers and filled with sugar cane and candy.

Wading or bathing in the water on St. John's Day is a tradition that many see as symbolic of John the Baptist's role in baptizing Jesus. In Puerto Rico, for example, San Juan Day is observed by gathering at the beaches to eat, dance, drink, build bonfires, and bathe in the Caribbean. Over the years, the religious significance of the event has been overshadowed, and today bathing in the water is believed to bring good luck in the coming year.

St. Peter's Day
June 29

St. Peter was one of Jesus's original twelve apostles. According to tradition, St. Peter and St. Paul were both martyred on June 29. For this reason their names have been linked in various observances around the world.

As the patron saint of fishermen, St. Peter's Day is celebrated in fishing villages and ports all over the world. Perhaps the largest American celebration takes place in Gloucester, Massachusetts, where St. Peter's Fiesta has been celebrated by the Italian-American fishing community for

several decades. The life-sized statue of St. Peter donated by an Italian-American fishing captain in 1926 provides a focal point for the celebration, and the Sunday morning procession carrying this statue from St. Peter's Club to an outdoor altar erected on the waterfront is still the highlight of the two-day festival. The Mass that follows is usually celebrated by the Roman Catholic archbishop of Boston, who also officiates at the Blessing of the Fleet that afternoon. Other festival events include fishing boat races, concerts, fireworks, and a "greasy-pole" contest in which competitors try to retrieve a red flag from the end of a well-greased spar suspended over the water.

In Malta, the feast of St. Peter and St. Paul is a harvest festival known as Mnarja. In Peru, the Dia de San Pedro y San Pablo is celebrated in fishing villages. Processions of decorated boats carrying an image of the St. Peter are common, and sometimes a special floating altar is set up, with decorations made out of shells and seaweed. In Valparaiso, Chile, this sort of procession has been going on since 1682. In Trinidad fishermen first go out to catch fish to give to the poor and as they return, the Anglican priest blesses them and the sea. Then the partying begins. After the priest leaves, bongo and bele dances are done to honor St. Peter.

Sint Pieter (as he is called in Belgium) is honored each year on June 29 by Belgian fishermen, mariners, and others who are exposed to the dangers of the sea because he walked across the water to reach Jesus. The Blessing of the Sea ceremony is performed at Ostend, Blankenberge, and other seaport towns on the Sunday following the saint's day. After a special service is held, a procession of clergy, church dignitaries, and seamen carry votive offerings, flowers, and garlands down to the shore. Then the priests board the boats and go out to bless the waves.

Another festival related to the fishing industry takes place on a weekend near St. Peter's day—the last weekend in June. The Blessing of the Shrimp fleet is a traditional two-day gala in Bayou La Batre, Alabama. The event celebrates the tiny town's major industries. Bayou La Batre is one of the top seafood producers in the nation, bringing in about $300 million annually. Boat building is the other major industry, producing about $400 million each year. On the day of this celebration, the two industries join in the blessing of the fleet by the priest of St. Margaret's Roman Catholic Church. Fifty to one hundred festively trimmed boats parade down the bayou (which serves as the main street of the town). The ceremony originated in the late 1940s and attracts up to 25,000 people annually. Also included in the weekend's events are contests in oyster shucking, crab picking, gumbo making, and shrimp heading.

July

Feast of the Most Precious Blood
July 1

In the Roman Catholic Church, July is the month of the Most Precious Blood. During the month, many Christians venerate the blood of Jesus, which, they believe, possesses life-giving power. In 1849, Pope Pius IX established the festival on the first Sunday in July. Later, Pope Pius X moved the feast to the first day of July.

St. James's Day
July 25

The Apostle James the Great was martyred by Herod in 44 C.E. Also known as Santiago, he is the patron saint of Spain. His feast day is celebrated in the Western Church on July 25, the anniversary of the day on which, according to Spanish tradition, his body was miraculously discovered in Compostela, Spain, after being buried there for 800 years. A church was built on the site, which later became the town of Santiago de Compostela, once a popular place of pilgrimage. St. James's Day is still celebrated in Compostela with a week-long festival that features a mock-burning of the 12th century cathedral and an elaborate fireworks display.

Reek Sunday
The last Sunday in July

Reek Sunday is observed as a day on which Irish pilgrims ascend Croagh Padraig, the steep mountain in County Mayo named for Ireland's patron saint (St. Patrick).

Volunteers of America Founder's Day
July 28

Members of the Volunteers of America, an offshoot of the Salvation Army, honor the birth of their founder Ballington Booth who was born on July 28, 1859.

August

Feast of the Transfiguration (Transfiguration of Jesus)
August 6

This holiday commemorates the revelation of Jesus's divinity to Peter, James, and John on Mt. Tabor. According to the Biblical account recorded in three of the Gospels, Elijah and Moses appeared to Jesus and the three apostles during a visit to the mountain. The name "transfiguration" refers to changes in Jesus's physical appearance during the event. The story in Matthew, Mark, and Luke reports that Jesus's face shone, and his clothing became bright white. The feast, which is very old, was extended throughout the Church in 1457 by Pope Callistus III.

Assumption of the Blessed Virgin
August 15

Assumption Day is observed in honor of the belief that the body of the Virgin Mary, the mother of Jesus, did not suffer decay, but was translated into heaven upon her death. The belief was not official dogma of the Catholic Church until 1950 when Pope Pius XII endorsed it. It is, however, one of the oldest solemnities observed by the Church, dating back to at least the seventh century, when its celebration was already established in Jerusalem and Rome.

It is possible that Assumption Day is a Christianization of an earlier pagan harvest festival and, in some places, it is still called the Feast of Our Lady of the Harvest.

Related to Assumption Day, Marymass Fair is held in Irvine, Ayrshire, Scotland on the third of fourth Monday in August. It takes its name from the Feast of the Assumption, which coincides with Old Lammas Day and was celebrated locally by dances around bonfires. The fair, which dates back to at least the twelfth century, is famous for its horse races, believed to be the oldest in Europe.

Queenship of Mary
August 22

This Roman Catholic observance is classed as a memorial. It commemorates Mary as Queen of heaven, angels, and mankind. Universal observance of the memorial was ordered by Pope Pius XII in the encyclical *Ad Ceali Reginam*, October 11, 1954. The original date of the memorial was May 31.

St. Bartholomew's Day
August 24

Saint Bartholomew was an apostle and martyr of the first century. In some places in Germany, the day's activities include pastoral activities, such as a shepherds' dance and a water-carriers' race in which contestants must balance a pail of water on their heads and pour it into a tub at the finish line.

Martyrdom of St. John the Baptist
August 29

The Martyrdom of St. John the Baptist has been celebrated by Christians since the fourth century. The observance started at Sebaste (Samaria), where the Baptist was believed to have been buried.

St. John the Baptist was beheaded by King Herod after denouncing Herod's marriage to Herodias, the wife of

Herod's half-brother Philip (Luke 3:19–20), an illegal union according to Jewish law. Herodias's daughter by a former marriage, by legend called Salome, pleased Herod so much with her dancing that he swore to give her whatever she wanted. At her mother's urging she asked for the head of John the Baptist on a platter (Matthew 14:3–12).

According to tradition, Herod, grief-stricken over having let himself be maneuvered into killing a good and innocent man, later had the head concealed within the palace walls to spare it any further indignities. The head remained there until after the discovery of the holy cross by St. Helena, an event which drew many pilgrims to Jerusalem. Two pilgrims found the head after St. John appeared to them in a vision.

African Methodist Quarterly Meeting Day
The last Saturday in August

This large annual gathering in Wilmington, Delaware, celebrates the establishment of the African Union Methodist Protestant Church (A.U.M.P.) in 1813, popularly referred to as the "Mother Church" for African-Americans. The A.U.M.P. Church had its origins in the congregation of Wilmington's Asbury Methodist Church which had denied its black members the right to fully participate in services. Under the leadership of Peter Spencer, 41 members of Asbury's congregation broke away from the Church in 1805, establishing Wilmington's first black congregation.

In the early days of the Big August Quarterly, participants from Delaware and surrounding states, many of whom were slaves, gathered together. They would hear and deliver revival messages, sing gospel hymns, and reunite with friends and family. Although the size of the gathering has diminished since its beginnings, the Big August Quarterly has recently enjoyed a resurgence of interest, and now offers an opportunity for participants to enjoy traditional cuisine and musical entertainment while mingling with fellow church members.

September

Feast of San Estevan
September 2

This festival is the annual harvest dance and feast day in the Native American pueblo of Acoma, New Mexico. Acoma was established in the twelfth century and is the oldest continuously inhabited community in America. Home to roughly fifty year-round residents, Acoma Indians from nearby villages return annually for the feast day and celebration.

A Mass and procession begin the festivities as a statue of San Estevan, the pueblo's patron saint, is taken from the church to the plaza. There, a variety of ritual dances are performed throughout the day.

Sante Fe Fiesta
The weekend after Labor Day

This festival combines religious and secular traditions in what is said to be the oldest such event in the United States. Dating to 1712, it recalls the early history of Sante Fe, New Mexico. The Spanish conquistadores were ousted from Santa Fe in 1680 by a Pueblo Indian revolt. The Spanish, led by Don Diego de Vargas, peacefully regained control in 1693. De Vargas had promised to venerate La Conquistadora, the small statue of the Virgin Mary now enshrined in St. Francis Cathedral, if she granted them success. In fulfillment of that promise, de Vargas held the first procession in her honor in 1712.

The celebration begins with an early morning Mass on the Friday following Labor Day. After this, a grand procession takes place with figures representing Vargas and the fiesta queen, la reina, on horseback, leading the Caballeros de Vargas to the Plaza. On Friday night, a forty-four-foot fabric and wood effigy of Zozobra or Old Man Gloom is burned. Thousands of spectators shout "Burn him!" as the effigy pleads for mercy. Fireworks announce the end of Gloom; the crowds then proceed to the Plaza to embark on two days of dancing, street fairs, a grand ball, and a parade with floats satirizing local politicians. The fiesta ends on the following Sunday with an evening Mass of thanksgiving and a candlelight procession to the Cross of Martyrs overlooking Santa Fe.

Feast of the Nativity of the Blessed Virgin Mary
September 8

The birth of the Virgin Mary is one of only three births celebrated by the Christian Church. (The births of John the Baptist on June 24 and Jesus on December 25 are the other two.)

The date of September 8 became widely accepted for this celebration during the seventh century although there seems to be no concrete evidence that this is the actual date of Mary's birth.

Coptic New Year
September 11

Members of the Coptic Orthodox Church, the native Christian Church in Egypt, celebrate the New Year on September 11 because it is the day on which the Dog Star, Sirius, reappears in the Egyptian sky, signalling the flooding of the Nile and the beginning of a new planting season. Church martyrs are also commemorated.

Red vestments and altar clothes are used, and the red date serves as a food of special significance. Its red color signifies the martyrs' blood, the white meat symbolizes their purity of heart, and the hard pit represents their steadfast faith. The Coptic New Year is also celebrated outside of Egypt by people of Egyptian descent.

Triumph of the Holy Cross
September 14

This Christian feast commemorates significant events relating to the cross on which Christ was crucified. These events include: the 326 C.E. discovery of fragments of the cross by St. Helena, mother of Constantine; the consecration of the basilica which was constructed in honor of the cross nearly 10 years after St. Helena's discovery; and the recovery around 628 C.E. of a major portion of the cross that had been taken from Jerusalem by the Persians. The feast originated in Jerusalem and spread through the East before being adopted in the West. General adoption followed the building at Rome of the Basilica of the Holy Cross in Jerusalem, so called because it enshrined what was believed to be a major portion of the true cross.

Mary as Our Lady of Sorrows
September 15

This Roman Catholic memorial recalls the sorrows experienced by Mary in her association with Christ: the prophecy of Simeon, the flight into Egypt (Matthew 2:13–21), and the three-day separation from Jesus (Luke 2:41–50). Also remembered are four incidents connected with the Passion: her meeting with Christ on the way to Calvary, the crucifixion, the removal of Christ's body from the cross, and his burial (Matthew 27:31–61; Mark 15:20–47; Luke 23:26–56; John 19:17–42). A Mass and Divine Office of the feast were celebrated by the Servites, especially in the 17th century. In 1817 Pope Pius VII extended the observance to the whole Church.

St. Matthew's Day
September 21

St. Matthew was an apostle, evangelist, and martyr of the first century. He is traditionally recognized as the author of the Gospel that bears his name.

Michaelmas (St. Michael and All Angels)
September 29

The Feast of St. Michael the Archangel on September 29 is observed by the Roman Catholic, Anglican, and Lutheran Churches, on the date when the first church in Italy was dedicated to him. This Christian feast is a traditional English quarter day, whose customs included bringing the herds down from the summer high pastures, eating roast goose, going back to school, and lighting bonfires. Many of these appear to be customs also associated with the fall equinox.

Also honored on this day are the other archangels, Raphael and Gabriel. Originally each archangel was commemorated on a separate day, but the days were combined and moved to Michaelmas by the Roman Catholic church in 1969.

October

Rally Day
During September or October

In liturgical Protestant Churches, Rally Day marks the beginning of the church calendar year. It typically occurs during the end of September or beginning of October. Participation in the day varies considerablly among Protestant Churches. Some customs associated with it are: the giving of Bibles to children; promoting children from one Sunday school grade to the next; welcoming new members into the Church; and, the formal presentation of Church goals for the coming year.

Guardian Angels Day
October 2

Guardian Angels Day is a feast, classed as a memorial, observed by Roman Catholic Churches. It commemorates the angels who assist people in doing good and protecting them from spiritual and physical dangers. A feast in their honor celebrated in sixteenth-century Spain was extended to the whole Church by Pope Paul V in 1608. In 1670, Pope Clement X set October 2 as the date of observance. Earlier, guardian angels were honored liturgically in conjunction with the feast of St. Michael.

Mary as Our Lady of the Rosary
October 7

The Virgin Mary is commemorated on this Roman Catholic memorial day by recalling the mysteries of the Rosary which recapitulate the events of her life and the life of Christ. The feast was instituted to remember a Christian victory over invading Islamic forces at Lepanto on October 7, 1571, and was extended throughout the Church by Pope Clement XI in 1716.

St. Luke's Day
October 18

Saint Luke, a companion of St. Paul, is recognized as the author of two canonical works: one of the four Gospels and the book of the Acts of the Apostles.

Table 7.5. Alphabetical List of Christian Holidays

Holiday	Date(s)
Advent	Beginning on the Sunday closest to November 30 and continuing through December 24
African Methodist Quarterly Meeting Day	Last Saturday in August
Aldersgate Experience	The Sunday nearest to May 24
All Saints' Day	November 1
All Souls' Day	November 2
Allen, Richard, Birthday of	February 11
Annunciation of the Lord	March 25
Ascension Day	Forty days after Easter
Ash Wednesday	Six and one-half weeks before Easter
Assumption of the Blessed Virgin	August 15
Baptism of the Lord, Feast of the	Sunday following Epiphany
Barnaby Bright *see* St. Barnabas's Day	
Barnaby Day *see* St. Barnabas's Day	
Bible Sunday	Last Sunday in November
Blessing of Animals	Sunday nearest to January 17
Candlemas *see* Presentation of Jesus	
Carling Sunday *see* Mothering Sunday	
Carnival	Variable, Ending with Shrove Tuesday.
Childermas *see* Holy Innocents' Day	
Children's Day	Second Sunday in June
Christ the King, Feast of	Last Sunday in August or October
Christmas Day	December 25
Christmas Eve	December 24
Circumcision, Feast of the	January 1
Close Sunday *see* Quasimodo Sunday	

Holiday	Date(s)
Conversion of St. Paul	January 25
Coptic New Year	September 11
Corpus Christi	Thursday after Trinity Sunday
Day of the Three Wise Men *see* Epiphany	
Dedication of St. John Lateran	November 9
Easter Vigil *see* Holy Saturday	
Easter	First Sunday after the Pascal moon; between March 22 and April 25
Epiphany Eve	January 5
Epiphany	January 6
Family Week	First Sunday in May
Fasching	Three days preceding Ash Wednesday
Feast of Annunciation of the Blessed Virgin Mary, Feast of *see* Annunciation of the Lord	
Feast of Kings *see* Epiphany	
Feast of the Most Holy Body of Christ *see* Corpus Christi	
Festival of the Christian Home *see* Family Week	
Footwashing Day	Sunday in early summer
Fox, George, Death of	January 13
Good Friday	Friday before Easter
Green Thursday *see* Maundy Thursday	
Guardian Angels Day	October 2
Holy Family, Feast of the	Sunday after Epiphany
Holy Innocents' Day	December 28
Holy Name Day *see* Circumcision, Feast of the	
Holy Saturday	Eve of Easter
Holy Thursday *see* Maundy Thursday	

Table 7.5. Alphabetical List of Christian Holidays, continued

Holiday	Date(s)
Immaculate Conception of Mary, Feast of the	December 8
Immaculate Heart of Mary, Feast of the	Saturday following the second Sunday after Pentecost
Innocents' Day see Holy Innocents' Day	
King, Martin Luther, Jr., Birth of	Third Monday in January
Laetare Sunday see Mothering Sunday	
Lent	Forty days before Easter (exclusive of Sundays)
Long Barnaby see St. Barnabas's Day	
Low Easterday see Quasimodo Sunday	
Low Sunday see Quasimodo Sunday	
Lucia Day see St. Lucy's Day	
Luciadagen see St. Lucy's Day	
Luther, Martin, Birthday	November 10
Magna Carta Day	June 15
Mardi Gras	Tuesday before Ash Wednesday
Martyrdom of St. John the Baptist	August 29
Mary as Our Lady of Sorrows	September 15
Mary as Our Lady of the Rosary	October 7
Maundy Thursday	Thursday before Easter
Michaelmas	September 29
Mid-Lent Sunday see Mothering Sunday	
Moravian Love Feast	December 24
Most Precious Blood, Feast of the	July 1
Mother Seton Day	December 1
Mothering Sunday	Fourth Sunday of Lent

Holiday	Date(s)
Nativity of Our Lord see Christmas	
Nativity of St. John the Baptist	June 24
Nativity of the Blessed Virgin Mary, Feast of the	September 8
Old Christmas Day	January 6
Palm Sunday	Sunday preceding Easter
Passion Thursday see Maundy Thursday	
Pentecost	Seventh Sunday after Easter
Plough Monday	Monday after Epiphany
Posadas	December 16–25
Presentation of Jesus	February 2
Presentation of the Blessed Virgin Mary, Feast of the	November 21
Psachal Thursday see Maundy Thursday	
Purification of the Blessed Virgin Mary see Presentation of Jesus	
Quadragesima	First Sunday of Lent
Quasimodo Sunday	Sunday after Easter
Queenship of Mary	August 22
Race Relations Sunday	Sunday nearest February 12
Rally Day	During September or October
Reek Sunday	Last Sunday in July
Reformation Day	October 31
Refreshment Sunday see Mothering Sunday	
Resurrection Sunday see Easter	
Rogation Days	Monday, Tuesday, and Wednesday preceding Ascension Day
Rogation Sunday	Fifth Sunday after Easter
Rose Monday	Monday before Lent

Table 7.5. Alphabetical List of Christian Holidays, continued

Holiday	Date(s)
Rose Sunday *see* Mothering Sunday	
Rural Life Sunday *see* Rogation Sunday	
Sacred Heart of Jesus	Friday after Corpus Christi
St. Andrew's Day	November 30
St. Barnabas's Day	June 11
St. Bartholomew's Day	August 24
St. James's Day	July 25
St. John the Evangelist's Day	December 27
St. Lucy's Day	December 13
St. Luke's Day	October 18
St. Mark's Day	April 25
St. Matthew's Day	September 21
St. Matthias's Day	February 24
St. Michael and All Angels *see* Michaelmas	
St. Nicholas's Day	December 6
St. Patrick's Day	March 17
St. Peter's Day	June 29
St. Philip and St. James's Day	May 1
St. Simon and St. Jude's Day	October 28
St. Stephen's Day	December 26
St. Thomas's Day	December 21
Saints, Doctors, Missionaries, and Martyrs Day	November 8
Salvation Army Founder's Day	April 10
San Estevan, Feast of	September 2
Sante Fe Fiesta	Weekend after Labor Day

Holiday	Date(s)
Shere [Sheer] Thursday *see* Maundy Thursday	
Soil Stewardship Sunday *see* Rogation Sunday	
Solemnity of Mary *see* Circumcision, Feast of the	
Thanksgiving	Fourth Thursday in November
Three Kings' Day *see* Epiphany	
Transfiguration of Jesus, Feast of the	August 6
Trinity Sunday	First Sunday after Pentecost
Triumph of the Holy Cross	September 14
Twelfth Day *see* Epiphany	
Twelfthtide *see* Epiphany	
Twelve Days of Christmas	December 25 through January 5
Universal Week of Prayer	First Sunday through the second Sunday in January
Vartanantz Day	Thursday preceding Ash Wednesday
Visitation of the Virgin Mary to Elizabeth *see* Visitiation, Feast of the	
Visitation, Feast of the	May 31 or July 2
Volunteers of America Founder's Day	July 28
Whitsunday *see* Pentecost	
Williams, Roger, Arrival of in the New World	February 5
World Day of Prayer	First Friday in Lent

St. Simon and St. Jude's Day
October 28

Because St. Jude is believed to have been martyred with St. Simon in Persia, where they had gone to preach Christianity, their feast is celebrated jointly on October 28, thought to be the date on which their relics were moved to old St. Peter's basilica. Aside from the fact that they were both apostles, little is known about Simon and Jude. The New Testament refers to "Judas, not Iscariot" to distinguish Jude the Apostle from the Judas who betrayed Jesus.

As the patron saint of hopeless causes, St. Jude's Day is observed particularly by students, who often ask for his help on exams.

Feast of Christ the King
Sunday before Advent begins in the Roman Catholic Church; the last Sunday in August in the Protestant Church

Christians celebrate the kingship of Jesus over the earthly authority on this holiday. Pope Pius XI originally instituted the feast December 11, 1925. In 1937, the National Council of Churches designated the last Sunday in August for its celebration.

Reformation Day
October 31

On October 31, 1517, Martin Luther posted his ninety-five theses on the Wittenberg church door. His proposals were intended to spark discussion within the Roman Catholic Church about what Luther saw as doctrinal error; instead, he started one of the most influential and far-reaching movements in the history of Christianity—the Reformation. Luther's ideas swept across Europe, inspiring many to break from Rome and begin their own churches. The Protestant Churches that were a result of this event observe October 31 as the anniversary of their beginning. The Lutheran Church celebrates the Sunday prior to Reformation Day as Reformation Sunday.

November

All Saints' Day
November 1

All Saints' Day is observed by Roman Catholic, Anglican, and many Protestant Churches to honor all of the Christian saints, especially those who do not have their own feast days. The celebration can be traced to the fourth century when groups of martyrs and other saints were honored on a common day, the first Sunday after Pentecost. Around 610 C.E., the Pantheon, a pagan temple at Rome, was consecrated as a Christian church for the honor of Our Lady and the martyrs. This event was celebrated annually on May 1. In 835 C.E., Pope Gregory IV combined the two celebrations and, in accordance with Pope Gregory I's policy of toleration for pagan tradition, moved the feast to November 1 to coincide with the pagan Festival of the Dead (see Samhain in Chapter 19).

Observed as a religious and national holiday in 36 nations of the world, All Saints' Day is a Holy Day of Obligation for Roman Catholics in the United States.

All Souls' Day
November 2

From the earliest days of Christianity, the faithful prayed for the dead. By the sixth century, Benedictine monasteries were holding a service on Pentecost to commemorate deceased members of the order. In 998 C.E., St. Odilo of Cluny moved the date of this memorial to November 2, which became the standard throughout the Christian Church. Although some Protestant Churches observe All Souls' Day, it is essentially a Roman Catholic and Anglican holy day.

On All Souls' Day, many Christians honor their ancestors by visiting the graves of relatives. The evening of November 1 is often called All Souls' Eve and is observed by the decoration of family graves and lighting of candles as a remembrance of the dead.

Saints, Doctors, Missionaries, and Martyrs Day
November 8

Saints, Doctors, Missionaries, and Martyrs Day is observed by the Anglican Churches as a counterpart to the Roman Catholic feasts of All Saints and All Souls. The date was established in 1928 commemorate all unnamed saints.

Dedication of St. John Lateran
November 9

This Roman Catholic observance is classed as a feast and it commemorates the first public consecration of a church (the Basilica of the Most Holy Savior) by Pope Sylvester on November 9, 324 C.E. The church and the Lateran Palace were the gift of the Roman Emperor Constantine. Since the 12th century it has been known as St. John Lateran, in honor of John the Baptist, after whom the adjoining baptistery was named. The church was rebuilt by Pope Innocent X (1644-55), reconsecrated by Pope Benedict XIII in 1726, and enlarged by Pope Leo XIII (1878-1903). This basilica is highly regarded throughout the Roman Rite.

Birthday of Martin Luther
November 10

Martin Luther's birthday, November 10, 1483, is commemorated by Lutheran Churches and German Protestants.

Feast of the Presentation of the Blessed Virgin Mary
November 21

Although no one is certain of the origin of this feast, the Greek Orthodox Church officially began celebrating the Presentation of the Blessed Virgin in the eighth century; the Roman Catholic Church instituted the observation later in the Middle Ages. The feast commemorates events related in the apocryphal Book of James of the presentation of the three-year old Mary in the Temple consecrating her to God's service.

Thanksgiving
The fourth Thursday in November

Thanksgiving Day in America traditionally commemorates the survival of the Pilgrims at the Plymouth, Massachusetts settlement. After their journey from England to North America, the settlers endured a terrible winter and an epidemic that threatened the existence of the colony. The Pilgrims were saved by native Indians who taught them how to plant crops in their new home; so, when the first bountiful harvest came in, the Pilgrims and Indians joined together to share in the goodness of the land.

Although many days of thanks have been declared and observed, the last Thursday in November was set aside by Abraham Lincoln as a day to remember the goodness of God to the United States. In 1939, Franklin D. Roosevelt changed this date to the fourth Thursday in November, although some states still observe the holiday according to Lincoln's proclamation.

Often, people attend church services on Thanksgiving morning. They may participate in a local parade, and then gather with family members for a meal usually consisting of stuffed turkey, mashed potatoes, yams, cranberry sauce, and pumpkin pie.

In Canada, Thanksgiving is normally celebrated on the second Monday in October, coinciding with Columbus Day.

Bible Sunday
The last Sunday in November

Bible Sunday is observed in many Protestant Churches in America as a day honoring the Christian Scripture.

CHAPTER 8

Christianity: Orthodox Expressions

Overview of Christian Orthodoxy

What Is Orthodoxy?

The Orthodox Church is the second largest Christian community, exceeded only by the Roman Catholic Church. Sources estimate nearly 250 million followers worldwide. The word "orthodox" comes from a Greek term that simply means "right belief." Several factors serve to distinguish the Orthodox Church from other Christian communions.

Members of the Orthodox Church possess a strong sense of historical continuity with the early church, drawn to the idea of *paradosis*, or tradition. This is evidenced in the fixed liturgical forms used throughout Orthodoxy. Though the Roman Catholic Church likewise shares a connection to early Christianity, the Orthodox Church claims that it remained faithful to the earliest witness while the Roman Church left the fold through various theological and pastoral innovations.

The Orthodox Church recognizes only seven ecumenical councils as having binding authority. These include Nicea I (325), Constantinople I (381), Ephesus (431), Chalcedon (451), Constantinople II (553), Constantinople III (681), and Nicea II (787). The Synod in Trullo (692) is considered by the Orthodox Church as sharing the ecumenical authority of Constantinople III, although it was concerned with disciplinary canons rather than definitions of doctrine.

In contrast to belief in Roman Catholicism and Protestantism, the Orthodox Church insists that the Holy Spirit proceeds from the Father alone. This conflict, known as the *filioque* controversy (from the Latin word meaning "and the Son"), was one of the factors leading to the Great Schism of 1054.

The Orthodox Church uses icons, which are images of Jesus Christ, Mary, or other religious figures. A strong emphasis is placed upon the incarnation of the Son of God, and this is seen to have consequences in prayer. Icons, therefore, become instruments in prayer—windows through which the faithful may catch a glimpse of the divine reality.

Infants are baptized into the Orthodox Church by triple immersion and are immediately anointed with oil in the sacrament of Chrismation. After this they are given their first Holy Communion. The Eucharistic bread is leavened.

Orthodox clergy are permitted to marry, provided they do so before their ordination. This is in contrast to their Roman Catholic counterparts. The Orthodox Church also tends to allow greater lay participation in missionary and educational work than do Roman Catholic Churches. Similar to the Roman Church, however, the Orthodox only ordain men.

A Patriarch has historically been the bishop of one of the Roman Empire's regional capitals and therefore had formal authority over the churches in their region. Orthodox Christians are under the authority of the Patriarchs of Constantinople, Alexandria, Antioch, and Jerusalem. At the Council of Chalcedon, the bishop of Constantinople was recognized as second in honor and equal in rank to the Pope of Rome. The title Ecumenical Patriarch, which he bears, reflects his status as bishop of the imperial capital and senior bishop of the Eastern Roman empire, and, since the breach with Rome, the senior authority of the Orthodox Church.

The Relationship between God and the Christian People

Orthodox Christians hold to many belief common among other traditional Christian expressions: People have been made in the image of God and given the freedom to obey or disobey him. Because the first man,

Adam, disobeyed God, all humans have inherited the consequences of his sin. These consequences result in the inevitability of our own sin and the punishment of death because of it. Everybody has but one life to live, and the consequences of their free choices made during life determine their eternal destiny. This does not mean that individuals can earn their way into heaven by works. Rather, it means that salvation is a free gift given by God and that, in response to Christ's loving sacrifice, humanity needs not only to receive that gift but to live in a godly manner. Both the spiritual and the physical work together for the glory of God. Salvation is a matter of placing one's faith in Jesus Christ, believing in his resurrection, entering into communion with him, becoming more and more like him, and receiving assurance from the Spirit.

The Orthodox Church's approach to salvation is sometimes known as deification. The theological refrain often quoted is "God became human in order that humans might become God." At it suggests, there is an especially strong link between the understanding of salvation and the doctrine of the incarnation. Human nature was created to be in communion with God in love. Through Jesus Christ coming to earth, that can once again be realized.

Rather than focus on a system of rewards and punishments, the Orthodox Church sees heaven as a relationship with God wherein those who embrace Christian teachings enjoy loving communion. Those who reject Christian teachings will experience God as a consuming fire. There is no system of purgatory as in Roman Catholicism.

Authorities and Sacred Writings

The Orthodox Church has two great sources of authority. They are the Holy Scriptures and holy tradition. The Scriptures are the writings of both the Old and New Testaments. The Old Testament contains all the books in the three sections of the Hebrew Bible: the Torah, the Prophets, and the Writings. As with the Roman Catholic Church, the Orthodox Church also recognizes a collection of books known variously as the Apocrypha or Pseudopigrapha. The New Testament is comprised of the same canon that both Roman Catholics and Protestants recognize.

For the Orthodox believer, the use of the Old Testament in liturgical texts is very important in that it serves as an introduction to the saving message of the New Testament. The prophecies and writings of the Prophets pointed to the coming of the Messiah, whose story is detailed in the New Testament. It is the New Testament that reveals both the human and divine nature of Jesus

Christ and his sacred teachings that all humans are called to follow.

Holy tradition, of which Holy Scripture is a part, includes writings of the apostles, martyrs, saints, and fathers of the Church as well as the liturgical and sacramental traditions handed down through the ages. The oral tradition of the early church as well as the decisions of the ecumenical councils also serve as collective wisdom and experience to form this second great source of sacred authority.

History of Orthodoxy

For centuries both the Orthodox and Roman Catholic Churches functioned as two branches of the same Christian tree. But disagreements led to brief separations that would last anywhere from fifteen to fifty years until they resumed their union again. From 863 to 1054 C.E., however, a series of events occurred that was to lead to the Great Schism. During this period, little to no communication took place between the churches.

Several factors were ultimately responsible for the split between the Orthodox and Roman Churches. They engaged in controversy over the use of images. There was conflict over the procession of the Holy Spirit, known as the *filioque* controversy. The Orthodox Church taught that the Holy Spirit proceeded from the Father alone whereas the Roman Church believed that the Spirit proceeded from the Father and the Son. The Patriarch of Constantinople and the Pope of Rome were unwilling to be subservient to each other. There was no sharp definition of the boundaries between territories ruled by Rome and Constantinople, and as a result frequent struggles arose over administration of border areas. And differences abounded with regards to issues such as the marital status of clergy, whether or not the clergy should be clean shaven, and if unleavened or leavened bread should be used in the Eucharist (communion).

When Patriarch Michael Keroularios (Latin spelling is Cerularius) closed the Latin churches in Constantinople, papal legates were sent bearing letters rebuking his actions. Despite the Byzantine emperor's efforts to make peace, Michael treated the representatives with contempt. On July 16, 1054 C.E., Cardinal Humbert placed a bull of excommunication on the altar of Hagia Sophia (the domed basilica of Constantinople which was completed in 537 and dedicated to Christ as the "Holy Wisdom").

The split was solidified by the sacking of Constantinople in 1204 by the Crusaders. Following this event, from 1204 to 1261 C.E., the Crusaders forced the Patriarchs of Antioch and Jerusalem to abandon their positions and imposed cruel governance over Constantinople, pillaging its resources and causing its eventual downfall.

In 1438 an attempt was made at reuniting the Churches at the Pseudo-Synod of Ferra-Florence. In reality, the gathering was little more than an attempt to control the Orthodox Church, forcing its representatives to sign a statement of reunion against their will. Although the rekindled alliance was proclaimed on July 6, 1439, it was denounced by a synod in Constantinople in 1451. Two years later, Constantinople fell ending any sincere effort at reconciliation with Rome. In many ways, the history of the Orthodox Church is one of greater suffering from the hands of the Christian West than from the Muslim East.

Orthodoxy Today

Orthodox Worship and Practices

At every Sunday worship service in Orthodox Churches the faithful recite the Creed. It contains the basic summary of doctrinal truths to which Orthodox Christians adhere. The Creed consists of the twelve articles of the Nicene-Constantinopolitan Creed, called the Pistevo.

The Divine Liturgy, the central worship service of the Orthodox Church, is celebrated each Sunday morning and on all holy days. It is the means by which humans achieve union with Jesus Christ and community with each other through the sacrament of Holy Communion.

There are seven sacraments in the Orthodox Church. They are considered the visible means by which the invisible grace of the Holy Spirit is imparted. Four sacraments are obligatory: Baptism, Chrismation (anointing with holy oil), Confession, and Holy Communion. Three are optional: Matrimony, Holy Orders (ordination), and Unction (anointing the sick).

The Orthodox Church calendar begins on September 1st and ends on August 31st. Every day is sacred. Therefore the Church venerates at least one saint or sacred event in the life of the Church each day of the year. Several major feast days are annually observed as well, with Easter, which is also called Pascha, being the most important.

As church buildings have become smaller in the modern era, the liturgical life has become more compressed, accompanied by a shift towards greater symbolism. Modern Orthodox services have several parts. Opening the Liturgy of the Word is the first procession, or Lesser Introit. Here the Gospel book is carried out from the altar through the nave and back again, signifying Christ's coming to us as the Word of God. At the beginning of the Eucharistic half of the service is the Great Entrance, or Major Introit. What used to be an entrance into the church from outside where the bread and wine were prepared has been reduced to a solemn transfer of the bread and wine from the sanctuary, out through the nave, then back again to be placed on the altar. This symbolizes Christ being led to his sacrifice and prefigures his coming to the believer in the sacrament of his body and blood. These foreshadowings are fulfilled in two later ritual appearances from behind the sanctuary chancel: the procession of the deacon with the Gospel lectionary reading, and the entrance of the presiding celebrant to distribute in communion the consecrated gifts.

Major Ethnic Groups within Orthodoxy

In the Orthodox Church the community plays an important role in maintaining ethnic identity and preserving cultural heritage. Complex networks of groups have developed historically from the movement of individuals, families, and whole communities from one geographical location to another. Theologically, however, each Orthodox community needs to be acknowledged as sharing in the inheritance of the Orthodox Church's mission, although how that mission is carried out may vary from church to church.

Several Orthodox congregations are currently recognized by the Ecumenical Patriarchate as fully independent. They include Constantinople, Alexandria, Antioch, Jerusalem, Russia, Serbia, Romania, Bulgaria, Georgia, Cyprus, Greece, Poland, Albania, Slovakia, the Czech Republic, and the Ukraine. Through massive emigration in the last century from Greece and the Near East to the West, the term "Eastern" no longer applies when referring to the Orthodox Church. Virtually all Orthodox nationalities are represented in the United States. Some of these include:

Greek

The Greek Orthodox Church is the largest of the American Orthodox communities, with nearly two million representatives and about 475 parishes. It is under the ecclesiastical and spiritual jurisdiction of the Ecumenical Patriarch of Constantinople. The first Greek Orthodox Christians arrived in America in 1768. The first Greek Orthodox community was founded in 1864 in New Orleans by a small group of merchants, and the first permanent community was founded in New York City in 1892.

Russian

The Russian Orthodox Church was the first Orthodox presence in North America. Two Russian explorers sighted the coast of Alaska on July 15, 1741, and five days later the first Orthodox Liturgy in America was celebrated. In 1794 eight monks founded a Russian Orthodox monastery on Kodiak Island and by 1840 a bishop was appointed to Alaska. In 1872 his seat of authority was moved to San Francisco and in 1905 the Russian Orthodox Church in America moved its headquarters to New York City. Before the Bolshevik Revolution in 1914, the majority of Orthodox immigrants to America were poor and had little education. But the wake of the Russian Revolution brought many people able to communicate Russian Orthodoxy to the west on a scholarly level. The Russian Orthodox Church is now the second largest congregation in America.

Antiochian

In the Roman Empire, Antioch was third in rank of importance, after Rome and Alexandria. The followers of Jesus were first called Christians in Antioch, and Peter established his seat there before going to Rome. Like Alexandria, and frequently in direct opposition to it, Antioch became a center of Christian learning with a strong emphasis on sound interpretation of the Bible. But whereas the Alexandrian Church promoted an allegorical understanding of Scripture, the Antiochian community held more faithfully to a literal rendering. Historically many important leaders and thinkers have been produced by the Antiochian church. These include John Chrysostom, Theodore of Mopsuestia, Nestorius, Severus, and Peter the Fuller. Many Antiochian Christians immigrated to America in the late 19th century, with the first society organized in 1895 in New York City. Today the Antiochian Orthodox community numbers more than 450,000 in 159 parishes throughout the United States and Canada.

Armenian

The Armenian Orthodox tradition, sometimes known as Gregorian, from St. Gregory the Enlightener, is currently split in matters of jurisdiction but not in matters of faith. In 1834 a small number of immigrants pursuing university degrees began arriving in America. In 1891, the first Armenian Church was built, in Worcester, Massachusetts. Today there are close to one million Armenians in the United States and Canada. Some of the major centers include Boston, Detroit, New York, and Philadelphia. Recent immigration from the former Soviet Union is also causing the Armenian Orthodox population to swell in places such as Glendale, CA, Kansas City, MO, Hartford, CT, Fargo, ND, Erie, PA, Chicago, IL, Jacksonville, FL, Nashville, TN, and St. Louis, MO.

——— " ———

"Come receive the unwaning light and glorify Christ who is risen from the dead." — from the Easter Vigil Service

——— " ———

Orthodox Calendars

The History and Development of the Religious Calendar

In the Orthodox Church holidays and feast days are determined by two different calendars, the Julian Calendar and the Gregorian Calendar. The former is attributed to the Roman Emperor Julius Caesar, and bears his name. The latter came about in the sixteenth century in an effort to correct the discrepancy between calendar time and calculated astronomical time. It added thirteen days back into the year and was named for Pope Gregory XIII, who commissioned the work.

Old and New Calendars

Throughout the centuries the Julian Calendar has been in use in both the Christian East and West. The introduction of the Gregorian Calendar fueled the ever increasing fire of animosity between the two Churches. Even though many in the East recognized the inadequacies of the Julian Calendar, leading some to go so far as to devise new calendars for themselves, it nevertheless remained in use throughout the Byzantine period and beyond.

When the Gregorian Calendar was introduced, Pope Gregory tried to convince the Orthodox to accept it, but they refused, primarily on the grounds that it would alter the dating of Easter. Canon 7 of the Council of Nicea (325) set clear regulations for the dating of Easter. To adopt the Gregorian Calendar would mean having Easter coincide with the Jewish Passover, something clearly against the canonical stipulations.

Orthodox Churches continued to use the Julian Calendar until May of 1923 when an "Inter-Orthodox Congress" was convened in Constantinople by the Ecumenical Patriarch Meletios IV. Not all Orthodox Churches were represented. Though invited, the Churches of Alexandria, Antioch, and Jerusalem did not attend. The Church of Bulgaria was never asked to come. Only the Orthodox Churches of Cyprus, Greece, Romania, and Serbia participated. Even then, no unanimous decision was reached regarding the calendar of choice. It has only been in recent years that the Churches of Alexandria, Antioch, Constantinople, Cyprus, Greece, Poland, Romania, and, in 1968, Bulgaria, voted to adopt the new Gregorian Calendar. The Churches of Jerusalem, Russia, and Serbia continue to adhere to the old Julian Calendar.

Calendar Problems among the Orthodox Churches

Utilization of the different calendars across different Orthodox Churches has not been without its problems. Those who have adopted the new calendar celebrate Christmas on December 25 along with the vast majority of other Christian Churches. The Orthodox Churches that continue to use the old calendar, however, celebrate Christmas thirteen days later, on January 7. The same difference in feast days happens with regards to Epiphany. Those following the new calendar observe Epiphany on January 6, whereas those following the old calendar wait until January 19.

These differences in feast dates for the new and old calendars are uniform except when it comes to Easter. The most important feast of the year, Easter, or Pascha, is calculated by all Orthodox Churches using the dates on the old Julian Calendar. Regardless of when the rest of Christendom celebrates Christ's resurrection, the Orthodox Church observes it together. The only exception to this rule is the Orthodox Church of Finland, which, making up less

Figure 8.1. Icons are stylized images used to help focus a worshipper's attention. ("The Lady of Kazan" in a Russian cathedral, Library of Congress, Prints and Photographs Division, Frank and Frances Carpenter collection LC-USZ62-132527.)

than two percent of the predominantly Lutheran population, observes Easter according to the new Gregorian Calendar for practical reasons.

It was necessary to make corrections to the old Julian Calendar, but the calculation of Easter continued to be based upon it so as to not violate any of holy canons. Nevertheless, this compromise was incapable of preventing the schism of "Old Calendarists" which ensued. As has happened throughout the history of Christendom, strong opposition followed in the wake of reformation. What made this reformation different from many others, though, was that it was initiated from within the Orthodox Church and was supported wholeheartedly by the state. Still, there was great resistance to the adoption of the new Gregorian Calendar, especially in Greece. Groups of "Old Calendarists" refused to abide by the Church's decision and continued to follow the old Julian Calendar for all feast days, be they movable or immovable, arguing that the canons ratified by the Ecumenical Councils were established using this earlier calendar. Nothing less than a new Ecumenical Synod, they claimed, had the authority to institute such widespread change. Because of their blatant refusal to acknowledge and follow the authority of the Church, the "Old Calendarists" were excommunicated by the Patriarchate of Constantinople. To this day "Old Calendarists" continue to exist and maintain a hierarchy of their own consisting of both monasteries and parishes, despite the attempts of civil authorities to suppress them.

Establishing and Determining Dates for Easter

The method of determining the date of Easter in the Orthodox Church was established at the First Ecumenical Council, at Nicea, in 325 C.E. According to its ruling, Easter Sunday should fall on the Sunday that follows the first full moon after the vernal equinox. If the full moon appears on a Sunday, Easter is observed the next week.

The difference in establishing the date of Easter between the Orthodox Church and other Christian Churches lies in the dating of the vernal equinox. All believe that when the Council of Nicea established the date for Easter, the vernal equinox happened on March 21. At that time the Julian Calendar was being used. But has already been shown, the Gregorian Calendar added thirteen days to make up for those that had been lost due to inaccuracies in the Julian Calendar. As such, the Gregorian Calendar still recognizes the vernal equinox as occurring on March 21. Currently in America we follow the Gregorian dating. Without adding thirteen days to the year, however, the original, Julian dating for the vernal equinox is later. March 21 on the Julian Calendar falls on April 3 on the Gregorian.

The Orthodox Church continues to base its calculations for Easter on the Julian Calendar. In essence this means that Orthodox Easter cannot be celebrated before April 3.

The date of Passover is also important in determining the date of Easter for the Orthodox Church and other Christian communions. Originally, the Jews celebrated Passover on the first full moon following the vernal equinox. Christians began to celebrate Easter on the first Sunday after that. Easter was always the first Sunday after Passover. But with sacking of Jerusalem in 70 C.E. and other tragic events that led to the scattering of the Jews, Passover began to occasionally take place before the vernal equinox. This happened because many of these dispersed Jews became dependent on local pagan calendars for calculating Passover. It wasn't long before most Christians ceased to regulate the observance of Easter by the Jewish holy day. Their intent was to preserve the original practice of observing Easter following the vernal equinox.

As one alternative to calculating Easter by the Passover, Paschal cycles were devised. In time, the Orthodox Church adopted a nineteen year cycle, whereas the Roman Church used an eighty-four year cycle. Inevitably the use of these two variant Paschal cycles gave way to differences between the Orthodox and Roman Churches regarding the observance of Easter. The conflicting dates between the Julian and Gregorian Calendars for the vernal equinox increased the differences. Ultimately, it is the combination of these variables which accounts for the differing date of Orthodox Eastern when it varies from the rest of Christendom.

Establishing Dates for Movable Celebrations

According to Byzantine practice, the Orthodox ecclesiastical year begins on the first of September and is divided between movable and immovable holy days. The movable feast days are determined by the date of Easter. There are times when the date of Orthodox Easter coincides with that of other Christian Churches, but there are also times when it occurs as much as five weeks later. As a compromise to those who opposed using the new Gregorian Calendar, all movable feast days that are dependent upon the dating of Easter are still calculated using the old Julian Calendar.

The Twelve Great Feasts

On the Orthodox Calendar, there are twelve great feasts that are next in importance after Easter. Three of these

feasts, Palm Sunday, the Ascension, and Pentecost, are movable. Of the twelve feasts, eight are devoted to Christ and four to the Virgin Mary.

Fast Periods and Days

In the Orthodox Church fasting includes abstinence from meat, fish, dairy products, olive oil, and wine. Total abstinence from all food or drink is reserved for the time of preparation before Holy Communion. Although observed in the monasteries and by the very devout, many Orthodox Christians today find the rigid rules for observing a fast difficult to uphold for the length of time prescribed. Upon consultation with one's spiritual director or approval of the local church hierarchy, deviation from the norm is permitted.

Table 8.1. The Twelve Great Feasts

Feast	Date
The Nativity of the Virgin Mary	September 8
The Elevation of the Life-giving Cross	September 14
The Presentation of the Virgin Mary in the Temple	November 21
Christmas	December 25
Epiphany	January 6
The Presentation of Christ in the Temple	February 2
The Annunciation	March 25
Palm Sunday	the Sunday before Easter
The Ascension	40 days after Easter
Pentecost	50 days after Easter
The Transfiguration	August 6
The Repose, or Dormition, of the Virgin Mary	August 15

Throughout the Orthodox liturgical year there are four main fast periods. Two of them, the Great Fast, or Lent, and the Fast of the Apostles, have movable dates of observance.

Individual fast days include the fast of the Elevation of the Holy Cross (September 14), the Beheading of St. John the Baptist (August 29), and the eve of Epiphany (January 5), as well as all Wednesdays and Fridays. However, other than Epiphany Eve there is no fasting between Christmas and Epiphany, nor any fasting during the tenth week of Easter, the week after Easter, or the week after Pentecost.

How the Current Orthodox Liturgical Calendar Works

There are five main elements to the Orthodox liturgical calendar: the daily cycle, the weekly cycle, the Paschal cycle, the cycle of fixed feasts, and the cycle of eight tones.

In contrast to practice in many other Christian Churches of starting the liturgical year with the first Sunday in Advent, the Orthodox liturgical year begins on September

Table 8.2. Periods of Fasting

Fast	Dates
Christmas Fast	forty days, from November 15 to December 24
Great Fast	begins on a Monday seven weeks before Easter until Easter
Fast of the Apostles	varies in length from one to six weeks, beginning eight days after Pentecost and ending on June 28, the eve of the feat of Saints Peter and Paul
Fast of the Repose of the Virgin Mary	from August 1 to 14

1. In the Ecumenical Patriarchate this is observed as the Day of the Environment, with the role in the salvation of the world of the Theotokos, the mother of God, being emphasized. The Nativity of the Virgin Mary on September 8 and her Dormition on August 15 come at opposite ends of the liturgical year. Other than those included among the twelve great feasts, the other Marian feast day is December 9, the Conception of the Virgin by St. Anne.

March 25, the Annunciation, is another major feast of the Theotokos, but it is also a feast of the Conception of Christ and begins a series of feasts of the Lord. The Nativity of the Lord, as well as the Visit of the Magi, is observed in the Orthodox Church on December 25. The Circumcision of Jesus falls on January 1, the feast of Saint Basil the Great. For the Orthodox Christian, Epiphany, or Theophany as it is sometimes known, is January 6 and commemorates Christ's baptism. The feast of the Transfiguration is held on August 6.

The Paschal cycle begins four weeks before Lent, on the Sunday of the Pharisee and the Publican. Lent itself begins on Pure Monday and ends on Lazarus Saturday, the day before Palm Sunday. The Passion, the Mystical Supper, the Agony, Betrayal, Trial, Sufferings, Death, Burial and Glorious Resurrection, the Assumption into heaven of the Lord, and the Sending of His Holy Spirit upon the Apostles are all celebrated in the feasts of the Paschal cycle. The cycle ends with Pentecost Sunday, the feast of the Holy Trinity, and the Sunday of All Saints.

In addition to the special feast days of the Lord or of Mary, every day on the Orthodox Calendar commemorates some saint. These may be saints venerated by all of Christendom, Latin Church saints from early centuries, saints particular to a specific locale, or the Righteous, or Dikaios, of the Old Law. Somewhat anachronistically, the Maccabees are commemorated as though they were Christian martyrs. The Maccabees were the family of Mattathias who, in 167 B.C.E., led the Jewish revolt against Antiochus IV Epiphanes. Even some Latin Church saints from after the Great Schism are recognized, and some Latin feasts, such as Corpus Christi, are observed.

In the medieval period of the Church, all music was organized on the basis of a system of eight tones. These continue to have not only musical significance but a calendrical significance as well. Beginning the first Sunday after Easter, St. Thomas Sunday, each successive week uses the texts and music of the next of the eight tones for its offices. Each day of the week has its distinctive hymns and verses for each of these eight tones. The book which contains the texts for each day's services for all eight tones is called the Parakletike.

⬛ ⬛ ⬛

Orthodox Holidays

Weekly

Sunday

Orthodox Christians observe Sunday as a day for communal worship. This practice originated with the first century followers of Christ. Although they were predominantly Jewish and used to meeting on the Jewish Sabbath, Saturday, they began meeting on Sundays in remembrance of Jesus's resurrection.

Several other Christian ritual practices are drawn from Jewish sources as well. One such example is the Eucharist, or Communion or Lord's Supper as it is sometimes known. It is the focal point of many Sunday services. The Jewish Passover Seder forms the basis of this Christian ritual of bread and wine, observed in memory of Jesus's last meal with His disciples.

Annually

September

Church New Year
September 1

Whereas many Christian groups in the west observe the start of the ecclesiastical year with the beginning of the Advent season, the Orthodox Church starts its ecclesiastical year on this date.

Feast of the Nativity of the Theotokos (Mother of God) and Ever-Virgin, Mary
September 8

The birth of the Virgin Mary is one of only three births celebrated by the Orthodox Church. John the Baptist (June 24) and Jesus (December 25) are the other two. Although there is no strong evidence that September 8 is the actual date of Mary's birth, it became widely accepted for this celebration during the seventh century.

Elevation of the Holy Cross
September 14

This Christian feast commemorates several historical events relating to the cross on which Christ was crucified. According to tradition, St. Helena, the mother of Emperor Constantine, discovered fragments of the cross in 326 C.E. This is the first event remembered. Another is the consecration of the basilica that was constructed in honor of the cross nearly a decade after Helena's

discovery. A third moment recalled during the feast is the recovery in 628 C.E. of a major portion of the cross that had been taken from Jerusalem by the Persians. The feast of the Elevation of the Holy Cross originated in Jerusalem.

St. Gregory the Illuminator
September 30

Born around 257 C.E., St. Gregory the Illuminator is celebrated in the Orthodox Church as the one who established Christianity in Armenia, although he was not the first to introduce Christianity in that country. Armenians maintain that both Bartholomew and Thaddeus preached the gospel there earlier.

Married with two sons, Gregory defended Christianity to King Trdat, who initially persecuted him. In time, however, the King embraced the faith, making Christianity the national faith of Armenia. This happened during the reign of Emperor Diocletian, giving Armenia the right to her claim as being the first Christian state. Upon Gregory's death he was buried at Thortan, and a monastery was built near his grave. His relics were later moved to Constantinople and eventually brought back to Armenia.

October

St. Thomas's Day
October 6

St. Thomas was dubbed "Doubting Thomas" because he wouldn't believe that Jesus had risen from the grave until he had touched Jesus's wounds for himself. But Thomas was also the first to call Jesus, "My Lord and my God."

Thomas became one of the most important disciples in the early church. When the apostles left Jerusalem to preach to the people of other nations, as Jesus had instructed them to do, tradition says Thomas traveled eastward toward India. In Kerala, the smallest state in India, the Malabar Christians claim St. Thomas as the founder of their church. For them his feast day is a major celebration. Thomas is the patron saint of India and Pakistan. His feast is also observed on the Sunday after Easter.

St. James the Brother of the Lord
October 23

St. James was an apostle and martyr of the first century. He was one of Jesus's disciples and became a leader in the Church of Jerusalem. St. James's feast day is observed because of his influence in the early Jerusalem Church.

St. Demetrios
October 26

St. Demetrios is one of the most popular saints celebrated in the Orthodox Church and is the patron of numerous churches. He was born in Thessalonica in 270 C.E. In a very short time, Demetrios became a high-ranking officer in the Roman army, but considered himself a soldier of Christ first and a soldier of the emperor second. The Emperor Maximian did not appreciate the sentiment and in time set up a gladiatorial contest between Christianity and paganism, challenging any Christian to fight against his athletic giant.

When Nestoras, a fellow Christian, was chosen to fight against the pagan champion, Demetrios prayed for him. Nestoras won. Recognizing that Demetrios's prayer was the inspiring power behind Nestoras's victory, the emperor had Demetrios executed by the spear on October 26, 306.

In ancient times, the life of St. Demetrios was commemorated with celebrations that lasted for months. Often these festivities were accompanied by the trading and exchanging of goods. Merchants, traders, philosophers, and artists would gather from all around to deal and trade and celebrate. Thessalonica still hosts Greece's largest international trade exhibition every year, in honor of St. Demetrios.

November

St. Michael and All Angels
November 8

The archangel Michael is mentioned several times in the book of Daniel, where he is described as the guardian of the Israelites. In the New Testament he is represented in the book of Jude as disputing with the devil over the body of Moses and in the book of Revelation as fighting in heaven against the dragon, "he that is called the devil and Satan." Also honored on this day are the other archangels, Raphael and Gabriel.

St. Philip
November 14

St. Philip, a native of Bethsaida on Lake Genesareth, was an apostle and martyr of the first century. He was a disciple of John the Baptist and was eventually called by Jesus. Philip not only obeyed the call but brought Nathaniel as a disciple as well.

Advent
November 15–December 24

In the Orthodox Church, Advent begins on November 15 in preparation for the Feast of the Nativity of our Lord. Orthodox Christians use the season of Advent as a time for fasting, meditation, and preparation before Christmas. It is, therefore, often referred to as Little Lent, because it mirrors the disciplines utilized during Great Lent in preparation for Easter.

St. Matthew
November 16

St. Matthew, also known as Levi, was a tax-collector in Capernaum, gathering duties for Herod Antipas and hated by the Pharisees and many of his Jewish brethren. After Jesus called him to be a disciple, however, Matthew became an apostle, evangelist, and martyr of the first century. He is traditionally recognized as the author of the Gospel that bears his name. St. Matthew is represented under the symbol of a winged man, carrying in his hand a lance as a characteristic emblem.

Feast of the Presentation of the Theotokos (Mother of God) and Ever-Virgin, Mary
November 21

Although the origin of this feast is uncertain, the Orthodox Church officially began celebrating the Presentation of the Virgin Mary in the eighth century. The feast commemorates events related in the apocryphal Book of James where three-year old Mary was presented in the Temple, consecrating her to God's service.

St. Catherine
November 25

Only eighteen years old, Catherine confronted the Emperor Maximinus for persecuting Christians, challenging his worship of false gods. Astounded by her audacity but unable to counter the wisdom of her arguments, he summoned numerous scholars to talk with Catherine in an effort to discredit her. Catherine won the debate, and was so eloquent that many of her adversaries declared themselves Christians and were subsequently put to death. This infuriated Maximinus so much that he had Catherine scourged and imprisoned. But the empress was eager to see her, and after visiting Catherine in the dungeon she believed in God, was baptized, and, like the earlier scholars, was promptly martyred. Numerous people continued to come to faith in Christ through Catherine's witness, so the emperor had her beheaded. According to tradition, angels carried her body to Mount Sinai where a church and monastery were later built in her honor.

December

St. Barbara and St. John of Damascus
December 4

These two saints are greatly revered in the Orthodox Church. Barbara was the daughter of a rich heathen named Dioscorus. While he was away, she had three windows placed in her bath-house as a symbol of the Holy Trinity. Upon his return, Barbara confessed herself to be a Christian and was immediately beaten by her father and dragged before the provincial prefect who had her tortured and condemned to death by beheading. Dioscorus carried out the sentence but as punishment was struck by lightning on his way home. St. Barbara has often been depicted as standing in a tower with three windows, carrying the palm of a martyr in her hand.

St. John was born in Damascus around 676 C.E. and is revered as much for his ability to collect and synthesize existing theological precepts as for his originality. He is considered by many as the precursor of the Scholastics, those Church figures who sought to harmonize philosophy and theology into one system for the rational demonstration of theological truth, seeking to better understand the faith by way of knowledge and reason. Others regard him as the first Scholastic, with his *Orthodox Faith* as the first work of Scholasticism.

St. Nicholas's Day
December 6

Besides his reputation for generosity, compassion, and humility, St. Nicholas was a representative and active member of the First Ecumenical Council in Nicea in 325 C.E. During that time he was serving as bishop of Myra, in what is now Turkey. One of the legends surrounding him is that he saved three sisters from being forced into prostitution by their poverty-stricken father by throwing three bags of gold into their room, thus providing each of them with a dowry. This may be the source of St. Nicholas's association with gift-giving.

Holy Theotokos (Mother of God) and Ever-Virgin, Mary
December 9

In contrast to the Roman Catholic doctrine of the Immaculate Conception, Orthodoxy proclaims that Mary was conceived and born like every other human. In giving birth to Christ, however, she preserved her virginity so she is often called the Ever-Virgin. The Orthodox Church observes the normal conception of the Holy Theotokos (Mother of God) by St. Anna, mother of Mary, on this day.

Feast of the Forebearers of Christ
Second Sunday before Christmas

Orthodox Churches celebrate the second Sunday before Christmas as the feast day of the Forebearers of Christ, beginning with Adam and Eve, the parents of the human race. Numerous customs are observed in leading up to

Christmas. One Slavic observance is that on Christmas Eve the entire house must be swept clean, all borrowed items returned, all tools put away, no lint or unfinished work is allowed to be seen, and no task is started than cannot be finished before nightfall. In both the Greek and Middle Eastern traditions the faithful fast all day in preparation for receiving Holy Communion at the Christmas Liturgy late on Christmas Eve.

Feast of the Nativity of Our Lord
December 25

Christmas is the day on which Christians celebrate the birth of Jesus Christ. It was originally commemorated by Orthodox Christians on the Feast of Epiphany, January 6. The Armenian Orthodox Church continues to celebrate the Nativity then. By 354 C.E., the Christmas Feast had taken hold in the West on December 25, and since the fifth century most Orthodox Churches have also celebrated the Nativity on that day. However, some Orthodox congregations, called "Old Calendarists" because of their use of the Julian calendar which is 13 days behind the Gregorian calendar, honor the birth of Christ on January 7.

Synaxis of the Holy Theotokos (Mother of God) and Ever-Virgin, Mary
December 26

A synaxis is a gathering or an assembly, and often refers to any religious function where people are gathered together, centered on a meeting place. The synaxis of the Holy Theotokos is the feast day where Orthodox Christians remember the flight into Egypt. According to the Gospel of Matthew, King Herod, ruler in Palestine at the time of Christ's birth, wanted to seek out and kill the infant Jesus. But Joseph, the husband of Mary, was warned in a dream of the impending danger and took his family to Egypt for safety until the king had died. This feast commemorates the safe journey of the Holy Family and their gathering in Egypt for asylum until the danger had past.

St. Stephen's Day
December 27

On this day about the year 35, St. Stephen became the first Christian martyr. Stephen was the first of the seven deacons appointed by the apostles to assist in the distribution of alms, as recorded in the book of Acts. His success aroused the hostility of the Jews, who accused him of blasphemy. In his defense, Stephen testified that they had killed Christ, who was the prophet announced by Moses. This so enraged them that they sentenced him to be stoned to death. Stephen died confessing Christ and asking for the forgiveness of his persecutors.

Holy Innocents' Day
December 29

This day is dedicated to the memory of the male children in Bethlehem who were slaughtered by King Herod in his attempt to kill the infant Jesus.

January

St. Basil's Day
January 1

Born in 329 C.E. into a family of saints, Basil became the Bishop of Caesarea and one of the most distinguished Doctors of the Church. One set of grandparents, his parents, his two brothers and one sister were all canonized. He was a staunch defender of Orthodoxy against the heresies of the fourth century. Along with his friend Gregory Nazianzus and his brother Gregory of Nyssa, Basil is part of the trio known as the Cappadocian Fathers, although St. Basil surpassed the other two in practical genius and actual achievement.

Feast of Epiphany
January 6

This feast recognizes the manifestations of the divinity of Christ. It is one of the oldest Christian feasts, originating in the second century before the official recognition of Christmas. At first, Epiphany recognized the birth of Jesus, the visitation of the Magi to Christ, and the baptism of Jesus by John the Baptist. The first two of these commemorations were transferred to Christmas when the Orthodox Church adopted that feast between 380 and 430. The current central feature of the Orthodox observance of Epiphany is the declaration of Christ's divinity at His baptism and at the beginning of His public life.

In the Orthodox Church, Epiphany is also associated with the Blessing of the Waters. On this day, in honor of the baptism of Christ, a large container of water in each church is blessed and small bottles of holy water are distributed to the congregation. In the United States, a service is often held at the banks of a local stream or river which the priest blesses. Around the world, the tradition of diving into the river to retrieve crosses thrown there by the priest has been practiced for centuries. It is believed that those retrieving the crosses will be especially blessed.

Three Hierarchs
January 30

The Three Hierarchs are sometimes called the Cappadocian Fathers. They are the brothers St. Basil the Great and St. Gregory of Nyssa, along with their close friend, St. Gregory Nazianzus. Basil died in 379 C.E., and during his life he served as bishop of Caesarea and was influential in early eastern monastic movements. Gregory of Nyssa, Basil's younger brother, died in 395 and served as bishop of Nyssa, writing prolifically on many theological and pastoral topics. Gregory Nazianzus died in 389 and served as bishop of both Sasima and later Constantinople, where he preached powerfully for the cause of Orthodoxy. Together these three became staunch defenders of the Orthodoxy established at the First Ecumenical Council of Nicea and were highly instrumental in the development of doctrine concerning the Trinity.

February

Triodion
70 days before Easter

The season of Triodion includes a four-week period of preparation preceding Great Lent as well as Great Lent itself. The name Triodion comes from the name of the Service Book used during this period.

Presentation of Christ in the Temple
February 2

This day commemorates Jesus's presentation in the Temple which was in accord with the prescriptions of Mosaic Law and Mary's forty-day purification following the birth of her child. According to the Gospel of Luke, this is also when Jesus was first publicly proclaimed as the Messiah by the prophets Anna and Simeon in the temple courtyard.

March

Meatfare Sunday
Second Sunday before Lent

Sometimes called the Sunday of the Last Judgment, Meatfare Sunday is traditionally the last day on which meat may be eaten until Easter.

First Saturday of Souls
Second Saturday before Lent

From the earliest days of Christianity, the faithful prayed for the dead. Saturdays were traditionally dedicated as times for this work, following the leading of St. John of Damascus, who wrote, "The Sabbath (Saturday) in Hebrew means 'rest,' since on that day God rested from His work. We make a remembrance of the deceased on that 'day of rest' for they are 'resting' from all their earthly cares." When the Orthodox Christian makes intercession to God for the souls of the departed, they pray that God might grant them eternal rest since, according to the Scriptures, to enter God's rest means to join Him in an eternal life of happiness.

In keeping with this, since the ninth century the Orthodox Church has established a special day for the dead called Souls Saturday. In fact, there are several All Souls Saturdays throughout the ecclesiastical year. Prayers for these special days of observance and prayer are taken from a book called the *Synaxarion*.

Cheesefare Sunday
Sunday before Lent

Sometimes called Forgiveness Sunday, Cheesefare Sunday is the last day on which cheese, milk, dairy products, and fish may be eaten. Sometimes it is characterized by dancing. At sunset, people attend the evening service of Forgiveness Vespers during which the priest and congregation exchange mutual forgiveness for their sins.

Second Saturday of Souls
Saturday before Lent

During the ninth century when the *Triodion*, the liturgical book used during the Easter season, was compiled, Second, Third and Fourth Saturdays of Souls were also dedicated for the commemoration of the dead. These were added for a number of reasons. First, they make provision for remembrance of the dead since in the Liturgy of the Presanctified Gifts, a ritual prescribed for Great Lent, there is no such condition. Second, the days remind the faithful of their own mortality and make the penitential exercises of Great Lent all the more meaningful. Third, they give the believer an opportunity to practice good deeds in behalf of the faithful who have died.

Great Lent
Seven weeks before Easter

Great Lent is a period of introspection and penitence observed by Christians in preparation for the celebration of Easter. The tradition of prayer, fasting, and self-denial was initially practiced only for three days before Easter, beginning with Holy Friday. In the late sixth century, however, Great Lent was established at forty weekdays by Gregory the Great. The significance of the length of days may reflect the importance of the number forty in the Bible. Moses fasted for forty days on Mt. Sinai. The Israelites wandered for forty years in the wilderness. Elijah fasted for forty days. And perhaps most importantly, Jesus went forty days without food after His baptism and prior to the onset of His public ministry.

In the Orthodox Church the second Sunday before Lent is Meatfare Sunday and is the last day meat may be eaten

until Easter. The Sunday before Lent is Cheesefare Sunday and is the last day on which dairy products and fish may be eaten before Easter. These observances are meant to help ease the faithful into the fast.

Clean Monday
Monday after the beginning of Lent

Clean Monday is the Monday that begins the season of Great Lent. It is so named because Orthodox Christians are called upon to begin the holy season with "clean hearts and good intentions." It is also because the season of Great Lent is regarded as a time for when Christians should clean up their spiritual house, coming to terms with their lives and rededicating themselves to a more holy and righteous way of living. Clean Monday is a day of strict fasting. The believer is permitted to take no food from midnight to noon and no meat all day long. They are also expected to spend extra time during the day in prayer and reading the Bible, a practice that should continue throughout Great Lent.

St. Theodore (Third Saturday of Souls)
First Saturday of Lent

Another Saturday of Souls dedicated to remembrance of the dead, this feast day also serves to remember St. Theodore, who was a monk and bishop of Anastasiopolis in Galatia. From early in his life Theodore was so committed to prayer that he would often go without food in order to spend more time in church. At various times he shut himself in his mother's cellar, a make-shift hermitage of sorts, and also lived for a while in a cave under a nearby, run-down chapel. His desire for isolation eventually led him to live in a cave in a mountain. Theodore's life was extremely austere, living only on a sparse diet of vegetables on wearing an iron girdle about his body. Though consecrated bishop, Theodore was able to leave the position after ten years and spend the remainder of his life as a monk, at one point curing the emperor's son of elephantitis.

Sunday of Orthodoxy
First Sunday of Lent

In the Orthodox Church the First Sunday of Lent commemorates the eighth century victory of the Orthodox over the iconoclasts, who were destroying and condemning the use of icons. The *Synodicon*, a text that proclaims the appropriateness of using icons in public and private worship and prayer, is read on this day.

Sunday of St. Gregory Palamas
Second Sunday of Lent

St. Gregory was born in Constantinople around 1296 C.E. After his father's death, he and several other members of his family became monks, entering a monastery on Mt. Athos. He is remembered by Orthodox Christians because of his important theological and spiritual positions. Gregory believed that although God is ultimately unknowable, humanity can experience His power through the sacraments and mystical experience, both only possible because of the Incarnation of Christ. A concerted focus on the Son of God makes one open to God's work in the believer's life.

Sunday of the Holy Cross
Third Sunday of Lent

The third Sunday of Lent is spent in extensive fasting and prayer, contemplating the Cross on which Christ was crucified. It calls the believer to consider his or her own mortality but more importantly the provision of Christ in His passion and subsequent resurrection.

Sunday of St. John Climacos
Fourth Sunday of Lent

St. John was born in 525 C.E. in Syria and died on Mt. Sinai on March 30, 606. Although his education was extensive, he chose early in his life to abandon a scholastic career and instead enter a life of solitude. Because the region around Mt. Sinai was known for the holiness of the monks who inhabited it, John went to a monk there named Martyrius and began practicing various Christian virtues under his guidance. When Martyrius died, John withdrew to a hermitage and for twenty years lived in isolation, studying the lives of the saints and becoming one of the most learned doctors of the Church.

When he was seventy five years old, several monks of Sinai persuaded him to become their leader. He served them with great wisdom and his fame spread. The pope, St. Gregory the Great, wrote to recommend himself to his prayers and send him a large sum of money for the hospital of Sinai where numerous pilgrims often stayed. Only fours years into his leadership, John resigned his charge and returned to his hermitage.

Though surnamed Scholasticas, St. John is often called St. John Climacos, meaning "of the Ladder." This refers to his most important work, *The Ladder of Divine Ascent*, which is a cornerstone of spiritual struggle and growth. Divided into thirty parts, or steps, it presents a picture of all the Christian virtues and contains numerous parables and historical touches drawn principally from the monastic life.

Sunday of St. Mary of Egypt
Fifth Sunday of Lent

Born around 344 C.E., St. Mary of Egypt is seen as an example of extreme repentance and humility. At the age

of twelve she left her home and moved to Alexandria, where for over seventeen years she lived the life of a prostitute. At the end of that time, she boarded a ship with pilgrims bound for Jerusalem, hoping to provide herself more opportunities for financial gain. Upon arrival in Jerusalem, she was caught up in a crowd observing the Feast of the Elevation of the Cross and making its way to the church where a portion of the Cross was kept. Upon reaching the church doors, however, she found herself repelled by some invisible force and unable to enter. Retiring to a corner of the churchyard, Mary was struck by remorse for the sinfulness of her life, and when her eyes fell upon a statue of the Virgin Mary she pledged that if the Holy Mother of God would help her find the way to salvation, she would renounce forever the ways of the world and do whatever was asked.

Mary immediately sensed a forgiveness of her years of sin and committed herself to a life of solitude and prayer. She lived alone for forty-seven more years, eating only herbs. At that time a priest and monk named Zosimus, who had gone into the desert to observe the Lenten fast, met her and learned from her the story of her life. For Orthodox Christians, Mary of Egypt continues to be an example of forgiveness and piety that can come from repentance and commitment to God.

Feast of the Annunciation
March 25

Formerly known as Annunciation of the Virgin Mary, this holiday commemorates the manifestation of the Archangel Gabriel to the Virgin Mary, announcing that she was chosen to be the mother of Jesus. A movable feast in Protestant and Roman Catholic Churches, it is not moved in the Orthodox Church, although it is celebrated a bit differently when it falls during Holy Week. Orthodox Christians began observing the feast around 430 C.E.

April

Lazarus Saturday
Saturday before Palm Sunday

In Orthodox Churches, the Saturday before Palm Sunday is set aside to honor Lazarus, who was raised from the dead by Jesus. Palms are blessed either at the evening vesper service or during the morning Liturgy and the branches are distributed to the worshippers, who take them home and display them above their icons. The raising of Lazarus serves as a reminder to the faithful of the universal resurrection of believers. In Greece, Romania, and the former Yugoslavia, Orthodox Christians sing songs, carry palm or willow branches from house to house, and act out the story of Christ raising Lazarus from the dead. In return they receive gifts of fruit and candy.

Palm Sunday
Sunday before Easter

Called Willow Sunday in some Slavic countries where palms are not traditionally available due to cold climates and great distances from warmer countries, Palm Sunday commemorates the day on which Jesus rode into Jerusalem greeted by a cheering crowd, crying, "Hosanna! Blessed is He that comes in the name of the Lord!" The people of Jerusalem believed the Messiah would be an earthly conqueror who could set them free from Roman rule, and they saw Jesus as this leader. So they honored Him by waving palm branches, a traditional symbol of victory, which they then spread in the street for Him to ride over. Orthodox Christians continue to observe Palm Sunday as a day to give praise and glory to Christ as the Savior who conquered death and the grave.

Paschal Thursday
Thursday before Easter

Paschal Thursday, or Footwashing Thursday, commemorates Jesus's institution of the Eucharist during the Last Supper. Part of the remembrance of Jesus's last evening with His disciples involves His washing the disciples' feet. Christians have celebrated it since the middle of the fourth century, practicing the ceremonial foot-washing in imitation of Jesus, who washed His disciples' feet before the Last Supper as a sign and example of humility and love.

Holy Friday
Friday before Easter

The Friday before Easter is a major observance for all Christians. On the afternoon of Holy Friday, Orthodox Christians observe the solemn service of Great Vespers. It concludes the remembrance of the events of Christ's passion and leads the believer toward watchful expectation, contemplating the mystery of the Lord's descent into Hades, the theme of Holy Saturday. This service is often called the Apokathelosis, a name derived from the liturgical re-enactment of the removal of Christ from the Cross.

The service has two dramatic liturgical actions. First is the Apokathelosis, or un-nailing of Jesus. Second comes the Procession of the Epitaphios, referring to an icon depicting the burial of Christ encased within a large embroidered cloth. During that ceremony the church elders process to a shrine carry a cloth depicting Jesus's dead body, where it is placed in a symbolic tomb. In addition, a series of three hymns of praise, each with many verses, is sung for the crucified Lord in anticipation of His resurrection.

Holy Saturday
Night before Easter

Throughout Holy Saturday, the Orthodox Christian contemplates the mystery of Jesus's descent into Hades. Then, at midnight, the Easter vigil begins when in a completely darkened Church the priest comes forth from the altar bearing the Paschal candle and proclaims, "Come receive the unwaning light and glorify Christ who is risen from the dead." After the faithful light their candles from the one light, the priest then leads in an outdoor procession. After the proclamation of the resurrection and many renditions of the Paschal hymn, "Christ is risen from the dead, trampling down death by death, and upon those in the tomb bestowing light," the priest knocks a series of three times on the church doors, symbolizing the three days Christ spent in the tomb, and declares Jesus's resurrection and

Figure 8.2. The form of cross used by Orthodox churches features three horizontal bars, instead of one as is used by many western churches. The top bar represents the inscription that was placed above Jesus during the crucifixion; the lower bar, which is slanted, represents the foot rest. The cross is sometimes adorned showing the letters "IC" and "IX." The letters are an abbreviation for "ISOUS CHRISTOS" which is Greek meaning Jesus Christ.

sovereignty. The doors are then swung open by the one person left inside the Church to answer the knocks. Worshippers re-enter a now fully lit Church and continue the resurrection service and liturgy.

Easter
The first Sunday after the first full moon on or following the vernal equinox

Easter, or Pascha, the most important holiday of the Christian faith and one of the earliest observances of the Church, celebrates the resurrection of Christ from the dead. It has always been regarded as the chief and most joyous observance within Christendom. Orthodox Christians continue to greet one another on this day with the salutation, "Christ is risen!" Easter's importance may be seen by the Christian calendar and the long period of preparation of Great Lent that precedes it, the special observances during Holy Week, and the weeks that follow. The ceremonies, customs, and rituals surrounding this mystery extend from Easter Sunday until the feast of Pentecost fifty days later.

In the early church, Easter was the great day of baptism. This came about based on the understanding that plunging the believer beneath the baptismal waters and then having them rise again from it re-enacted the death and resurrection of Jesus.

Many traditions have grown up around the celebration of Easter. One of these is the Easter egg. Long a symbol of new life, resurrection, and immortality in much of Europe, the egg was easily adopted by Christians as a part of the Easter iconography. In the Orthodox Church the traditional red eggs derive from an event in the life of St. Mary Magdalene when she approached the Emperor to tell him of her new-found faith, and in his presence the egg she was carrying as a gift to him turned red to confirm her proclamation of Jesus Christ.

Bright Week
Week after Easter

The week after Easter in the Orthodox Church is known as Bright Week, or Renewal Week. It is observed as a special time of celebration for the resurrection of Jesus Christ. It is called Bright Week for two reasons. First, the Orthodox Christian recognizes that all of creation is renewed by the Lord and Savior, Jesus Christ. Second, the catechumens who were baptized on Easter Sunday wear their new white robes all week, signifying their purity.

St. Thomas's Day
Sunday after Easter

St. Thomas was dubbed "Doubting Thomas" because he wouldn't believe that Jesus had risen from the grave until he had touched Jesus's wounds for himself. But

Thomas was also the first to call Jesus, "My Lord and my God." His feast is observed on October 6 as well.

St. George's Day
April 23

Little is known with certainty about the life or martyrdom of St. George, although he probably suffered at or near Lydda in Palestine, shortly before the reign of Emperor Constantine. Known in England since the eighth century, and patron saint of England from the time of Edward III, St. George received special veneration during the Crusades when Richard I's soldiers were inspired by visions of him. St. George is commemorated through the Orthodox Churches and is one of the most revered saints in the Church.

St. James the Son of Zebedee
April 30

James was the son of Zebedee and the elder brother of the apostle John. Like his brother and in partnership with saints Peter and Andrew, he was a fisherman in Galilee. At the call of Jesus, Scripture says James "forsook all and followed Him." He was present at the Transfiguration and in Gethsemane. He also was nicknamed, along with his brother, as Boanerges, "Sons of Thunder."

Before his death, James preached in Spain, and after his martyrdom his body was taken to Compostella, a city in the northwest corner of that country. After Rome and Jerusalem, his shrine became the most popular place of pilgrimage in Christendom and his symbol, a scallop shell, became the badge of medieval pilgrims.

May

Ascension
Forty days after Easter

This holiday commemorates the ascension of Jesus back to heaven after His resurrection from the dead. It is celebrated forty days after Easter Sunday because the Biblical account in the Acts of the Apostles indicates that Jesus spent forty days with His disciples after His resurrection. During the forty days, He instructed them on how to carry out His teachings. Then, on the fortieth day, He took them to the Mount of Olives near Jerusalem and ascended to heaven as they watched. According to oral tradition, the observance of this day is one of the oldest celebrations of the Christian Church, dating to 68 C.E.

Fourth Saturday of Souls
49 days after Easter

This is another day to remember and pray for the faithful who have died.

Pentecost
Fifty days after Easter

Pentecost is a moveable celebration held on the seventh Sunday after Easter. According to the biblical book of Acts, it was the day on which the Holy Spirit descended on the Apostles in a form likened to tongues of fire, accompanied by a sound like a rushing wind. According the Holy Spirit then empowered St. Peter and the other believers with him to witness to Jews in Jerusalem. Three thousand conversions were reported in one day.

The name Pentecost comes from the word for fifty used by Greek-speaking Jews. It was the name of the celebration held fifty days after Passover. In the Orthodox Church it is marked by the wearing of green vestments.

Holy Spirit Day
Monday after Pentecost

The Orthodox Church is strongly Trinitarian, and on this first Monday after Pentecost it celebrates the third person of the Trinity, the Holy Spirit. Orthodox Christians believe that humanity is created in God's image but has been corrupted through sin. But because of the death and resurrection of Jesus Christ, death is conquered, and through the Holy Spirit new life is given to the faithful. One factor that distinguishes the Orthodox Church from the Roman Catholic Church is its belief that the Holy Spirit proceeds from God the Father through God the Son. Roman Catholic doctrine regards the Holy Spirit as proceeding from the Father and the Son. This distinction came to be known and the Filioque Controversy and was one of the reasons behind the Great Schism of 1054 C.E.

Table 8.3. Alphabetical List of Orthodox Holidays

Holiday	Date(s)
Advent	November 15–December 24
All Saints' Day	First Sunday after Pentecost
Ascension	Forty days after Easter
Birth of St. John the Baptist	June 24
Bright Week	Week after Easter
Cheesefare Sunday	Sunday before Lent
Church New Year	September 1
Clean Monday	Monday after the beginning of Lent
Easter	The first Sunday after the first full moon on or following the vernal equinox
Elevation of the Holy Cross	September 14
Feast of Epiphany	January 6
Feast of the Annunciation	March 25
Feast of the Dormition of the Theotokos (Mother of God) and Ever-Virgin, Mary	August 15
Feast of the Forebearers of Christ	Second Sunday before Christmas

Holiday	Date(s)
Feast of the Nativity of Our Lord	December 25
Feast of the Nativity of the Theotokos (Mother of God) and Ever-Virgin, Mary	September 8
Feast of the Presentation of the Theotokos (Mother of God) and Ever-Virgin, Mary	November 21
Feast of the Transfiguration	August 6
First Saturday of Souls	Second Saturday before Lent
Fourth Saturday of Souls	49 days after Easter
Great Lent	Seven weeks before Easter
Holy Friday	Friday before Easter
Holy Innocents' Day	December 29
Holy Saturday	Night before Easter
Holy Spirit Day	Monday after Pentecost
Holy Theotokos (Mother of God) and Ever-Virgin, Mary	December 9
Lazarus Saturday	Saturday before Palm Sunday

All Saints' Day

First Sunday after Pentecost

All Saints' Day is to honor all of the Christian saints, especially those who do not have their own feast days. From the earliest days of Christianity martyrs were honored on the days of their death. Initially it was customary to solemnize the anniversary of a martyr's death at the place of martyrdom. Therefore neighboring churches began to interchange feasts and transfer relics or to join together for a feast. Frequently groups of martyrs suffered on the same day, so joint commemoration was common.

During the persecution of Diocletian so many believers were martyred that it became impossible to assign a different day to each. In response, the Church assigned a common day for them all, feeling that every martyr should be venerated. The earliest trace of such a feast day comes from Antioch, when it occurred on the Sunday after Pentecost. Such a custom is also mentioned in the writings of St. Ephrem the Syrian in 373 C.E. and in a homily of St. John Chrysostom in 407. The Chaldean Orthodox Calendar, which dates from 411 also lists All Saints' Day as being honored on the first Sunday after Pentecost. Orthodox Christians continue to observe All Saints' Day on the first Sunday after Pentecost although many other Christian traditions today celebrate All Saints' Day on November 1.

Sts. Cyril and Methodios

May 11

Saints Cyril and Methodios were brothers, Methodios born in 826 C.E., and Cyril one year later. While they were

---

Table 8.3. Alphabetical List of Orthodox Holidays, continued

Holiday	Date(s)
Meatfare Sunday	Second Sunday before Lent
Palm Sunday	Sunday before Easter
Paschal Thursday	Thursday before Easter
Pentecost	Fifty days after Easter
Presentation of Christ in the Temple	February 2
Second Saturday of Souls	Saturday before Lent
St. Barbara and St. John of Damascus	December 4
St. Basil's Day	January 1
St. Catherine	November 25
St. Demetrios	October 26
St. George's Day	April 23
St. Gregory the Illuminator	September 30
St. James the Brother of the Lord	October 23
St. James the Son of Zebedee	April 30
St. Matthew	November 16
St. Michael and All Angels	November 8
St. Nicholas's Day	December 6
St. Peter and St. Paul	June 29

Holiday	Date(s)
St. Philip	November 14
St. Stephen's Day	December 27
St. Theodore (Third Saturday of Souls)	First Saturday of Lent
St. Thomas's Day	October 6
St. Thomas's Day	Sunday after Easter
St. Vladimir	July 15
Sts. Constantine and Helen	May 21
Sts. Cyril and Methodios	May 11
Sunday of Orthodoxy	First Sunday of Lent
Sunday of St. Gregory Palamas	Second Sunday of Lent
Sunday of St. John Climacos	Fourth Sunday of Lent
Sunday of St. Mary of Egypt	Fifth Sunday of Lent
Sunday of the Holy Cross	Third Sunday of Lent
Synaxis of the Holy Theotokos (Mother of God) and Ever-Virgin, Mary	December 26
Three Hierarchs	January 30
Triodion	70 days before Easter

living in a monastery, they received word from Constantinople that the Khazar people had requested someone to come and be their Christian teacher. Cyril was selected, and his brother accompanied him. While successfully working among the people, a group of Moravians from Germany sent request for a teacher who could conduct the Divine Liturgy in their Slavonic tongue. Because of their familiarity with the language, Cyril and Methodios were selected. In preparation for this work, Cyril invented an alphabet and, with the help of Methodios, translated the Gospels and all necessary liturgical books into Slavonic. In time, Methodios was named archbishop of the Archdiocese of Moravia and Pannonia. Before his death on April 6, 885, he completed a translation of all the Holy Scriptures into the Slavonic language. Saints Cyril and Methodios are celebrated in the Orthodox Church as the missionary brothers who brought Christianity to the Slavs.

Sts. Constantine and Helen
May 21

The Emperor Constantine and his mother Helen are commemorated in the Orthodox Church for establishing and keeping Christianity in the Roman Empire. Helen is also remembered for finding the cross of Christ in the third century, an event celebrated on the feast of the Elevation of the Holy Cross.

June

Birth of St. John the Baptist
June 24

St. John the Baptist, forerunner to Christ, was born six months before Jesus. His mother Elizabeth and father Zachariah were well past childbearing age, and when the angel announced that they would have a son Zachariah did not believe it. He was made mute for his disbelief, such that at John's birth he was not able to say what he was to be named but had to write the name down. This feast commemorates the Baptist's birth.

St. Peter and St. Paul
June 29

St. Peter was one of Jesus's original twelve apostles, and is often listed as first in rank. St. Paul was unmatched in his evangelistic efforts within the early church and is responsible for writing many of the letters that are found in the New Testament. According to tradition, St. Peter and St. Paul were both martyred on June 29. For this reason their names have been linked in various observances around the world and the Orthodox Church celebrates the day as a combined day for Saints Peter and Paul.

July

St. Vladimir
July 15

St. Vladimir was the first Russian ruler to embrace Christianity. He was born in 956.

Today the Orthodox Church celebrates St. Vladimir as the Prince who established Orthodox Christianity in his realm. After he became a Christian, Vladimir took upon himself the conversion of his subjects. He ordered statues of pagan gods to be thrown down, chopped to pieces, and burned. These acts impressed the people with the helplessness of their gods, and upon being told that they should follow Vladimir's example and become Christians, they agreed. Vladimir eventually established churches and monasteries throughout Russia. In 989 he erected the large Church of St. Mary Ever Virgin and in 996 the Church of the Transfiguration, both in Kiev. He established schools, introduced ecclesiastical courts, and became known for his mildness and for his zeal in spreading the Orthodox faith. His wife died in 1011, having borne him two sons who also became saints, Boris and Gleb. St. Vladimir died in Berestova on July 15, 1015.

August

Feast of the Transfiguration
August 6

This feast commemorates the transfiguration of Jesus on Mt. Tabor, when Peter, James, and John all were witnesses to His divinity. According to the Biblical account as recorded in three of the Gospels, Elijah and Moses appeared to Jesus and the three apostles during a visit to the mountain. The name "transfiguration" refers to changes in Jesus's physical appearance during the event, when His face shone and His clothing became bright white.

Feast of the Dormition of the Theotokos (Mother of God) and Ever-Virgin, Mary
August 15

The Feast of the Dormition (or "falling asleep") of the Theotokos is observed in the Orthodox Church in honor of the belief that the body of the Virgin Mary, the mother of Jesus, did not suffer decay but was translated into heaven upon her death. This feast is sometimes called the Assumption. Such a belief is one of the oldest solemnities observed by the Church, dating back to at least the seventh century when its celebration was already established in Jerusalem and Rome.

CHAPTER 9

Christianity: Non-Trinitarian and Non-Traditional Expressions

Overview of Other Christian Expressions

Groups of Christians claiming to possess special knowledge or be in receipt of additional revelation have existed throughout the course of Christian history. As early as the second century, some groups claimed to possess special understanding. These people were called Gnostics, a word derived from the Greek word for knowledge. Marcion (in the second century) and Mani (who founded the Manichees in the third century) are both examples of founders of movements claiming to have received special knowledge apart from the writings and traditions recognized by the main body of Christian believers.

In the modern era, many diverse movements—with memberships ranging from a few individuals to millions—continue in this tradition, holding to views that are not endorsed by the more traditional branches of Christianity, such as Roman Catholicism, Protestantism, and Orthodoxy. Some reject the doctrine of the Trinity (a concept developed to explain the three personalities—Father, Son, and Spirit—that comprise the traditional Christian view of God). Some seek to combine the basic Christian message with elements from other faiths. Others incorporate newly received revelation, and some reject traditions that have been established through centuries of Church history in favor of practices believed to be closer to those of the early Church.

This chapter includes information about a few well-known examples of non-trinitarian and non-traditional churches. Many—but certainly not all—of these groups follow the calendar system used by other Christian groups and observe major Christian holidays (primarily Christmas and Easter) in addition to dates important to their own unique histories and viewpoints.

◨ ◨ ◨

Christian Science

History and Overview

The Church of Christ, Scientist (Christian Science) was founded by Mary Baker Eddy in the nineteenth century. In search of better health, Eddy began an extensive investigation of a number of popular therapies in the 1840s. Then in February 1866, she was healed of the effects of a life-threatening accident by turning to the Gospel accounts of Jesus's healings. Following that experience, Mary Baker Eddy began to develop the scientific system of healing she would later call Christian Science.

Eddy began an intense study of the Bible and established a successful healing practice. This early period culminated with the publication of the first edition of *Science and Health with Key to the Scriptures* in 1875. This book continues to be in demand today by spiritual seekers; to date, over 10 million copies have been sold.

In 1879 Eddy founded the Church of Christ, Scientist, "to commemorate the word and works of our Master [Jesus Christ], which should reinstate primitive Christianity and its lost element of healing." The Mary Baker Eddy Library for the Betterment of Humanity, which opened in September 2002, evolved in response to a renaissance of interest in the life of Eddy and the public's growing interest to know how to heal spiritually.

Christian Science Holiday

Thanksgiving
Fourth Thursday in November

In conjunction with the secular observance of Thanksgiving in the United States, a Thanksgiving service is held at all branch Churches of Christ, Scientist, throughout the world. The celebration includes Bible lessons, hymns, and testimonies where participants speak of God's blessings.

◈ ◈ ◈

Church of Jesus Christ of Latter-Day Saints (Mormonism)

Overview

The Church of Jesus Christ of Latter-Day Saints (Mormonism) was founded by Joseph Smith in 1830. Smith claimed to have received visions from God and angelic visitations. According to Mormon teaching, Smith received from an angel an ancient record engraved on metal plates which he translated and published as the *Book of Mormon*. Mormons hold the *Book of Mormon* and the *Bible* in equal esteem. Mormon teaching asserts that true Christian authority did not survive past the first generation of apostles.

Relationship between God and the Mormon People

Mormons believe God is the Heavenly Father who created the universe. All people lived with Him as spirit children prior to birth into this world. Only those who receive the atoning sacrifice of Jesus Christ can return to live with God after death. This requires faith in Jesus, baptism from an ordained priest, and the process of repentance. Repentance includes confession of sin, asking God for forgiveness, seeking to make restitution when possible, and living by the commandments.

Authorities and Sacred Writings

Along with the *Bible* and the *Book of Mormon*, the Church of Latter-Day Saints also accords merit to *The Doctrine and Covenants* and *The Pearl of Great Price*, books containing more of Joseph Smith's revelations.

They are considered as authoritative as the *Bible* and the *Book of Mormon*.

Other writings are considered important, but not divinely authoritative. These include *History of the Church*, *Journal of Discourses*, and *Lectures on Faith*. Mormons also believe that God continues to speak to living prophets. The Church President is regarded as a living prophet.

History

Joseph Smith lived in Fayette, New York when he organized the Mormon Church. He moved several times due to religious opposition and was killed in Carthage, Illinois in 1844 along with his older brother, Hyrum, when religious protestors stormed the jail in which the two were being held. Brigham Young succeeded Smith as President and led the Mormon people into the area of Salt Lake City, Utah. After arriving there in 1847, he helped 70,000 people immigrate into settlements throughout the western United States.

In 2003, the Church of Jesus Christ of Latter-day Saints reported 11.7 million members worldwide.

Mormon Holidays

Founding of the Church of Jesus Christ of Latter-Day Saints
April 6

On April 6, 1830, Joseph Smith and the first five of his followers organized the Church of Jesus Christ of Latter-Day Saints under New York state law.

Aaronic Priesthood Commemoration
May 15

In a visitation from John the Baptist on May 15, 1829, Joseph Smith and Oliver Cowdery received instructions for renewing the priesthood of Aaron. These directions included baptizing and laying on of hands to ordain men into the priesthood. Because only an ordained priest can give the authority of the priesthood to another man, each priest can trace that authority back to these two men. This date is remembered with father and son campouts organized by local temples.

Birthday of Brigham Young
June 1

Brigham Young, second President of the Church of Jesus Christ of Latter-Day Saints and the leader who brought the beleaguered Mormons to refuge in Utah, was born on June 1, 1801.

Martyrdom of Joseph and Hyrum Smith
June 27

Joseph Smith, founder of the Church of Jesus Christ of Latter-Day Saints, and his brother Hyrum were shot to death by a mob in Carthage, Illinois on June 27, 1844. The date is commemorated by the Church of Jesus Christ of Latter-Day Saints.

Hill Cumorah Pageant
Begins the third weekend in July

The Hill Cumorah Pageant revolves around a Mormon play performed in July at the Hill Cumorah, near Palmyra, New York. The work recounts Joseph Smith's

Figure 9.1. Moroni is a resurrected messenger who visited Joseph Smith and prepared him to receive divine revelation. He is depicted as a herald, and his likeness stands atop many Mormon temples.

finding of the book engraved on golden plates that Mormons believe he translated as the *Book of Mormon*. The Pageant takes place over a nine-day period (excluding Sunday and Monday) beginning on the third weekend in July. The event involves as many as five hundred participants and attracts tens of thousands of spectators. It is billed as the largest outdoor pageant in the United States.

Pioneer Day
July 24

On July 24, 1847, the first Mormon settlers arrived in the valley of the Great Salt Lake. Under the leadership of Brigham Young, they had traveled from Nauvoo, Illinois after the murder of Joseph Smith, the founder of their faith. The site of the original settlement is now Salt Lake City, Utah. Thousands of Mormon pioneers followed the original group, settling not only in Utah, but also in Idaho, Arizona, Nevada, Wyoming, New Mexico, Colorado, Canada and California. The anniversary of the founding of the Salt Lake City settlement is observed by Latter-Day Saints worldwide.

Holy Spirit Association for the Unification of World Christianity (Unification Church)

History and Overview

The Holy Spirit Association for the Unification of World Christianity (Unification Church) has its roots in the early twentieth century in Korea. The Unification Church was introduced to the United States by the Rev. Sun Myung Moon. At first growth was slow, but in the 1970s the movement gained a rapid influx of converts.

A document regarded as scripture, *Divine Principle*, presents revelation concerning the Messiah and church history. Unification teaching maintains that God sent Jesus as the foretold Messiah, but the Jewish people of his time did not accept him, and he was killed. The will of God was that he should have been accepted and that, if he had been, physical and spiritual salvation would have been established, thereby making a second coming unnecessary. By going the way of the Cross, Jesus established spiritual salvation.

Physical salvation—the establishment of God's kingdom on earth—awaits the second coming. Many Unificationists believe that Moon fulfills the requirements of the second Messiah.

Unification Holidays

God's Day
January 1

God's Day is one of five major holidays celebrated by the Unification Church. The holiday was established in 1968 as a joyful commemoration of God's desire to bless his children. Unlike the other Unification holidays, God's Day always falls on a fixed day.

Unification holiday services are attended by invited participants. The ceremonies include ritual bowing, special prayers, a benediction, and the sharing of food. In preparation for the service, food gifts are set on elaborately prepared tables. The amount of food and its arrangement is related to a designated number having special significance. The True Parents (the Rev. Sun Myung Moon and his wife) preside over the service; in their absence pictures are hung behind empty chairs. Other holiday activities may include the giving of testimonies, sporting events, and participating in traditional Korean games.

True Parents' Birthday
Usually in February

True Parents' Birthday is one of four major movable feasts observed by members of the Unification Church. It is a day on which Unificationists celebrate the birthdays of their True Parents—the Rev. Sun Myung Moon and his wife.

Parents Day
Approximately March 1

Parents Day is a movable feast. It is a day on which Unificationists celebrate their origins and look forward to the restoration of humanity. The observance of Parents Day was initiated on March 1, 1960 by the Rev. Sun Myung Moon.

Day of All Things
Approximately May 1

Day of All Things is a movable feast. It is a day on which Unificationists celebrate the restoration of the environment and cosmos. The observance of the Day of All Things was initiated on May 1, 1963 by the Rev. Sun Myung Moon.

Children's Day
Approximately October 1

Children's Day is a movable feast. It is a day on which Unificationists remember that all people have the potential to become members of the True Family which is headed by the True Father, the Rev. Sun Myung Moon. The observance was established on October 1, 1960 by Moon.

Jehovah's Witnesses

History and Overview

The Jehovah's Witness movement began in the early 1870's with a small Bible study group in what is now Pittsburgh, Pennsylvania. By the year 1879, the group began to publish their first monthly newsletter and other informative literature. Publishing information so that it can be shared with others remains an important aspect of the group's activities today.

The name, Jehovah's Witnesses, is taken from a passage in the Old Testament found in Isaiah 43, in which God says his name is Jehovah. This courtroom scene, which is interpreted to represent the world, serves as the scriptural basis for why they witness door to door in more than two hundred and thirty countries.

Jehovah's Witnesses live by a high moral standard that is derived from the Bible which also serves as the basis for their doctrines. God is the creator of all things. Jesus, the first of His creations, is inferior to Him. Because the first couple (Adam and Eve) failed God's direction to rule over all of creation, God's purposes for the earth were not fulfilled. In order for man to live righteously as God had intended, Jesus Christ died on a stake to pay the ransom for disobedience. He was then raised from death as an immortal spirit person.

Traditional Holy Days Not Observed

Among Jehovah's Witnesses, all days are held in equal esteem. For this reason, no particular day is set aside as a "Sabbath" day. Regular gatherings are held, however, on various days throughout the week both in "Kingdom Halls" and in private homes. The meetings feature talks, study, and discussion.

Christmas, Easter and birthdays are not celebrated among Jehovah's Witnesses because there is no scriptural basis for observing them. Many of the traditions of these holidays are considered pagan in origin and, therefore, they are not sanctioned by God.

Jehovah's Witnesses Holiday

The Lord's Evening Meal (Memorial of Christ's Death; Anniversary Supper)
Nisan 14

The only annual celebration among Jehovah's Witnesses is the anniversary memorial of Jesus's death. It is held in conjunction with the Jewish observance of Passover, on Nisan 14 according to the Jewish calendar. The service, akin to a communion service, commemorates Jesus's last meal with his disciples before his death.

Swedenborgian Church (Church of the New Jerusalem)

History and Influence

Swedenborgianism began in England when in 1787 a group of followers formally established the Church of the New Jerusalem, based on the teachings of Emanuel Swedenborg (1688–1772), a Swedish theologian and scientist. He taught that the Bible was the inspired word of God, containing both an historical record and a deeper, spiritually directed account of each person's journey to faith. In that way scripture functioned as a living and active source, speaking directly to the faithful about their spiritual growth and demonstrating the way to live better, more fulfilled lives.

Swedenborg taught that there is one God, known by many names, and that Jesus Christ is Lord. People are spirits clothed with material bodies that perish at death while the individual continues to live on in a spiritual body according to the kind of life led on earth. The responsibility of each person is to put their belief into practice. If the faithful do this, spreading the love of Jesus, they will be saved regardless of their particular belief.

By the early 1800s, the first church in America was established and a periodical stating many of Swedenborg's teachings was published. Growth was furthered by the work of missionaries who ministered among wilderness pioneers. One such missionary was known for planting fruit trees with the purpose of giving him an opportunity

to spread Swedenborgianism throughout the west, handing out publications every chance he got. This man was John Chapman, better known as Johnny Appleseed.

Swedenborgianism places a high value on education, and the impact of such an approach on the American intellectual atmosphere is not insignificant. Ralph Waldo Emerson included many Swedenborgian tenets into his work, using many specific terms, making eighty references to Swedenborg's works, and even publishing an essay entitled Swedenborg, or the Mystic. Other Transcendentalists such as Bronson Alcott and Henry James, Sr. expressed an affinity for the church's teachings, as did many eighteenth and nineteenth authors, including Honore de Balzac, William Blake, the Brownings, Samuel Taylor Coleridge, and Edgar Allan Poe.

Social reform is another important value of Swedenborgianism, with its mission not only to teach spiritual truths but to teach and practice spiritual freedom, not only in spiritual, but in social, moral, and political matters as well. Whereas the church officially took no dogmatic stance on the concerns of the day, it did advocate reflection and responsibility in its members concerning social issues.

Swedenborgian Worship and Practices

At the center of a Swedenborgian sanctuary is the open Bible. This serves to call the faithful to consider the resurrection of Jesus, the word of God, and the truths contained within the word. The Swedenborgian church holds this symbolism as very important.

A typical Swedenborgian service may include the minister, wearing clerical robes, entering the sanctuary and opening the large copy of the word on the altar. This symbolically serves to invite the Lord to be fully present in what follows. Some hymns, responsive readings, and a unison scripture recitation set the theme for the service. After a brief message for the children, they are dismissed while a lesson from the writings of Emanuel Swedenborg is read. A sermon follows, with prayer and a blessing concluding the service. The goal is to make one's theology a part of one's life, experiencing God in all things.

At various times throughout the year, the congregation may celebrate the Lord's Supper in a manner consistent with many Christian traditions. They also participate in special services such as baptisms, weddings, confirmations, home dedications, and memorial or resurrection services.

———— " ————

One member of the Swedenborgian church, John Chapman, was known as Johnny Appleseed.

———— " ————

Swedenborgian Holiday

New Church Day
Sunday nearest June 19

In addition to the holidays celebrated by many Christian traditions, including Easter, Christmas, and others, the Swedenborgian church also recognizes New Church Day on the Sunday nearest June 19th. Many times a pageant is given or a non-traditional service is held to commemorate the revelation to Emanuel Swedenborg of the Lord's Second Coming through Swedenborg's teachings.

❖ ❖ ❖

Unitarian Universalism

History and Overview

The Unitarian Universalist faith has its origins in two separate faith traditions: the Universalist Church, which was organized in 1793; and the Unitarian Church, which was organized in 1825. Though widely overlapping in many areas of belief, the two movements were initially separate. Major differences included varying beliefs regarding the importance of the *Bible* and how God's role in man's salvation was understood. Members of each church were also often separated by socioeconomic status. As time passed, however, these distinctions began to blur, and in 1961 the Unitarian Universalist Association (UUA) was formed. Today more than one thousand congregations make up the UUA.

Unitarian Universalists in the United States look to the Massachusetts settlers and the founders of the republic as their spiritual ancestors. Many influential figures from American history are counted among the Unitarian faithful, including John Adams, Louisa May Alcott, Susan B. Anthony, Clara Barton, Ralph Waldo Emerson, Oliver Wendell Holmes, Adlai Stevenson, and Whitney Young. Early Universalists, though less well known, also contributed to the development of the young nation. These include John Murray, Elhanen Winchester, Hosea Ballou, and Dr. Benjamin Rush.

Each Unitarian Universalist congregation is self-governing, adopting its own bylaws, electing its own officers, and approving its own budget. Every member is encouraged to be an active part of church activities, which may include adult education classes, daycare centers, church school, family events, lectures and forums, and study or support groups.

What the Unitarian Church Believes

Although Unitarian Universalism has its roots in both Jewish and Christian traditions, members believe that personal experience, conscience, and reason should be the final authorities rather than any traditionally honored person, book, or institution. Adherents believe that religious insights should be evaluated by each individual, freely searching for truth. As a noncreedal religion, Unitarian Universalism has no statements of belief to which all must assent.

The church believes that religious wisdom is always changing because human understanding of life, death, and the world around us is never complete. Revelation is, therefore, continuous, and the insights of prophets, sages, and teachers throughout the years and around the world are all honored.

Within Unitarian congregations members focus on acceptance and on encouragement toward spiritual growth; people believe in the right of conscience and the use of democratic processes within the congregation and within society at large. Unitarian Universalists affirm several guiding principles, which were formally adopted as the Unifying Principles of the Unitarian Universalist Association in 1985. These include the inherent worth and dignity of all people; justice, equity, and compassion in human relations; the concept of working toward peace and liberty for all; a respect for the interdependent web of all existence, of which all people are a part; and the importance of a free and responsible search for truth.

Sources of Influence

Unitarian Universalists draw upon many beliefs and different types of knowledge from all cultures. The actions and thoughts of various men and women who have challenged the powers and structures of evil serve as examples for others to follow. Religions and philosophies from around the world provide wisdom that inspires the ethical and spiritual life of Unitarian Universalists. For example:

- The Judeo-Christian tenet of loving one's neighbor as one's self offers practical guidance.

- The results of scientific endeavors guide and inform reason.

- Earth-centered traditions that celebrate the sacred circle of life teach about living in harmony with nature.

Varying Church Calendar

Because each congregation is self-governing and Unitarian Universalism is a noncreedal religion, there is no master calendar governing church celebrations. Each local church determines which events will be recognized each year based upon its own needs and interests.

The holidays listed in this chapter are thus representative, not universally observed, and not inclusive of all that could be honored. In fact, a great number of other days are celebrated by individual Unitarian Universalist congregations around the world, including birthdays of important world and religious leaders, anniversaries of significant world events, and nature-based observances. Many of the traditional Christian and Jewish holidays are celebrated by Unitarian Universalist congregations along with the holidays of some of the other major world religions. Celebrations of member unity are also practiced by some congregations. The dates of many of these celebrations are variable and may be adjusted according to the needs of the individual congregations.

Representative Unitarian Universalist Holidays

World Peace Day and the Universal Hour of Peace
January 1

The inherent worth and dignity of all individuals is an important tenet of the Unitarian Universalist faith, leading to a consequent focus upon promoting peace among all peoples. World Peace Day is a day set aside for meditation for peace throughout the world. The Universal Hour of Peace may be observed as part of this day, from 7:00 to 8:00 A.M.

World Religions Day
January 20

This day honors the Unitarian Universalist belief that the differing world religions are merely different paths to one universal truth.

Earth Day
April 22

This day celebrates the importance of respect for the earth and environment. It relates to the Unitarian Universalist focus on respect for the interdependent web of existence, of which all people are a part.

National Day of Prayer
First Thursday in May

This holiday focuses upon the importance of freedom of religion and of expression. It is honored in conjunction with the National Day of Prayer celebrated by many traditional Christian denominations in the United States.

Celebration of Unifying Principles
June 21

This day commemorates the adoption of the seven unifying principles of the Unitarian Universalist faith and provides an opportunity for reflection upon those principles.

Fast for a World Harvest
November 21

The Unitarian Universalist idea of providing adequately for all people is an important component of the belief in the inherent worth of all people. As a reflection of that belief, this day calls the faithful to fast and commit to action to help prevent deaths from malnourishment worldwide.

Human Rights Day
December 10

This day commemorates the establishment of the Universal Declaration of Human Rights, and celebrates the Unitarian Universalist belief in the fundamental human rights of all peoples of the world.

Figure 9.2. Many Unitarian congregations begin their services by lighting a flame inside a chalice. The flaming chalice has become a symbol of Unitarianism.

▨ ▨ ▨

United Church of God, an International Association

Overview

The United Church of God, an International Association derives its name from the New Testament example of consistently referring to the Church established by Jesus Christ as the Church of God. It is a worldwide association of congregations that adhere to the teachings and customs of those early Christians described in the book of Acts. The various national bodies of its congregations are united in their conviction that the *Bible* alone—in contrast to traditions adopted after the time of the original apostles—defines the criteria for their religious customs and beliefs. Consequently, the religious celebrations observed by United Church of God congregations are those commanded directly and explicitly in the *Bible*, including the seventh-day Sabbath. Observance of nationally or locally established non-religious holidays is left to the discretion of each member—providing such extra-biblical holidays do not incorporate the celebration of scripturally forbidden motifs.

God's Master Plan of Salvation, Couched in a Harvest Analogy

The dates of seven biblically ordained festivals are set on the Hebrew lunar calendar according to the Old Testament harvest seasons—two in the spring, one in early summer and four in the fall. They are viewed as figuratively representing the seven most important aspects of God's master plan of salvation—that is, the spiritual harvest of repentant individuals to eternal life.

The meaning of each festival instituted formally in the days of Moses is expanded significantly in the New Testament to reflect the work and mission of Jesus Christ in completing the spiritual harvest assigned to him by God the Father; therefore, they are understood as also distinctively Christian celebrations.

United Church of God Holidays

Passover
Nisan 14

The first observance of this festival was on the occasion of ancient Israel's exodus from Egypt, when only those households that splashed the blood of sacrificed lambs on their doorposts were spared the death of their firstborn sons. According to the New Testament, those ancient sacrificial lambs were symbolic of Jesus as the Messiah—who, following his death and resurrection, is also designated as the "firstborn from the dead" (quotations taken from the King James Version of the *Bible*).

Jesus's death made him the Christian's true and permanent Passover lamb, sacrificed for the remission of sins. This act constituted God's first vital step in his plan for humankind's redemption. The Christian Passover is an annual reminder that reconciliation with God through Christ's sacrifice is the first step toward salvation. All aspects of God's plan pictured by subsequent biblical festivals are dependent upon that sacrifice.

Jesus personally instituted the proper time and manner to observe the Christian Passover. Years later, Paul confirmed that this time and form of Passover observance had remained the standard practice of the Christian community in the apostolic age, and the United Church of God continues to follow Jesus's example and instructions for this ceremony.

The Christian Passover is observed shortly after sunset on the evening that begins the 14th day of the first month in the Hebrew calendar. This occurs one day prior to the Jewish Seder, which commences the Jewish Passover season.

Festival of Unleavened Bread
Beginning on Nisan 15

This seven-day festival immediately following the Passover, in which unleavened bread is eaten rather than normal leavened bread, was ordained initially as the annual anniversary of ancient Israel's deliverance from Egyptian bondage. It memorialized God's emancipation of the Israelites from physical slavery to lead them toward the even greater freedom of citizenship in their own physical land of promise. In the New Testament an even more significant emancipation is explained: the Christian's emancipation from sin.

In compliance with biblical instructions from Paul, the United Church of God continues to observe this festival celebrating the fact that once followers are delivered from the penalty of death through Christ's sacrifice they can receive special help from him to begin the process of purging sin from their lives and replacing it with the sincerity and truth that he taught. Since Jesus also refers to himself as the "Bread of Life," observance of this festival signifies a lifetime commitment to emulate his sinless or "unleavened" life. This spiritual transformation of one's character is the second step in God's plan of salvation.

Pentecost
Sivan 6

The next festival is Pentecost, observed 50 days following the Sabbath during the Festival of Unleavened Bread.

Jewish tradition initially associates it with the occasion of God's giving of the Ten Commandments. Its New Testament significance becomes clear from the events of Acts 2:1-4 when the Holy Spirit was first given to the Church.

Pentecost is the anniversary of Christ's servants—members of the Church of God—having their lives transformed spiritually by the Holy Spirit. It is this Spirit that continues guiding them into a more thorough understanding of God's truth, thereby significantly changing their lives. Paul explained that without the Spirit no one truly belongs to Christ, nor is truly a member of His Church. This is why the festival of Pentecost is a cherished celebration for the United Church of God and represents the third vital step toward salvation, the receiving of God's Holy Spirit.

Feast of Trumpets
Tishri 1

Anciently the Feast of Trumpets was celebrated with the ceremonial sounding of trumpets. Its Christian significance is found in the biblical book of Revelation where the second coming of Jesus Christ to set up his kingdom on earth is said to occur at the sounding of the seventh or "last" trumpet. At that time, the New Testament tells us, those who have died in Christ will be resurrected and, along with all Christians still living, will be changed instantly into immortal spirit beings. The United Church of God observes this festival in anticipation of Christ's return, the fourth vital step in God's great spiritual-harvest plan.

Day of Atonement
Tishri 10

The Day of Atonement, observed by fasting and a special assembly, is somewhat similar to the Passover in that Jesus Christ as the Passover is also the Atonement. In ancient Israel the emphasis for this festival was on the yearly cleansing of the entire nation of sins committed in ignorance. Its future application is for the spiritual cleansing of the whole world.

To thoroughly cleanse humanity from sins committed in ignorance, God first must banish Satan because he has been the primary cause of humanity's spiritual ignorance and blindness. Therefore, one of Christ's first acts, at his second coming will be to bind and banish Satan for 1,000 years. Once this is done, the reconciling of the entire world through the atoning sacrifice of Christ can begin in earnest. This is the fifth step in God's master plan.

Feast of Tabernacles
Tishri 15–21

With deception and confusion out of the way, Christ will begin filling the entire world with the true knowledge of God and his ways. This is represented by the next biblical festival, the seven-day Feast of Tabernacles. It pictures the 1,000-year rule of Christ as the King of Kings and the great general harvest of humanity to eternal life. This is the sixth major step in God's master plan.

Last Great Day
Tishri 22

A separate, biblically unnamed, one-day festival called the Last Great Day immediately follows the Feast of Tabernacles. The last event in God's plan of salvation mentioned in the Bible is the Great White Throne Judgment that immediately follows the 1,000 year reign of Christ. This festival, therefore, represents the conclusion of God's final judgment concerning the destiny of human beings, which is the seventh and last step in God's plan.

CHAPTER 10

Islam

Overview of Islam

What Is Islam?

The word Islam is an Arabic word that means surrender to God. Its other meanings include peace, safety, and health. The central focus of Islam is a personal commitment and surrender to Allah, the Arabic word for God. In Islam, the concept of Allah is universal and eternal. Allah is the same in every religion and throughout the history of humankind. A person who follows Islam is called a Muslim, which means one who surrenders or submits to Allah's will.

The message of Islam was brought by Muhammad, who was born around 570 C.E. and died in 632 C.E. Muhammad is considered a prophet of Allah.

Muslims recognize that a line of prophets—including Adam, Abraham, Moses, Jesus, and Muhammad—preached the monotheistic message of Islam. Twenty-nine prophets are mentioned specifically in the *Qur'an* (the holy book of Islam), but the *Qur'an* also mentions that there existed many more prophets throughout history. Among some Muslims, there is a belief that there were over 200,000 prophets, most of whom did not have their stories told in the *Qur'an*. Muhammad is considered the last of these prophets.

Islam is not just a religion of belief; it is a religion of action. Five specific deeds are required of followers; these are called *The Five Pillars of Islam*. They are:

1. *Shahadah*—confession of faith. Every Muslim is expected to declare before others at least once in his or her life: "There is no God but Allah and Muhammad is his Prophet (some translations use slightly different words such as: Messenger, Servant, Slave, Apostle). The declaration must be made vocally and freely, without coercion, and with heartfelt assent.

2. *Salat*—prayer/worship. Muslims are expected to pray at five specific times throughout the day: Before sunrise; early afternoon; late afternoon; after sunset; and before going to bed or at the time when no light can be seen in the sky. Prayers involve specific recitations and postures, and they must be made facing in the direction of the Ka'bah in Mecca, Saudi Arabia (which is to the southeast of the United States). The Ka'bah is a cube-shaped structure that serves as Islam's central shrine.

3. *Sawm*—fasting. All Muslims who are physically able are expected to abstain from eating, drinking, smoking, sexual relations, and any negative behavior, habits, and conduct from dawn until sunset during the entire Islamic month of Ramadan, the ninth month of the Muslim calendar.

4. *Zakat*—charity. Every Muslim is expected to pay zakat. Zakat, originally a charity instituted by Muhammad to help the poor, is used to help provide social services, spread Islam, pay debts, and ransom captives. Zakat is 2.5 percent of a person's annual savings and property, apart from personal dwellings and household items. In the past, payment was mandatory, and it was collected by governments. Although some Muslim governments do still collect and administer zakat, in other areas it is often treated as a voluntary charitable offering. According to Muslim belief, however, a property is not purified or legitimate unless the zakat has been paid.

5. *Hajj*—pilgrimage. Every Muslim who is physically able and has the financial means to accomplish it is expected to make a pilgrimage to the Ka'bah in Mecca once in his or her life.

The Relationship between Allah and Muslims

The Muslims worship God, known as Allah. The name Allah is derived from the Arabic phrase *al-ilah*, which means the one without any partner. Muslims believe people and all of creation exist to serve Allah, and serving Allah means to be his representative in the world. Although Allah is compassionate and righteous, he is master; people are his servants. Serving Allah, however, is a fulfilling experience and does not equate with the humiliation suffered by the slaves of human masters.

Allah is one God, but he has infinite attributes that describe his qualities and the expanse of his powers. Even reciting these attributes is considered a part of worship. In the *Qur'an*, 99 specific attributes are mentioned. However, Muslims understand that Allah's attributes have no limits, and the *Qur'an* mentions divine attributes that are not part of the 99 attributes. Some of the attributes of Allah are: "The Great," "The Merciful," and "The Disposer."

In addition to their devotion to Allah, Muslims believe in a final judgment in which humanity will be raised to appear before Allah. They will be sent to live in paradise or hell according to their deeds, intentions, and Allah's mercy. Islamic tradition has many different ways of understanding salvation. The most common understanding is that humans are responsible and accountable for their deeds, but salvation can only be attained through Allah's mercy. The Muslim concept of divine judgment also extends to the fates of nations. Muslims believe that Allah's judgment upon nations affects history as it unfolds.

Islam also teaches that there are angels that convey Allah's words to his messengers and prophets. Angels are beings created for the purpose of worshipping and serving Allah.

Demons also exist in Islam. The chief of the demons is called Iblis (sometimes called Shaitan or Satan). Iblis was a jinn, a creation that was close to the angels and even joined them in their worship of Allah. However, when Allah created Adam, Iblis sinned by refusing to accept Adam. Iblis then tempted Adam and Eve to sin, and he tempts humans now to do evil things. Although Iblis is also Allah's servant, he is the enemy of humanity because he compels humans to turn away from their innate desire to serve Allah. From the Islamic perspective, demons are not some terrible enemy of God locked in an eternal struggle for supremacy. Instead, demons are the constant whispering in human hearts that makes people forget Allah and become preoccupied with their own desires.

Authorities and Sacred Writings

The Qur'an

The *Qur'an* (also sometimes spelled *Koran* or *Alcoran*) is the holy book of Islam. According to Islamic belief, the *Qur'an* was revealed to Muhammad by Allah over a period of twenty-three years. Authorship of the *Qur'an* is attributed to Allah, and not to Muhammad; Muhammad merely received it. Muslims believe that because it originated with Allah, the *Qur'an* is infallible.

The word *Qur'an* comes from the word *qaraa*, which in Arabic means to read or to recite. Initially the word *qur'an* was applied by Muhammad to refer to a revelation. Later, the term was broadened to refer to the book in which the revelations were recorded.

The *Qur'anic* messages were delivered to Muhammad by the chief of Allah's messenger angels, Jibril (also called Gabriel in Christian literature and sometimes spelled Jibreel). Jibril delivered the *Qur'anic* passages; Muhammad received the revelations in pure Arabic, which was his native tongue. Because Muhammad could not read or write, he directed the recitations to be written down by his followers and many of those followers committed them to memory. The entire text was delivered in this way over a 23-year period.

After Muhammad's death, the finalized text of the *Qur'an* was compiled from oral and written sources around 650 C.E. It consists of 114 chapters, or suras. The shortest chapter contains 3 verses; the longest, 286. The text addresses a variety of topics including religious, social, commercial, and legal matters. It is poetic in nature. Muslims believe that the *Qur'an* transmitted to Muhammad is an exact copy of an original that exists in heaven; therefore, translations from the original Arabic are not considered exact renderings but simply interpretations of the meaning of the *Qur'an*. Once the *Qur'an* is translated, its exact meanings are distorted because of the choices translators have to make about words. Muslims believe that the *Qur'an* is not only a book in the sense of a readable text, it is the container of a divine message.

The Sunna and the Hadith

The Sunna refers to the "example of the prophet." Within it the collected remembrances of what Muhammad did or said regarding a number of issues not specifically addressed in the *Qur'an* are recorded. It covers the life of Muhammad and tells about activities within the early Islamic community. Muslims consider Muhammad as the living interpreter of the *Qur'an*, and thus the Sunna contains instructions for living according to the *Qur'an*.

The Sunna was transmitted in oral and written forms until approximately the 9th century when it was collected and set down in a standardized format. The *Hadith* is the book in which the Sunna is compiled, however, the Sunna is broader than the *Hadith*. Muslims believe the *Hadith* contains the sayings of Muhammad, and the

Sunna is his way. Different sects within Islam honor different canonical collections of the *Hadith*. Those held by the Sunnis were compiled beginning in the ninth century C.E., and those held by the Shi'ites were compiled during the tenth and eleventh centuries. The Muslims developed a method to ensure the *Hadith*'s accuracy. This process is known as isnad, the chain of transmission detailing the people involved in relaying the *Hadith* until it was recorded in writing.

Although the *Hadith* is considered an important source of instruction, it is not considered infallible. Together, the *Hadith* and *Qur'an* form the *Shari'ah*, or law (or more literally, way).

The Ijtihad and Ijma

Two other sources of authority in Islam are the ijtihad and the ijma. Ijtihad refers to the opinion of a responsible individual. Its doctrinal use permitted an authorized person to use reasoning in establishing an appropriate response to a situation not covered in the *Qur'an* or *Hadith*. Some schools of thought in Islam place strict limitations on the use of the ijtihad; others seek to expand its influence. The ijma refers to the consensus of the Islamic community. It is reached through time as opinions are accepted or rejected by the community as a whole.

History of Islam

Pre-Islamic Conditions in the Arabian Peninsula

In the centuries before the proclamation of Islam, the Arabian peninsula consisted of a desert terrain, which was inhabited predominantly by nomadic tribes. Several cultural centers had been established on the coastlines and around some oases, but between the cities wandering peoples followed the water. The harsh geographical conditions made the peninsula a place unconquered by foreign invaders but also not unified by its Arabian inhabitants.

The existing religious system included the worship of gods, goddesses, and other spirits often associated with water sources and other natural phenomenon. The establishment of shrines dedicated to the various gods and the performance of pilgrimages to important places was common. Despite the Arabian people's lack of faith in a monotheistic religion, there remained a concept of Allah. There was no idol named Allah, but there was an idol named Lat. Some claimed that by worshipping the female deity Lat, they could become closer to Allah.

One tribe, the Quraysh, settled in a valley near Mecca (also called Makkah, Bakka, or, more anciently, Macoraba).

Mecca was home to a popular shrine called the Ka'bah, which included a black stone thought by some to be a meteorite. The many clans of the Quraysh tribe placed their shrines to their own preferred deity inside the Ka'bah. The Quraysh flourished in Mecca due to its favorable position in relation to popular trade routes of the era. As a result, by the sixth century the tribe had become one of the strongest in the region. It was into this tribe that Muhammad was born.

Muhammad

The precise date of Muhammad's birth is unknown but most sources place it between 570 and 580 C.E. Muhammad's early life was difficult. His father died before his birth, his mother died when he was six, and his grandfather died when he was eight. He was sent to live among the nomads during his infancy and early childhood, as was customary then to provide the open, healthy environment of the desert and to learn the pure form of the Arabic language. Muhammad was raised by an uncle, Abu Talib, and led the trading caravans. During his time of service among the nomadic Bedouin people in the desert he learned the pure Arabic language and other skills that would serve him later in life.

As a young adult, Muhammad went to work for a widow 25 years his senior named Khadijah. At her suggestion, the two married. Their union resulted in six children: two sons who died during childhood and four daughters who survived. One daughter, Fatimah, became the best known for her role in propagating the faith.

The Call of Islam

In 610 C.E., when Muhammad was about 40 years old he received a visionary revelation from God calling him to turn away from the polytheistic practices that predominated in the region and believe in one God, Allah. The revivalistic message focused on restoring the monotheism of Abraham, the Jewish patriarch. According to Islamic doctrine, Abraham was not a Jew by faith, but a man of pure faith whose monotheistic belief had been distorted throughout the centuries. Muhammad's mission was to call people back to one God, Allah. After the first revelation, the prophetic messages continued coming to him over a period of twenty-three years until 632 C.E., the year of his death. Muhammad passed the messages along by preaching to those who would listen.

During the early years of Muhammad's proclamations, he had few followers. Although small in number they were devoted and played an important role in spreading Islam during its first century. They included his wife Khadijah; his cousin Ali (who was the son of the uncle who had raised him); Muhammad's friends, Abu Bakr,

Umar, and 'Uthman; and a slave named Zaid, who was Muhammad's adopted son and played a relatively minor role in spreading the faith.

The Hijrah

In accordance with his understanding of the messages he received from Allah, Muhammad preached against the traditional religious practices that were conducted at the Ka'bah. The early Muslims identified that Muhammad's message had to do with the purification of their hearts and that he wished to turn them from their selfish and cruel practices toward merciful, loving, and just behavior. Serving the many pilgrims who came to the shrine, however, was a major industry in the city. As a result, Muhammad's preaching was resented by many of the people in Mecca. As Muhammad's preaching efforts intensified, they were viewed as a threat to the local economy. While his uncle and wife were alive, Muhammad was personally protected as a result of clan loyalties, but the persecution of his followers began.

Some of Muhammad's followers who lacked protection from powerful family members emigrated to Ethiopia in Africa, where they were given protection by the Christian ruler. These followers represented the first hijrah (or emigration), and their actions set the stage for the Great Hijrah to Medina that was to follow. When Muhammad's uncle and wife both died in 620 C.E., he too was without family protection and began to suffer abuses at the hands of his contemporaries.

In 622 C.E. Muhammad and his followers left Mecca and migrated to a city called Yathrib, which was located approximately 300 miles (482 km) to the northeast. Yathrib was selected because a delegation from it had invited Muhammad to come and serve as a political leader. Yathrib was later renamed Madinat al-Nabi, which means "city of the prophet," and is modernly called Medina.

This movement, or emigration, was called the Great Hijrah (from the Arabic word meaning abandon or leave behind). It is the event that marks the beginning of the Islamic community (called the Muslim Umma), an event so important it serves as the epoch of the Islamic calendar. Islamic years are numbered with the designation of A.H. (*anno hegirae*, literally "in the year of the hijrah," or more simply in English, "after hijrah").

Wars between Medina and Mecca

In Medina, Muhammad rose in power and gained many more followers. After Muhammad became established in Medina, his opponents in Mecca, fearful of the growing influence of Islam, initiated hostilities. Clashes between the two communities escalated. In 624 C.E., two

years after the Great Hijrah, a force of approximately 300 Muslims defeated a large Meccan invasion force of 950. The Muslims viewed their victory in the face of overwhelming numbers as a sign of Allah's favor.

In 630 C.E. Muhammad entered Mecca and gave a general amnesty to its inhabitants. They responded by accepting Islam in large numbers. When Mecca surrendered to Muhammad he also took over the ancient shrine of the Ka'bah and rededicated it to Allah, ousting all its idols.

The Death of Muhammad

Muhammad died of a fever in 632 C.E. According to Islamic teaching, the end of his life signified the end of the prophetic era. Muhammad is sometimes called the Seal of the Prophets, signifying that no further prophets would come to the human race.

Abu Bakr

Following Muhammad's death, successors arose from among his followers to lead the Muslim people. They were called Caliphs (also sometimes spelled Khalifahs, which means successor or one who is behind another). The caliphate selection process was based on popular acceptance.

Abu Bakr, one of Muhammad's closest companions, was selected as the first Caliph. One of the difficulties he faced was keeping the Islamic community unified. Muhammad had instituted the practice of collecting alms (called zakat) from the various tribes with which he had formed covenants. Some of these tribes felt that the covenant period ended with Muhammad's death, and that payments would be no longer due. Abu Bakr enforced the covenants on the basis that they had been made between the tribes and Allah, not Muhammad. There were also two individuals, considered false prophets by religious leaders, who emerged at that time in eastern and north central Arabia and led the rebellion against the Caliphs. By keeping the wavering tribes within the Islamic fold, the community remained intact.

Abu Bakr served as Caliph until his death two years later. Another of his major accomplishments was overseeing the compilation of the *Qur'anic* recitations.

Umar

Umar ibn Al-Khattab, another close companion of Muhammad, succeeded Abu Bakr. He served as Caliph for ten years from 634 until 644 C.E. when an enemy assassinated him. In 639 C.E. Umar established the Islamic calendar and designated the epoch (year 1) as the year of the Great Hijrah. Umar also expanded the Muslim territory. Under his leadership the Muslims conquered all of Iraq, which constituted western Persia, Syria, and Palestine, as well as Egypt.

'Uthman ibn 'Affan

'Uthman ibn 'Affan succeeded Umar as Caliph. He was selected on the basis of his conversion to Islam during Muhammad's early years in Mecca and his close companionship with the prophet. 'Uthman was also married to Muhammad's daughter Ruqaiyyah, and upon her death, he married another of the prophet's daughters, Umm Kulthum.

'Uthman's principal accomplishments included compiling the *Qur'an* and overseeing its distribution throughout all Islamic communities. In conjunction with this effort, 'Uthman ordered the destruction of all unofficial versions of the *Qur'an*. The unofficial versions did not necessarily contradict the *Qur'an*, but were merely incomplete personal copies or were arranged in a different order. This act of destroying the unofficial versions angered some factions.

Some Islamic adherents disliked 'Uthman because he favored his own clan and appointed his relatives to most of the powerful positions in government, which was in contradiction to the egalitarian, merit-based system of Muhammad. The result of 'Uthman's policy was corruption and abuse of power in Syria, Egypt, and Iraq. This led to rebellion and his tragic death. 'Uthman's tenure as Caliph ended abruptly when he was assassinated in 656 C.E. by an Egyptian delegation.

Ali

Ali became the fourth Caliph. He was a son-in-law of Muhammad (married Muhammad's daughter Fatimah) and also a cousin of Muhammad. During his Caliphate, Ali moved the Islamic capital to an area in the territory now in modern-day Iraq. He was assassinated in 661 C.E. Ali was martyred at the hands of Abdul-Rahman ibn Muljim, a member of a group called the Kharijites. This Bedouin group was aligned with Ali when he was fighting against Muawiyya, a nephew of the third Caliph 'Uthman. Suddenly, they shifted their loyalty and declared that they would fight against both Ali and Muawiyya believing that if they eliminated Ali, Muawiyya, and 'Amr ibn al-'Aas the civil war would end. They assigned three assassins for the three leaders, but only ibn Muljim succeeded in his scheme.

Islamic Community Splits

The events following Ali's death led to a split in the Islamic community. Followers of Ali believed that only descendants of Ali had the right to be Caliphs. As a result, they disavowed the first three Caliphs who were companions of Muhammad and not his descendants.

The split resulted in the formation of two groups, who today comprise almost all Muslims: the Shi'ites, who hold to the doctrine of the House of Ali; and the Sunni, who recognize the legitimacy of the first four Caliphs and do not hold the House of Ali doctrine. Currently, the largest body of orthodox Muslims are Sunni.

After Ali's demise, his son Hasan was acknowledged as the leader. However, in an attempt to stop the civil war, Hasan made a deal with Muawiyya. The deal was that Muawiyya's son Yazid would not succeed him. But Muawiyya did not keep his word and appointed his son as successor. After Hasan's death, Ali's other son Husayn decided to accept the invitation of the people of Kula, Iraq, to assume their leadership.

Sunni Muslims did not recognize Husayn's authority. Instead, they acknowledged the leadership of Muawiyya. Muawiyya, founder of the Umayyad dynasty, established his capital in Damascus in Syria. After Muawiyya's death, his son Yazid claimed the Caliphate.

Yazid took Husayn's acceptance of authority in Iraq to be an act of rebellion and sent a force to fight against him. Husayn fought against Yazid's forces with only his extended family. A battle between Husayn's followers and the Umayyads occurred in 680 C.E. Husayn and his followers were defeated, and Husayn was killed at Karbala. The day continues to be remembered by Shi'ites with mourning.

Rise in Islamic Power and Culture

Despite the differences between the two factions, the reach of Islam continued to spread. Muslims gained religious influence and political power. Orthodox practices became established and further aspects of the law were defined.

During the eighth century, changes in political leadership brought the first influx of non-Arab followers. In 711 C.E. an Islamic army entered Spain and conquered the Iberian Peninsula. Their advance was stopped by the French at the Battle of Tours in 732 C.E. To the east, the Arabian armies made their first advance toward the Indian subcontinent in 712 C.E. The Punjab and regions beyond were later annexed in the eleventh and twelfth centuries. As Islam rose in power, its influence spread, and Islamic communities emerged in northern Africa, Europe, Turkey, Persia, and the island nations of Southeast Asia.

During the medieval centuries (generally considered the ninth through thirteenth centuries C.E.), Islamic culture also flourished. Academies were established in Baghdad, Cairo, and Andalusia. Great strides were made in the areas of the natural and social sciences, mathematics, and philosophy.

Shifts in Political Power

Islam's political power in Baghdad fell to the Mongols in 1258 C.E., and in the fifteenth century, the Muslims were ousted from Spain. These losses, however, were offset by growing power in Turkey and the rise of the Ottoman Empire. The Turkish army succeeded in carrying Islam into Eastern Europe, to areas currently occupied by the Balkan states, Albania, Bulgaria, and the former Yugoslavia. By the seventeenth century Islam was well established in a region that stretched from southeastern Europe, through the Near and Middle East, across the regions surrounding the Black Sea, and into India and western China.

Toward the end of the Turkish Ottoman Empire, increasing power in Europe led to colonialism. As a result, many Muslim lands lost their autonomy to Europeans, especially in India, Africa, the Middle East, and Southeast Asia. This shift in political power led to much anti-Western sentiment.

Wahhabis

During the eighteenth century, reform movements within Islam began to surface. Some people believed that the loss of autonomy was a result of Allah's dissatisfaction with the Muslim community. One of the first of these efforts at reformation was initiated in modern-day Saudi Arabia.

In the eighteenth century Muhammad Ibn 'Abd al-Wahhab (1703–1787 C.E.) began a movement aimed at bringing social and moral reform to Islamic communities. He rejected the concept of ijma (consensus) and sought to purge what he considered to be non-Islamic influences from the Muslim community. He spoke out against proscribed things such as worship of graves and saints and mixing of local customs with religion. Muslims consider the words Wahhabi or Wahhabism to be derogatory terms.

Additional Reforms

The emphasis on returning Islam to its fundamental roots in an effort to regain Allah's favor, however, led to more revivalistic movements during the nineteenth and twentieth centuries. Jamal al-Din al-Afghani (1838–1897 C.E.) was a writer and an activist who traveled through Muslim territories urging reconstruction of Muslim thought. Other reformers rose to prominence by promoting the concept of the jihad, which means struggle against injustice or oppression or to defend one's community from aggression. According to Islamic belief, although individuals should not be coerced into converting to Islam, armed struggle is legitimate to change unjust government. Once political institutions were transformed, the affected populations would be enabled to embrace Islam.

Islam Today

Muslims around the World

During the early years of Islam, the faith spread throughout the Arabian Peninsula into regions that are today occupied by Saudi Arabia, Syria, Iraq, and Jordan. Contrary to popular opinion, however, Muslims are not just Arabs. Muslims—followers of Islam—are found in many different ethnic groups all over the globe. In fact, Arabs make up less than 20 percent of Muslims.

According to some estimates there are more than one billion Muslims worldwide with major populations found in the Middle East, North and sub-Saharan Africa, Turkey, Central Asia, and Southeast Asia. In Europe and the United States, Islam is the second largest religious group with some 7 million adherents in the United States alone (Christianity is the largest). Other countries with significant Muslim populations include France, Britain, West Germany, and Canada.

Worship

A Muslim house of worship is called a mosque (or masjid, an Arabic word meaning place of prostration). Because Islam does not allow images, mosques contain no representations of Allah or Muhammad. They are typically decorated in abstract patterns such as geometric figures, swirling designs that evoke feelings of infinity, or stylized calligraphic inscriptions of passages from the *Qur'an*.

The central feature of a mosque is the prayer hall in which Muslims gather to pray. Although private prayers may be offered in the mosque at any time, the largest gathering occurs on Friday afternoons. Because Muslims must face Mecca when they pray, one wall usually has an ornately decorated niche, called a mihrab, which indicates the direction within the hall to face for prayer. Other important but not essential components of the mosque include the minarets (exterior towers from which the call to worship is made), the minbar (a platform from which the Imam or prayer leader may give instruction or teaching), and an area for performing ritual washing, called wudu.

Services at the mosque begin with the call to worship made by a man called the muezzin. (In some modern countries, the call to worship may be made by a recording.) Although women are permitted to attend the Friday services, their presence is optional. Men are required to be present. The wudu is performed before the prayers are offered. Prayers consist of a series of mandated recitations and postures.

Sects

Sunni

There are two main sects within Islam: Sunni and Shi'ite. Sunni Muslims are the majority (estimated at about 80 percent). They recognize the authority of the first four Caliphs, including Ali, and they believe that the Sunna (the example of the Prophet Muhammad) is interpreted through the consensus of the community.

Sunni Muslims recognize the validity of six collections of documents said to contain reports of Muhammad's actual words and deeds. These form the basis of their *Qur'anic* interpretations and governance of their communities.

Shi'ite

Shi'ite Muslims look to special teachers, called Imams. The Imams are the direct descendants of Muhammad through Fatimah and Ali. These individuals are believed to be inspired and to possess secret knowledge. Shi'ites, however, do not recognize the same line of Islamic leaders acknowledged by the Sunnis. Shi'ites hold to a doctrine that accepts only leaders who are descended from Muhammad through his daughter Fatimah and her husband Ali. Many Shi'ite subsects believe that true Imams are errorless and sinless. They receive instruction from these leaders rather than relying on the consensus of the community.

The largest group of Shi'ites is called the Twelvers. The Twelvers believe that there were twelve infallible leaders beginning with Ali and continuing in a chain until the tenth century C.E. when the last disappeared. Twelvers expect the twelfth leader who is alive but in hiding to return and bring justice to the world.

The Ismailis, another Shi'ite subsect, are one of the smallest groups within Islam. Their origins date back to an eighth century dispute over who was the legitimate successor to Jafar al-Sadiq, the sixth Imam. The Ismailis, who believe that the Imam is an incarnation of Allah, await the return of the seventh and last Imam on Judgment Day. During the twelfth century a small group of Ismailis, known as the Assassins, earned a reputation for attacking Sunni religious and political leaders (thus, their name entered the modern vocabulary). Modern Ismaili groups are centered in India, Pakistan, Iran, Yemen, East Africa, and Canada.

Sufi

Sufism, a mystical movement within Islam, originated before the eighth century among pious Muslims who wanted to focus on developing a meaningful inner spiritual life. They sought direct, ecstatic communion with Allah. Sufi practices were personal and spontaneous and included recitation and meditation, which led to ecstatic experiences that produced intimate knowledge of Allah.

An early Sufi leader, al-Hallaj, was executed in Baghdad for heresy in 922 C.E. Later Sufis, however, were more successful in blending orthodox Islamic doctrine with their mystical pursuits. By the twelfth century, Sufi brotherhoods, or schools, existed throughout the Islamic world. Founders of Sufi schools were called Shaikhs and they were regarded as saints. When a Shaikh died, his role would pass onto one of his followers. The Sufis often served the poor and sought to bring spiritual enlightenment to their followers.

There are three different categories of modern Sufi: traditional Muslims for whom Sufism represents an added focus of spiritual dimension in ritual worship; people who practice spiritual spontaneity and eschew rules and morals; and those who seek ecstatic experiences with Allah.

Figure 10.1. A mihrab is an ornately decorated niche on the interior wall of a mosque that indicates the direction in which people should face for prayer (toward Mecca). The designs are abstract patterns, geometric figures, and stylized calligraphic inscriptions in Arabic. This photograph, taken by Abdullah Frères sometime between 1880 and 1893, shows the mihrab of the Kebir Cami (Great Mosque) in Turkey. (Library of Congress, Prints and Photographs Division, Abdul Hamid II Collection, LC-USZ62-81550.)

◈ ◈ ◈

The Islamic Calendar

A Lunar Calendar

The *Qur'an* is the holy book of Islam, revealed through the prophet Muhammad to his followers. Muslims believe that the *Qur'an* exists in heaven with God and that Muhammad transmitted a copy of it to his disciples. It is to this heavenly authority that the Muslims look for their calendar. In the *Qur'an* (IX, 36–37), Allah revealed to Muhammad that the calendar of Islam should follow the lunar cycle.

The Thirty-Year Cycle

The Islamic lunar calendar is based on a thirty-year cycle. It consists of twelve lunar months that alternate between twenty-nine and thirty days. The calendar operates on a thirty-year cycle in which an extra day is added to the last month of years 2, 5, 7, 10, 13, 16, 18, 21, 24, 26, and 29.

The eleven days that are added to the cycle compensate exactly for the .03059 days the moon gains in each average month of 29.5 days. Thus, the Islamic calendar stays perfectly in phase with the moon. However, because the Islamic year is 354 or 355 days long, it is about 11 days short of the solar year. As a result, there are about thirty-three Islamic years for every thirty-two solar years. This means that the months of the Islamic calendar pass through all the seasons every thirty-three years, and on the common civil calendar, Islamic festivals will seem to move backward by eleven days from year to year.

The Epoch of the Muslim Era

The emigration of Muhammad is the epoch of the Muslim Era. In 622 C.E., Muhammad migrated from Mecca to Medina, an event which is known as the Great Hijrah. The epoch of the Muslim Era is based on his arrival in the city of Medina. The era officially began at sunset on Muharram 1, 622 C.E. (which would have fallen on July 16 according to the Western civil calendar). The second Caliph, Umar I, formally designated Muharram 1 to be the beginning of the year some time during his reign (634–644 C.E.).

Throughout the Muslim world, the Era of the Hijrah (A.H.) or Muslim Era is used privately, and many nations use it as the authorized method for reckoning time. Countries that officially recognize the Muslim Era include Saudi Arabia, Yemen, and the principalities of the Persian Gulf. In Egypt, Syria, Jordan, and Morocco, both Muslim and Common Eras are sanctioned.

Still other Muslim countries use a combination of the two systems. Around 1088 A.H. (1677 C.E.), Turkey, for example, designated March 1 as the New Year, adopted the solar year and Julian months, but kept the Muslim Era. In the nineteenth century, the Turkish Empire accepted the Gregorian calendar, and in the twentieth century, the Common Era.

Another country that adopted a combined system is Iran. During the reign of Reza Shah Pahlavi (1925–1942 C.E.), the solar year was incorporated into a calendar with Persian month names and the Muslim Era. March 21 is the beginning of the Iranian year. Thus, the Iranian year 1349 began on March 21, 1970.

Months, Weeks, and Days

Like the Hebrew month, the Islamic month begins when two witnesses report seeing the crescent of the new moon. Their claim is verified by a qadi (judge) and a mufti (interpreter of Muslim law). The mufti declares the beginning of a new month. Also like the early Hebrews, Muslims faced the problems of cloudy nights and poor communication, which posed a hindrance to the timely and efficient declaration of a new month. Each town or community would assume responsibility for declaring the beginning of the month. This caused confusion because the months would start on different days from one location to the next. In modern times, Muslims are increasingly using scientific calculations for establishing the appearance of the new crescent moon. In the United States, this effort is specifically led by the Islamic Society of North America (ISNA).

Table 8.1. The Twelve Islamic Months

1. Muharram
2. Safar
3. Rabi al-Awwal
4. Rabi al-Thani
5. Jumada al-Ula
6. Jumada al-Akhira
7. Rajab
8. Sha'ban
9. Ramadan
10. Shawwal
11. Dhu al-Qa'dah
12. Dhu al-Hijjah

All Muslim calendars are composed of seven-day weeks and twenty-four hour days. The names for the days vary from place to place except for the weekly holy day, Al Jumah, literally, "the day of gathering." In terms of the Western civil calendar, Al Jumah falls on Friday and marks the beginning of the Islamic week. Days in the Muslim system run from sunset to sunset.

———— " ————

"There is no God but Allah and Muhammad is his Prophet." — Islamic confession of faith.

———— " ————

Table 8.2. The Islamic Holiday Cycle

Muharram

1	Awwal Muharram
10	Ashura
10	Yevmi Ashurer
10	Husayn Day

Safar

~	Mandi Safar
14–16	Shah Abdul Latif Death Festival
18–19	Data Ganj Baksh Death Festival

Rabi al-Awwal

12	Mawlid al-Nabi

Rajab

27	Laylat al-Miraj

Sha'ban

15	Shab-Barat

Ramadan

1–30	Fast of Ramadan
27	Laylat al-Qadr
30	Lantern's Festival

Shawwal

1–3	'Id al-Fitr

Dhu'al-Hijjah

8–13	Pilgrimage to Mecca (Hajj)
10	Al-'id al-Kabir
10–12	'Id al-Adha

Islamic Holidays

Daily

Salat (Prayers)
Five times a day

Muslims are required to pray five times a day: just before sunrise (just at the first break of daylight), early afternoon (just after the sun reaches its zenith), late afternoon, after sunset, and before retiring at night (after all daylight is gone from the sky). Designated prayers are offered in units; each unit consists of specific postures, prayers, and *Qur'an* recitations. The postures involve standing, genuflection, prostrations, and sitting. All prayers are offered facing in the direction of the Ka'bah in Mecca. Although these prayers are intended to be congregational and not private, individuals are not required to attend a mosque to participate in the daily prayers. There are also extra daily prayer cycles that are optional.

Tahajjud (Night Vigil)
After midnight

Tahajjud prayers are individual devotional prayers made after midnight. Unlike the mandated daily cycle of prayers, Tahajjud prayers are optional.

Weekly

Salat-ul-Jumu'ah (Friday Prayers)
Friday

Early afternoon prayers on Fridays typically represent the main Muslim gathering of the week. In addition to the regular prayers designated for the hour, a sermon (called a khutbah) or other form of teaching may be offered. Unlike weekly holy day observances in Christianity and Judaism where the entire day is marked by a cessation of regular activities, the Muslim Friday services take place during a pause in the regular workday pattern. The establishment of Friday as the day for special gatherings is based on the belief that Adam was both created and received into Paradise on Fridays.

Annual

Muharram

Muharram
First month of the Muslim calendar

Muharram was designated as the first month in the Islamic year by Umar, the second Caliph. At the beginning of a new year, Muslims repent, regret, and abandon the sins of the past and determine to make a new start. The first and tenth days of the month (described below) have special significance.

Awwal Muharram (New Year's Day)
Muharram 1

Awwal Muharram is the Islamic New Year celebration. It is observed as a holiday in nineteen countries. The day commemorates the migration of Muhammad from Mecca to Medina in 622 C.E. Muhammad's journey, called the Great Hijrah, came about as a result of hostility toward his teachings and the scarcity of converts in Mecca. In Medina, Muhammad was welcomed, and Islam gained a solid following. Because of the significance of this event, Muslims count their era from this date.

Ashura (Ashoora)
Muharram 10

Muhammad initially instituted the observance of Ashura as a two-day fast on Muharram 9 and 10. It is still observed as an optional fast by Sunni Muslims.

The significance of the tenth day of Muharram is linked with several observances that vary among the different sects of Islam. Events associated with the day include: the creation of the heavens, land, and seas; the creation of Adam; the day of Noah's departure from the Ark after the great flood; the day Moses was saved from Pharaoh in Egypt; and, looking to the future, the tenth day of Muharram is the day on which Allah's final judgment will take place.

Yevmi Ashurer (Day of Sweet Soup or Porridge)
Muharram 10

Turkish Muslims celebrate Muharram 10 in memory of Noah's departure from the Ark onto Mount Ararat and God's covenant with Noah never to destroy the earth by flood again. Because they must share Allah's gifts with others, everyone makes ashurer, which is a sweet soup or porridge made of boiled wheat, dried currants, grain, and nuts, similar to that supposedly made by Noah and stored in the bins of the Ark. Each person is assigned a day to invite his neighbors to come and share it.

Husayn Day (Hosay Festival)
Muharram 10

Among Shi'ite Muslims, Muharram 10 is observed as Husayn Day (also spelled Husain or Hussein) in honor of Husayn ibn Ali (son of Ali). Husayn, the grandson and, according to Shi'ite belief, legitimate successor of Muhammad, was killed in a battle on October 10, 680 C.E.

(61 A.H.). Husayn represents a righteous person under persecution, and the Shi'ites draw inspiration from his example.

The holy day of mourning includes fasting, praying, and the singing of elegies. Some Shi'ite communities also participate in reenactments of the battle and conduct processions in which Husayn's standard is carried. Passion plays called *ta'ziya* (a word that means consolation) are produced in Iran, Iraq, Pakistan, India, and other areas with large Shi'ite populations.

In Trinidad and Tobago, however, where the remembrance of Husayn's death was first celebrated in 1884, the traditional procession of mourning has been mixed with various European, African, and Indian rituals to form a celebration that is far from somber. Called the Hosay Festival, the observance features popular processions held between February and March in the towns of St. James, Curepe, Tunapuna, Couva, and Cedros.

The festival in Trinidad and Tobago usually begins with a procession of flags symbolizing the beginning of the battle of Karbala, in which Husayn and his brother were killed. On the second day dancers wearing Tadjahs—small minaretted tombs made of bamboo, colored tissue, tinfoil, crepe paper, mirrors, and coconut leis—parade through the streets to the accompaniment of drummers in a ritual that is reminiscent of Carnival.

Figure 10.2. A Tazia—a temporary structure representing Husayn's tomb or mausoleum—is carried in a procession on Husayn Day in commemoration of the fallen hero's death during the Battle of Martyrs. Husayn, the grandson and, according to Shi'ite belief, legitimate successor of Muhammad was killed on October 10, 680 C.E. (61 A.H.). Husayn represents a righteous person under persecution, and the Shi'ites draw inspiration from his example.

The highlight of the festival occurs on the third night, when the large Tadjahs, some of which are six feet tall, are carried through the streets. There are also two moons, representing Husayn and his brother, carried by specially trained dancers. These large crescent-shaped structures are studded with sharp blades and carried on the dancers' shoulders. At midnight, the two moons engage in a ritual embrace to a chorus of cheers from the onlookers.

Safar

Mandi Safar
Occurs during the month of Safar

Mandi Safar is a Muslim bathing festival unique to Malaysia. The observance was originally believed to commemorate the last time Muhammad was able to bathe before his death. Muslims wearing bright colors visit beaches for a religious cleansing of the body and soul with water. There is no mention of the rite in the *Qur'an* (the Muslim holy book), and orthodox Muslims consider it nothing more than a picnic. It continues as a merry holiday. The best-known gathering places are the beaches of Tanjong Kling near Malacca and the beaches of Penang.

Shah Abdul Latif Death Commemoration
Safar 14–16

Shah Abdul Latif was a Sufi poet (1689–1752) who lived in Sind, now a province in modern-day Pakistan. He was one of the most beloved of Pakistan's mystic Sufi poet-musicians. He is best remembered as the author of the *Risala*, a collection of romantic poetry in the Sindhi language. The heroes and heroines in his work have become symbols of the oppression of Sind by foreign occupiers.

At Latif's death festival (called an urs, which means a wedding signifying union with Allah, the Beloved) a huge fair takes place outside the poet's shrine. There are wrestling matches (a popular entertainment in Sind), transvestite dances, a circus, theater, and numerous food and souvenir booths. Inside the shrine the atmosphere is quiet, and there is devotional singing by well-known Sind groups. The main event of the urs is a concert at which the annual Latif Award is presented to the best performers. None of these celebrations have any association with Islamic religious practices.

Data Ganj Baksh Death Festival
Safar 18–19

Data Ganj Baksh, which means "He Who Gives Generously," was the name given to Syed Ali Abdul Hasan Bin Usman Hajweri (also spelled Ali Hujwiri or al-Hujwuri), a scholar and author who lived most of his life in Lahore (now in modern-day Pakistan), and died in 1072. He wrote *Kashful Majhab* (or *Kashf al-mahjub*), the oldest Persian treatise on Sufism. It is a text on the fundamentals of Sufism and it reviews Islamic mysticism, linking each famous master to a particular doctrine.

Ali Hujwiri is one of the most popular saints in Pakistan, and every day hundreds of pilgrims pray at the Mausoleum of Data Ganj Baksh in Lahore, Pakistan asking for blessings and favors. At his death festival (called an urs), thousands throng to the shrine for celebratory activities and prayers.

Rabi al-Awwal

Mawlid al-Nabi (Birthday of Muhammad; Bara Wafat)
Rabi al-Awwal 12

Mawlid al-Nabi, meaning birthday of the prophet, is not universally celebrated by all Muslims. Some Islamic communities refrain from participating in the festival because Muhammad himself did not celebrate his own birth. The custom of celebration, however, dates back to the tenth century in Egypt. In India, the feast of Mawlid al-Nabi, or Bara Wafat, is celebrated with enthusiasm.

Muhammad was born on the twelfth day of Rabi al-Awwal, which in the Western calendar fell on April 12, 571 C.E. He was born at Mecca in Arabia, during a period of moral chaos and great corruption. Muhammad spent much of his time in prayer, meditation, and seclusion where he received revelations from Allah. For twenty-three years, from the time he was forty years old until his death, Muhammad succeeded in establishing a religion based on the revelations he had received and brought a political cohesiveness to the Arab tribes that had not been previously experienced.

On the day of Mawlid, the Prophet's teachings are repeated, the holy *Qur'an* is read and recited, and religious meetings are held in the mosques. The devotees keep a night vigil, spending their time in prayer and reading the *Qur'an*. They invite friends and relatives to a feast and give donations to the poor.

Rajab

Laylat al-Miraj (Lailat al Miraj; Isra' and Mi'raj; Night Journey; Ascension of the Prophet)
Rajab 27

This celebration commemorates Muhammad's night journey to Jerusalem from Mecca in 620 C.E. and his ascension into heaven. According to the *Qur'an*, one night during the tenth year of his prophecy, the angel Jibril

Table 8.3. Alphabetical List of Islamic Holidays

Holidays	Date(s)
Al-'id al-Kabir	Dhu al-Hijjah 10
Ascension of the Prophet *see* Laylat al-Miraj	
Ashoora *see* Ashura	
Ashura	Muharram 10
Awwal Muharram	Muharram 1
Bara Wafat *see* Mawlid al-Nabi	
Birthday of Muhammad *see* Mawlid al-Nabi	
Data Ganj Baksh Death Festival	Safar 18-19
Day of Light *see* Lantern's Festival	
Day of Sweet Soup or Porridge *see* Yevmi Ashurer	
Eidul Adah *see* 'Id al-Adha	
Eidul Fitr *see* 'Id al-Fitr	
Fast of Ramadan	Ninth month of the Islamic lunar year
Feast of Breaking the Fast *see* 'Id al-Fitr	
Feast of Sacrifice *see* 'Id al-Adha	
Hajj *see* Pilgrimage to Mecca	
Hosay Festival *see* Husayn Festival	
Husayn Day	Muharram 10
'Id al-Adha	Dhu al-Hijjah 10-12
'Id al-Fitr	Shawwal 1-3
Id as-Saghîr *see* 'Id al-Fitr	
Isra' and Mi'raj *see* Laylat al-Miraj	
Lai-Lai-Tu-Gadri *see* Lantern's Festival	
Lailat al Miraj *see* Laylat al-Miraj	

Holidays	Date(s)
Lailat Alqadr *see* Laylat al-Qadr	
Lantern's Festival	Ramadan 30
Laylat al-Miraj	Rajab 27
Laylat al-Qadr	Ramadan 27
Laylat il-Qader *see* Laylat al-Qadr	
Laylat-ul-Bara'h *see* Shab-Barat	
Lelé-I-Kadir *see* Laylat al-Qadr	
Mandi Safar	During the month of Safar
Mawlid al-Nabi	Rabi al-Awwal 12
Muharram	First month of Muslim calendar
New Year's Day *see* Awwal Muharram	
Night Journey *see* Laylat al-Miraj	
Night of Destiny *see* Laylat al-Qadr	
Night of Determination *see* Laylat al-Qadr	
Night of Forgiveness *see* Shab-Barat	
Night of Power *see* Laylat al-Qadr	
Nuzulul Qur'an *see* Laylat al-Qadr	
Pilgrimage to Mecca	Dhu al-Hijjah 8-13
Sallah *see* Al-'id al-Kabir	
Seker Bayram *see* 'Id al-Fitr	
Shab-Barat	Sha'ban 15
Shah Abdul Latif Death Festival	Safar 14-16
Sugar Feast *see* 'Id al-Fitr	
Yevmi Ashurer	Muharram 10

woke Muhammad and traveled with him to Jerusalem on the winged horse, Burak. There he prayed at the site of the Temple of Solomon with the Prophets Abraham, Moses, Jesus, and others. Then, carried by Jibril, he rose to heaven from the rock of the Temple Mount, where the Dome of the Rock sanctuary now stands. In heaven, Muhammad received instructions from Allah regarding the five daily prayers observed by all Muslims.

Muhammad's journey provides inspiration, particularly to the mystical Sufis. In it, Sufis see a foreshadowing of the possibility of the relationship between Allah and his servants in which the servant could experience an annihilation of self in order to experience the presence of Allah.

The holiday is observed by some Muslim groups as a festive gathering at which the story of Muhammad's experience is retold and food is shared. Other Muslims choose to not celebrate the occasion.

Sha'ban

Shab-Barat (Night of Forgiveness; Laylat-ul-Bara'h)
Sha'ban 15

Shab-Barat (or Shab-i-Barat) is the evening on which Muslims, especially Indian and Pakistani followers, entreat Allah for forgiveness of their dead. The devout often spend the night in mosques praying and reading the *Qur'an*. Muslims visit graveyards to pray for the souls of their friends and ancestors. Allah's mercy is celebrated by fireworks displays, the illumination of the outside of mosques, and provision of food for the poor.

This time is also known as Laylat al-Bara'ah, or the Night of Forgiveness. It is a time of preparation for Ramadan through intense prayer. Muslim belief indicates that this is the night on which sins are absolved.

Ramadan

Ramadan (Fast of Ramadan)
Ninth month of the Islamic lunar year

During the month of Ramadan, Muslims commemorate Muhammad's reception of the divine revelations recorded in the *Qur'an*. The *Qur'an* itself mandates this observance and provides explicit instructions for following the month-long fast, which was first instituted in 2 A.H. (624 C.E.).

The first day of Ramadan occurs when the new crescent moon is sighted. It is the holiest period during the Islamic year, and ends when the new moon is sighted for the next month. The Festival of Breaking Fast immediately follows the Fast of Ramadan and is a time of rejoicing, gift-giving, and celebration.

During Ramadan, Muslims observe a strict fast from food, water, beverages, sexual activities, and smoking from sunrise to sunset. The fast is one of the Five Pillars of the Islamic faith, and is considered a time of introspection and intensified devotion to Allah.

Each day, believers rise early and eat a light meal, called a Suhur, before dawn. They fast through the day, then after prayers they break the fast with an evening meal. In some places the end of the fast is announced by the firing of a cannon.

In addition to fasting from food, smoking (smoking at any time is discouraged), alcohol (alcohol is a banned activity at any time and a sin for Muslims), and sexual activities, Muslims particularly avoid sins such as lying, promise breaking, and anger during the daylight hours of Ramadan. In addition, an extra set of prayers, called the Tarawih, may be added to the fifth set of daily prayers. Although most Muslims are expected to fast during Ramadan, the *Qur'an* does make provisions to excuse those who are unable to fast due to reasons such as illness, pregnancy, menstruation, and travel. Some pious Muslims elect to stay in the mosque for the last ten days of Ramadan.

Laylat al-Qadr (Night of Power; Night of Destiny; Night of Determination; Laylat il-Qader; Lailat Alqadr; Lelé-I-Kadir; Nuzulul Qur'an)
Ramadan 27

One night during the last ten days of Ramadan (most often Ramadan 27), is set aside for special attention. Known as the Laylat al-Qadr, or Night of Power, it marks the very first revelation of the *Qur'an*. It is observed by spending the night in worship. This night is believed to be the time when Allah establishes the events to occur in the coming year. Islamic scholars point out that Ramadan 27 is a belief that may or may not be correct. Each of the last 10 days of Ramadan could be the Night of Power, although it is believed to fall on an odd-numbered day.

Islamic teaching states that Allah revealed the entire *Qur'an* (Muslim holy book) to Muhammad through a series of revelations spanning twenty-three years. These began in 610 C.E. when the angel Jibril first spoke to him. The revelations continued throughout the remainder of his life. Islamic children begin studying the *Qur'an* when they are very young, and they celebrate when they've read all 114 chapters for the first time. Many adults and young people try to memorize the entire *Qur'an*.

According to custom, the night of Ramadan 26 is the precise date on which Muhammad received the first revelation of the *Qur'an*; however, the common belief that this day occurred on the 26th or 27th day of Ramadan has no Islamic base. Some researchers speculate that the date originated in Manicheism where the death of Mani is celebrated on the 27th of the fasting month.

Lantern's Festival (Day of Light; Lai-Lai-Tu-Gadri)
Ramadan 30

Lantern's Festival, an observance originating in Freetown, Sierra Leone, during the 1930s, occurs near the end of the month-long fast of Ramadan. The custom of parading with lanterns originated with a trader known as Daddy Maggay. The original lanterns were simple handheld paper boxes, lit from within and mounted on sticks. They were carried through the streets of Freetown in celebration of the day Allah sent the *Qur'an* to earth (the twenty-sixth day of Ramadan, also known as the Day of Light, or Lai-Lai-Tu-Gadri).

As the years passed, the celebration—and the lanterns—grew larger. Heavy boots, originally worn as protection, came to be used to produce drum-like rhythmical beats on the paved streets since some Muslims discourage using drums. Maggay's group was called bobo, the name for the distinctive beat. Neighborhood rivalries, based on competition in lantern-building, often erupted in violence. By the 1950s the Young Men's Muslim Association had taken over the festival in hopes of reducing the violence through better organization. The lanterns—which by that time were elaborate float-like structures illuminated from within and drawn by eight-man teams or motor vehicles—were divided into three categories for judging: Group A for ships; Group B for animals and people; and Group C for miscellaneous secular subjects. Prizes were awarded to the top three winners in each group, based on creativity and building technique.

Shawwal

'Id al-Fitr (Feast of Breaking the Fast; Eidul Fitr; Id as-Saghîr; Seker Bayram; Seker Bayrami; Sugar Feast; often referred to simply as Id—pronounced "Eid")
Shawwal 1–3

This three-day festival, also known as Breaking of the Fast, marks the end of the month-long fast of Ramadan. It begins when the new moon is first seen. It is a festival of thanksgiving, offering thanks to Allah for the blessing of enjoying the month of Ramadan.

'Id al-Fitr is a festival of great cheer, rejoicing, and festivity. Muslims wear their new or best clothes and shoes and offer mass prayers in mosques or in specially designated spaces outside, called musallas. After prayers there is a religious lecture from an Imam and warm greetings. According to Islamic tradition, 'Id al-Fitr marks the last day during which a Muslim can pay the Zakat al-Fitr, or charity.

In many Muslim communities around the world, the whole day of 'Id is spent in festivities and exchanging sweets, good wishes, and visits. Children often receive presents, and 'Id greeting cards may be sent. Many village squares have carnival rides, puppet shows, and candy vendors. In Indonesia, Thailand, and Malaysia, the festival is called Lebaran, or Hari Raya. In Turkey, where it is called the Candy Festival, or Seker Bayrami, children are given candy or money wrapped in handkerchiefs. In Pakistan the special treat associated with 'Id is saween, a very fine spaghetti cooked in milk and sugar and sprinkled with almonds, pistachios, and dates. In the spirit of benevolence that characterizes the celebration, the poor and needy are also given food, money, and clothes. People also visit their loved ones and ask their forgiveness as part of the 'Id.

In modern times it has become customary to have one's non-Muslim friends visit to foster understanding between different ethnic groups. Muslims in turn visit Chinese friends during Lunar New Year, Hindus during Dewali, and Christians at Christmas.

Dhu al-Hijjah

Pilgrimage to Mecca (Hajj)
Dhu al-Hijjah 8–13

At least once in a lifetime, every Muslim man or woman (if she is accompanied by a male protector) with the means and the opportunity to do so is expected to make a pilgrimage to Mecca, the city in modern-day Saudi Arabia where Muhammad was born. It is one of the Five Pillars (fundamental duties) of Islam and must be performed during the special pilgrimage season. The *Qur'an* says the founder of this pilgrimage was Abraham. The pilgrims wear two sheets of seamless white cloth and perform elaborate rites at the Grand Mosque of Mecca and in the immediate vicinity. All together, the rites require about six days to complete.

The focal point of the pilgrimage is the Ka'bah, a fifteen-foot-high stone structure that stands in the center court of the Grand Mosque of Mecca. It consists of one room without windows and is shaped like a cube. Islamic tradition states the Ka'bah was built by Abraham and Ishmael. In one corner of the structure of the Ka'bah is the Black Stone, believed to have been brought by the angel Jibril. The Black Stone serves as a symbol of eternity because of its durability, and pilgrims traditionally kiss it before starting the circumambulation around it. The Ka'bah symbolizes the place of worship of the one God and its shape represents simplicity and a sense of infinity. It is kept covered with a dark cloth decorated with embroidery.

Pilgrims must perform specific rites during their pilgrimage. These include walking around the Ka'bah seven times, walking between two hills near it seven times, marching to Mina (three miles away), marching to Arafat (another six miles) to seek forgiveness from God, walking or driving back to the Ka'bah, offering a sacrifice, and walking around the Ka'bah a final time. At Mina, there is also a symbolic stoning of Satan represented by three stone pillars at Mina. This reenacts

Figure 10.3. The Ka'bah is the central shrine in Islam. It is located in Mecca, the city where Muhammad was born, which is in modern-day Saudi Arabia. The building is cube shaped and black, decorated with embroidered fabric. It houses the Black Stone, which is believed to have been brought by the angel Jibril. One of the requirements under Islamic law dictates that every Muslim who is physically able and has the financial means to accomplish it make a pilgrimage to the Ka'bah. A person who has made the pilgrimage earns the right to use the title Hajji.

the experience of Abraham when he was about to sacrifice his son and was tempted three times by Satan.

It is not uncommon for two million or more Muslims to participate in the pilgrimage, which has led Saudi Arabia and other countries to explore new methods for freezing, preserving, and distributing the meat that is produced by so many sacrifices. At the end of the pilgrimage, it is customary to visit the tomb of Muhammad at Medina before returning home.

Returning pilgrims are met by family and friends who have rented taxis and decorated them with palm branches and the families' best rugs. The pilgrim's house has been decorated with palm-leaf arches and sometimes outlined with lights. The doorways will also have designs suggesting the journey. A feast and party called The Feast of Sacrifice finish the welcome home. A person who has made the pilgrimage earns the right to use the title Hajji.

Al-'id al-Kabir (Sallah; Salah)
Dhu al-Hijjah 10

Al-'id al Kibar is the major Islamic festival marking the end of the Hajj or pilgrimage season. In Nigeria the festival is called Sallah (or Salah) where it is celebrated with pomp and ceremony. People throng together in their best regalia. Processions of nobles on horseback are led by the emir (a ruler or chief) to the prayer grounds. After a prayer service, the emir, dressed in white and carrying the historic Sword of Katsina, is seated on a platform. Groups of men take turns galloping up, reining in so their horses rear up at the last moment, and salute the emir. He raises the sword in response. Later, there is entertainment by musicians, acrobats, jesters, and dancers. Niger and some other African countries also celebrate the day with elaborate festivities.

'Id al-Adha (Feast of Sacrifice; Eidul Adah; Baqr 'Id)
Dhu al-Hijjah 10–12

This three-day festival commemorates Abraham's obedience to God in nearly sacrificing his son Ishmael. Muslims maintain that it was Ishmael who was the son of promise and thus it was Ishmael who was nearly sacrificed but saved by God at the last moment. (This contrasts with the Jewish and Christian accounts maintaining that Isaac was the son of promise and the object of the intended sacrifice.) Ishmael is believed to be the ancestor of all Arabs.

To commemorate the miraculous provision of a sacrifice in Ishmael's place, goats, cows, camels, and rams are offered to Allah at this time. The sacrifice of an animal also symbolizes that man's position in the creation is far higher than any beast, and any sacrifice, however great, is a small thing for the sake of Allah.

In India and Pakistan the festival is also known as Baqr 'Id. Baqr 'Id is observed by Muslims who go to the mosques in the morning to offer prayers to Allah, and then return home to sacrifice the animal at home. In keeping with the Islamic practice, the meat is divided into three portions: one for the needy, one for family and friends, and one for own self. Some prefer to give away all the meat to the needy. The cooked meat becomes part of the family meal that ensues. The holiday is traditionally a time of peace, charity, and goodwill. As part of this, many people reach out to the poor, needy, and sick with money and gifts.

CHAPTER 11

The Bahá'í Faith

Overview

What Is the Bahá'í Faith?

The Bahá'í faith is one of the newest world religions. It was founded in Iran during the nineteenth century by Mírzá Husayn-'Ali Núrí, who is known by the title Bahá'u'lláh ("The Glory of God" in Arabic). A "Bahá'í" is a follower of Bahá'u'lláh. Bahá'u'lláh claimed to be the latest divine messenger in a line of prophets that included Abraham, Krishna, Moses, Zoroaster, Buddha, Christ, and Muhammad. The Bahá'í theme is one of fulfillment: the great teacher, long expected in other traditions, had arrived to bring world peace.

The central message of Bahá'u'lláh's religion is unity—of people and of religions. Bahá'ís believe that all the world religions have been "dispensations" of one religion, successively revealed to humanity by divine messengers or "Manifestations" of God. Bahá'ís believe that that humanity is one and call for an end to all prejudice based on race, religion, ethnicity, class, and nationality. They also uphold the equality of men and women. Other basic principles include the belief that each person has the responsibility to investigate religious truth independently, that religion and science should be in accord, that spiritual principles should be applied to solve social and economic problems, and that just structures of international governance should be created that will protect the human rights of all peoples and maintain peace.

The Relationship between God and the Bahá'í People

The Bahá'í faith teaches that there is one God, who is the creator of all, who is all-powerful and all-knowing. While human beings cannot know God directly—as the divine essence itself is inaccessible—they can know about God through the great spiritual teachers, or "Manifestations of God," sent by God approximately every thousand years. These divine messengers reaffirm and renew the eternal spiritual and moral principles shared by all religions. They also bring specific social laws designed to address the needs of society in different times and places. Their revelations have given rise to the great world civilizations and together form a progressive, but unified, revelation from God. Bahá'ís do not believe that the revelation of Bahá'u'lláh is the final one, but that after a thousand years there will be another revelation.

According to the Bahá'í teachings, human beings were created to know and to worship God. Recognition of the Manifestation of God and living in accordance with his teachings are the central duties of the covenant between God and the individual soul. The human soul is created at conception and is eternal. The purpose of physical life is to strive to develop divine attributes and spiritual qualities such as love, trustworthiness, generosity, compassion, justice, and mercy, and to reflect them in every aspect of life. Thus the arts, crafts, and all work performed in the spirit of service are accounted as worship. After death the soul continues its journey of return to God on a spiritual level of existence. Bahá'ís do not believe in reincarnation.

Authorities and Sacred Writings

The Bahá'í sacred scriptures include the writings of Bahá'u'lláh, the Báb, and 'Abdu'l-Bahá. Bahá'u'lláh wrote numerous volumes in his lifetime, including book-length works, prayers, meditations, and letters. His writings are referred to as "Tablets." His *Kitáb-i-Aqdas* (The Most Holy Book), revealed in 1873, contains the laws intended to govern Bahá'í society, as well as moral principles, exhortations on a wide range of subjects, and statements addressed to the kings and rulers of the time. It establishes the most important of the Bahá'í holidays. Other major writings include the *Kitáb-i-Íqán* (Book of Certitude), which explains the doctrine of progressive revelation, and *The Hidden Words*, a collection of short aphoristic statements on moral and ethical subjects. *The Seven Valleys and the Four Valleys* describes the stages in the mystic journey of the soul. Bahá'u'lláh's letters to the rulers of his time are collected in *The Summons of the Lord of Hosts*. In the *Book of the Covenant*, Bahá'u'lláh's Will and Testament, he named his son 'Abbás Effendi, known as 'Abdu'l-Bahá ("Servant of Bahá") as his successor.

'Abdu'l-Bahá holds a unique status for Bahá'ís. Although not considered a prophet, he is regarded as the "perfect exemplar" of his father's teachings and his writings have scriptural status. In his own Will and Testament he named his grandson Shoghi Rabbani, known to Bahá'ís as Shoghi Effendi, as Guardian of the Bahá'í faith and infallible interpreter of the Bahá'í writings.

The Bahá'í community is governed by democratically elected councils of nine members at the local, national, and international level. There are 182 National Spiritual Assemblies and 11,746 Local Spiritual Assemblies worldwide. The international Bahá'í council is the Universal House of Justice, with its seat at the Bahá'í World Centre in Haifa, Israel.

History of the Bahá'í Faith

The Báb

The Bahá'í era is considered to begin in 1844 with the announcement by Siyyid 'Alí-Muhammad, a pious young merchant from Shiraz, Iran, that he was the "Báb" ("Gate") of God and the Promised One of Islam. The Báb, however, said that the purpose of his revelation was to prepare the way for another divine messenger even greater than himself, "Him whom God will make manifest" (in Arabic, "Man Yuzhiruhu'lláh")—similar to the way that John the Baptist was the forerunner of Jesus.

In the next six years, the Báb's religion spread throughout Iran, gaining thousands of followers, known as Bábís. His teachings, which instituted changes in Islamic law, were regarded as heretical by the Islamic clergy, and it determined to exterminate the Bábí movement. The government and religious authorities imprisoned the Báb, and thousands of Bábís were brutally persecuted and massacred.

In 1848, at a gathering called the Conference of Badasht, the Bábís began to realize that their religion was more than a reform movement within Islam. The complete break with Islam and its traditions was symbolically demonstrated by the action of Quratu'l-Ayn, known as Táhirih ("Pure One"), the sole woman among the first disciples of the Báb, who stunned the assembly by appearing before them with her face unveiled.

In 1850 the civil and religious authorities ordered the Báb to be put to death by firing squad. The commander of the Armenian regiment ordered to execute him was a Christian who was reluctant to kill the Báb. When the smoke from the 750 rifles of the firing squad cleared, the Báb was not there. The bullets had only cut the ropes binding him, and the Báb was found back in his room, completing an unfinished conversation. The Armenian commander refused to carry out the order again and another regiment was found, this time killing the Báb.

Bahá'u'lláh

The martyrdom of the Báb did not put an end to the movement, however. One of the Bábí leaders was Bahá'u'lláh, who came from a wealthy noble family of Mazandaran, Iran. He had rejected the life of the court for a life of charitable works and was known as the "Father of the Poor." Bahá'u'lláh was one of the Bábís imprisoned in 1852 in a subterranean dungeon in Tehran. While there, he received a revelation that he was the one promised by the Báb. Bahá'u'lláh did not disclose this knowledge publicly at first. In 1853, along with his family, he was exiled from his native land to Baghdad, in the Ottoman Empire. In April 1863, just before departing from Baghdad for Istanbul, he declared his prophetic mission to a small group of followers.

Despite repeated persecution including imprisonment and banishment to ever more remote regions, Bahá'u'lláh continued to attract followers, sympathizers, and visitors. He was further exiled to Edirne and in 1868 he was sent to be imprisoned in the penal colony of Acre, near Haifa. He resided in the environs of Acre until his death in 1892 at the age of 74.

During those years, although a prisoner, Bahá'u'lláh continued to proclaim his message and to write Tablets including some of the most important of the Bahá'í holy texts, including the *Kitáb-i-Aqdas* and messages to the rulers of his time, telling them to treat their subjects with justice, to reconcile their differences, and to bring about world peace.

'Abdu'l-Bahá

After the death of Bahá'u'lláh, his eldest son, 'Abdu'l-Bahá, became the leader of the Bahá'í faith. During the first years of 'Abdu'l-Bahá's leadership, he was still a prisoner of the Turkish government. After the Young Turk Revolution, 'Abdu'l-Bahá was set free. In 1911 He traveled to Europe and North America, visiting cities as far West as San Francisco, to introduce Western audiences to the teachings of his father. 'Abdu'l-Bahá died in 1921 and in his own Will and Testament named his eldest grandson, Shoghi Effendi, as the Guardian of the Bahá'í faith and the authorized interpreter of its scriptures.

Under the leadership of Shoghi Effendi, the administrative structure of Bahá'í councils set out in the writings of the founders of the Bahá'í faith was systematically established, and the religion gradually spread around the world. Shoghi Effendi translated many of the Bahá'í writings into English and was responsible for the construction of the gardens, shrines, and the first of the monumental buildings of the Bahá'í World Centre on Mount Carmel and in the Acre area. He died in London in 1957. By 1963 a sufficient number of National Spiritual Assemblies (56) had been established in order to hold the first election of the Universal House of Justice, the international governing council whose creation had been prescribed in the Bahá'í writings.

The Bahá'í Faith Today

In only a century and a half, the Bahá'í faith evolved from a small movement into an independent world religion. By the beginning of the twentieth-first century, there were an estimated 5 million Bahá'ís living in some 235 countries and territories, in 127,555 localities worldwide, representing over 2,100 ethnic, racial, and tribal groups.

Because many Bahá'í teachings concern the application of spiritual principles to social development issues,

Figure 11.1. Terraces approaching the Shrine of the Báb, Mount Carmel. © 2003 Bahá'í World News Service. Reprinted by permission. The Bahá'í faith began in 1844 when Siyyid 'Alí-Muhammad announced that he was the "Báb" ("Gate") of God and the Promised One of Islam. The gold-domed Shrine of the Báb is a place of Bahá'í pilgrimage.

including education, agriculture, justice, human rights, and consultative decision making, the Bahá'í community is actively engaged in thousands of social and economic development projects worldwide. This process accelerated significantly in the last two decades of the twentieth century. The Bahá'í International Community is accredited to the United Nations Economic and Social Council as a nongovernmental organization with consultative status and actively participates in United Nations activities and conferences.

An event of great religious significance to Bahá'ís occurred on May 22, 2001, with the inauguration of the newly completed terraced gardens that extend outward from the mausoleum of the Shrine of the Báb on Mount Carmel as well as new administrative buildings of the World Centre of the Bahá'í faith. The inaugural events were attended by more than 3,000 Bahá'ís from all over the world.

Persecution by the Muslim clergy continued, however, especially in Iran, where the government has continued to regarded the religion as a heretical sect of Islam and therefore subject to extermination. In the twentieth century, Bahá'ís in Iran were repeatedly persecuted. They were denied the right to work or attend school because of their beliefs, and their homes and property were confiscated. Some were imprisoned and executed. After the Islamic Revolution of 1979, more than 200 Bahá'ís, men and women, were put to death for refusing to recant their belief; thousands more fled the country.

Worship

The Bahá'í writings prescribe daily obligatory prayer, which may be chosen from three prayers revealed by Bahá'u'lláh, and the recitation of the Greatest Name—"Alláh-u-Abhá" ("God is Most Glorious" in Arabic) ninety-five times. In addition to the obligatory prayer, Bahá'ís also practice individual devotion, including prayer, study, and meditation on passages of scripture. Bahá'í communities hold devotional meetings, open to all, which include prayers and passages from sacred texts. The Bahá'í writings call for a House of Worship, or "Mashriqu'l-Adhkár" ("Dawning Place of the Mention of God" in Arabic), to be established in each locality. The House of Worship is intended to serve as the spiritual hub of community service institutions. In the House of Worship itself, nondenominational services are held using the scriptures of the world religions. Currently there are Bahá'í Houses of Worship on every continent, the most recently completed ones in India and Western Samoa.

Bahá'ís who are able to do so make pilgrimages to Bahá'í holy places associated with the lives of the central figures of the religion. Currently pilgrimages are only possible to the holy places at the Bahá'í World Centre in and around Haifa and Acre.

◙ ◙ ◙

The Bahá'í Calendar

A Solar Calendar

The Bahá'í calendar was established by the Báb in his writings and later confirmed by Bahá'u'lláh with some modifications and additions. Bahá'u'lláh set the year 1 of the Bahá'í era at the Báb's declaration in 1844 C.E. (1260 A.H.). Thus, for example, the year 2000 C.E. was the year 157 B.E. (Bahá'í Era).

The Bahá'í calendar is based on the solar year. It begins on the spring equinox in the Northern Hemisphere (normally March 21) and contains nineteen months of nineteen days each. The months are named for divine attributes or qualities, and the same nineteen names are also used as to designate the nineteen days of the month. For example, the Bahá'í New Year falls on the first day of the first month, or the day of Bahá of the month of Bahá. Table 11.1 lists the month and day names of the Bahá'í calendar.

Four intercalary days—five in leap years—are added to keep the calendar in accord with the solar year. These intercalary days, called Ayyám-i-Há, are inserted before the last month of the Bahá'í year, which is also the period of fasting.

Weeks and Days

In addition to months and days, each day of the seven-day week also has a name. In a manner similar to the Western civil calendar in which the days of the week are observed concurrently with but independently of the days of the month, the Bahá'í week days are acknowledged in order irrespective of the month days. The days of the Bahá'í week are shown in Table 11.2.

The Bahá'í day begins and ends at sunset. Therefore, the night that precedes a holiday is accounted as part of that day. Although not currently in effect in most parts of the world, Friday is designated in the Bahá'í scriptures as the day of rest.

Table 11.1. The Bahá'í Month and Day Names

Month Begins on Gregorian Date	Number and Bahá'í Name	Meaning
March 21	1. Bahá	Splendor
April 9	2. Jalál	Glory
April 28	3. Jamál	Beauty
May 17	4. 'Azamat	Grandeur
June 5	5. Núr	Light
June 24	6. Rahmat	Mercy
July 13	7. Kalimát	Words
August 1	8. Kamál	Perfection
August 20	9. Asmá'	Names
September 8	10. 'Izzat	Might
September 27	11. Mashíyyat	Will
October 16	12. 'Ilm	Knowledge
November 4	13. Qudrat	Power
November 23	14. Qawl	Speech
December 12	15. Masá'il	Questions
December 31	16. Sharaf	Honor
January 19	17. Sultán	Sovereignty
February 7	18. Mulk	Dominion
February 26	Ayyám-i-Há	Intercalary Days
March 2	19. 'Alá'	Loftiness

Table 11.2. The Bahá'í Week

Day	Name	Meaning
Saturday	Jalál	Glory
Sunday	Jamál	Beauty
Monday	Kamál	Perfection
Tuesday	Fidál	Grace
Wednesday	'Idál	Justice
Thursday	Istijlál	Majesty
Friday	Istiqlál	Independence

——— " ———

The Greatest Name "*Alláh-u-Abhá*" (which means "God is Most Glorious") is recited in prayer.

——— " ———

Bahá'í Holidays

With a few exceptions (obligatory prayer and the simple ceremonies for marriages and funerals), the Bahá'í faith has no rituals or ceremonies. Thus there are no fixed customs for observing Bahá'í holidays. Practices vary considerable among communities around the world and often include diverse cultural expressions. Holidays are often observed by holding gatherings where prayers and passages from the Bahá'í writings, are read—or, if in Persian or Arabic, chanted—including special Tablets revealed for certain holidays. Festive holidays also may include music, singing, social activities, fellowship, and hospitality or feasting. According to the Bahá'í writings, the holy days are also an occasion to show thanks to God for his blessings, including initiating projects of community service. There are nine holy days on which work is suspended and Bahá'í children are excused from school.

Monthly

Nineteen-Day Feast
The first day of each of the nineteen months of the Bahá'í calendar

On the first day of each of the nineteen months of the Bahá'í year, in each locality the Bahá'í community gathers for the Nineteen-Day Feast. The Feast has three parts: a devotional service consisting of prayers and readings from the sacred writings; a meeting of the Bahá'í community for consultation on local affairs; and a social occasion with hospitality and fellowship.

Annually

Festival of Naw-Rúz
March 21 (Bahá 1)

Naw-Rúz is the Bahá'í New Year's Day. It is observed on the spring equinox (normally March 21, but on March 22 if the equinox occurs after sunset). The holiday also marks the end of the 19-day fast. Naw-Rúz is a joyous holiday often celebrated with community and family gatherings and hospitality.

Festival of Ridván
April 21-May 2 (Jalál 13–Jamál 5)

During this, the holiest period of the Bahá'í year, Bahá'ís commemorate the twelve days in 1863 which Bahá'u'lláh spent in the Najíbíyyih Garden near Baghdad, just before his departure for Istanbul. It was here that he first disclosed to some of his followers that he was the Promised One whose coming had been foretold by the Báb. The location came to be known to Bahá'ís as the Garden of Ridván ("Paradise"). Bahá'u'lláh established this as the "Most Great Festival" in the *Kitáb-i-Aqdas* and specified that the first, ninth, and twelfth days of Ridván should be observed as holidays when work is suspended. The first day of Ridván is observed at 3:00 p.m. on April 21. The annual elections of the administrative councils of the Bahá'í community take place during the Ridván period.

Declaration of the Báb
May 23 ('Azamat 7)

On the evening of May 22, 1844, in Shiraz, the Báb revealed his mission to his first disciple, Mullá Husayn Bushrú'í. The Declaration of the Báb is observed two hours after sunset on May 22 and is one of the nine holy days on which Bahá'ís do not work and children are excused from school. The House of the Báb in Shiraz, in which the Declaration occurred, was a place of pilgrimage for Bahá'ís but it was demolished by the Iranian authorities in 1979.

Ascension of Bahá'u'lláh
May 29 ('Azamat 13)

Each year, Bahá'ís observe the anniversary of the passing of Bahá'u'lláh, which occurred at Bahjí, near Acre, at 3:00 A.M. on May 29, 1892. The Ascension of Bahá'u'lláh was established as a holiday by 'Abdu'l-Bahá. It is commemorated by gatherings for prayers and readings from the Bahá'í scriptures, in particular the Tablet of Visitation. (The term "ascension" refers to the spirit, not the body). This solemn holiday is one of the days on which work is suspended and children are excused from school.

Race Unity Day
The second Sunday in June (Núr)

Race Unity Day was established in 1957 by the National Spiritual Assembly of the United States as a Special Event Day to focus attention on the problem of racial prejudice as the "most vital and challenging issue" facing America. Gatherings are held on this day to promote the oneness of humanity.

Martyrdom of the Báb
July 9 (Rahmat 16)

At about noon on July 9, 1850, the Báb was executed by a firing squad in the barracks square of Tabriz, Iran, by order of the civil and religious authorities. After his death, his followers concealed his body and eventually transported it to the Holy Land, where in 1909 it was interred in a sepulchre, the gold-domed Shrine of the

Báb, on Mount Carmel, which is now a place of Bahá'í pilgrimage. Bahá'ís commemorate the Martyrdom of the Báb by gathering together at about noon to hold a worship service including readings from the Bahá'í writings. It is a solemn holiday on which Bahá'í s do not work and children are excused from school.

Birth of the Báb
October 20 (Ilm 5)

On October 20 Bahá'ís commemorate the birth of Siyyid 'Alí-Muhammad, the Báb, the prophet-forerunner of the Bahá'í faith. In the Muslim lunar calendar, which was in effect at the time (since the Bahá'í era did not begin until 1260 A.H./1844 C.E.), his birthday occurred on Muharram 1, 1235 A.H. In that calendar, the birthdays of

the Báb and Bahá'u'lláh fell on consecutive days. Bahá'u'lláh refers to these holidays in the *Kitáb-i-Aqdas* as the "Festival of the Twin Birthdays" and specifies that if they occur during the month of fasting, the fast is to be suspended for these two days. Eventually the international Bahá'í governing council, the Universal House of Justice, will decide whether these days are to be celebrated on the lunar or the solar calendar. At present, in most places, the Birth of the Báb is observed on October 20. Bahá'ís do not work or go to school on this holiday.

Birth of Bahá'u'lláh
November 12 (Qudrat 9)

On November 12 Bahá'ís celebrate the birthday of Bahá'u'lláh, the founder of their faith. In the Muslim lunar calendar, which was in effect at the time (since the Bahá'í era did not begin until 1260 A.H./1844 C.E.), his birthday occurred on Muharram 2, 1233 A.H. In that calendar, the birthdays of Bahá'u'lláh and the Báb fell on consecutive days. Bahá'u'lláh refers to these holidays in the *Kitáb-i-Aqdas* as the "Festival of the Twin Birthdays" and specifies that if they occur during the month of fasting, the fast is to be suspended for these two days. Eventually the international Bahá'í governing council, the Universal House of Justice, will decide whether these

---

Table 11.3. Bahá'í Holiday Cycle

March

21 .... Festival of Naw-Rúz

April

21–May 2 ... Festival of Ridván

May

23 .... Declaration of the Báb
29 .... Ascension of Bahá'u'lláh

June

~ .... Race Unity Day

July

9 .... Martyrdom of the Báb

October

20 .... Birth of the Báb

November

12 .... Birth of Bahá'u'lláh
26 .... Day of the Covenant
28 .... Ascension of 'Abdu'l-Bahá

January

~ .... World Religion Day

February

26–Mar 1 .... Ayyám-i-Há

March

2–20 .... Period of the Fast

Table 11.4. Alphabetic List of Bahá'í Holidays

Holidays	Date(s)
Ascension of 'Abdu'l-Bahá	November 28
Ascension of Bahá'u'lláh	May 29
Ayyám-i-Há	February 26–March 1
Birth of Bahá'u'lláh	November 12
Birth of the Báb	October 20
Day of the Covenant	November 26
Declaration of the Báb	May 23
Martyrdom of the Báb	July 9
Naw-Rúz, Festival of	March 21
Period of the Fast	March 2–20
Race Unity Day	Second Sunday in June
Ridván, Festival of	April 21–May 2
World Religion Day	Third Sunday in January

days are to be celebrated on the lunar or the solar calendar. At present, in most places, the Birth of Bahá'u'lláh is observed on November 12. Bahá'ís do not work or go to school on this holiday.

Day of the Covenant
November 26 (Qawl 4)

On this date each year, Bahá'ís observe the appointment of Bahá'u'lláh's eldest son, 'Abdu'l-Bahá, as his successor and the Center of his Covenant. Because 'Abdu'l-Bahá's birthday falls on the day of the Declaration of the Báb (May 23), 'Abdu'l-Bahá specified that his own birthday should not be celebrated because the day should be devoted to the Báb's anniversary. However, in response to the request from believers to designate a day to observe in 'Abdu'l-Bahá's honor, he established the Day of the Covenant. It is not obligatory to refrain from work on this holiday.

Figure 11.2. Many Bahá'í people recognize a nine-pointed star as a symbol of their faith. The number nine occurs often in Bahá'í writings and is incorporated in many ways. For example, the Bahá'í community is governed by councils of nine members and there are nine holy days on which work is suspended and Bahá'í children are excused from school.

Ascension of 'Abdu'l-Bahá
November 28 (Qawl 6)

'Abdu'l-Bahá died on November 28, 1921, at about 1 a.m., in Haifa. He is buried in one of the chambers of the Shrine of the Báb on Mount Carmel This solemn occasion is commemorated annually by Bahá'ís who hold memorial gatherings at the time of his passing to read prayers including the Tablet of Visitation of 'Abdu'l-Bahá. It is not obligatory to refrain from work on this day. (The term "ascension" refers to the spirit, not the body.)

World Religion Day
The third Sunday in January (~Sultán)

In 1950, the National Spiritual Assembly of the Bahá'ís of the United States established this date as a Special Event Day to focus on the oneness of religion and the harmony of spiritual principles, and to emphasize the role of religion in achieving unity on a global level. Today World Religion Day is observed in many Bahá'í communities around the world and is an occasion for holding interfaith gatherings and prayer services drawing together people from many different faiths.

Ayyám-i-Há
February 26 through March 1 (Ayyám-i-Há)

In the *Kitáb-i-Aqdas*, Bahá'u'lláh established Ayyám-i-Há, the four intercalary days (five in leap years) that are inserted between the eighteenth and nineteenth months of the Bahá'í calendar. The period of Ayyám-i-Há is a time for giving praise to God, performing acts of service and charity to the poor and needy, gift giving, feasting, hospitality, and inner preparation for the Bahá'í fast which occurs during the nineteenth month.

The Fast
March 2-20 ('Alá' 1–19)

During the nineteenth month, the last month of the Bahá'í year, Bahá'ís from the ages of 15 to 70 observe a fast in which they do not eat or drink from sunrise to sunset. Although believers abstain from food and drink, the focus of the fast is on detachment from desires and on inner purification. People who must do heavy labor, as well as the elderly, the ill, travelers, and pregnant and nursing mothers, are exempted from the requirement to fast.

CHAPTER 12

Hinduism

Overview of Hinduism

What is Hinduism?

The word Hindu is derived from the Sanskrit term Sindhu (or Indus) which meant river. It referred to people living in the Indus valley in the Indian subcontinent. Many scholars regard Hinduism as the oldest living religion.

Hinduism has no founder, one universal reality (or god) known as Brahman, many gods and goddesses (sometimes referred to as devtas), and several scriptures. It is a religion of diversity within an established tradition founded on writings called the *Vedas*. It encompasses a multitude of sects who venerate selected gods or goddesses (or their consorts or children) in any one of their various or multiple manifestations. Although Hindu adherents practice their faith differently and venerate different gods (devtas), they share a similar view of reality and look back on a common history.

Some concepts that are part of the Hindu heritage include transmigration of the atman (a concept similar to that of the self, soul, or spirit) and karma. Transmigration of the atman, also called reincarnation, means that a person's atman goes through a succession of lives. Depending on the type of karma, or according to the form of Hinduism, previous lives may include animals and even plants. The cycle of rebirths, called samsara (also sometimes spelled samskara), continues without end until spiritual purity is achieved. Upon reaching this level of perfection, the person's atman is liberated from samsara and becomes one with Brahman, the ultimate universal reality. The term moksya (also sometimes spelled moksha) is used to describe the achievement of freedom from samsara.

The means by which perfection and liberation are achieved vary among different groups of Hindus but they focus on the elimination of karma. Karma is produced by a person's actions in life. Good actions lead to the accumulation of good karma; bad actions lead to the accumulation of bad karma. A person's karma determines several features of their next rebirth: what level of society they will be born into, how long their life will be, and what experiences they will encounter. Good and bad karma, however, both lead to rebirth. To become freed from karma, a Hindu must attain a level of detachment in which no karma is accumulated or follow a precise code of conduct that eliminates karma.

To eliminate karma, some Hindus practice yoga, a system of mental and physical disciplines in which a heightened state of consciousness is sought through attention to body posture, breath control, and focused mental concentration. Others may follow a path of devotion to one of many personal gods or goddesses. Some stress the importance of specific actions, deeds, or occupations. Other Hindus seek the attainment of spiritual knowledge learned from a teacher, called a guru. Many Hindus recognize four separate stages of life: during the first stage a youth begins to study under the guidance of a guru; the second stage involves duty to family and the community; during the third stage detachment is sought; and the fourth stage prepares for what lies beyond the current life.

From the concepts of karma and rebirth a belief in social stratification, called the caste system, developed. The caste system is a hierarchical organization that governs many things about a person's life including occupation and marriage partner. Hindu tradition teaches that castes were originally established according to profession, but later they came to represent stations in life into which one was born. The highest class (called the Brahmins) comprises priests, scholars, and professionals. The next level, the Ksatriyas consists of rulers and soldiers. The third level, the Vaishyas, are merchants and farmers. The lowest class, the Sudras, are peasants and servants.

Within these four major groups there exist approximately 3,000 subcasts.

The Relationship between the Gods (Devtas) and the Hindu People

The Hindu pantheon includes approximately 33 million gods. Some of these are held in higher esteem than others.

Over all the gods, Hindus believe in one absolute high god or universal concept. This is Brahman. Although he is above all the gods, he is not worshipped in popular ceremonies because he is detached from the day to day affairs of the people. Brahman is impersonal. Lesser gods and goddesses (devtas) serve him. Because these are more intimately involved in the affairs of people, they are venerated as gods.

The most honored god in Hinduism varies among the different Hindu sects. Three of the most popular are Vishnu, Shiva, and Sakti. Hindus may consider these three as different gods or as different expressions of god.

Vishnu is a good, benevolent god. Laksmi, the goddess of fortune, is his wife. He is known through his ten incarnations (called avataras). These are:

- Matsya, the Fish, who saved the first man from the flood

- Kurma, the Tortoise, upon whose back Mount Mandara rested when the ocean was churned so the gods could look for lost ambrosia

- Varaha, the Boar, who rescued the earth after a demon threw it into an ocean

- Narasimha, the Man-Lion, who killed the demon Hiranyakasipu

- Vamana, the Dwarf, who freed the earth, air, and sky from the dominion of demons

- Parashu Rama, Rama of the Axe

- Rama, King of Ayodhya, hero of the epic *Ramayana* who freed Sri Lanka by killing the demon Ravana

- Krishna, a mischievous but beloved manifestation, whose dialogue with Arjuna is presented in the *Bhagavad Gita*

- Buddha, the founder of Buddhism, the last avatara in history

- Kalkin, an awaited savior—an expected incarnation of the future who will bring judgement to the earth and restore the golden age

Of these, the two primary incarnations of Vishnu were as Rama and as Krishna. Some Hindus believe that Jesus of Nazareth and Muhammad were also incarnations of Vishnu. In this way they create a unification of religions.

Shiva represents destruction and regeneration, rebirth and renewal. He has a dual aspect of good and bad and is often accompanied by evil spirits. To his followers, he is loving. He is associated with storms and has authority over diseases and healing herbs. Shiva can often be recognized in artistic renditions of him by his blue neck. In the *Rig Veda* he is called Rudra. Other names by which he is known are Pashupati (or Pashupa; Protector of Cattle), Sambhu, and Sankara.

Sakti, the wife of Shiva, is a mother goddess (devi). She has both benevolent and horrifying aspects. Her forms are Durga (also known as Kali) and Parvati (also known as Uma). Durga is a harsh form that in the past was worshipped with blood sacrifices, both animal and human. Parvati is a mild form of the goddess, a beautiful, passionate lover and virtuous wife.

Other major Hindu gods include Brahma, Ganesa, Indra, Skanda, and Hanuman. Brahma is not the same as the universal Brahman. Brahma, however, is the creator god credited with fabricating the earth. Saraswati is his consort. She supervises the work of musicians, writers, and students. Ganesa, a son of Shiva, is a deity with an elephant head and human body who helps remove obstacles. According to legend, after Ganesa's head was turned to ashes, Shiva took the head of Indra's elephant to give to Ganesa. Indra is a warrior god credited with saving the world from the cosmic serpent. Skanda, another son of Shiva, is often portrayed with six heads. Hanuman, a monkey god, was Rama's helper. He is considered a guardian. In his honor, monkeys are protected in India.

Authorities and Sacred Writings

The Vedas

Hinduism has no priesthood or hierarchical structure similar to that seen in some other religions, such as Christianity. Hindus acknowledge the authority of a wide variety of writings but there is no single, uniform canon. The oldest of the Hindu writings are the *Vedas*. The word "veda" comes from the Sanskrit word for knowledge. The *Vedas*, which were compiled from ancient oral traditions, contain hymns, instructions, explanations, chants for sacrifices, magical formulas, and philosophy.

The *Rig Veda* is a collection of 1028 hymns to the Vedic gods and goddesses (devtas and devis). It dates from approximately 1500–1200 B.C.E. and is the oldest surviving literature for any of the world's living religions. The *Rig Veda* is also the oldest surviving literature in any of the Indo-European languages. Other Vedic works include the *Sama Veda* (hymns for chanting), the *Yajur Veda* (for sacrifices), and the *Atharva Veda* (incantations and sacrifices.)

Ritual and philosophy books based on the four *Vedas* are *Brahmanas* and *Aranyakas*. *Brahmanas* dates between 800–600 B.C.E. It provides a commentary on the *Vedas* and explains Vedic mythology. *Aranyakas* dates from approximately 600 B.C.E.

The *Upanisads* are also books in the Vedic tradition. They consist of doctrinal texts written between 800–300 B.C.E and include dialogues between a teacher and student or between sages. The discussions focus on ritual, commentary, and philosophy.

The Epics

Another set of sacred books include the *Great Epics* which illustrate Hindu faith in practice. The *Epics* include the *Ramayana* the *Mahabharata*, and the *Bhagavad Gita*.

The *Ramayana* (which means life of Rama) presents a story about Vishnu in his avatara of Prince Rama. The tale recounts his exploits and the rescue of his wife after she is taken captive by a demon, Ravana. The epic story contains seven books and comprises 24,000 verses. Its central focus is on human virtues.

The *Mahabharata* (which means War Poems of the Bharata) is a compilation of legends that present accounts of a civil war among the potential heirs to an ancient kingdom. It is the longest epic, comprising 18 books, called parvas, and totaling 100,000 verses. The central focus of the *Mahabharata* is on human virtues and vices.

The *Bhagavad Gita* (which means Song of God) is another book of the *Mahabharata* and is perhaps the most widely read of all the Hindu scriptures. It contains a sermon delivered by Krishna to warriors preparing for battle. The shortest of the three Hindu epics, it consists of 700 verses in 18 chapters. Important elements in the *Bhagavad Gita* include the worship of Krishna as an incarnation of Vishnu, a discussion of the nature of atman and Brahman, ways to achieve moksa (freedom from the cycle of rebirth), comparative philosophies, and the moral and religious duties of the different castes.

Law Codes, Puranas, and Tantras

Other sacred books include the *Law Codes* and the *Purnas*. The *Law Codes* offer societal regulations. The *Manyu-Smriti* (Laws of Manu) was developed around 100 B.C.E. It provides comprehensive laws governing things such as marriages, funerals, the duties of kings, and caste regulations. The *Puranas* are verses dating from 500–1000 C.E. that further develop classical Hindu mythology and provide genealogies for various gods and heros.

The *Tantras* comprise a set of writings dating from about the seventh century to the 14th century C.E. They focus on feminine power and include information about spiritual matters, disciplines, and rituals to harness sensual energies for the attainment of moksa.

History

The Aryan People

Modern Hinduism is based on the beliefs of people who established themselves in the Indus Valley (northwestern region of the Indian subcontinent) between 2500 and 1700 B.C.E. Called the Aryans, they were taller and of lighter skin than the native population. The word Aryan is derived from Sanskrit and it means "noble people." Most of the information available about the ancient Aryans comes from the Hindu sacred books.

The Caste System

The Aryans lived in semi-nomadic tribal groups, each with its own warrior chief called a rajah. The people were divided among three castes based on professions: priests, leaders and soldiers, and common people, a system similar to the feudal system of medieval Europe. A lower fourth class, called the Sudras, consisted of dark-skinned, non-Aryan, indigenous people.

The strictures of the caste system and abuses perpetrated by those of the higher castes led to discontent. Between 400–500 B.C.E. several scholars interpreted and simplified Hinduism (according to their view of Hinduism) and thus became distinct religions. Two of the most notable were founded by Gautama Buddha (Buddhism) and Mahavira (Jainism). Jainism never acquired a sufficient number of followers to pose a threat to traditional Hinduism, but Buddhism won many converts including the leader of the Indian empire, Chandragupta Maurya (c. 321–297 B.C.E.).

Rather than abandon the caste system, however, Hindu society enlarged it. Beginning around 300 B.C.E. the original divisions underwent a series of subdivisions based on occupational groups. The presence of numerous individual groups, called jatis, increased the segregation between people at all levels of society.

Societal Changes

Asoka, the last emperor of the Maurya dynasty died in 232 B.C.E. and the era that followed was marked by turbulence and conquest. By the end of the second century

B.C.E., the Indian empire had diminished in power and new kingdoms had gained prominence in the northern regions of the Indian subcontinent. During the uncertain times of the era, people returned to their ancient beliefs, revitalized their complex legal system, and empowered the Brahmin (priestly) caste.

The Gupta dynasty dates from approximately the fifth century C.E. It marked a time when both Buddhism and Hinduism flourished in India, but Hindu practices prevailed. The role of Hindu priests, under the emperor's patronage, was elevated. The practice of venerating a particular god or gods rose, primarily in the southern portion of the region and with particular emphasis on Vishnu and Shiva (alternate spellings are Visnu and Siva). The bhakti movement, which is marked by devotion to god, devtas, and saints, traces its beginnings to this era in southern India. Its spread into other regions occurred slowly, reaching northern India during the eleventh century.

Different Schools of Hinduism

During the following centuries, Brahminical forms of Hinduism rose in popularity. Elaborate temples were built and dedicated to the gods, particularly to Vishnu and Shiva. Worship of gods increased as literature helped spread knowledge of them. Different schools of Hinduism also began to differentiate themselves.

Sankara, born in 788 C.E.,was a philosopher, mystic, and poet. Some believed him to be an incarnation of Shiva. Sankara founded the Advaita Vedanta school of Hinduism and taught that the physical world was an illusion; the only true reality was Brahman. He also believed that the human soul and Brahman were merged into oneness when moksa was achieved. His views emphasized the unity of Brahman (the universal reality) and atman (the human soul).

Contrasted with Sankara's teachings are those of Ramanuja (1017–1137 C.E.). Ramanuja founded a school of Hinduism called Vishisht Advaita. He believed that the physical world was not an illusion and that a person's soul was not identical with Brahman. He promoted individual devotion as the proper way of worshipping.

Madhva (1197-1280) started the Dvaita school of Hinduism. He believed that Brahman and atman were different and remained separate even after a person achieved release from the cycle of rebirth.

Foreign Influences

Beginning with the 13th century, Hindu society came in more frequent contact with other cultures. The Muslim Moghul dynasty became established in the northwestern part of the Indian subcontinent. By the sixteenth century, contact with European culture, particularly Christianity, technology, and education, brought new ideas about social reforms.

British rule, established in 1757 in Calcutta brought further reforms to ancient practices including changes in child marriage laws (created in an effort to thwart Muslim invaders), the lessening of caste distinctions, and the abatement of some of the human misery associated with the lower casts and "outcastes."

Social and Religious Reforms

Ram Mohan Roy (1772–1833) was a social reformer who advocated an educational system and the abolishment of sati (the practice of burning a widow on her husband's funeral pyre which was instituted during the Muslim invasion to prevent the widow from becoming a slave or concubine of the Muslims). Roy also founded the Brahmo Samaj (Congregation of Brahman) which emphasized humanism and promoted the belief that faith should be founded on reason.

Another Hindu reformer of the nineteenth century, Ramakrishna (1836–1886) believed that god could be found through any religion and that all religions were merely different paths to the same ultimate reality.

Figure 12.1. Krishna is one of the most popular avataras of Vishnu.

One of the best known figures during the years before India's independence was Mahatma Gandhi (1869–1948). Born Mohandas Karamchand Gandhi, he was given the title Mahatma which means "great soul." Gandhi's religious focus was based on the *Bhagavad Gita* from which he developed the belief that the intention of life was for purposeful action. He advocated non-violence and non-cooperation with foreign rulers. He promoted the cause of the "untouchables" and called them "Harijan" (Children of God). Gandhi's vision and efforts helped create the Independent Republic of India in 1947. (Discrimination on the grounds of "untouchability" was outlawed in India in 1950.)

Gandhi was assassinated on January 30, 1948. Some Hindus believe he was an avatara (incarnation) of Vishnu.

Hinduism Today

The Hindu People

Although the largest number of Hindus live in India, significant numbers also live in Africa, Europe, Latin America, North America, and in the Pacific Islands. Population estimates vary widely from 400 million or 500 million to over one billion.

Hindu Worship

Temples and shrines are common throughout India. Typically they contain an image which is called a murti. For some Hindus the murtis are representative of concepts. For others, the murtis are actual gods. They are bathed, dressed, and carried in processions. Music and dances are provided for their entertainment. Festivals celebrate special events or reenact mythic legends.

In the temples, worship is typically not congregational (although in some places a form of congregational worship does exist). Priests, who are specialists in the performance of specific rituals, make offerings on behalf of the worshippers. Typical offerings are of flowers, food, or money which the worshipper gives to the priest to offer to the god. A token portion of the offering may be returned. Individual worshippers perform other rituals such as walking around the murti. Prayers and bowing may be performed. A mantra may be recited. Mantras are believed to represent a god in sound. The "om" syllable that is often chanted represents Brahman. Some temples are built in conjunction with a body of water (either natural or constructed) where worship often involves bathing.

The act of worship is called a puja. It can occur in a private home or in a temple. One of the most important aspects of Hinduism is individual worship which is conducted in private homes. Most houses devote either a room or a portion of a room as the family shrine which contains an image of the god the family venerates. Worship includes anointing the image or representation of the god, lighting incense, placing flowers, reciting sacred texts, and meditation.

Hindu Sects

Hindu sects are called sampradayas. Initiation into a sampradaya often involves wearing some kind of identifying mark, learning a mantra (sacred verbalization), following a particular guru, and applying devotion to a specific god or goddess (devta or devi). Some of the most popular sampradayas are Vaishnava (devotees of Vishnu), Saivite (devotees of Shiva), Rama Cults (devotees of Rama), and Krishna Cults (devotees of Krishna). The term "cult" used to describe these sects refers the shared culture of rites and beliefs among the devotees; it does not indicate an unorthodox position or a judgement that it is in any way unconventional or spurious.

Vaishnavas

Vaishnavas are devotees who honor Vishnu as the supreme god in the Hindu pantheon. Many Vishnu sampradayas appeared between the fifth and twelfth centuries C.E. and attracted people from the lower castes.

The Sri Vaishnavas, considered to be among the oldest of the Viashanava Sampradayas, claim that Vishnu and his wife, Laksmi, founded their sect which is marked for its personal worship of the god and goddess. Another Vaisnava sect, the Nimbarki Sampradayas hold a doctrinal position describing the similarities and differences between the human atman and the divine.

Saivites

Saivites are devotees of Shiva. The first Shiva sects appeared during the first and second centuries C.E. They focused on the manifestation of Shiva as Pashupati, (Protector of Cattle). During the following centuries other Shiva sects developed. Some worshipped the ambiguous deity by indulging in wine and performing ritual sexual intercourse. By the seventh century, the worship of Shiva had assumed a less controversial nature and included elements such as meditation and penance. Worship of the "linga," a symbolic representation of Shiva's phallus, continues to play an important role in honoring Shiva.

Rama Cults

Rama cults first appeared during the centuries of Muslim incursion into traditionally Hindu lands (beginning in the eighth century, but with its main push beginning in the eleventh century). Many Rama cults tended to elevate Rama to the position of supreme deity rather than merely as a manifestation of Vishnu.

Krishna Cults

Madhwaguariya Samparadayas, a subsect of Vaishnavas, honor Krishna and worship him through the recitation of his name. The Hare Krishna movement, well known in the United States, has its roots in Madhwaguariya Samparadaya.

Caitanya, a scholar from Bengal who was born during the 15th century, became a follower of Krishna. He assumed the name Krishna Caitanya, which means "he whose consciousness is Krishna." He sought moksa (liberation from the cycle of rebirth) through the adoration of Krishna and the constant repetition of his name. After several centuries and through generations of followers the movement became established in the United States in 1966 as the International Society for Krishna Consciousness (ISKCON). The sect attained popularity through its association with singer George Harrison of The Beatles.

Figure 12.2. Ganesa, a son of Shiva, is a deity with an elephant head and human body. He is honored as one who helps remove obstacles and is the god of prosperity, wisdom, learning, prudence, success, and power. According to legend, after Ganesa's head was turned to ashes, Shiva took the head of Indra's elephant to give to Ganesa. Ganesa has four hands, one of which is held out in blessing, and is accompanied by his mount, the rat.

⊡ ⊡ ⊡

The Hindu Calendars

Many Methods of Measuring Time

There is no single Hindu calendar. Various Hindu sects define the month differently. The varying definitions of the lunar month caused a division in the Hindu religion. The boundaries of the contending groups seem to fall along geographical lines. In northern India, the lunar month begins with the full or waning moon, while Hindus in the south of India measure the month from the new or waxing moon.

The confusion caused by the use of two methods of measuring the month has resulted in the celebration of holidays on different dates by the Vishnu and Shiva sects of Hinduism. This happens because the waxing half of the month (from the new to the full moon) falls in the same month in both regions, but the waning half falls in different months. Therefore any festivals that take place in the waning half of the month can fall up to thirty days apart in the north and south.

Common Components

Despite regional differences, the Hindu calendars share some common components. To make the two systems as compatible as possible, Hindus number the two halves of the months separately. The months are divided into two periods of approximately fifteen days called pakshyas, or "fortnights," in which the days are numbered from one to fifteen. Each of the days in the fortnight is consecrated to a deity in the Hindu pantheon.

The calendars contain both solar and lunar aspects. The solar component is based on a sidereal year (not the tropical year used in the West). The sidereal year marks a complete orbit of the earth around the sun by observing the precise positioning of stars; the tropical year is based on the progression of the sun from equinox to equinox.

By relying on sidereal calculations, the Hindu calendar months perfectly correspond to the signs of the zodiac. Month names among the Hindu calendars vary according to the dialects of the regions, but the names of the astrological signs are consistant throughout the country.

The solar months are based on the celestial movement of the sun and stars along the ecliptic. A new month begins when the moon enters a new celestial sign. Each month and sign has an arc of 30° along the ecliptic, but the months vary in actual length between 27 and 32 days.

Table 12.1. Days of the Hindu Fortnight

Day	Name	Consecrated to
1	Pratipada	Brahma
2	Dvitiya	Vidhatr
3	Tritiya	Vishnu
4	Chaturthi	Ganesa or Yama
5	Pañcami	Moon
6	Shashti	Karttikeya
7	Saptimi	Indra
8	Ashtami	Sakti or the Vasus
9	Navimi	Sakti or the Serpent
10	Dashami	Dharma
11	Ekadashi	Vishnu or Rudra
12	Dvadashi	Sun
13	Trayodashi	Shiva
14	Chaturdashi	Ganesa or Yama
15	Purnima (full moon)	Devas
	Amavasaya (new moon)	Devas

A Lunar Component

Like many other religious calendars, the Hindu calendars also have a lunar component. The Hindu lunar calendar consists of twelve 30-day months with one month intercalated about every three years. Whenever two new moons occur within one solar month (months based on the zodiacal signs), the intercalary lunar month is added. The normal month in which the two new moons occurred has "nija" added to the end of its name. The intercalated month is named for the normal month but "adhika" is added to the end. The normal months of the Hindu lunar calendar are named for the solar month in which they begin.

Hindu Eras

In addition to marking the passing of lunar and solar months and years, Hindu mythology describes long eras called yugas. The current era, called the Kali Yuga, began in 3102 B.C.E. It is considered to be the most decadent of the Yugas.

There are four Yugas which begin with perfection and go through successive stages of deterioration. After the fourth yuga, the Kali Yuga, time is interrupted while the cosmos is recreated and begins again. A cycle of four Yugas, called a Maha Yuga, lasts 4,320,000 years. According to some Hindu belief systems, 1,000 Maha Yugas comprises one day in the life of the creator, Bramha.

Table 12.2. The Hindu Year

Season	Means	Months in Season	Gregorian Equivalents
Vasanta	Spring	Vaisakha / Jyestha	April–May / May–June
Grisma	Summer	Asadha / Sravana	June–July / July–August
Varsa	Rains	Bhadrapada / Asvina	August–September / September–October
Sarad	Autumn	Kartika / Margasira	October–November / November–December
Hemanta	Winter	Pausa / Magha	December–January / January–February
Sisira	Dews	Phalguna / Caitra	February–March / March–April

Table 12.3. The Length of the Yugas

Kruga (Sat) Yuga
1,728,000 years

Treta Yuga
1,296,000 years

Dwapar Yuga
864,000 years

Kali Yuga
432,000 years

Table 12.4. The Hindu Holiday Cycle

Date(s) .... Holiday

Vaisakha—Waxing (April–May)

1	Vaisakhi
1–10 days	Pooram
3	Akshya Tritiya
3	Parasurama Jayanti
3–24	Chandan Yatra
5 or 10	Sankaracarya Jayanti
9	Janaki Navami
14	Narsimha Jayanti

Vaisakha—Waning

New Moon	Mata Tirtha Snan

Jyestha—Waxing (May–June)

6	Sithinakha (Cake Festival)
8	Jyestha Ashtami
10	Ganga Dussehra
11	Nirjala Ekadashi
Full Moon	Snan Yatra
Full Moon	Buddha Jayanti

Jyestha—Waning

13	Vata Savitri

Asadha—Waxing (June-July)

2	Ratha Yatra
11	Hari-Shayani Ekadashi
15	Guru Purnima

Sravana—Waxing (July–August)

1–15 waning	Sravani Mela
3	Hariyali Teej
5	Nag Pañcami
7	Tulsidas Jayanti
11	Putrada Ekadashi
15	Narieli Purnima
15	Raksa Bandhana
15	Jhulan Latra

Sravana—Waning

11	Kamada Ekadashi
14	Ghanta Karna

Bhadrapada—Waxing (August–September)

~	Tirupati Festival
~	Gokarna Aunsi
~	Onam
3	Haritalika Teej
4	Ganesa Caturthi
5	Rishi Pañcami
14	Anant Chaturdashi

Bhadrapada—Waning

6	Halashashti
8	Janmashtami
8	Radha Ashtami
14–Asvina	Indra Jatra

Asvina—Waxing (September–October)

~	Laksmi Puja
1–10	Durga Puja
10	Dussehra
15	Sharad Purnima
15	Kojagara
15	Valmiki Jayanti

Asvina—Waning

1–14	Pitra Visarjana Amavasya

Kartika—Waxing (October–November)

~	Kartika Snan
~	Skanda Shashti
1	Govardhan Puja
2	Bhaiya Duj
6	Surya Shashti
11	Devathani Ekadashi
15	Kartika Purnima
15	Puskar Mela

Kartika—Waning

4	Karwachauth
5 days	Tihar
13	Dhan Teras
14	Narak Chaturdashi
15	Dewali

Table 12.4. The Hindu Holiday Cycle, continued.

Date(s) .... Holiday

Margasirsa—Waxing (November–December)

11	Gita Jayanti
11	Vaikuntha Ekadashi
15	Dattatreya Jayanti

Margasirsa—Waning

8	Bhairava Ashtami
11	Vaitarani

Pausa—Waning (December–January)

8	Rukmini Ashtami
12	Swarupa Dwadashi

Magha—Waxing (January-February)

~	Makar Sankranti
3 days	Pongal
3–12 days	Thaipusam (Thai Poosam)
5	Vasant Pañcami
8	Bhishma Ashtami
15	Magha Purnima
15	Minakshi Float Festival

Magha—Waning

4	Sakata Chauth
15	Mauni Amavasya

Phalguna—Waxing (February–March)

11	Amalaka Ekadashi
14	Holi
15	Dol Purnima

Phalguna—Waning

14	Mahashivarati
~	Gangaur

Caitra—Waxing (March–April)

1	Gudi Parva
1	Ugadi Parva
1–9	Vasanta Navaratra
7	Caitra Parb
8	Sitala Ashtami
8	Ashokashtami
9	Ramanavami
10 days	Panguni Uttiram
10 days	Caitra Purnima
15	Hanuman Jayanti

◼ ◼ ◼

Hindu Holidays

Semi-monthly

Ekadashi
Eleventh day of each waxing and waning moon

Ekadashi is the Sanskrit word for "eleventh." In all, 24 Ekadashi (eleventh-day) fasts are observed during the course of a year, but some are of relatively greater importance. (See also Amalaka Ekadashi, Devathani Ekadashi, Hari-Shayani Ekadashi, Kamada Ekadashi, Nirjala Ekadashi, Putrada Ekadashi, and Vaikuntha Ekadashi.) Each Ekadashi is held in honor of a different Hindu legend and has specific religious duties associated with it.

On all Ekadashi fasts, rice eating is prohibited because a demon is said to dwell in rice grains on the eleventh day. According to Hindu legend, a demon was born of the sweat that fell from Brahma's head. Brahma sent it to inhabit the rice grains eaten by people on Ekadashi and to become worms in their stomach.

Every 210 Days

Galungan
Every 210 days

Galungan is a Bali Hindu festival commemorating the Balinese New Year. The ten-day event is celebrated throughout the Indonesian island province of Bali every 210 days. (The Balinese festival calendar follows a 210-day cycle.) The Balinese religion mixes traditional Balinese thought with Hindu practices and beliefs.

During the festival, Balinese believe that the gods come to earth. Small thrones are set up in temples as symbolic seats for the gods to occupy. Activities include rituals; cock-fights (a combination of sport and gambling); offerings of foods, fruit, and flowers made to the temple by the women; and card games, music, and dancing.

Annual Holidays

Vaisakha (April-May)

Vaisakhi (The Hindu New Year; Baisakhi)
First day of the waxing half of Vaisakha

The Vaisakhi festival marks the beginning of the Hindu New Year. It derives its name from the Hindu month of Vaisakha. On this day early in the morning people bathe in sacred rivers such as the Ganges, pools, or wells, then dress in festive clothes, and visit shrines and other places of worship to offer prayers. It is also customary to exchange gifts.

This northern Indian festival is also observed in Punjab with special enthusiasm and fervor. The people of Punjab perform special dances, sing folk songs accompanied by rolling drums, exchange greetings, and enjoy feasts and merrymaking.

Vaisakhi marks the beginning of a month-long bathing tradition held during Vaisakha. The pilgrimage to the only shrine of Badrinath, in the Himalayas, also commences from this day. Many Hindus believe that charities done during Vaisakha are especially meritorious; thus, people generously give money, grains, and other items to the poor and the Brahmans. Observers of Baisakhi also fast, chant the glories of the Lord, and practice other pious activities.

Pooram
During Vaisakha

One of the most spectacular festivals of southern India, this is a 10-day celebration in Trichur, Kerala, dedicated to Shiva. People fast on the first day of the festival and the rest of the days are devoted to fairs, processions, and fireworks displays. The highlight of the pageantry comes when an image of the deity Vadakkunathan (Shiva) is taken from the temple and carried in a procession of richly caparisoned elephants. The Brahmans riding them hold colorful ceremonial umbrellas and whisks of yak hair and peacock feathers. The elephants lumber through the pagoda-shaped gateway of the Vadakkunathan temple and into the village while drummers beat and pipers trill. Fireworks light the skies until dawn.

Akshya Tritiya
Third day of the waxing half of Vaisakha

Observance of Akshya Tritiya consists of both fasting and festivities. "Akshya" literally means undecaying or exempt from decay. The piety and devotions done on this day are believed to never decay and to secure permanency.

On Akshya Tritiya, a fast is observed and Vishnu, along with his consort Laksmi, is worshipped with holy Ganges water, tulsi leaves (basil), incense, flowers, lamps, and new clothes. Brahmans are given food in charity. Bathing in the Ganges or other waters is considered a sign of devotion.

Also on this day, the passes of Sri Badrinarayan in the Himalayas open after the long, snowy winter. Devotees worship Badri with food offerings in their homes and temples.

Akshya Tritiya is also believed to be the first day of Satya-Yuga, the "golden age."

Parasurama Jayanti
Third day of the waxing half of Vaisakha

According to Hindu mythology, Parasurama (Rama with an Ax) destroyed the evil Ksatriya kings and princes 21 times, including the thousand-armed warrior, Arjuna. Parasurama became manifest in the world in the beginning of the Treta Yuga (the second age). Parasurama Jayanti (Parasurama's birthday) is observed with fasting, austerities, and prayer. It is also a day to worship Lord Vishnu, of whom Parasurama is believed to be the sixth incarnation. To Hindus, Parasurama represents filial obedience, austerity, power, and brahmanic ideals.

Chandan Yatra
Beginning on the third day of the waxing half of Vaisakha and lasting twenty-one days

On each of this festival's twenty-one days, images of Hindu deities are taken out in procession to nearby water tanks, where they are rowed in decorated boats to the accompaniment of music and dance. This summer festival is celebrated at Puri, Orissa, Bhubaneshwar, Baripada, and Balanga.

Sankaracarya Jayanti
Fifth day (southern India) or tenth day (northern India) of the waxing half of Vaisakha

This birth anniversary celebration honors Adi Sankaracarya, one of the greatest saint-philosophers of India who symbolizes India's cultural and emotional integrity and unity. Sankaracarya, believed to be an incarnation of Shiva, revived Brahmanism and took Vedanta philosophy to new heights. Historians believe he lived between 788 and 820 C.E., but Hindu tradition places him in 200 B.C.E.

Sankaracarya was a native of Malabar in the Indian state of Kerala. He worked many miracles and died at the age of 32. He is the reputed author of many original philosophical works and commentaries on the Upanisads, Vedanta Sutras, and *Bhagavad Gita*. He has been called the "Vedanta Guru," and his philosophy is equally accessible to both the learned and the layman. He composed many popular hymns, and urged people to devote themselves to God in any of his forms and incarnations. The Hindu custom is that Sankaracarya Jayanti is a fit occasion to study his works, to fast, to meditate, and to rededicate oneself to the service of the Lord.

Janaki Navami
Ninth day of the waxing half month of Vaisakha

Sita, heroine of the Hindu epic poem *Ramayana* whose name means "furrow," is supposed to have sprung on this day from a furrow plowed by King Janaka in a field. Janaka took her up and raised her as his own child. She is also called A-Yonija, "not born from the womb." She was actually the goddess Laksmi in human form, incarnated in the world. Many Hindus believe that she reflects the idealized Indian woman as an embodiment of self-sacrifice, purity, tenderness, fidelity, conjugal affection, and other virtues. Some believe that Sita appeared in Janaka's field on the eighth day of the waning half of Phalguna (February-March), and they fast on that day.

Narsimha Jayanti
Fourteenth day of the waxing half of Vaisakha

According to Hindu mythology, this is the day on which Vishnu appeared as the Narsimha, or Man-Lion, to free the world from the demon king, Hiranyakasipu. Hiranyakasipu had forbidden prayer and worship to Hari (Vishnu), and substituted worship and prayer to himself. He was very much annoyed to discover his own son Prahlada was an ardent devotee of Vishnu, and tortured Prahlada to convert him, but the child remained unmoved in his devotion to the god. The king tried to kill Prahlada by trampling him under elephants, by throwing him down precipices, and by other means, but without success.

One day Hiranyakasipu was so enraged that he rushed to kill Prahlada with his own sword, asking the child, "Where is your savior?" Instantly Vishnu stepped out of a nearby pillar in the form of Narsimha, half lion, half man, and tore Hiranyakasipu to pieces.

On this day, people fast, meditate on Narsimha, and seek his grace to have devotion like that of Prahlada. To Hindus, Narsimha symbolizes the omnipresence of god, his deep concern and love for the devotees, and the victory of good over evil. People often demonstrate the sincerity of their devotion by giving cows, grains, gold, robes, and other goods to the poor and the Brahmans as acts of charity on this day.

Mata Tirtha Snan (Mother's Day)
New Moon

One of the most widely celebrated festivals in Nepal, Mata Tirtha Snan (or Mother's Day) falls in the first month, Vaisakha (also spelled Baisakh; April/May), of the Nepali Year. It is also called Mata Tirtha Aunsi because it falls on the night of the new moon night.

Jyestha (May-June)

Sithinakha (Cake Festival)
Sixth day of the waxing half of Jyestha

On this day Hindus honor the birth of the god Kumara (also known as Skanda) the god of war. Kumara was the first-born son of Shiva. He has six heads because he was nursed by the Karttikas, six women who as stars comprise the Pleiades. For this reason he is also called *Karttikeya* meaning "son of Karttikas." The six heads also represent the six senses (including extrasensory perception). He also has a large following under the name *Subrahmanya*, meaning "dear to the Brahmanas."

Most Hindus observe this day with a ritual purification bath followed by processions to the temples to honor Kumara. It is also considered a good opportunity to clean out wells and tanks. According to tradition, the snake gods are off worshipping on this day, so it is safe to enter their habitats.

In Nepal, eight different kinds of cakes, made from eight different grains, are offered to Kumara on his birthday, and for this reason Sithinakha is sometimes referred to as the Cake Festival. Lotus-shaped windmills are often set on rooftops at this time, to symbolize the end of bad times and the onset of holier days.

Jyestha Ashtami
Eighth day of waxing half of Jyestha

Jyestha Ashtami is celebrated by the people of Khir Bhawani in Kashmir in honor of their patron goddess, also named Khir Bhawani. People come from the adjoining hill areas to assemble at the shrine, offer prayers and worship at the foot of the goddess, and sing hymns and songs in praise of Bhawani. Khir (rice boiled in milk) is prepared as a food offering. The beautiful marble shrine overlooks a pool formed by spring waters, which change color from rosy red, turquoise green, lemon pale, sky blue, milky white, or pure white. It is located 25 kilometers from Srinagar, and 5 kilometers from Ganderbal and is visited by hundreds of Kashmiri Hindus daily.

Ganga Dussehra
Tenth day of the waxing half of Jyestha

According to Hindu mythology, the Ganges River in India originally flowed only in heaven. In the form of a goddess, Ganga, the river was brought down to earth by King Bhagiratha in order to purify the ashes of his ancestors, 60,000 of whom had been burned under a curse from the great sage Kapila. The river came down reluctantly, breaking her fall on the head of Shiva so that she wouldn't shatter the Earth. By the time she reached the Bay of Bengal, she had touched the ashes of the 60,000 princes and fertilized the entire region.

Ganga Dussehra commemorates the Ganges's descent to earth in Hashta Nakhsatra. Literally the word Dussehra means "that which takes away ten sins." People get up early in the morning and go to the Ganges to bathe in holy waters. When the Ganges is inaccessible, they bathe in some nearby tank, pool, river, or the sea, chanting

"Har Har Gange! Har Har Gange!" thus invoking the Ganges and offering her prayers and worship. At places where the Ganges flows, such as Rishikesh, Hardwar, Garh Mukteshwar, Prayag, and Varanasi, its banks are overcrowded with worshipers. Many Hindus believe that a bath in the Ganges on this day is of great religious merit and washes away all sins.

The very name of the Ganges is sacred to Hindus. Samples of its waters are kept within sealed pots in Hindu homes where, some believe, the water remains unpolluted even if it is kept for many years. Holy Ganges water thus kept is used on sacred days to sanctify places and is given to a dying person with tulsi leaves (basil) to facilitate the soul's peaceful separation from the body.

Nirjala Ekadashi
Eleventh day of the waxing half of Jyestha

Nirjala Ekadashi is a complete fast; even water is not taken. Because the month of Jyestha is very hot and the day is long, observing a fast without water is an extreme act of pious austerity. Both men and women observe the fast and offer puja (worship) to Vishnu to ensure happiness, prosperity, and forgiveness of transgressions and sins. Panchamrit (also spelled Pancamrata) is prepared by mixing together milk, ghee (clarified butter), curds, honey, and sugar. It is then offered to the image of Vishnu, which has been draped in rich clothing and jewels, with a fan placed beside it. Hindus meditate on Vishnu as the Lord of the Universe and worship the deity with flowers, lamps, water, and incense. In the evening worshippers venerate Vishnu while holding durva grass in their hands. The night is spent in meditation and prayer.

Some Hindus believe that faithful observance of the fast and other rituals on this day ensures happiness, salvation, longevity and prosperity. Clothes, grains, umbrellas, fans, and pitchers filled with water are given in charity to the Brahmans according to the ability of the giver.

Snan Yatra
Full-moon day of Jyestha

On this occasion, a grand bathing festival is held in Orissa. Images of the Lords Jagannatha, Balabhadra, Subhadra, and Sudarshan are brought in a grand procession to the bathing platform for their ceremonial baths. With the recitation of mantras from the Vedas, 108 pots of consecrated waters are poured upon the deities. Then, the deities are ceremonially attired before they retire into seclusion for fifteen days. It is an occasion of great rejoicing and merrymaking.

Buddha Jayanti (Baishak Purnima)
Full-moon day of Jyestha

Many Hindus honor Buddha as an incarnation of Vishnu. This day is dedicated to Lord Buddha's birthday, enlightment, and Nirvana. Many ceremonies are held especially in Lumbini, Buddha's birthplace.

Vata Savitri
Thirteenth day of the waning half of Jyestha

The fast of Vata Savitri is generally observed on this date, but at some places it is observed on the full moon of Jyestha. It is meant only for married women, who keep this vow for the sake of the longevity and well-being of their husbands.

Asadha (June-July)

Ratha Yatra
Second day of the waxing half of Asadha

Ratha Yatra is a festival honoring Jagannatha, Lord of the Universe, a form of Krishna. It is celebrated throughout India but the biggest festival commemorating it is held at the Jagnnatha Temple in Puri in Orissa, one of the largest Hindu temples in India. During the festival, wooden images of Jagannatha, Balabhadra (his brother), and Subhadra (his sister) are taken in procession in three huge chariots or carts that look like temples and are called *raths*. The main chariot carrying Jagnnath measures 45 feet high, 35 feet square, and is supported by 16 wheels, seven feet in diameter. At the termination of the ceremony the chariot is disassembled and its materials used to manufacture religious relics.

The images go from the Jagannatha Temple to be bathed at Gundicha Mandir, a temple about a mile away; the gods are installed there for a week before being brought back to the Jagannatha Temple. This is a popular festival because all castes are considered equal, and everyone has to eat the food prepared by low caste men at the shrine.

The festival of Puri is famous worldwide, and thousands of devotees participate in this spectacular event. The imposing twelfth-century Jagannatha shrine, 60 kilometers from Bhubaneshwar, is situated on Nilachala mountain. It is one of the four great Hindu holy places (the others being Badrinath, Dwarka, and Rameshwaram). For a devout Hindu, a pilgrimage to Jagannatha Puri is a lifelong ambition. Many Hindus believe that a three-day sojourn to Puri will free a pilgrim from future births and deaths.

Hari-Shayani Ekadashi
Eleventh day of the waxing half of Asadha

Hari-Shayani Ekadashi is the day when Lord Hari (Vishnu) retires to sleep on the bed of Shesha Nag in the

Ksirsagar. According to a popular Hindu religious belief, Hari slumbers during the four months of the rainy season, which begins on the 11th of the waxing fortnight of Asadha. The rainy season is known as "Chaturmas," and during this period such activities as marriage and the thread ceremony are prohibited.

Guru Purnima (Vyasa Purnima; Asadha Purnima)
Full-moon day of Asadha

The purnima, or full moon day, or Asadha is set apart for the veneration and worship of the Guru. In the Hindu hierarchy or respect, the gods come first and teachers come second. In ancient days students received their education in Ashrams and Gurukuls. The students would worship their teachers on this day, pay their fee, and give them presents according to their means and capacity. Devotees and disciples fast and worship their gurus to seek their blessings.

The day is also known as Vyasa Purnima because Rishi Vyasa was a great guru. Vyasa (or Veda-Vyasa), the son of Rishi Parashar and Satyavati, is also known as Krishna Dwaipayna. He is said to have compiled the four Vedas, the *Mahabharata*, and the 18 Puranas.

Sravana (July-August)

Sravani Mela
During Sravana

Festivities associated with this festival include a grand fair, held in Bihar at Deoghar. Throughout the month, devotees pick up water from the holy Ganges at Sultanganj, carry it on their shoulders to Deoghar, and offer it on linga (phallic symbol of Shiva).

Hariyali Teej (Tij; Green Teej; Teej; Hari Tritiya)
Third day of the waxing half of Sravana

On this day women of all ages make merry. Daughters and daughters-in-law are given gifts. Swings are hung in the houses and gardens, and the women enjoy them throughout the day. The preparation of sweets is also a highlight in each home. Hariyali Teej is celebrated on a large scale in Uttar Pradesh and especially in Braj Mandal.

Nag Pañcami (Bhratri Panchami)
Fifth day of the waxing half of Sravana

Nag Pañcami is a Hindu festival celebrated throughout India and Nepal. It is dedicated to the sacred serpent,

Figure 12.3. During Ratha Yatra huge, temple-shaped chariots carry images of Jagannatha, Balabhadra, and Subhadra in a procession.

Ananta, on whose coils Hindus believe Vishnu rested while he was creating the universe. According to Hindu belief, snakes can bring wealth and rain, and unhappy ones can cause a home to collapse. Cobras and snakes are worshipped with milk, sweets, flowers, lamps, and sometimes sacrifices. Images of snake deities painted on walls or made from silver, stone, or wood are bathed with milk and water, then they are worshipped with the reciting of mantras. Worshippers observe a fast on this day, but the Brahmans are fed. In return for their piety, people are assured protection against snake bites in the future. One particular custom associated with Nag Pañcami is that digging in the earth is prohibited, because serpents live underground, (which is believed to be the netherworld) and digging may hurt or annoy them.

Because snakes are also worn by Shiva, hundreds of snakes are released at the Indian Shiva temples in Ujjain, where Shiva lived after destroying a demon, and in Varanasi, considered the religious capital of the Hindu faith. In Jodhpur, India, huge cloth Nagas, or "cobras," are displayed.

Nag Pañcami is also observed as Bhratri Panchami, and some Hindu women fast and worship snakes to guard their brothers against snake-bites.

Tulsidas Jayanti
Seventh day of the waxing half of Sravana

According to Hindu belief, the saintly poet Tulsidas was contemporary with Akbar the Great. He was born to Brahman parents but was orphaned. St. Narharidas, after receiving instructions from God in a dream, raised and educated Tulsidas. Tulsidas married and started living the life of a householder, but chance words of his wife awakened his ardent devotion to God, and he became a sanyasi and began to live at Varanasi. There he wrote his well-known *Ramacharitra Manas* and a dozen other books. His masterpiece *Ramayana* was written in the language of the common people for their benefit and is revered by devout Hindus. His example of sanctity and the magic of his writings have had a far-reaching impact for the spiritual uplifting of the masses—comparable to the teachings of hundreds of gurus. He and his works are so greatly revered that tradition regards him as Valmiki reborn.

Many Hindus believe that Tulsidas died on the same day that he was born; on that day, a fast is kept, and works of charity are done. The *Ramayana* is read and recited, Brahmans are fed, and Lord Rama, along with his consort Sita and devotee Hanuman, is worshipped with great religious fervor. In literary and social circles, discussions, lectures, seminars, and symposiums are organized on Tulsidas's teachings, life, and works.

Putrada Ekadashi
Eleventh day of the waxing half of Sravana

Putrada Ekadashi is observed by couples without children in order to produce a son. Some Hindus believe that fasting and piety on this day will ensure conception of a boy while also destroying the sins of the aspirants. Like other Ekadashis, it is dedicated to Vishnu.

A fast is observed, Vishnu is worshipped and meditated upon, and the Brahmans (priests learned in the Vedas and sacred religious lore) are fed and given robes and money. At night the aspirants sleep in the room where Vishnu was worshipped. In addition, they are encouraged to observe Kamada Ekadashi in the waning half of the month of Sravana. Kamada Ekadashi is known as the wish-fulfilling Ekadashi.

Narieli Purnima
Full moon day of Sravana

Narieli Purnima is celebrated in order to appease the fury of the sea god Varuna. Marking the end of the monsoon season, it is primarily observed by sailors, fishermen, and others living in the coastal areas of south India, who offer coconuts to the sea on this occasion. If the sea happens to be far away, this ritual may be carried out at a nearby water source.

Raksa Bandhana (Brother and Sister Day; Avani Avittam)
Full moon day of Sravana

The word "Raksa" means protection, and as a ritual of protection, Hindu women and girls tie a thread bracelet around their brothers' wrists to guard them against evil during the ensuing year. Sisters also feed their brothers with sweets, dried fruits, and other delicacies. The brothers give their sisters gifts of money, clothes, and other valuable things and promise to protect them in return.

Priests and Brahmans also tie threads around the wrists of their patrons to receive gifts. They recite a mantra or sacred formula to charge the thread with the power of protection.

In southern India, the day is called Avani Avittam. A holy thread is charged and a libation of water is offered to the ancestors and rishis. The new thread is worshipped with saffron and turmeric paste before being worn, and the old one is discarded in the water. The day is specially significant for a Brahman boy who has recently been invested with a holy thread to remind him of its religious significance. Vedas are also read and recited on this day.

Jhulan Latra
Full moon day of Sravana

In Orissa, a festival of Lord Jagannatha is celebrated. In a lavishly decorated swing, Lord Jagannatha is asked to relax to the accompaniment of music and dance. The celebration is particularly observed in the Jagannatha temple at Puri and other shrines for a week preceding the Sravana Purnima (full moon). The full-moon day of the month marks the festival's culmination.

Kamada Ekadashi
Eleventh day of the waning half of Sravana

The Kamada Ekadashi is known as the wish-fulfilling Ekadashi. Like other Ekadashis, it is dedicated to Vishnu.

Ghanta Karna (Festival of Boys)
Fourteenth day of waning half of Sravana

This day commemorates the death of Ghanta Karna, or "Bell Ears," a monster who wore jingling bells in his ears so that he'd never have to hear the name of Vishnu. In Hindu mythology he caused death and destruction wherever he went, until a god in the form of a frog persuaded him to leap into a well, after which the people clubbed him to death and dragged his body to the river to be cremated.

Also known as the Festival of Boys because young boys play a primary role in the celebration of Ghanta Karna's death, this day is observed in Nepal by erecting effigies at various crossroads and making passers-by pay a toll. After they've spent the day collecting tolls and preparing for the Ghanta Karna funeral, the boys tie up the effigy with a rope and throw it in the river. Sometimes the effigy is set on fire before being thrown in the water. Young girls hang tiny dolls on the effigy of Ghanta Karna to protect themselves from the monster.

Children also sell iron rings on this day and use the money to buy candy. It is believed that those who have iron nails in the lintels of their homes or are wearing an iron ring will be protected from evil spirits in the coming year.

Bhadrapada (August-September)

Tirupati Festival
Ten days during Bhadrapada

A grand festival, held at Tirupati, the seat of Lord Venkteshwara, a manifestation of Lord Vishnu. The festival lasts for ten days and during it devotees congregate to seek Lord Venkteshwara's blessings for material and spiritual gains.

The shrine at Tirupati, one of the richest temples in the world, is situated on the seven Tirumala hills, which correspond to the seven hoods of the snake god Adishesha, who forms the bed of Vishnu in the cosmic ocean. Because of these seven picturesque hills, Venkteshwara is also known as the "Lord of the Seven Hills."

Tirupati is considered an essential pilgrimage center for every devout Hindu. It is tradition that devotees, whether men or women, shave their hair off as a votive offering for a vow fulfilled. Parents bring their very young children to perform their first tonsure (the act of clipping the hair) at the feet of the Lord.

Gokarna Aunsi (Father's Day)
During the dark fortnight of Bhadrapada

The most auspicious day to honor one's father is Gokarna Aunsi. It occurs during the dark fortnight of Bhadrapada (in August or in early September). It is also known as Kuse Aunsi.

Onam
Four days in the Malyalan month of Chingam (August-September)

According to legend, Bali was permitted by Vamana (the fifth incarnation of Vishnu) to visit his lost kingdom and subjects once a year; this visit is celebrated by his devotees on Onam. To welcome their ancient king Bali, the people of the Indian state of Kerala tidy up their houses and environs, decorate the houses with flowers and leaves, and arrange grand feasts and many types of amusements. The spectacular snake-boat races mark the crowning glory of these games.

A clay image of Vamana is worshipped on this day in temples and houses, and youngsters are given gifts by the elders. On the second day of the festivity, Bali is believed to visit his kingdom in Kerala. Bali is also called Mahabali, and his capital was Mahabalipuram, near Madras.

Haritalika Teej
Third day of the waxing half of Bhadrapada

Observed by Hindu women, the Haritalika fast honors the goddess Parvati and her consort Shiva, and their statues are worshipped ritually. Parvati, the daughter of Himalaya and Mina, desirous of having Sankara (Shiva) as her husband, performed extraordinary feats of magic and thereby married him. From that day onward married women have worshipped the divine couple, keeping a strict fast to ensure their conjugal happiness and prosperity. Unmarried girls fast to gain suitable husbands of their choice. Brahmans receive charity, unmarried girls are fed, and aspirant women tell the story of

Haritalika among themselves and break their fast in the evening. The next morning the sun is worshipped and offered water.

Ganesa Caturthi (Ganesha Chaturthi; Ganesha Chata)
Fourth day of the waxing half of Bhadrapada

This lively Hindu festival honors Ganesa, the elephant-headed god of prosperity, wisdom, learning, prudence, success, and power. He is also known as Vighnesha, or remover of obstacles. Ganesa is propitiated at the start of every activity, whether it be a journey, marriage, initiation, house construction, writing of a book or even a letter.

Hindus generally believe that Ganesa is a great scribe and learned in religious lore and scripture. It was Ganesa who, at the dictation of the seer Vyasa, wrote the *Mahabharata*. He is also the Lord of Ganas, Shiva's hosts. Ganesa bears a single tusk; holds in his four hands a shell, a discus, a goad, and a lotus; and is always accompanied by his mount, the rat. Ganesa is a great lover of sweets and fruits.

On Ganesa Caturthi, the images of Ganesa are worshipped with sweet balls, water, new clothes, incense, flowers, scent, betel leaf, and naivaidyas (food offerings). His mantra is repeated as he is meditated upon and worshipped. Food offerings are later distributed as charity. Brahmans are fed and given gifts. Clay figures of Ganesa are worshipped during this festival and then immersed in sea, river, pool, or some other water. Around Bombay, a spectacular week-long festival ends with the immersion of Ganesa's sculpted likeness in the waters at Chowpatty Beach to ensure well-being on both land and sea. In Maharashtra this festival is observed with great religious fervor, pomp, and gaiety, and Ganesa statues are taken out in grand processions before immersion in the sea. In Nepal the day, called Ganesha Chata, celebrates a bitter dispute between Ganesa and the moon goddess. Therefore, the Nepalese try to stay inside on this night and close out the moonlight.

Rishi Pañcami
Fifth day of the waxing half of Bhadrapada

The Sapta Rishis (seven seers, or mental sons of Brahma) are honored on this day with piety and acts of devotion. The seven are: Bhrigu, Pulastya, Kratu, Pulaha, Marichi, Atri, and Vasistha. Although the day is primarily observed by women, a man can also participate for the well-being and happiness of his wife.

An earthen or copper pitcher filled with water is sanctified with cow dung and an eight-petalled lotus is made on it. After the pitcher is installed on an altar, the seven seers are worshipped with betel leaf, flowers, camphor, and a lamp. Devi Arundhati, the wife of Rishi Vasishtha (a model of conjugal excellence) is also worshipped along with the seven sages.

Anant Chaturdashi
Fourteenth day of the waxing half of Bhadrapada

On this day, Hindus worship and meditate upon Vishnu. A fast is observed and fruits, sweets, and flowers are offered to Vishnu in worship. An unrefined thread colored in turmeric paste and having 14 knots is also tied on the upper right arm while meditating. Hindus believe that this ensures protection against evil and brings prosperity and happiness.

According to Hindu belief, the Pandava princes in exile observed this fast on the advice of Krishna to regain their lost kingdom and prosperity. As a result, they defeated the Kauravas and regained their kingdom, wealth, reputation, and happiness.

Halashashti (Balarama Shashti)
Sixth day of the waning half of Bhadrapada

Halashashti is a festival commemorating the birth of Krishna's older brother, Balarama. Balarama's weapon was a plough, so it is also the day on which the farmers and peasants of India worship the hala, or plough. They apply powdered rice and turmeric to the plough's iron blade and decorate it with flowers. A small piece of ground is sanctified and plastered with cow dung. In it, a small pool of water is created. Branches of plum, fig, and other fruit trees are then planted.

In observance of the day, some Hindu women fast to ensure happiness, prosperity, and longevity of their sons. Only buffalo milk and curds are eaten. Unmarried girls observe the Chandra Shashti on this day, and their fast is terminated by the rising of the moon.

Janmashtami (Krishnastami; Krishna's Birthday)
Eighth day of the waning half of Bhadrapada

Janmashtami, one of the most important Hindu festivals, commemorates the birth of Krishna, the eighth avatara (or incarnation) of Vishnu. The birthday of Krishna, the direct manifestation of Vishnu himself, is celebrated in all parts of India with great enthusiasm. Krishna's life is described in great detail in the Puranas. He is known as "the supreme universal truth, the supreme dwelling, the eternal person, divine prior to the gods, unborn, omnipresent."

The Janmashtami celebrations start with an early morning bath in sacred waters and prayers. The climax occurs at midnight with the rising of the moon, which signifies Krishna's divine birth. A strict fast is kept and broken only after the birth of Krishna at midnight. The piety and fast observed on this day ensure the birth of many good sons, and salvation after death.

Temples and homes are decorated, and scenes depicting Krishna's birth and his childhood pranks are staged with both animate and inanimate models. The Krishna child's image is put into a richly decorated swing and rocked with tender care all day. At night, after the birth, a small image of toddling Krishna is bathed in the Charnamrita, amidst the chanting of hymns, blaring of the conches, ringing of bells, and joyous shouting of "Victory to Krishna!"

In Mathura, where Krishna was born, there are performances of Krishna Lila, folk dramas depicting scenes from Krishna's life. In the state of Tamil Nadu, oiled poles called "ureyadi" are set up, a pot of money is tied to the top, and boys dressed as Krishna try to shinny up the pole and win the prize while spectators squirt water at them. In Maharashtra, where the festival is known as Govinda, pots containing money and curds and butter are suspended high over streets. Boys form human pyramids climbing on each others' shoulders to try to break the pot. These climbing games reflect stories of Krishna, who as a boy loved milk and butter so much they had to be kept out of his reach.

In Nepal, a religious fast is observed on Krishnastami, and Krishna's temple at Lalitpur is visited by pilgrims. People parade in a procession around the town and display pictures of Krishna.

Radha Ashtami
Eighth day of the waning half of Bhadrapada

Radha Ashtami celebrates the birth of Radha, an incarnation of Laksmi. Some Hindus believe that Radha, the favorite mistress and consort of Krishna during his Vrindavana days, is a symbol of the human soul drawn to the ineffable god Krishna, or the pure divine love to which the fickle lover returns.

On this day, after early morning baths, the image of Radha is bathed in Panchamrita, and then richly adorned and ornamented before being offered food and worship. A fast is kept on this day and charity distributed.

Indra Jatra
Beginning the end of Bhadrapada until early Asvina

Indra Jatra is the most important festival of Nepal, combining homage to a god with an appearance by a living goddess. The festival, lasting for eight days, is a time to honor the recently deceased and to pay homage to the

Hindu god Indra and his mother Dagini so they will bless the coming harvests. It also commemorates the day in 1768, during an Indra Jatra ("jatra" means "festival"), that Prithwi Narayan Shah (1730–1775) conquered the Katmandu Valley and unified Nepal.

Legend says that Indra, the god of rain and ruler of heaven, once visited the Katmandu Valley in human form to pick flowers for his mother. The people caught him stealing flowers. Dagini, the mother, came down and promised to spread dew over the crops and to take those who had died in the past year back to heaven with her. The people then released Indra and they have celebrated the occasion ever since.

Before the ceremonies start, a 50-foot tree is cut, sanctified, and dragged to the Hanuman Dhoka Palace in Katmandu. It represents Shiva's linga, the phallic symbol of his creative powers and shows he has come to the valley. As the pole is erected, bands play and cannons boom. Images of Indra, usually as a captive, are displayed, and sacrifices of goats and roosters are offered.

Three gold chariots are assembled in Basantpur Square, outside the home of the Kumari, the living goddess and vestal virgin. The Kumari is a young girl who was selected to be a goddess when she was about three years old, and she will be replaced by another girl when she begins to menstruate. Two boys playing the roles of the gods Ganesa and Bhairab emerge from the Kumari's house to be attendants to the goddess. Then the goddess herself appears in public for the first time, walking on a carpet so her feet don't touch the ground. The crowds go wild. The king bows to the Kumari, and the procession moves off to the palace where it stops in front of the 12-foot mask of the Bhairab. This is the fearsome form of Shiva in Nepal and is displayed only at this time. The Kumari greets the image and rice beer pours from its mouth. Those who catch a drop of the beer are blessed, but even more are those who catch one of the tiny live fish in the beer.

In the following days the procession moves from place to place around Katmandu. Masked dancers perform every night at the Hanuman Dhoka square dramatizing each of the earthly incarnations of Vishnu. On the final day of the festival the great pole is carried to the river.

Asvina (September-October)

Laksmi Puja
During Asvina

The annual festival in honor of the Hindu goddess Laksmi is held in the autumn, when Hindus of all castes ask for her blessings. Lights shine from every house, and no one sleeps during the celebrations.

Laksmi is traditionally associated with wealth, prosperity, and good luck. In later Hindu literature, she appears as the dutiful wife of the god Vishnu and is typically portrayed massaging his feet while he rests on the cosmic serpent, Shesa. She remains a popular Hindu goddess in India, where she is worshipped especially by merchants, who ask her to grant them wealth and success.

Durga Puja (Festival of Victory)
During the waxing half of Asvina

This Hindu festival of the Divine Mother is a ten-day holiday in India honoring the ten-armed Durga, wife of Shiva. Also known as the Festival of Victory, Durga Puja honors Durga's conquest of the demon Mashishasura.

On the first lunar day of the waxing half of Asvina, an earthen pitcher, filled with water and its mouth covered with green leaves and an earthen lid, is installed with an invocation of Ganesa, the god of learning and wisdom. A clarified butter lamp (ghee lamp) is always kept burning before the installed pitcher during the celebration. Durga is then invoked and worshipped with ceremonial rites. Daily readings of the *Durgasaptasati, Devi Bhagvat Purana,* and *Devi Mahatmya* sections of the *Markandeya Purana* are part of the celebrations as well. Unmarried girls below the age of ten are also worshipped and given gifts during these nine days. The aspirants sleep on the ground and keep a strict fast all these days. On the final day of the festival, people wear young barley sprouts in their hair and visit older relatives to seek a blessing.

In Bengal, Durga Puja is celebrated with great excitement and festivity. Huge puja (worship) pavilions with ten-armed Durga figures are constructed for this purpose. Durga, the beautiful but fierce goddess, rides her lion, killing the demon Mahisasura. She holds in her hands the gods' special weapons: Vishnu's discus, Shiva's trident, Varuna's conch shell, Agni's flaming dart, Vayu's bow, Surya's quiver, Indra's thunderbolt, Kubera's club, and a garland of snakes from Shesha. During the celebrations music, dance, drama, and poetry are performed. The images of the goddess Durga are taken on the final day in triumphal processions to the river, where they are ceremonially immersed.

Dussehra (Dashara; Vijay Dashami; Dasain)
Tenth day of the waxing half of Asvina

This Hindu festival celebrates Rama's victory after a ten-day struggle against Ravana (king of the demons) as told in the epic story of the *Ramayana*. Rama is worshipped, prayed to, and meditated upon to obtain his blessings and favor. In the past, kings often marched their forces against their enemies on this day.

During the ten days of the celebration, the battle is reenacted in puppet shows and in traditional plays. In addition, elaborate and joyous processions depicting various scenes of the *Ramayana* in the form of tableaus take place through bazaars and main streets. On the last day of the festival, huge mannequins representing Ravana, his brother Kumbhakrna, and his son Meghnatha are stuffed with brilliant fireworks, raised at various open grounds, and set afire. This climactic event marks the termination of the festival.

Sharad Purnima
Full moon day of Asvina

The Hindu moon god, Hari, is honored on this day. Hari is also the lord of herbs, seeds, Brahmans, waters, and Naksatras (or Constellations). Some Hindus believe that on Sharad Purnima, amrit (an elixir) is showered on the earth by moonbeams.

A custom associated with Sharad Purnima is the collection of amrit. Khir, milk thickened with rice and mixed with sugar, is prepared in the temples and homes, and offered to Hari amidst the ringing of bells and chanting of hymns. The mixture is kept in the moonshine all night so that it may absorb the amrit falling from the moon. At night the moon god is worshipped and offered food. The next morning the khir is given to the devotees.

Kojagara
Full moon day of Asvina

The word "Kojagara" is a combination of two terms, "Kah" and "jagara", which means "who is awake?" It is an exclamation of the goddess Laksmi, who descends to the earth this night, and blesses with wealth and prosperity all those who are awake. Hence, the night is spent in festivity and various games of amusement to honor the goddess. It is a harvest festival and is celebrated throughout India. Laksmi is worshipped and a night vigil is observed.

Valmiki Jayanti
Full-moon day of Asvina

This festival celebrates the birthday of the Ai Kavi (the "first Poet") Valmiki, whom Hindus believe to be the author of the Sanskrit *Ramayana*. A contemporary of Rama, the hero of the *Ramayana*, Valmiki himself is represented as taking part in some of the scenes he relates. He received the banished Sita into his hermitage and educated her twin sons Kusha and Lava. The invention of the "Shloka" (epic meter) is attributed to Valmiki.

Valmiki received his name because when immersed in meditation he allowed himself to be overrun with ants like an anthill. Members of many disadvantaged Indian classes claim they are descended from Valmiki. On his birthday he is worshipped and prayed to, and his portraits are taken out in festive processions through the main bazaars and streets.

Pitra Visarjana Amavasya (Pitra Paksha)
During the waning half of Asvina

This fourteen-day ceremony is a time for honoring ancestors by making special offerings of food and water, especially khir (rice boiled in milk) to deceased relatives by their surviving family members. These sacrifices, called Sraddha, symbolically supply the dead with strengthening nutriment after the previous funeral ceremonies have endowed the ethereal bodies. One Hindu belief is that until Sraddha has been performed, the deceased relative is a restless, wandering ghost and has no real body. Only after the Sraddha does he attain a position among the Pitris, or Divine Fathers, in their blissful abode called Pitri-Loka.

Brahmans (priests, members of the highest Hindu caste) are often invited to partake of these special foods in the belief that they will ensure that the offerings reach the souls of departed family members. According to custom, a Sraddha is most desirable and efficacious when done by a son, so the eldest son or senior member of the family typically performs the rituals associated with this festival. On the last day of the fortnight, called Amavasya (the new moon), oblations are offered to all ancestors whose day of death is unknown.

Kartika (October-November)

Kartika Snan
During Kartika

Among the 12 months of the year, some are regarded as especially holy and sacred, and as such they are most suitable for acts of piety. These are Vaisakha (April-May), Kartika (October-November), and Magha (January-February).

Throughout the month of Kartika, the early morning bath in a sacred river, stream, pond, or at a well is considered highly meritorious. On the sacred rivers like the Ganges and Yamuna, a month-long bathing festival is held. Some people set up tents along the river banks for this purpose, and at the termination of the festival return to their distant homes. During the month, aspirants observe strict continence, have regular early morning baths in the sacred streams, take a single simple meal every day, and spend their time in prayer, meditation, and other acts of piety and devotion.

Hindu women in villages and towns get up early in the morning and visit the sacred streams in groups, singing hymns, and after their baths visit the nearby temples. They fast and hang lamps in small baskets from the bamboo tops of their homes or on the river banks. These sky lamps are kept burning through Kartika to light the path of departed souls across the sky.

Tulsi leaves offered to Vishnu in Kartika (October-November) are said to please him more than the gift of a thousand cows. The Tulsi plant is sacred and cultivated specially in homes and temples. It is considered the wife of Vishnu and shown according respect. It is offered daily puja (worship) by Hindu women in the evening with lamps. Tulsi leaf is put in the mouth of a dying person along with Ganges water to facilitate an easy departure. Hindus believe that watering, cultivating, and worship of the Tulsi plant ensures happiness. When its leaves are put into any water, it becomes as holy as Ganges water.

Since Tulsi is Vishnupriya (beloved of Vishnu), their marriage is celebrated on the 11th day of the waxing half of the month of Kartika (October-November). On this day the image of Vishnu is richly decorated and then carried to the place where the Tulsi plant is grown, and the marriage ritually solemnized. Fasting is also observed on this day.

Skanda Shashti
During the Tamil month of Tulam (October-November)

Skanda, the second son of Shiva, is also known as Karttikeya or Subramanya. According to Hindu mythology, Shiva cast his seed into fire, and it was afterwards received by the Ganges, which "gave birth" to him. The boy was fostered by Krittika (Pleiades) and has six heads. He was born for the purpose of destroying Taraka, a demon whose austerities had made him a formidable opponent to the gods. The festivities of Skanda Shashti celebrate Taraka's defeat.

In south India there are six holy places associated with Skanda's life and work. At these places Skanda Shashti is celebrated with great fervor, and thousands of devotees congregate at each temple to seek the lord's blessings. Hymns are sung, psalms chanted, people fed, and scenes from his life dramatized. The festivity begins six days before the Shashti. Lord Subramanya is worshipped during these days, and devotees make pilgrimages to different Subramanya shrines. A common Hindu belief is that the devotion observed on this day ensures success, prosperity, peace, and happiness.

Govardhan Puja
First day of the waxing half of Kartika

Govardhan Puja is celebrated in northern India on the day following Dewali. The day is associated with an event of Krishna's life where he lifted the Govardhan Mountain (in Vrindavana) on his little finger for seven days to protect the cows and people of Vrindavana against the deluge of rain sent by the enraged Indra, god of the heavens and rains. People by the thousands from all over India visit, worship, and circumambulate Mount Govardhan on this day. Those who cannot come to Vrindavana worship at home with great devotion and give gifts to Brahmans. Cows and bulls are also decorated and worshipped.

Bhaiya Duj (Yama Dvitiya)
Second day of the waxing half of Kartika

Celebration of Bhaiya Duj honors the affection between brothers and sisters. Married women invite their brothers to their homes, apply tilaks (colorful paste) on the men's foreheads, tie a colored thread round their right wrists, pray for their prosperity and longevity, and then feed them sweets and other delicacies. In return the women receive valuable gifts. Unmarried girls do so at their parent's homes.

Bhaiya Duj is also called Yama Dvitiya in commemoration of the affection between Yama and his sister Yami. Sisters observe a strict fast and pray to Yama for their brother's longevity, good health, and happiness. Yama's sister, Yami (also known as Yamuna) is also worshipped.

Surya Shashti
Sixth day of the waxing half of Kartika

Observance of Surya Shashti includes a continual three-day fast for married Hindu women with children. Women participating in the fast abstain from taking even water, yet they worship the sun with offerings of food and water and keep a night vigil.

The next day the aspirant women bathe before sunrise, worship the rising sun, and break their fast. Brahmans are also fed and given gifts on this day. Hindu women believe that the fast and piety observed on this day ensure the good health, longevity, and happiness of their children and husbands.

Devathani Ekadashi
Eleventh day of the waxing half of Kartika

Devathani Ekadashi is a rural festival observed with much jollity in the countryside. It celebrates the waking of Vishnu. Hindus believe that Vishnu's eventually triumphant battle with the great demon Shankhasura was so exhausting that he and the other deities went to sleep for a period of four months. Each year, Vishnu slumbers from the 11th day of the waxing half of Ashadha (June-July) till the tenth day of the waxing half of Kartika (October-November), then awakes on the 11th day.

During the months of sleep, ceremonies such as marriages or the thread ceremony are not observed.

On Devathani Ekadashi Hindu women fast, worship Vishnu, and sing hymns in praise of various gods and goddesses around a fire. New products from the fields, including sugarcane and waternuts, may be eaten for the first time. From this day onward marriages and other ceremonies can be held.

Kartika Purnima
Full moon day of Kartika

Hindus celebrate Kartika Purnima in honor of the day when Vishnu incarnated himself in a fish form called the Matsya Avatara. The reason he appeared as a fish was to save Vavaswata, the seventh Manu and the progenitor of the human race, from destruction by a deluge. Charities done and piety observed on this day are believed to earn high religious merit. Bathing in the Ganges, or in other holy water, is considered to be of special religious significance. People fast, practice charities, and meditate on the gods.

It is also believed that Sankara killed the demon Tripurasura on this day, for which he is also called Tripurari. Shiva is worshipped on this occasion and giving a bull (Shiva's mount) as a gift to a Brahman is thought to be of great religious significance. Big cattle fairs are also held at various places.

Puskar Mela
Full moon day of Kartika

A camel fair and one of the best known of the Hindu religious fairs (melas) is held annually at Puskar, the place where it is said a lotus flower slipped out of Lord Brahma's hands. Water sprang up where the petals fell and created the holy waters of Puskar Lake. A temple to Brahma on the shore of the lake is one of the few temples in India dedicated to Brahma. Puskar is in the state of Rajasthan, a vast desert area dotted with oases and populated with wild black camels.

Karwachauth
Fourth day of the waning half of Kartika

Karwachauth is observed by married Hindu women in order to ensure prosperity, sound health, and their husband's longevity. Married women keep a strict fast and do not take even a drop of water. They get up early in the morning, perform their baths, and wear new and festive clothes.

Shiva, Parvati, and their son Karttikeya are worshipped with ten Karuwas (the small earthen pots with spouts) filled with sweets. The Karuwas are given to daughters and sisters along with gifts. At night, when the moon appears, the women break their fast after offering water to the moon. The story of Karwachauth is told and heard among the women. Sometimes a Brahman priest tells this story and receives gifts in return. Married women receive costly gifts from their husbands, brothers, and parents on this occasion. They touch the feet of their mother-in-law and other elderly women of the family and seek their blessings.

Tihar
During the waning half of Kartika

A five-day Hindu festival in Nepal that honors different animals on successive days. The third day of the festival is the most important day because the goddess Laksmi visits every home that is suitably lit for her. It is known throughout India as Dewali (see below).

On the first day of the festival, offerings of rice are made to crows, thought to be sent by Yama, the god of death, as his "messengers of death." The second day honors dogs, since in the afterworld dogs will guide departed souls across the river of the dead. Dogs are fed special food and adorned with flowers. Cows are honored on the morning of the third day; they, too, receive garlands and often their horns are painted gold and silver.

The fourth day is a day for honoring oxen and bullocks, and it also marks the start of the new year for the Newari people of the Katmandu Valley. On the fifth day, known as Bhai Tika, brothers and sisters meet and place tikas (dots of red sandalwood paste, considered emblems of good luck) on each other's foreheads. The brothers give their sisters gifts, and the sisters give sweets and delicacies to their brothers and pray to Yama for their brothers' long life. This custom celebrates the legendary occasion when a girl pleaded so eloquently with Yama to spare her young brother from an early death that he relented, and the boy lived.

Dhan Teras (Dhanvantri Trayodashi)
Thirteenth day of the waning half of Kartika

Two days prior to Dewali, Dhan Teras, or Dhanvantri Trayodashi, is observed with great mirth and rejoicing. Dhanvantri, the physician of the gods, who appeared at the churning of the ocean, is worshipped on this day, especially by physicians. He is the father of Indian medicine, and Ayurveda is attributed to him. He is also called Sudhapani, because he appeared from the ocean carrying nectar in his hands.

People rise at dawn, bathe, don new robes, and fast. In the evening, an earthen lamp is lit before the door of every house and the fast broken. It is considered an auspicious day to purchase new utensils.

Narak Chaturdashi
Fourteenth day of the waning half of Kartika

The day after Dhan Teras is celebrated as Narak Chaturdashi. It is dedicated to Yama, the god of Naraka or Hell. Bathing at dawn on this day is considered of great religious merit; in fact, some texts assert that Hindus believe those who bathe on this day after sunrise have their religious merit destroyed. Therefore, the devout rise early in the morning to bathe.

After the bath, libations are offered to Yama three times to please and appease him. The hope of those who sacrifice is that he may spare them the tortures of death. A fast is observed and in the evening lamps are offered to Yama. Some Hindus believe that piety observed on this day in honor of Yama liberates them from the possible tortures of hell.

Dewali (Divali; Deepavali; Festival of Lights)
Fifteenth day of the waning half of Kartika

Dewali, or the Festival of Lights, is an important and popular festival which marks the New Year and is celebrated throughout India. Hindus believe that this great festival of lights symbolizes the human urge to move toward the light of truth from the darkness of ignorance and unhappiness. The climax of the five-day festival falls on the last day of the waning half of Kartika.

The customs observed during Dewali are associated with several legends. One myth says that on this day Laksmi, the goddess of wealth and good fortune, roams about and visits the houses of people. Therefore people clean their homes and businesses, decorating them lavishly as they prepare to welcome the goddess. It also commemorates the triumph of Rama over Ravana, the ruler of Sri Lanka who had kidnapped Rama's wife. Also on this day, Krishna is said to have killed the demon of Narkusura.

A few days before the festival, houses are whitewashed and cleaned. The courtyards, the gates, and the place of worship are decorated with flowers and intricate colored paperwork. The theme of illumination serves as one of the festival's primary features, and at night people place earthen lamps and candles on the edges of roofs and windows and along rivers and driveways. According to custom, these lights help the goddess Laksmi find her way to houses to distribute her gifts of prosperity. The word "dewali," from which the festival derives its name, means "a row or cluster of lights."

Dewali is celebrated with gift exchanges, fireworks, and festive (typically vegetarian) meals. Sweets are prepared and exchanged, and people ask forgiveness of one another for any wrongs committed. In the evening, Laksmi is worshipped.

Margasirsa (November-December)

Gita Jayanti
Eleventh day of the waxing half of Margasirsa

Gita Jayanti honors the birthday of the Bhagavad Gita, a Sanskrit poem relating a dialogue between Krishna and Arjuna found in the Hindu epic *Mahabharata*. Some texts assert that on this day Krishna taught Arjuna the sacred lore of the *Gita* on the battlefield of Kurukshetra, and thus made available to the whole human race the Song Celestial. The day is celebrated by reading and reciting passages from the *Gita* and by holding discussions on its philosophical aspects. It is also a day on which Hindus fast, worship Krishna, and resolve to put more effort into their study of the *Gita*.

The *Gita* has been a great source of strength, inspiration, and wisdom to Hindus through the centuries. Many Hindus believe that the *Gita*, as a voice of the Supreme, is not merely scripture, but a great song of universal spiritual uplifting, always to be studied and pondered, for it illumines the path to perfection and purity, which can be followed even while doing one's worldly duties. It urges all to perform actions while remaining united with God at heart.

Vaikuntha Ekadashi
Eleventh day of the waxing half and the eleventh day of the waning half of Margasirsa

Vaikuntha Ekadashi is celebrated in southern India. Devotees observe a fast, keep vigil the whole night, and have meditation sessions. A gateway in the temple is thrown open on this day for aspirants to pass through, signifying their entrance into heaven or vaikuntha.

Dattatreya Jayanti
Full-moon day of Margasirsa

Dattatreya Jayanti, observed all over India, is a celebration in commemoration of Dattatreya's birth. Dattatreya, son of Rishi Atri and Anusuya, is identified with Brahma, Vishnu, and Shiva, for it is believed that portions of these deities were incarnated in him.

One legend explains that Anusuya was an exceptionally devoted and virtuous wife. The wives of Brahma, Vishnu, and Shiva decided to test her virtue by sending their husbands, disguised as beggars, to ask her to give them alms while in the nude. Anusuya avoided the trap by transforming them into babies and suckling them. When her husband returned from his morning bath and discovered what had occurred, he turned the babies into one child with three heads and six hands. The wives begged for their husbands' return, and when Anusuya restored them to their original forms, Anusuya, Rishi

Atri, and their son Dattatreya were blessed. Dattatreya had three sons, Soma, Datta, and Durvasa, to whom a portion of the divine essence was also transmitted.

On Dattatreya Jayanti people rise early in the morning and bathe in sacred streams. They fast and spend the day in meditation, prayer, and worship. They meditate on the life of Dattatreya and read sacred works attributed to him, which include *Avadhuta Gita* and *Jivanmukta Gita*. The image of Dattatreya is worshipped with flowers, lamps, incense, and camphor, and the aspirants resolve to follow in Dattatreya's footsteps.

Bhairava Ashtami
Eighth day of the waning half of Margasirsa

Bhairava is a manifestation of Shiva: a terrifying character worshipped to obtain success, prosperity, the removal of obstacles, and recovery from illness. One of the Bhairava's characteristics is that he punishes sinners with a danda (staff or rod); thus, he is also called Dandapani. Another of Bhairava's names, Swaswa, comes from the legend that he rides a dog. "Swaswa" means "He whose horse is a dog."

On Bhairava Ashtami, people worship Bhairava and his mount with sweets and flowers. The dogs are fed milk, sweets, and other such delicacies. At night, aspirants keep vigil and spend the time telling stories of Bhairavanath. Dead ancestors are offered oblations and libations.

Vaitarani
Eleventh day of the waning half of Margashirsha

Aspirants observe a fast and other prescribed rituals. In the evening a black cow is worshipped. She is bathed in fragrant water, sandal paste is applied on her horns, and food is offered to her. Brahmans are also given gifts of food, clothes, and a cow made of either gold or silver.

A cow is worshipped and offered food on this day because the river Vaitarani (the Hindu Styx) can only be crossed with the aid of a cow. The river, said to be filled with all kinds of filth, blood, and moral offenses must be crossed by departed souls before the infernal regions can be entered. Many Hindus believe that a cow given to Brahmans transports the dead over the river. Thus, cows are given in charity to Brahmans when there is a death in the community.

Pausa (December-January)

Rukmini Ashtami
Eighth day of the waning half of Pausa

Vaishnavite Hindus believe that Rukmini was born on this day. Rukmini was Lord Krishna's principal wife and queen. She bore him a son, Pradyumna. According to the

Harivansha Purana, she was sought in marriage by Krishna, with whom she fell in love, but her brother Rukmin had betrothed her to Sisupala, king of Chedi. On her wedding day, as she was going to the temple, Krishna saw her, took her by the hand, and carried her away in his chariot. They were pursued by Sisupala and Rukmin, but Krishna defeated them, took her safely to Dwarka, and married her.

On Rukmini Ashtami a strict fast is observed by both married and unmarried women, and married women are honored. Rukmini, Krishna, and Pradyumna are worshipped. A Brahman priest is also fed and given dan-dakshina on this day. Middle-class Hindus believe that observance of this fast ensures conjugal happiness and prosperity, and also enlists the help of Rukmini in finding good husbands for unmarried girls.

Swarupa Dwadashi
Twelfth day of the waning half of Pausa

The vow of Swarupa Dwadashi is observed by women desiring physical beauty, happiness, and healthy children. On the preceding day (the Ekadashi, which is the eleventh day), aspirant women ritually tell stories relating to Lord Vishnu. On Dwadashi they keep a strict fast, place an image of Vishnu in a vessel full of sesame, and worship it. Afterward, oblations are offered in the fire, Brahmans are fed and given charity, and the fast is broken.

Magha (January-February)

Makar Sankranti (Magh Sankranti; Uttarayana Skranti)
During the Hindu month of Magha; commences upon the sun's entrance into Capricorn on or about January 14

This three-day Hindu festival, generally falls around January 14 according to the Gregorian calendar. It is celebrated as Pongal in the south (see below), but in the north it is observed as Makar Sankranti or Uttarayana Sankranti. The beginning of the period, when the sun travels northward, is considered highly favorable for activities.

On this day Hindus bathe in the Ganges and other holy streams. At Ganga Sagar, where the Ganges enters the sea, a grand fair and festival is held. Devotees in large numbers reach Sagar Island in boats, and bathe there.

Makar Sankranti is a very significant day. The first batch of corn from the new harvest is cooked and offered to the Sun and other deities. The poor are fed and given clothes and money. In the morning, people offer libations to their dead ancestors and visit temples.

In Assam this day is called Magha Bihu or Bhogali Bihu, the festival of feasts. Bonfires are lit, and the round of feasts and fun continues for about a week.

In Nepal the celebration of the sun's movement back toward the Northern Hemisphere is called Magh Skranti. The Nepalese people visit holy bathing spots during their festival. Some actually bathe in the shallow water, but the weather is usually chilly and most are content to splash water on their hands and faces and sprinkle it on their heads. People also spend the day sitting in the sun and massage each other with mustard oil, which is also used by mothers to bless their children. Foods traditionally served on this day include *khichari*, a mixture of rice and lentils; sesame seeds; sweet potatoes; spinach; and home-made wine and beer. Traditional gifts for the priests are a bundle of wood and a clay fire pot.

Pongal
During Magha; mid-January

Pongal is a three-day festival in honor of the sun, earth, and the cow. The celebration takes place in southern India on Sankranti and marks the beginning of the sun's northern course. This occasion for rejoicing and merry-making takes place when the sun passes to Capricorn from Sagittarius.

The first day is Bhogi-Pongal, the Pongal of joy. On this day, people exchange visits, sweets, and presents, and enjoy a leisurely day. The second day is dedicated to the sun. As part of the traditional celebration, people rise early in the morning, and the woman of the house puts rice to boil in milk, which makes a sweet treat. As soon as the rice begins to simmer, the family shouts together, "Pongal! Pongal!" ("It boils!"). The sweet rice is then offered to Surya, the sun god, and a portion of it is given to the cows. The family then enjoys the treat as well. On this day of the festival, people often greet one another with the phrase "Has it boiled?" to which the response is "Yes, it is boiled."

The third day, Mattu Pongal, is the Pongal of the cows. Cows and oxen are worshipped and proudly paraded around the village. Their horns are painted in various colors, and garlands of leaves and flowers are hung around their necks. On this day the cows are allowed to graze anywhere they like, without any restraint.

Thaipusam (Thai Poosam)
Three to 12 days in Magha

Thaipusam marks the birthday and victory of the Hindu god Subrahmaniam (known as Lord Murugar) over the demons. It is a time of penance and consecration to the god, usually involving self-mortification in a test of mind over pain. The dramatic festival is celebrated in India,

Malaysia, Sri Lanka, Singapore, South Africa, Mauritius, and elsewhere.

In Malaysia, the festival is a public holiday in the states of Perak, Penang, and Selangor. In Georgetown, Penang, a statue of Subrahmaniam—covered with gold, silver, diamonds, and emeralds—is taken from the Sri Mariamman temple along with his consorts, Valli and Theivanai. It is placed in a silver chariot and carried in a grand procession to his tomb in the Batu Caves near the capital city of Kuala Lumpur. The statue is carried up 272 steep steps and placed beside the permanent statue kept there. The next day about 200,000 people begin to pay homage, while movies, carrousels, and other entertainments are provided for their amusement.

Among the Tamil people of Mauritus, devotees, both male and female, abstain from meat and sex during the sacred 10 days before the festival. Each day they go to the temple (kovil) to make offerings. In Port Louis, at Arulmigu Sockalingam Meenaatchee Amman Kovil, Murugar and his two consorts are decorated differently each day to depict episodes in the deity's life.

On the eve of the Tamil celebration, devotees prepare the kavadees (wooden arches on wooden platforms) and decorate them with flowers, paper, and peacock feathers. They may be built in other shapes, such as a peacock or temple, but the arch is most common.

The next morning, priests pour cow milk into two brass pots and tie them to the sides of each kavadee. Fruits, or jagger (a coarse, brown sugar made from the East Indian palm tree), may also be placed on the platform. Then religious ceremonies are performed at the shrines to put the bearers in a trance.

When ready, penitents have their upper bodies pierced symmetrically with vels, the sacred lance given to Lord Subrahmaniam by his mother, Parvati; some also have skewers driven through their cheeks, foreheads, or tongues. The procession then begins, with the devotees carrying the kavadees on their shoulders. Some penitents draw a small chariot by means of chains fixed to hooks dug into their sides; some walk to the temple on sandals studded with nails.

Groups of young men and women follow, singing rhythmic songs. Each region may have 40 to 100 kavadees, but in places like Port Louis there may be 600 to 800. At the temple, the kavadee is dismounted, the needles and skewers removed by the priest, and the milk in the pots is poured over the deity from head to foot. The penitents then go out and join the crowds.

Some believe carrying the kavadee washes away sins through self-inflicted suffering; others say the kavadee symbolizes the triumph of good over evil.

Vasant Pañcami
Fifth day of the waxing half of Magha

This Hindu festival honors Saraswati, goddess of learning, eloquence, and the arts. During this holiday season, people wear bright yellow clothing to represent the mustard plant whose blossoms herald the coming of spring. The day of Vasant Pañcami is celebrated with music, dancing, and kite-flying.

In West Bengal, Saraswati is known as the goddess of speech, learning, wisdom, fine arts, and sciences. She is credited with the invention of the Sanskrit language and the Devnagari script. Celebrations of Vasant Pañcami in West Bengal include a procession in which images of her graceful figure are carried to the river for a ceremonial bath, and books and pens are placed at her shrine.

Bhishma Ashtami
Eighth day of the waxing half of Magha

On this day, Bhishma is offered libations with barley, sesame, flowers, and Ganges water.

In Hindu mythology Bhishma was the son of King Shantanu. The king decided he wanted to marry a beautiful young maiden named Satyavati, but her parents would not permit it because Bishma was heir to the throne. This meant that if King Shantanu and Satyavati had sons, the boys could not inherit the kingdom. To allow the marriage to go forward, Bhishma vowed never to marry, nor have children of his own, nor to accept the crown. Shantanu then married Satyavati, and she bore him two sons.

The two sons died without producing any offspring, but Satyavati had two grandchildren by a son who had been born before she married the king. Bhishma ended up raising these two and taking charge of the training of their children, who were known as the Kauravas and the Pandavas.

In the battle that was eventually fought between the two groups of offspring, Bhishma sided with the Kauravas. According to Hindu mythology, he was so badly wounded during the fighting there was barely a space of two fingers' width on his body that had not been pierced by an arrow. He did not die immediately, however, because he had been allowed to choose the time of his death. He waited on his death-bed of arrows for 58 days. As he waited to die, Bhishma delivered many religious discourses. He later became the model for modern ascetics who lie on nail-studded beds. Bhishma is considered a great example of self-denial, loyalty, and devotion.

Magha Purnima
Full moon day of Magha

Magha is one of the four most sacred months and Hindus believe that bathing in the Ganges on the purnima (full moon day) is of high religious merit. When the Ganges is not accessible, one may bathe in any holy stream, river, tank, or pond. Fasting is also observed and charities are done. Early in the morning, libations are offered to dead ancestors, and clothes, food, and money are given to the poor. Gifts are also given to Brahmans according to one's means and capacity.

Minakshi Float Festival
Full moon day of Magha

The Float Festival is celebrated at Madurai, which is famous for its majestic Minakshi Temple. Minakshi is the fish-eyed goddess, and it is another name of Parvati. The major part of the Minakshi temple was built during the reign of Tirumala Nayak (1623-55), whose birthday falls on Magha Purnima.

On this day, images of Minakshi and Lord Sundareshwara (Shiva) are mounted on floats and taken to Marriamman Teppakulam, Sarovar, east of Madurai. The deities are displayed on richly decorated and illuminated floats that are drawn back and forth across the water to the accompaniment of music and devotional songs. Afterwards they are returned to Madurai.

The waters on which the deities are displayed are confined in a pool called a tank which is fed by underground channels from the river Vaigai. A shrine stands on an island in the center of the tank. It was built in 1641 by King Tirumala Nayak. The float festival is very popular, and thousands of pilgrims and devotees from all parts of India congregate to see it.

Sakata Chauth
Fourth day of the waning half of Magha

Ganesa is honored with a fast on this day, believed to be the day of his birth. The fast is observed by both men and women. After the early morning bath, a pitcher and Ganesa statue are installed and worshipped with sweets and balls made of jaggery and sesame seeds. The moon god and Rohini are also worshipped ritually and offered food. At night, with the rising of the moon, the fast is broken. The moon is worshipped and offered water (arghya). The day-long fast is believed to ensure wisdom, a trouble free life, and prosperity.

Mauni Amavasya
Fifteenth day of the waning half of Magha

The month-long bathing and fasting associated with the month of Magha ends with the observance of Mauni Amavasya, when Lord Vishnu is worshipped and the peepal tree (*Ficus religiosa*) circumambulated. A complete silence is observed. If the day falls on Monday, then its auspiciousness increases.

Hindus believe that piety and devotion on this day at Prayag, the place where the Ganges, Yamuna, and Saraswati are confluent, is highly meritorious. Aspirants come and live there for a full month and practice prescribed rituals and ceremonial sacrifices known as "Kalpa-Vas." Through the entire month, religious discourses and services are held for aspirants. Observers take one simple meal a day or ingest only fruit and milk.

Phalguna (February-March)

Amalaka Ekadashi
Eleventh day of the waxing half of Phalguna

On Amalaka Ekadashi the Alma tree (*Emblica officinalis*) is worshipped. Hindus believe in taking a respectful attitude toward all things, whether trees or beasts, rivers or deities, animate or inanimate, because the one Universal Spirit pervades all. It is this concept of God or Reality that underlies the worship of trees. In addition, according to Hindu thought, Vishnu lives in the Alma tree.

An Alma tree is ceremonially bathed and watered and then worshipped. A fast is observed and Brahmans are given gifts. Amalaka Ekadashi also marks the beginning of the Holi festival.

Holi (Holika Dahan)
Fourteenth day of the waxing half of Phalguna

Holi is one of the four most popular festivals in India, observed by all Hindus without any distinction of caste, creed, status, or sex. It celebrates the burning of Holika, an evil sorceress who once tormented all of India and marks the end of winter and the advent of the spring season. The two-day festival is most notable for the freedom and loss of inhibition practiced by the people.

On the first night of the festival, a bonfire is constructed in the evening. Before the fire is lit, a worship ceremony is performed in which water and grains are offered, then people dance around the fire. Throughout the evening, images of Holika are burned, drums are pounded, horns are blown, and people shout.

The next day many people interact by splashing colored water and throwing colored powder on their friends, relatives, neighbors, and even passersby. Noisy and colorful processions are made through the bazaars and streets. Other people celebrate the day with songs, music, floral decoration, and by splashing perfumed water. Sweets and visits are exchanged, and cold drinks prepared at home are served liberally. People forget all enmity and embrace each other, with warmth and love, and renew their friendship. New corn is baked and eaten on this day for the first time in the season.

There are several myths about the origin of the festival of Holi. According to one Puranic myth, an evil king, Hiranyakasipu, had a good son, Prahlada, who was sent by the gods to deliver the people from the oppressive rule of the king. This angered the king so greatly that he ordered the death of the child. The sister of the king was an evil witch named Holika, who claimed to be impervious to fire. So to kill Prahlada, Holika snatched the child and jumped into a great bonfire. Prahlada, however, was rescued from the flames by Krishna and it was Holika who was destroyed. Holi commemorates this event and symbolizes the triumph of good over evil.

Dol Purnima
Full moon day of Phalguna

Dol Purnima is a Bengali festival dedicated to Krishna. An image of Krishna, richly adorned and smeared with colored powder, is taken out in procession in a swinging cradle decorated with flowers, leaves, colored clothes, and papers. The procession proceeds forward to the accompaniment of music, sounding of conch shells, trumpets, and shouts of "Jai!" (victory).

Dol Purnima is also significant because it is the birthday of Chaitanya Mahaprabhu (1485–1533), also known as Gauranga, the Vaishnava saint who popularized modern Sankirtana. Followers of the Chaitanya School of Vaishnavism believe Chaitanya himself was a manifestation of Krishna.

Mahashivarati (Great Night of Shiva; Shiva Chaturdashi of Phalguna)
Fourteenth day of the waning half of Phalguna

Mahashivarati is a major Hindu festival marked by worship services at all temples where Shiva is honored throughout India. Devotees by the thousands collect at Shiva shrines and spend the entire night practicing devotion and piety, meditating, and reading and reciting Shiva scriptures. The linga (phallic) symbol of Shiva is worshipped with Ganges water, milk, curds, honey, and clarified butter (ghee). Betel leaves, dhatura fruit, aak, and flowers, are also offered to Shiva.

Special puja (worship) celebrations are held at Varanasi, Tarkeshwar, Baidyanath, Walkeshwar, Rameshwaram, and Ujjain. At Pashupatinath in Nepal a grand celebration is held and adherents keep a strict fast and do not take even a drop of water.

According to Hindu teaching, Shiva is a great and powerful god, one of the Hindu Trinity. As Mahadeva, he is worshipped by various gods including Brahma and Vishnu. He is Mahakala the destroyer dissolving everything into nothingness, but also, as Sankara, restores and reproduces that which has been destroyed. His linga (phallus) symbolizes this reproductive power. As a Mahayogi, or great ascetic, he combines in himself the highest perfection of austere penance and abstract meditation. In this form he is a naked ascetic, digambra "clothed with the elements." He is also called Chandrashekhra, "Moon Crested"; Girisha, "Mountain Lord"; Mahakala, "Great Time"; Pashupati, "Lord of the Beasts"; and Vishwanath, "Lord of the Universe."

Gangaur
Two weeks after Holi

Gangaur is primarily an eighteen-day Hindu women's festival that begins the day after Holi and culminates two weeks later. It is a great local festival in Rajasthan, but is also celebrated in many parts of northern India.

During the festival both married women and unmarried girls worship the goddess Gauri (the most fair and benign aspect of the goddess Durga, the consort of Shiva) with durva grass, flowers, fruits, and bright brass pots filled with fresh water. The married women seek Gauri's blessings for conjugal happiness, while the unmarried pray for a suitable handsome husband and future marital prosperity.

On the final day of the Gangaur festival, Hindu women keep a strict fast, worship the goddess, wear colorful clothes and ornaments, and exchange sweets. The wooden or earthen images of the goddess are taken through the main streets and bazaars in procession with decorated elephants, camels, horses, chariots, dancers, and musicians.

Caitra (March-April)

Gudi Parva
First day of the waxing half of Caitra

Gudi Parva, or Padva, marks the beginning of preparations for the Hindu New Year, and is mainly celebrated in Maharashtra on Caitra Pratipada. People arise early in the morning, tidy up their houses, have baths, and wear festive and new clothes. Women decorate their houses, a silk banner is raised and worshipped, and then greetings and sweets are exchanged.

Ugadi Parva
First day of the waxing half of Caitra

Ugadi Parva is a Hindu festival that ushers in the New Year for the inhabitants of Andhra. On this day, people visit one another, enjoy feasts, and wear new clothes. The festive day begins with ritual bathing and prayers, and continues late into the night. Some Hindus believe that both Brahma's creation of the world and Lord Vishnu's first incarnation as Matsya (the fish) occurred on this day. Brahma is especially worshipped on this day.

Vasanta Navaratra
Nine nights preceding Ramanavimi during the month of Caitra

Navaratras are observed twice a year. Vasanta Navaratra occurs in the Hindu month of Caitra (March-April), preceding Rama Navami; the second Navaratra fast occurs in the month of Asvina (September-October) preceding Dussehra. The name of the fast means "nine nights." The purpose of Navaratra is to propitiate the goddess Durga and to seek her blessings. The methods by which Navaratra is kept vary regionally.

Caitra Parb
Eight days prior to the full-moon day of Caitra

Caitra Parb is a festival held by the tribes in Orissa, India. It starts eight days before the Purnima (full moon). Throughout the celebrations people fast, dance, and hunt. Heads of the families pay homage to their forefathers in the presence of the "Jani," or village priest, and every member of the family attends in festive new costumes. Animal sacrifice is a main feature of the festival, which also signals the beginning of the mango season.

Sitala Ashtami
Eighth day of the waxing half of Caitra

Sitala Ashtami is a festival honoring the Hindu goddess Sitala. She is the goddess of smallpox and her blessings are invoked for protection against the disease. Sitala is depicted as roaming the countryside riding an ass. She is identified with the devil or Durga in her role as the goddess of smallpox. On this day, which is either a Monday or Friday, Hindu women visit the Sitala shrine in the morning, and offer rice, homemade sweets, cooked food, and holy water mixed with milk. At several places colorful fairs are held on this occasion near the shrine of Sitala and there is a lot of merry-making, songs, dance, feasting and brisk buying and selling.

Ashokashtami
Eighth day of the waxing half of Caitra

This festival of Lingaraja at Bhubaneshwar is based on the Car Festival of Jagannatha at Puri, also known as Ratha Yatra. The protege of Lingaraja is taken out in a giant wooden chariot to the Rameshwar temple, about two kilometers from the Lingaraja temple, and returned after four days. Ashokashtami is a major local festival witnessed by thousands of devotees and spectators.

Ramanavami (Ram Navami; Rama Navami)
Ninth day of the waxing half of Caitra

The Hindu festival of Ramanavami celebrates the birth of Rama, who was the first son of King Dasaratha of Ayodhya. According to Hindu belief, the god Vishnu was incarnated in ten different forms, of which Rama was the seventh. He and his wife, Sita, are venerated by Hindus as the ideal man and wife. Because Rama is the hero of the great religious epic poem, the *Ramayana*, Hindus observe his birthday by reciting stories from it. They also flock to the temples, where the image of Rama is enshrined, and chant prayers, repeating his name as they strive to free themselves from the cycle of birth and death.

In Ayodhya, the birth place of Rama, great celebrations are held; the temples are decorated, the *Ramayana* is read and recited, and a fair is held. At other places icons of Rama, along with Sita and Hanuman, are richly adorned and worshipped, and other acts of devotion and piety are observed. Chanting the holy name of Rama and lectures and discourses on Rama's life and teachings are common features of the celebrations. People take vows to devote themselves more to their spiritual and moral evolution on this occasion. Many Hindus believe that Ram-Nam is a great magic formula (mantra) that should be repeated, recited, and meditated upon frequently.

Panguni Uttiram (Meenakshi Kalyanam)
Ten days including the full moon day of Caitra

The full moon day of Caitra is the day on which the Hindu god Shiva married the goddess Meenakshi at Madura, Indonesia. The 10-day Hindu festival that follows also celebrates the marriage of Subramanya to Theivanai, adopted daughter of Indra.

Panguni Uttiram is a popular festival in Malaysia, where the worship of Subramanya is widespread. There are fairs on the temple grounds and processions in which Hindu gods and goddesses are carried through the streets in chariots. In Kuala Lumpur, Subramanya and his consort are taken from the Sentul temple in an elaborately decorated chariot through the city streets. Free meals are served throughout the day to visitors.

In Singapore, Panguni Uttiram is a two-day festival held at the Sri Veeramakaliamman Temple. There is a procession of Subramanya on the first day, and special pujas (worship ceremonies) are held at the temple on the second day. At Bukit Mertajam, a fire-walking ceremony is held.

In India, the festival is known as Meenakshi Kalyanam. Garlands, marigolds, and other offerings presented at the temple are devoted to Meenkashi in Madurai. Figures representing the god and his wife are then adorned with ceremonial robes and later carried in chariots.

Caitra Purnima
Ten days in Caitra

In southern India, Caitra Purnima is also considered sacred to Chitra Gupta. On this day, Chitra Gupta,

Yama's assistant, is worshipped. Some Hindus believe that it is Chitra Gupta who maintains the accounts of good and bad actions in this world, and that people are rewarded or punished accordingly hereafter. At Kanchipuram, near Madras, the image of Chitra Gupta is taken out in a procession and devotees bathe in the holy waters of the River Chitra, which flows from the nearby hills.

Hanuman Jayanti
Full-moon day of Caitra

The monkey-god Hanuman is worshipped all across India, either singularly or together with Rama because he played a central role in the great Hindu epic the *Ramayana* in which he helped Rama rescue his wife Sita from the demon Ravana. Hanuman is depicted in the form of a monkey with a red face who stands erect like a human.

On his birth anniversary (jayanti), Hanuman is celebrated with great religious fervor. People visit Hanuman's shrines, fast, offer prayers and puja (worship), and read the *Ramayana* and the Hanuman *Chalisa*. Statues of Hanuman are given new coats of vermillion mixed with clarified butter and then richly decorated. Fairs are sometimes held at places near the shrines.

Hanuman is regarded by Vaishnavites as one of the greatest embodiments of strength, speed and agility, learning, and selfless service to Lord Rama. On Hanuman Jayanti, Vaishnavites observe a strict fast, meditate on Hanuman and his lord Rama, practice charity, and spend the day repeating his glories and adventures.

Every 12 Years

Kumbha Mela (Pitcher Fair)
Every 12 years on a date calculated by astrologers (one was held in 2001)

The Kumbha Mela festival is marked by mass immersion rituals by Hindus near the city of Allahabad (the ancient holy city of Prayag) in north-central India. Millions of pilgrims gather to bathe at the confluence of the Ganga (Ganges) and Yamuna Rivers, which is also where the mythical river of enlightenment, the Saraswati, flows. The bathers wash away the sins of their past lives and pray to escape the cycle of reincarnation. Sadhus (or holy men) carry images of deities to the river for immersion. The most ascetic sadhus, naked except for loincloths and with their faces and bodies smeared with ashes, go in procession to the waters, escorting images borne on palanquins. The Ganges is not only a sacred river but is the source of all sacred waters. The junction of the three

rivers at Allahabad is called the "sangam" and is considered by some to be the holiest place in India.

The mela (a word that means "fair") is thought to be the largest periodic human gathering in the world. During its duration a vast tent city appears, temporary water and power lines are installed, and ten pontoon bridges are laid across the Ganges. Movies of Hindu gods and heroes are shown from the backs of trucks, and plays recounting Hindu mythology are performed. Merchants lay out all manner of goods.

The story behind the mela is that Hindu gods and asuras (or demons) fought for a Kumbha (or pitcher) carrying amrit, the nectar of immortality. The god who seized the Kumbha stopped at Prayag, Hardwar, Nasik, and Ujjain on his way to paradise. The journey took 12 days (longer than earthly days), and therefore the mela follows a 12-year cycle.

A purification bathing ceremony called the Magh Mela is also held each spring in Allahabad. It is India's biggest yearly religious bathing festival. Although the Magh Mela attracts about a million people, the Kumbha Mela dwarfs it.

Masi Magham
Full moon day February-March

The Masi Magham festival is observed every 12 years during the full moon in February or March, although a smaller festival takes place annually. Hindus flock to Kumbakonam, in southern India, to bathe in the Maha-Magha tank, where the waters of nine holy rivers are said to be mixed: the Ganges, the Yumma, the Godavari, the Saraswati, the Narmada, the Cauvery, the Kumari, the Payoshni, and the Sarayu. Bathing in the sacred tank (or pool) purifies them of their sins.

The Masi Magham festival is also a time for gift-giving, particularly in support of charitable institutions. One way of measuring the size of one's gift to the poor is to give one's weight in gold, a custom known as Tulabhara. Sometimes the gold collected in this way is used to renovate the 16 temples that have been built over the years near the site of the sacred tank.

In Malaysia, the Masi Magham is a two-day festival celebrated by the Chettiyar (a Tamil merchant caste) community in Malacca. The image of Subramanya, a Hindu god, is taken in procession to the temple known as Sannasi Malai Kovil, formerly the home of a famous ascetic who had the power to heal. Oratorical contests are held and dramas are staged at the temple. At the end of the day, the statue is taken back through the streets of Malacca to Poyyatha Vinayagar Kovil, where it remains for another year.

Table 12.5. Alphabetical List of Hindu Holidays

Name	Date(s)
Akshya Tritiya	Third day of the waxing half of Vaisakha
Amalaka Ekadashi	Eleventh day of the waxing half of Phalguna
Anant Chaturdashi	Fourteenth day of the waxing half of Bhadrapada
Asadha Purnima *see* Guru Purnima	
Ashokashtami	Eighth day of the waxing half of Caitra
Avani Avittam *see* Raksa Bandhana	
Baisakhi *see* Vaisakhi	
Baishak Purinma *see* Buddah Jayanti	
Balarama Shashti *see* Halashashti	
Bhairava Ashtami	Eighth day of the waning half of Margasirsa
Bhaiya Duj	Second day of the waxing half of Kartika
Bhishma Ashtami	Eighth day of the waxing half of Magha
Bhratri Panchami *see* Nag Pañcami	
Brother and Sister Day *see* Raksa Bandhana	
Buddah Jayanti	Full moon in Jyestha
Caitra Parb	Eight days prior to the full-moon day of Caitra
Caitra Purnima	Ten days in Caitra
Cake Festival *see* Sithinakha	
Chandan Yatra	Beginning on the third day of the waxing half of Vaisakha
Dasain *see* Dussehra	

Name	Date(s)
Dashara *see* Dussehra	
Dattatreya Jayanti	Full-moon day of Margasirsa
Deepavali *see* Dewali	
Devathani Ekadashi	Eleventh day of the waxing half of Kartika
Dewali	Fifteenth day of the waning half of Kartika
Dhan Teras	Thirteenth day of the waning half of Kartika
Dhanvantri Trayodashi *see* Dhan Teras	
Divali *see* Dewali	
Dol Purnima	Full moon day of Phalguna
Durga Puja	During the waxing half of Asvina
Dussehra	Tenth day of the waxing half of Asvina
Father's Day *see* Gokarna Aunsi	
Festival of Boys *see* Ghanta Karna	
Festival of Lights *see* Dewali	
Festival of Victory *see* Durga Puja	
Ganesa Caturthi	Fourth day of the waxing half of Bhadrapada
Ganesha Chata *see* Ganesa Caturthi	
Ganesha Chaturti *see* Ganesa Caturthi	
Ganga Dussehra	Tenth day of the waxing half of Jyestha
Gangaur	Two weeks after Holi
Ghanta Karna	Fourteenth day of waning half Sravana

Table 12.5. Alphabetical List of Hindu Holidays, continued

Name	Date(s)
Gita Jayanti	Eleventh day of the waxing half of Margasirsa
Gokarna Aunsi	During the dark fortnight of Bhadrapada
Govardhan Puja	First day of the waxing half of Kartika
Great Night of Shiva *see* Mahashivarati	
Green Teej *see* Hariyali Teej	
Gudi Parva	First day of the waxing half of Caitra
Guru Purnima	Full-moon day of Asadha
Halashashti	Sixth day of the waning half of Bhadrapada
Hanuman Jayanti	Full-moon day of Caitra
Hari Tritiya *see* Hariyali Teej	
Hari-Shayani Ekadashi	Eleventh day of the waxing half of Asadha
Haritalika Teej	Third day of the waxing half of Bhadrapada
Hariyali Teej	Third day of the waxing half of Sravana
Hindu New Year *see* Vaisakhi	
Holi	Fourteenth day of the waxing half of Phalguna
Holika Dahan *see* Holi	
Indra Jatra	Beginning the end of Bhadrapada until early Asvina
Janaki Navami	Ninth day of the waxing half month of Vaisakha

Name	Date(s)
Janmashtami	Eighth day of the waning half of Bhadrapada
Jhulan Latra	Full moon day of Sravana
Jyestha Ashtami	Eighth day of waxing half of Jyestha
Kamada Ekadashi	Eleventh day of the waning half of Sravana
Kartika Purnima	Full moon day of Kartika
Kartika Snan	During Kartika
Karwachauth	Fourth day of the waning half of Kartika
Kojagara	Full moon day of Asvina
Krishna's Birthday *see* Janmashtami	
Krishnastami *see* Janmashtami	
Kumbha Mela	Every 12 years on a date calculated by astrologers
Laksmi Puja	During Asvina
Magh Sankranti *see* Makar Sankranti	
Magha Purnima	Full moon day of Magha
Mahashivarati	Fourteenth day of the waning half of Phalguna
Makar Sankranti	Commences upon the sun's entrance into Capricorn, at the winter solstice
Masi Magham	Every 12 years on the full moon in February or March
Mata Tirtha Snan	New moon in Vaisakha
Mauni Amavasya	Fifteenth day of the waning half of Magha
Meenakshi Kalyanam *see* Panguni Uttiram	

Table 12.5. Alphabetical List of Hindu Holidays, continued

Name	Date(s)
Minakshi Float Festival	Full moon day of Magha
Mother's Day see Mata Tirtha Snan	
Nag Pañcami	Fifth day of the waxing half of Sravana
Narak Chaturdashi	Fourteenth day of the waning half of Kartika
Narieli Purnima	Full moon day of Sravana
Narsimha Jayanti	Fourteenth day of the waxing half of Vaisakha
Nirjala Ekadashi	Eleventh day of the waxing half of Jyestha
Onam	Four days in the Malyalan month of Chingam
Panguni Uttiram	Ten days including the full moon day of Caitra
Parasurama Jayanti	Third day of the waxing half of Vaisakha
Pitcher Fair see Kumbha Mela	
Pitra Paksha see Pitra Visarjana Amavasya	
Pitra Visarjana Amavasya	During the waning half of Asvina
Pongal	During Magha (mid-January)
Pooram	10 days during Vaisakha
Puskar Mela	Full moon day of Kartika
Putrada Ekadashi	Eleventh day of the waxing half of Sravana
Radha Ashtami	Eighth day of the waning half of Bhadrapada
Raksa Bandhana	Full-moon day month of Sravana

Name	Date(s)
Ram Navami see Ramanavami	
Rama Navami see Ramanavami	
Ramanavami	Ninth day of the waxing half of Caitra
Ratha Yatra	Second day of the waxing half of Asadha
Rishi Pañcami	Fifth day of the waxing half of Bhadrapada
Rukmini Ashtami	Eighth day of the waning half of Pausa
Sakata Chauth	Fourth day of the waning half of Magha
Sankaracarya Jayanti	Fifth day (south) or tenth day (north) of the waxing half of Vaisakha
Sharad Purnima	Full moon day of Asvina
Sitala Ashtami	Eighth day of the waxing half of Caitra
Shiva Chaturdashi of Phalguna see Mahashivarati	
Sithinakha	Sixth day of waxing half of Jyestha
Skanda Shashti	During the Tamil month of Tulam
Snan Yatra	Full-moon day of Jyestha
Sravani Mela	During Sravana
Surya Shashti	Sixth day of the waxing half of Kartika
Swarupa Dwadashi	Twelfth day of the waning half of Pausa
Teej see Hariyali Teej	
Thai Poosam see Thaipusam	

Table 12.5. Alphabetical List of Hindu Holidays, continued

Name	Date(s)
Thaipusam	Three to 12 days in Magha
Tihar	During the waning half of Kartika
Tij *see* Hariyali Teej	
Tirupati Festival	Ten days during Bhadrapada
Tulsidas Jayanti	Seventh day of the waxing half of Sravana
Ugadi Parva	First day of the waxing half of Caitra
Uttarayana Skranti *see* Makar Sankranti	
Vaikuntha Ekadashi	Eleventh days of the waxing and waning halves of Margasirsa
Vaisakhi	First day of the waxing half of Vaisakha (about April 13)

Name	Date(s)
Vaitarani	Eleventh day of the waning half of Margashirsha
Valmiki Jayanti	Full-moon day of Asvina
Vasant Pañcami	Fifth day of the waxing half of Magha
Vasanta Navaratra	Nine nights preceding Ramanavimi during the month of Caitra
Vata Savitri	Thirteenth day of the waning half of Jyestha
Vijay Dashami *see* Dussehra	
Vyasa Purnima *see* Guru Purnima	
Yama Dvitiya *see* Bhaiya Duj	

CHAPTER 13

Jainism

Overview of Jainism

What Is Jainism?

Jainism originated in India around the same time that Buddhist thought developed. Jains believe in a sequence of reincarnations: Animals must become human, and lay people must become monks in order to attain salvation from the world. Salvation, called mokhsa, is attained by liberating the soul from the contamination of matter (karma). This liberation results in omniscience and bliss for eternity.

One of the fundamental doctrines of Jainism is the separation of living matter (called jiva) and non-living matter (called ajiva). In order to achieve freedom from karma, Jains must completely avoid harming any living thing and practice perfect asceticism. Three concepts govern the affairs of the Jain people. These are known collectively as the Triratna (Three Jewels) and consist of right faith, right knowledge, and right conduct.

The primary focus of the religion is on nonviolence and asceticism. Jains believe that all life is sacred and that cruel actions darken the soul and thwart the ability to achieve freedom from karmic matter. Some Jain monks and nuns wear cloths across their mouths to keep them from accidentally destroying insect life. Some carry brushes to help remove insects from their path and are strict vegetarians. Monks vow to abstain from killing, stealing, lying, sexual activity, and possessing personal property.

The name Jain comes from the Sanskrit word, Jina, which means Conqueror. The conquerors honored by the Jains are people who have overcome and won enlightenment. The name Jinas also applies specifically to 24 spiritual guides from history and the legendary past who are collectively called the Tirthankaras (which means ford-markers). Each of the Tirthankaras achieved liberation, and by his model taught others how to do the same.

Jainism teaches that the universe is eternal—it was not created, it has no beginning, and will have no end. It passes through cycles during which civilizations rise and fall, men attain large size and life-spans lengthen. In each cycle, 24 Tirthankaras appear. The last (24th) Tirthankara was Vardhamana Mahavira who lived about the same time as Buddha. Jain sects place the date of his death in 527 B.C.E., and some researchers place the event in 477 B.C.E. Mahavira taught a path of passionless detachment and, according to Jain teaching, had achieved omniscience (knowledge of all things) before he started preaching.

The Relationship between the Gods and the Jain People

There is no personal god in Jainism. Although several gods and goddesses are recognized (and a few of them are also included in the Hindu pantheon), they take a subordinate position to the 24 Tirthankaras.

The first Tirthankara to appear in the current cycle of degenerative ages was Risabha. The timing of his birth, placed him at a point in the era that was closer to an idealistic age. Risabha is credited with establishing the first Indian emperor, founding human social conventions (such as marriage), and developing the caste system. According to tradition, he lived more than 600,000 years.

Historical evidence exists for Parsva, the twenty-third Tirthankara, who lived approximately 250 years before Mahavira. Jains believe that his disciples joined with Mahavira. Jains thus believe that Mahavira did not found a new religion, but that he provided guidance to a tradition that was already established.

In addition to the Tirthankaras, some sects of Jains also venerate heavenly beings called yaksas (male) and yaksis (female). Some of these have similarities with Hindu gods and others serve as protectors, guardians, or servants of the Tirthankaras and the Jain community.

Sacred Writings

The two main sects of Jains acknowledge different canons of scripture. Both sects recognize original texts which were compiled into twelve books called angas and transmitted orally for several centuries. Efforts at establishing canonical lists of writings is aimed at recovering portions of the original texts.

The Svetambara sect established the canon of writings it considered as scripture through a series of councils that culminated in the sixth century. The complete canon currently contains 45 texts. The Digambara sect, not represented at the councils, independently established their own canon. The Digambara scriptures include works by Kundakunda, the Siddhanta texts by Virasena and Jayasena, and Gommatasara by Nemichandra. Tatvarthasutra of Umaswati is accepted by both sects.

The types of documents include rules for conduct and doctrinal dissertations. One important document, the *Kalpa Sutra*, dates from the second century B.C.E. The *Kalpa Sutra* describes the lives of the Jinas, and it is often recited at major festivals in the Svetambara sect.

Other books of Jain writings, while not considered sacred, have been influential. These texts include historical narratives, religious and moral teachings, medicinal and other secular sciences, and poetry. Other important writings include commentaries and biographies of Jain monks.

History

Jainism, in its current form, began during the sixth century B.C.E. Its founder was Vardhamana Mahavira. The designation Mahavira is a title rather than a given name; it means Great Hero.

Mahavira was born in northern India into a family of the warrior caste. He was trained in the tradition of a spiritual guide named Parsva, who Jains consider the 23rd Tirthankara. Mahavira is revered as the twenty-fourth Tirthankara.

According to Jain teaching, Mahavira's mother Trisala (also known as Priyakarini) had a series of miraculous dreams heralding his birth and signifying his importance. Beginning at the age of 30, he gave up all his possessions and followed a path of austerity for more than 12 years. Mahavira then achieved enlightenment and became a Jina (conqueror) while meditating under an Ashoka tree after two and a half days of fasting.

Accounts of Mahavira's life after his enlightenment vary among the Jain sects. According to Digambaras, he also stripped himself of all his clothes and went naked afterwards. Svetambara Jains believe that Indra (a god from the Hindu pantheon) presented him a white robe to wear, which was discarded after some time. Both sects agree that he did not wear any clothes during his career as a Tirthankara.

Mahavira lived 30 years after his enlightenment and gathered many disciples. At the age of 72 he died and attained mokhsa (liberation from the material world). Although the account of specific events of Mahavira's life, especially those that occurred after his enlightenment, are a point of division among the two major sects of Jainism, both recognize the same set of the five most important phenomenon from his life: his conception; his birth; his renunciation of the world; his enlightenment; and his attainment of nirvana.

After Mahavira's death, one of his disciples, Indrabhuti, received enlightenment and became a leader in the Jain community. Another of his disciples, Gosala, left the bounds of the tradition and established a sect called the Ajivika, which enjoyed a small following for several centuries and then eventually died out.

Figure 13.1. Mahavira, the founder of Jainism in its current form, is revered as the twenty-fourth and last Tirthankara of the current cycle. Tirthankaras (which means ford-markers) are spiritual guides who achieved liberation and taught others how to do the same. Jains believe that Mahavira did not found a new religion, but that he provided guidance to a tradition that was already established.

About 200 years after Mahavira's death, a council was held to establish official Jain doctrines. Consensus was not achieved, and ultimately the events that transpired during the century following the council led to the development of separate Jain sects in distinct geographic areas. The two sects were called the Digambaras and the Svetambaras. Other councils held in subsequent centuries were predominantly represented by members of the Svetambara sect and focused on establishing the canon of Jain scripture.

Although never a majority faith in India, the Jains developed into a sizable and well-respected community. Between the eleventh and sixteenth centuries, elaborate shrines were constructed in several cities. Jain temples continue to be built today. There are about 200 major pilgrimage centers. Two temples on Mount Abu in Rajasthan and the colossal statue of Bahubali at Sravanbelgola in Karnataka are among the best known examples of Jain pilgrimage centers.

Jainism Today

The Jain People

The Jains are a small but influential community in India. Their numbers include many of India's industrialists and businessmen.

There are approximately four million Jains worldwide. The largest Jain community is in western India centered in Gujarat, Rajasthan, Mysore, Madhya Pradesh, and Maharashtra. Other smaller communities exist in the United Kingdom, Canada, and the United States. In North America there are an estimated sixty Jain centers affiliated with Jain Associations in North American (JAINA) that serve about 80,000 Jains. These centers accommodate all Jain sects.

The Jain community retains many of the characteristics organized by Mahavira. In India, it consists of four ranks of members: monks, nuns, lay men, and lay women. Many communities outside India, however, do not have monks and nuns.

Worship

Jain temple activity is not considered worship in the traditional sense. It is more closely associated with contemplation. Images of the Tirthankaras, called murtis, serve as the focal points in Jain temples to assist laypeople in their worship. Worship includes making offerings to the images by pouring a specially prepared solution (which is sometimes made from milk, curds, clarified butter, sugar, and flowers) over the image and then washing it with pure water. In addition to bathing the images of the Tirthankaras, worshippers wave lamps, and sing devotional hymns. Some sects do not use flowers, and about a third of the Jains belong to sects that do not use any idols.

Sects

There are two main sects of Jainism, each with its own texts. They differ primarily in the areas of discipline and practice rather than in areas of belief.

Digambaras

Digambaras ("sky-clad" sect) are the dominant form of Jainism in southern and central India. They believe that total nudity is required of monks. This prohibition of clothing for monks extends into worship as well. Digambaras believe that images of the Jinas should not be clothed.

Digambaras claim the possession of oral teachings passed down from Mahavira and subsequently preserved in their writings. One belief that separates Digambaras from other Jains is the position that only men can achieve liberation from the cycle of rebirths. Another unique belief centers on the life of Mahavira following his enlightenment. According to Digambara understanding, after Mahavira experienced enlightenment he did not become involved in human relationships or routine activities such as eating, drinking, or talking. They believe that he lived solely on divine provisions.

Svetambaras

The Svetambaras ("white-clad" sect) represent the dominant form of Jainism in western India. They believe that, because of the current condition of the universe, it is not practically possible for monks to be naked. In accordance with this belief, Svetambaras worship images of the Jinas which they also cover with clothes and adorn with jewelry.

Svetambara Jains possess written texts which they claim were based on Mahavira's original teaching. They believe that men and women alike can achieve liberation from the cycle of rebirths and that the nineteenth Tirthankara, Malli, was female. In contrast with the Digambaras, Svetambaras believe that, after his enlightenment, Mahavira continued to live as an ordinary mortal.

Sthanakvasis and Terapanthi

Sthanakvasis emerged as a subsect of the Svetambaras during the seventeenth century. They differentiated themselves in how worship was practiced. The Sthanakvasis have no temples and do not worship before images. Another sect, called Terapanthi, is an offshoot of the Sthnakvasis.

⊞ ⊞ ⊞

The Jain Calendar

A Lunisolar Calendar

The Indian calendars generally have lunar months, but the duration of an average year is a sidereal year. The dates of most all the Jain festivals and fasts are calculated using such a lunisolar calendar. In northern India, the beginning of the month occurs at the full moon. This means that the first fortnight is waning. People in southern India typically mark the beginning of the month at the new moon and the first fortnight is waxing. Jains begin the new year in the autumn with the Diwali festival commemorating the liberation (achievement of Nirvana) of their founder, Nataputta Mahavira.(The Hindu new year generally occurs in the spring, however in Gujarat, the Hindu new year also starts with Diwali.)

Mahavira's achievement of Nirvana (at his death) in 527 B.C.E. also serves as the epoch for the Jain calendar. Diwali 2004 C.E., for example, begins the year 2531 V.N.S. (Vira Nirvana Samvat).

Figure 13.2. Some Jain monks and nuns wear a folded cloth, called a muhpatti, across their mouths to keep them from accidentally destroying insect life.

Cyclical Eras

The Jain concept of how time cycles through progressive and regressive eras also differs from that of the Hindus. Jains believe that a complete cycle of time consists of twelve separate units. Of these, six represent deteriorating conditions and six represent improving conditions. The third and fourth units of both half-cycles represent times when neither extreme predominates. Only during these units can the Tirthankaras be born.

Currently, the earth is experiencing the fifth unit in the declining part of the time cycle. Risabha, the first Tirthankara of the current age, is said to have been born during the third unit; Mahavira was born at the close of the fourth. Each of the last two units in the declining half-cycle has a duration of 21,000 years.

Table 13.1. The Jain Calendar

Month Names	Gregorian Equivalent
Kartika	October-November
Margasira	November-December
Pausa	December-January
Magha	January-February
Phalguna	February-March
Caitra	March-April
Vaisakha	April-May
Jyestha	May-June
Asadha	June-July
Sravana	July-August
Bhadrapada	August-September
Asvina	September-October

Table 13.2. The Jain Holiday Cycle

Date	Holiday
Kartika, waning 15	Diwali
Kartika, waxing 5	Jnana Panchami
Pausa, waning 10	Birth of Parsvanath
Magha, waning 14	Nirvana of Risabha
Caitra, waxing 13	Birth of Mahavira
Vaisakha, waxing 3	Aksaya Trtiya
Asadha	Caturmas begins
Bhadrapada, waning 13–5	Partyshana Parva
Bhadrapada, waxing 5–10	Dasa Laksana Parvan
Bhadrapada, waxing 14	Anata-Chaturdashi
Asvina, waning 1	Ksamavani

Jain Holidays

Kartika (October–November)

Diwali
Fifteenth day of the waning half of Kartika

The Jains celebrate Diwali as Lord Mahavira's day of final liberation (the achievement of Nirvana). At great Jain shrines like Pavapuri in Bihar, and Girnar in Gujarat, special puja (worship) festivals are held, sacred scriptures read and recited, and Lord Mahavira worshiped. Additionally, Lakshmi, goddess of wealth and good fortune, is honored by many Jains on the night of Diwali.

Diwali also serves as the beginning of the new year in the Jain calendar.

Jnan Panchami (Day for Honoring the Books)
Fifth day of the waxing half of Kartika

This day is for worship of knowledge in form of books. The books are taken out of storage, cleaned and worshipped. Jains have a very high regard for books, Indian's oldest libraries at Patan and Jaisalmer have been preserved by Jains.

Pausa (December–January)

Birth of Parsvanath
Tenth day of the waning half of Pausa

The birth of Parsvanath, an Indian teacher who lived approximately 250 years before Mahavir, is commemorated by Jains. Jains believe that Mahavira did not originate a new religion, but that he reforumlated one that was previously established.

Magha (January–February)

Nirvana of Risabha and Mauni Amavasya (Day of Silence)
Fourteenth and fifteenth day of the waning half of Magha

The Nirvana day of the first Tirthankara Risabha is celebrated by a special worship. In South India this festival is called Jinaratri, and processions are taken out. On the next day (amavasya) a day of silence is observed by devout Svetambara Jains.

Caitra (March–April)

Birth of Mahavira (Mahavir Jayanti)
Thirteenth day of the waxing half of the Hindu month of Caitra

Jains celebrate the birth of Vardhamana Jnatiputra, called Nataputta Mahavira (Mahavira means Great Hero), a sixth century B.C.E. religious reformer and founder of Jainism in the current form.

Jain pilgrims from all over India congregate at the ancient Jain shrines at Girnar and Palitana in Gujarat and at Mahavirji in Rajasthan. Pawapuri and Vaishali in Bihar are the other such centers. A grand festival is held at Vaishali, Mahavira's birthplace, and it is known as Vaishali Mahotsava.

Chariot processions with the images of Mahavira are taken out, rich ceremonies in the temples are held, fasts and charities are observed, Jain scriptures are read, and at some places fairs are held.

Vaisakha (April–May)

Aksaya Tratiya
Third day of the waxing half of Vaisakha

Svetambaras Jains honor a fast on Aksaya Tratiya. According to Jain teaching, the first Tirthankara observed a fast and after fasting was given some sugar cane juice to break the fast. This holiday commemorates his breaking of the fast.

Asadha (June–July)

Caturmas
June through September

Jain monks and nuns are required to be wanderers, not staying in one place for a long time. They observe a retreat during the rainy season in India, however. It involves a curtailment of travel. During the rainy season roads become hard to travel. Also traveling may cause the unnecessary killing of many small insects that come out during the season. This season is also marked by interaction between the monks and the laity and frequent fasting.

Bhadrapada (August–September)

Partyshana Parva (Paryushan; Pajjo-Savana)
Thirteenth to the fifth day of the waning half of Bhadrapada

The day of Paryshana (the fifth day of the waning half of Bhadrapada) is celebrated by both Svetambaras and Digambaras. The Svetambara (white-clad) celebrate a festival that lasts eight days culminating in an annual meditation on the last day. It takes place during the rainy season and is marked by recitations from the *Kalpa sutra* (Jain sacred writings) including the section that describes the birth of Mahavira.

The festival signifies a man's emergence into a new world of spiritual and moral refinement from that of a gross and depraved world. The ten cardinal virtues cultivated during this festival are forgiveness, charity, simplicity, contentment, truthfulness, self-restraint, fasting, detachment, humility, and continence. During the festival all of the virtues are lectured upon by the Jain saints and their cultivation stressed.

During this celebration many devout Jains fast, eating only once a day, worship the Tirthankaras, and try to take in the qualities and virtues of the great Jain saints and preachers. A few Jains fast for all eight days. This is also an occasion of self-analysis and criticism. Jains ask one another for forgiveness during this festival for offenses done knowingly or unknowingly, helping to restore lost relations and friendships. On the final day of the festival people can confess their sins and receive pardon. This is traditionally done by exchangeing letters and cards with friends and family members. At the end of the festival, an image of one of the Tirthankaras is carried in a procession.

Dasa Laksana Parvan (Time of the Ten Characteristics)
Fifth to thirteenth day of the waxing half of Bhadrapada

Dasa Laksana Parvan is a Digambara (sky-clad) Jain observance which starts with the Paryushan. It typically occurs during the rainy season and lasts ten days. The scripture readings focus on different portions of the holy text describing the ten characteristics to which Jains aspire. The ten characteristics are: forbearance, gentleness, uprightness, purity, truth, restraint, austerity, renunciation, lack of possession, and chastity.

Anata-Chaturdashi
Fourteenth day of the waxing half of Bhadrapada

Anata-Chaturdashi is a day of special worship observed by Digambara (sky-clad) Jains to mark the end of the Dasa Laksana Parvan festival. Many places observe it with special temple processions.

Asvina (September-October)

Ksamavani (Request for Forgiveness)
First day of the waning half of Asvina

Ksamavani is the day for requesting forgiveness from all, and for forgiving all for all past offences. Ksamavani is observed by the Digambaras; Sventambaras request forgiveness on the annual Paryushan day.

Table 13.3. Alphabetical List of Jain Holidays

Holidays	Date(s)
Aksaya Trtiya	Third day of the waxing half of Vaisakha
Anata-Chaturdashi	Fourteenth day of the waxing half of Bhadrapada
Birth of Mahavira	Thirteenth day of the waxing half of Caitra
Birth of Parshvanath	Tenth day of the waning half of Pausa
Caturmas	June through September
Dasa Laksana Parvan	Fifth to thirteenth day of the waxing half of Bhadrapada
Day for Honoring the Books *see* Jnan Panchami	
Day of Silence *see* Nirvana of Risabha	
Diwali	Fifteenth day of the waning half of Kartika
Jnana Panchami	Fifth day of the waxing half of Kartika
Ksamavani	First day of the waning half of Asvina
Mahavir Jayanti *see* Birth of Mahavira	
Nirvana of Risabha	Fourteenth day of the waning half of Magha
Pajjo-Savana *see* Partyshana Parva	
Partyshana Parva	Thirteenth to the fifth day of the waning half of Bhadrapada
Paryushan *see* Partyshana Parva	
Request for Forgiveness *see* Ksamavani	
Time of the Ten Characteristics *see* Dasa Laksana Parvan	

CHAPTER 14

Sikhism

Overview of Sikhism

What Is Sikhism?

Sikhism, an independent faith, developed during the fifteenth century in India. The word Sikh comes from the Sanskrit word shishya, which means disciple or student. The faith is also sometimes called Gurmat, which means "the *Guru*'s doctrine." Sikhs believe that God was the original *Guru* (*Guru* means divinely inspired prophet or teacher) and that he chose to reveal his message to the first Sikh *Guru*, Nanak. Sikhs believe that their *Guru*s were prophets sent by God to lead people into truth. They emphasize equality among people of different castes, practice Kirat Karni (a doctrine of laboring), and follow the precepts of charity.

Sikhism resembles both Islam and Hinduism, but is not directly associated with either. Similar to Hindus, Sikhs believe that the human soul progresses through a series of births and rebirths and that its ultimate salvation occurs when it breaks free from the cycle. Sikhs, however, reject the Hindu pantheon and do not participate in bathing rituals. Instead they worship one God who they believe is the same God of all religions, including Allah of Islam. Unlike Muslims, however, they shun fasting and pilgrimages.

The Sikhs can be distinguished from their Hindu neighbors by the distinctive turbans they wear. The largest population center of Sikhs is in the Punjab area of northwestern India. Many members of the faith hope they will eventually win sovereignty.

The Relationship between God and the Sikh People

For Sikhs, God is a personal creator with whom people can have individual relationships. God is eternal, without form, and indescribable, but he is willing to reveal himself in visible ways. He is present everywhere in creation and in the human heart. According to Sikh teaching, religious rituals of both the Hindu and Islamic faiths serve only to keep their adherents bound in the reincarnation cycle. Sikhs call God Nam (literally, Name). Other names by which he is known are Akal Purakh (the Eternal One) and Raheguru (Wonderful Lord).

Service to God is one of the primary human tasks. It may be performed by reading from the Sikh sacred writings, by helping maintain a house of worship, or by assisting in the preparation and service of a meal (called a langar) that traditionally follows a Sikh worship service. God may also be served by offering hospitality to anyone irrespective of their caste or religion.

Authorities and Sacred Writings

The Sikh holy scriptures are called the *Guru Granth Sahib* (*Guru* means divinely inspired teacher; *Granth* means book; *Sahib* means revered). A more ancient name is *Adi Granth*, which means first or original book. The *Guru Granth Sahib* was compiled by the fifth Sikh *Guru*, Arjan, and revised by Gobind Singh, the tenth *Guru*. It contains hymns composed by the *Guru*s.

On special occasions such as festivals and certain ceremonies, the *Guru Granth Sahib* may be read continuously in its entirety, a process that takes about 48 hours. Such a complete reading is called an Akhand Path. On other occasions, such as at weddings and funerals, parts of the book may be read. These partial, non-continuous readings are called Sidharan Paths.

Within the Sikh temple (called a gurdwara), the *Guru Granth Sahib* is displayed on a special platform called a Palki. It is elaborately arranged with embroidered cloths and set on special cushions. At night it is moved to a room of rest.

Two other important but non-canonical Sikh books are the *Dasam Granth* (book of the Tenth) and the *Nit nem*.

The *Dasam Granth* consists of a collection of writings including popular prayers, devotional hymns, biographical narratives, and poetry attributed to the tenth *Guru*, Gobind Singh. The *Nit nem* is a collection of sacred songs excerpted from the *Guru Granth Sahib*. It is used primarily in homes for private worship. When not in use, Sikhs honor it by wrapping it in cloth.

Sikhs do not have an established priesthood. Gobind Singh abolished the Sikh priesthood because he believed that priests would become egocentric and corrupt. Although individual gurdwaras may employ specially trained people to care for the *Guru Granth Sahib*, all Sikhs are free to read from their holy scriptures either in the temple or in their homes.

In addition, there is no one person to whom all Sikhs look for guidance in religious matters. The Sikh community is called the Panth, and collective decisions may be made by the Panth for the entire community. The Shiromani Gurdwara Parbandhad Committee, whose members are elected, provides guidance for all the gurdwaras in the Punjab. Individual local gurdwaras elect their own committees to oversee local matters.

History

Guru *Nanak*

Sikhs originated with *Guru* Nanak, who was born in Talvandi (which is now located in Pakistan) in 1469 C.E. Talvandi was later renamed Nankana Sahib in his honor. Although born into a Hindu family, Nanak was influenced by Islamic teachings, particularly those of the Sufis (a mystical sect within Islam).

According to Sikh teaching, Nanak began to ask questions about spiritual matters at the age of five. As a young man, he sought out the company of holy men and wandering ascetics. Then, at the age of 30, he had a mystical experience with God in which he received a mission to teach people about God and how to practice devotion.

Nanak's teachings combined elements from both the Islamic and Hindu faith systems. He advocated reforms such as the abolition of idol worship and caste regulations. He promoted liberalized social practices and preached the name of God as a potent means of spiritual realization. Nanak also encouraged his followers to work hard and pursue normal family relations (instead of celibacy).

Nanak traveled throughout India, toward each of the four compass points, to proclaim his message to both Hindu and Islamic audiences. His companions included Mardana, a Muslim musician, and Bala, a Hindu peasant.

Upon the approach of his death, Nanak appointed one of his disciples to succeed him as *Guru*.

Successive Gurus

Under the supervision of ten successive *Guru*s, Sikh doctrines developed over a 200-year period. Upon the death of a *Guru*, religious leadership passed to the person considered to be the most worthy candidate. The first four *Guru*s were unrelated; the last six were from the same family.

The second Sikh *Guru*, Angad (1504–1552) began to follow Nanak after being inspired by the divine message he received upon hearing one of Nanak's hymns being sung. Angad is remembered for his work to consolidate Nanak's followers, for compiling and writing hymns, and for building temples.

The third *Guru*, Amar Das (1479–1574) converted from Hinduism to Sikhism when he was 60 years old. He devoted the remaining years of his life to serving Angad, and at the age of 73 was appointed to be his successor. Amar Das reorganized the Sikh community into units called manjis and instituted the custom of assembling the entire community for special occasions. Amar Das is also remembered for initiating communal meals (based on a tradition originating with Nanak) and teaching on the equality of mankind. He appointed Ram Das to be his successor.

Ram Das (1534–1581), the fourth Sikh *Guru*, was a son-in-law of Amar Das. His name was originally Bhai Jetha but upon his appointment as *Guru* it was changed to Ram Das, which means "God's servant." The focal points of his teachings were sincere worship, hard work to earn one's living, and charity. Ram Das also spoke out against the Hindu practice of sati (burning a widow on her husband's funeral pyre), and he championed the right of widows to remarry. In addition, Ram Das established Amritsar as a place of worship. He is credited with beginning preparations for the eventual construction of the Sikh Golden Temple. Ram Das appointed his youngest son to succeed him.

Arjan (1563–1606) was the fifth *Guru*. Although he is best remembered for building the Golden Temple at Amritsar, he also oversaw the construction of gurdwaras in other places including Taru Taran, Kartarpur, and Sri Hargobindpur. In addition, Arjan compiled hymns and teachings of the previous *Guru*s into the *Adi Granth*, which later became the *Guru Granth Sahib*, the Sikh sacred scriptures.

Although the events of his life were important, his death marked a turning point in Sikh history. In 1606, Argan was taken captive by the Mughal Emperor Jehangir. (The

Mughal dynasty ruled over portions of India between 1526 and 1858.) After five days of torture, Arjan was put to death for refusing to convert to Islam. Arjan submitted to the ordeal peacefully, but he left instructions for his successors to take up arms to defend the innocent.

Har Gobind (1595–1644), Arjan's only son, became the sixth *Guru*. Under his leadership the Sikhs began the militaristic tradition with which they are currently associated. It is said that Har Gobind wore two swords, one signifying spiritual power and the other worldly power. He trained a small army and created the Nishan Sahib (the Sikh's national flag). The Nishan Sahib is triangular in shape with an orange (or saffron) background. The emblem shows two kirpans (swords), a khanda (a double-edged sword), and a circle that symbolizes the unity of God.

In 1609, Har Gobind built the Akal Takhit, which means "throne of the divine." The building in Amritsar faces the Golden Temple and serves as the Sikh high court. It also provides a nightly resting place for the copy of the *Guru Granth Sahib* that is used in the Golden Temple.

Figure 14.1. One of the 5Ks to which Sikh's adhere is "kesh" — uncut hair. Sikh men keep their hair wrapped in a distinctive turban.

Important decisions for the entire Sikh community are made at Akal Takhit. The building was destroyed in a military action in 1984 but was subsequently rebuilt.

Har Raj (1630–1661), the seventh *Guru*, was raised to his office when he was fourteen years old. He retained a small army and taught that the hymns of the *Gurus* should not be changed. He also taught against the show of miraculous power, which he felt was contrary to God's will.

Har Krishan (1656–1664), the youngest son of Har Raj, became the eighth *Guru* when he was only five years old. He fell ill with smallpox at the age of eight. Before his death, he named his great-uncle (a son of Har Gobind) to be his successor.

The ninth *Guru*, Teg Bahadur (1621–1675) was appointed *Guru* at the age of 43. He was martyred at the age of 54. His death resulted from fighting against the Mughals and refusing to convert to Islam. A gurdwara was erected to mark the place of his death in Delhi. After Teg Bahadur died at the hands of invaders, Sikhs focused more intently on building their military.

The tenth, and last of the human *Gurus*, Gobind Singh (1666–1708) was established in his position when only nine years old. His life was marked by constant fighting against Mughal armies. He died in 1708 after being stabbed by an assassin. He is best remembered for founding the Khalsa and installing the *Adi Granth* (which became the *Guru Granth Sahib*) as perpetual *Guru* to the Sikh community.

The Khalsa

The Khalsa (which means, literally, "belonging only to the divine") is a spiritual brotherhood with military significance open to all baptized Sikhs. The Khalsa refers to the collective body of all Sikhs who partake in a special initiation ceremony in which they vow to lead a life of spiritual discipline and uphold the highest ideals of Sikh principles. Its members wear the Five Ks:

- *kesh,* uncut hair (Sikhs believe that because growing hair is natural it should not be cut off from the body; wearing a turban to cover the hair is mandatory for Sikh men and optional for Sikh women);

- *kangha,* a comb that holds the hair in place;

- *kirpan,* a ceremonial sword (a symbol of a Sikh's duty to uphold justice, commonly worn on the body under clothing);

- *kara,* a steel bracelet (it is worn on the right wrist, the steel represents strength; the round shape symbolizes continuity);

- *kachh,* an undergarment (part of the military uniform that also symbolizes sexual restraint).

Members of the Khalsa also abstain from beef, pork, alcohol, tobacco, hemp, and opium.

According to Sikh teaching, the Khalsa was created by Gobind Singh in 1699 on Baisakhi Day when the Sikhs were assembled at Anandpur (approximately 175 miles east of Amritsar) for a festival. During the gathering, Singh brandished his sword and asked if any among those assembled were prepared to die for the religion and for their leader. When one man came forward, he was taken into a tent with the *Guru.* The *Guru* came back out of the tent with blood on his sword and again asked if anyone was willing to die for him and for the Sikh faith. Another man came forward. The process was repeated five times. After the fifth man entered the tent, all five were presented—alive—to the crowd. They were wearing special uniforms and earned the title Panj Pyares (five beloved ones). These five were the first five members of the Khalsa, a brotherhood of people willing to give their lives for their faith.

Sikhism after Gobind Singh

After Gobind Singh's death other leaders emerged within the Sikh community but no single person stood as a sole spiritual leader. One of the most well-known Sikh leaders was Ranjit Singh (1780–1839). He led Sikh defiance against British attempts to conquer the Punjab along with the rest of India.

Eventually, however, the Punjab did fall. In 1849, the British annexed the Punjab area and recruited Sikhs into the British army. This action paved the way for Sikh migration into other British lands including Hong Kong and Singapore and eventually to other countries such as the United States and Canada.

During the latter part of the nineteenth century and the early part of the twentieth century many Sikh struggles were focused on the effort to define Sikh identity and achieve autonomy. In 1870, the Singh Sabha was established to help schools in the Punjab and to increase the strength of the people through education and knowledge of literature.

The Struggle for Autonomy

In 1919, following World War I, British rulers in India controlled Sikh houses of worship and other shrines. They issued orders forbidding Sikhs to assemble for the celebration of Baisakhi because they feared an uprising. The Sikhs did assemble and were subsequently attacked. In the fighting that followed, more than 1,500 people were killed. In 1925, the Gurdwaras Act placed oversight of Sikh holy places under the Indian Government.

British rule ended in 1947, and India was divided into separate countries. Part of the Punjab, the Sikh homeland, became part of Pakistan, which was under Islamic rule. As a result, many Sikhs emigrated to India and to other parts of the world.

Sikhism Today

The Sikh People

Sikhism is one of the youngest organized religions and the fifth largest in the world today. An estimated 20 million Sikhs live around the world, the vast majority of them dwelling in northwestern India. The largest Sikh population outside India is in Britain. Other substantial Sikh communities exist in the United States and Canada with smaller population centers in Singapore, Hong Kong, Thailand, East Africa, Iran, Malaysia, Fiji, and Australia.

Worship

Sikhs participate in family worship and attend temples called gurdwaras. The word gurdwara means "*Guru*'s door," or more figuratively, "house of God." Temples do not contain images; they contain the Sikh sacred scripture,

Figure 14.2. The Sikh insignia contains two kirpan (curved swords), a khanda (double-edged sword), and a circle which stands for unity. The Sikh Flag, called the Nishan Sahib, consists of the insignia on a triangular flag with an orange background.

the *Guru Granth Sahib*, which is revered and kept on a cushion under a canopy.

Worship is traditionally conducted in the Punjabi language, although in places outside of India, part of the service (such as some of the hymns and prayers) may be conducted in English. A granthi (reader) serves as the custodian of the *Guru Granth Sahib*.

In India, Sikh temples are open to worshippers all day long but typically two daily services are held, one in the morning and another in the evening. They consist of singing or recitation and the distribution of Karah parshad, a consecrated food made from flour, clarified butter, and sugar. The Karah parshad symbolizes equality. Outside India where Sikh communities are smaller, services are held on a weekly basis.

Sikh temples also provide free food to all people who come, including members of the Sikh community, visitors, and travelers. Every gurdwara contains a community kitchen called a langar (which means kitchen of the *Guru*) where the meal is prepared.

True worship, however, is not marked by attendance at the gurdwara but by a lifestyle. Sikhs also consider an upright manner of living and personal love and devotion to God as forms of worship.

Sects

During the nineteenth century two Sikh offshoots developed. Primarily in response to British rule, they both focused their efforts on holding fast to the Sikh national identity.

Nirankari

Nirankari means "worshippers of the Formless One." They were founded by a former Hindu, Dayl Das (1783–1853). The Nirankari emphasized the centrality of the *Guru Granth Sahib* in naming and marriage ceremonies but they also honored another book, the *Hukam-nama* (Book of Ordinances). Most Nirankari Sikhs are centered in eastern Punjab.

Namdhari

The Namdhari (name-bearing) sect was founded by Baba Balak Singh (1816–1884) in the nineteenth century. Singh instituted new baptismal rituals and promoted strict disciplines. He emphasized the centrality of the *Gurus'* teachings, advocated adherence to religious authorities, and denied the perpetual authority of scripture. Unlike other Sikhs who believe that Gobind Singh appointed the *Guru Granth Sahib* as *Guru*, the Namdharis believe Gobind Singh went into hiding and that Baba Balak Singh was his successor.

◩ ◩ ◩

The Sikh Calendars

A Lunar Calendar

The Sikh calendar is a lunar calendar that is based on the moon's movement from one zodiac sign into the next rather than on the phase of the moon. The dates of some festivals, however, are based on the phase of the moon. The beginning of a new month is called the Sangrand. It is announced in the Sikh house of worship (gurdwara) but it is not a festival day.

Sikh festivals are marked on a special calendar called the Sikh Gurpurab Calendar. A gurpurab is a date commemorating births, deaths (and martyrdoms), or other important events associated with the lives of the ten Sikh human *Guru*s or with the Sikh scriptures, the *Guru Granth Sahib*. The Gurpurab Calendar also notes the anniversary dates of historic incidents that are important to the Sikh faith.

The Sikh Gurpurab Calendar begins with the month of Chait (March/April). The Sikh New Year celebration, however, falls on the first day of the second month, Basakh.

Intercalations

The Sikh have used several calendars since their religious tradition began. Over time, the lunar calendar, called the Bikrami calendar, was used predominantly. The Bikrami calendar consisted of twelve months averaging 29½ days. This yields a year that is approximately eleven days shorter than the solar year. To keep the lunar calendar in line with the solar seasons, the Sikh calendar intercalated an extra lunar month whenever two new moons occur within the same solar month. The thirteenth lunar month then took the name of the solar month in which it fells. The names of the regular twelve lunar months are listed in the *Guru Granth Sahib*.

Calendar Reform

The solar component of the Bikrami calendar, however, did not correspond exactly to the natural solar year—every seventy years a discrepancy equal to one day accrued. To resolve this problem, two calendars were developed that would accurately match the natural solar year: the Nanakshai Calendar, which is based on *Guru* Nanak's birth, and the Khalsa Calendar, which is based on the founding of the Khalsa. In 1999 c.e., the Sikhs adopted the Nanakshai Calendar. Although choice carried some controversy, it is now used to observe all Sikh religious holidays, and is becoming increasingly popular especially among Sikh communities outside India.

The Nanakshai calendar is devised in a manner that maintains consistency with the western calendar so that holidays always fall on the same day of the year. It begins with the month of Chait (Chait 1 falls on March 14) and contains five months of 31 days and seven months of 30 days. The last month usually contains 30 days, but in leap years, an extra day is added.

The Nanakshai calendar counts years from *Guru* Nanak's birth in1469 C.E. The year 536 NANAKSHAI begins in the year 2004 C.E.

Table 14.1. The Nanakshai Calendar

Month Name (Alternate Spelling)	Gregorian Equivalent	Days in month
Chait (Chet)	March/April	31
Basakh (Vaisakhi)	April/May	31
Jaith (Jeth)	May/June	31
Har (Harh)	June/July	31
Sawan	July/August	31
Bhadro (Bhadon)	August/September	30
Asun (Asu)	September/October	30
Katik	October/November	30
Magar (Maghar)	November/December	30
Poh	December/January	30
Magh	January/February	30
Phagan (Phagun)	February/March	30/31

Table 14.2. The Sikh Holiday Cycle

Chait (March/April)
1 .... Scriptural New Year
1 .... Hola Mohalla

Basakh (April/May)
1 .... Baisakhi (Birth of the Khalsa)
1 .... *Guru* Nanak's Day

Har (June/July)
2 .... Martyrdom Anniversary of *Guru* Arjan

Sawan (July/August)
8 .... Birthday of *Guru* Har Krishan

Bhadro (August/September)
17 .... Installation of Sri *Guru Granth Sahib*

Asun (September/October)
25 .... Birthday of *Guru* Ram Das

Katik (October/November)
~ .... Divali

Magar (November/December)
11 .... Martyrdom Anniversary of *Guru* Teg Bahadur

Poh (December/January)
~ .... Lohri
23 .... *Guru* Gobind Singh's Birthday

Magh (January/February)
~ .... Maghi

Sikh Holidays

Weekly

Diwan (Weekly Worship)
Often on Sunday, but some Sikh communities choose other days of the week

Sikhs observe a weekly gathering at their gurdwaras (houses of worship). These gatherings include prayers, reading from their holy scriptures, the *Guru Granth Sahib*, and singing or reciting hymns. A teaching or sermon based on the scripture readings is often given.

After the service, Sikhs share a communal meal called a langar. The meal is served to all, including non-Sikhs, free of charge and irrespective of caste distinctions. The tradition of serving a communal meal was instituted by the first Sikh *Guru*, *Guru* Nanak and promoted into general acceptance by the third *Guru*, *Guru* Amar Das.

Annually

Chait (March/April)

Scriptural New Year
Chait 1

Sikh scriptures establish Chait as the first month of the New Year. The Nanakshai calendar fixes this date so that it falls on March 14 according to the western civil calendar.

Hola Mohalla
Chait 1

The observance of Hola Mohalla (a term that means attack and counterattack) was instituted in 1700 C.E. by *Guru* Gobind Singh. He assembled the Sikhs in Anandpur to take part in military exercises so that they would be prepared to fight for their defense if necessary.

Sikhs celebrate the day with a three-day festival that includes fairs and carnival processions. Demonstrations of horsemanship and swordsmanship along with traditional children's games are typical features of the event. In addition to games of physical skill, Sikhs also enjoy presentations of singing and poetry reading.

The Nanakshai calendar marks the observance of Hola Mohalla on Chait 1, however many Sikh communities continue to honor the traditional date during Phagan according to the Hindu calendar.

Basakh (April/May)

Baisakhi (Birth of the Khalsa)
Basakh 1

This Sikh celebration of the New Year is observed on the first day of the second month. It coincides with the spring harvest. Using the Nanakshai calendar, the date for Baisakhi corresponds with April 14 on the western civil calendar.

The observance of the Baisakhi holiday was first instituted by *Guru* Amar Das, the third Sikh *Guru*, in 1567. At a Baisakhi gathering in 1699 under the leadership of the tenth *Guru*, Gobind Singh, the Sikh brotherhood of the Khalsa was formed. As a result, the day is also marked as the birth of the Khalsa, and it is a traditional day on which initiates are baptized into the Khalsa.

Other traditions associated with Baisakhi include visiting gurdwaras (houses of worship) for prayers and the singing of hymns, changing the wrappings on the flag post at the gurdwaras, and participating in parades. In addition, a large fair is held at the Golden Temple in Amritsar, the central shrine of Sikhism.

Guru Nanak's Day (Guru Parab)
Basakh 1

This festival celebrates the birth of *Guru* Nanak, the founder of Sikhism. He was followed by nine other *Guru*s, in succession, under whom Sikhism gradually developed. Many of Nanak's hymns form part of the *Guru Granth Sahib* (the Sikh scriptures).

Guru Nanak was born in 1469 at Talwandi (about 45 km away from Lahore), now known as Nankana Sahib. At Nankana Sahib there is a beautiful shrine and a holy tank. On *Guru* Parab, a grand fair and festival is held.

The birth of Nanak is also observed in other parts of India and in other Sikh communities around the world. Frequently the celebration will cover a three-day period beginning two days before the designated date. During the first two days a ceremony called an Akhand Path begins. The Akhand Path is an uninterrupted, continuous reading of the entire *Guru Granth Sahib*. The reading is timed so that it ends on the birthday celebration day. Other activities include prayers, lectures, singing of hymns, processions, and the distribution of free meals.

The Nanakshai calendar marks the observance of *Guru* Nanak's on Basakh 1, however many Sikh communities continue to honor the traditional date, the full-moon day in Katik (October-November).

Har (June/July)

Martyrdom Anniversary of Guru *Arjan*
Har 2

Guru Arjan was the fifth Sikh *Guru* and the first martyr. Jehangir, the Emperor of the Mughal Empire, unsuccessfully sought to have *Guru* Arjan convert to Islam. After five days of torture, Arjan was put to death in 1606. Although Arjan accepted his death peacefully, he left instructions for his successor, his son Har Gobind, to permit the Sikhs to take up arms to protect the innocent. The anniversary of Arjan's death is remembered with services in the gurdwaras (houses of worship) and with readings from the *Guru Granth Sahib* (Sikh scriptures).

Sawan (July/August)

Birthday of Guru *Har Krishan*
Sawan 8

Har Krishan was the eighth of the ten human Sikh *Gurus*. He is sometimes called the Child *Guru* because he was only five years old when he succeeded his father and assumed the position of *Guru*. Har Krishan served as *Guru* for only three years. He died from smallpox at the age of eight. The anniversary of his birth, or gurpurab, is celebrated with services in the gurdwaras (houses of worship) and with readings from the *Guru Granth Sahib* (Sikh scriptures).

Bhadro (August/September)

Installation of Sri Guru Granth Sahib
Bhadro 17

Three days before his death in 1708, *Guru* Gobind Singh selected his successor. Rather than choosing a human follower, as had been done by his predecessors, he selected the Sikh scriptures, the *Adi Granth*. The *Adi Granth* was renamed the *Guru Granth Sahib* and became installed as the eleventh, perpetual *Guru* to the Sikhs.

The anniversary of the installation of the *Guru Granth Sahib* is observed with ceremonies in the gurdwaras (houses of worship). These often include readings, singing of hymns, lectures, and the distribution of free meals. A continuous reading of the entire *Guru Granth Sahib* that takes approximately three days to complete may also be conducted. The installation anniversary is also a popular day for Sikhs to rededicate themselves to their faith.

Asun (September/October)

Birthday of Guru *Ram Das*
Asun 25

Guru Ram Das, the fourth Sikh *Guru*, was the son-in-law of the third *Guru* (Amar Das). Upon his selection to succeed his father-in-law his name was changed from Bhai Jetha to Ram Das meaning "God's servant." The gurpurab commemorating his birth is celebrated in Sikh gurdwaras (houses of worship) with prayers, the singing of hymns, and with readings from the *Guru Granth Sahib* (Sikh scriptures).

Katik (October/November)

Divali (Diwali)
During Katik

Divali is a Sikh adaptation of the Hindu celebration Dewali. It features an assembly in Sikh temples, called gurdwaras. The origin of the Sikh observance of the festival dates to the sixteenth century C.E. when *Guru* Amar Das declared that all Sikhs should gather together to receive the *Guru's* blessing on the Hindu celebration of Divali.

Some historical events served to make the date more auspicious. In 1577 C.E., the foundation for the famous Golden Temple at Armritsar was laid on Divali. In 1619 C.E. the temple was illuminated on Divali to provide a special homecoming to *Guru* Har Gobind when he returned to Amritsar following his release from jail. Sikhs continue the tradition of illuminating the Golden Temple on Divali. Lights are also used to decorate homes and businesses, and the Divali celebration often includes a fireworks display.

Magar (November/December)

Martyrdom Anniversary of Guru *Teg Bahadur*
Magar 11

Guru Teg Bahadur was the ninth of the ten human Sikh *Gurus*. His death resulted from fighting against the Mughals and refusing to convert to Islam. The anniversary date of his martyrdom is honored with services in the gurdwaras (houses of worship) and with readings from the *Guru Granth Sahib* (Sikh scriptures).

Poh (December/January)

Lohri
During Poh

The traditional Indian festival of Lohri (which is not a Sikh religious observance) marks the end of winter.

Bonfires are lit, and people dance and sing folk songs around the fire. Traditional sweets are made of sesame, ground nuts, and puffed rice. Lohri is celebrated with great enthusiasm and merrymaking in cities, towns, and villages alike. It is a traditional time for unmarried women to pray for a happy marriage.

Guru *Gobind Singh's Birthday*
Poh 23

Guru Gobind Singh was born in 1666 at Patna. He was the tenth and last of the human *Gurus*. Instead of appointing a human successor, Gobind Singh installed the Sikh scriptures, the *Guru Granth Sahib*, to be an eternal *Guru* to the Sikh community.

Singh's birth is celebrated by Sikhs in India and around the world. The festivities are similar to those that mark the birth of *Guru* Nanak, the first Sikh *Guru*. They also often include the three-day continuous reading of the *Guru Granth Sahib* called the Akhand Path ceremony.

Magh (January/February)

Maghi
During Magh

This Sikh observance commemorates an event that occurred during the seventeenth century when *Guru* Gobind Singh struggled against the Mughal army at Anandpur. Forty of his followers who fought against the Mughal army were killed. The forty were blessed by the *Guru* and he proclaimed that their actions had enabled them to achieve liberation from the cycle of rebirth.

Maghi is a day that honors these men, now called the Forty Immortals. Sikhs observe the holiday by visiting gurdwaras (houses of worship) and listening to the recitation of sacred hymns.

Table 14.3. Alphabetical List of Sikh Holidays

Holiday	Date
Baisakhi	Basakh 1
Birth of the Khalsa *see* Baisakhi	
Divali	during Katik
Guru Gobind Singh's Birthday	Poh 23
Guru Har Krishan's Birthday	Sawan 8
Guru Nanak's Day	Basakh 1
Guru Parab *see Guru* Nanak's Day	
Guru Ram Das's Birthday	Asun 25
Hola Mohalla	Chait 1
Installation of Sri *Guru Granth Sahib*	Bhadro 17
Lohri	during Poh
Maghi	during Magh
Martyrdom Anniversary of *Guru* Arjan	Har 2
Martyrdom Anniversary of *Guru* Teg Bahadur	Magar 11
Scriptural New Year	Chait 1

CHAPTER 15

Buddhism

Overview of Buddhism

What Is Buddhism?

Buddhism, one of the largest four religious families in the world, is based on the teachings of Siddhartha Gautama who came to be known as Buddha, or "The Enlightened One."

The Life of Buddha

Siddhartha Gautama was born in Lumbini Grove—an area that is modernly located in Nepal in the foothills of the Himalayas between India and Tibet. Mahayana Buddhist traditions and many Western scholars place his birth around 563 B.C.E., but Theravada Buddhists give the date 624 B.C.E. He was a prince of the Sakya clan and several legends surround his birth. According to one legend, his mother, Queen Maha Maya, dreamed she saw a white elephant descend from the mountains bearing a lotus when he was conceived. Her dream signified that the child she was to bear would be special. Queen Maha Maya was not to live to know of her son's future for she died shortly after his birth. His father, King Suddhodana, tried to protect him from suffering because astrologers had predicted that the young Gautama could be a great ruler, but if he saw suffering he would become a religious leader instead.

Gautama was raised in luxurious surroundings and protected from the sufferings of the world. On an excursion into the countryside, however, he met a meaningful series of situations: a diseased man, an aging man, and a corpse. From these encounters Gautama understood the suffering of illness, the suffering of growing old, and the fact that death was the ultimate end of life. He also saw a fourth person, a religious beggar, who radiated peace and joy. This experience led to Gautama's decision to become a wandering ascetic.

At the age of 29, Gautama renounced his princely life, his wife, and his infant son to search for a path that would offer relief from universal human suffering. For six years he practiced severe austerities, including eating very little and nearly starving. Ultimately, he came to realize that self-mortification would not provide a solution to the problem of suffering. He sat down under a tree, now called the Bodhi tree (or Bo Tree), and vowed not to move until he achieved enlightenment.

While meditating, he was tempted and attacked by Mara, the personification of evil, and the so-called "daughters" of Mara: Tanha (desire), Raga (lust), and Arati (aversion). After several unsuccessful attempts, Mara left. Many Buddhists interpret the temptation in psychological terms and see the assault as the surfacing of impurities that had still been in Gautama's mind.

Afterwards, while sitting in deep meditation, Gautama achieved enlightenment, or the great awakening from delusion. The basis of his enlightenment was the understanding that desire lay at the root of human problems and suffering. Gautama's enlightenment occurred at Bodh Gaya in 528 B.C.E. (589 B.C.E. according to Theravada texts).

The experience of enlightenment accorded Gautama a new title, the Buddha (Enlightened One). The Buddha's first sermon was delivered to five companions, in the Deer Park in Sarnath. Here, he delivered his first sermon, and set in motion the Wheel of Law or Maha-Dharmachakra Pravartan. and it detailed the Four Noble Truths and the Noble Eightfold Path (Table 15.1).

In the years that followed, Buddha laid down rules of ethics, condemned the Hindu caste system, and promoted the equality of men and women. Buddha's teachings emphasized that the aim of Buddhist practice was to free oneself from deep-rooted habits of and delusionary thinking that ultimately led to suffering. Enlightenment in Buddhism is thus seen as an awakening from the unconsciousness of delusionary thinking. The Buddha taught a large numbers of disciples to continue his work before his death in 483 (or 544) B.C.E.

Buddhists recognize four important places in the life of the Buddha—Lumbini where he was born, Bodh Gaya, the place of his enlightenment, Deer Park in Sarnath where he delivered his first sermon, and Kushinagar where he departed his mortal body. All these locations are in the Ganges Valley of northern India and are important pilgrimage sites for modern Buddhists.

Buddhist Concepts

The Buddha taught that earthy human life is characterized by suffering or Dukka. The cause of suffering is craving or desire (Trishna or Raga). According to the Buddha, suffering can be overcome by reaching a level of detachment or enlightenment (called bodhi) and thereby achieving Nirvana. The word nirvana means "blown out." It implies that desire has been extinguished and that a changeless state which is the true reality has been attained. Buddhist teachings state that the concept of the self is itself a delusion and the eradication of ego and its cravings enables the true bliss that has come to be known as Nirvana. The achievement of Nirvana can only be attained through the development of moral attributes, meditating, and gaining wisdom over many incarnations and life times.

The term samsara refers to the continual cycle of birth, death, and rebirth to which a person is bound by karma. Karma is the entity that binds a self to its former existences, its present existence, and its future existences; it comes from deeds. Bad deeds produce bad karma, called papa karma. Papa karma leads to sickness, poverty, an untimely death, and rebirth as a demon, ghost, animal, or resident of hell. Good deeds produce good karma, called punya karma. Punya karma leads to a long life, good health, prosperity, and rebirth into one of twenty-two heavenly realms. To live as a god in heaven, however pleasurable, is not the ultimate goal. Instead, Buddhists seek to escape the cycles of samsara and ultimately reach Nirvana.

To eliminate desire and attain Nirvana, Buddhists follow a path called The Middle Way, avoiding both the extremes of hedonism (self-centered participation in unrestrained sensual delights) and asceticism (self-denial). The Buddhist path involves an effort of the self, which is comprised of the body, feelings, perception, impulses, and consciousness. The Buddhist concept of self does not include a component similar to the Christian "soul" or Hindu "atman."

Both monks and laity play important roles in the pursuit of Nirvana. Monks provide teaching and inspiration; lay people honor and support the monks. To help people in their quest for Nirvana, the Buddhist community comprises three resources, called the Triratna (or Three Jewels): (1) Buddha, who found enlightenment and taught it to others; (2) dharma, teaching about truth; and (3) sangha, the local assembly of monks. (Sangha can also refer to the entire Buddhist community of monks, nuns, and laity.)

The Buddha's dharma refers to his doctrinal position. It is summarized in a statement called The Four Noble Truths. The truths are: (1) the truth and reality of suffering; (2) suffering is caused by desire; (3) the way to end suffering is to end desire; and (4) the Eightfold Path shows the way to end suffering.

The Eightfold Path consists of (1) right view or right understanding; (2) right thoughts and aspirations; (3) right speech; (4) right conduct and action; (5) right way of life; (6) right effort; (7) right mindfulness, and (8) right contemplation.

The Relationship between Buddha and the Buddhist People

Buddha is not a god. There is neither a transcendent, nor personal god in Buddhist teaching. There is no ultimate principle or reality that upholds or animates the material world. A Buddha can be any human who has achieved enlightenment. Gautama himself was preceded

---

Table 15.1. The Four Noble Truths and the Eightfold Path

The Four Noble Truths

1. There is suffering.
2. Suffering results from desire.
3. The way to end suffering is to end desire.
4. The Eightfold Path shows the way to end suffering.

The Eightfold Path

1. Right view or right understanding
2. Right thoughts and aspirations
3. Right speech
4. Right conduct and action
5. Right way of life
6. Right effort
7. Right mindfulness
8. Right contemplation

by previous Buddhas, and contemporary Buddhists anticipate the coming of an individual known as the Maitreya, or future Buddha.

There are many paths to Nirvana. Some Buddhists focus their energies on meditation and self-understanding; some believe that actions and good deeds lead to Nirvana; others believe that the true path is found through the veneration of one or more of the Buddha's manifestations.

Authorities and Sacred Writings

The Sutras

The sutras are records of the teachings and conversation of the Buddha. Different sects of Buddhism acknowledge different canons of sacred writings but they draw on the same basic traditions. The Mahayana Buddhist texts were written in Sanskrit and date back to the first century B.C.E. The Theravada Buddhist texts, called the Pali Canon (because they are written in an ancient dialect related to Sanskrit known as Pali), are believed by adherents to contain Gautama's actual words. After the Buddha's death, his teachings were orally transmitted

---

Table 15.2. Buddhist Writings

Theravada Buddhism

Tipitaka (Three Baskets)

  Sutta Pitaka (Basket of Discourses)

  Vinaya Pitaka (Basket of Disciplines)

  Abhidhamma Pitaka (Basket of Higher Teachings)

Milinda-panha (Questions of Milinda)

Visuddhi-magga (The Way of Purification)

Mahayana Buddhism

Tripitaka (Three Baskets)

  Sutra Pitaka (Basket of Discourses)

  Vinaya Pitaka (Basket of Disciplines)

  Abhidharma Pitaka (Basket of Higher Teachings)

Prajna-paramita Sutras (Perfection of Wisdom Discourses)

Sad-dharma-pundarika Sutra (Sutra of the Lotus of the True Dharma)

Sukhavati-vyuha (Vision of the Pure Land)

---

down the centuries and were not committed to a written record till the first century B.C.E. The first adherents of the Buddha met at the Cave of the Seven Leaves in Rajagaha for three months after his parinibanna (entry into Nirvana) and began the task of codifying his teachings to ensure its correct interpretations for future generations. Three of the Buddha's closest adherents, Ananda, Mahakashyapa, and Upali were each charged with what would eventually become parts of the Tripitaka.

The *Tripitaka* (Sanskrit) or *Tipitaka* (Pali) is the foundational document for Buddhist teachings. The title means "three baskets" and it contains three separate volumes (with slightly different titles for Theravada and Mahayana Buddhism). The first basket, called "Basket of Discourses" and the second, "Basket of Discipline," contain similar information for the two main branches of Buddhism. The third, "Basket of Higher Teachings," deals with monastic discipline, theories of the self, transmigration or reimbodiment, and philosophy. For each branch of Buddhism, its content reflects the specific doctrines of the sect. A list of selected Buddhist texts for both Theravada and Mahayana Buddhism is given in Table 15.2.

For some Buddhists, canonical texts exist only in ancient languages and translation is forbidden. For others, translation is an on-going process. Other Buddhist groups view the canon as still open and new teachings may yet be added.

Sangha

The Buddhist community, called a sangha, is made up of laypeople and monks (or monks and nuns). Monastics vow to maintain celibacy and are permitted to own only eight prescribed items (a robe, an alms bowl, a belt, a razor, a needle, a filter with which to strain water, a staff, and a toothpick). In keeping with the first of the so-called Five Precepts of Buddhism against the taking of life, most monastics are also vegetarians. In some Theravada communities such as Thailand, laypeople provide food, shelter, and clothing for the monks. These acts of giving are part of the Theravada tradition of "merit" where giving is seen as being part of the karmic lore. According to the Six Perfections (the Six Paramitas), generosity and charity is the foremost virtue, and acts of giving can reduce selfishness and suffering. For their part, monastics engage themselves in studying, meditating, and teaching. Many orders are also actively engaged in charitable works, disaster relief and cottage industries.

The Spread of Buddhism

During the third century B.C.E. an Indian leader, Asoka (the last ruler in the Indian Maurya Dynasty) converted to Buddhism from Hinduism and became an example of an ideal ruler. He embraced Buddhist teachings because of remorse over the human suffering caused by his military conquests. Under his patronage monastic orders were restored and supported, ancient burial mounds were renovated, and new ones were built. The burial mounds, called stupas, served to honor kings and great religious leaders of the past. He also established government ministries to help the impoverished rural population. According to legend, Asoka sent his son and daughter as missionaries to Sri Lanka where they established a Buddhist Sangha (community).

According to Buddhist legend, King Devanampiyatissa of Sri Lanka was chasing a deer in the forest of Mihintale when someone called out his name. He looked up and saw a figure in a saffron-colored robe standing on a rock with six companions. The robed figure was the holy patron of Sri Lanka, Arhat Mahinda, the son of Emperor Asoka of India. Mahinda converted King Devanampiyatissa and the royal family, and they in turn converted the common people. Mahinda, who propagated the faith through works of practical benevolence, died in about 204 B.C.E.

The spread of Buddhism continued in other regions as well. During the third century B.C.E., Buddhism reached southeast Asia, an area that remains predominantly Theravada Buddhist. Buddhism reached China during the first century B.C.E. where the faith commingled with existing Confucian and Taoist philosophies.

The practice of making images of the Buddha (called rupas) also began during the first century B.C.E. Some common features of the popular statues were long ear lobes, representing spiritual wisdom, and wheel patterns on the feet, signifying one who restarts the dharma or wheel of teaching.

During the first century of the common era, another movement within Buddhism developed. It involved veneration of the Buddha called Amitabha, the celestial Buddha. According to Mahayana texts, Amitabha established a heaven (celestial home) for people who wished to be reborn there. The paradise he created, called the Pure Land, was devoid of suffering, aging, and death. People who were reborn into the Pure Land could benefit from Amitabha's teaching and gain sufficient merit to step up into Nirvana. Under traditional Buddhist teaching, being born into a heavenly realm did not lead to nirvana. Descent back to earth in a human form was the only path by which Nirvana was attainable. In addition to creating the Pure Land, Amitabha provided the means by which people could attain it. The simple expression of faith through the recitation of a formulaic prayer offering homage to Amitabha Buddha assured a follower a place in the Pure Land.

Buddhism was introduced to Korea from China during the fourth century C.E. Tradition is that the teachings were first brought to the northern Korean kingdom of Koguryo by a Chinese monk. Some years later Buddhism was introduced by another central Asian monk to the southwestern kingdom of Paekchae. From Korea, legendary sources state that a statue of the Buddha and several Buddhist texts were introduced to the court of the Japanese emperor Kimmei in October, 538 C.E. Within fifty years during the successive reigns of the Empress Suiko and Emperor Shotoku, Buddhism would become firmly established in Japan. Buddhism in Japan commingled with existing Shinto beliefs resulting in many forms of Buddhism that focused on personal experience and intuition.

By the reign of King Songtsen Gampo (born in approximately 557 C.E.) Tibet had developed a written script that enabled the translation of Indian-language Buddhist texts into Tibetan. In the ensuing centuries, almost the entire canon of Indian Buddhist texts was translated into Tibetan. This, along with the arrival of great Buddhist teachers such as Padmasambhava, Vairocana, Santaraksita, and Vimalamitra in the eighth century C.E. facilitated the spread of Buddhism in Tibet.

Buddhism Today

The Buddhist People

Buddhism, a diverse faith, has a long, 2500-year history and a global presence. During the late twentieth century, it claimed an estimated 500 million followers. Most of these were located in Asia, but other places around the world, including North America and Europe, now have significant populations of adherents from different sects. In some countries, Buddhism is the official national religion. These include Tibet, Sri Lanka, Burma, and Thailand.

Practice

Buddhist people do not worship Buddha in the same sense that other religions worship gods. Many Buddhists regard Buddhism as a practice involving self-monitoring, discipline, and compassion rather worship. The Buddha and lesser Buddhas known as Bodhisattvas are regarded not as gods or transcendent beings, but as exemplars whose potentials have been realized. Veneration, in the sense of acknowledging the worthiness of Buddhas and Bodhisattvas, involves lighting incense and, depending on cultural origins, the placement of flowers, fruits, food, and water in front of the images of the Buddha and Bodhisattvas. Bowing and prostration before an image or shrine symbolize respect for the Buddha and surrender or yielding to the higher possibilities inherent in all beings.

Buddhist temples typically have statues of Buddha in different manifestations as well as those of the different Bodhisattvas. These statues may also depict the Buddha or Bodhisattvas with specific hand gestures, called mudras. Mudras have long been associated with meditation and yoga practices in India. In Buddhism, these gestures are signifiers of different Buddhist concepts. When an individual uses a certain gesture, it is said that the hand or hands send specific messages to the mind and body energy system. When Buddhists look at statues of the Buddha or Bodhisattvas, they generally understand immediately the significance of a particular pose. For example, a statue of the Buddha with his hands folded in his lap signals his engagement in what is known as the Dhyana Mudra, or the gesture of meditation.

Meditation plays a central a central role in Buddhist cultivation toward enlightenment. Along with study and knowledge, Buddhists are taught that there must also be contemplation of what is acquired through knowing and meditation. The purpose of meditation is to bring about a mental clarity that enables the individual to cut through layers of false perceptions, ideas, and assumptions that prevent her or him from seeing the true nature of reality. The Buddha was once asked if he were a god or an angel. He replied that he was "awake" —a person who had achieved a heightened state of perceiving reality.

Buddhists recognize eight levels of meditation, the first four of which involve differing levels of consciousness. The other four levels operate at a plane at the karmic level above consciousness. Some Buddhists may also use pictures or designs, called yantras, as an aid to help focus visually during meditation.

Buddhist Schools and Sects

Over the centuries following the Buddha's entry into Nirvana, two major traditions evolved within Buddhism to form the Mahayana and Theravada traditions. Many Buddhists acknowledge the veracity of different paths and do not judge the correctness of one path in comparison with others. Other Buddhists, however, make distinctions of preference among the many paths.

Mahayana

The term Mahayana means "Great Vehicle." It connotes the ability to carry many passengers beyond suffering to Nirvana. The Mahayana branch is the largest school of Buddhism and it offers many different paths. Mahayana Buddhism is practiced mainly in China, Japan, Korea, some parts of Southeast Asia, and Central Asia.

One of the distinctions between Mahayana and Theravada Buddhism is in the concept of a Bodhisattva. Mahayana Buddhists use the term to refer to someone who is qualified to be a Buddha but who has chosen to pass up Nirvana in order to help others. Bodhisattvas are bound by certain vows: generosity, virtue, patience, meditation, and wisdom. People who become Bodhisattvas are venerated as saints, and they are able to help others attain enlightenment. Theravada practitioners believe, however, that only individuals themselves can be responsible for their enlightenment.

Theravada

Theravada is the oldest form of Buddhism. The word Theravada, or "Lesser Wheel" is sometimes translated as "The Doctrine of the Elders." Adherents of the Theravada branch of Buddhism assert that its traditions are the most accurate representation of the Buddha's teaching. Mahayana texts pejoratively call it the "Little Vehicle" (Hinayana) because it limits the number of those who can achieve Nirvana to the monks. Theravada is the most commonly found form of Buddhism in countries such as Thailand, Myanmar, and Sri Lanka.

Theravada Buddhists place emphasis on the exemplars and teachings of the *arahats*, or monks, who were the first followers of the Buddha. These are also individuals who followed the Eightfold Path and reached spiritual perfection.

Temples are centers of various religious and secular activities in Theravada Buddhism. Temples provide a place where monastics live and serve as a shrines where rituals are carried out. Temples in Southeast Asia are also sometimes hospices for the terminally ill, aged, or refugees. Some temples have temple schools which may serve as the only schools in the area. In countries such as Thailand where all males serve as monks at one point of their lives, particularly during the monsoons, temples serve as retreats where lay people are able to study Buddhist texts and meditate.

Tibetan Buddhism

Tibetan Buddhism is a form of Mahayana called Vajrayana ("Diamond Vehicle"). It is defined not only by Buddhist teachings but also by Tibetan indigenous religious traditions of shamanism and animism. These practices, conducted by shamans known as shen (gshen) or bonpo (bon po), are known as *Bon* or *Bon chos*. Tibetan Buddhism also incorporates folk practices known as *mi chos*.

Tibetan Buddhism is characterized by its numerous schools. The most well-known schools today include the Nyingma School, the Kagyu School, the Sakya School, and the Gelug or Gandenpa School. The Dalai Lamas of Tibet have historically been members of the Gelug School.

Tibetan Buddhists also venerate Avalokiteshvara, who is known as Chenrezig, a Bodhisattva whom they believe is incarnated in the Dalai Lama. The Dalai Lama is held in such esteem that he is considered the fourth jewel of Buddhism (the traditional three are the Buddha, the Buddha's doctrine, and the Buddhist community).

There are a number of rituals and implements that are unique to Tibetan Buddhism. These include the use of a mandala as a focal point for meditation. Mandalas can be made of paper, textiles, or colored sand. Designs vary from geometric forms to those which incorporate images of demons, animals or Bodhisattvas. Prayer wheels and prayer flags are also unique to Tibetan Buddhism. Other ritual implements include a scepter, known as the dorje (also known as the Vajra or Thunderbolt); the hand bell or drill bu; the phurpa, or "magic dagger" that is believed to conquer evil; the kapala, or cup made from a skull; and the curved chopper.

Tibetan Buddhists also recite mantras or sacred chants. The Sanskrit word, mantra, can literally be translated to mean "protection of the mind." Repetition of mantras is meant to dispel negative karma and the generation of negative or confusing thoughts. Mantras may also be written on paper that is inserted into either mechanical prayer wheels or hand-held prayer rattles. When the mantra is chanted the wheel is turned with each turn of the wheel representing one repetition of the mantra.

Political events of the twentieth century have had an impact on Tibetan Buddhism. Tibet was invaded by the Chinese in 1949, and the Dalai Lama has been in exile since 1959 when he and many of his ministers along with approximately 100,000 Tibetans escaped across the Himalayas. The Dalai Lama has lived since then in exile in Dharmsala, India. Today there are some 80,000 Tibetans in India, 30,000 in Nepal, and 3,000 in Bhutan. Much of the Tibetan culture has been suppressed, but festivals are still observed in a modest way in Tibet and by Tibetans in exile.

Chinese Buddhism

Buddhism was introduced to China in the first two centuries of the common era but did not begin to find popular acceptance until the fourth century. The blending of indigenous Chinese philosophies and Buddhist philosophies led to the creation of schools of Buddhism in which compatible beliefs merged.

Translation of Buddhist texts by the Chinese monastic An Shih-kao was undertaken as early as 148 C.E. Recognizing the tendency of the Chinese to regard foreigners as "barbarians" An Shih-Kao and other Chinese translators employed a task termed ko-i, or "matching concepts," meaning that pre-existing Taoist terminology was used to aid in translating Indian and Buddhist terms. Buddhist teachings were thus rendered more acceptable to the Chinese. The resulting form of Chinese Buddhism thus came to be co-mingled with existing Chinese folk religions, Confucian teachings, and Taoist practices.

The Tiantai school of Buddhism, which asserts that many skillful means can lead people to enlightenment, was compatible with the ancient Chinese belief that the harmony of different things was good. Buddhism continued to thrive in China along with Confucianism, Taoism, and other folk religions, until the Cultural Revolution (1966–1976) sought to suppress religious expression.

Japanese Buddhism

There are many Japanese Buddhist schools and sects based on the Mahayana tradition.

Tendai Buddhism, introduced into Japan from China around the ninth century C.E., focused on attaining salvation from the world through meditation and faith. Followers of Tendai obscured the difference between Buddhas and Bodhisattvas. They also incorporated rituals

Figure 15.1. Buddha received Enlightenment while seated under the Bodhi tree.

and secret teachings into their practices. From Tendai Buddhism, many other sects developed.

Shingon Buddhism (which means "True Word") uses symbol, ritual, and sacred mantras to express the mystery at the heart of the universe. One of the principles in Shingon is that an individual's own Buddha nature is identical with the Buddha's teaching. It was introduced to Japan during the ninth century C.E. from China and became popular among Japan's warrior class, the samurai. The central focus of Shingon is on the Buddha of Infinite Light and it also incorporates the veneration of other gods.

Pure Land Buddhism is the largest Buddhist school in Japan. It is also called Jodo-shu. It involves a faith in Amitabha Buddha (Buddha of Boundless Light). Practitioners believe that salvation can come from repeating Amitabha's name. The form of Pure Land Buddhism practiced in the United States is the form that comes closest to the traditional Western understanding of religion. The basis for the Pure Land doctrine is that salvation comes from a transference of merit from the Buddha to an unworthy follower. Emphasis is placed on the importance of family and community involvement. A celebration of Amitabha is observed by this sect on the fifteenth day of each month. Another type of Pure Land Buddhism, True Pure Land (Jodo Shinshu), emphasizes that faith is expressed in passivity.

Nichiren Buddhism is a Japanese nationalistic form of Buddhism marked by heightened devotion to Buddha, doctrine, and scripture. It is named for its founder who studied Tendai Buddhism in the middle thirteenth century C.E. Nichiren denounced practitioners of Pure Land Buddhism and Zen Buddhism for placing their trust in anything but the *Lotus Sutra*. In homage to the sacred text, he developed a mantra, which Nichiren followers chant.

Zen Buddhism

Zen Buddhism with its emphasis on meditation is said to have begun with a lesson given by the Buddha himself where he sat in silence holding a lotus. None of his followers save one understood what he was trying to convey.

Zen Buddhism, as it is known today, had its roots in China where it was developed by an Indian monastic known as Bodhidharma in the 6th century C.E. Bodhidharma is said to have sat for nine years facing a wall in deep meditation He came to be known as the first patriarch of Ch'an Buddhism which later came to be known as Zen when it was transported to Japan.

After World War II, Americans encountered Zen Buddhism through the writings of D.T. Suzuki. Zen Buddhism was further introduced in America by writers and artists of the Beat generation such as Ginsberg, Kerouac, Burroughs, and Synder, and later popularized in the 1960s by the counterculture movement in the United States. Zen Buddhism is perhaps more familiar today to Westerners than many other schools of Buddhism.

Unlike the more esoteric and ethereal Mahayana orientation, Zen absorbed the asceticism and highly disciplined outlook of bushido, or the code of the samurai warriors. This asceticism includes the goal of achieving freedom from the individual self. The theory is that extreme self-denial builds a tension that can be used to break through to an instant revelation of oneness. The ability to achieve enlightenment suddenly (satori) is unique to Zen.

Zen adherents seek to develop their own intuition. Practitioners use koans to center their meditation. The word koan comes from the Chinese term kung-an meaning "public announcement." Koans are questions or narratives that are deliberately paradoxical so as to evade rational analysis. Koans are usually posed by a teacher evoke insight from the student. Some of the earliest koans date back to the twelfth century.

Zen Buddhists regard meditation as the study of the self in order to be rid of the self. Although Zen meditation may be performed while doing simple tasks, sitting meditation, or zazen, is a unique form used in Zen and is the focus of Zen practice. There are several positions a person may adopt in Zen meditation. These include the lotus position with each foot placed on the opposite thigh and the half-lotus where the left foot is place on the right thigh. In both positions, the hands are placed on the lap in the dhyana mudra (cosmic meditation) position. In Japan, Zen practitioners sometimes use the seiza position where the individual meditates in a kneeling position with feet tucked under the thighs and hands in the cosmic mudra position. In all Buddhist schools, practitioners use some form of cushions or mats for meditation. Zen practitioners use mats or thin cushions, known as zabutons, and round supporting cushions known as zafu.

The Triratna (or Three Jewels):

(1) Buddha, who found enlightenment and taught it to others;

(2) Dharma, teaching about truth; and

(3) Sangha, the local assembly of monks or the entire Buddhist community.

🔲 🔲 🔲

Buddhist Adaptations of Regional Calendars

Based on Hindu Roots

Buddhism is derived from Hinduism in much the same way that Christianity is derived from Judaism. As a reform of Hinduism in India, Buddhism met with a varying degree of receptivity in different countries. Buddhism bears the marks of its Hindu ancestry in its time reckoning systems. Similarities between the two calendars include the lunar and astrological base and intercalations.

Buddhists and Hindus also hold similar views on the cyclical character of time. Buddhists view time as an extension of the ever-repeating sequences in nature: day follows day; the moon waxes and wanes; the seasons repeat year after year. In Buddhist history, there is no story of the first creation or ultimate destruction of the universe, only a cycle of expansion, decline, and rest.

A Variety of Lunar Calendars

Because Buddhist calendars are not associated with a specific civil calendar, the variances among geographical locations are even more pronounced than differences in Hindu calendars. For example, the method for determining the date of the new year is not uniform among Buddhist sects. Some Buddhist calendars begin the new year, Wesak, with the full moon in Taurus, which is believed to be the date of the Buddha's birth, enlightenment, and passing on. In contrast, the Tibetan Buddhists, whose calendar has been heavily influenced by the Chinese calendar, begin their new year at the full moon nearest to the midpoint of the sign Aquarius. In Vietnam, the new year, called Tet Nguyenden, begins at the new moon in Capricorn.

Development of Regional Calendars

As Buddhism spread outside of India following the death of the Buddha (Siddhartha Gautama) around 483 B.C.E., the two dominant traditions, Mahayana and Theravada, became prominent in separate regions. The Theravada tradition spread to the south and southeast Asia while the Mahayana tradition became established in east Asia. The conquest of northwest India (in the area known today as the Punjab) by Alexander the Great in 327 B.C.E. led to the spread of Buddhist teachings to the West

Different regions developed different holidays and calendars. Holidays honoring diverse manifestations of the Buddha, such as the Medicine Buddha, became a part

of some calendars. The Buddha of Boundless Light, or Amitabha, is honored by followers of Pure Land Buddhism and is celebrated on the fifteenth day of each month. There are also special days dedicated to the Bodhisattvas: Kuan Yin the Bodhisattva of Compassion (Kannon in Japan, Tchenrezig in Tibet) is the best loved Bodhisattva in east Asia and parts of southeast Asia. Her birthday in March is widely celebrated in Taiwan, and April 15 is usually set aside as the day for Kuan Yin's Ritual of Compassion. In the United States, some popular Zen Buddhist holy days are observed. Also, many religious festivals of the new host lands became incorporated into the Buddhist calendar. One such festival is the Chinese Ch'ing Ming, or Festival of Pure Brightness. This ancient Chinese observance, held in honor of the dead, has become an established Buddhist holiday in China.

Dates for Buddhist Holidays

For convenience, the holidays listed in this book are shown in Gregorian months. Where practical notations about their order in terms of lunar cycles are also given. Although some Buddhist communities follow the fixed dates that appear on the Gregorian calendar, many others calculate holiday dates on the basis of a lunar calendar. There is, however, no single lunar calendar that serves as a model for all Buddhists. In practice many of the holidays listed are observed on different and widely varying dates. Month names in the Buddhist calendar also vary considerably depending on the community, nation of origin, and type of Buddhism.

Figure 15.2. A mandala is used among Tibetan Buddhists as a focal point for meditation. The mandala depicted here was made of sand, signifying impermanence. Copyright © Melitta Tchaicovsky.

Table 15.3. Buddhist Holiday Cycle

Dates .... Holidays

January
1–3 .... Oshogatsu
~ .... Chinese New Year

February
~ .... Losar
~ .... Monlam Chenmo

March
1–14 .... Omizutori Matsuri
~ .... Magha Puja
20 or 21 ...... Spring Higan

April
~ .... Vesak
13–14 .... Songkran

May
~ .... Poson
~ .... Sanghamitta Day

June
~ .... Airing the Classics
~ .... Esala Perahera

July
~ .... Hemis Festival
6 .... Birthday of the Dalai Lama
~ .... Waso
13–15 .... Obon Festival
~ .... Marya

August
15 .... Floating Lantern Ceremony

September
2 .... Shinbyu
~ .... Vatsa
23 or 24 ...... Autumnal Higan

October
5 .... Bodhidharma Day

November
19 .... Tazaungdaing
~ .... Festival of Lights

December
8 .... Rohatsu or Boddhi Day

Note: Dates marked with a ~ are variable. They are placed in their approximate sequence.

Buddhist Holidays

Weekly

Uposatha Days

The Theravada Buddhist tradition of weekly festivals developed out of the customary monks' practice of gathering at every new moon and full moon. Although Uposatha gatherings at the full moon and new moon are still the most important, gatherings at quarter moons are also observed. On the Uposatha days, lay people come to the temples, make offerings to the monks, and venerate the image of Buddha.

Monthly

Jizo Ennichi
Twenty-fourth day of each month

It is customary for Japanese Buddhists to express their devotion to Ksitigarbha Jizo on the twenty-fourth day of each month in a devotional practice known as Jizo Ennichi.

Ksitigarbha Jizo is a Bodhisattva, or "Buddha-to-be," who is highly regarded by Buddhists in Japan as well as in China, where he is known as Ti-t'sang. Among Japanese Buddhists, Ksitigarbha is known as the protector of children and women in labor. All over Japan, there are shrines to Jizo who is also venerated for his ability to put out fires, ensure good rice harvests, finding lost objects, and curing illnesses. Jizo is also recognized as the rescuer of children who die and are sent to a sort of hell known as saino kawara where they are punished for having caused their parents to grieve. Jizo shrines in Japan are also sometimes adorned with children's clothes offered by sorrowing parents. As children who die are known as mizuko, or "watery children," shrines where Jizo is venerated as the rescuer of dead children are known as mizuko Jizo shrines.

Jizo is also believed to play a role in receiving and welcoming the faithful when they die. He is usually depicted in monk's robes, holding a staff with six rings in his right hand and an orb or pearl in his left hand. The rings on his staff which symbolizing the six dimensions of existence in the realm of desire also serve as a rattle to arouse individuals out of their delusionary state. The pearl symbolizes the precious truths of the dharma or Buddhist teachings. His statue is most often found outside the temple, where he can guide both the dead and the living. Shrines in his honor are often set up along the roadside, since he protects travelers as well.

Annual

January

Oshogatsu (Ganjitsu; Japanese New Year's Day)
January 1-3

This Japanese New Year's Day celebration is also known as the "festival of festivals." Government offices, banks, museums, and most businesses are closed during its duration from January 1 through January 3.

Preparations begin in early December, when cities start decorating the streets with pine branches, plum branches, and bamboo—known traditionally as the three friends of winter. Small pine trees with bamboo stems attached, representing longevity and constancy, are traditionally placed in the home. For weeks before the New Year celebration, people clean house and purchase new clothes for their children, exchange gifts and pay off personal debts.

On New Year's Eve, many people don traditional kimonos and walk through the streets as they visit shrines. The ancient tradition of tolling the great bells in the Buddhist temples at midnight ends the day of celebration. Priests strike the bells 108 times as a reminder of the 108 human frailties or sins in Buddhist belief. At the end of the bell tolling ceremony, the impure desires of the old year have been driven away.

New Year's Day celebrations begin early, at four a.m., with the practice of worshiping in four directions. Traditionally, the Japanese emperor looked in all four directions asking for peace and abundant crops during the coming year. Other New Year's Day traditions include saying prayers at the household altar and eating specially prepared New Year food known as osechi-ryori. Items of New Year food are each symbolic of hopes for the coming year such as good health, prosperity or longevity. Foods included in osechi ryori include sweet omelet, chestnuts mashed with sweet potatoes, sake shrimp and herring roe.

Chinese New Year (Yuan Tan)
Generally between January 21 and February 19, beginning on the first day of the first full moon.

The Chinese New Year is a festival involving family celebrations, ancestral veneration, religious duties, and celebration. It is a 15-day festival and each day has a special significance. Preparations and observances may actually begin a week earlier when different gods, including the Kitchen God, return to the Jade emperor to report on the conduct of humans during the previous year. The send-off rituals may include burning of paper money—travel expenses for the gods, and in the case of the household Kitchen God, smearing his lips with honey or sugar so that he will issue a "sweet" report to the Jade Emperor.

On the first actual day of the New Year, family members present new year wishes to one another. In Chinese households, the first day of the new year is also a day to welcome the gods of heaven and earth and to pay ritual respects to ancestors, parents, and grandparents. Traditional greetings include *kung-his fatt chai* meaning congratulations and much prosperity. Red envelops containing money known as *hung pao* or *lai his* are given to children after they have wished their elders long life and happiness. Traditionally, only married persons are permitted to give these red envelopes, as one is not considered to be a human being until one is married. The youngest child in the family wears a special cap depicting the eighteen Buddhist saints.

On the second day, new year wishes are given to neighbors. The second day is sometimes celebrated as the birthday of all dogs, and humans are expected to be especially kind to them. In old China, the second day of the new year was the day wives were permitted to return to their ancestral homes.

The third and fourth days of the new year are generally reserved for sons-in-laws to visit their in-laws and pay their respects. In folklore, the third day was also the day mice were permitted to marry. Historically, humans historically retired early so the household mice could have their wedding festivities undeterred by people.

The fourth day of the new year is usually held to be significant as it marks the return of the Kitchen God Tsao Chun. Having been symbolically sent to heaven before the new year by having his effigy burnt, his return is marked by the establishment of a new altar with his fresh image in a place of honor in the kitchen. The return of the Kitchen God also marks the end of freedom to live unfettered, as Tsao Chun begins his duty of monitoring human behavior.

The fifth day of the new year is known as *powu* or the day to welcome back the God of Wealth. The day is usually spent at home as it is believed that going outdoors on the day of the God of Wealth's return would be infortuitous. Visitations to friends and relatives are therefore permitted on the sixth to tenth days of the new year. The seventh day of the new year is regarded as the birthday of all humans and the wish that all humans enjoy longevity and prosperity, noodles (for long life) and fish (for wealth) are generally eaten. The Jade Emperor is honored with offerings in homes and temples on the ninth day.

Feasting and celebrations continue for remaining days and the new year festivities conclude on the fifteenth day with the Lantern Festival.

February

Losar (Tibetan New Year)
Usually in February

The Tibetan calendar is based on a lunar cycle. Like the Chinese calendar, each year is symbolized by an animal. The twelve year cycle of animals are identified as the year of the rat, ox, tiger, rabbit, dragon, snake, horse, ram, horse, bird, dog, and pig. In turn, each year is designated "feminine" or "masculine" depending on configurations with the five elements of water, fire, wood, metal or earth.

Tibetans observe a form of Buddhism known as Lamaism or Lama Buddhism. This involves belief in evil spirits, magic, and the spirits of nature. Many of the traditions surrounding the celebration of Losar, or the New Year, are associated with these beliefs.

Prior to the new year, houses are whitewashed and thoroughly cleaned to chase away bad memories from the old year; a little dirt from the house is saved and thrown in a crossroads where spirits are believed to dwell. On the last day of the old year, usually the 29th day of the last month, all vestiges of the old year including accumulated misdeeds must be cleared for the new year. Monks ceremoniously drive out evil spirits by performing a mask dance known as *cham*. The dances, which portray the struggle between good and evil, are performed in a deep meditative state to the accompaniment of music performed by temple orchestras. Cham is meant to exorcise all the negative elements of the old year and to ensure positive circumstances in the new year. Pyramids made of butter with figures representing the ills of the previous year are erected. These are know as *zor torma* and are burnt as a way of excising the evils of the past.

Certain foods are prepared for Losar. These include pastries known as *khapse* which are used as offerings on family altars. Gifts of khapse and scarves known as *khata* are also given as presents. Tibetans also partake of a so-called "nine-ingredients" soup called *gutuk*. Tradition also dictates that one has to have nine bowls of nine-ingredients soup. The soup usually has dumplings which are filled with different ingredients symbolizing trends for the coming year. Each person leaves a spoonful of soup which is then collected and placed in a pot. To this a piece from the each person's clothing, ashes from the family hearth, hair, and nails are added. A human effigy made of dough is placed atop the pot and the pot is carried outside to a crossroads where it is burned. This ritual too is meant to symbolize the exorcising of past evils.

Another ritual during Losar involves throwing a pinch of roasted barley known as *tsampa* into the air to ensure good harvests for the coming year. Other celebrations continue with consumption of a fermented drink known as *chang* and thick buttered tea.

On the first day of the new year, people place water and offerings on their household shrines early in the morning. The three-day celebration is a time of hospitality and merrymaking, with feasts, dances, and archery competitions. Although much of the Tibetan culture has been suppressed since the Chinese invasion in 1950, the festivals are still observed in a modest way in Tibet and by Tibetans in exile.

Tibetan exiles in India celebrate Losar by flocking to the temple in Dharmsala where the Dalai Lama lives. On the second day of the new year, he blesses people by touching their heads and giving them a piece of red and white string. People tie the blessed string around their necks as a protection from illness.

In Bodhnath, on the eastern side of Katmandu, Nepal, crowds of Tibetan refugees visit the stupa to watch lamas perform rites. Copper horns are blown, there are masked dances, and a portrait of the Dalai Lama is displayed.

Monlam Chenmo (The Great Prayer Festival)
Usually begins in February; fourth through twenty-fifth day of the first lunar month of the Tibetan calendar

Monlam Chenmo or the Great Prayer Festival is the ten-day Tibetan festival that follows the Losar, or New Year, celebration. Started in the fifteenth century by Tsongkhapa, the reformist monk, the festival ensures that the new year will be successful and prosperous. In the past, celebrants thronged to Lhasa's famous Jokhang Monastery where monks created enormous butter sculptures of Buddhist heroes. A procession around the Barkor, the old city of Lhasa, carried a statue of Maitreya, the future Buddha.

Celebration of the festival ceased when the Chinese denounced religious observances in 1959, but it was revived in 1986 and has been practiced since on a smaller scale.

March

Omizutori Matsuri (Water Drawing Festival)
March 1-14

The Omizutori Matsuri is a ritual of purification that has been observed at the Buddhist Todaiji Temple in Nara (Akita Prefecture) in Japan since the twelfth century. This time of meditative rituals is characterized by the drone of devotees reciting sutras and the sound of blowing conchs echoing from the temple. The climax of the festival occurs on March 12 when young monks in the gallery of the temple shake off burning pieces from pine-branch torches. Observers attempt to catch the sparks, believing them to have supernatural power against evil. Water is drawn from the sacred wells and offered to Kannon (Kuan Yin) the principle Bodhisattva of the temple.

The Water Drawing ceremony commences at 2 a.m. on March 13. Ancient music plays as monks carry buckets to a well and the first water drawn for the year is offered to the Buddha. The monks then perform a dramatic fire dance to the beating of drums which signals the end of the festivities.

Magha Puja (Maka Buja, Full Moon Day; Four Miracles Assembly; Sangha Day)
~*March 6; Full moon night of the third lunar month*

Magha Puja commemorates Buddha's meeting with 1,250 of his followers in the Bamboo Grove at Rajagaha in the last year of his life. It is also known as Sangha Day to because it commemorate what it means to be part of sangha, or community, of Buddhists. The Buddhist community includes the fourfold sangha of lay men and women and monks and nuns. Tradition also states that the day marks the event where the Buddha predicted his death, which came three months after the meeting. The day is sometimes called the Four Miracles Assembly because of the four miracles that occurred during the auspicious meeting. These miracles were: (1) all the disciples were enlightened; (2) the meeting was not predetermined; (3) all disciples independently arrived at Veluvan Monastery in Rajagriha, India, by coincidence; and (4) the sangha, brotherhood of monks, was established.

The day is remembered by bringing offerings to the temple when the full moon is visible. The offerings often include items such as candles, incense, and lotus. Other activities associated with the day include sermons, chanting, and freeing captive birds and fish. After sunset, monks lead followers in walking three times around the chapels of monasteries. Each person carries flowers, glowing incense, and a lighted candle in homage to the Buddha. In Laos, the ceremonies are especially colorful at Vientiane and at the Khmer ruins of Wat Ph near Champasak.

Spring Higan (Shunbun-no-Hi)
March 20 or 21

The Higan festival and the seven-day period surrounding it marks both the spring and autumnal equinoxes when day and night are of equal length. The word means the "other shore," and refers to the spirits of the dead reaching Nirvana after crossing the river of existence. Thus, Higan celebrates the spiritual move from the world of suffering to the world of enlightenment and is a time for remembering the dead, visiting, cleaning, and decorating their graves, and reciting sutras (Buddhist prayers). A week of Buddhist services is observed in Japan. A similar observance is held at the autumnal equinox. Japanese folklore maintains that on the day when day and night are of the same duration the Buddha returns for a week to redeem lost souls.

Higan appears to have been decreed an officially recognized holiday in 805 C.E., and the Emperor of Japan offers prayers to his forbears on this day. Food offerings are also made during Higan. Food associated with Higan is known *ohagi*. It is made from or soft rice and sweet bean paste. No meat is permitted in Higan food offerings.

April

Vesak (Wesak; Buddha's Birthday; Waicak, Vesakha Puja; Buddha Jayanti; Phat Dan Day; Buddha Purnima; Full Moon of Waso; Vixakha Bouxa; Feast of the Lanterns)
April 8; or the full moon day of the Hindu month of Vaisakha

Vesak is the holiest of Buddhist holy days. In Theravada Buddhist countries, it marks three anniversaries: Buddha's birth, his enlightenment, and his death, or attaining of Nirvana. In Japan and other Mahayana Buddhist countries, it commemorates Buddha's birth and the other two anniversaries are usually observed on separate days—the enlightenment on December 8, and the death on February 15. Vesak is a public holiday in many countries, including Thailand, Indonesia, Korea, and Singapore. In addition to the popular name of Vesak (or Wesak), it is known by many other names including Waicak, Vesakha Puja (Thailand), Buddha Jayanti (Nepal and India), Phat Dan Day (Vietnam), Buddha Purnima (India), Full Moon of Waso or Kason (Burma), Vixakha Bouxa (Laos), and sometimes it is called the Feast of the Lanterns.

The celebration differs from country to country, but in general activities are centered on Buddhist temples, where people gather to listen to sermons by monks. In the evening, there are candle-lit processions around the temples. Homes are also decorated with paper lanterns and oil lamps. In honor of the virtue of showing kindness to all living things, some countries practice a tradition of freeing caged birds on this day. In some areas, food booths are set up along streets. In Burma, people water the Bodhi tree with blessed water and chant prayers around it.

Lumbini, the isolated birth place of the Buddha (prince Siddhartha Gautama), is one of the most sacred pilgrimage destinations for Buddhists, especially on Vesak. A stone pillar erected in 250 B.C.E. by the Indian emperor

Ashoka designates the birthplace, and a brick temple contains carvings depicting the birth. Another center of celebration in Nepal is the Swayambhunath temple, built about 2,000 years ago. On Vesak it is constantly circled by a procession of pilgrims. Lamas wearing colorful silk robes dance around the stupa (temple) while musicians play. On Vesak, the temple's collection of mandalas (geometrical and astrological representations of the world) and rare embroidered religious scrolls called "thangkas" are displayed.

Sarnath, India, is the place where the Buddha preached his first sermon. A big fair and a procession of relics of the Buddha highlight the Vesak celebrations there. Bodh Gaya (or Buddh Gaya) in the state of Bihar is also a site of special celebrations. It was here that Siddhartha Gautama sat under the Bodhi tree, attained enlightenment, and became known as the Buddha, meaning the "Enlightened One."

Songkran (Pi Mai; Thai Buddhist New Year)
April 13–14; during the sixth or seventh moon of the Thai calendar

The Thai Buddhist New Year takes place in the spring. The festivities surrounding the day take place over a three-day period (April 12–14) and are religious as well as secular. In the religious ceremonies, images of the Buddha are bathed in water and, like the Hindu Holi festival from which the tradition is derived, people splash each other with water as they walk through the street. Respect is shown to older people, however, as the young honor them by sprinkling water on their hands or feet rather than splashing them indiscriminately.

Figure 15.3. The procession of the Sacred Tooth in Sri Lanka.

May

Poson (Dhamma Vijaya; Full Moon Day)
May-June; full moon day of the Hindu month of Jyestha

The Poson festival celebrates the arrival of Buddhism to Sri Lanka (formerly Ceylon) where it is second in importance only to Vesak (the celebration of Buddha's birth). While the holiday is celebrated throughout Sri Lanka, the major ceremonies are at the ancient cities of Anuradhapura and Mihintale. There, historical events involving Arhat Mahinda (the holy patron of Sri Lanka who was a convert to Buddhism from Hinduism and the son of Emperor Asoka of India) are reenacted, streets and buildings are decorated and illuminated, and temples are crowded. In Mihintale, people climb to the rock where Arhat Mahinda delivered his first sermon to the king. An important part of the festival is paying homage to the branch of the Bodhi Tree brought to Sri Lanka by Mahinda's sister, Sanghamitta. This is the tree that Gautama sat under until he received enlightenment and became the Buddha.

Sanghamitta Day
May or June; full moon day of the Hindu month of Jyestha

In Sri Lanka, the Buddhist community commemorates an event from 288 B.C.E. Princess Sanghmita (daughter of India's Emperor Asoka) presented King Devanamipiya with a sapling from the Bo Tree under which Buddah received enlightenment. The sapling was planted in Anuradhapura and is currently reputed to be the oldest documented tree in existence. It is a popular place of pilgrimage.

June

Airing the Classics
June or July; sixth day of the sixth lunar month

Buddhist monasteries in China observe the sixth day of the sixth lunar month by examining the books in their library collections to make sure that they haven't been damaged. It commemorates the time when the boat carrying the Buddhist scriptures from India was upset at a river crossing, and all the books had to be spread out to dry. Setting aside a special day for "Airing the Classics" is important in tropical climates, where books are more susceptible to mold and insects.

Esala Perahera
June or July; full moon day of the Hindu month of Asadha

In Sri Lanka, the temple at Kandy has a relic reputed to be a tooth of the Buddah. The Esala Perahera celebration originated in the fourth century when the king of Kandy declared that the tooth be paraded annually so people could honor it. During the festival a decorated elephant carries the tooth out of the temple while actors, dancers, and other elephants form a parade. Each successive night of the nine-day festival more participants join the parade.

Hemis Festival
Usually in June or July

This three day Buddhist festival occurs at the Hemis Gompa (monastery) in the mountainous northern Indian state of Ladakh. The festival celebrates the birthday of Guru Padmasambhava, the Indian Buddhist mystic who introduced Tantric Buddhism to Tibet in the eighth century. Tradition says he was a native of Swat (now in Pakistan), an area noted for magicians.

The ceremonial aspects of the day include dancers in elaborate robes and heavy masks swirling to the music of symbols, drums, and pipes as they enact the battle between good and evil spirits. Fairs are set up around the monastery where local artisans sell their crafts.

The highlight of the festival is the Devil Dance of the monks. Demon dancers are costumed as satyrs, many-eyed monsters, fierce tigers, or skeletons, while lamas portraying saints wear miters and opulent silks and carry pastoral crooks. These good lamas, ringing bells and swinging censers, scatter the bad lamas, as they all swirl about to the music of cymbals, drums, and 10-foot-long trumpets. The dance is a morality play, a battle between good and evil spirits, and also expresses the idea that a person's helpless soul can be comforted only by a lama's exorcisms.

July

Birthday of the Dalai Lama
July 6

The Dalai Lama is the spiritual and political leader of Tibet and Tibetan Buddhism. The observance of the Dalai Lama's birthday is always held on July 6. The birthday is observed today by exiles in India with incense-burning ceremonies to appease the local spirits, family picnics, and traditional dances and singing.

The name Dalai means "ocean," and it was given to the ruling lama in the sixteenth century by the Mongol leader Altan Khan. The title suggests depth of wisdom. The present Dalai Lama, who was enthroned in 1940 at the age of five, is the latest in the line that began in the fourteenth century. Each Dalai Lama is believed to be the reincarnation of the preceding one, and when a Dalai Lama dies, Tibetan lamas search throughout the country for a child who is his reincarnation.

Waso (Vassa; Buddhist Monsoon Retreat)
Three months beginning around July 23

The rainy monsoon season of three months is traditionally a time of retreat for Buddhist monks. The practice may have begun in order to keep the monks, who typically wandered around the countryside, from walking on rice plants during the critical part of their growing season.

In observance of Waso, monks stay in monasteries and their followers bring offerings of food and gifts. The permitted gifts, however, must be items from among a list of only eight things a monk is permitted to own (a robe, an undergarment, a belt, a begging bowl, a water strainer, a blade, a needle, and a mat.)

The months in the Waso season are considered a time of restraint and abstinence. Weddings are not celebrated, and people try to avoid moving to new homes. Many young men in countries such as Thailand where every male serves once as a monk during his lifetime, enter the priesthood during the retreat period. As a result, many ordinations take place. The new young monks have their heads shaved and washed with saffron. Then they are given yellow robes. During this period, lay people also attend the monasteries for instruction and meditation.

The end of the Monsoon Retreat is marked with a joyful celebration. Lamps and lights are kept alight in homes for three days; processions to pagodas occur in the evening. From the full moon that marks the end of the Monsoon Retreat until the next full moon, is a traditional time to bring new robes to monks. Each community may set aside a special day on which the offering of robes is presented.

Obon Festival (Festival of the Dead)
July 13–15 or August 13–15

The date of the Japanese Obon Festival varies from region to region, although it is always celebrated in either July or August. According to Japanese Buddhist belief, the dead revisit the earth during this time; thus Buddhist families participate in special religious services and hold family reunions to honor the dead.

The festival begins with the lighting of small bonfires outside of homes to welcome the spirits of ancestors. A ceremony to summon the dead begins with the striking of a gong thirty-three times and the names of the dead are read aloud. A traditional meal of vegetables, rice cakes, and fruit is placed on an altar known as a *budsudan* for the spirits who are included in family activities as if they were physically present. On the final day of the festival, another bonfire is lit outside to guide the spirits back to the netherworld. The climax of the Obon Festival is the Bon-Odori which comforts the souls of the dead. During this event, the town is lit with paper lanterns. As a closure to the festival, paper floats with lighted candles are set on rivers or on the sea symbolizing the departure of the souls of loved ones again into the world of the dead.

Obon is an important Japanese festival and is observed throughout the world wherever there are Japanese communities. In the United States, elaborate Obon celebrations take place in Chicago and various locations in California.

Marya
July or August; third day of waning half of the Hindu month of Sravana

According to Buddhist legend, when Gautama sat down under the Bo tree to await Enlightenment, Mara, the Buddhist Lord of the Senses and satanic tempter, tried a number of strategies to divert him from his goal. Disguised as a messenger, Mara brought the news that one of Gautama's rivals had usurped his family's throne. Then he scared away the other gods who had gathered to honor the future Buddha by causing a storm of rain, rocks, and ashes to fall. Finally, he sent his three daughters, representing thirst, desire, and delight, to seduce Gautama—all to no avail.

In the city of Patan, Nepal, a procession on this day commemorates the Buddha's triumph over Mara's temptations. A procession of 3,000 to 4,000 people, carrying gifts—usually butter lamps—for Lord Buddha, moves through the city from shrine to shrine. Some wear masks and others play traditional Nepalese musical instruments. The devil dancers and mask-wearers in the parade often pretend to scare the children who line the streets by suddenly jumping out at them.

August

Floating Lantern Ceremony (Toro Nagashi)
August 15

The Floating Lantern Ceremony, a Buddhist ceremony held in Honolulu, Hawaii, commemorates the end of World War II. This festival is part of the annual Buddhist Bon season during which the spirits of dead ancestors are entreated and welcomed back to earth with prayers, dances, offerings, and the ceremony of setting afloat several thousand colorful paper lanterns bearing the names of the dead.

September

Shinbyu
September 2

Shinbyu is a Buddhist initiation ceremony that is observed in Myanmar. Parents provide a feast for their sons who wear headdress and robes. After the meal, the boys are taken to the temple, their heads are shaved, and they enter the monastery for a period of time typically ranging from three days to three months.

Vatsa (Ho Khao Slak)
Three months beginning around September 22

In Laos the observation of the Buddhist Rains Retreat is called Vatsa or Ho Khao Slak. It begins later in the year than the traditional season observed in many other Buddhist communities. Customs associated with the day are also slightly different. In Laos, people draw the name of a monk in the monastery and bring him a gift of food, flowers, or one of the eight essential items a monk is permitted to own. Also, some parents give toys and candy to their children. At the end of the festival, boat races are held on the rivers in Laos at Vientiane, Luang Phabang and Savannakhet.

Autumnal Higan
September 23 or 24

The Autumnal Higan is a week of Buddhist services observed in Japan at the autumnal equinox, when day and night are of equal length. A similar observance is held at the spring equinox.

October

Bodhidharma Day
October 5

Bodhidharma was a Buddhist teacher during the sixth century C.E. Although his teachings were not consolidated until the eighth century, he is still considered the founder and patriarch of Zen Buddhism. Many Zen monasteries observe this day in his honor with an all-day sitting.

November

Tazaungdaing
November 19

In Burma (now officially called Myanmar) Burmese Buddhists honor the robe that Buddha's mother wove for him. The commemoration is observed by girls who enter weaving competitions to make an entire robe. Another festival activity is the offering of new robes to the monks to replace the soiled robes they have worn throughout the rainy season.

Festival of Lights (Ganden Ngamcho)
November or December; twenty-fifth day of the tenth Tibetan lunar month

This Tibetan festival commemorates the birth and death of Tsongkhapa (1357–1419), a saintly scholar, teacher, and reformer of the monasteries, who enforced strict monastic rules. In 1408 he instituted the Great Prayer, a New Year rededication of Tibet to Buddhism; it was celebrated without interruption until 1959 when the Chinese invaded Tibet. He formulated a doctrine that became the basis of the Gelug (meaning "virtuous") sect of Buddhism. It became the predominant sect of Tibet, and Tsongkhapa's successors became the Dalai Lamas, the rulers of Tibet.

During the festival, thousands of butter lamps (dishes of liquid clarified butter called ghee, with wicks floating in them) are lit on the roofs and window sills of homes and on temple altars. At this time people seek spiritual merit by visiting the temples.

December

Rohatsu (Boddhi Day; Buddha's Enlightenment)
December 8

Zen monasteries honor Buddha's enlightenment with an arduous retreat typically lasting a week. Among other Buddhist schools, commemoration of Buddha's enlightenment is observed as Boddhi Day.

Table 15.4. Alphabetical List of Buddhist Holidays

Holidays	Date(s)
Airing the Classics	6th day of the 6th lunar month
Autumnal Higan	September 23 or 24
Birthday of the Dalai Lama	July 6
Boddhi Day *see* Rohatsu	
Bodhidharma Day	October 5
Buddha Jayanti *see* Vesak	
Buddha Purnima *see* Vesak	
Buddha's Birthday *see* Vesak	
Buddha's Enlightenment *see* Rohatsu	
Buddhist Monsoon Retreat *see* Waso	
Chinese New Year	First day of the first full moon
Dhamma Vijaya *see* Poson	
Esala Perahera	Full moon day of the Hindu month of Asadha
Feast of the Lanterns *see* Vesak	
Festival of Lights	Twenty-fifth day of the tenth Tibetan lunar month
Festival of the Dead *see* Obon Festival	
Floating Lantern Ceremony	August 15
Four Miracles Assembly *see* Magha Puja	
Full Moon Day *see* Magha Puja	
Full Moon Day *see* Poson	
Full Moon of Waso *see* Vesak	
Ganden Ngamcho *see* Festival of Lights	
Ganjitsu *see* Oshogatsu	
Hemis Festival	Usually in June or July
Ho Khao Slak *see* Vatsa	
Japanese New Year's Day *see* Oshogatsu	
Losar	Usually in February
Magha Puja	Full moon night of the third lunar month
Maka Buja *see* Magha Puja	
Marya	Third day of waning half of the Hindu month of Sravana

Holidays	Date(s)
Monlam	Chenmo Fourth through twenty-fifth day of the first Tibetan lunar month
Obon Festival	July 13–15 or August 13–15
Omizutori Matsuri	March 1–14
Oshogatsu	January 1–3
Phat Dan Day *see* Vesak	
Pi Mai *see* Songkran	
Poson	Full moon day of the Hindu month of Jyestha
Prayer Festival *see* Monlam	
Rohatsu	December 8
Sangha Day *see* Magha Puja	
Sanghamitta Day	Full moon day of the Hindu month of Jyestha
Shunbun-no-Hi *see* Spring Higan	
Shinbyu	September 2
Songkran	April 13–14
Spring Higan	March 20 or 21
Tazaungdaing	November 19
Thai Buddhist New Year *see* Songkran	
Tibetan New Year *see* Losar	
Toro Nagashi *see* Floating Lantern Ceremony	
Vassa *see* Waso	
Vatsa	Three months beginning around September 22
Vesak	April 8; or the full moon day of the Hindu month of Vaisakha
Vesakha Puja *see* Vesak	
Vixakha Bouxa *see* Vesak	
Waicak *see* Vesak	
Waso	Three months beginning around July 23
Water Drawing Festival *see* Omizutori Matsuri	
Wesak *see* Vesak	
Yuan Tan *see* Chinese New Year	

CHAPTER 16

Taoism, Confucianism, and Chinese Folk Religions

Overview of Chinese Religious Thought

The Development of Chinese Religious Principles

The religions of ancient China, though diverse, often shared similar concepts and components. One of these was a view that things in the natural world—earth, sky, stars, and waters, and including humans, animals, and plants—were interrelated. Correspondences and dissonances among them had effects that could be recognized and used for benefit. The human role in the cosmos was one of responsibility. Ritual actions, whether performed by the shaman, the sage, or the emperor, ensured that seasons would change, that crops would grow, that epidemics would abate, and that human fertility would be protected.

The ebb and flow of human life and the cyclical patterns observed in nature gave rise to a concept of intertwined opposites. These are defined in Chinese culture as "yin" and "yang." Yin represents cold and darkness; yang represents heat and light. They are viewed as opposites but complementary parts of a whole—both emerging from and existing within the other.

From nature, the ancient Chinese also developed the concept of *chi* (also sometimes spelled qi) which was perceived to be the vital energy that fills the universe. Chi, interacting with the five elements—wood, fire, earth, metal, and water—is seen as the animating force that is present in nature. Whether something is considered yin or yang depends on the extent to which chi emanates from a combination of any of the five elements.

All things in the universe are seen to be permeated by either yang energies or yin energies. Those things that are infused with yang are seen as masculine, positive, warm and active. Conversely, things that are thought to be yin are characteristically feminine, negatively charged, cool, and passive. Human actions at all levels are governed by the imperative to maintain a balance between yang and yin. Consequently, Chinese dietary habits, medicine, and practices, such as feng shui and tai chi, are all governed by the principle aim of maintaining a balance with the yin and yang energies, thus effecting a harmonious relationship between nature and human societies.

The Role of Ancestors and Gods

Another widespread component of Chinese religious thought focuses on the role of ancestors. Ancestors are members of the family who have died. They are often consulted through divination, honored as if still present, and appeased through rituals to avoid trouble. Practices surrounding the veneration of ancestors include funeral rites in which a deceased family member is officially numbered among the ancestors. Additionally, wood inscribed with the name of the deceased is kept on a family altar. Offerings of incense, food, and tea are also placed on the family altar. Unappeased spirits of the dead, from both within and outside the family, are feared as ghosts and are placated in different rituals.

In addition to organized religious traditions, a myriad of folk religions also existed throughout Chinese history. Many local observances focused on specific gods who were sometimes honored in homes as well as in rural temples. By the tenth century local deities, called city gods (*chenghuang*), were often publicly worshipped. Typically they were understood to possess powers over nature, and their adherents often included people who also observed other traditions, such as Taoism or Buddhism.

Some cults were forced into hiding by government sanctioned persecution; others became more widely accepted.

The gods of historic Chinese folk religion continue to play important roles in contemporary Chinese religious thought. These include gods of the natural world (such as the earth, sky, sun, moon, water, and wind) and gods of human endeavors (such as the gods of scholars, business, and midwifery). Other gods include those who are protectors of specific domains, such as the twin guardian gods who stand at the entrances of buildings or the god of the kitchen and his wife who occupy a place of honor in many Chinese homes.

At different historical periods, a supreme god was recognized. During the Shang Dynasty (approximately 1500–1040 B.C.E.) a reigning deity, called Shang-ti, ruled over the lesser gods of nature but was not intimately involved in the lives of men. During the Chou Dynasty (approximately 1040–256 B.C.E.), the supreme god was called T'ien. His role in human affairs was closer to that of an ancestor.

The Imperial Cult

The Chinese ideal of a hierarchical society, as articulated by Confucius, led to an official state cult of the emperor in which the ruler, called the Son of Heaven, was seen as possessing divine ancestors. He was responsible for performing specific rituals, and his actions affected the fortunes of his empire. During the Han Dynasty (206 B.C.E.–220 C.E.) the cult of the emperor reached its full expression. Beneficial events, such as good harvests, were attributed to the virtue of the emperor; catastrophic events, such as droughts and floods, were blamed on the emperor.

The Ming (1368–1644) and Ching Dynasties (1644–1912) were especially well known for their assertion of the imperial cult. In Beijing, the Imperial Palace (also known as the Forbidden City), was oriented so that its major buildings faced south signifying the sun's goodness and holiness. Ching emperors performed a ritual sacrifice to the earth at the summer solstice on a special square altar in the northern portion of the Palace grounds. Other sacrifices were made at the beginning of each of the four seasons and at the end of the year. A spring plowing ceremony conducted in the Temple of Agriculture and overseen by the emperor, marked the start of the farming season.

Secularism and Atheism

In the middle of the 19th century, the religious face of China changed. A reformer, Hong Xiuquan (1814–1864), influenced by Christian literature, asserted that he was a younger brother of Jesus. He began a civil war, called the T'ai-ping Rebellion, which crusaded against idolatry and promoted the causes of land reform and egalitarianism (a belief that all people should have the same political and social rights). After more than 15 years and the loss of an estimated 20 million lives, the T'ai-ping Rebellion was defeated. Its legacy helped usher in an age of secularism.

The Chinese Communist Party, under the leadership of Mao Tse-tung (also sometimes spelled Mao Zedong), came to power in 1949, and China became an atheistic state. Temples, images of ancestors, and sacred books were burned. The Cultural Revolution (1966–1976) sought to silence the nation's religious voice. Beginning in the 1980s (following Mao's death in 1976), however, religious expression was once again more accepted. Seminaries were reopened, religious periodicals published, and temples rebuilt.

Overview of Confucianism

Confucian beliefs and practices are based on the teachings of Confucius, a Chinese sage from approximately the fifth century B.C.E. The primary Confucian focus is on human relationships. The five relationships defined by Confucius are: (1) between a ruler and a subject; (2) between a father and a son; (3) between a husband and wife; (4) between the eldest son and his siblings; and (5) between peers.

Whether Confucianism is properly classified as a philosophy or a religion is a source of debate. Although Confucius expressed a belief in heaven, he did not consider himself a divine messenger, and he did not promote the worship of any specific god or gods.

One of the central principles of Confucianism is noble conduct. In contrast to Christianity with its premise that all humans are born sinful, Confucius taught that humans are essentially good, but prone to negative behaviors. Education and vigilance are, therefore, the means of ensuring a standard of ethical conduct that would be the hallmark of stable societies.

Confucius felt that the ethics of his era had declined from the ideals of the previous dynasty (Chou 1040–256 B.C.E.) which he elevated as an example and a standard. His precepts were based on perpetuating the established traditions of the past.

Several key elements in Confucian teaching are the concepts of li, hsiao, i, and jen:

- Li, the observance of social ritual, is essential as a means of ensuring that all individuals behave in terms of a commonly accepted code of appropriateness. Confucius's ideal society was a hierarchical society, and Li was the means of ensuring that individuals knew their place in society and would behave accordingly. Confucius felt that knowing how to behave when addressing others or when interacting with others in the hierarchical social order would prevent chaos or confusion.

- Hsiao (also spelled xiao), which means filial piety, refers to the respect children feel toward their parents and ancestors. Confucius felt that a child's relationship with his or her parents set the stage for relationships with others. Hsiao also implied loyalty, courage, and trustworthiness.

- I, which means propriety, was demonstrated in friendships through mutual obligations and accountability.

- Jen, or human virtue, was viewed as the natural result of right living and the primary source of all goodness and integrity. Jen may be translated as empathy toward others or the ability to place oneself in another's place. Confucius thought that this ability would prevent people from committing acts against others that they would not want committed against them. It was the sum of li, hsiao, and i. Jen encompassed the love of people one to another.

Confucius believed that the combination of these four elements would result in a person becoming a perfect "junzi" or virtuous gentleman. A junzi exhibits five honorable traits: charity, justice, propriety, wisdom, and loyalty. Confucius's political ideals emphasized that those chosen to rule should be selected on the basis of their virtues rather than on their social position.

Table 14.1. Major Chinese Dynasties

Approximate Dates	Name
1500–1040 B.C.E.	Shang
1040–256 B.C.E.	Chou
221–206 B.C.E.	Ch'in
206 B.C.E.–220 C.E.	Han
581–618 C.E.	Sui
618–907 C.E.	T'ang
960–1279 C.E.	Song
1279–1368 C.E.	Yuan
1368–1644 C.E.	Ming
1644–1912 C.E.	Ching (Manchu)
1949 C.E.	Beginning of Communism

The Relationship between Confucius and the People

Confucius made no claims of divinity and there is neither a central god nor secondary deities in Confucianism. Instead, Confucius advocated an alignment with T'ien (translated as the mandate of heaven) by perfecting one's moral conduct and culture.

Authorities and Sacred Writings

Confucius did not write his teachings down. The books that are held in esteem by Confucians include classics of his day and books of his teachings written down by his followers. The works of Confucius include:

- A collection called the *"Four Books"* compiled primarily during the T'ang Dynasty (seventh through tenth centuries C.E.).

- *Lun-yu* (*The Analects*), a collection of the sayings of Confucius, attributed to Mencius, a disciple of Confucius's grandson, Tzu-ssu (also spelled Zi Si).

- *Ta-hsueh* (*The Great Learning*), an ancient ritual collection that explained the relationship between individual spiritual development and society.

- *Chung Yung* (*The Doctrine of the Mean*) ascribed to Confucius's grandson, a treatise on human nature and the moral order of the universe.

- *Meng-tzu* (*The Book of Mencius*), a collection of the sayings of Mencius.

Other important books in Confucianism include texts that were existent in Confucius's era and from which he is reputed to have taught. Called the Five Classics these are:

- *Shu Ching* (*The Book of History*)

- *Shih Ching* (*The Book of Odes*)

- *I Ching* (*The Book of Changes*)

- *Ch'un Ch'ui* (*Spring and Autumn Annals*)

- *Li Chi* (*The Book of Rites*)

History

Confucius (a Latinized form of the Chinese name or K'ung-fu-tzu) lived from approximately 551 to 479 B.C.E. during a turbulent age in Chinese history marked by warring feudal states. He lived in the state of Lu, which is now located in the Shandong Province. During his lifetime, Confucius taught approximately 3,000 students and had fewer than 100 disciples. Two later followers of Confucius expanded his teachings, influence, and fame: Mencius (371–289 B.C.E.; also spelled Meng-tzu) and Hsun-tzu (300–230 B.C.E.; also spelled Xunzi).

Mencius was a follower of Confucius's grandson. His teachings focused on ending the warring among the feudal states of his era. Mencius believed that a virtuous leader would be acknowledged by heavenly mandate and, as a result, would be acknowledged by the people. To Confucius's original teachings, Mencius added the concept that every human possesses innate goodness. Mencius also supported the rights of the people to rebel against governments that did not conform to Confucian ideals.

Hsun-tzu, the third great Confucian philosopher, did not agree with Mencius about the natural condition of the human being. He believed that goodness was not innate, but that it had to be taught. He also had a different concept of heaven. He believed that it existed as a separate entity from the human world. He taught that people interested in pursuing goodness needed to do so without divine guidance.

During the Han Dynasty (206 B.C.E.–220 C.E.), the emperor Han Wu-ti adopted Confucianism as the official doctrine of the state. He commanded that it be taught in universities. He established the tradition of using Confucian sacred writings as the basis for civil service examinations.

After the collapse of the Han dynasty, however, other traditions in China emerged to challenge the authority of Confucianism. These included Taoism and Buddhism. Eventually Buddhism, perceived as a foreign religion, fell into disfavor and Chinese leaders of the Song dynasty once again embraced Confucian ideals.

Song leaders reestablished the study of the Confucian classics. At the same time, some metaphysical elements of Taoism and Buddhism were incorporated. The Confucianism that emerged came to be called Neo-Confucianism by Western analysts. Neo-Confucianism held that an underlying universal principle bound people together with the cosmos and provided guidance in everyday life. During the Song Dynasty, the practice of using Confucian texts as a basis for civil service examinations was re-instituted, and it continued until the close of China's imperial age in the early twentieth century.

Confucianism Today

In China, the importance of Confucianism diminished in the wake of Communism. Communist leaders condemned Confucianism on the grounds that its rites and practices were elitist and an impediment to needed social change. Since the death of Mao Tse-tung in the 1970s, however, there has been a revived interest in Confucianism and renewed attention to ceremonies honoring Confucius's birth.

Worship

Confucius did not promote himself as divine. He did, however, advocate a limited number of things which were worthy of veneration. These included heaven, men of greatness, and the teaching of sages. In the past, some Confucians worshipped him in temples. During the twelfth century it was common practice to make offerings to T'ien (heaven), to local gods, and to the spirits of Confucius and his disciples. In more modern times, temples continue to exist, but Confucius is no longer worshipped. Some people continue to make pilgrimages to his tomb, but the main body of Confucianism is centered on correct mores and virtues. Worship involves the choices of everyday life rather than rites.

Confucian Schools of Thought

During the course of its development, three primary schools of Confucianism developed.

School of Principle

The School of Principle, founded by Chu Hsi (1130–1200 C.E., also spelled Zhu Xi) focused on intellectual study. It included the belief in a concept called the Great Ultimate (T'ai-chi) and a principle of physical matter called chi. According to the school's doctrines, a person who understood the nature of things reduced the chi in the mind. This permitted insight into universal truths which enabled the enlightened person to acquire virtue.

Figure 16.1. The *I Ching* uses eight trigrams, comprised of three lines each following patterns of solid and broken lines.

School of the Mind

The School of the Mind focused on intuition. Its concepts can be dated to the eleventh and twelfth centuries, but its practices did not become popular until the late fifteenth century under the leadership of Wang Yang-ming (1472–1529). In contrast with the School of Principle, which taught that the mind contained chi (matter), the school of the Mind taught that the mind did not contain matter, which meant that the mind was basically good. As the school developed following Wang's death, it focused on more subjective principles and incorporated a Zen-like style of meditation.

School of Practical Learning

The School of Practical Learning developed during the late seventeenth century in response to the collapse of the Ming Dynasty. Confucian scholars felt that the dynasty's downfall was the result of misapplied Confucian principles. It rejected the mysticism related to the School of Principle and the subjectivity of the School of the Mind and instead focused on objective analysis.

Overview of Taoism

In contrast with the Confucian ideal that an individual should strive to conform to the expectations of society, Taoism promoted the idea that an individual should harmonize with the inherent patterns of the universe. Three important components of Taoism are the concepts of Tao, wu-wei, and yin and yang.

The Tao (the Way) refers to the reality that gives order to the physical world. The Tao expresses the undefinable manner of the cosmos.

To conform to the Tao, a person must practice "wu-wei," which is sometimes loosely translated as "do nothing." The principle, however, does not mean the same thing as the phrase "do nothing" might be commonly understood in English. Rather wu-wei embodies a "not doing" in the sense of making no unnatural struggle against the natural order. The effortlessness of nature is seen as the result of the congruent rather than oppositional movement of elements in the natural world. Similarly, wu wei is the practice of aligning oneself to the flow of events instead of acting in opposition to them.

Yin and yang represent opposite energies that work together to form harmony. Yin and yang are traditionally symbolized by a stylized circle divided equally into two colors (traditionally dark and light) by a curved line. Each portion of the circle contains a smaller circle of the opposite color.

Some Taoists are primarily philosophical Taoists. They seek to achieve humility and a mystical quiet for the purpose of gaining inner understanding. Philosophical Taoists seek harmony with the ultimate reality that permeates the universe.

Philosophical Taoism, blended with Chinese folk practices, yielded a spiritual Taoism with complex rituals and gods. Religious Taoists worship traditional gods and seek immortality. Some Taoists use magic and ritual to control nature. The ancient five elements (earth, wood, fire, metal, and water) are each associated with correspondences to colors and directions. Five sacred mountains are honored: Heng Shan (in the north) T'ai Shan (in the east—the most popularly visited of the five); Heng Shang (in the south); Hua Shan (in the west) and Sung Shan in the center.

Divination also plays an important role. The classical text *I Ching* (*Book of Changes*) serves as a tool for interpreting the meaning of Hexigrams. Hexigrams are formed by combining two Trigrams. A Trigram is formed by a series of three lines, broken and unbroken, representing yin (broken) and yang (unbroken). Different patterns of lines yield one of eight different Trigrams. By combining sets of Trigrams, a total of 64 different Hexigrams can be drawn.

The Relationship between the Gods and the Taoist People

Taoism developed a pantheon of gods typically representative of qualities and attributes but also incorporating mythological and historical figures. These were often described in groups of threes such as the "Heavenly One," "Earthly One," and "Great One," who were honored by Taoists of the early Han Dynasty.

Later Taoists recognized a supreme ruler called The First Principle, an eternal deity, who is the source of all truth but who does not interact directly in human affairs. The highest god who interacts with people is called the Jade Emperor (Yu-huang). He rules over subordinate gods in the hierarchy of heaven. The Jade Emperor's jurisdiction includes lesser gods, buddhas, people, ghosts, and demons.

Authorities and Sacred Writings

The collection of Taoist scriptures is called the *Tao-tsang*; it comprises more than 1,400 separate texts which were compiled over a period of 1,500 years.

One of the most important is the *Tao-te Ching* (The Way and Its Power), which is attributed to Lao Tzu. The word "Tao" in the title refers to the Tao, a way or a path, or alternately a way of behaving or teaching. The word "te" refers to virtue or power.

Other books important to Taoists include:

- *The Three Caverns*, a collection of texts dating from the fifth century including esoteric knowledge, talismans, and rituals.

- *Chuang Tzu*, a collection of parables and allegories attributed to Chuang-tzu, considered to be a formal presentation of Taoist philosophy.

- *T'ai-p'ing* (*Classic of the Great Peace*), a work that dates from the seventh century C.E. and looks forward to an era of peace and the coming of a messiah-like figure.

History

Traditionally, the development of Taoism is traced to Lao Tzu (c. 551–479 B.C.E.), a Chinese philosopher and mystic. According to Taoist belief, Lao Tzu decided to leave civilization because of its declining condition. On his way to the frontier (between China and Tibet) he was asked by the guard of the border to write down his teaching. The resulting book was called the *Tao-te Ching*. Some modern researchers doubt that Lao Tzu was a single individual and instead attribute the work ascribed to him to a group of philosophers who contributed to it over an extended period of time.

Chuang-tzu (c. 369–286 B.C.E.) was an early follower of the philosophies described by Lao Tzu. The book bearing his name is one of the classics in the Tao collection of revered writings. Chuang-tzu, who criticized the political leaders of his era, promoted the cause of intuition over reason and the use of figurative language over logic.

When the Han Dynasty rose to power in the second century B.C.E., China entered an era of relative political calm. A religious reformer near the end of the Han Dynasty, Chang Tao-ling, was instrumental in refocusing Taoism as a religion. Claiming he had seen Lao Tzu in a vision, he organized a sect called the Celestial Masters (which is also known as the Heavenly Masters or the Celestial Teachers). Practices of the Celestial Masters included making offerings of cooked vegetables instead of blood sacrifices, confession of sins, and healing.

In the second century C.E. following a civil war in western China and during the Wei dynasty, Taoists affiliated with the Celestial Masters combined with an alchemist movement seeking to find an illusive elixir able to provide immortality. They were followed by other groups who received revelations from gods and divine messages associated with magical practices.

In the middle of the fifth century C.E. *The Canon of the Yellow Court*, a text used for meditation, helped to unify the many diverse and separate Taoist groups. This led to the development of a Taoist movement in which adherents recognized many shared beliefs, rituals, and festivals. Taoists priests served as mediators between people and spirits and other supernatural forces.

Taoism Today

In modern China, religious Taoism is less common than philosophical Taoism, but its presence continues to play an important role.

Worship

Taoist worship combines elements from nature and ancestor worship. Ceremonies and rituals vary according to the god or gods being honored. Priests are viewed as experts in the performance of rituals. Common ritual elements include the burning of paper charms and exorcisms for the healing of sickness. The use of incense represents spirits rising up to be with the gods. Mountains are viewed as sacred places where people can come in contact with the gods, and temples are often stylized to represent mountains.

Sects

Of the many Taoists sects to emerge during the religion's development, two continue to enjoy popularity. The Heavenly Masters school of Taoism predominates in southern China. Its priesthood is perpetuated through heredity and its emphasis is on the use of talismans. The Perfect Truth sect is more popular in the north. It incorporates concepts such as fasting and meditation.

Figure 16.2. The yin-yang symbol represents opposing but equal forces.

◈ ◈ ◈

The Chinese Lunar Calendar

A Lunisolar Calendar

As in many other Eastern religious calendars, the Chinese calendar emphasizes the ebb and flow of nature's patterns. In addition to charting the course of the year, the Chinese Lunar Calendar serves as a tool for divination.

Oracle bones, estimated to be from the 14th century B.C.E. Shang dynasty, provide details about one of the oldest and most accurate timekeeping systems known. The ancient Chinese followed a calendar that predicted a lunar cycle of 29½ days and intercalated a month of 29 or 30 days seven times during a 19-year period, yielding a solar year of 365¼ days. The ancient calendar fell into disfavor, however, and was replaced by another that used the sun's position to determine the timing of intercalated months.

Yin and Yang

The concepts of yin and yang also play an important role in the Chinese understanding of the calendar. Yin and yang, conceptual yet complementary opposites, provide the harmony and necessary balance to keep the cosmos ordered. They are born at opposite points in the year and establish the basis of the ever-cycling sequence of years and also parallel the rhythms of life.

Yang is born at the winter solstice and strengthens and grows during the spring. The yang half of the year represents the human experiences of adolescence and entering maturity. Yin is born at the summer solstice and strengthens and grows during the summer. The yin half of the year represents old age and renewal or rebirth.

Religious Calendar

Although the solar calendar is currently used as the official calendar in China, many people still follow the lunar calendar for religious purposes. Most dates for major festivals are calculated on the basis of the lunar calendar. The first day of the month corresponds with the new moon and the fifteenth of the month marks the full moon. Similar to the ancient methods of intercalation, the Chinese lunar calendar is synchronized to the solar calendar by the addition of an extra month whenever the sun fails to progress to the next zodiac sign during the course of a month. This occurs in seven of every nineteen years.

Taoist Divinatory Eras

In addition, Taoists use the calendar in divination. Although the twelve animals representing the constellations of the Chinese zodiac are well-known in the West,

their use is considered too simple to be accurate by religious Taoists. (The twelve are: rat, ox, tiger, hare, dragon, snake, horse, sheep, monkey, rooster, dog, and pig.) Instead, a complex system based on ten celestial signs called "stems" and twelve earth signs called "branches" is used. Stems and branches are combined to form sixty different pairs. These are associated with differing levels of power and energy.

Three sixty-year cycles, each with its own energy pattern, combine to form a larger unit of time equal to one hundred and eighty years. Within this larger period, a separate sequence also operates. Called the Nine Cycles, it comprises nine repetitions of a twenty-year pattern.

Table 14.2. Chinese Holiday Cycle

First Lunar Month (January–February)

1	Lunar New Year (Throughout East Asia)
9	Making Happiness Festival (Folk)
15	Lantern Festival (Folk)
18	Star Festival (Folk)

Second Lunar Month (February–March)

~	Monkey God Festival (Taoist)

Third Lunar Month (March–April)

4 or 5	Qing Ming Festival (Folk)
23	Matsu Festival (Taoist; Buddhist; Folk)

Fourth Lunar Month (April–May)

~	Chongmyo Taeje (Confucian)
8	Tam Kung Festival (Taoist)
8–9	Birthday of the Third Prince (Taoist)

Sixth Lunar Month

13	Birthday of Lu Pan (Taoist)

Seventh Lunar Month (July–August)

15	Festival of Hungry Ghosts (Taoist; Buddhist; Folk)

Eighth Lunar Month (August–September)

~	Monkey God Festival (Taoist)
15	Mid-Autumn Festival (Folk)

Ninth Lunar Month (September–October)

1–9	Festival of the Nine Imperial Gods (Taoist; Buddhist)
~	Confucius's Birthday (Confucian)

Tenth Lunar Month (October–November)

1	Sending the Winter Dress (Folk)

Twelfth Lunar Month (December–January)

~	Winter Solstice (Folk)
~	Ta Chiu (Taoist)
23	Kitchen God Festival (Taoist; Folk)

The symbol ~ indicates a date that is not fixed on the Chinese lunar calendar.

⊞ ⊞ ⊞

Taoist, Confucian, and Other Chinese Religious Holidays

First Lunar Month (January–February)

Lunar New Year (Spring Festival; Yuan Tan; Tet; Sang-Sin; Je-sok)
First day of the first lunar month

Celebrations marking the beginning of the new year are the most important and the longest of all Chinese festivals. They are observed by Chinese communities throughout the world. The festival, believed to date back to prehistory, marks the beginning of the new lunar cycle. It is also called the Spring Festival, since it falls between the Winter Solstice and Vernal Equinox.

In China the first day of the new lunar year was formerly called Yuan Tan ("the first morning"), but the name was changed when the Gregorian calendar was officially adopted by the Republic of China in 1912. To differentiate the Chinese new year from the Western new year, January 1 was designated Yuan Tan. Today in China and in other Eastern nations, January 1 is a public holiday, but the Lunar New Year (Spring Festival) is the much grander celebration.

The Lunar New Year has certain variations from country to country, but they all include offerings to the household god(s), house-cleaning and new clothes, a large banquet, ancestor worship, and firecrackers. Preparations begin during the preceding month and include making traditional food, cleaning houses, settling debts, and buying new clothes. It is also customary to paste red papers with auspicious writings on the doors and windows of homes.

The high point of the festival occurs on the eve of the new year. Family members return home to honor their ancestors and enjoy a feast. The food served has symbolic meaning. Abalone, for example, promises abundance; bean sprouts, prosperity; and oysters, good business. It is also a night of colossal noise. Firecrackers explode and rockets whistle to frighten away devils. An old legend says that the lunar festival dates from the times when a wild beast (a nihn; also the Cantonese word for "year") appeared at the end of winter to devour many villagers. After the people discovered that the beast feared bright lights, red, and noise, they protected themselves on the last day of the year by lighting up their houses, painting objects red, banging drums and gongs, and exploding bamboo "crackers." The explosions go on until dawn, and continue sporadically for the next two weeks.

On the first day of the new year, household doors are thrown open to let good luck enter. Families go out to visit friends and worship at temples. Words are carefully watched to avoid saying anything that might signify death, sickness, or poverty. Scissors and knives are avoided for fear of "cutting" the good fortune. Brooms are also not used lest they sweep away good luck. Dragon and lion dances are performed, with 50 or more people supporting long paper dragons. There are acrobatic demonstrations and much beating of gongs and clashing of cymbals.

An ancient custom is giving little red packets of money (called hung-pao or lai see) to children and employees or service-people. The red signifies good fortune, and red is everywhere at this time.

Families stay home on the third day of the festival because it is regarded as a day of bad luck. On the fourth day, local deities return to earth after a stay in heaven and are welcomed back with firecrackers and the burning of spirit money. According to legend, the seventh day is regarded as the birthday of all humans. The ninth day is the birthday of the Jade Emperor, the supreme Taoist deity. He is honored with firecrackers. In most Asian countries, people return to work after the fourth or fifth day of celebration.

In Taiwan, New Year's Eve, New Year's Day, and the two days following are public holidays, and all government offices, most businesses, restaurants, and stores are closed. The closings may continue for eight days.

Celebrations vary from country to country and region to region. In Vietnam, where the holiday is called Tet, the ancestors are believed to return to heaven on the fourth day, and everyone has to return to work. On the seventh day, the Cay Nev is removed from the front of the home. This is a high bamboo pole that was set up on the last day of the old year. On its top are red paper with inscriptions, wind chimes, a square of woven bamboo to stop evil spirits from entering, and a small basket with betel and areca nuts for the good spirits.

In Taiwan the festival is called Sang-Sin. Small horses and palanquins are cut from yellow paper and burned to serve as conveyances for the kitchen god. The New Year's feast is first laid before the ancestor shrine. About seven o'clock, after the ancestors have eaten, the food is gathered up, reheated, and eaten by the family. The greater the amount of food placed before the shrine, the greater will be the reward for the new year. After the banquet, oranges are stacked in fives before the ancestor tablets and household gods. A dragon-bedecked red cloth is hung before the altar. The dragon is the spirit of rain and abundance, and the oranges are an invitation to the gods to share the family's feasting.

In Korea, Je-sok (or Je-ya) is the name for New Year's Eve. Torches are lit in every part of the home, and everyone sits up all night to "defend the New Year" from evil spirits. In modern Seoul, the capital, the church bells are rung 33 times at midnight. A traditional food is duggook soup, made from rice and containing pheasant, chicken, meat, pinenuts, and chestnuts.

Making Happiness Festival (Tso-Fu Festival)
Ninth day of the first lunar month

The Making Happiness Festival is celebrated in Taiwan soon after the beginning of the Lunar New Year. The Happiness Master, headman, chief medium, and other villagers "invite the gods" by collecting a number of gods who normally dwell in various shrines and private homes and bringing them to the temple, accompanied by a hired band, children, gongs, and banners. Mothers of newborn sons pay their respects to the Heaven God by presenting hsin-ting ping ("new male cakes"). The following day they distribute these cakes to every household except those occupied by other new mothers. Elaborate sacrificial rites are performed in the temple and a special feast is held for villagers over 60 years of age, other important guests, and women who have given birth to sons during the year. At the end of the festival, the gods that have been brought to the temple are returned to their shrines.

Lantern Festival (Yuan Hsiao Chieh; Yuen Siu)
Fifteenth day of the first lunar month

Beginning on the thirteenth and fourteenth days of the new year, shops hang out lanterns in preparation for the Lantern Festival which falls the day of the first full moon of the new year. It marks the conclusion of the new year celebration.

According to one legend, the Lantern Festival originated with the emperors of China's Han dynasty (206 B.C.E.–220 C.E.) who paid tribute to the universe on that night. Because the ceremony was held in the evening, lanterns were used to illuminate the palace. The Han rulers imposed a year-round curfew on their subjects, but on this night the curfew was lifted, and the people, carrying their own simple lanterns, went forth to view the fancy lanterns of the palace.

Another legend holds that the festival originated because a maid of honor (named Yuan Hsiao, also the name of the sweet dumpling associated with the day) in the emperor's household longed to see her parents during the days of the Spring Festival. The resourceful Dongfang

Shuo decided to help her. He spread a rumor that the god of fire was going to burn down the city of Chang-an. The city was thrown into a panic. Dongfang Shuo, summoned by the emperor, advised him to have everyone leave the palace and also to order that lanterns be hung in every street and every building. In this way, the god of fire would think the city was already burning. The emperor followed the advice, and Yuan Hsiao took the opportunity to see her family. There have been lanterns ever since.

Star Festival
Eighteenth day of the first lunar month

When the Lunar New Year celebration is over, a day is set aside for men to worship the Star Gods. To the Chinese, the stars and planets are the homes of sainted heroes who have the power to influence the course of human destiny. Women are traditionally forbidden to participate in the ceremony, which consists of setting up a small table or altar in the courtyard of the house with a simple food offering (usually rice balls cooked in sugar and flour). Two pictures are placed on the altar, one of the Star Gods and another of the cyclical signs associated with them. In a sealed envelope is a chart of lucky and unlucky stars. The master of the house makes a special prayer to the star that presided over his birth and lights the special lamps, made of red and yellow paper and filled with perfumed oil, that have been arranged around the altar. They burn out quickly, after which each son of the house comes forward to honor his own star by relighting three of the lamps. If their flames burn brightly, it means he will have good luck in the coming year.

Second Lunar Month
(February-March)

Monkey God Festival
Celebrated on February 17 and September 12

Tai Seng Yeh, the popular Monkey God, is honored on both February 17 and September 12. According to Taoist belief, Tai Seng Yeh sneaked into heaven and acquired miraculous powers. He is thought to cure the sick and absolve the hopeless. He is the godfather of many Chinese children.

In Singapore, Taoist mediums go into a trance to let the god's spirit enter their bodies. Then, possessed, they howl and slash themselves with knives, and scrawl symbols on scraps of paper that are grabbed by devotees. There are also puppet shows and Chinese street opera performances at Chinese temples. The festival also may include demonstrations of fire walking.

Third Lunar Month (March-April)

Qing Ming Festival (Ch'ing Ming; Festival of Pure Brightness; Cold Food Day; Han Sik-il; Han Shih)
Fourth or fifth day of the third lunar month

The Qing Ming Festival is a Confucian celebration that dates back to the Han Dynasty (206 B.C.E. to 220 C.E.). It is computed as 105 days after the Winter Solstice, Tong-ji. Its purpose is to honor the dead, and it is now a Chinese national holiday.

Qing Ming is observed by the maintenance of ancestral graves; the presentation of food, wine, and flowers as offerings; and the burning of paper money at the graveside to provide the ancestors with funds in the afterworld. Traditional Chinese belief holds that the afterlife is quite similar to this life, and that the dead live below ground in the Yellow Springs region. In ancient China, other festivities of the day included playing Chinese football and flying kites. Today, people picnic and gather for family meals.

The day is also called Cold Food Day because, according to an ancient legend, it was taboo to cook the day before. In Korea, the holiday's name is Han Sik-il; in Taiwan it is Han Shih. The Taiwanese observance includes a symbolic ritual of maintaining the home of one's ancestors. This is accomplished using strips of yellow paper about three inches long by two inches wide which are stuck in the ground by the grave. After this is completed, prayers and food offerings are made.

Matsu Festival (T'ien-hou Festival)
Twenty-third day of the third lunar month

Matsu (or Ma-cho or Mazu; also known as T'ien-hou), the Chinese Goddess of the Sea, is venerated on the day set aside to honor her birth. Fishermen honor her for protecting them from storms and disasters at sea. People pay homage to her at the Meizhou Mazu Temple on Meishou Island, in other Chinese communities, and on Taiwan.

On Taiwan, the most famous Matsu celebration site is the Chaotien Temple in Peikang, Taiwan's oldest, biggest, and richest Matsu temple, built in 1694. During the festival, a carnival-like atmosphere prevails, with watermelon stalls, cotton candy stalls, sling-shot ranges, parades of the goddess and other gods, altars for sacrifices of food and incense, and firecrackers. It has been estimated that 75 percent of all firecrackers manufactured on Taiwan are exploded in Peikang during the Matsu Festival. The festival is attended by hundreds of thousands of people, many of whom make pilgrimages from the town of Tachia about 60 miles north and spend a week visiting about 16 Matsu temples along the route.

A story is told that Matsu, a girl from the Hokkien Province in China, took up the fishing trade to support her mother after her fisherman father died. One day she died at sea, and because of her filial devotion, she came to be worshiped as a deity. During World War II, when American planes started to bomb Taiwan, many women prayed to Matsu, and it is said that some women saw a girl dressed in red holding out a red cloth to catch the falling bombs.

The origins of the festival are uncertain. According to one Chinese legend, the goddess was born in about 960 C.E. and, because she never cried in the first month of her life, was named Lin Moniang (moniang means "quiet girl"). She began to read when she was eight, studied Buddhist and Taoist scriptures, became a believer in Buddhism at 10, studied magic arts when she was 12, and at 28 achieved nirvana and became a goddess. She is worshiped because she is believed to have performed many miracles during her life. Courts in successive dynasties issued decrees to honor her with such titles as "Holy Princess" and "Holy Mother."

Figure 16.3. One component of Chinese religious thought focuses on the role of ancestors. Ancestors are members of the family who have died. Practices surrounding the veneration of ancestors include funeral rites in which a deceased family member is officially numbered among the ancestors. Additionally, wood inscribed with the name of the deceased is kept on a family altar.

Fourth Lunar Month (April-May)

Chongmyo Taeje (Royal Shrine Rite)
First Sunday in May

This rite is a Confucian memorial ceremony held at Chongmyo Shrine in Seoul, Korea, to honor the Yi kings and queens of the Choson Dynasty (1392–1910). The shrine, in a secluded garden in the center of Seoul, houses the ancestral tablets of the monarchs. Each year elaborate rites are performed to pay homage to them, and a number of royal descendants, robed in the traditional garments of their ancestors, take part. The rites are accompanied by court music and dance. The ceremony is a grand expression of the widespread Confucian practice of honoring ancestors, either at home or at their graves.

Tam Kung Festival
Eighth day of the fourth lunar month

Tam Kung is a popular god among fisherfolk. Taoists believe his powers were apparent when he was only 12 years old. Although his greatest gift was controlling the weather, he could also heal the sick and predict the future. Residents of the Shau Kei Wan area believe he saved many lives during an outbreak of cholera in 1967. His birthday is marked with a grand procession, Cantonese opera, and lion and dragon dances.

Birthday of the Third Prince
Eighth and ninth days of the fourth lunar month

The Third Prince is a Taoist child-god. Taoists believe he rides on the wheels of the wind and fire and can work miracles. A festival in his honor is held in Singapore. Chinese mediums in trances dance, slash themselves with spiked maces and swords, and write charms on yellow paper with blood from their tongues. There is also a street procession of stilt-walkers, dragon dancers, and Chinese musicians.

Sixth Lunar Month (June-July)

Birthday of Lu Pan
Thirteenth day of the sixth lunar month

Lu Pan, the Taoist patron saint of carpenters and builders is honored on the day set aside to commemorate his birth. According to tradition, Lu Pan was born in 507 B.C.E. An architect, engineer, and inventor, Lu Pan is credited with inventing the drill, plane, shovel, saw, lock, and ladder. His wife is said to have invented the umbrella. Because his inventions are indispensable to building, it is common practice at the start of major construction projects for employees to have feasts, burn incense, and offer prayers to Lu Pan so that he may protect them and the construction work from disaster.

In Hong Kong, people in the construction industry observe Lu Pan's birthday with celebratory banquets to give thanks for their good fortune in the past year and to pray for better fortune in the year to come. They also pay their respects at noon at the Lu Pan Temple in Kennedy Town.

Seventh Lunar Month (July-August)

Festival of Hungry Ghosts
Full moon or 15th day of seventh lunar month; July-August

The Festival of the Hungry Ghosts is celebrated by both Taoists and Buddhists. Its origins probably date back to the sixth century and Confucius. It is observed in China and throughout the rest of eastern Asia.

According to Chinese legend, the souls of the dead are released from purgatory during this time to roam the earth. This makes it a dangerous time to travel, get married, or move to a new house. Unhappy and hungry spirits, those who died without descendants to look after them or who had no proper funeral, may cause trouble and therefore must be placated with offerings. Offerings are made by people who burn paper replicas of material possessions like automobiles, furniture, clothing, and paper money ("ghost money") believing that this frees these things for the spirits to use. Offerings of food are placed on tables outside people's homes. Prayers are said at Chinese temples and in Chinese shops and homes. The festival also includes open-air performances of street opera, called wayang, and puppet shows.

Eighth Lunar Month (August-September)

Mid-Autumn Festival (Moon Cake Festival; Chung Ch'iu; Hangawi; Ch'usok; Trung Thursday; Tiong-chhiu Choeh.)
Fifteenth day of the eighth lunar month

The Mid-Autumn Festival celebrates the birth of the moon goddess. The festival is a national holiday in China and observances occur throughout the Far East and in Asian communities all over the world. In Korea, it is called Hangawi or Ch'usok; in Vietnam Trung Thursday; in Hong Kong Chung Ch'iu; and in Taiwan Tiong-chhiu Choeh.

Several traditional activities are associated with the festival including family reunions, exchanging presents, feasting, and eating moon cakes. Some people also pray to the moon for protection, family unity, and good fortune.

Table 14.3. Alphabetical List of Chinese Holidays

Holidays .... Date(s)

Birthday of Lu
    Pan (Taoist) .... Thirteenth day of
        the sixth lunar month

Birthday of the Third
    Prince (Taoist) .... Eighth and ninth
        days of the fourth
        lunar month

Ch'ing Ming
    see Qing Ming Festival
Ch'usok *see*
    Mid-Autumn Festival
Chongmyo Taeje
    (Confucian) .... First Sunday in May
Chung Ch'iu *see*
    Mid-Autumn Festival
Cold Food Day
    see Qing Ming Festival
Confucius's Birthday
    (Confucian) .... September 28
Festival of Hungry
    Ghosts (Taoist; Folk) .... Full moon day of the
        seventh lunar month
Festival of Nine Imperial
    Gods (Taoist) .... First nine days of the
        ninth lunar month
Festival of Pure
    Brightness *see*
    Qing Ming Festival
Han Shih *see*
    Qing Ming Festival
Han Sik-il *see*
    Qing Ming Festival
Hangawi *see*
    Mid-Autumn Festival
Je-sok
    see Lunar New Year
Kitchen God Festival
    (Taoist; Folk) .... 23rd night of the
        twelfth lunar month
Lantern Festival (Folk) .... Fifteenth day of the
        first lunar month
Lunar New Year
    (East Asia) .... First day of the first
        lunar month
Making Happiness
    Festival (Folk) .... Ninth day of the first
        lunar month
Matsu Festival
    (Taoist; Folk) .... 23rd day of the
        third lunar month

Holidays .... Date(s)

Mid-Autumn Festival
    (Folk) .... Fifteenth day of the
        eighth lunar month
Monkey God Festival
    (Taoist) .... February 17 and
        September 12
Moon Cake Festival *see*
    Mid-Autumn Festival
Qing Ming Festival (Folk) ... Fourth or fifth day
        of the third lunar
        month
Royal Shrine Rite
    see Chongmyo Taeje
Sang-Sin
    see Lunar New Year
Sending the Winter Dress
    (Folk) .... First day of the
        tenth lunar month
Spring Festival
    see Lunar New Year
Star Festival (Folk) .... 18th day of the first
        lunar month
Ta Chiu (Taoist) .... About December 27
Tam Kung Festival
    (Taoist) .... Eighth day of the
        fourth lunar month
Teacher's Day *see*
    Confucius's Birthday
Tet *see* Lunar New Year
T'ien-hou Festival
    see Matsu Festival
Tiong-chhiu Choeh
    see Mid-Autumn
    Festival
Tong-ji *see* Winter Solstice
Trung Thursday *see*
    Mid-Autumn Festival
Tso-Fu Festival
    see Making Happiness
    Festival
Tung Chih
    see Winter Solstice
Winter Solstice (Folk) .... About December 21
Yuan Hsiao Chieh
    see Lantern Festival
Yuan Tan *see*
    Lunar New Year
Yuen Siu
    see Lantern Festival

There are varying legends associated with the origin of the festival, which is thought to date back to the ninth century. One story tells of a rabbit who can be seen on the dark side of the full moon. The rabbit, who makes a potion for immortality, is honored on this day which is believed to be his birthday, and moon cakes were made to feed the rabbits. Another version says that the day marks the overthrow of the Mongol overlords in ancient China; the moon cakes supposedly hid secret messages planning the overthrow. Another version of the day's origin is that the day is a harvest festival, and it occurs at a time when the moon is brightest.

Ninth Lunar Month (September-October)

Festival of the Nine Imperial Gods
First nine days of the ninth lunar month

As celebrated today in Singapore, the Festival of the Nine Imperial Gods derives from an ancient Chinese cleansing ritual. The festival begins with a procession to a river or the sea to invite the Nine Imperial Gods to descend from the heavens into an urn filled with burning benzoin. The urn is then carried to the temple and put in a place where only Taoist priests and Buddhist monks are allowed to enter. Nine oil lamps representing the gods are hung from a bamboo pole in front of the temple. They are lowered and then raised again to signify that the gods have arrived. The ground below the lamps is purified every morning and afternoon with holy water. Worshippers enter the temple by crossing a specially constructed bridge, symbolizing the belief that they are leaving the evils of the past year behind.

Chinese operas known as wayang shows—some of which take two or more days to complete—are often performed during the nine days of the festival. On the ninth day, the sacred urn with the burning ashes is brought out of the temple and taken in procession back to the water's edge, where it is placed in a boat. The observers wait for the boat to move, indicating that the gods have departed—but what often happens is that other boats turn on their engines to churn up the water and send the gods on their way.

Confucius's Birthday (Teacher's Day)
September 28

Confucius, perhaps the most influential man in China's history, is honored on a day set aside to commemorate his birth. In Taiwan, the day is a national holiday. In Qufu, Shandong Province, China, the birthplace of Confucius, there is a two-week-long Confucian Culture Festival. In Hong Kong observances are held by the Confucian Society at the Confucius Temple at Causeway Bay near this date.

Commemorations in Taiwan take the form of dawn services at the Confucian temples. The Confucius Temple in Tainan built in 1665 is the oldest Confucian temple in Taiwan.

Tenth Lunar Month (October-November)

Sending the Winter Dress
First day of the tenth lunar month

By tradition, on this day the Chinese send winter garments to the dead. They are not real items of clothing but paper replicas packed in parcels bearing the names of the recipients. The gift packages are first exhibited in the home; the actual sending of the garments takes place in a courtyard or near the tomb, where they are burned.

Twelfth Lunar Month (December-January)

Winter Solstice (Tung Chih; Tong-ji)
During the twelfth lunar month; about December 21

The Chinese god T'ien is honored at the Winter Solstice. According to tradition, the ancient emperors of China would present themselves before the god at the Forbidden City in the capital of Beijing to offer sacrifices on behalf of the people. Modernly, the festival is commemorated on the longest night of the year. People visit temples and serve feasts in their homes to honor deceased family members.

Ta Chiu
During the twelfth lunar month; about December 27

Ta Chiu is a Taoist celebration of renewal. During the observance, gods and ghosts are summoned. Images of all patron saints are gathered in one place and people make offerings. A priest then reads the names of living persons to be recognized by the ceremony. These are fastened to a paper horse and burned so that the smoke can rise to heaven.

Kitchen God Festival
Twenty-third night of the 12th lunar month

The Kitchen God Festival occurs during preparations for the new year. According to legend, at this time Zao Wang (which means "the Lord Who Watches over the Hearth") prepares for his journey to report to the Jade Emperor, who is supreme over all the gods. Zao Wang's mission is to tell the Jade Emperor about everyone's behavior. To send their Kitchen God on his way, households burn paper money and give him offerings of wine. To make sure that his words to the Jade Emperor are sweet, they also offer tang kwa, a dumpling that finds its way to the mouths of eager children.

CHAPTER 17

Shinto

Overview of Shinto

What Is Shinto?

The name Shinto was first employed during the sixth century C.E. to differentiate indigenous religions in Japan from faith systems that originated in mainland Asia (primarily Buddhism and Confucianism). The word is derived from two Chinese characters, *shen* (gods) and *tao* (way). Loosely translated, Shinto means "way of the gods." Its roots lie in an ancient nature-based religion. Some important concepts in Shinto include the value of tradition, the reverence of nature, cleanliness (ritual purity), and the veneration of spirits called *kami*. Strictly speaking, *kami* are not deities. The literal translation of the word *kami* is "that which is hidden."

Kami (which is both the singular and plural term) are honored, but do not assert their powers upon humans in the traditional manner deities or gods in other religions. People may be descended from the *kami*, and *kami* may influence the course of nature and events. The *kami* can bestow blessings, but they are not all benign. *Kami* are present in natural things such as trees, mountains, rocks, and rivers. They are embodied in religious relics, especially mirrors and jewels. They also include spirits of ancestors, local deities, holy people, and even political or literary figures.

The human role is to venerate the *kami* and make offerings. The ultimate goal of Shinto is to uphold the harmony among humans and between people and nature. In this regard, The principle of all *kami* is to protect and sustain life.

One of the most important human tasks is to maintain ritual purity. While other religions are concerned with sin, Shinto adherents are more concerned about contamination. Washing before coming into the presence of the *kami* is essential, and purity helps a person ascend towards the level of the gods.

The Relationship between the **Kami** *and the* *Shinto People*

The *kami* exist in all of nature, but in some places and at some times their presence is more manifest. Places marked for their geographic beauty, such as rock formations and waterfalls, are especially noted for the presence of local *kami*. As a result, some of the most picturesque areas in Japan boast Shinto shrines. The *kami* are also present when the weather changes, such as when storms brew.

In addition to the myriad of *kami* that inhabit the land of Japan, the Japanese people also recognize some *kami* of greater importance who serve as the gods and goddesses responsible for establishing and directing the course of the nation's development. According to Shinto legend, the first gods were born of the union between the first male and the first female who emerged from creation. Three of the most important deities were generated spontaneously by the male while he was washing in the sea. Amaterasu, the sun goddess, came from his left eye. Tsukiyomi, the moon god, came from his right eye; Susano-o, the god of the summer wind, came from his nostrils.

According to an ancient story, Susano-o, a temperamental god, frequently angered and insulted his sister. In one instance, she locked herself in the Rock Cave of Heaven and refused to come out. An assembly of 800 spirits gathered to extricate the goddess. They hung a mirror in a tree and performed loud, raucous dances. When Amaterasu emerged to investigate, the spirits roped off the Cave preventing her from returning to it. In remembrance of this event, the mirror continues to play a central role in Shinto and is often the focal point of a shrine.

Authorities

Priests

The central authorities in Shinto are the priests. Traditionally the duties of the priest were passed through heredity lines, but in modern times, priests are trained on the basis of recommendation. The priests' duties include communicating with the *kami* and ensuring that ceremonies are properly carried out. Each individual priest is responsible for becoming ritually pure before performing required rites. Preparations include special bathing (ablutions), dietary rules, and sexual abstinence.

Books

Shinto does not have a single collection of sacred texts analogous to the Christian *Bible* or Islamic *Qur'an*. Instead, several important books provide information and guidance.

- *Kojiki* (*Records of Ancient Events*), compiled during the early eighth century C.E. under imperial command, is based on oral traditions. The text consists of three sections. The first section describes the mythic founding of Japan; the second and third sections include histories of the first emperors including time up to the reign of Empress Suiko in the early seventh century.

- *Nihongi* (*Chronicles of Japan*), comprising thirty books, covers ancient Japanese history through the end of the seventh century C.E.

- *Engishiki* (*Chronicles of the Engi*) contains ritual and ceremonial instructions along with prayers for sacred services.

History

Shinto grew out of the ancient worship of spirits in nature such as heaven, earth, mountains, rivers, seas, islands, and forests. It began with the age of the *kami*. *Kami* were formed when the cosmos materialized out of chaos. The most important *kami* was the Sun Goddess Amaterasu. The relationship between Amaterasu and her brother, the god Susano-o, shaped the early history of Japan.

Amaterasu sent her grandson to the Japanese islands to establish rule because she was dismayed with the disorder that existed under the rule of Susano-o's son. When her grandchild, Ninigi, descended to the earth, the age of human history began. His great-grandson, Jimmu Tenno was the first Japanese emperor of Japan. The traditional date for Jimmu's ascent to the throne is 660 B.C.E. (although many Western scholars place the date between the first century B.C.E. and the first century C.E.).

Because of this legendary history, emperors in Japan are viewed as having divine descent. Upon their ascension to power, they are given three symbols of the goddess Amaterasu: a mirror, jewels, and a sword. Early emperors

were also believed to possess shamanistic powers and they served as a spokesperson for the gods. One early Japanese leader, Queen Himiko, who reigned during the late second and early third century, was reputed to serve the spirits and hold special powers over people.

By the time of the fourth and fifth centuries, the Japanese political system and the worship of the *kami* were closely interrelated. Rulers believed that the *kami* held power, influence, and protection. As the political system developed, the priesthood also became more organized.

Beginning in the sixth century C.E., the Japanese people began to come into greater contact with the people of mainland Asia. Religions from China, in particular Buddhism, Confucianism, and Taoism, were introduced and foreign concepts blended with ancient veneration of the *kami*. By the early ninth century, Buddhist and Shinto doctrines had merged to form Ryobu Shinto (Shinto of Two Kinds). The sect also incorporated some Confucian elements.

Buddhist temples often included shrines to local *kami*, and shrines contained Buddha figures. By the tenth century, two Shinto *kami* were identified as Buddhist bodhisattvas (incarnations). In the following years, more of the *kami* became identified with bodhisattvas. Shinto also had a profound effect on Japanese Buddhism. Several Buddhist schools developed out of syncretism with Shinto thought, but eventually Shinto practices faded as Buddhist customs rose in popularity.

Beginning in the eleventh century, Japan's cultural stability became threatened and fighting among feudal lords intensified. The emperor retained official status as the head of the Japanese government due to his divinity, but real power shifted to military rulers called shoguns.

During the thirteenth century, when stormy seas prevented a Mongol invasion of Japan, the preeminence of Shinto gods was asserted. By the fifteenth century, a doctrine with a nationalistic emphasis emerged. The *kami* were seen as fundamental and other Buddhist and Confucian manifestations were viewed as merely offshoots of the *kami*.

The seventeenth century saw the establishment of the Tokugawa Shogunate (1603–1867). Under its leadership the superiority of Japanese culture over Chinese culture was proclaimed. In a revival of Shinto, an effort was made to purify the ancient faith by purging Buddhist and Confucian elements. The National Learning Movement (Kokugaku) was formed to focus the attention of the Japanese people on developing an unadulterated Japanese ideology.

The rule of the shoguns came to an end following a civil war in the middle nineteenth century. In 1868 Emperor Meiji, asserting his divine right to rule, reorganized Japan's government according to its historic form and instituted changes that led to the establishment of State Shinto as the official religion of Japan.

With the rise in power of State Shinto, unauthorized sects were banned and persecuted. Eventually, the national government, under economic pressure from foreign governments, permitted some freedom of religion and officially recognized thirteen sects. According to many analysts, State Shinto became a tool used by the government for political purposes rather than a religion in the traditional sense.

Following Japan's defeat in World War II, State Shinto fell into disarray. The terms of Japan's surrender included a requirement that the emperor renounce his claims to divinity and that religious movements be severed from government control. The imperial family, however, continues to honor personal rituals as part of the country's traditional heritage.

Shinto Today

People

Despite the fall of the nationalistic State Shinto, other forms of Shinto continued to be practiced. By the early 1990s, there were more than 80,000 Shinto shrines in Japan. Estimates of the number of adherents varied widely, however, from 3 to 110 million. The lower figures reflected the number of people who identified Shinto as their primary or exclusive religion; the larger figures included people who participated in Shinto ceremonies, the vast majority of them also professing other religions (predominantly Buddhism). Most Shinto adherents live in Japan, but small communities also exist in Europe, Latin America, North America, and in the Pacific island nations.

Worship

Shinto shrines provide a place were people can go and worship or petition the *kami*. Shinto shrines are known in Japanese as *yashiro* as opposed to *tera* meaning temple. However, *Yashiro* may be dedicated to either Shinto or Buddhist entities. Shrines are also sometimes referred to as *miya* or "honorable houses" as shrines in ancient times were the most important houses in a village. Shrines are sometime dedicated to trios of *kami* such as the Iwashimizu-Hachiman shrine, for instance which is dedicated to Emperor Ojin, his mother the Empress Jingo, and the Princess *kami* Himegami.

The traditional architecture of shrines includes an approach over a pond or body of water. A typical shrine is located in a grove or other place of natural beauty. The body of water leading to the shrine is usually spanned by a sacred bridge or *shin kyu*. Crossing this bridge symbolically signifies leaving the secular world for the sacred space. Pathways leading to shrines are often lined with lanterns.

Once a person crosses the bridge she or he enters the shrine compound. Shrine roofs are generally made of thatched cypress bark. Before approaching the building housing the *kami*, adherents line up in an area known as the *haiden* or veration area before coming up to the actual area where the *kami* are placed.

The *torii* gate is perhaps the most unique feature of Shinto shrines. Like the sacred bridge, the gate way symbolically demarcates the sacred area from the profane areas. *Torii* gates are placed in different locations with regard to shrines. Some are placed at the entrance to a shrine, others are placed directly in front of the building which houses the *kami*, and others a located a long way off from the shrines themselves. Torii gates usually consists of two pillars or columns with two cross beams at the top.

After entering the *torii* gate one usually walks down a path called the *sando* which leads up to the shrine. It is customary to wash ones hands and mouth before approaching the shrine and there is usually a ladle and baisin of water for this purpose placed at the entrance. Shrines are usually guarded at the entrance by a pair of stone statues called *koma-inu*, or lion dogs.

Other elements found in many shrines include a place for ritual washing, a place to hang tablets with prayers and petitions, a platform where offerings can be made, and a place to house the sacred object in which the *kami* lives. The dwelling of the *kami* is typically located in an inner shrine, which only a priest may enter. The sacred object is frequently a mirror which represents Amaterasu.

In the modern era, many Shinto shrines are kept by priests who also have full time secular jobs. People who visit the shrines come to make offerings and venerate the *kami* with ritual bows and claps. During festival times, people may also make offerings of votive candles and buy special charms for good luck. Folded paper talismans or pieces of paper tied to trees help summon opportunity, dispel misfortune, and empower prayers.

Shinto rituals also often involve offerings of food and drink and performances of music and dance. Practitioners believe that the *kami* receive the gifts and in return bestow blessing on the givers. The priest may use a branch from a sakaki tree (a type of evergreen) to sprinkle water over worshippers to indicate the *kami*'s blessing.

Major festivals are often marked by processions in which portable shrines carry the *kami* through the streets. The practice is believed to distribute the *kami*'s blessings throughout an entire community.

In addition to shrine worship, many practicing Shintoists have small shrines in their homes. These family shrines, called *kami*danas, consist of a sacred space where holy objects, candles and offerings are kept. They also typically include an amulet or some other representation of the *kami* being honored.

In some areas of rural Japan, mediums who communicate with the *kami* are common. The mediums, called *miko*, are typically female. Other holy people recognized by Shintoists include male and female ascetics who perform healing rituals and provide other spiritual services.

Sects

There are several Shinto sects currently recognized in Japan. They are classified into two major categories: Shrine Shinto and Sect Shinto. Another group, Confucian Shinto, also exists. It combines aspects of traditional Shinto with Confucian ethical principles and the metaphysical doctrines of the Neo-Confucians.

Shrine Shinto

The largest group of Shintoists are classified as belonging to the Shrine Shinto tradition. Followers venerate the *kami* historically recognized in Japan. During the era prior to World War II, many of the shrines were controlled by the government, but since that time the shrines have been restored to the priests. One of the best known shrines is located in Ise, and it is devoted to the sun goddess, Amaterasu.

Sect Shinto

Sect Shinto incorporates numerous small individual groups that operate independently. Many of the groups so classified trace their origins to the nineteenth century as people with perceived shamanic powers and supernatural experiences gathered followers. The types of groups include mountain sects (who venerate the *kami* of mountains), faith healing sects, and purification sects. The purification sects believe that individuals must maintain ritual purity in order to preserve physical and mental health.

The largest group within Sect Shinto is Tenrikyo (Heavenly Reason). It was established during the nineteenth century by two women who claimed divine encounters. The sect's teachings focus on mental and spiritual healing and the omnipresence of a divine spirit.

⧈ ⧈ ⧈

Japanese Lunar Calendar and Modern Reforms

The Japanese Lunar Calendar

There are many similarities between the ancient Japanese and Chinese lunar calendars. One of the primary differences was in dating methods. Chinese calendars counted years based on the Chinese emperor's reign, and Japanese calendars reckoned their years based on the reign of the Japanese emperor.

There were also minor differences in recognizing the precise stage of the moon. These may have been attributable to differences in longitudes rather than differences in the underlying theories. The Japanese lunar calendar began each month with the new moon. The full moon occurred on the fifteenth day. The first full moon to occur after the winter solstice marked the beginning of a new year. In order to keep the lunar and solar cycles in harmony, intercalary months were added in seven years of every 19-year cycle. The twelve normal months of the year were named according to agricultural cycles.

Used for Divination

The ancient Japanese also used the calendar for divination. A complex system of ten celestial signs called "stems" and twelve earth signs called "branches" were used in combination to form a cycle consisting of sixty

Table 17.1. Ancient Japanese Month Names

Name	Meaning
MuTsuki	Harmony
KisaRagi	Change of Dress
YaYohi	Grass Grows Dense
UTzuki	Plant Rice
SaTsuki	Rice Sprouts
MiNaTzuki	Put Water in the Field
FuTzuki	Letters
HaTzuki	Leaves
NagaTsuki	Autumn
KaNaTzuki	Gods
ShimoTsuki	Falling Frost
ShiHasu	Winter

units. These units applied to cycles of sixty days and were used to divine "lucky" and "unlucky" days. Interest in divination and the perceived need to accurately predict auspicious times from inauspicious ones initially led to resistance against efforts to reform the Japanese calendar.

Calendar Reform

By the late seventeenth century, the Japanese calendar was approximately two days out of step with astronomical observations. Although some minor adjustments were made, it was not until the Gregorian calendar was adopted in 1868 that Japan's calendar achieved modern precision.

In modern times, three different calendars work in conjunction to order the timing of Shinto festivals: the solar calendar, which begins with the new year on January 1; the lunar calendar which begins with the first full moon after the winter solstice; and the Chinese almanac which charts lucky and unlucky days for the year.

Table 17.2. Shinto Holiday Cycle

January
1–3 .... Ganjitsu

February
3 or 4 .... Setsubun
8 .... Hari-Kuyo

March
3 .... Hina Matsuri

May
5 .... Children's Day
15 .... Aoi Matsuri
~18 .... Sanja Matsuri

June
14 or 15 ...... Rice Planting Festivals
17 .... Lily Festival

July
17 .... Gion Matsuri

October
20 .... Ebisu Festival

November
15 .... Shichi-Go-San

December
31 .... Omisoka

Shinto Holidays

January

Ganjitsu (Japanese New Year)
January 1–3

The Shinto observance of the Japanese new year is focused on activities at shrines. Shrines and homes are typically decorated with symbolic emblems such as bamboo (representing sincerity), pine (constancy), and early-blooming plum blossoms (renewed life). Traditionally, the bamboo, pine and plum are known as "The Three Friends of Winter." Other decorations include paper talismans to avert evil and bring good luck. Many people travel to visit a shrine and attend a morning ceremony or watch the sun rise.

February

Setsubun (Bean-Throwing Festival)
February 3 or 4

Setsubun occurs on the last day of winter according to Japan's lunar calendar. Observed in all major temples and shrines, it marks the beginning of spring. The day is celebrated by attending public ceremonies at temples and shrines in which beans are thrown to people who have gathered. The beans are thrown to drive away evil spirits, and catching one is considered good luck. Sardine heads are also used to ward off evil. People hang them in doorways because evil spirits dislike their smell.

Hari-Kuyo (Festival of Broken Needles)
February 8

This memorial service for needles is held throughout Japan. The ceremony of laying needles to rest dates back to at least the fourth century C.E. Today the services are attended not only by tailors and dressmakers but also by people who sew at home. Traditionally, a shrine is set up in the Shinto style, with a sacred rope and strips of white paper suspended over a three-tiered altar. On the top tier are offerings of cake and fruit, on the second tier there is a pan of tofu, and the bottom tier is for placing scissors and thimbles. The tofu is th important ingredient; people insert their broken or benet needles in it while offering prayers of thanks to the needles for their years of service. Afterwards, the needles are wrapped in paper and laid to rest in the sea.

Hina Matsuri (Girl's Day; Doll Festival, Mom-No-Sekku; Peach Blossom Festival)
March 3

In homes where there are daughters, a stepped altar lined with dolls is usually set up. Ideally, there are eight steps each lined with *hina ninngjyow,* or "princess dolls." These dolls represent noble ladies from Japan's history. An empress doll is usually placed on the top-most step of the shrine. Little girls wear colorful kimonos and parties are usually held where girls and their friends gather together. Some of the traiditional foods associated include popped rice (hina arare), a pink rice cake (hina mochi), and a non-alcoholic drink called ama sake.

May

Children's Day (Kodomo No Hi)
May 5

On Children's Day, children are blessed in Shinto shrines by having a priest wave white paper streamers over their heads. Originally, May 5 was designated Boy's Day, but since 1948, this day has been reserved to celebrate both boys and girls. The tradition on this day is to fly a carp-shaped banner for each boy in the family. The carp symbolizes strength, courage, and determination.

Aoi Matsuri (Hollyhock Festival)
May 15

One of the three major festivals of Kyoto, Japan, Aoi Matsuri is believed to date from the sixth century. The festival's name derives from the hollyhock leaves adorning the headdresses of the participants; legend says hollyhocks help prevent storms and earthquakes. The festival owes its present form to the time in the Heian period (792–1099 C.E.) when imperial messengers were sent to the Kyoto shrines of Shimogamo and *Kami*gamo after a plague (or a flood) that came about because the shrines were neglected.

Today the festival, which was revived in 1884, consists of a re-creation of the original imperial procession. Some 500 people in ancient costume parade with horses and large lacquered oxcarts carrying the "imperial messengers" from the Kyoto Imperial Palace to the shrines to honor the god who protects the city.

Sanja Matsuri (Three Shrines Festival)
Weekend near May 18

The Sanja Matsuri is one of the most spectacular festivals in Tokyo, Japan. It is held to honor Kannon, the goddess of mercy (who is known as Kuan-yin in China), and the three fishermen brothers who founded the Asakusa Kannon Temple in the 14th century. The word Sanja means "three shrines," and matsuri is the Japanese term for festival.

According to legend, after the three brothers discovered a statue of Kannon in the Sumida River, their spirits were enshrined in three places. The annual festival has been held since the late 1800s on a weekend near May 18. Activities are focused on the Asakusa Temple and Tokyo's Shitamachi (downtown area).

More than 100 portable shrines (called mikoshi), which weigh up to two tons and are surmounted by gold phoenixes, are paraded through the streets to the gates of the temple. Carrying them are men in happi coats (traditional short laborers' jackets) worn to advertise their districts. There are also priests on horseback, musicians playing "sanja-bayashi" festival music, and dancers in traditional costume. On Sunday, various dances are performed.

June

Rice Planting Festivals
June 14 or 15

There are many rituals associated with the growing of rice in Japanese farming communities. Shinto priests are often asked to offer prayers for a good harvest season. The local *Kami* are also honored. In many rural celebrations, young women in costume perform rituals including planting seedlings while singing rice-planting songs to the accompaniment of pipes and drums. Sometimes women light fires of rice straw and pray to the rice god.

Figure 17.1. Amaterasu is the Shinto Sun Goddess

Table 17.3. Alphabetical List of Shinto Holidays

Holidays	Date(s)
Aoi Matsuri	May 15
Bean-Throwing Festival *see* Setsubun	
Children's Day	May 5
Doll Festival *see* Hina Matsuri	
Ebisu Festival	October 20
Festival of Broken Needles *see* Hari-Kuyo	
Ganjitsu	January 1-3
Gion Matsuri	July 17
Girl's Day *see* Hina Matsuri	
Hari-Kuyo	February 8
Hina Matsuri	March 3
Hollyhock Festival *see* Aoi Matsuri	
Japanese New Year *see* Ganjitsu	
Kodomo No Hi *see* Children's Day	
Lily Festival	June 17
Mom-No-Sekku *see* Hina Matsuri	
Omisoka	December 31
Peach Blossom Festival *see* Hina Matsuri	
Rice Planting Festivals	June 14 or 15
Sanja Matsuri	Weekend near May 18
Setsubun	February 3 or 4
Seven-Five-Three Festival *see* Shichi-Go-San	
Shichi-Go-San	November 15
Three Shrines Festival *see* Sanja Matsuri	
Year's End *see* Omisoka	

One of the better-known rice planting festivals occurs on June 14 in Osaka where thousands congregate to observe a group of young kimono-clad women plant rice and sing in the sacred fields near the Sumiyoshi Shrine. Working rhythmically to the music, the young women appear to be participating in a dance rather than the hard work of planting.

Lily Festival
June 17

The Lily Festival is a shrine celebration. Lilies are gathered in preparation for the festival and the temple priest offers a bouquet of lilies on the altar. The lilies are then blessed by seven women who wear white robes and perform a special dance. Afterwards, the lilies are mounted on a float and taken out in a procession. The lily dance marks the end of the rainy season, and the paraded lilies signify the purifying of the air.

July

Gion Matsuri
July 17

Gion Matsuri is the best-known festival in Japan and the biggest in Kyoto. It honors Susano-o, the brother of Amatersau (the sun goddess). Many smaller Gion festivals are held in other places throughout Japan in honor of the local *kami*.

The Gion Matsuri festival began in the year 869 C.E. when hundreds of people died in an epidemic that swept through Kyoto. The head priest of the Gion Shrine, now called the Yasaka Shrine, mounted 66 spears on a portable shrine, took it to the Emperor's garden, and the pestilence ended. In gratitude to the gods, the priest led a procession in the streets. Except for the period of the Onin War (1467–77), which destroyed the city, the procession has been held annually ever since.

There are events related to the festival throughout July but the main event is the parade of elaborate, carefully preserved floats on July 17. These gigantic floats include 29 hoko ("spears") floats and 22 smaller yama ("mountains") floats. The immense hoko weigh as much as 10 tons and can be 30 feet tall; they look like wonderfully ornate towers on wheels. They are decorated with Chinese and Japanese paintings and even with French Gobelin tapestries imported during the 17th and 18th centuries. Just under their lacquered roofs musicians play flutes and drums. From the rooftops of the floats two men toss straw good-luck favors to the crowds. The hoko roll slowly on their big wooden wheels, pulled with ropes by parade participants. Yama floats weigh only about a ton, and are carried on long poles by teams of men. Life-size dolls on platforms atop each float represent characters in the story the float depicts.

October

Ebisu Festival
October 20

The Ebisu Festival honors Ebisu, one of seven Shinto gods of good luck and the patron deity of tradesmen. Although he has a limited following in Tokyo where the shrine is located, a popular fair is held on the preceding day to provide people with items needed to participate in the commemoration. People buy wooden images of Ebisu, good-luck tokens, and large, white, pickled radishs (known as bettara).

November

Shichi-Go-San (Seven-Five-Three Festival)
November 15

This festival, possibly with roots in antiquity when children frequently died at a young age, honors children who have attained the ages of seven, five, and three. The children are attired in special dress (wearing kimonos) and presented at the shrine. There they are purified, and the priest prays to the tutelary deity for their healthy growth. At the end of the ceremony the priest gives each child two little packages: one containing cakes in the form of Shinto emblems (mirror, sword, and jewel), and the other with sacred rice to be mixed with the evening meal. Parents also give other gifts. Afterwards, there are often parties for the children. One custom is the giving of a special pink hard candy, called "thousand-year candy," which symbolizes hopes for a long life. Because Shichi-Go-San is not a legal holiday in Japan, families observe the ceremony on the Sunday nearest November fifteenth.

December

Omisoka (Year's End)
December 31

The last day of the year serves as a day to prepare for the new year. Home and shrine altars are purified and rededicated. Some people also visit and tend to the graves of their ancestors. By making things clean, the spirits of the *kami* are honored.

Figure 17.2. A torii gate marks the entrance to a Shinto temple or sacred place.

CHAPTER 18

Native American Religions

Overview of American Indian Tribal Religions

What Are Tribal Religions?

Many different Nations of American Indians live throughout North and South America. In the United States, there are over five hundred Nations with federal recognition. Hundreds more exist without federal status. Each tribe has its own religious traditions. Although many elements are shared in common, every tribe employs a unique blend of features that distinguish its faith from that of others. In some instances the dissimilarities are slight; in others, the distinctions are more profound. As with other religious families, variations exist in basic beliefs, mythic content, customs, and ritual ceremonies.

Despite this diversity, some general statements can be made. Most American Indian religious systems seek to create or uphold the harmony between humans and nature. In addition, some of the religions incorporate similar beliefs about the existence of spirits (especially guardian spirits), practices related to taboos (prohibitions based on something's sacred status or perceived danger), animal ceremonialism, and spiritual medicine.

Many tribes recognize an Ultimate or Supreme Being, called Creator or Great Spirit, who is distant and not directly involved with the day-to-day affairs of humans and animals inhabiting the earth. In some cases, this Supreme Being is viewed as a single deity, in others as a force comprised of more than one expression. It is not uncommon for the concept of the Supreme Being to be linked with that of a cultural hero, such as a legendary benefactor who provided vital societal knowledge (for example, farming techniques) or who functioned as the progenitor of the tribe.

A female deity, sometimes known as Grandmother Spider but also called by a variety of other names, is revered by some tribes. Another deity often honored, but not equal to Creator, is one typically possessing grandiose intentions and a tendency for committing blunders. This spirit is known as the Trickster or Coyote among some tribes. Among Algonkian tribes he is known as Nanabusho.

Supernatural experiences, typically manifested as dreams or visions, are another important component of many American Indian tribal religions. Such events, believed to be divinely inspired, are interpreted as guidance to the individual or to the entire tribe. New instructions and innovative practices received through such visions have led to increased diversity in religious expressions and resulted in variances even among clans of the same tribe.

Sacred Traditions and Authorities

Oral Traditions

Native American tribal religions possessed no commonly held canonical texts analogous to the Christian *Bible* or Islamic *Qur'an*. Histories, myths, and legends were—and continue to be—passed on by oral tradition. Although the accounts of the past carry some authority, they are subject to change and reinterpretation as new visions are received.

It is a misconception, however, that the lack of a common cannon was due to the lack of a writing system. Several Native American tribal people had written languages well before the nineteenth century when Sequoyah first developed inscriptions for a Cherokee syllabary. Hieroglyphic writing was used by the Maya people for nearly a millennium, and other Native American languages, including the Lenne Lenape (Delaware) and Shawnee, also had writing systems.

Authorities

Depending on the tribe, authority is often shared by a tribal chief and a religious leader. Religious leaders include medicine men and women and others who are specialists in seeing visions. The term "shaman" is sometimes misused in reference to American Indian medicine people; the term is more appropriately applied to Asian religions.

Medicine people learn their trade from older practitioners, and they are skilled in using the curative powers found in natural substances. A medicine man (or woman) is also believed to possess supernatural powers, including the ability to heal. This is not unlike healing concepts found in other religious families, such as the laying on of hands or focused, positive thoughts.

Medicine people and others within a tribe or clan often maintain medicine bundles. These bundles include a collection of symbolic objects. Some of the objects are believed to possess supernatural power; some represent clans within the tribe. The specific items in a collection vary significantly between tribes (and even among individuals within the same tribe or clan). Examples can include feathers, bones, teeth, herbs, rocks, and hair. Other articles included in the bundle may be items important to the individual in meditation and prayer. In the past, precise rituals usually governed the opening of a bundle for a religious event. More modernly, bundles are also opened for teaching. In some tribes, bundles were, and continue to be, passed from one generation to the next. In others, individuals are responsible for collecting items and assembling their own bundles.

People who serve as specialists in dream interpretation or in seeing visions play an important role in many tribes. The means by which visions and dreams are induced are varied. In some tribes sweat lodges are used for mental, physical, and spiritual healing. Many tribes allow a number of individuals to participate. Others, such as the Shawnee, allow only the healer and the patient. Other means used to induce trances for the purpose of identifying spirits responsible for diseases or calamities include prolonged isolation, deprivation of food and water, self-inflicted harm, and the use of psychotropic plants. Perhaps the most well-known of these is peyote, a species of spineless cactus containing alkaloid mescaline. This plant is a sacrament of the Native American Indian Church.

History

The history of Native American cultures dates back thousands of years into prehistoric times. According to many scholars, the people who became the Native Americans migrated from Asia across a land bridge that may have once connected the territories presently occupied by Alaska and Russia. The migrations, believed to have begun between 60,000 and 30,000 B.C.E. continued until approximately 4,000 B.C.E. This speculation, however, conflicts with traditional stories asserting that the indigenous Americans have always lived in North America or that tribes moved up from the south.

The historical development of religious belief systems among Native Americans is unknown. Most of the information available was gathered by Europeans who arrived on the continent beginning in the sixteenth century C.E. The data they recorded was fragmentary and oftentimes of questionable accuracy because the Europeans did not understanding the native cultures they were trying to describe and the Native Americans were reluctant to divulge details about themselves.

Some beliefs incorporated in ancient stories contain elements similar to those found in other places around the polar region. For example, many tribes shared creation stories with parallel elements and a comparable view of the cosmos. The cosmos was often seen as being layered with the heavens above and the underworld beneath. Although the number of heavens and the number of underworlds varied, the earth was located in the middle.

In some traditions, the different levels of the cosmos were connected by a tree, called the World Tree, which was represented in ceremonies by a pole. In a similar Norse legend, the earth was one of nine worlds connected by a World Tree. Modern followers of Asatru (Northern European Paganism) view the traditional May Pole as a representation of the mystic tree. (See Chapter 19–Paganism, for a more complete description of Asatru beliefs and practices.)

Developmental Patterns

Many modern researchers note that religious practices of individual tribes appear to have been closely related to means employed in the procurement of food. Based on this premise, Native American religions can be grouped into two fundamental patterns: religions among agricultural tribes and religions among hunting tribes. Agricultural tribes often focused their attention on rain and crop cycles, and the ceremonies that evolved were suited for permanent settlements. Among hunting tribes, the religious focus centered on animals and spirits. These ceremonial practices were suited to a nomadic existence. Although this simple differentiation between hunters and growers helps explain patterns, in practice many tribes participated in aspects of both.

Perhaps one of the religious artifacts most familiar to people of European ancestry is the ceremonial pipe (also called a calumet pipe or peace pipe). Among some tribes, tobacco is burned as a sacrificial offering. It is also believed that the smoke produced by tobacco in the pipe carries prayers to the Creator. Among some tribes the decoration of the pipe itself serves to convey meaning: white feathers signified peace, red feathers meant war.

Another common form of religious expression involved animal-related ceremonies. Animal ceremonialism includes the ritual honoring of an animal to appease its spirit and to thank it for sacrificing itself to the hunter for food. This type of ceremony is most often performed with kinds of animals that are (or were) hunted, especially bears. Another interpretation is that the ritual pays homage to animals so that other animals, anticipating similar honors, will make themselves available.

In northern areas, some tribes believed that masters presided over the spirits of some types of animals, typically animals that served as a food source or that provided other significant benefits to the social structure. The masters were responsible for controlling hunts and ensuring that hunters were worthy of their quarry. Spirit names and their allied animals varied in different areas. For example, one master of the spirits found among the Inuit Indians (commonly called Eskimos), was a goddess known as Sedna. Sedna, who was part animal and part fish, watched over the sea mammals.

Contact with Europeans

The coming of Europeans to the American continents made a pivotal impact on Native populations. In many cases early European settlers were viewed by Native Americans as a curiosity: European technology was interesting but cultural traditions were confusing. Europeans established themselves in permanent settlements from which movement would be difficult if local resources were depleted. In addition, the newcomers were often unprepared to cooperate with nature and its cycles.

Despite their peculiarities, the Europeans proved to be persisting and oppressive neighbors. They introduced catastrophic communicable diseases, especially smallpox and influenza. These illnesses, along with war and murder, contributed to the deaths of millions of North American Indians. Changes in land use caused disruptions in traditional Native cultural patterns, and European notions of religion discounted the value of Native beliefs. Intensive missionary efforts converted thousands of Native Americans to Christianity and impacted the faith systems of many thousands more.

In 1799 C.E., a prophet of the Seneca (part of the Iroquois nation), called Handsome Lake (Ganio 'Daí Io), called for cultural reform and intertribal cooperation. His message serves as the basis for a tradition called Gaiwiio (Good Message). Handsome Lake advocated family and tribal life. He opposed sorcery and the drinking of alcohol, which had been unknown to Native Americans until the Europeans arrived. His half-brother Cornplanter (Kaiiontwa'ko) also advocated temperance and called for the restoration and preservation of Iroquois religious traditions. Tenskwatawa (Open Door), the brother of Tecumseh, and other American Indian religious leaders in North America (known as Turtle Island among some Native nations) also advocated shunning European religious or cultural influences and returning to traditional ways.

Tensions Mount

Conflicts between people of European ancestry and Native Americans continued. During the early nineteenth century, the newly established United States began implementing the practice of removing tribes from their ancestral lands. The Removal Act of 1830 displaced Indian Nations from the Southeast to Oklahoma. The Cherokees, who were removed from their homeland in Georgia, endured a forced march that is remembered as The Trail of Tears. An estimated 4,000 died as a result of insufficient food supplies, a lack of blankets and warm clothing, and from illnesses. Other tribes who were similarly moved from their traditional lands included the Creek, Chickasaw, Choctaw, and Seminoles. Shawnee, Delaware, Seneca, Mingo, Miami, and many other Algonkian and Iroquoian People likewise suffered a forced disruption of their ancient ways. As a result of these events, many Nations lost their entire cultures, languages, and religions. A rift was also created between federally recognized and unrecognized tribes in America.

A shift in government policy during the late nineteenth century focused efforts on assimilating Americans Indians into White society instead of segregating them. The Dawes Act of 1887 granted property rights to individual Native American people instead of communally to tribes. The Act was intended to encourage Indians to abandon previously held nomadic lifestyles and become settled farmers. Instead, it resulted in the transfer of much valuable Indian land to new White owners.

The practice of sending Native American children to boarding schools was another example of attempted cultural change. Boys and girls were removed from their traditional ways and had their hair cut according to White standards. They were dressed in uniforms and taught new "civilized" skills. Harsh punishments, sometimes even resulting in death, were dealt out to those who persisted in their old cultural patterns or who continued to speak native languages.

As tensions between Indians and Whites escalated, the Natives became increasingly interested in reestablishing their religious traditions. Prophecy, revelations, and promises of restored power attracted attention. Several movements, such as the Ghost Dancers and the Native American Church, became established during the turbulent years of the late nineteenth century.

In 1924, by an act of Congress, Native Americans were granted rights of citizenship in the United States. Part of the motivation for this decision was to reward the thousands of American Indians who served and died in World War I. In 1934, the Indian Reorganization Act encouraged tribes to organize their own governments. By the end of the century, however, many controversial issues between Whites and Native Americans remained unresolved. Many are still unresolved.

Native American Tribal Religions Today

People

The vast majority of American Indians living today in the United States find themselves in situations completely removed from the traditions of their ancestors. The practice of confining Native people to reservations meant that status could not be attained by customary means and ancient cultural practices were divorced from their relevance. The loss of hunting lands and agricultural grounds led to economic collapse for the Native Nations.

According to the U.S. Census Bureau, in 2000 more than half a million people identified themselves as solely American Indian or Alaska Native (with no other racial heritage); 3.5 million more identified themselves as American Indian or Alaska Native with one or more other races. 3.1 million people claimed a specific tribal affiliation. Nearly 700,000 indicated they were Cherokee, and almost 300,000 identified themselves as Navajo. Other tribes with more than 50,000 individuals were the Choctaw, Blackfeet, Chippewa, Muscogee, Apache, and Lumbee.

The U.S. government holds more than 55 million acres in trust for use by recognized tribes and other Native American groups. The Trust lands, located in 35 states, include reservations, pueblos, rancherias, and Native Alaskan villages. Census data for 2000 indicate that 538,300 American Indians and Alaska Natives live on reservations. The largest tribal nation (in terms of both population and size of reservation) was the Navajo: 175,200 people lived within the Navajo nation's 15 million acres.

Worship

A growing number of Americans Indians have maintained, or are returning to, their old religious ways. Others have embraced an amalgamation of Christian and Indian spiritual traditions. In several places increased pride in native languages and religions continue to emerge and give new vitality to ancient rites. Some have begun to look to their common heritage as indigenous people rather than to the practices of individual tribes. Legal changes were needed to accommodate these faith expressions. Some Native American practices, such as participation in the Sun Dance, were previously deemed illegal by the U.S. government. The American Indian Religious Freedom Act (AIRFA) of 1978 restored to Native people the right to celebrate this and other ceremonies without fear of reprisal.

Dances

The form of religious expression most closely associated with the Western concept of worship often is found within the context of a dance ritual. In some dances participants wear distinct regalia to invoke the spirit of a represented animal or bird. Specific dances reflect certain prayers.

Powwows

Another type of ceremonial practice found among many different tribes is the powwow. Powwows feature gatherings during which ceremonies and other community activities are conducted. The purpose often includes paying homage to spirits with ritual music and dance. Some powwows are observed at specified times and others are assembled on the basis of need, such as in response to a famine or epidemic. Today powwows are found across the country. They are typically held during the warm months.

Ceremonial Places and Structures

Religious ceremonies take place in a variety of locations according to what is readily available. Many occur in a ceremonial circle outdoors, others within structures— some constructed for religious activities and others serving for community purposes as well.

Among the Delaware, the Long House is a structure used for ceremonies. The name can also be used for the ceremonies themselves. A Long House is a rectangular building with a roof that is open in the middle to allow ventilation from ceremonial fires burning within. A large pole, reminiscent of the World Tree and carved with an image depicting the Great One, extends from the floor upwards through the roof. The walls represent the four compass points, the floor signifies the earth, and the opening in the roof is associated with the spirit world. Ceremonies include counter-clockwise circumambulations of the structure's interior.

Some eastern Shawnee Bands hold ceremonies inside enclosed circular structures that sit directly on the ground with no flooring so that dancers make direct contact with the earth. A center pole, surrounded by a smoke hole, supports the roof. The entrance is on the East side with an altar opposite it. The interior reflects a clan's animal totems and may also include agricultural representations or food items on some occasions.

Another type of sacred structure, called a kiva, is found in the American Southwest among the Pueblo Indians. The kiva is an underground room, cylindrical or rectangular in shape. It represents the womb of the earth, out of which the two-legged (humans) emerged. The walls of a kiva are typically decorated with sacred representations and depictions of everyday village life. The ceremonies may be restricted to selected participants on behalf of the entire tribe.

Among traditional Navajo (Diné) people, religious ceremonies are conducted in a hogan. A hogan consists of a round room with a door facing the east. Men and women sit on different sides (women on the north; men on the south). Visitors in attendance sit on the west side. Some ceremonies may use elaborate sand paintings that serve in a manner akin to altars. Although the paintings can take hours to complete, they are not permanent. They are destroyed when the ceremony for which they were created is concluded.

Religious Movements

Ghost Dance

The Ghost Dance movement grew out of two elements. Its first appearance occurred in the 1860s when it was introduced by Wodziwob, a Paiute Indian, as a dance that would usher in a return to the old ways. This version began to fade in the 1870s but was revived in 1889 by another Paiute, Wovoka, from the Walker River Reserve, Nevada. Information about this second form of the Ghost Dance spread rapidly and reached the Plains tribes. The Sioux embraced the Ghost Dance but not related teachings on peace and non-violence. The Ghost Dance movement then culminated in anti-White sentiments that led to U.S. military action against the Dakota Sioux Indians and their chief, Sitting Bull, in 1890. Many Indians who believed that wearing special clothing would make them invulnerable to bullets died at Wounded Knee on December 29, 1890. Wovoka's version of the Ghost Dance, however, continued. He died in 1932 and some followers continued his teachings until the 1960s.

Pan-Indianism

Pan-Indianism, a movement of the twentieth century with roots in the Ghost Dance, sought to recreate ancient tribal religions into a unified expression. Following an era of intense cultural conflict with Whites, it grew out of an effort to define a shared identity and common expressions from history. Some of the desire for a unity and collective expression was the natural result of multiple tribes living in close proximity after the Removal.

Native American Church

The Native American Church developed out of a movement led by Quanah Parker, a Comanche leader, seeking to revive traditional ways. The Church received its first charter from the state of Oklahoma in 1918 and by 1930 counted membership estimated at nearly half the Indian population.

Following a tradition that has existed for 7,000–10,000 years in Mexico and North America, the Native American Church uses peyote (the cactus Lophophora williamsii) as a sacrament. The cactus button contains alkaloid mescaline which produces hallucinations (it is not, however, related to the mescal bean Sophora secundiflora). Consumption of a tea made from peyote causes nausea, which is followed by a euphoric feeling, heightened sensory awareness, and visions. The use of peyote remains controversial, especially in locations where local traditions did not incorporate its use. In some places visions may be achieved through fasting and isolation instead of by the use of peyote.

American Indian Movement (AIM)

Organized in the summer of 1968 in Minnesota, the American Indian Movement (AIM) began as a militant civil rights group. Its initial motivation was to protest police brutality, inadequate housing, soaring unemployment rates, poor education for Indian children, open racism demonstrated by the local welfare system against the American Indian clients, and federal government misbehavior in regard to Native policies.

During the past twenty-five years, the Movement has taken on organizing and creating opportunities for people across North America. AIM's headquarters are located in Minneapolis with chapters in many cities and Indian Nations. The American Indian Movement is a spiritual and cultural movement with no formal membership.

——— " ———

"Our people know of Christmas, and for that reason, sometimes if that certain moon for midwinter ceremony becomes close to Christmas, we move it back to the next moon, because they say that the earth is too noisy then. So the creator may not hear us."

— Handsome Lake (1913)

——— " ———

⊠ ⊠ ⊠

Seasonal Cycles

Among Native American tribes, time was viewed as a cyclical, rather than a linear, phenomenon. Instead of beginning at a point in the distant past and progressing toward culmination, time was understood as an extension of the repetitive patterns in nature.

According to archaeoastronomists, in Mesoamerica the Mayan and Aztec societies developed a sophisticated calendar for tracking time periods analogous to weeks and months as well as ceremonial cycles, solar years, and longer 52-year units. The Mayan Long Count Calendar extended to more than 5,000 years.

In North America time was marked by tabulating events on animal skins, counting sticks, and other methods. Although time periods such as days, months, seasons, and years were recognized, they were not interrelated. They were counted and tracked independently.

The period of a day, a single cycle of daylight and night, was observed as a basic unit, but there is no historical evidence that days were named. Months were recognized as a cycle of the moon's phases. These often began at the new moon, but among some tribes, months were reckoned based on the moon's position relative to the sun. The days of the month were sometimes counted in a progression leading from a new moon to the full moon and then to the next new moon. One method for counting the days of the month was to relate each day to a specific body part (joint or bone) from the small finger of the right hand, up to the head (at the full moon), and then in reverse order down the left side until the next new moon.

The counting of seasons was typically related to changes in weather patterns rather than the passing of moons. The number of seasons varied between four and five.

Years were marked by the cycling of seasons, not by a fixed number of days. Some tribes counted the passing of twelve moons in a year, and a few tribes practiced intercalating a moon at different times. The Zuni Indians (New Mexico) used names for the moons. The first six were colors; the second six were directions.

Despite the consistency in recognizing the basic cycle of a year, its beginning was observed at different times in different areas. The equinoxes (vernal or autumnal) were used in some places. Among the Hopi, the New Year began in November. The Creek Indians began their new year in the summer, but the precise date varied among individual settlements.

Time-Keeping Artifacts

One of the most basic devices for keeping track of time consisted of bundles of sticks. Each bundle contained a specified number of sticks, one of which would be removed on a daily basis. These types of bundles served to count down days until an event.

Notched sticks were sometimes employed to mark years after an important incident. However, these were most often used as mnemonic devices for recalling events in a series for story-telling, instead of counting.

Pictographs used by some tribes also marked the passing of years. One of the best known objects of this kind is a buffalo robe that begins in the year 1800 C.E. and is marked for 71 years.

Some tribes used devices called medicine wheels to trace the path of the sunrises and sunsets along the horizon. The wheels, made of stone and placed in a circle, were used as a type of calendar to determine certain significant dates with an astronomical basis, such as the summer solstice.

The Ceremonial Cycles

Although traditional calendars were not used, ceremonial cycles often related to the patterns observed during the solar year. The Tewa (a Southwestern Pueblo people in New Mexico) ceremonial calendar consists of two parts identified as winter and summer. The Tewa society is similarly divided into two units, called moieties. One moiety is identified with the winter cycle and the other with the summer cycle. The chief of each moiety rules for half of the year. Within each half-year cycle, a progressive series of rituals serves to bring supernatural assistance to the seasonal work being performed.

The Kwakiutl (who call themselves Hwak-wake-wakw) live in the Pacific Northwest on Vancouver Island. Their year is also divided into two halves, summer and winter. During the summer (called basux), people live in isolated areas for hunting and fishing and have limited opportunity for contact. In the winter (called tsetseqa) people return to their homes, and many ceremonies take place in the village.

The Hopi Indians also observe a ceremonial calendar in which the year is divided into two parts. According to tradition during one half of the year the katchinas (nature, ancestral, and guardian spirits) live in the village and reveal themselves to the people through ceremonial dances. During the other half of the year, the katchinas separate themselves from the village and return to live in their homes in the mountains. The Kachina season begins around the time of Winter Solstice, as people begin to prepare the ground for planting, and it closes in late July with the bringing in of the first harvest.

◈ ◈ ◈

Holidays Observed by Indigenous American People

Although many groups of American Indians honor different holidays and follow different seasonal cycles, the holidays listed are combined in one chronological list so that common themes may be more easily identified.

Great New Moon Ceremony (Cherokee New Year) (Cherokee)

New Moon in October

Cherokee stories tell that the world was created in the autumn, and the Great New Moon Ceremony is a celebration of the Cherokee New Year. The ceremony marks the end of nature's productive season and serves as a time of thanksgiving to the Earth and to the Great Spirit. Seven men are selected to be in charge of the ceremony and seven women are selected to prepare food for the feast. Seven days before the main council's prediction of the new moon, hunters gather game for the feast. On the evening before the main festival, women in the community perform a religious dance. On the day of the new moon, several activities occur, including dancing, a purification ceremony, giving offerings, praying, and a feast. The purification ceremony involves going to a river and immersing seven times in the water. As part of the purification ceremony, a sacred crystal is used to predict health for the next year. During the feast, each family gives produce. Corn, beans, and pumpkins are among the most common offerings.

The Chief Dance (Cherokee)

New Moon in October every 7th year

The Chief Dance is celebrated once every seven years in conjunction with the Great New Moon Ceremony. During the Chief Dance, the chief leads people in a dance of thanksgiving. The people then acknowledge the chief as the leader of all the clans. People are also reminded of the one true chief, the Great Spirit-Creator.

Atohuna (Friends Made; Cementation Ceremony) (Cherokee)

10 days after the Great New Moon Ceremony

Also called the Cementation Ceremony, Atohuna deals with the relationships between different people. The celebration has several purposes, making friends, uniting people with the creator, purifying the body and mind, and reconciling between people who have quarreled in the last year. The ceremony offers a brand new start to its participants. The fresh beginning is symbolized by replacing the old sacred fire with a new one. The new fire brings forgiveness to conflict and new bonds of eternal friendship. The fire keeper and his assistants build

Figure 18.1. Medicine wheels are created by placing rocks on the ground. They serve as focal points for prayer and meditation, but they are also aligned to mark astronomical events.

Table 18.1. Pueblo Feast Days

The Pueblo people have lived in the area currently identified as the southwestern portion of the United States for many centuries. Each Pueblo is an independently governed community. Although some aspects of their religious ceremonies remain secret, dances are often open to the public on feast days. In addition to the dances and other traditional components, feast day elements may also reflect Latino and Catholic influences, such as honoring the feast day of a Pueblo's patron saint.

Date	Holiday/Dance (Pueblo)
January 1	Turtle Dance (Taos Pueblo)
January 6	King's Day (most Pueblos)
January 22	Evening Firelight Dances (San Ildefonso Pueblo)
January 23	San Ildefonso Feast Day (San Ildefonso Pueblo)
February 2	Candelaria Day (San Felipe and Picuris Pueblos)
Late February	Deer Dances (Santa Clara and San Juan Pueblos)
March 19	St. Joseph Day (Laguna Pueblo)
Easter Weekend	Basket and Corn Dances (most Pueblos)
Easter	Bow and Arrow Dance (Zia Pueblo)
May 1	Feast of San Felipe (San Felipe Pueblo)
May 3	Santa Cruz Feast Day (Cochiti Pueblo)
May 3	Blessing of the Fields and Corn Dance (Taos Pueblo)
June 1	Blessing of the Fields and Corn Dance (Tesuque Pueblo)
June 13	San Antonio Feast Day (Sandia and Taos Pueblos)
June 13	Comanche Dance (Santa Clara Pueblo)
June 24	San Juan Feast Day (Taos Pueblo and many others)
June 29	San Pedro Feast Day (Santa Ana Pueblo)
July 4	Maiden's Puberty Rites (Mescalaro Apache Pueblo)
July 4	Waterfall Ceremonial (Nambe Pueblo)
mid July	Annual Powwow (Taos Pueblo)
July 14	San Buenaventura Feast Day (Cochiti)

Date	Holiday/Dance (Pueblo)
July 26	Santa Ana Feast Day (Laguna, Santa Anna, and Taos Pueblos)
August 2	Nuestra Senora de Los Angeles Feast Day (Jemez Pueblo)
August 4	Santo Domingo Feast Day (Santo Domingo Pueblo)
August 10	Feast of San Lorenzo (Picuris and Acoma Pueblos)
August 12	Santa Clara Feast Day (Santa Clara Pueblo)
August 15	San Antonio Feast Day (Laguna and Zia Pueblos)
August 28	San Augustine Feast Day (Isleta Pueblo)
September 2	San Estevan Feast Day (Acoma Pueblo)
September 4	San Augustine Feast Day (Isleta Pueblo)
September 8	Nativity of the Blessed Virgin Mary (Laguna and San Ildefonso Pueblos)
September 19	San Jose Feast Day (Laguna Pueblo)
September 30	Feast of San Geronimo (Taos Pueblo)
October 4	Feast of San Francisco (Nambe Pueblo)
October 17	Sts. Margaret and Mary Feast Day (Laguna Pueblo)
November 12	San Diego Feast Day (Jemez and Tesuque Pueblos)
December 12	Nuestra Senora de Guadalupe Feast Day (Pojoaque, Santa Clara, and Tesuque Pueblos)
mid to late December	Various Christmas observances and dances (many Pueblos)
late December	Harvest Dance (Laguna Pueblo)

Note: Dates are approximate and subject to change.

a new sacred fire and fast for seven days before the festival. The Atohuna festival lasts for four days and includes activities such as dancing, a blood adoption ceremony, cementation ceremony, a cleansing ritual, and fasting on designated days. According to tradition, two men publicly exchange clothes one piece at a time and then become brothers for life. The cleansing ritual involves the people going to the water and immersing seven times to forgive transgressions. Each participant in the festival is assigned different tasks such as hunting game, food preparation, leading dances, playing music, and cleaning the council house area.

Wuwuchim (Hopi)
Eve of the new moon in November

Wuwuchim is the new year for Hopi Indians. Observed by the Hopi people in northeastern Arizona, it is the most significant of the Hopi rituals because it serves to establish the rhythms for the year to come.

Over a four-day period, priests offer prayers, songs, and dances for a prosperous and safe new year. Other traditions include dances performed by men of the tribe costumed in embroidered kilts. Their dance is accompanied by the creation-myth chants of priests from the Bear Clan.

Shalako Ceremonial (Pueblo)
Late November or early December

The Pueblo Indians at the Zuni Pueblo in southwestern New Mexico celebrate this impressive ceremonial dance in the fall of each year. Intended to commemorate the dead and entreat the gods for good health and weather in the coming year, the ceremony involves all-night ritual dances and chants, and the blessing of houses. The dance features towering masked figures with beaks who represent the rainmaker's messengers. They wear kachina regalia that is ten feet tall. As they move from house to house through the Pueblo, the dancers make clacking noises to indicate the houses receiving blessings. They stop at the designated houses, remove their masks, perform chants, and share food with the inhabitants. Others taking part in the ceremony represent rain gods, whip-carrying warriors, and the fire god.

Soyal (Hopi)
On or near the Winter Solstice

Among the Hopi Indians, the Soyal period was observed for the purpose of helping the sun turn from its departure and begin its return. The rituals associated with Soyal were held in the kiva (ceremonial rooms) and marked by fasting and silence.

Guatemalan Winter Solstice (Palo Voladore) (Mayan)
December 21

In Guatemala, Mayan Indians honor the sun god they worshipped long before they became Christians with a dangerous ritual known as the *palo voladore*, or "flying pole dance." Three men climb to the top of a 50-foot pole. As one of them beats a drum and plays a flute, the other two each wind a long rope attached to the pole around one foot and jump. If they land on their feet, it is believed that the sun god will be pleased and that the days will start getting longer.

Bounding Bush (Cherokee)
Winter

The Bouncing Bush Ceremony is a joyous celebration of thanksgiving. Thanks are given to the Great Spirit and his helpers who are acknowledged as the source of the year's blessings. Activities include dancing, feasting, and giving offerings. Dances are held for four nights, and for the first three nights, they end at midnight. On the fourth night, a feast held before the dance, and the dancing

Figure 18.2. Kachina dolls represent spirits that live among the Hopi people for part of the year.

continues until near daybreak. During the celebration, participants offer tobacco and pine needles into the sacred fire as offerings of thanks.

White Dog Feast (Iroquois Midwinter Ceremony, Great Feather Dance) (Iroquois)
January

The White Dog Feast, dedicated to Teharonhiawagon (the Master of Life) is the longest and most important Iroquois ritual. It occurs in mid-winter, normally in January. It signifies renewal for the tribe, provides relief from the long winter, and marks the Iroquois New Year.

The feast incorporates the sacrifice of a dog and an offering of tobacco. These are necessary to ensure the return of spring and the rebirth of life. A white dog is strangled so that no blood is shed or bones broken. It is decorated with ribbons, feathers, and red paint and hung from a cross-pole for four days. On the fifth day, it is taken down and carried to the longhouse or assembly hall, where it is placed on the altar and burned. A basket containing tobacco is also thrown on the fire, its smoke rising as incense.

The Great Feather Dance is performed on the sixth day as a way of giving thanks to the Creator for the crops. The False Face Dance, during which a pair of masked "uncles" would visit Iroquois homes and scatter ashes, is also performed during the White Dog Feast. Ashes were also blown directly on sick people in a curing ritual. Other components of the festival include a dream-guessing game, a gambling game, and an activity where children impersonate wood spirits and beg for maple sugar candy.

Kwakiutl Winter Ceremonial (Kwakiutl)
Winter

The Kwakiutl people live along the western coast of the North American continent between Vancouver (Canada) and Alaska (United States). The winter season includes many rituals based on legendary events that occurred during the creation of the universe. Dances, masks and costumes evoke images of life, wealth, and death.

Alacitas (Aymara)
January 24

In South America (Bolivia) the Aymara people honor their god of prosperity, Ekeko, with a fair. Ekeko is depicted as a little man with a big belly, an open mouth, outstretched arms, and wearing a backpack. Miniature replicas of Ekeko are sold, as well as miniature items of food, clothing, and other goods that the Aymaras would like to have. They believe that if they fill one of Ekeko's packs with these miniature objects, he will bring them

Table 18.2. Cycle of Native American Holidays

Date(s)	Holiday
New Moon in October	Great New Moon Ceremony (Cherokee)
New Moon in October every 7th year	The Chief Dance (Cherokee)
10 days after the Great New Moon Ceremony	Atohuna (Cherokee)
Eve of the new moon in November	Wuwuchim (Hopi)
Late November or early December	Shalako Ceremonial (Pueblo)
Winter Solstice	Soyal (Hopi)
Winter Solstice	Guatemalan Winter Solstice (Mayan)
January	White Dog Feast (Iroquois)
Winter	Bounding Bush (Cherokee)
Winter	Kwakiutl Winter Ceremonial
January 24	Alacitas (Aymara)
February	Midwinter Dream Festival (Iroquois)
After new moon in February	Powamu Bean Dance (Hopi)
March	Maple Dance (Iroquois)
New moon in March	First New Moon of Spring (Cherokee)
First thunder	Thunder Dance (Iroquois)
Early Spring	Eagle Dance (Navajo and Others)
March or April	Planting Dances (Iroquois)
Memorial Day Weekend	Ute Bear Dance (Ute)
Summer Solstice	Sun Dance (Navajo and Others)
June	Strawberry Festival (Iroquois)
June or July	Green Corn Ceremony (Cherokee)
July 3–7	Seminole Green Corn Dance (Seminole)
July 26	Niman Dance (Hopi)
early to mid August	Ripe Fruits Ceremony (Cherokee)
Summer	New Corn Dance (Iroquois)
Mid to late August	Snake-Antelope Dance (Navajo)
Mid to late August	Flute Ceremony or Snake Dance (Navajo)
Late summer	Creek Green Corn Ceremony (Creek)
Late September	Lakon (Hopi and Navajo)
Late September	A Good Crop Dance (Navajo)
First weekend of October	Shiprock Navajo Nation Fair (Navajo)

the real things they represent. The name of the fair is derived from the word meaning "buy me."

Midwinter Dream Festival (Iroquois)
February

The Midwinter Dream Festival is one of the most sacred Iroquois festivals. During the festival, dreams are shared, their meanings guessed, and specialists in dream interpretation are consulted.

Powamu Bean Dance (Hopi)
Sixteen days beginning after the new moon in February

The Powamu festival is celebrated annually by the Hopi Indians who live at the Walpi Pueblo in northeastern Arizona. It commemorates the final step in creation and serves to purify the year to come. The entire observance lasts sixteen days, eight days are dedicated to preparation and eight days are dedicated to rituals.

The Hopi Indians believe that for six months of the year, ancestral spirits called the katchinas leave their mountain homes and visit the tribe, bringing health to the people and rain for their crops. During the Powamu Festival, the Hopi people celebrate the entry of the Sky Father (also known as the Sun God) into the pueblo by dramatizing the event. The Sky Father, represented by a man wearing a circular kachina mask surrounded by feathers and horsehair with a curved beak in the middle, is led into the pueblo from the east at sunrise. He visits the house and kiva of the chief, performs certain ceremonial rites, and exchanges symbolic gifts.

Kachina representations, often made of cottonwood, are given to the young girls at the Bean Dance to teach them traditional Hopi ways. The most widely known kachina is probably the Hemis Kachina, which can be identified by its tableta headdress. Another is Salako, which is tall and dressed in feathers.

Maple Dance (Iroquois)
Date determined by Council; often in March

Maple Dance is celebrated at the time of making maple syrup and sugar. Council determines the date, which varies according to weather but is soon after sap begins to run. The festival includes singing, dancing, and the offering of tobacco to a ceremonial fire.

First New Moon of Spring (Cherokee)
First new moon in March

The First New Moon of Spring starts the planting season and includes ceremonies to help ensure the new crop's success. When the seven principal councilors determine when the new moon will occur, a messenger is sent out to announce the upcoming celebration. Like the Great New Moon Ceremony, seven men are put in charge of the festival, seven are in charge of food preparation, and hunters are designated to gather game for a feast. On the first evening of the festival selected women perform the friendship dance. On the second day, all the people go to the water for a purification ceremony. On the third day, all the people fast. On the fourth day, all the people perform the friendship dances. As part of the ceremony, the fire keeper relights the sacred fire and all home fires are put out and relit from the new fire. This symbolizes the renewal of life from Mother Earth.

Thunder Dance (Wasaze) (Iroquois)
First thunder of the year

The Iroquois Thunder Dance honors the spirit of Thunder. When the first thunder of the year is heard, usually in early spring, a council is called to set the time for the dance. Dancers congregate outside the council house and the dance begins immediately after opening remarks are made by the chief or priest. The spirit of Thunder is thanked for past services and people pray for continued favors. Music features war songs because the spirit of Thunder is believed to enjoy them. Tobacco is burned as an offering.

Eagle Dance (Navajo and Others)
Early Spring

Many North American Indians associate the eagle with supernatural powers, especially thunder and rain. The Jemez and Tesuque pueblos in New Mexico celebrate the Eagle Dance in the early spring. Two dancers, male and female, wear feathered caps with yellow beaks and wings made from eagle feathers as they circle each other while emulating the movements of the eagle. During the Comanche Eagle Dance, a dancer imitates the eagle, who legend tells is the young son of a chieftain who turned into an eagle when he died. Dancers in the Iowa tribe's Eagle Dance carry an eagle feather fan in their left hands, while the Iroquois eagle dance features feathered rattles and wands.

Planting Dances (Iroquois)
During March and April

Among the Iroquois nations, various dances occur during the spring crop planting season. A specific dance is associated with the planting of each individual crop or with the blessing of the seeds. The events are scheduled according to crop needs and weather conditions. In most cases, a tobacco offering and feast are included, along with a prayer of appreciation or honor which is offered by the tribe's medicine person.

The Cornplanting Dance, which lasts about four or five hours, focuses on securing divine favor and help with

Table 18.3. Alphabetical List of Native American Holidays

Holiday	Date(s)
Alacitas (Aymara)	January 24
Atohuna (Cherokee)	10 days after the Great New Moon Ceremony
Bounding Bush (Cherokee)	Winter
Cementation Ceremony *see* Atohuna	
Cherokee New Year *see* Great New Moon Ceremony	
Chief Dance (Cherokee)	New Moon in October every 7th year
Creek Green Corn Ceremony (Creek)	Late summer
Eagle Dance (Navajo and Others)	Early Spring
First New Moon of Spring (Cherokee)	First new moon in March
Flute Ceremony or Snake Dance (Navajo)	Middle to late August
Friends Made *see* Atohuna	
Good Crop Dance (Navajo)	Late September
Great Feather Dance *see* White Dog Feast	
Great New Moon Ceremony (Cherokee)	New Moon in October
Green Corn Ceremony (Cherokee)	June or July
Guatemalan Winter Solstice (Mayan)	December 21
Home Dance *see* Niman Dance	
Iroquois Mid-Spring Festival *see* Strawberry Festival	
Iroquois Midwinter Ceremony *see* White Dog Feast	
Kwakiutl Winter Ceremonial	Winter

Holiday	Date(s)
Lakon (Hopi and Navajo)	Late September
Maple Dance (Iroquois)	March
Midwinter Dream Festival (Iroquois)	February
New Corn Dance (Iroquois)	Summer
Niman Dance (Hopi)	July 26
Palo Voladore *see* Guatemalan Winter Solstice	
Planting Dances (Iroquois)	March and April
Powamu Bean Dance (Hopi)	Sixteen days beginning after the new moon in February
Ripe Fruits Ceremony (Cherokee)	Early to mid August
Seminole Green Corn Dance	July 3–7
Shalako Ceremonial (Pueblo)	Late November or early December
Shiprock Navajo Nation Fair (Navajo)	First weekend of October
Snake-Antelope Dance (Navajo)	Middle to late August
Soyal (Hopi)	On or near the Winter Solstice
Strawberry Festival (Iroquois)	Typically in June
Sun Dance (Navajo and Others)	Summer Solstice
Thunder Dance (Iroquois)	First thunder of the year
Ute Bear Dance	Memorial Day weekend
Wasaze *see* Thunder Dance	
White Dog Feast (Iroquois)	January
Wuwuchim (Hopi)	Eve of the new moon in November

the spring planting process. People are encouraged to participate in tilling the ground and thus earn the a share in the coming year's provisions.

The Bean Dance is the only dance in which physical contact between dancers is permitted. Dancers holding hands represent the climbing bean vine.

Ute Bear Dance (Ute)
May, Memorial Day weekend

The Ute Bear Dance has its roots in an ancient ceremony of the Southern Ute Indians. Originally the ritual was held in late February or early March, at the time of the bears' awakening from their hibernation. It stemmed from the belief that the Utes were descended from bears, and the dance was given both to help the bears coming out of hibernation and to gain power from them, since bears were believed to cure sickness and to communicate with people in the Spirit World. Today the dance is largely a social occasion and it is held on the Sunday and Monday of Memorial Day weekend in Ignacio, Colorado.

Sun Dance (Navajo and Others)
Summer Solstice

Many North American Indian tribes hold ritual dances of thanksgiving in honor of the sun and its life-giving powers. Many tribes also view the sun as an expression of the Supreme Being's power. Early European immigrants to North America frequently misunderstood rituals honoring the sun for this role, and thought that the sun itself was the object of worship. Although the Sun Dance is often observed in conjunction with the summer solstice, in some places it is timed to coincide with the harvest. Specifics vary among tribes, but the rituals often emphasize individual bravery and courage.

The Sioux celebration is sometimes considered to be one of the most spectacular examples of the Sun Dance. In preparation, a tree is cut and raised to represent the connection between the heavens and earth. Tepees are set in a circle, representing the cosmos. The dance lasts from one to four days. During this time, participants, who abstain from food and drink, decorate their bodies in symbolic colors: red for sunset; blue for sky; yellow for lightning; white for light; and black for night. They wear loincloths, wristlets, and anklets, and carry a bone whistle made from an eagle wing. The dance also may involve self-laceration or hanging from the tree-pole with feet barely touching the ground. One goal of the dance is to experience a vision. After the dance, participants have a steam bath and are given food and water.

Among other groups of Plains Indians, the Sun Dance may also include ritual participation in a re-telling of the creation story. The event focuses on restoring the harmony between people and the environment.

Another group with a Sun Dance tradition is the Southern Ute tribe (in Ignacio, Colorado) whose annual two-day ritual is held beginning on the Sunday following July 4. The dancers who perform the ceremony are chosen from those who dream dreams and see visions. They fast for four days before the dance. One aspect of the ceremony involves chopping down a tree, stripping its bark, and then dancing around it. The Utes version of the Sun Dance does not incorporate self-torture.

The Iroquois observance of the Sun Dance differs from that of many others. Although its purpose is still to honor the sun, the ceremony does not occur at a specified time. Any person who feels the ceremony is necessary may call for it. On the agreed-upon date, people gather at noon. Arrows are shot toward the sun with accompanying war cries. Tobacco is offered in a ceremonial fire, and a priest chants specified rites.

Strawberry Festival (Iroquois Mid-Spring) (Iroquois)
When the strawberries are ripe (typically in June)

The Strawberry Festival is one of several annual festivals held by Iroquois Indians. The people congregate at Tonawanda, N.Y., in their longhouse to hear a lengthy recitation of the words of the Seneca prophet Handsome Lake (Ganio 'Daí Io; 1735–1815) calling for cooperative farming, abstention from hard drink, abandonment of witchcraft and magic, the prohibition of abortion, and other instructions. This prophecy forms the basis of today's Longhouse religion.

Following the recitations and speeches are ceremonial dances accompanied by chants and the pounding of turtle-shell rattles. Lunch follows, with a strawberry drink and strawberry shortcake. The Iroquois say, "You will eat strawberries when you die," because strawberries line the road to heaven.

Green Corn Ceremony (Cherokee)
June or July

The Cherokee Green Corn Ceremony is held when the new corn is ripe enough to eat, however, the new corn is not to be eaten until after the ceremony. Before the ceremony, a messenger is sent out to notify the people regarding when the ceremony will take place. As he travels, the messenger takes one ear of corn from the field of a different clan, gathering seven ears in total. Upon the messenger's return, the chief and his seven councilors fast for six days and then begin the ceremony on the seventh. The ceremony is one of thanksgiving, and it includes the relighting of the sacred fire, dancing, feasting, and story telling. The chief dedicates the new corn to the Creator and the priest makes offerings of the first-fruits of corn to the sacred fire.

Seminole Green Corn Dance (Seminole)
July 3–7

This four-day festival is observed by the Seminole Indians in the Florida Everglades region. It serves as a ritual to welcome the new year. The celebration includes feasting and traditional games. Dances include the catfish dance and the alligator dance. On the evening of the third day the Green Corn Dance is performed to give thanks for the harvest.

Niman Dance (Home Dance) (Hopi)
July 26

The Niman dance is a summer-time ritual marking the home-going of the "kachinas" (mountain-dwelling, supernatural beings who are believed to live among the Hopi people from mid-winter to mid-summer). The ceremony honoring their departure serves to bring health and rain. Up to 75 dancers representing the katchinas spend an entire day singing and dancing. Children receive traditional gifts: Kachina dolls are given to girls, and boys receive bows, arrows and rattles.

Ripe Fruits Ceremony (Cherokee)
40 to 50 days after the Green Corn Ceremony [early to mid August]

The Ripe Fruits Ceremony is another thanksgiving ceremony thanking the Creator for the harvest of ripe fruits. Before the ceremony, honorable women perform a religious dance and decide when the festival will take place. A committee is appointed to be in charge of the ceremony, hunters are sent to gather game, and an arch is built with green branches on the ceremonial grounds. During the festival, a special tea, called a "Black Drink" is used for cleansing and purifying. Dancing and feasting were also part of the festival. The celebration lasts for four days and is held outdoors. The Ripe Fruits Ceremony marks the end of the Cherokee national cycle of ceremonies.

New Corn Dance (Iroquois)
Summer

Among the Iroquois, the season's first corn is honored with the New Corn Dance. The principal dish served at the accompanying feast is succotash, made with corn, lima beans, squash, and venison or beef.

Snake-Antelope Dance (Navajo)
Middle to late August

Among the Hopi Indians, the Snake-Antelope Dance is held in alternate years during the last dry week in August.

It occurs over a period of several days during which snakes are gathered, bathed in a solution made from the yucca plant, and blessed. The purpose of the dance is to help bring rain. Hopi Snake Priests wearing loin cloths, body paint, feathers, and carrying rattles, enter the kiva for the ceremony. Hopi Mesas, Arizona Hopi Pueblo dancers wearing loin cloths, fox fur tails, body paint, moccasins, and carrying feathers, perform in the Snake Dance.

The dance begins when the Snake and Antelope priests come out of the kiva (a special ceremonial room) where secret rituals are held, and perform a dance around the enclosure where the snakes are confined. Then they divide into groups of three, each consisting of a carrier, a hugger, and a gatherer. The carrier takes a snake in his mouth, the hugger puts his left hand on the carrier's shoulder, and the gatherer does the same thing to the hugger. Together they circle the area four times. Then the carrier releases the snake and the gatherer retrieves it. Eventually the snakes are set free enabling them to carry out their mission and summon the rain.

Flute Ceremony or Snake Dance (Navajo)
Middle to late August

The Flute Ceremony is held once every two years by the Hopi people. Its observance alternates with the Snake-Antelope ceremony. It begins with a procession and concludes with flute music and song. The timing of the ceremony serves to commemorate the sun's journey to its summer home. Its purpose is to help the crops reach maturity and to bring rain. The Apache also celebrate rain dances as needed.

Snake dances are common among Indian tribes. Snake dances and Flute ceremonies are not open to public participation or observation.

Creek Green Corn Ceremony (Creek)
Late summer

The Muscogee-Creek Indians observe a religious harvest festival, not open to the public, in late summer on the ceremonial grounds in Okmulgee, Oklahoma. Each tribal group conducts its own Green Corn Ceremony on one of 12 such Creek ceremonial grounds in the state.

The dances for the ceremony are performed to the rhythm of turtle and gourd rattles. Women are designated "shell-shakers," and they dance in groups of four with shells (or sometimes today with juice cans filled with pebbles) around their ankles. Children are included in ceremonies from infancy as women dancers with babies carry them into the ceremonial circle. One dance, known as the ribbon dance, honors women and is performed only by women and girls.

Other elements of the festival are stickball games and cleansing ceremonies, but the affair is essentially religious. To worship the Great Spirit, Creeks perform rituals relating to wind, fire, water, and earth.

Lakon (Hopi and Navajo)
Late September

Lakon is the most important of three harvest ceremonials performed among the Hopi people. (The other two are called Marawu and Owaqlt.) Ritual activities are done primarily by women and the rites serve to remind the people that life is temporary and that they must comply with the Creator's plans.

Preparations for Lakon begin during the planting time of year when designated women and one man (chosen to perform ceremonial tasks that only men are permitted to do) enter the kiva (special ceremonial room). There they fast, pray, and sing for eight days. The observance of Lakon concludes with another eight-day ritual held at harvest time, the precise dates are determined by the position of the sun.

A Good Crop Dance (Navajo)
Late September

Similar to the Hopi harvest ceremony of Lakon, some Apache tribes participate in a harvest dance called A Good Crop Dance. In a similar fashion, the Taos Pueblo in New Mexico celebrates the Fiesta of San Geronimo at harvest time, reflecting the Catholic influence in the area.

Shiprock Navajo Nation Fair (Navajo)
Usually the first weekend of October

Also known as the Northern Navajo Fair, this harvest fair began in 1924 and is considered the oldest and most traditional of Navajo fairs.

The fair coincides with the end of an ancient nine-day Navajo healing ceremony called the Night Chant. The rituals involved in the Night Chant are complex and only portions are open to public attendance.

Other events of the fair include an all-Indian rodeo and inter-tribal powwow, a livestock show, a carnival, the Miss Northern Navajo Pageant, exhibits by Indian artisans, and a parade on Saturday morning.

CHAPTER 19

Paganism

Overview of Pagan and Neo-Pagan Religious Expression

What Is Paganism?

The term Paganism covers a variety of religions that share some common elements. These include nature worship, magic and divination, a belief in some kind of reincarnation, and a reverence for Goddesses and Gods (who may be viewed as abstract qualities or as literally existing). Most commonly these deities are drawn from the Celtic, Germanic, Norse, Greco-Roman, and Egyptian pantheons. For example, the Greek nature god Pan and the Celtic deity Cernunnos serve as prototypes for the Pagan Horned God; and Gaia, the Greek female spirit of the earth, becomes Mother Earth.

Modern pagan practices revive and reconstruct rituals based on interpretations of ancient mythologies. Although the rituals vary and individual groups may use different names, most pagans share a common set of eight holidays: the winter solstice; the spring equinox; the summer solstice; the fall equinox; and four days marking the midpoints between the solstices and equinoxes (traditionally February 1; May 1, August 1, and November 1).

Magic, often spelled "Magick" in order to distinguish it from the work of stage performers, is one of the most basic elements of Paganism. Magick is the practice of changing reality to conform to the magickian's will. Pagan magickians employ a variety of techniques to effect these changes. Some magick workings are highly ritualized and ceremonial, involving elaborate props and preparation. Others are performed in a casual atmosphere using little more than visualization or simple rhymes or chanting to focus will. Magick is seen by Pagans as evidence of the influence of unseen forces on the physical world, these forces are believed to originate in Divinity, in nature, and in themselves. Pagans practice Magick to reaffirm their connection to these forces.

The best known types of Pagans are Wiccans, Druids, the Asatru (consisting of Odinists and followers of other Northern European traditions), and Goddess Worshipers. Of these, the Wiccans probably have the greatest numbers. The groups, however, are not all mutually exclusive and practitioners in one may also be practitioners in another.

Authorities and Sacred Writings

The basic tenets of Paganism are typically taught by experience rather than authority. Different groups of pagans relate to authority in different ways. Among Wiccans it is common for the High Priest or Priestess to be considered as one among equals rather than as one with superior status. Typically, each coven operates independently in a democratic fashion. Other groups have a more clearly delineated line of prominence, but there is no one ultimate authority for all Pagans.

The types and kinds of writings held in esteem by Pagan groups and the level of that esteem vary. These may include official collections of ancient myths and a *Grimoire* (book of ceremonial magic). A group's *Grimoire* may be codified in a precise form or exist as an informal guideline. Two groups, each called The Odinic Rite, exemplify the difference. One group possesses *The Book of Blots* containing the final, authoritative version of all ceremonies; the other possess *The Book of Blotar of the Odinic Rite* which contains guidelines for rituals and other ceremonies. In Wicca, the *Book of Shadows*, includes rites, spells, chants, dances, and other elements of the religion, but there is no one definitive version of the *Book of Shadows*. In some Wiccan covens, each member compiles her or his own personal book.

Other subjects addressed in contemporary Pagan books include theology, ancient artifacts, Runes, and myths. These books, although not canonical, help individual pagans understand the complex interactions between themselves and the religious path they follow.

The History of Paganism

The history of modern paganism has been debated both within the Pagan community and outside it. Some claim that its traditions have been preserved by clandestine pagan groups and handed down secretly through generations of Christian dominion; they see folk customs and tales as being vestiges of a long religious heritage. Others suggest that the "ancient traditions" are twentieth century constructions for which folk customs and tales have provided inspiration for the imagination.

Whether Paganism is a continuation of an ancient religion or a modern innovation, events in European history helped produce a culture able to accept it as an alternate to mainstream religion in the middle and late twentieth century.

Historical Evidence

Researchers believe that ancient British society included people who were perceived as being exceptionally wise or who possessed healing powers. These people may have served their community in a capacity similar to that of a priest or priestess by overseeing spiritual events, like births, weddings, and funerals. Or, they may have served their communities in a more secular role, similar to that of a doctor. The historical record does not provide evidence that they worshipped the deities worshiped by modern Pagans. Nevertheless, modern Pagans (sometimes referred to as neopagans) view these ancient wise ones as their forbearers.

In the early centuries of the Common Era (C.E.), old religious practices were lost as Christianity gained political power and spread through northern Europe. In some instances, the old blended with the new. In other instances, the new persecuted the old and drove it either underground or to extinction.

One of the most perplexing issues in Pagan history relates to the European witch trials (1450-1700 C.E.). The witch trials, historically well-documented, are events that certainly occurred. But the question, "Who was burned?" lacks a definitive answer. Some historians have argued that the unfortunates were practitioners of an ancient pagan religion. Others believe that the "witches" who were burned were innocents selected for political or hysterical reasons.

Irrespective of which view most accurately described the historical event, several popular books on witchcraft written during the late nineteenth and early twentieth century asserted that actual witches had been burned. These witches were said to have been followers of an ancient religion that worshipped a female deity.

Magical Societies

In addition to popular belief in a goddess-based type of witchcraft, growing interest in magic and the occult also played a part in paving the way for modern Paganism.

The desire to control nature by magic and to manipulate events to one's own benefit has long been part of human history. In many cultures, legends of individual magicians can be found. In addition, several religions have magical offshoots, such as the Qabbalah. (Qabbalah is a form of mystical Judaism with roots in the early Christian era that became popular during the thirteenth century in Spain. Its followers use magic to achieve knowledge of God.)

Beginning with the seventeenth century, however, magical groups began to form. These magical societies included Rosicrucians, an occult group formed to impart secret wisdom, and Freemasons, a secret fraternal order established during the early 1700s from a consolidation of old stonecutters guilds. By the dawn of the twentieth century, many of these groups were operating with multiple levels of initiation into ritual practices and secrets, similar to modern Wiccan covens.

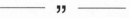

The Goddess is referred to as the triple goddess and she manifests herself in three attributes: as the beautiful young Maiden; the Mother; and the old woman or Crone.

Figure 19.1 The triple aspects of the Goddess are often represented by the moon in three phases. The waxing crescent (left) represents the maiden, the full moon (center) represents the mother, and the waning crescent (right) represents the crone.

Poets and Other Authors

At the same time interest in magic increased, literary figures turned their attention to Pagan images. These included Robert Burns (Scottish poet, 1759–96), John Keats (English poet 1795–1821), and William Butler Yeats (Irish poet and dramatist 1865–1939). Drawing on ancient legend and cultural symbols, such writers found fertile ground with fairies and giants and other supernatural beings. They glorified pagan images, sometimes in opposition to Christian conventions or governmental authorities. The popularity of their ideas helped usher in a cultural atmosphere ready for magic and sexual freedom, two of the major components of modern Paganism.

The Beginnings of Modern Druidry and Wicca

The two most commonly known modern Pagan groups, Wicca and Druidry, can trace their beginnings to specific people and events. Revivals of Druidry began during the 18th century among Christians who saw Druids as monotheistic decedents from one of the Lost Tribes of Israel. The Ancient Order of Druids was founded in London in 1781. As societal interest turned to the occult and the patriarchal tendencies of the first Druid revivalists were softened, Druidry emerged as a Pagan religion due largely to the influence of a leader in the order named Ross Nichols.

Gerald Gardner, a contemporary of Nichols, is recognized as a founder or a co-founder of Wicca. Gardner, a Freemason, Rosicrucian, spiritualist, and a member of the Druid order, published the first Wiccan publication in 1949. In 1951, when the remaining laws against witchcraft in Britain were repealed, the way for the current Wiccan revival was opened.

Paganism Today

In the 1960s, Paganism became more organized and open to the public, partly because of Wicca's connections to the emerging feminist movement. This led to a surge in popularity during the 1980s when regional and national festivals were held that attracted hundreds and sometimes thousands of participants. Charlotte Hardman, one of the co-authors of *Paganism Today* (Thorson, 1995) estimates that the number of pagans in the United States is between 50,000 and 100,000 and the number in the United Kingdom is somewhere between 30,000 and 50,000.

According to some observers, the increasing popularity of Pagan religions may be tied to the effects of increased urbanization. As people become more and more inhabitants of cities, they long for the simpler times and have a deep desire to become re-connected with the things of nature.

Nature plays a central role in Pagan rites. Modern Pagan ritual ceremonies often take place within the context of a circle. This is typically done outside when circumstances permit. Among some groups being out of doors and in direct contact with the ground is essential, for others it is optional. The circle itself may be physically drawn or symbolically represented. The sacred items and symbols present will vary depending on the Goddess(es) or God(s) being honored, the season, and the needs of the group.

Wiccans

Wiccans, one of several groups known as witches, honor the Goddess (frequently identified with the earth and the moon) and the God (identified with the sun and with vegetation). They celebrate both lunar and solar festivals although some groups place greater emphasis on lunar phases and typically conduct their rituals under the moon (that is, at night). Some Wiccan rites remain private and open only to the attendance of the initiated, but an increasing number of Wiccan groups are holding open rituals. Initiation is often done by degrees, with between three and seven ranks. In some groups much is made of these ranks and initiates must undergo specific training and wait a year and a day between the levels of initiation into the deeper mysteries of the craft. In other groups initiation is not emphasized.

The annual Wiccan holiday cycle lends itself to many metaphysical interpretations. One of these is patterned after the human life cycle. The Great Mother Goddess and her consort, called the Horned God, give birth to the Divine Child of the new year at the winter solstice. At Beltane (or May Day) the Sacred Marriage and sexual union of the Goddess and God is celebrated. The deity dies at Mabon (the autumnal equinox) to be reborn at the winter solstice.

The Wiccan year is divided into two segments, based on solar changes. During one half of the year, as days grow longer, the sun is seen as waxing or increasing in power. In the other half of the year the sun wanes as its visible hours decrease. Each half of the year is associated with an aspect of the God. As the Oak King he presides over the abundance of the waxing year, and as the Holly king he rules the decline of the waning year. The Holly King represents the death aspect and the Oak King represents the aspect of rebirth.

The Goddess is referred to as the triple goddess and she manifests herself in three attributes: as the beautiful young Maiden; the Mother; and the old woman or Crone. These aspects are based on the phases of the moon as well as archetypes from mythology. Diana, Demeter, and Hecate fill the roles of Maiden, Mother, and Crone in Greek myths.

Druids

Although Druids hold many things in common with Wiccans their celebrations are more closely tied to the sun. Their festivals are conducted during the day where the sun serves as a symbol of spiritual light. Some Druids conduct their rites in private but many are public.

Like the Wiccan holiday cycle, the annual cycle within Druidry typically follows a human life pattern. For example, the British Druid Order follows the mythical story of Lleu Llaw Gyffes who was born at the Winter Solstice, named at Candlemas, and armed at the Spring Equinox. His bride-to-be, Blodeuedd, was created on the Eve of May. The Summer solstice marked the zenith of his power. Lleu Llaw Gyffes married Blodeuedd on Lammas and died at the hands of the Lord of Winter on Samhain, his spirit to be reborn again at the Winter Solstice.

The Asatru

The Asatru include groups that honor Northern European deities (Germanic and Scandinavian). Groups that specifically honor the God Odin are referred to as Odinists. They tend to be ecologically concerned and some distinguish themselves from other Pagan groups because they do not use an altar to separate themselves from the ground during their worship rituals.

Within the Asatru, some groups follow the traditional primary eight Pagan holidays. Others, however, do not. Instead they observe the solstices and equinoxes (four in total) along with other specified monthly festivals.

Goddess Worshippers

Goddess worship involves the veneration of a Goddess who is manifest in many forms. It differs from other Pagan groups who esteem both Goddesses and Gods.

Goddess worshippers follow the annual cycle of death and rebirth as depicted in the mythological story of Persephone (also called Kore) and her mother, Demeter. In the story Persephone is taken to be the wife of the God of the underworld—symbolic of her death—and her mother, grief-stricken, withholds fruitfulness from the world. A bargain is struck and Persephone walks on the world for six months during which the earth blooms. She returns to the underworld for six months and the earth suffers autumn and winter, awaiting rebirth in the spring.

———— " ————

Magick is the practice of changing reality to conform to the magickian's will.

———— " ————

Pagan Calendars

Lunar and Solar Cycles

Pagan groups observe both lunar and solar cycles. For convenience, these are typically reconciled to the western civil calendar either by re-naming the twelve months (January through December) or by observing 13 lunar months and overlapping the beginning and ending moon where necessary.

The first month or moon of the year varies among the different groups. One of the most commonly used starting points of the year is the winter solstice—a time when the waning sun yields to the waxing sun. Other dates used as starting points include the spring equinox (when the growing season begins) and Samhain (a time when the death that leads to new life is celebrated).

Pagans claim one of the oldest calendar systems. The assertion is based on an artifact estimated to be 30,000 years old—a piece of bone with holes arranged in a manner suggesting counting in a series of sevens. The sequence may represent three cycles of the moon's phases from new to full, the approximate equivalent of a season.

Days

The measure of a day varies among modern pagan groups. Some prefer the common practice of beginning and ending a day at midnight. Others follow the example from ancient Greece and begin the day at dawn. For others, the day begins at sunset.

The way a day is determined affects the celebration of some festivals. In groups that celebrate a day beginning at sundown a holiday (day) and its eve (night before) will be seen as a single festival that was conceived on the eve, underwent gestation during the night and was fully birthed at dawn. For those who see the day beginning at midnight or dawn, the eve (or day before a festival) may be thought of as separate festival or as part of a two-day event.

Because of the relationship between some rituals, their magic, and events in nature, local time can be an important element. For example, the exact moment of sunrise or noon will vary depending on a locality's longitude. In some Pagan groups, awareness of the precise local time is important. In others, festivals and rituals are held when convenient at a time close to an astronomical event, such as delaying the celebration of a solstice until the weekend.

The Wheel of the Year

For most Pagans, the concept of the Wheel of the Year, describes the turning of day to day, moon to moon, and season to season in a cycle that is continually repeated. Within the cycle some days are set aside as notable days. Similar to the notable days of many other religions, some of these days are "fixed" (that is they occur on the same calendar date every year) and some are "moveable" (their date of observance changes).

A common set of eight major notable days, called Sabbats, are shared by many Pagan groups. These Sabbats consist of four movable days, called Quarter Days, and four fixed days, called Cross-Quarter Days. The Quarter Days occur in conjunction with the sun's movements. (They are celebrated on the winter solstice, spring equinox, summer solstice, and autumn equinox.) The Cross-Quarter Days occur at the midpoints between the Quarter Days. (They are celebrated on February 1, May 1, August 1 and November 1.) The Sabbats of prime importance differ from group to group. In general, the quarter days tend to be more important to solar-dominated (that is, male) groups, such as Druids and Odinists. The cross-quarter days are more important to lunar-oriented (that is, female) groups, such as Wiccans and Goddess Worshipers.

Although most modern Pagan groups observe the Sabbats, they are known by different names. Table 19.1 presents some of the most familiar names for the celebrations.

The Lunar Cycles

In addition to observing the Sabbats, many groups within modern paganism also observe celebrations in conjunction with the moon. In Wiccan circles, lunar observances are called Esbats.

Table 19.1. Common Names for the Eight Pagan Sabbats

Sabbat	Occurs
Yule	Winter solstice
Imbolg (or Brigid)	February 1
Ostara	Spring equinox
Beltane (or May Day)	May 1
Litha (or Midsummer)	Summer solstice
Lammas (or Lughnasadh)	August 1
Mabon	Autumnal equinox
Samhain	November 1

Within the solar year there are approximately 13 lunar cycles. Some Pagan groups observe the full moon; others observe the new moon (when no moon is visible). Because the lunar and solar cycles do not precisely coincide, a specific solar calendar may contain 12 full moons and 13 new moons, or 13 full moons and 12 new moons.

There are three commonly employed methods of reconciling the discrepancy between the lunar and solar cycles. For some the choice of celebrating a moon when it is new or full changes from year to year depending on which will yield 13 celebrations. For others, the last new or full moon may also be celebrated as the first. The third method moves the celebration of the 13th moon (when necessary) to a designated date prior to the winter solstice irrespective of the actual phase of the moon.

Various Calendar Systems

The Celtic Tree Calendar

One of the most popular calendar systems employed by modern Pagan groups is the Celtic Tree Calendar, developed by Robert Graves in the 1950s. Graves, in his *White Goddess*, presents a Tree Calendar (Table 19.2.), based on the eighteen-letter Gaelic alphabet. These are known as the Ogham runes and they are made with a pattern of slash marks either vertically or horizontally across or beside a base line. They represent thirteen consonants and five vowels. The thirteen consonants (B, L, N. F, S, H, D, T, C, M, Ng, G, and R) each correspond with a lunar month and its associated tree. The five vowel runes (A, O, E, U, and I) represent five seasons termed Rebirth, Spring, Summer, Autumn, and Death.

Graves's calendar uses the thirteen consonants of the tree alphabet as names of months and the five vowels as markers of quarter days. This configuration creates a calendar of thirteen 28-day months, plus an extra day (two in leap years) to make up the 365 days of a year. Although there is no plausible evidence that any such calendar was ever in general use in ancient Britain, it has been adopted by the Pagan movement and Pagan playwrights have composed special dramas based on the symbolism of the tree calendar for use in the celebration of their eight Sabbats.

The Asatru Calendar

Members of pagan groups worshipping the Northern European deities grouped together under the label Asatru. Asatru years are counted from the time Odin received the Runes: 250 B.C.E. Thus, 2004 C.E. is equivalent to 2254 R.E. (Runic Era). Month names of the Asatru are shown in Table 19.3.

The Goddess Calendar

The Goddess Worshippers observe an annual progression of 13 months named in honor of various goddesses. The year begins after the Winter Solstice. The sequence of months is shown in Table 19.4.

Table 19.2. The Celtic Tree Calendar

Date on the Western Calendar	Date on the Tree Calendar
December 23	Day of the Yew and Silver Fir (vowels: Idha, Yew; Alim, Silver Fir)
December 24	First day of the Birch (Rune=Beth)
January 21	First day of the Rowan (Luis)
February 18	First day of the Ash (Nion)
March 18	First day of the Alder (Fearn)
March 21	Day of the Furze (also known as Gorse) (vowel: Onn)
April 15	First day of the Willow (Saille)
May 13	First day of the Hawthorn (Huath)
June 10	First day of the Oak (Duir)
June 22	Day of the Heather (vowel: Ura)
July 8	First day of the Holly (Tinne)
August 5	First day of the Hazel (Coll)
September 2	First day of the Vine (Quert)
September 22	Day of the Aspen (vowel Eadha)
September 30	First day of the Ivy (Gort)
October 28	First day of the Reed (Ngetal)
November 25	First day of the Elder (Ruis)

Table 19.3. The Asatru Calendar

Gregorian Month Name	Asatru Month Name
January	Snowmoon
February	Horning
March	Lenting
April	Ostara
May	Merrymoon
June	Fallow
July	Haymoon
August	Harvest
September	Shedding
October	Hunting
November	Fogmoon
December	Wolfmoon

Table 17.4. The Goddess Calendar

Month Names	Approximate Gregorian Equivalents
Hestia	December/January
Birdhe	January/February
Moura	February/March
Columbina	March/April
Maia	April/May
Hera	May/June
Rosea	May/June/July
Kerea	June/July
Hseperis	July/August
Mala	August/September
Hathor	September/October
Cailleach	October/November
Astrea	November/December

Table 19.5. The Pagan Holiday Cycle

December (beginning with the winter solstice)
~22 .... Yule
~23 .... New Year for Trees
~ .... The Day that Is Not a Day
~ .... Saturnalia
31 .... Hogmany

January
~6 .... The Twelfth Night
~7 .... St. Distaff's Day
~ .... Up-Helly-Aa

February
1 .... Imbolg
1 or 2 .... Gaelic Fire Festival
~ .... Homstrom
14–15 .... Lupercalia

March
~22 .... Ostara
~22 .... Iduna and Summer Finding

April
1 .... All Fool's Day
21 or 22 ...... Earth Day
30 .... Walpurgis Night

May
1 .... Beltane

June
~21 .... Midsummer Eve
~22 .... Litha

July
~3 .... Dog Days (until August 11 or 15)
31 .... Lammas Eve

August
1 .... Lammas
17–25 .... Odin's Ordeal and the Discovery of
the Runes
~ .... Carnea

September
~22 .... Mabon
~22 .... Winter Finding

October
31 .... Oidhche Shamhna

November
1 .... Samhain
5 .... Guy Fawkes's Night
11 .... Old Halloween

December (before the winter solstice)
~21 .... The Mother Night

◩ ◩ ◩

Pagan Holidays

Monthly

Esbats

Full moon of each month; sometimes at the new moon and sometimes at both the full and new moons, depending on the custom of a particular coven

Many modern Wiccan covens hold regular meetings, referred to as Esbats, on the most convenient evening nearest the full and/or new moon. Esbat rituals typically use color, nature symbolism, candles, and symbolic acts to enhance the significance of the attributes of a particular moon. Rituals serve as a form of worship, a means of teaching, an aide to meditation, and a form of communication between the practitioner and the Goddesses and Gods. Esbat meetings are sometimes open only to initiates, and in some groups they are specifically intended to develop members who are in training for the priesthood of the religion.

Beginning with the full moon closest to the winter solstice, the names of the 13 moons of the year are:

First moon: Oak Moon (Tree month name: Birch Moon)

Second moon: Wolf Moon (Tree month name: Rowan Moon)

Third moon: Storm Moon (Tree month name: Ash Moon)

Fourth moon: Chaste Moon (Tree month name: Alder Moon)

Fifth moon: Seed Moon (Tree month name: Willow Moon)

Sixth moon: Hare Moon (Tree month name: Hawthorne Moon)

Seventh moon: Dyad Moon (Tree month name: Door Oak Moon

Eighth moon: Mead Moon (Tree month name: Holly Moon)

Ninth moon: Wort Moon (Tree month name: Nut-Hazel Moon)

Tenth moon: Barley Moon (Tree month name: Vine Moon)

Eleventh moon: Wine Moon (Tree month name: Ivy Moon)

Twelfth moon: Blood Moon (Tree month name: Reed Moon)

Thirteenth moon: Snow Moon (Tree month name: Elder Moon)

Some groups may prefer to celebrate the full moons according to their traditional rural American names. Although these names may vary, some of most commonly used are:

January: Wolf Moon

February: Snow Moon

March: Worm Moon or Sap Moon

April: Pink Moon or Grass Moon or Egg Moon

May: Flower Moon or Planting Moon

June: Hot Moon or Strawberry Moon

July: Buck Moon or Thunder Moon

August: Sturgeon Moon or Corn Moon or Grain Moon

September: Harvest Moon

October: Hunter's Moon

November: Beaver Moon or Frosty Moon

December: Cold Moon or Long Night Moon

Because there are approximately 13 lunar cycles in one solar year, it is possible for an occasional month to have either two new moons or two full moons. When a month has two full moons, the second full moon in that month is called the Blue Moon.

Maniblot
Full moons

Similar to esbats which are observed primarily by Wiccans, Maniblot rituals are observed by the Odinshof, a group devoted to the teachings of Odin.

Eight times per year

Sabbats
Quarter Days (Spring equinox, Summer solstice, Fall equinox, and Winter solstice) and Cross Quarter Days (February 1, May 1, August 1, and November 1)

The eight Sabbats are the major holidays celebrated by members of the various Pagan religions that have flourished in the United States since the mid-1960s. The Sabbats may sometimes be displaced from their traditional date in order to fall closer to that of a specific pagan

festival. For example, the Eleusinian Mysteries in Greece were celebrated just after the full moon that fell closest to the fall equinox. Thus, if September 22 falls midweek, a coven observing the Greek traditions will often move its Sabbat to a weekend nearer the full moon.

Among covens meeting regularly for an Esbat at each moon during the year, a Sabbat is observed by means of a special ritual that is inserted into the middle of the coven's ordinary ritual. Hence, there is a set of eight such special rituals in a coven's liturgical manual or *Book of Shadows*.

Since 1970, the outdoor celebration of Sabbats in the United States has increased in popularity on both the local and national level. Although local gatherings may attract a few dozen to a few hundred people, there is now an annual cycle of festivals—approximately one for each Sabbat in each major region of the United States (for example, New England, southern California, the upper Midwest, or the Southeast)—regularly attended by thousands of Pagan adherents. The Sabbat Ritual typically focuses on an aspect of the Goddess and her consort and combines drama, poetry, music, costume, and dance. The working of a newly written Sabbat Ritual is usually the climax of a festival.

Bonfire Nights
Dates usually falling near each of the eight Sabbats

In Britain there were many traditional nights during the year when a bonfire would be lit and danced around. Most of them fall on or near the dates for the eight Sabbats of the "Wheel of the Year." The specific list of bonfire nights is: Twelfth Night; Imbolg (or the Gaelic Fire Festival); Ostara; Walpurgis Night (May Eve); Midsummer Eve; Lammas Eve; and Oidhche Shamhna ("Vigil of Samhain" or Halloween).

Quarterly

Quarter Days
Spring equinox, Summer solstice, Fall equinox, and Winter solstice

During the middle ages, British landowners collected quarterly rents on or near the equinoxes and solstices. Eventually these days became known as quarter days, and they continued to be used into the early modern age.

Because of their association with the solstices and equinoxes, the quarter days have also gained religious connotations. In England, the quarter days are called: Lady Day (March 15), Midsummer Day (June 24), Michaelmas (September 29), and Christmas Day (December 25). In Scotland, the names and dates were slightly different. Candlemas fell on February 2; Whitsunday was observed on the seventh Sunday after Easter; Lammas was on August 1; and November 11 marked the celebration of Martinmas.

The observation of these days waned through the nineteenth century but has seen a resurgence in the twentieth century because of the increased popularity of the modern Pagan movement. The Quarter Days recognized by Pagans are Ostara (spring equinox, about March 22), Litha or Midsummer (summer solstice, about June 22), Mabon (fall equinox, about September 22), and Yule (winter solstice, about December 22).

Cross-Quarter Days
February 1, May 1, August 1 and November 1

The cross-quarter days are the four traditional Celtic festivals celebrated by Pagans along with the quarter days. Together they make up the "Wheel of the Year." These holidays "cross" the quarter days (the solstices and equinoxes) about halfway in between. The most common names are Imbolg (February 1), Beltane (May 1), Lammas (August 1), and Samhain (November 1).

Figure 19.2. The Holly King is an aspect of the Horned God, the consort of the Goddess. Artwork by Joanna Powell Colbert, www.jpc-artworks.com.

Annually

December
(beginning with the winter solstice)

Yule (Alban Arthuan)
Winter solstice; around December 22

Yule, or the Winter Solstice, is a Quarter Day. It marks the beginning of many Pagan calendars. In the Celtic Tree Calendar, the Silver Fir, symbolic of birth, and the Yew, symbolic of death, are honored together on this day.

Yule is the longest night of the year and the day when the waning (lessening) sun yields to the waxing (growing) sun signifying rebirth or resurrection and the beginning of a new cycle. The Ancient Romans celebrated the winter solstice as Sol Invictus (The Undefeated Sun).

In many Pagan traditions, the concept of rebirth is expressed through the birth of a Divine Child. The celebration may include a vigil on the eve of Yule in anticipation of the birth. The child born at Yule is given different names in different legends. In Egyptian mythology the child is Horus; in Greco-Roman it is Apollo; in Norse it is Balder; in Phoenician it is Baal; and in Celtic it is Bel.

The Yule Sabbat ritual usually focuses on the themes of the returning light, the birth of the new king, and the giving of presents, which was a pagan custom long before Christianity. Yule also represents the crossing of the year from its waning period into its waxing period, and some groups celebrate this with a mock combat between the Oak and Holly Kings. Mistletoe, a plant sacred to the Druids, is also traditionally gathered at Yule (and again at Midsummer).

One of the better known customs associated with Yule is the burning of the Yule log. The Yule log, a large piece from the trunk of an oak tree, may be burned according to the practice employed by a particular Pagan group. In one method, the piece is marked into four sections, one for each season of the year. At the beginning of each season, a fire is kindled to burn a portion of the log and people prayed to their gods for blessings on the season. In other practices, the log is burned only at Yule but a portion is left unburned and kept throughout the year. The unburned portion serves as an amulet of protection and is used to kindle the next year's Yule log, symbolic of the continuity of the cycle from one year to the next.

Another ritual associated with Yule among Wiccans is replacing and lighting altar candles which were extinguished at the preceding Samhain. The new candles serve to symbolize the sun's return.

New Year for Trees
Day after the winter solstice; around December 23

This day is observed by some Pagans who use Robert Graves's tree calendar. The New Year for Trees begins the day after the winter solstice. (See also the Jewish celebration of Bi-Shevat occurring on the fifteenth day of Shevat.)

The Day that Is Not a Day (The Extra Day of the Year; Time that Is Not a Time)
Day after the winter solstice; around December 23

In the Celtic Tree Calendar, the day following the winter solstice is the extra day of the year. The concept of magical time between times, when it is not one time or another is celebrated. It is a day of liberation.

Saturnalia
Late December

The ancient Roman festival of Saturn (the father of the gods) was celebrated in late December, just about the same period now observed as the "Christmas season" in the United States. It was marked by "reversals": cross-dressing, Lords of Misrule, the rich serving the poor, and so on, as is still practiced to some extent in the German Fasching traditions. Many Pagans celebrate a revived Saturnalia as part of their Yule festival.

Hogmany
December 31

Hogmany originated in Northern England and Scotland. It was observed primarily by children who dressed in sheets, visited neighboring houses, recited rhymes, and received special cakes.

Some modern Pagans observe Hogmany as a day sacred to the solar deity, Hogmagog (or Magog). Participants, sometimes dressed up as animals, burn special sticks for protection against evil spirits. The spirits driven away represent any remaining ill from old year, thus making certain that only good welcomes in the new year.

January

The Twelfth Night
Early January

The Twelfth Night, counted from Yule, marks the ending of the Yuletide cycle of celebrations. By tradition, all Yule decorations around the house must be removed.

Mystical drama associated with the Twelfth Night depicts Persephone (Kore) preparing to rise from the underworld back into the world of the living.

St. Distaff's Day
Early January

Traditionally, St. Distaff's Day was the day after the "Twelfth Day." In the Christian calendar, the Twelfth Day (Epiphany) falls on January 6. As a result, St. Distaff's day is sometimes observed on January 7th; however, some prefer to observe St. Distaff's Day on January 12 (the Twelfth Day of January).

The "St. Distaff" honored is not a person. A distaff is a tool used to hold the wool or flax when spinning yarn. St. Distaff's Day marked the day when regular work resumed after the Yuletide break. It is observed by some modern pagans as a day to honor household gods.

Up-Helly-Aa
Last Tuesday in January

Up-Helly-Aa is an old Norse fire festival revived in 1889, during the first modern wave of Paganism. It is observed with reconstructed pagan rituals, including the burning of a Viking ship, at Lerwick in the Shetland Islands. The festival is also known as Antinmas, a name which may be derived from the Old Norse for "ending of the holy days."

February

Imbolg (Imbolc; Oimelc; Oimelg; Brigid; Brigantia; Gwyl Fair)
February 1

Imbolg, is the first Cross-Quarter Day of the year (the other three are Beltane—May 1, Lammas—August 1, and Samhain—November 1). The day is sometimes called Brigid, named for both the Irish goddess Brigid (also known as Bride, Bridget, Bridhe; patron of poets and daughter of the Dagda) and the Irish Saint Bridget, a historical figure who shares many of the goddesses' qualities and attributes. The Imbolg Sabbat is usually devoted to celebrations of light, poetry, and the overflowing bowl. It marks the time when the Goddess sheds her guise as the old hag (or crone) and becomes the bride.

A ritual often associated with Imbolg is the placing of the "Brides Bed." By tradition, the last sheaf of grain harvested in the fall was believed to contain the spirit of the grain. This sheaf was saved, made into a human figure, and symbolically dressed with cloth. On Imbolg this figure is placed in a small basket and kept by the front door where it remains until Samhain. The "Brides Bed" by the door serves as a protective amulet and marks the home as a Pagan home. After Samhain, the grain is returned to nature either by scattering it as seed or by giving to the birds.

Gaelic Fire Festival (Candlemas)
February 1 or 2

The Gaelic Fire Festival (or Candlemas) is one of the traditional bonfire nights. It is sometimes observed as part of the Imbolg celebration rather than as a separate festival. (Firecraft is one of threefold attributes the associated with the Goddess Brigid; the others are healing and poetry.) Fires may be kindled as bonfires or through the ritualistic lighting of candles. The symbolic intent is that the old fire is extinguished and a new fire for the new year is kindled and blessed. This new fire symbolizes purity. Dried greens that were used to decorate for Yule are sometimes burned in the fire.

Homstrom
Usually the first Sunday of February

Homstrom is a Swiss festival celebrating the end of winter. One tradition associated with the day is the burning of a straw man symbolizing Old Man Winter. Homstrom is occasionally observed by Swiss-American communities on the first Sunday in February. It is reminiscent of the February 1 Celtic mid-winter festival of Imbolg (Brigid).

Lupercalia
February 14-15

With roots in ancient Roman Paganism, Lupercalia was a festival sacred to Faunus, the fertility god overseeing agriculture and flocks. On the first day of the festival, preparations for Lupercalia were made when men drew lots to select a female partner for the following day. Priests of Faunus, dressed in goatskin loincloths, struck women on their palms with thongs in a ceremony related to fertility. Some researchers believe that Lupercalia is the basis for modern-day Valentines traditions.

March

Ostara (Eostre; Alban Eilir)
The vernal (spring) equinox, about March 22

Ostara, the spring-equinox holiday, is one of the four Pagan Quarter Days. The other three are Litha (the summer solstice which is also known as Midsummer), Mabon (the fall equinox), and Yule (the winter solstice).

At Ostara the waxing daylight and waning night are again equal. The light, which is growing stronger than the darkness, is honored. Fires are set to commemorate the return of spring and honor the God and Goddess.

Ostara is also celebrated as a time of fertility and conception. In some Wiccan traditions, it is marked as the time when the Goddess conceives the God's child which will be born at the Winter solstice.

In Goddess mystical drama, Persephone (Kore) returns from the underworld to be reunited with her mother (Demeter). Celebrations commemorate the relationship between mothers and daughters and the bond between all women.

Many of the familiar secular symbols surrounding spring and the Christian observance of Easter have pagan roots. For example, eggs and rabbits both signify fertility.

Iduna and Summer Finding
Near the spring equinox

Among observers of Northern European Paganism, two festivals surround the spring equinox. Iduna is sacred to the Norse Goddess Iduna, who represents the half of the year in which the light overcomes the darkness. Summer Finding is observed as a day sacred to the God Thor. It marks the beginning of the farming season.

April

All Fool's Day (Festival of Fools)
April 1

All Fool's Day customs are popular in many communities and are so wide-spread they have become secularized. Some researchers theorize that the practice of setting one day aside to play tricks and practical jokes is a way to cope with the authority that rules the rest of the year. Although many festival celebrations begin on their eve and continue through the next day, All Fool's Day, begins in the morning and continues only until noon.

On All Fool's Day, Northern European Pagans honor the god Loki, who was known as a trickster.

Earth Day
April 21 or 22

Earth Day is a day on which the Mother Earth Goddess, Gaia (her Roman name), is honored. Modern environmental groups have chosen this day on which to encourage environmental responsibility.

Walpurgis Night (May Eve)
April 30

Walpurgis Night, one of the eight fire festivals, is dedicated to the German Goddess Walpurga. The night is considered a time of magic. Festivals are marked by revelry in anticipation of the coming summer. One ritual custom, that of leaping through or over the fire, is symbolic of purifying oneself. Some groups with Portuguese and Spanish roots, observe Walpurgis Night as a festival of the dead.

May

Beltane (Beltaine, May Day, Calan Mai)
May 1

Beltane is one of the four Cross-Quarter Days (the others are Lammas—August 1, Samhain—November 1, and Imbolg—February 1). The name Beltane is made of two parts: Bel is the name of the Celtic god; and tane (or tain) is a Celtic word meaning fire. Beltane is also the Irish Gaelic name for the month of May.

Beltane, or May Day, appears to have been a festival celebrating the beginning of the good weather season in northern Europe: when herdsmen could safely take the herds to the high summer pastures, and when wild fruits and berries began to grow and ripen. It celebrates the full blossoming of spring, the fertility of the Earth, and the rebirth of the flowers.

European folklore is full of May Day customs, many of them being folk-magic rituals for young women to use to reveal their future husbands. The wedding theme is also found in some Wiccan circles where Beltane marks the marriage of the Goddess and the Horned God. In some areas, the election of a May Queen is reminiscent of this sacred these Nuptials. Out of respect for the deities, however, May is considered an unlucky time for mortal marriages. As a result, June is a popular month for traditional weddings.

In Roman Catholic assemblies, the month of May was dedicated to Mary, and May Day was the traditional day for crowning the Blessed Virgin statues. It is often claimed that in the Middle Ages Mary was substituted for the pagan goddess to whom May was originally sacred.

One of the best known traditions associated with Beltane is the Maypole. Dancers circle the Maypole holding ribbons attached to the top. The dancers spiral inward as they dance, symbolizing the dual themes of death and resurrection. Odinists may see the Maypole as a representation of the World Tree that connects the nine worlds.

Other traditions associated with May include all-night outings to look for flowering branches and other prizes, picking flowers, making and exchanging wreaths, and kindling the Beltane fire.

Depending on the preferences of the people conducting the ceremony, the Beltane fire may be kindled on Walpurgis Night (May Eve) or on Beltane (May 1). By tradition, the Beltane fire contains bundles of nine different types of wood chosen for their symbolism and associated attributes. For example, hazel nuts are considered symbolic of wisdom, so adding hazel to the Beltane fire will bestow wisdom during the coming year.

June

Midsummer Eve
The evening before the summer solstice, about June 21

Midsummer Eve, celebrated in Shakespeare's *A Midsummer Night's Dream*, is noted for revivals of supposedly ancient rituals and the burning of bonfires. By tradition, the midsummer fire must lit by friction between fir and oak (fir representing rebirth and oak signifying magical power). Some groups, however, prefer to use modern utensils to light the fire but maintain the symbolism by using fir and oak in the kindling.

In the British Isles, Midsummer Eve is observed by the Ancient Order of Druids (founded in 1781) and various other British Druid orders, some of whom stay up all night to observe the Midsummer sunrise at Stonehenge. (The National Heritage will allow Druids into Stonehenge but limits the access of other Pagans and tourists.)

Figure 19.3. Dancing around the Maypole has heralded the beginning of spring for centuries. It remains a popular tradition associated with Beltane.

Litha (Midsummer, Alban Hefin)
Summer solstice, on or about June 22

Litha is one of the four Quarter Days. The other three are Ostara (spring equinox, about March 22), Mabon (fall equinox, about September 22), and Yule (winter solstice, about December 22).

The summer solstice occurs on the longest day of the year when the sun reaches its full power. The day is one of special significance among some Druid groups who gathered at Stonehenge to celebrate the Light which reaches its highest point at noon on the day of the solstice.

For many other Pagan groups, the day symbolizes maturity and fullness. One tradition holds that a fire kindled on Litha carries smoke that blesses. Some customs include burning sunwheels, carrying torches, or swinging burning brands. Midsummer is the day when the year moves from its waxing aspect into its waning period, and is sometimes celebrated with a dramatization of the transfer of power from the Holly King to the Oak King aspect of the God. It is also a customary day for harvesting mistletoe which may be used as an amulet of protection.

July

Dog Days
July 3–August 11 or 15

This time period represents the hottest part of the year. According to ancient Roman tradition it is ruled over by the star Sirius, called the Dog Star. The determination was made because the star rose about the same time as the sun. Because the star was one of the brightest in the sky, people assumed that it added its heat to the heat of the sun. Among the Asatru, Sirius is known as Loki's Brand.

Lammas Eve
July 31

Lammas Eve, the night before Lammas is one of the eight traditional bonfire nights when special fires are kindled. The Lammas Eve fire may be burned as part of the Lammas Sabbat.

August

Lammas (Lughnasadh; Gwyl Awst)
August 1 (in some traditions July 31-August 1)

Lammas is one of the four Cross-Quarter Days (the other three are Samhain—November 1, Imbolg—February 1, and Beltane—May 1) and the first of three harvest festivals (the other two are Mabon and Samhain). The day is thought to have been a precursor of Thanksgiving in America and Canada's Harvest Festival.

Lammas celebrates the first harvest which is typically the grain harvest. In many Pagan traditions, grain symbolizes the concepts of death and resurrection, and although the festival focuses on the joy of harvest, it is also a day for mourning the loss of loved ones. One custom associated with the day is the baking of bread. The festival, originally celebrated as the Gule of August, became somewhat Christianized because of the practice of blessing the loaves. The name Lammas is a shortened form of "loaf mass."

Lughnasadh is an alternate name for the festival with a more Pagan origin. Lugh is the Celtic god of wisdom, and at Lughnasadh the Goddess is seen in her aspect as a pregnant mother. The Sabbat is usually celebrated outdoors during a weekend camp-out if possible. The ancient "games of Tara" are reenacted or an appropriate drama is performed.

Odin's Ordeal and the Discovery of the Runes
August 17-25

This holiday season of nine days commemorates Odin's crucifixion on the World Tree, called the Yggdrasil, and his resulting discovery of the Runes. According to the legend, Odin (the chief Norse deity) sacrificed himself and hung on the Yggdrasil, the tree that links the nine worlds together. (The manifest world inhabited by human beings is but one of the nine worlds.) After nine days and nine nights he received the Runes. The Runes are ancient alphabetic characters that can be used in divination.

Carnea
August

Carnea is an ancient Greek festival that was one of the three principle religious celebrations observed in Peloponnesus, Cyrene, and Magna Graecia of antiquity. Dating as far back as 676 B.C.E., the festival honored Apollo Karneios, the god of fertility and herding. Carnea derived its name from the month of Carneus (August) and primarily celebrated a bountiful harvest. The ritual celebration featured young men called *staphylodromoi* ("grape-cluster-runners") who pursued other celebrants draped in garlands presumably made of grape vines. Successful capture of the garland-bearing participants indicated a good omen.

In addition to entreating the god Apollo to ensure a good harvest, the Carnea was intended to secure the god's aid in battle. Ironically, military engagement was prohibited during the Carnea. Some historians have suggested that

Table 19.6. Alphabetical List of Pagan Holidays

Holidays	Date(s)
Alban Arthuan *see* Yule	
Alban Eilir *see* Ostara	
Alban Elfed *see* Mabon	
Alban Hefin *see* Litha	
All Fool's Day	April 1
All Hallows' Eve *see* Oidhche Shamhna	
Beltaine *see* Beltane	
Beltane	May 1
Brigantia *see* Imbolg	
Brigid *see* Imbolg	
Calan Mai *see* Beltane	
Candlemas *see* Gaelic Fire Festival	
Carnea	During August
Day that Is Not a Day	The day after the winter solstice; around December 23
Dog Days	July 3–August 11 or 15
Earth Day	April 21 or 22
Eostre *see* Ostara	
Eve of Samhain *see* Oidhche Shamhna	
Extra Day of the Year *see* Day that Is Not a Day	
Festival of Fools *see* All Fool's Day	
Festival of the Dead *see* Samhain	
Gaelic Fire Festival	February 1 or 2
Guy Fawkes's Night	November 5
Gwyl Awst *see* Lammas	
Gwyl Fair *see* Imbolg	
Halloween *see* Oidhche Shamhna	
Halomas *see* Samhain	
Hogmany	December 31
Homstrom	Usually the first Sunday of February
Iduna and Summer Finding	Near the spring equinox
Imbolc *see* Imbolg	
Imbolg	February 1
Lammas	August 1 (in some traditions July 31-August 1)
Lammas Eve	July 31

Holidays	Date(s)
Litha	Summer solstice, on or about June 22
Lughnasadh *see* Lammas	
Lupercalia	February 14–15
Mabon	Autumnal (fall) equinox, about September 22
Martinmas *see* Old Halloween	
May Day *see* Beltane	
May Eve *see* Walpurgis Night	
Midsummer Eve	The evening before the summer solstice, about June 21
Midsummer *see* Litha	
New Year for Trees	The day after the winter solstice; around December 23
Nos Galan Gaeof *see* Samhain	
Odin's Ordeal	August 17-25
Oidhche Shamhna	October 31
Oimelc *see* Imbolg	
Oimelg *see* Imbolg	
Old Halloween	November 11
Old November Day *see* Old Halloween	
Ostara	The vernal (spring) equinox, about March 22
Samhain	November 1
Saturnalia	Late December
St. Distaff's Day	Early January (about January 7)
The Mother Night	Eve of the winter solstice
The Twelfth Night	Early January (about January 6)
Time that Is Not a Time *see* Day that Is Not a Day	
Up-Helly-Aa	The last Tuesday in January
Vigil of Samhain *see* Oidhche Shamhna	
Walpurgis Night	April 30
Winter Finding	Autumnal equinox
Yule	Winter solstice; around December 22

the smashing defeat of the Spartan forces by the Persians at Thermopylae may have been prevented if the main Spartan army had not been immobilized in honor of the Carnea.

September

Mabon (Alban Elfed)
Autumnal (fall) equinox, about September 22

Mabon is one of the four Quarter Days (the other three are Yule—winter solstice, Ostara—spring equinox, and Litha—summer solstice). It marks the second point in the year when the days and nights are equally long. At spring (Ostara), however, the waxing sun rises to pre-eminence; at Mabon, the waning sun rules.

Mabon marks a time when harvests are gathered and seeds stored for the next year. It is the second of three harvest festivals (the others are Lammas and Samhain) and it focuses on the fruit harvest.

When the autumnal equinox does not exactly coincide with a date that is convenient for the Pagan festival, Mabon may be displaced from its traditional date and observed at another time. For example, the Eleusinian Mysteries in Greece were celebrated just after the full moon that fell closest to the fall equinox; hence, if September 22 falls midweek, many covens that favor the Greeks will move their Mabon Sabbat to a weekend nearer the full moon.

In some Wiccan traditions, a coven's leadership will be transferred from the High Priestess to the High Priest, symbolic of the seasonal change from the time of year when the Goddess rules to the time of year ruled by the God, represented as the Horned Lord. As the earth rests, the Goddess rests and is not visibly manifest in nature during the coming season.

Winter Finding
Autumnal equinox

Among observers of Northern European Paganism, the autumnal equinox is observed as a day sacred to the God Frey, the Norse god of fertility.

October

Oidhche Shamhna (Vigil of Samhain; The Eve of Samhain; All Hallows' Eve; Halloween)
October 31

Some Pagans following the tradition of beginning a holiday celebration on the eve before the day (similar to the Jewish tradition of observing a day from sunset to sunset) begin their Samhain observances on the night more popularly known as Halloween (a shortened form of All Hallows' Eve, or the evening before All Saints' Day).

To the ancient Celts, and among some modern Pagan groups, Samhain Eve marked the end of the old year and Samhain the beginning of the new. As a result, the night is remembered as a time between the years, a time when the separation between the world of the living and the world of the dead is very thin. It is a favored night for divination and one of the eight traditional bonfire nights when special fires were kindled.

According to ancient Celtic belief the boundary between this world and the netherworld of fairies, gods, spirits, and magic was at its thinnest on the Vigil of Samhain. As a result, passage between the two dimensions was easier than at any other time. Visitations from the spirits of one's own departed ancestors, divine beings, or demons were believed to be possible, but not desirable. Many of the customs that developed surrounding this night were directed toward understanding and appeasing these spirits, thus protecting one's family from their influences.

Halloween is a popular holiday in the United States because of the custom of "trick-or-treating," in which children dressed as ghosts, witches, and monsters go from house to house begging for treats. According to some, the costumed children represent the spirits of dead ancestors, fairies, and other supernatural beings who demand to be bribed with a treat to keep from working a trick on the inhabitants of the house. Other traditions associated with the Vigil of Samhain include setting places at the table for the dead, leaving food by the fireside, and wearing masks representing the Goddesses and Gods, spirits of the dead, or animal spirits.

Some pagan groups may choose to distance themselves from the commercial popularity of the secular observance of Halloween by displacing their Samhain celebrations to another day, such as the closest weekend, the closest new or last quarter moon, or a sign in nature, such as the first frost.

November

Samhain (Halomas, Festival of the Dead, Nos Galan Gaeof)
November 1

Samhain (pronounced "Sa-oo-en") is one of the four Cross-Quarter Days (the other three are Imbolg—February 1, Beltane—May 1, and Lammas—August 1) and the third harvest festival (the other two are Lammas and Mabon). The Samhain harvest is one of animals, when animals were traditionally slaughtered in preparation for the coming winter.

Samhain marks a turning point in the pagan year when death rules and the darker side of life is honored. A transition from light to dark, from physical to spiritual, takes place. In some Wiccan covens the Horned God rises to predominance; and to signify this, the Priestess may step aside yielding her position to a Priest.

The Sabbat Rituals of Samhain are focused on honoring the dead: celebrating life in death, calling out the names of those who have passed on, remembering what they did in life, and asking the gods to grant them a worthy rebirth. Some Wiccan covens observe a tradition of extinguishing altar candles at the end of the Samhain Sabbat; they are not re-lit until Yule, when the new year is reborn. The Goddess is seen in her aspect of the crone (hag), or destroyer.

Among Druids, Samhain is an important time for divination. Traditionally Druids were asked by kings to look into the future to discover events of the year to come.

Guy Fawkes's Night
November 5

Guy Fawkes's Night is observed primarily in England as a day of deliverance from Roman Catholic domination but it is thought to be related to more ancient tradition of burning the effigies of evil spirits. Some modern Pagans celebrate Guy Fawkes's Night by lighting bonfires and burning effigies representing the sadness and ills from the year gone by.

Old Halloween (Old November Day; Martinmas)
November 11

In 1752 Britain adopted the Gregorian calendar which dropped ten days from the calendar and caused a discrepancy in dating. As a result the date for the Eve of Samhain (or Halloween) was moved. Some groups prefer to observe the date according to the old calendar. In the Christian church calendar, November 11 is called Martinmas Day.

December
(before the winter solstice)

The Mother Night
Eve of the winter solstice

Among observers of Northern European Paganism, the winter solstice is one of the most sacred days of the year. It is devoted to Odin, Ing, and Erda. Asatru followers believe that dreams on The Mother Night foretell events of the coming year.

CHAPTER 20

Western African Religions and Their New World Expressions

Yoruba

Overview of Yoruba Religious Traditions

The Yoruba people are indigenous inhabitants of Nigeria, Africa. They are a cultural group currently occupying parts of western Nigeria and Benin. The city of Ile Ife, in southwestern Nigeria, serves as the religious center and seat of divine authority.

According to traditional Yoruba belief, all power in the universe emanates from a supreme being, Olodumare. Olodumare, known as the owner of everlasting abundance, among many other praise names, holds all power and is the giver of all life. Olodumare is the mystical remote source of all things and is not identified by gender. All that exists, including supernatural divine realities and natural earth realities are part of Olodumare.

As the supreme almighty source, Olodumare is directly involved in the affairs of the earth through a complex core of sub-divinities called orisa. The orisa are authoritative divine emissaries and serve as intermediaries between the people of earth and Olodumare. They are the major objects of veneration and ritual obligation.

The names and number of orisa varies according to national and local custom, but they number in the hundreds. Some are more nationally known while others may be only venerated according to localized custom. One of the most commonly honored orisa is Orisa-nla, also called Obatala. Orisa-nla was responsible for creating the earth and forming the first human beings. Differing mythological accounts of creation exist, and some versions include a second orisa, called Oduduwa, who assisted Orisa-nla when the original plans went awry.

Other important orisa include Orunmila (a deity associated with divination) and Esu (a trickster orisa associated with positive and negative features).

Esu guides the destiny and fate of all things. It is destiny that contains constructive and destructive elements. Esu thus represents the universal principle of polarity. Esu also plays an important role in communicating between people and spirits. Because he serves as a mediator, he is summoned first in all ceremonies.

Another orisa, Ogun, is associated with war, iron, and labor. The pantheon of orisa also includes female divinities. Two of the most widely known are water deities. Yemonja, known as the mother of fish, represents the ocean and original life forms. Osun originates in the township of Osogbo. She is associated with rivers, human emotions, sensuality, luxury, brass, gold, and merriment.

In addition to the hierarchal order of orisa, the Yoruba people also honor several types of ancestor spirits. Communities commonly revere deified cultural spirits who played significant historical roles; individual families pay homage to their worthy ancestors.

Authorities

The Yoruba religion is based on oral traditions that predate Christianity. Beliefs and practices are preserved by passing history, customs, and traditions from one generation to the next. Authority for interpreting events and establishing proper conduct of ethics and morals, rests with a bureaucratic structure of rulers who function in both religious and political realms.

The oni is the central figurehead assisted by cabinet members with various functions. The oba presides over the people within a geographic area, similar to a governor in western society, with ruling authority over a region or state. Under him are those with authority over smaller regions. Each city or town has its own complex ruling body similar to a western municipal government. Ultimately each family is presided over by a family head, called the olori ebi, who directs both religious activity and the day-to-day affairs of family members.

In addition to the socio-political hierarchy of rulers, important religious figureheads serve within specific spheres of influence. These include: mediums and mediators who communicate with the orisa and the souls of ancestors; traditional specialized priests and priestesses who use consecrated objects to consult and interpret the central dogma and employ ancient divine methods to reveal human destiny and recommend action; traditional medicine specialists who work with combined natural and supernatural influences to help bring healing power; and a hierarchy of priests and priestesses who tend to various shrines and oversee the performance of specific community and home rituals.

History

The origins of Yoruba religious practices extend back into pre-history and little is known with certainty. The city of Ile Ife, currently located in Nigeria, is believed to be the place at which the world was created. The first recorded Yoruba king, Oduduwa, ruled in Ile Ife. In stories of the past, the kings of all surrounding territories received their authority from the reigning king in Ile Ife.

Islam was introduced to western, sub-Saharan Africa during the seventeenth century. It was followed by Christianity in the nineteenth century. Both foreign religions produced intensive missionary efforts, and their overall precise impact on indigenous traditions is not well known. Some researchers speculate that the concept of Olodumare as a supreme god originated as a result of contact with the monotheistic traditions; others believe that the Yoruba understanding of Olodumare pre-dates foreign contact and represents the native cosmology.

Yoruba Today

Estimates regarding the number of Yoruba people vary from five to 16 million. The largest number live in Nigeria, but smaller communities exist in Ghana, Togo, and Benin. During the transatlantic slave trade people from the Yoruba tribes were relocated in large numbers primarily in the island of Cuban. Their descendants there are identified religiously by the name Santeria. In Brazil, another place where many people were relocated, they are called Candomblé.

People

Although many of the Yoruba people live in cities, the primary occupation is sedentary hoe farming. Cities are often surrounded by farmland and workers travel between their homes and the fields. Many religious practices and customs focus on agricultural themes.

Worship

Yoruba worship involves the proper performance of rituals. Several specialized types of priests fill various spiritual roles:

- An elegun is a person who experiences spiritual possession that results in ecstatic states during which communication takes place.

- An egungun is a dancer who wears a special costume and concealing mask that is believed to be endowed with spiritual power from the ancestors.

- A babalawo is a priest ordained to the order of the divinity Orunmila. A babalawo is skilled in the interpretation and application of the central dogma called Ifa.

- The Ifa corpus is a complex traditional system use to diagnose and forecast. It is considered to be the word or will of Olodumare and the orisa.

- An oloogun works with the babalawo to cure sickness.

- An awolorisa is a priest ordained to a patron divinity. An awolorisa uses a different traditional method to diagnose and forecast and is also involved in various types of ritual performance.

Overview of Santeria (Lukumi)

Afro-Cuban Santeria is a religion that originated in Nigeria where it is known as Ayoba or Yoruba. The Yoruba and their descendents in Cuba are traditionally known by two regional names—Lukumi and Arara. The common contemporary names used are Santeria and Regla de Ocha. In modern usage the term Santeria refers to saint worship. Regla de Ocha means rule of orisa or Regla Lukumi—way of Lukumi. The name Lukumi comes from the Yoruba word Olukumi which means "we are friends," and it refers to the people and culture that developed in Cuba from Yoruba traditions.

Although the name Santeria is commonly used in modern times, it is controversial. The word Santeria comes from a Spanish term that was used historically during the Inquisition for a deviant Catholic. Santero also means artisan carver of Catholic saint figures. These terms became used to denote slaves after they were forcibly baptized and monitored by the Roman Catholic Church.

Early twentieth century scholars identified the religion as one that combines western Yoruba elements with Spanish Roman Catholic characteristics. The religion is not a merger, however. Its central dogma, form of veneration, language, music, rituals, ceremonies, icons, and deities are Yoruba. A cultural syncretism, however, is noticeable in Cuba. An unknown number of people mix their beliefs in varied forms while others do not. What actually occurs may be broadly described in three ways:

1. People who follow either the Roman Catholic faith or the Ayoba/Lukumi faith without syncretic elements.

2. Primarily Catholic people who incorporate varying degrees of Ayoba/Lukumi practices as a secondary resource.

3. Primarily Ayoba/Lukumi people with a superficial reliance on Catholic or multiple faiths.

In Santeria a priest or priestess is traditionally called olosha or olorisha which means an extension of orisa. A general member of the religion is called a santero, although at times the term may be used to refer to a priest or priestess. The traditional term for any person baptized in the Afro-Cuban Lukumi religion is omorisa, which means child of orisa.

Table 20.1. Selected Orisas and Equivalences to Roman Catholic Saints

Orisa	Saint
Elegbara/Esu	St. Anthony, Niño de Atocha
Ogun	St. Peter
Oshosi	St. Norbert
Obatala	Virgin of Charity
Oshun	Virgin Caridad del Cobre
Oya	St. Teresa/Candelaria
Orishaoko	St. Isidro Labrador
Babalu Aiye	St. Lazarus
Erinle	St. Michael the Archangel
Ibeji	Sts. Cosums and Damien
Orunmila	St. Francis of Assisi
Shango	St. Barbara
Yemaya	Virgin of Regla
Oduduwa	St. Manuel

Followers of Santeria believe in one almighty creator God, called Olodumare who is viewed as the omnipotent, omnipresent source of everything. Olodumare is served by spiritual emissaries called orisas. As a result of the cultural fusion in Cuba, the orisas were associated with Roman Catholic saints when an equivalence could be made. Some of these equivalences are shown in Table 20.1.

History of Santeria

In Cuba and Brazil, predominantly Catholic countries, the Yoruba and their descendents were forcibly baptized because adoption of the Catholic faith was a requirement for legal entry. In colonial Cuba, all African indigenous religions were outlawed, and over time the dehumanization and rehumanization process of slaves into Spanish and Portuguese societies caused a cultural syncretism and religious juxtaposition.

Within the framework of the Cuban Catholic church, African ethnic societies called cabildos were allowed to be formed. The cabildos functioned as social and religious organizations in which members aided each other. Church holidays were celebrated by the cabildos with African traditions, especially drumming and dancing.

The orisas that had been honored in Africa were paired with saints of the church. According to some researchers, the initial impetus for the matching of orisas with saints may have been to promote secret worship of the African spirits. Some church records suggest, however, that syncretism was originally promoted by the church as means of conversion. Over time, the conversion process was not complete. Modern members of the population follow either faith or mix both religions in varying degrees. Moreover in the minds of the worshippers, the distinctions between the orisas and the saints remain in a juxtaposition that is distinctly African.

When Cuba gained its independence from Spain the cabildos also gained independence from the Catholic church. They formed individual groups called reglas (which means path or way) based on the African ethnicity of the group's members. Some scholars believe that the religion called Santeria may have emerged from the reglas as an autonomous faith.

After the revolution in 1959, many Cubans left the island and migrated to North and South America. Included in their number were oloshas (santeros) who carried their faith with them into exile.

Santeria Today

Since its beginnings, Santeria was forced to survive in a culture that imposed strong social stigmas, and at times it has been outlawed or tolerated reluctantly. As a result there is little certainty regarding the number of followers. The largest Santeria (Lukumi) population center is believed to be in the Caribbean islands, particularly in Cuba and Puerto Rico. In the United States the largest populations are located among Hispanic groups in New York City and Florida. According to some estimates in the early 1990s, there were approximately one million adherents in the United States. Cuba's estimates range from six to eight million members.

Afro-Cuban families are religiously diverse. Within an immediate and extended family unit, it is common to find a wide range of religious memberships. Some may practice Santeria (Lukumi), some may be spiritualists, and others may hold the Roman Catholic faith. The mix is held together by family tolerance and a cultural frame of thought. There is a belief that God the creator is everywhere, therefore, family comes first. Denominational views or divisive lines fall second to family values. Family members, therefore, cross over their particular religious affiliation and participate in another family member's religious celebration or day of observance. This tolerance among mixed family members makes it possible to practice differing religious expressions without conflict Moreover, both the Catholic and the Lukumi believe in patron saints or orisa.

An example of sharing religious expressions is found on St. Lazarus day, which is paralleled with the African orisa Babalu Aiye. In a religiously mixed family unit, a shared altar is prepared with icons and offerings honoring both. Members of the extended family and friends from all religious affiliations are invited to celebrate and honor simultaneously. Although the family and friends celebrate together, each person preserves his or her own understanding; celebrating together, therefore, does not indicate forfeiting a personal belief.

Worship

Worship in Santeria involves interaction and communication with the orisa. Some of the ways this takes place is through ceremonial ritual, prayer, divination, abstinence, thanksgiving, drumming in celebration, food, and sacrificial offerings. There is also a belief in orisa possession. At times, some rituals or events may cause divine possession where the orisa being summoned takes over the physical body of a devotee and directly communicates with participants.

The most controversial aspect of Santeria in north America involves the use of animal sacrifice. Generally, farm animals are used in offering ceremonies. Only specialized priests with years of apprenticeship perform offerings utilizing the traditional methods consistent with religious tenants. According to Santeria belief, animal sacrifice is required under special circumstances. There are two ways that animal offerings are determined—either prescribed by divination or directed by orisa possession. Animal offerings are believed to be integral for priesthood ordination ceremonies, exorcism of evil spiritual intrusion, thanksgiving, and healing rituals. Depending on the ritual nature, animals may be cooked and presented as an offering to the orisa or consumed as sacred food. In cases where animals are used for exorcism or healing rituals they are discarded in whole after the sacrifice. In a landmark decision, the United States Supreme Court upheld the right of Santeria priests to practice animal sacrifice.

Overview of Candomblé

Candomblé is a generalized name given to a diverse expression of African-based religious traditions in Brazil. Through the use of ethnic drum music, practitioners seek to manifest ancestral spirits within the community.

Like many other African-based sects in the New World, however, Candomblé also incorporated images of saints from Roman Catholicism. The orixa (the Brazilian form of orisa is traditionally spelled orixa) are often symbolized with small statues of the saints which are adorned in distinctive dress, and Olorun (the supreme being) is frequently equated with the Christian God.

History of Candomblé

The largest number of African slaves were transported to Brazil during the nineteenth century. The principal port of entry was located in Salvador da Bahia (often called Bahia). Communication and travel between Bahia and Africa were maintained by free blacks seeking to ensure that African religious traditions were preserved.

During the years of slavery, ceremonies were typically conducted in secret. Following the emancipation of Brazilian slaves in 1888, some gatherings were held in the open and others chose to remain concealed. The gatherings, organized into communities, centered around a local leader, most often a priestess. Although individual Candomblé centers shared a common heritage, they were also differentiated in practice. Some focused on maintaining the purity of African traditions; others freely incorporated Roman Catholic elements and even added some gods from the Native American culture to their pantheon.

Overview of Voodoo

Voodoo (also called Voudoun) is a faith that combines Western African elements with French Roman Catholic characteristics. The religion began in Haiti when African slaves from various tribes with diverse backgrounds were brought together under harsh conditions. Over time, the slaves developed a consolidated belief system with blended rituals to form the new religion.

The supreme being recognized by Voodoo practitioners is known as Bon Dieu. Other spiritual beings include ancestors (or the dead in general), twins, and a diverse pantheon of gods called loa that are typically associated with Roman Catholic saints.

The History of Voodoo

Western African religious thoughts and practices were introduced to the New World as a result of slave trading during the eighteenth and nineteenth centuries. Slaves, often forcibly baptized into Christian traditions, combined elements from their past culture with symbols from new religions to form syncretistic faith systems. Of these innovative faiths, Voodoo is one of the best known.

French rulers in Haiti outlawed Voodoo practices but the religion continued as an underground faith. From Haiti, it spread to other areas of the Caribbean, to Brazil, and to the United States, particularly in Louisiana.

During the nineteenth century in New Orleans, Voodoo enjoyed a period of popularity. Although most voodoo ceremonies were held in secret, the New Orleans authorities allowed slaves to dance in Congo Square on Sunday afternoons under the watchful eye of government authorities. One ritual, called the Calinda Dance, was performed on the eve of St. John's Day (June 23; St. John's Day was June 24) by a voodoo priestess. The dance imitated the undulations of a snake in a sensual way. In 1843 its performance was banned on the grounds that it was obscene.

Voodoo Today

The largest Voodoo population center is in Haiti but other communities, called société centers, exist in places such as New Orleans, Miami, and New York City.

Worship

Voodoo ceremonies take place within a group of initiated practitioners called a hounfort. Worship often entails the performance of dance rituals that may be conducted by a priest (called a houngan) or a priestess (called a mambo). During the ceremony drums help summon the spirits who enter dancers and cause ecstatic trance states during which prophecies may be delivered. Although many people commonly associate Voodoo with menacing sorcery, only a small minority of Voodoo practitioners participate in black magic rituals.

Seasonal Timekeeping and Roman Catholic Influences

Uncertain Origins

The origins of timekeeping systems in Western Africa are unknown. The cycling of days, as a natural phenomenon, was a progression observed by people all over the world. In different areas, however, the significance attributed to specific days and the number of days that comprised longer periods of time varied.

In tribal Africa, individual days and parts of days were often described according to the activity that was customary. For example, among one tribe in Central Africa the late afternoon/early evening hours were called by a name that meant "the cows come home." Among the Yoruba people, the days were numbered around agricultural cycles.

Months and Years

Archeological evidence from central Africa suggests that some tribes may also have observed months. Markings on bones have been interpreted by some researchers as representations of the waxing and waning periods of the moon. Notches seem to count 14 and 15 day periods from the first appearance of a waxing crescent moon to the full moon and from the full moon to the last crescent of the waning moon.

Although the passing of the solar year was noted, there is no evidence that ancient African societies used the zodiac constellations or planetary cycles in their timekeeping systems. There is also no evidence that written calendars were developed. It is possible, however, that calendars and information about celestial signs were transmitted orally and that the stories have been lost.

The year was probably marked as the passing of a cycle of seasons. The recognition of seasonal variations in rainfall and other patterns of relevance to agricultural communities served to relate human activities to environmental phenomenon. Festivals related to agriculture occurred at specified times in conjunction with activities related to the seasons. Many other festivals were held at times determined by divination according to need.

The Igbo people of Nigeria celebrated the coming of the new year around the time of the vernal equinox with a solemn ceremony marking the end of the old year and heralding the arrival of the new. The council of elders, who were responsible for setting the annual calendar, determined the exact hour at which the year ended.

Roman Catholic Influences

In the New World, the original Yoruba calendar did not survive. The most significant change may have been adjusting to a western new year and a seven day week system. Over time, the new generations, called Lukumi (or Santeria), lost the traditional calendar. It became necessary for them to reinterpret time and orisa days of observance. Once the entire society conformed to the western calendar, celebration and holy days were reconciled to fit in the best way possible.

The first of January became the New Year for the Lukumi (Santeria), making it the most important day of the year. Lukumi today parallel the Saint days as established by the colonial Roman Catholic Church of Spain. In most cases the orisa are honored on the same dates of the saints. The custom is to honor the orisa beginning the evening before leading to midnight and ending at midnight of the calendar saint day.

Table 20.2. Cycle of African-Based Holidays

Date(s) .... Holidays

January
1 .... Annual Forecast (Lukumi/Santeria)
1 .... Honoring Oduduwa (Lukumi/Santeria)

February
2 .... Honoring Oya (Lukumi/Santeria)

March
22 .... Honoring Orishaoko (Lukumi/Santeria)
~20 .... Ibu Afo Festival (Yoruba)
~ .... Bobo Masquerade (Yoruba)
~ .... Rara Festival (Voodoo)

May
Mid-May ... Ibeji Ceremony (Yoruba)
15 .... Honoring Orishaoko in some regions (Lukumi/Santeria)

June
~ .... Egungun Festival (Yoruba)
6 .... Honoring Oshosi (Lukumi/Santeria)
13 .... Honoring Elegbara/Esu (Lukumi/Santeria)
24 .... St. John's Day (Voodoo)
~ .... Eje (Yoruba)
30 .... Honoring Ogun (Lukumi/Santeria)

July
~ .... Pilgrimage of Saut D'Eau (Voodoo)

Date(s) .... Holidays

August
~ .... Gelede (Yoruba)

September
7 .... Honoring Yemaya/Yemonja (Lukumi/Santeria)
12 .... Honoring Oshun (Lukumi/Santeria)
24 .... Honoring Obatala (Lukumi/Santeria)
27 .... Honoring Ibeji (Lukumi/Santeria)
27 .... Cosmas and Damian Day (Candomblé)
29 .... Honoring Erinle (Lukumi/Santeria)

October
4 .... Honoring Orunmila (Lukumi/Santeria)
15 .... Honoring Oya in some regions (Lukumi/Santeria)

December
4 .... Honoring Shango in some regions (Lukumi/Santeria)
6 .... Honoring Shango (Lukumi/Santeria)
17 .... Honoring Babalu Aiye (Lukumi/Santeria)

The symbol ~ indicates a movable date.

Holidays Related to Western African Religions

Annual Forecast (Santeria/Lukumi)
January 1

The annual forecast is called *letra del año*. Priests ordained to the order of orisa Orunmila, known as babalawos, gather weeks in advance to employ the sacred Ikin (palm nuts) methodology of Ifa divination. Ifa serves as the pre-christian central dogma which the Lukumi use for guidance. The purpose of the gathering is to consult the oracle and attain divine instruction on a series of rituals for the community. The last series of rituals begin on December 30 and ending on January 1 with the annual forecast. The divine guidance is interpreted by the babalawos and a transcript is later distributed throughout the religious community.

The orisa Oduduwa is also honored on January 1 in relationship to his attributes of origins or beginnings of earthly life forms. At precisely midnight members of Lukumi typically light white candles and pour fresh water outside of the front door of their homes using prayers and petitions for the health, safety, and welfare, of family, friends, and the community at large. Additional rituals may be done according to each household's

Figure 20.1. Ifa divination uses a tray in which 16 palm or kola nuts are manipulated. A priest skilled in their interpretation is called a babalawo.

circumstance. Once the community becomes informed of the fortunes and misfortunes that may unfold during the new year based on the annual forecast, they begin to plan and engage the recommended ceremonies and rituals within a prudent time table.

Honoring Orisa Oya (Santeria/Lukumi)
February 2 (or October 15 in some regions)

Oya was the wife of king Shango. She is associated with warfare, whirl winds, and tornados. She also has a role in child birth. Most important, however, is her role as the divinity that transports the soul from earth back to its heavenly resting place upon human death. This makes Oya a divinity closely related to ancestor worship.

Oya is honored by the priests and priestesses ordained to her priesthood and by those who have her as their patron orisa. The tradition is to honor her beginning on the eve of her celebration day. An elaborate altar is made adorned with her icons, hand beaded materials, cloth with the associated colors of the orisa, flowers, and consecrated instruments associated with her worship. Oya's favorite food offerings are made and placed at the altar. Family members and friends gather in celebration to feast, pray, and honor her.

Ibu Afo Festival (Yoruba)
On or near March 20

The Igbo people of Nigeria celebrate their New Year's Eve around March 20 with a solemn ceremony marking the end of the old year and heralding the arrival of the new. The council of elders who fix the annual calendar determine the exact hour at which the year will end. When it arrives, a wailing noise signals the departing year, and children rush into their houses, lock the doors to avoid being carried away by the old year as it leaves, and bang on the doors to add to the din. As soon as the wailing dies down, the doors are thrown open and everyone greets the new year with spontaneous applause.

Honoring Orisaoko (Santeria/Lukumi)
March 22 (May 15 in some regions)

Orisaoko is the orisa of agriculture. He is connected to the annual forecast. A good harvest is viewed as prosperity for the community because it is associated with a good food supply, economy, and employment. The process of preparing the land, planting seeds, and the care of crops is associated with fertility. Therefore, orisaoko is also honored as a fertility orisa.

Orisaoko is honored outdoors. An altar is prepared on the ground. His icons are surrounded by plates, baskets, and gourds. Each is filled with raw beans, varied vegetables, fruits, and bean fritters. The celebration may include opening of a hole near the altar. The officiating priest begins the prayers, invocations, and hymns honoring the orisa followed by a multiple food offering to the earth in thanksgiving.

Bobo Masquerade (Yoruba)
Late March

The Bobo people of Burkina Faso celebrate the balance between the sun, the rain, and the earth. The god Dwo is honored in this festival that features painted masks and costumes. The event repels evil and maintains natural balance necessary for crops to thrive.

Rara Festival (Voodoo)
Holy Week in the Christian calendar; March or April

This Haitian celebration of spring with deep ties to voodoo incorporates some elements of Christianity and bears a superficial resemblance to Carnival celebrations. The festival occurs between Palm Sunday and Easter and features a procession and exhibition by a Rara band (also spelled Ra-Ra). Each Rara band consists of a musical group, a band chief, a queen with attendants, a women's choir, and vendors selling food.

The observance begins by calling on Legba (an old man, trickster spirit) who is the guardian of thresholds and crossroads. The group's leader often dresses like a jester and twirls a long baton known as a jonc. On Shrove Tuesday night, the Rara bands perform a Bruler Carnival in which they carry out the ritual burning of various carnival objects and then make a cross on their forehead with the ashes.

Ibeji Ceremony (Yoruba)
Mid-May

Among Yoruba people twins are called ibeji and people believe that twins have special powers. The Ibeji ceremony is conducted at a supper to which the mother of twins invites friends. If one of the twins is dead, a doll is substituted.

Ibeji is also the name of the twin-child orisa (divine being or saint) honored by people who practice Santeria. Ibeji is associated with the Roman Catholic saints Cosmas and Damien, Christian medical practitioners who were martyred under Diocletion in the early fourth century c.e.

Egungun Festival (Yoruba)
June

The Egungun is a secret society among the Yoruba people of Ede, Nigeria. The major Egungun festival takes place in June, when members of the society come to the market place and perform masked dances. The masks they wear represent ancestral spirits and may cover the whole body or just the face. It is considered dangerous to see any part of the man who is wearing the mask—an offense that was at one time punishable by death.

The masqueraders all dance simultaneously, although each has his own drum accompaniment and entourage of chanting women and girls. The festival climaxes with the appearance of Andu, the most powerful mask. It is believed that the spirits of the deceased possess the masqueraders while they are dancing, and although it promotes a feeling of oneness between the living and the dead, the festival also inspires a certain amount of fear.

Honoring Oshosi (Santeria/Lukumi)
June 6

Oshosi is a hunter orisa. His main symbol is a bow and arrow. Being the hunter he is viewed as the provider of

Figure 20.2. Egungun masquerade costume. Image provided by the Museum of African Art, New York, NY. Photo by Jerry L. Thompson. An egungun is a dancer who wears a special costume and concealing mask that is believed to be endowed with spiritual power from the ancestors. The Egungun masquerade is part of a Yoruba tradition that honors ancestors. The costumes consist of woven cloth in many layers. They may also contain shells and mirrors sewn on as decorations. Although the costumes share similar characteristics, there are stylistic differences among various groups or villages. Some costumes are tall, others wide. The costume shown here is a wide style. Others may be of more human proportions.

meats, furs, the capture and domestication of wild animals, and other items found in the wild. He is associated with the expert qualities of a hunter—precision, covert movements and camouflage, being sharp shooter, trap setting, and possessing the ability to subsist in the wild for long periods of time. Oshosi is also attributed with being an excellent warrior. Over time, the Lukumi have associated him with law enforcement work and incarceration. Traps and handcuffs have become part of his symbols.

Oshosi is an orisa of localized worship. His altar is made of tree branches and plants in simulation of a dense bush. The altar is adorned with gourds, dried meat, smoked fish, and hunting items like bow and arrow and spears. At the center of the altar his icon is seated over an elaborate cloth and surrounded by various types of food offerings. He is honored in thanksgiving with a feast of cooked meats, grains, and vegetables.

Honoring Elegbara/Esu (Santeria/Lukumi)
June 13

With the Christian influence came the misconception that Elegbara/Esu is equivalent to the devil or Satan. Yoruba and Lukumi do not have a concept that is the equivalent of such an entity.

Elegbara is a general name used for a group of more than one hundred orisa, each with distinctive characteristics and roles. In general attributes, he is an orisa of knowledge, associated with human rationality and irrationality. He is master of the known and unknown mysteries of heaven and earth. Elegbara is a messenger divinity who guides all living creatures through their respective destiny and fate. He is ever present in all fortune and misfortune, therefore, believed to be a trickster divinity who rules over life's crossroads.

Elegbara is honored with a altar made of tree branches, sweets, varied cooked foods, fruits, rum, and cigars. The altar is adorned with an elaborate red and black cloth. On his day, families with their children and friends gather in merriment. The ambiance is of a birthday party with music, laughter, jokes, dancing, and a feast with plenty of varied foods and sweets. Trick games and toys are at times used to entertain children. It is a thanksgiving in celebration of life.

St. John's Day (Voodoo)
June 24

A family of yellow-flowered plants, commonly called St. John's wort, is used by voodoo conjurors and folk medicine practitioners to ward off evil spirits and ensure good luck. In the southern United States, all species of the plant are called John the Conqueror root, or "John de Conker," and all parts of it are used: the root, leaves, petals, and stems. The plant's imagery is often mentioned in African-American folklore and blues music.

The leaves, and often the petals, contain oil and pigment-filled glands that appear as reddish spots when held to the light. According to legend, these spots are John the Baptist's blood, and the plant is most potent if rituals are performed on his birthday.

Eje (New Yam Festival) (Yoruba)
Late June

The Eje celebration among the Yoruba people is an elaborate harvest festival that takes place over a two-day period and consists of purification rites, presentation rites, divining rites, and thanksgiving rites.

The first day of the festival serves to prepare for the rites that will follow on the second day. A shrine to the sea god, Malokun, is erected and a scared space is purified. Yams are gathered and presented to Malokun as the people welcome the harvest. Rituals of thanksgiving occur during the night.

On the second day, the festival's focus shifts to ascertaining the future prospects of the community. In one divination rite, a recently harvested yam is divided into two parts. They are thrown on the ground, and if one lands face up and the other face down, this is considered a positive sign for the life of the community and the success of crops in the coming year. If both fall face down or face up, problems lie ahead.

Honoring Ogun (Santeria/Lukumi)
June 30

Ogun is a general name for a group of orisa similar to Elegbara. In general, he is attributed with human labor, iron work, making of weapons, the military, guarding of townships, and fierce warfare. His domain covers brutal force of destruction and the reshaping or reconstruction of all things—the ability to destroy things as they are and the ability to bring things back to life in a new form. Ogun represents the ways of primitive humankind and the modern era of civilization.

As a warrior orisa, Ogun is honored with an altar similar to Elegbara and Oshosi. It is made of trees simulating a bush. His icons are generally adorned with green and black cloth and hand beaded symbols. The common offerings are rum, honey, cooked beef and goat meat, palm oil, fruits, and custard. The thanksgiving celebration honors Ogun for health, safety, and employment throughout the year.

Pilgrimage of Saut D'Eau (Voodoo)
Early to mid July

This Haitian observance combines elements of Roman Catholic tradition and voodoo. It honors both Our Lady of Mount Carmel and Ezili Freda, the voodoo spirit of love. The pilgrimage begins with prayers of celebration and lasts six days. It concludes at the Church of Our Lady of Mount Carmel in Haiti.

Gelede (Yoruba)

Late August

This Yoruba festival honors witches in an effort to appease them so that they will do good and not evil. Two types of masked dancers perform. The Efe dance at night

in jest of people who may have foolishly irritated a witch. The Gelede dancers dance during the day; they wear masks resembling witches and try to please them.

Honoring Yemaya/Yemonja (Santeria/Lukumi)

September 7

Yemaya is a generic name for a group of ocean and sea orisa. A common name is yeye mo eja which means "mother of fish." Among the orisa she is a mother figure

---

Table 20.3. Alphabetical List of Western African-Based Holidays

Holiday	Date
Annual Forecast (Lukumi/Santeria)	January 1
Bobo Masquerade (Yoruba)	~ late March
Cosmas and Damian Day (Candomblé)	September 27
Egungun Festival (Yoruba)	~ June
Eje (Yoruba)	~ Late June
Gelede (Yoruba)	~ Late August
Honoring Babalu Aiye (Lukumi/Santeria)	December 17
Honoring Elegbara/Esu (Lukumi/Santeria)	June 13
Honoring Erinle (Lukumi/Santeria)	September 29
Honoring Ibeji (Lukumi/Santeria)	September 27
Honoring Obatala (Lukumi/Santeria)	September 24
Honoring Oduduwa (Lukumi/Santeria)	January 1
Honoring Ogun (Lukumi/Santeria)	June 30
Honoring Orishaoko (Lukumi/Santeria)	March 22
Honoring Orishaoko (Lukumi/Santeria)	May 15 in some regions
Honoring Orunmila (Lukumi/Santeria)	October 4
Honoring Oshosi (Lukumi/Santeria)	June 6
Honoring Oshun (Lukumi/Santeria)	September 12
Honoring Oya (Lukumi/Santeria)	February 2
Honoring Oya (Lukumi/Santeria)	October 15 in some regions
Honoring Shango (Lukumi/Santeria)	December 4 in some regions
Honoring Shango (Lukumi/Santeria)	December 6
Honoring Yemaya/Yemonja (Lukumi/Santeria)	September 7
Ibeji Ceremony (Yoruba)	~ Mid-May
Ibu Afo Festival (Yoruba)	~ March 20
Pilgrimage of Saut D'Eau (Voodoo)	~ early to mid July
Rara Festival (Voodoo)	~ Holy Week (March or April)
St. John's Day (Voodoo)	June 24

represented by various shades of blue colors, marine life, nutrients, conception, and early life forms. She is attributed with the characteristics of both the stern and the nurturing mother in charge of raising and protecting her family.

Yemaya is widely worshiped alongside the Catholic Virgin of Regla. Many mixed family units will merge the celebrations with the Lukumi and Catholic events honoring her. There is an old port area in Cuba called Regla where many freed and domestic slaves lived. This area has an important colonial history. The altar for Yemaya consists of a throne made of elaborate cloth combined with white and shades of blue. Her icon is adorned with beaded art and marine symbols. Food offerings are made of sugarcane syrup, shredded coconut, watermelon, palm oil, honey, fried pork chunks, green plantain chips, and blackeyed bean fritters. Offerings of foods and flowers are also taken to the ocean on her day.

Honoring Oshun (Santeria/Lukumi)
September 12 and September 8 in some regions

Oshun is a popular orisa who is worshiped alongside her Catholic counterpart. Her name is also generic representing a group of orisa associated with rivers. Some of her attributes are merriment, arteries and blood, sensuality, beauty and refinement, brass, gold, honey, and financial prosperity.

Oshun's altar is typically adorned with fine cloth in yellow, gold, and coral colors. Food offering of fine pastries, desserts, and well presented cooked meals are setup esthetically with great care. Flowers and pleasant scents are used throughout the sacred areas. At times when afforded, live violin music is played to entertained participants. Champaign, cider, and wine bottles are placed at the altar and later they are socially consumed. Bottles are given as gifts to guests with trays of fine desserts at the end of the celebration. Oshun is honored in thanksgiving for the merriment of children, family, friends, and prosperity.

Honoring Obatala (Santeria/Lukumi)
September 24

Obatala is a generic name for a group of male and female orisa, however, Obatala is commonly addressed in using male pronouns. Obatala is the orisa of whiteness, wisdom, peace, and purity. He is associated with the physical creation of mankind and is attributed in mythological accounts with being among the first orisa to inhabit earth. Among several symbols associated with him, the sun is most important.

Altars made of fine cloth always highlight the color white. Depending on the orisa within the obatala group, however, some accent color is added, such as red, purple, emerald green, or coral. The basic food offerings are bread roles, meringue, rice, boiled egg, white chocolate desserts, and varied fruits. The celebrations honoring Obatala are more naturally calm with the consumption of less spicy foods than other orisa events.

Honoring Orisa Ibeji (Santeria/Lukumi)
September 27

Ibeji is a generic name that corresponds to a group of seven twin orisa. Myths indicate that the original set of twins come from the marriage between Shango and Oya. However, among the Lukumi some twins are associated with Yemaya, Shango, and Oshun. Male twin figures are commonly dressed in Shango's red and white colors while females are dressed in Oshun's or Yemaya's colors. Ibeji are associated with childlike characteristics. Although they are highly regarded, their worship is localized.

The altar for Ibeji is usually split in half—red on one side and blue on the other. Mixed fruits and candy are presented in abundance covering the two-sided altar. A favorite food always present is cooked yellow rice and chicken. It, along with ripe plantains, becomes the main course meal for participants. Bananas are commonly placed around two figure icons representing the twins. The ambiance is lively, similar to celebrating a child's birthday.

Cosmas and Damian Day (Candomblé)
September 27

In Brazil, Cosmas and Damian (Christian medical practitioners who were martyred under Diocletion in the early fourth century C.E.) are regarded as the patron saints of children. They are honored by giving children candy. Brazilians of African descent link Cosmas and Damian with the sacred orixa Ibeji. Sometimes children receive a special dinner of okra, a vegetable that is associated with Ibeji.

Honoring Orisa Erinle (Santeria/Lukumi)
September 29

Mythology presents Erinle as a master hunter in the southwestern region of Nigeria and a colleague of orisa Oshosi. He eventually moved from his home town and lived near a river bank. Thus, he became associated with the orisa Oshun. Lukumi accounts also place him as being very knowledgeable about traditional medicine. In fact, the idea of the modern medical doctor is directly associated with Erinle. The duality of roles makes him an orisa of hunters but the emphasis is placed on medicine. Erinle is an orisa of localized worship of importance related to human health.

His altar is prepared in elaborate cloth with green and blue tones. Since he is an orisa of localized worship his celebration day is limited to those who have him as a patron orisa rather than one with a large gathering of participants. His favorite foods are fish and yams which are placed around the altar as offerings. The celebration is usually not elaborate, but it is an important thanksgiving related to human healing.

Honoring Orisa Orunmila (Santeria/Lukumi)
October 4

Orunmila is a divinity specialized in the interpretation of Ifa divination, the oracle which serves as a central dogma. He is a male orisa with female servants called apetebi. This orisa's priesthood order is comprised of males. As a divinity of divination he has a broad following. Orunmila is represented by objects he used on earth such as opele—a divination chain, kola nuts, and a divination tray.

His icons are adorned with elaborate yellow and green cloth, beaded art, and a fly whisk. Participants bring yams, coconuts, and candles which are placed on the floor around the icons. The custom is to kneel on a straw mat, present the offerings to Orunmila, and honor him with prayers and praises.

Honoring Orisa Shango (Santeria/Lukumi)
December 4 and December 6 in some regions

Recorded history has Shango as a king of Old Oyo in northern Nigeria. He is descendant of Oduduwa, which makes him a royal historical figure. Oyo was the political center of the Yoruba. As king he extended the empire to eastern territories of Dahomey. He was known as a stern ruler who brought prosperity to be people. As a leader and warrior, he represents the master of strategy and tactics. Shango was very masterful in the use of fire, hence he is classified as the divinity of fire, thunderstones, and lightening.

Shango is widely worshiped alongside his Catholic counterpart. Mass processions for both have been held every year dating back to colonial Cuba. His altar is usually designed with elaborate red and white cloth with accents simulating lightening. His favorite food offerings are yellow corn meal, okra, and bananas. The celebration usually includes varied foods, music, and an uplifting ambiance with a sense of refinement.

Honoring Babalu Aye (Santeria/Lukumi)
December 17

Babalu Aye is a generic name for a group of orisa related to health. He also became known and widely worshiped in some regions of Dahomey. His domain is polarized. On one hand he represents contamination and illness, while on the other, the ability to heal and avert illnesses. Babalu Aye is connected to Orisaoko the orisa of agriculture. It is the blessing of Babalu Aye that makes it possible to have a healthy crop.

Catholic and Lukumi alike gather in large numbers every year honoring this orisa. The celebrations are elaborate and dramatic. Lukumi gatherings include a lengthy cleansing ritual and offering of numerous raw grains and foods. Afterward, the participants in thanksgiving consume root vegetables, rice, beans, and cod fish.

CHAPTER 21

Ancient Wisdom, Metaphysical, Other Faith Communities

Chapter Overview

This chapter includes information about faith communities that honor wisdom embodied in—or received from—ancient masters, universal concepts, the human spirit, or other spiritual beings and entities. They seek to understand truth through means such as spiritualism, metaphysics, mysticism, and parapsychology. Many reveal their secrets only to the initiated.

The seven organizations listed here were chosen because they provide diverse examples of some of the most well-known or historically influential organizations in this group. For the most part, these faith communities use the Gregorian calendar for determining dates of important events.

⊠ ⊠ ⊠

Church Universal and Triumphant

Overview

The Church Universal and Triumphant is a religious organization that is based on the beliefs that spiritual beings and meditation can bring enlightenment to humanity.

In 1958, Mark Prophet (1918–1973) founded The Summit Lighthouse, which was later renamed the Church Universal and Triumphant. When Prophet was 17 years old, he was contacted by El Morya, a nineteenth-century mystic who helped to establish the Theosophical Movement. Prophet, who was raised as a Christian, sent El Morya away and didn't resume contact with him until many years later, when he became a messenger for El Morya on earth. Prophet also published a series of messages from El Morya called *Ashram Notes*.

According to Prophet's beliefs, El Morya was an Ascended Master. An Ascended Master is a being who has achieved perfection in trials on earth. Because the Ascended Masters pursued perfection and achieved a balanced karma, their cycle of rebirth was ended and they ascended to God. Prophet taught that Ascended Masters continue to enlighten humanity by offering insights, also known as dictations, to messengers in the Great White Brotherhood. The messengers of the Great White Brotherhood are said to be guiding all of humanity into a new age of human and planetary advancement, sometimes known as the Aquarian Age, the higher consciousness, or the New Age.

Church Universal and Triumphant members believe that Jesus, among others, is an Ascended Master. The Ascended Masters communicate to humans on earth through messengers and make predictions for the future. In addition to El Morya and Jesus, the Summit Lighthouse identifies Lord Lanto, Paul the Venetian, Serapis Bey, Hilarion, Nada, Saint Germain, Maha Chohan, and others as Ascended Masters.

After he became a messenger for El Morya, Mark Prophet founded The Summit Lighthouse in Washington, DC. In 1963, he married Elizabeth Clare Wulf (she was born in 1939). Elizabeth Prophet had a similar supernatural experience during adolescence, claiming to have been contacted by the Ascended Master Saint Germain, a seventeenth-century German alchemist who died in 1684. After her contact with Saint Germain, Elizabeth Prophet devoted her life to spreading his teachings and those of The Summit Lighthouse.

In 1966, The Summit Lighthouse moved its headquarters from Washington to Colorado Springs, Colorado, and later to California. In 1970, the Prophets founded a Montessori school based on the educational principles of Dr. Maria Montessori.

Mark Prophet died of a stroke in 1973, and after his death, he became known as the Ascended Master Lanello. According to Elizabeth Prophet, Mark Prophet's past lives were numerous, including, among others, Noah, Lot, Aesop, the disciple Mark, Lancelot, Louis XIV, Longfellow, and the Russian czarevitch Alexis Nikolayevich.

After Mark Prophet's death, Elizabeth Prophet (also known as Mother Prophet, World Mother, or simply Mother) renamed the organization the Church Universal and Triumphant (sometimes abbreviated as CUT). Although she faced some opposition in establishing herself as the leader of the church, she received dictations from the Ascended Masters that secured her position and she continues to lead the congregation today.

The Church Universal and Triumphant is currently located on a 32,000 acre ranch in Montana, from which conferences, publications, and radio and television programs are created to provide information about the Church Universal and Triumphant and further its teachings and the enlightenment of its members.

Relationship between People and God

Followers of the Church Universal and Triumphant believe that the creation of nature expresses the dual nature of God. All of creation is comprised of the physical lower self and the inner spiritual self, which is part of a higher, unchanging being. Humans seek to connect the lower physical self to the higher spiritual self through reincarnation.

Those who belong to the Church Universal and Triumphant perform religious activities known as "I AM." The beliefs of "I AM" involve receiving messages from Ascended Masters who have purified themselves through reincarnation. Another facet to the "I AM" belief is the practice of decreeing. In decreeing, a person prays by asserting that positive statements have already come true and demands that the cosmic powers of the universe make the affirmation come to pass. The "I AM" beliefs are derived from the Biblical passage of Exodus 3:14, in which God states his name as "I Am." The "I AM" philosophy in the Church Universal and Triumphant is modification of the theology of the Theosophy religious movement.

The founder of the "I AM" movement, Guy Ballard, was also contacted by Saint Germain, the same Ascended Master who later contacted Elizabeth Prophet during her adolescence. Ballard brought the "I AM" movement to prominence in America, and it was later adopted by Mark and Elizabeth Prophet for use in the Church Universal and Triumphant.

Believers in the Church Universal and Triumphant also purify themselves by calling on the violet flame. The violet flame provides a burst of spiritual energy that empowers believers to feel mercy, forgiveness, justice, and freedom. Living a proper lifestyle and calling on the violet flame enables believers to lead a balanced life, which results in the ascension of the soul to God. Once the soul is ascended, it is reunited with the "I AM" presence, which allows a believer to break free from the cycle of reincarnation.

Sacred Writings

Although followers of the Church Universal and Triumphant believe in Jesus, they believe that he was one of many Ascended Masters. Therefore, the *Bible* is just one sacred text from which they draw insight.

Believers also study the book about the Church Universal and Triumphant written by the Prophets, titled *Climb the Highest Mountain*, as well as other dictations provided by the Prophets and Ascended Masters.

Today

Today the Summit Lighthouse is a general organization that includes the religious movement called the Church Universal and Triumphant. Summit Lighthouse and the Church Universal and Triumphant sponsor conferences and workshops as well as maintain Summit University Press (a religious publisher) and Summit University.

According to Elizabeth Prophet, the Church Universal and Triumphant is an international organization with 200 groups in the United States (a church population of 3,000 in Montana alone) and a presence in 38 countries.

In 1990, Elizabeth Prophet predicted nuclear war would occur on April 23. As a result, members of the Church Universal and Triumphant from around the world traveled to the Montana ranch to pay for spaces in underground bunkers at the ranch. The state of Montana later ordered that the church could never again use the bunkers.

CUT Holidays

Anniversary of the Founding of Summit Lighthouse
August

In addition to regular prayer vigils and weekly services, followers of the Church Universal and Triumphant may celebrate the founding of the Summit Lighthouse by Mark Prophet.

◼ ◼ ◼

Eckankar

Overview

Eckankar has roots in the religious movements of Theosophy, Scientology, and ancient eastern wisdom. Eckankar (sometimes called the Religion of the Light and Sound of God) was founded in 1965 by Paul Twitchell (also known as Paulji or Peddar Zaskq). Eckankar means "co-worker with God." Followers of Eckankar believe that God (Sugmand) connects to the soul (Tuza) of each person through light or sound. The connection to God is known as the Eck or Eck current.

Twitchell, who was born in Kentucky during the early twentieth century, served in the U.S. Navy and was a professional reporter and journalist before founding the modern-day version of Eckankar. Twitchell was influenced by several spiritual leaders and movements. After joining the navy, Twitchell began exploring a variety of different religious groups, including the Self-Revelation Church of Absolute Monism. He later studied with Kirpal Singh, the founder of the Ruhani Satsang, a branch of the Radhasoami tradition, as well as L. Ron Hubbard, founder of the Scientology movement.

After a dispute, Twitchell broke ties with Singh and began offering lectures and workshops in San Diego, California. He declared himself the 971st ECK master, and on October 22, 1965, Eckankar was officially founded.

Twitchell was a prolific writer, publishing in periodicals and penning more than 60 books before his death in 1971. Twitchell was succeeded by Darwin Gross, the 972nd Living ECK Master. Many Eckankar followers felt that Gross was not a suitable successor to Twitchell. A power struggle between Gross and Harold Klemp resulted in Klemp being named the 973rd Living ECK Master in 1981. He continues to lead Eckankar believers today.

Relationship between People and God

Followers of Eckankar believe that each person is a particle of God sent into the world to gain spiritual experience. To gain spiritual experience, one must perform spiritual exercises. One such spiritual exercise involves chanting and meditating on the word hu (pronounced *hue*), which followers of Eckankar believe is an ancient and holy word for God. Through these spiritual exercises and religious study, a person is purified and comes in contact with the Holy Spirit (also known as ECK). Followers of Eckankar believe that the Holy Spirit absolves them of sin (called karma) and makes it possible for them to gain wisdom, charity, love, and freedom.

Members of Eckankar are encouraged to meditate and perform spiritual exercises for 20 to 30 minutes each day. Eckankar followers also believe that spiritual insight can be gained from dreams, and they are encouraged to keep journals to record their dream experiences.

Members of Eckankar are called ECKists or ECK chelas (students). A spiritual leader of Eckankar is called a Living ECK master, or Mahanta. Twitchell was the ECK master from 1965 until his death in 1971. Darwin Gross was the ECK master from 1971 to 1981, followed by Harold Klemp (also known as Sri Harold Klemp) from 1981 to present.

Eckankar members may also participate in Soul Travel, a process designed to bring a person to a higher spiritual consciousness. Soul Travel is taught by the Living ECK Master, and followers believe it allows them to experience other planes of spiritual existence. According to Eckankar belief, the planes of spiritual existence include the physical plane (senses), the astral plane (emotions), the causal plane (memories), the mental plane (the mind), and the etheric plane (intuition).

Eckankar members may also choose to work through levels of initiation, which mark an individual's level of spiritual progress.

Sacred Writings

Eckankar believers study the sacred text known as the *Shariyat-Ki-Sugmand*, which are comprised of twelve volumes in the spiritual worlds. The first two were transcribed by Paul Twitchell, founder of Eckankar. Eckankar followers may also study books written by Paul Twitchell, Harold Klemp, and other Eckankar leaders.

Today

The main spiritual center of Eckankar is the Temple of ECK, located in Chanhassen, Minnesota, which offers a public reading room, chapel, fellowship hall, and classrooms. The Temple of ECK also publishes the religious periodical, the *Eckankar Journal*.

Eckankar Holidays

Founder's Day
September 17

Eckankar followers honor and remember Paul Twitchell, the founder of Eckankar, on the anniversary of his death each year.

Spiritual New Year
October 22

An annual Eckankar spiritual seminar is held on or close to this date, which is a time of reunion and spiritual renewal for Eckankar followers.

◩ ◩ ◩

Pantheism

Overview

Pantheism is a philosophy that fuses religion and natural science. Believers of Pantheism feel that everyone and everything is part of the universe, including God. In Pantheistic belief, there is not a separate God; instead, God is united with everything in the universe. Two of the primary tenets of Pantheism are that the universe is divine and the earth is sacred.

In the same way, Pantheists do not believe that God designed the universe; instead, they uphold that the earth designed itself through evolution. Pantheists do not believe in a judgmental or all-knowing God, so there is no concept of sin against God or a deity. In Pantheistic belief, humans are the creators of ethics and morals. Pantheists believe in a respect for all living and non-living things, including respect for animal rights, the preservation of the diversity and growth of species, and an awareness of and dedication toward the maintenance of ecology.

There are several movements within Pantheistic belief. Christian Pantheists believe that the *Bible* (especially the words of St. Paul) supports Pantheism, and that the dwelling of the Holy Spirit within believers indicates that God is united with the universe. Scientific Pantheists deeply revere nature and embrace life, the body, and earth, but do not believe in supernatural deities or powers or an afterlife. People who believe in scientific Pantheism see death as a reunion with nature and the cosmos, as part of nature, and not something to be feared.

History

The term Pantheist was coined in 1705, but the philosophy of Pantheism has ancient roots dating back to the early Greeks. Early Greek philosophers espoused the Pantheistic belief that the universe is the only divine entity, and other early eastern religions such as Taoism, Buddhism, and Hinduism also supported the belief that the universe was divine.

During the early centuries C.E., Pantheism began to resemble a religion. An ex-Dominican monk named Bruno (late 1500s) and a Jewish philosopher named Spinoza (middle to late 1600s) identified ethical concerns and introduced religious ceremony to Pantheism. These traditions created a more formal foundation to the philosophies of Pantheism.

In 1705, an Irish writer named John Toland (1670-1721) was the first to name Pantheism. Toland also called for reform within the Pantheistic community by suggesting a network of secret societies to observe the Pantheist religion in his book *Pantheisticon*.

Many historical figures are believed to be Pantheists, including Marcus Aurelius, Albert Einstein, William Wordsworth, Ralph Waldo Emerson, Walt Whitman, and Oscar Wilde. Many followers of other religions, such as Taoism, Buddhism, Paganism, and Universalist Unitarianism, affirm the ideals of Pantheism.

During the late twentieth century, Paul Harrison (born in 1945), an English writer and consultant on population, environment, and development, founded the Scientific Pantheism movement. He later published a book about Pantheism and Scientific Pantheism called *The Elements of Pantheism*.

Today

Because many traditions and religions embrace the concepts and ideals of Pantheism, the exact number of Panthiests is unknown, but supporters claim it reaches into the millions. The branch of Pantheism known as Scientific Pantheism is much smaller; it identified 645 members from 43 countries in 1999.

Pantheists may celebrate any number of special days annually, including those of other religions, such as Hinduism, Buddhism, and Taoism. The Pantheist religion does not dictate what adherents should or should not celebrate. Instead, celebrations are left up the individual.

Pantheists may celebrate natural events that remind them of their connection to the universe and the earth, including the yearly solar cycle and the monthly lunar cycle. Pantheists may also celebrate at certain times in the year when there are the strongest falls of shooting stars. These occur as the earth crosses the orbit of clouds of meteors—especially the Perseids, peaking in mid-August, and the Geminids, peaking in the second week in December. Local Pantheist groups may hold viewing ceremonies to watch the natural display.

Pantheist Celebrations

Spring Equinox
on or about March 22

Pantheists in the northern hemisphere celebrate the spring equinox, which marks the beginning of growth in plants and breeding among animals.

Summer Solstice
on or about June 22

Pantheists hold annual ceremonies to celebrate the sun's highest point in the sky.

Perseid Meteor Shower
mid-August

In the middle of August, Pantheists may gather to watch the Perseid meteor shower, which occurs when the earth crosses the orbit of clouds of meteors.

Autumn Equinox
on or about September 22

Pantheists in the northern hemisphere celebrate the autumn equinox and the bounty of the summer's harvest.

Geminid Meteor Shower
second week of December

In the second week of December, Pantheists may gather to watch the Geminid meteor shower, which occurs when the earth crosses the orbit of clouds of meteors.

Winter Solstice
on or about December 22

The winter solstice indicates the birth of the solar year, and Pantheists may hold ceremonies to celebrate.

Ramtha's School of Enlightenment

Overview

Ramtha's School of Enlightenment (RSE) was founded in 1988 by J.Z. Knight, at the time a housewife in Tacoma, Washington. Ms. Knight's initial encounter with Ramtha occurred in February 1977 one Sunday afternoon without prior warning when she and her husband were making pyramids. Further encounters and experiences led to her channeling Ramtha, and the two began a unique teaching partnership. She first publicly operated as a channel in November 1978 to a small group in Tacoma and found an immediate public response. During 1979 she began to travel throughout the United States and overseas and allowed Ramtha to channel through her at two-day and evening events, termed Dialogues.

In his channeled messages, Ramtha has described himself as a person born among a group of survivors of ancient Lemuria. He grew up in the despised refugee community of Lemurians in Onai, the port city of Atlatia (better known as Atlantis), where he grew to hate the Atlatians. During his teen years, after much hardship and enslavement and following his mother's death, he left the city searching for revenge against the Unknown God of his people. Eventually he led a successful revolution.

He emerged as a warrior conqueror and throughout a long march conquered two-thirds of the then-known world.

According to his account, the course of his life changed following a near fatal assassination attempt. During his long convalescence he had time to contemplate the meaning of the Unknown God and found it in the life force all around him, and he wondered what it would be like to be this Unknown God. He learned to conquer his own barbaric emotions and transmuted them into a respect and understanding of humankind and a love of God in all life and in every individual. He never died but transformed his body and took it with him when he left the Earth. He has returned at a crucial time in history to teach the knowledge that he knew and what he now knows.

Through the Dialogues and the resultant books and tapes, Ramtha was able to engage his students intellectually, while inspiring them with knowledge and new ideas. In 1988 J.Z. Knight significantly changed direction by founding Ramtha's School of Enlightenment, where students, instead of simply listening to channeled messages, learned practices that allowed the teachings to be practically integrated into their lives.

At the school, Ramtha developed the original Dialogues into a unique teaching program of spiritual disciplines designed to help the students increase their self-awareness and quality of their life. His comprehensive system of thought provides a world-view, seen as an approach to reality that answers the many questions that have enraptured great philosophers and thinkers through the ages.

The keystone of Ramtha's message could be summarized as the calling of people to remember their divinity, the unlimited God potential that lives within everyone. He asserts that every thought, whether conscious or unconscious, shapes and creates reality, that human destiny is ultimately to make known (manifest) the unknown (that which is potential). He calls students to evolve beyond the self-created constraints of human limitation that have largely defined individual realities, and continually to rediscover the personal self in new, challenging, and adventurous ways that enrich the whole of life everywhere.

RSE Holidays

Ramtha's Appearance
In February

Ramtha first appeared to J.Z. Knight on the third Sunday in February 1977. It has been traditional for Ramtha to address his students on that day or close to that day and review their progress made throughout the year with further significant teachings.

Foundation Day
In conjunction with Easter Sunday

Ramtha's School of Enlightenment was founded on Easter Sunday 1988 at a Retreat held in Yelm, Washington, attended by students from around the world. The small city of Yelm, at the foothills of Mt. Rainier in Washington's green countryside, became the location of Ramtha's School of Enlightenment from that day forward. The RSE students remember this day each year with continuing classes and festivities.

Rosicrucianism

Overview

Rosicrucianism is a secret fraternal order with ancient roots. By studying Rosicrucianism, followers hope to gain specific knowledge of metaphysics, mysticism, philosophy, psychology, parapsychology, and science not taught by conventional educational systems or traditional religions.

The largest and most well-known order of Rosicrucianism in the United States is The Rosicrucian Order (or Ancient Mystical Order Rosae Crucis, AMORC), founded by H. Spencer Lewis (1883–1939). According to AMORC, Rosicrucian teachings allow people to find themselves, change their lives, and influence the universe. Rosicrucianism focuses on studying and exploring inner wisdom and the meaning of life.

Although AMORC members are not required to keep the information they learn about in private a secret, there is much mystery about the laws and principles of Rosicrucianism. People who study Rosicrucianism are not required to abandon previous beliefs or religions. The Rosicrucian Order states that it is not a religion or a code of beliefs; instead, it maintains that through practical teachings and study, a person can gain enlightenment and guidance toward living life.

According to AMORC philosophy, a person achieves success in life by creating positive mental images of their health, wellness, wealth, and happiness. Another primary belief of Rosicrucianism is that humans possess both physical and psychic senses, and in so doing are dual beings. Rosicrucianism and the study that accompanies the philosophy focuses on inner development; with an emphasis on intuition, the subconscious mind, independent thinking, self-esteem, self-confidence, and psychic or inner spiritual growth.

Rosicrucians believe that the wisdom taught by the Rosicrucian orders has been preserved and handed down through Rosicrucian schools for centuries. To current students of Rosicrucianism, this ancient wisdom is passed on through a series of correspondence courses, lectures, conferences, and group meetings. Improvements in mental imagery are made by studying monthly 6- to 8-page correspondence lessons called monographs. Although the monographs are sent in the mail, followers of Rosicrucianism can meet in local groups called lodges or orders to discuss concepts and ideas.

As a new person (called a neophyte) studies Rosicrucianism, he or she completes three degrees, also known as Atrium lessons. After completing this initial introduction to the philosophy, a person can choose to complete nine more degrees, which take a total of about 5 years to complete. The person may then enter what is known as the Temple, which confers nine more degrees. After the final Temple degree is completed, followers of Rosicrucianism continue to study and educate themselves about topics such as creative visualization, reincarnation, and karma. Followers of Rosicrucianism believe that study and learning should be a lifelong endeavor.

Leaders in the Rosicrucian Order include Grand Masters, Imperators, and Grand Imperators. Male members of the Rosicrucian Order are called Fratres; female members are called Sorores. Both men and women are welcome to study Rosicrucian teachings.

Sacred Writings

The AMORC does not have one particular sacred text, but the teachings and writings of H. Spencer Lewis are studied as part of the AMORC Rosicrucian education. The *Bible* is also studied as part of Rosicrucian study, but it is not believed to be the only source of knowledge about God and Jesus. Other Rosicrucian groups may study the texts and writings of their own fraternal order leaders.

History

Religious scholars debate the origins of Rosicrucianism, but it is traditionally believed to have roots in ancient Egypt. In Europe, Rosicrucianism was first mentioned in 1115 C.E. According to Rosicrucian legend, it wasn't until 1408 that the German-born Christian Rosenkreuz formed the Order of the Rose and Cross as the result of his travels and experiences in the Middle East. Various Rosicrucian groups have differing opinions about the validity of the existence of Christian Rosenkreuz. Some groups believe he existed, but others maintain that Rosenkreuz' experiences were part of a fictional story used to further Rosicrucian teachings.

Rosicrucianism had a resurgence in popularity during the seventeenth century, which is attributed to Johann Valentin Andreae, a German theologian and Lutheran pastor. In his writings, Andraea described the story of Rosenkreuz. Andraea also promoted reform within the Rosicrucian movement by suggesting that followers also study a combination of Christian pietism, Renaissance hermeticism, magic, and alchemy.

During the eighteenth century, the philosophy flourished in Britain with the establishment of Rosicrucian lodges consisting of like-minded individuals. In America, a small Rosicrucian order was established in Pennsylvania. Begun by Johann Jacob Zimmerman in England and called the Chapter of Perfection, this group of Rosicrucians hoped for Christ to return to earth with them when they settled in America in 1694. The Chapter of Perfection ended within a generation, but in 1858 Paschel Beverly Randolph founded the oldest Rosicrucian body in the United States, the Fraternitas Rosae Crucis located in Quakertown, PA, which is still in existence today.

In the early twentieth century, H. Spencer Lewis, formerly a Methodist artist from New Jersey and New York, founded the New York Institute for Psychical Research (also known as the Rosicrucian Research Society) to study the occult and Rosicrucian teachings. Lewis's study of British and European occults also influenced his use of the Rose Cross emblem, which is the current symbol of Rosicrucianism. After studying Rosicrucianism in Europe, Lewis returned to America and began holding meetings to discuss the philosophy. After 6 years of meetings, the Rosicrucian group formed the Ancient Mystical Order Rosae Crucis and began holding national conferences and offering correspondence courses.

In 1927, the headquarters of AMORC were moved to San Jose, California, where they reside today. Despite tremendous growth in membership, the AMORC experienced conflict with other Rosicrucian organizations. In 1928, the Fraternitas Rosae Crucis located in Quakertown, PA, challenged AMORC on the use of the term "Rosicrucian" in their name. Tensions still exist today between AMORC and other Rosicrucian orders in the United States.

In July 1934, AMORC established a Rosicrucian student research center, the Rose-Croix University of America, and in 1936, a planetarium was added to the educational facilities in San Jose. In 1939, the Rosicrucian Research Library opened its doors.

H. Spencer Lewis led AMORC as the Grand Imperator until his death in 1939. His son Ralph M. Lewis served as Grand Imperator from 1939 to 1987. An embezzlement scandal led to the removal of Gary L. Stewart as the next Grand Imperator in 1990. Stewart's replacement was Christian Benard, who currently serves as the AMORC's Grand Imperator.

In addition to continuing to offer Rosicrucian study programs via correspondence courses, AMORC also publishes *The Rosicrucian Digest*, *The Rosicrucian Forum*, and numerous books and periodicals to provide information and supplement one's Rosicrucian studies. The Rosicrucian Order also runs the Rosicrucian Egyptian Museum, which contains the largest collection of Egyptian artifacts in the United States.

Although exact membership numbers aren't known, religious scholars estimate that AMORC, the largest Rosicrucian body in the U.S., has at least 250,000 members. According to AMORC, membership exists in over 100 countries throughout the world.

The Rosicrucian Order maintains that many historical figures studied Rosicrucian teachings or participated in Rosicrucian orders, including Sir Francis Bacon, Leonardo da Vinci, Rene Descartes, Blaise Pascal, Isaac Newton, Benjamin Franklin, and Thomas Jefferson.

In addition to AMORC and the Fraternitas Rosae Crucis, noteworthy Rosicrucian orders include The Rosicrucian Fellowship, which is related to the philosophical teachings of Theosophy and astrology and was founded by Max Heindel; and the Ausar Auset Society, which applied the philosophy of Rosicrucianism to African-Americans and was founded by R.A. Straughn.

Rosicrucian Holidays (AMORC)

Rosicrucian Thanksgiving Ritual
mid-June

Each year, active members who have received the First Degree Initiation in a Rosicrucian lodge are eligible to attend this ceremony.

Memorial Ceremony
mid-September

A Rosicrucian official presides over this annual ceremony, which is open to the public as well as initiates of Rosicrucianism.

Scientology

Scientology is based on the writings of L. Ron Hubbard (1911–1986). During the 1930s and 1940s, Hubbard formed a theory of human mental development which he described in *Dianetics: The Modern Science of Mental Health*, published in May of 1950. According to Hubbard's teachings, the mind consists of two parts, an analytical part and a reactive part. The Reactive Mind was responsible for formulating abnormal behavior patterns on the basis of recorded perceptions of trauma called engrams. The focus of Dianetics and Scientology is a process known as auditing, through which participants discover and remove engrams. Hubbard continued his research and soon discovered that he was actually dealing with the human spirit. This led to the codification of the axioms that became the Scientology religion. Dianetics remains a sub-study within the larger subject of Scientology.

The first Church of Scientology was established in Los Angeles, California in 1954; a second was established in Auckland, New Zealand, the following year. Scientology churches soon followed around the world.

Since its creation, the Church of Scientology has experienced controversy and legal difficulty. During the 1960s the U.S. Food and Drug Administration confiscated devices called E-Meters (used to identify engrams) on the basis that they were not medically valid. The Church of Scientology ultimately won a court decision on religious grounds and the E-Meters were returned. In other instances, the church has faced suits from former members and from the U.S. Internal Revenue Service. These suits were resolved when the Internal Revenue Service formally granted non-profit religious recognition to Scientology churches in October of 1993.

Despite the controversies, the Church of Scientology experienced rapid growth. By the end of the 1990s, the organization reported an estimated world-wide membership of more than eight million.

Scientology Holidays

Birthday of L. Ron Hubbard (Founder's Birthday)
March 13

L. Ron Hubbard, founder of Dianetics and Scientology, was born March 13, 1911, at Tilden, Nebraska. This date is celebrated internationally by the Church of Scientology as the Founder's Birthday.

May 9 Day
May 9

The ninth of May is celebrated internationally by the Church of Scientology as its Founding Day. The date May 9, 1950, marked the date of publication of L. Ron Hubbard's *Dianetics: The Modern Science of Mental Health*, the foundation document of Scientology.

Auditors' Day
Second Sunday in September

Auditors' Day is observed by the Church of Scientology. The day honors all auditors (Scientology's spiritual counselors) and the central religious practice of auditing.

Founding of the International Association of Scientologists
October 7

Scientologists celebrate the founding of the International Association of Scientologists, which unites, supports and protects the Scientology religion and Scientologists all over the world.

Scientologists in particular geographic areas may also observe their own significant dates, such as the founding of the church in their area. Members of the Church also observe the traditional religious and national holidays in their countries.

Theosophical Society

Founded by Helena Petrovna Blavatsky (1831–91) and Henry Olcott (1832–1907), the Theosophical Society combined ancient European and Egyptian thought with Hindu and Buddhist elements. Blavatsky, a Russian-born aristocrat, developed a belief about the nature of the universe based on her participation in occult and psychic phenomenon coupled with secret revelations received from hidden spiritual guides in Tibet. She became acquainted with Olcott in 1873, and together they established the Theosophical Society in 1875.

The basic beliefs of the Society are that there is only one Universal Spirit behind all that exists and that the universe is cyclical in its development, reaching a zenith then diminishing into quiescence. All souls, or Monads, emanate from the Universal Spirit and are thus eternal and divine, but each must be enlightened once it becomes encased in matter—animal, vegetable, or mineral.

The cosmology presented by the Theosophical Society includes a hierarchically arranged pantheon of deities. The supreme deity, called God or Cosmic Logos, is expressed in a trinitarian formula of creator, preserver, and destroyer. Seven other rulers, called Planetary Logoi, hold dominion over all the stars. They are served by angelic beings called Devas.

Each human being is also viewed as possessing a hierarchically arranged multi-leveled self comprising seven types of bodies. These fall along a continuum from pure spirit to pure physical. Through a process of reincarnations, humans seek to eliminate the material aspects of themselves to become pure spirit. Supernatural guides assist in the process.

The popularity of the Theosophical Society in Europe and India increased under its second leader, Annie Besant (1847–1933). In the United States, William Judge ascended to the highest position. Ultimately followers of Besant and Judge formed two organizations: the Theosophical Society (loyal to Judge) and the Theosophical Society in America (loyal to Besant, with international headquarters in India).

Thesophical Holiday

Death of Helena Petrovna Blavatsky
May 8

Helena Petrovna Blavatsky, founder of the Theosophical Society, died on May 8, 1891. Theosophists around the world remember her on this day each year.

PART THREE

Appendices and Indexes

APPENDIX A

Sources for More Information

The following list describes internet and organizational resources for further information about calendars, religions, and holidays.

Calendars and Timekeeping

Calendar Converter
URL: http://www.fourmilab.ch/documents/calendar/

This website allows you to convert dates between the Gregorian, Julian, Hebrew, Islamic, Persian, Mayan, Bahá'í, Indian civil, and French Republic calendars as well as a number of others used in the technical fields. It also provides a brief description of the history and uses of each.

Calendar Home Page
URL: http://www.calendarhome.com

This page includes a calendar converter for the Julian, Gregorian, Hebrew, Islamic, Persian, Mayan, Bahá'í, Indian Civil, and French Republican calendars as well as a date calculator which will specify the number of days between any two dates. It also includes links to calendar websites in fourteen different categories, as well as a search engine.

Calendar Zone
URL: http://www.calendarzone.com

The religious portion of this site at http://www.calendarzone.com/Religious/ includes links to many religious calendar sites. The reform section at http://www.calendarzone.com/reform/ provides links to many sites related to calendar reform.

CalendarReform
URL: http://www.calendarreform.com

This site summarizes the calendar reform movement and offers viewers the opportunity to vote for their favorite version.

Calendars through the Ages
URL: http://webexhibits.org/calendars

This website offers a fascinating glimpse of the history of our calendar. It includes overviews of the history and development of our week and our year and a timeline of interesting calendar facts. It also includes a section on the history of daylight saving time.

Calendopaedia: The Encyclopaedia of Calendars
URL: http://www.geocities.com/calendopaedia

This site includes a chart comparing the organization of twenty-two different types of calendars. It also includes a short overview of each type, as well as an extensive amount of other calendar-related information.

Home Page for Calendar Reform
URL: http://personal.ecu.edu/mccartyr/calendar-reform.html

This website summarizes the history of the calendar reform movement and provides synopses of many of the current proposals for calendar reform. It also includes a number of links to calendar-related sites.

Interfaith Calendar
URL: http://www.interfaithcalendar.org

This site contains an interfaith calendar of the primary sacred times for many of the different world religions, as well as a brief summary of each of the faiths, broken down by families of religions. It also contains an alphabetic glossary of many of the interfaith calendar terms. A number of related links are also provided.

Measurement of Time
URL: http://www.npl.co.uk/time/time_measure.html

This website provides a brief overview of the measurement of time and a discussion of why an accurate measurement of time is important. It includes a brief discussion of the Gregorian and Julian calendars, Greenwich Mean Time, Universal Time, and atomic time scales. A useful bibliography of time-related resources is also included.

Official U.S. Time
URL: http://www.time.gov

The Time Exhibits portion of this site at http://www.time.gov/exhibits.html includes links to historical and technical information on calendars and time-keeping devices.

Sizes: Index to Time and Calendars
URL: http://www.sizes.com/time

This site provides an overview of a number of the world's calendars, as well as a listing of world eras, calendar units, time scales, and time zones.

Soul to Spirit (TM) Festival Calendar
URL: http://67.120.246.148/calendar/holiday_by_religion.asp

This site provides a listing of holidays by religion, date, and country. It also includes a listing of the lunar phases for the current year.

Today's Calendar and Clock Page
URL: http://www.ecben.net/calendar.shtml

This page provides a complete rundown of the various world classifications for today's date. It also provides a long listing of links to related sites, broken down by religion and type of calendar.

U.S. Naval Observatory
Astronomical Applications Department
URL: http://aa.usno.navy.mil/AAmap.html

This website provides data on world sunrise and sunset times, phases of the moon, and eclipses. The calendars and historical events section discusses world calendars, U.S. holidays, and the dating of Easter, as well as the Star of Bethlehem and problems in dating the Crucifixion.

Walk through Time
URL: http://physics.nist.gov/GenInt/Time/time.html

This site features a brief overview of timekeeping, from the earliest calendars and clocks to the present.

Worldwide Holiday and Festival Site
URL: http://www.holidayfestival.com

The Religions section of this page provides a listing of world holidays and festivals, broken down by country, religion, and current month.

Judaism

Jewish Reconstructionist Federation
7804 Montgomery Avenue, Suite 9
Elkins Park, PA 19027
Phone: 215-782-8500
Fax: 215-782-8805
Website: http://www.jrf.org

This site includes a resource list for those seeking more information on the Jewish holidays, including book lists and links to other sites. It also offers an overview of holidays in Israel.

Judaism 101
URL: http://www.jewfaq.org

The holiday portion of this site at http://www.jewfaq.org/holiday0.htm includes and overview of the major Jewish holidays. This site also features an introduction to Judaism and a search engine.

Orthodox Union
11 Broadway
New York, NY 10004
Phone: 212-563-4000
Fax: 212-564-9058
Website: http://www.ou.org

Especially of note at this site is the list of holidays at http://www.ou.org/chagim/default.htm.

Shamash: The Jewish Network
URL: http://shamash.org

This site is a clearinghouse for Jewish websites and discussion forums on the Internet. Especially note the extensive Judaism and Jewish Resources at http://shamash.org/trb/judaism.html and the calendar calculator at http://shamash.org/trb/yahr.

Union of American Hebrew Congregations
633 Third Avenue
New York, NY 1001-6778
Phone: 212-650-4000
Website: http://www.uahc.org

This is the official website of the central body of the Jewish Reform Movement in American Of special interest at this site is the holiday information at http://www.uahc.org/holidays/jcal.shtml.

United Synagogue of Conservative Judaism
155 Fifth Avenue
New York, NY 10010-6802
Phone: 212-533-7800
Fax: 212-353-9439
Website: http://www.uscj.org

Of special interest at this site is the section on holidays and candle lighting, which provides a calendar of major Jewish holidays and a calculator for determining the candle lighting times for cities and countries worldwide. A discussion of holiday foods and essays on several holidays are also provided.

Zoroastrianism

Avesta
URL: http://www.avesta.org

This site provides a complete text of the extant Avesta, the most ancient scriptures of Zoroastrianism. It also includes information about the Avestan language. A part of this website of special interest is the Zoroastrian Religious Calendar at http://www.avesta.org/zcal.html.

Federation of Zoroastrian Associations of North America
951 Jordan Crescent
Edmonton, Alberta, CANADA T6L 7A5
Website: http://www.fezana.org

This site provides a link to the *FEZANA Journal*, as well as a calendar of FEZANA events.

World of Traditional Zoroastianism
URL: http://zoroastrianism.com

This website explains the tenets of Zoroastrianism and provides links to a number of Zoroastrian sites.

World Zoroastrian Organisation
URL: http://www.w-z-o.org

This site includes a number of essays on Zoroastrian culture, religion, and customs.

Zarathushtrian Assembly
URL: http://www.zoroastrian.org

This page provides a variety of articles on Zoroastrianism. Of special interest are the articles on the Iranian New Year and the Precise Iranian calendar.

Christianity: Roman Catholic and Protestant Expressions

American Evangelical Christian Churches
P.O. Box 47312
Indianapolis, IN 46247-0312
Phone: 607-565-2891
Fax: 607-565-2891
Website: http://www.aeccministries.com

This is the official website of the American Evangelical Christian Churches.

Catholic Information Network
URL: http://www.cin.org

Of special interest at this site is its listing of Catholic saints' days and feast days, as well as its overview of the liturgical year.

Christian Classics Ethereal Library
Development Office, Calvin College
3201 Burton Street SE
Grand Rapids, MI 49546
Website: http://www.ccel.org

This site contains classic Christian books in electronic format.

The Mass.org, Liturgical Calendar Index
St. Ann's Media
P.O. Box 111
Scranton, PA 18504-0111
Phone: 570-941-0100
Fax: 570-941-0185
Website: http://www.themass.org/calendar.htm

This website contains a liturgical calendar index, in three-month blocks.

National Association of Evangelicals
P.O. Box 23269
Washington, DC 20026
Phone: 202-789-1011
Fax: 202-842-0392
Website: http://www.nae.net

This is the official website of the National Association of Evangelicals.

National Council of Churches
475 Riverside Drive, Suite 880
New York, NY 10115
Website: http://www.ncccusa.org

The history and mission of the National Council of Churches are summarized in this website, which also includes summaries of the organization's education and leadership ministries and justice, public witness, and unity resources. A search engine is also included.

United States Conference of Catholic Bishops
3211 4th Street, N.E.
Washington, DC 20017-1194
Phone: 202-541-3000
Fax: 202-541-3412
Website: http://www.usccb.org

Of special interest at this site is its liturgical calendar for the dioceses of the United States.

Contact Information for Some of the Largest Protestant Denominations

African Methodist Episcopal Church
500 8th Avenue South
Nashville, TN 37203
Phone: 615-254-0911
Fax: 615-254-0912
Website: http://www.ame-church.com

American Baptist Churches
P.O. Box 851
Valley Forge, PA 19482-0851
Phone: 610-768-2000 or 800-ABC-3USA
Fax: 610-768-2275
Website: http://www.abc-usa.org

Assemblies of God
1445 North Booneville Avenue
Springfield, MO 65802
Phone: 417-862-2781
Website: http://www.ag.org

Association Free Lutheran Congregations
3110 E. Medicine Lake Blvd.
Plymouth, MN 55441
Phone: 763-545-5631
Website: http://www.aflc.org

Baptist General Conference
2002 S. Arlington Heights Road
Arlington Heights, IL 60005
Website: http://www.bgcworld.org

Baptist Missionary Association
P.O. Box 73
Waxahachie, TX 75168
Phone: 972-923-0757
Website: http://bmaweb.net

Christian Church (Disciples of Christ)
130 East Washington Street
Indianapolis, Indiana 46204-3645
Phone: 317-635-3100
Website: http://www.disciples.org

Christian and Missionary Alliance
P.O. Box 35000
Colorado Springs, CO 80935-3500
Phone: 719-599-5999
Website: http://www.cmalliance.org

Christian Reformed Church in North America
2850 Kalamazoo Avenue SE
Grand Rapids, MI 49560
Phone: 616-241-1691 or 877-279-9994
Fax: 616-224-0803
Website: http://www.crcna.org

Church of God (Cleveland, TN)
2490 Keith Street
P.O. Box 2430
Cleveland, Tennessee 37320-2430
Phone: 423-472-3361
Fax: 423-478-7066
Website: http://www.churchofgod.cc

Church of God in Christ
Website: http://www.cogic.org

Churches of Christ
Website: http://church-of-christ.org

Church of the Brethren
1451 Dundee Avenue
Elgin, IL 60121
Phone: 800-323-8039 or 847-742-5100
Fax: 847-742-6103
Website: http://www.brethren.org

Church of the Nazarene
6401 The Paseo
Kansas City, MO 64131
Phone: 816-333-7000
Website: http://www.nazarene.org

Cumberland Presbyterian Church
1978 Union Avenue
Memphis, TN 38104
Website: http://www.cumberland.org

Episcopal Church, USA
815 Second Avenue
New York, NY 10017
Phone: 212-716-6000
Website: http://
www.ecusa.anglican.org

Evangelical Lutheran Church in America
8765 W. Higgins Road
Chicago, IL 60631
Phone: 773-380-2700 or 800-638-3522
Fax: 773-380-1465
Website: http://www.elca.org

International Pentecostal Holiness Church
P.O. Box 12609
Oklahoma City, OK 73157
Phone: 405-787-7110
Fax: 405-789-3957
Website: http://www.iphc.org

Lutheran Church-Missouri Synod
1333 S. Kirkwood Road
St. Louis, MO 63122-7295
Phone: 888-843-5267
Website: http://www.lcms.org

Mennonite Church USA
Phone: 1-866-2872
Website: http://www.mennonites.org

Moravian Church in America
P.O. Box 1245
Bethlehem, PA 18016
Phone: 610-867-0593
Fax: 610-866-9223
Website: http://www.moravian.org

National Association of Free Will Baptists
P.O. Box 5002
Antioch, TN 37011-5002
Phone: 615-731-6812 or 877-767-7659
Fax: 615-731-0771
Website: http://www.nafwb.org

North American Baptist Conference
1 So. 210 Summit Avenue
Oakbrook Terrace, IL 60181
Phone: 630-495-2000
Fax: 630-495-3301
Website: http://www.nabconference.org

Presbyterian Church in America
1700 North Brown Road, Suite 105
Lawrenceville, GA 30043-8122
Phone: 678-825-1000
Website: http://www.pcanet.org

Presbyterian Church – USA
100 Witherspoon Street
Louisville, KY 40202-1396
Phone: 502-569-5000 or 800-872-3283
Fax: 502-569-5018
Website: http://www.pcusa.org

Reformed Church in America
475 Riverside Drive, 18th Fl.
New York, NY 10115
Website: http://www.rca.org

Seventh Day Adventist Church
12501 Old Columbia Pike
Silver Spring, MD 20904-6600
Phone: 301-680-6000
Website: http://www.adventist.org

Southern Baptist Convention
901 Commerce Street
Nashville, TN 37203-3699
Phone: 615-244-2355
Website: http://www.sbc.net

United Church of Christ
700 Prospect Avenue
Cleveland, OH 44115
Phone: 216-736-2100
Website: http://www.ucc.org

United Methodist Church
Phone: 615-742-5400 #100 D68
Website: http://www.umc.org

Wesleyan Church
P.O. Box 50434
Indianapolis, IN 46250
Phone: 317-570-5100
Website: http://www.wesleyan.org

Wisconsin Evangelical Lutheran Synod
2929 N. Mayfair Road
Milwaukee, WI 53222
Phone: 414-256-3888
Website: http://www.wels.net

Christianity: Orthodox Expressions

Antiochian Orthodox Christian Archdiocese of North America
P.O. Box 5238
Englewood, NJ 07631-5238
Website: http://www.antiochian.org

Of special interest at this site is its listing of saints of the day at http://www.antiochian.org/liturgical.asp.

Armenian Church of America
630 Second Avenue
New York, NY 10016
Phone: 212-686-0710
Fax: 212-686-0245
Website: http://www.armenianchurch.org

This site includes a liturgical calendar at http://www.armenianchurch.org/worship/calendar/index.html.

Greek Orthodox Archdiocese of America
8 East 79th Street
New York, NY 10021
Phone: 212-570-3500
Fax: 212-570-3569
Website: http://www.goarch.org

This page features a calendar of saints and feasts at http://www.goarch.org/en/Chapel/calendar.asp.

Orthodox Church in America
P.O. Box 675
Syosset, NY 11791-0675
Phone: 516-922-0550
Fax: 516-922-0954
Website: http://www.oca.org

Of special interest at this site is its listing of feasts and saints of the church year.

Synod of Bishops of the Russian Orthodox Church Outside of Russia
75 East 93rd Street
New York, NY 10128
Phone: 212-534-1601
Website: http://www.russianorthodoxchurch.ws/english

This is the official website of the Russian Orthodox Church Outside of Russia.

Christianity: Non-Trinitarian and Non-Traditional Expressions

American Unitarian Conference
P.O. Box 331
Fenton, MI 48430-0331
Phone: 810-714-6087
Website: http://www.americanunitarian.org

This is the official website of the American Unitarian Conference.

Church of Christ, Scientist
Christian Science Plaza
175 Huntingdon Avenue
Boston, MA 02115
Phone: 617-450-2000
Website: http://www.tfccs.com

This is the official website of the Church of Christ, Scientist.

Church of Jesus Christ of Latter-Day Saints
Website: http://www.lds.org

This is the official website of the Church of Jesus Christ of Latter-Day Saints.

Jehovah's Witnesses
25 Columbia Heights
Brooklyn, NY 11201-2483
Website: http://www.watchtower.org

This is the official website of the Jehovah's Witnesses.

Swedenborgian Church of North America
11 Highland Avenue
Newtonville, MA 02460-1852
Phone: 617-969-4240
Fax: 617-964-3258
Website: http://www.swedenborg.org

This is the official website of the Swedenborgian Church of North America.

Unitarian Universalist Association
25 Beacon Street
Boston, MA 02108
Phone: 617-742-2100
Website: http://www.uua.org

This is the official website of the Unitarian Universalist Association.

Islam

Ahlul Bayt Digital Islamic Library Project
URL: http://www.al-islam.org

This site presents Islamic resources related to the history, law, practice, and society of the Islamic religion with particular emphasis on Twelver Shia Islamic school of thought.

Al-Qur'an was-Sunnah Society
URL: http://www.qss.org

A part of this website of special interest is "Establishing Ramadhan and Other Islamic Dates" at http://www.qss.org/articles/moon/text.html. This section cites scripture for the correct establishment of the month by natural astronomic observation to explain how new moons determine Islamic dates. This site also features an introduction to Islam, over 100 links to additional information, and a search engine.

Gregorian-Hijra Dates Converter
URL: http://www.rabiah.com/convert/

This page is a straightforward program that converts Gregorian dates to Hijri dates and vice versa. An introduction covers the history and motivation behind the lunar-based Islamic calendar.

Islam 101
URL: http://www.islam101.com

This educational site includes an introductory course on Islam and presents Islamic views on contemporary issues. Of particular interest is the section on the Islamic calendar at http://www.islam101.com/dawah/calendar.htm.

Islamic Society of North America
P.O. Box 38
Plainfield, IN 46168
Phone: 317-839-8157
Website: http://www.isna.net

This is the official website of the Islamic Society of North America.

Moonsighting.com
URL: http://www.moonsighting.com

This site includes an Islamic calendar for North America, a listing of important Islamic dates in North America, a discussion of the methods for determining the beginning of Islamic months, and a discussion of the methods of determining prayer times.

Bahá'í

Bahá'í Calendar
URL: http://www.fragrant.demon.co.uk/caltext.html

This site provides a brief overview of the Bahá'í calendar, with a short discussion of Bahá'í holidays. It also includes a Bahá'í date converter from the Gregorian calendar.

Bahá'í Faith
Bahá'í National Center
1233 Central Street
Evanston, IL 60201
Phone: 800-22-UNITE
Website: http://www.us.bahai.org

This site provides a brief overview of the Bahá'í faith. Included is a schedule of Bahá'í holy days.

Hinduism

Hindu Links
URL: http://www.hindulinks.org

This site contains links to almost 30,000 Hindu sites. Of special interest is the listing of significant Hindu dates in the calendar section of this site.

Hindu Universe
URL: http://www.hindunet.org

The Hindu Calendar, at http://hindunet.org/hindu_calendar/ has a full and detailed explanation of the Hindu calendar that includes the days, months, years and ages of Hindu history. Delving into the esoteric, the page also includes a daily ephemeris for use in a branch of Vedic astrology. Also included is a link to an essay on the Hindu concept of time.

Hinduism Simplified
URL: http://www.hindubooks.org/hinduism_simplified

This site includes a discussion of the Hindu calendar and how it differs from the Gregorian calendar, and also a brief summary of important Hindu festivals and fasts.

Online Hindu Vedic Calendar
URL: http://www.panchangam.com

This site offers an online Hindu Vedic calendar, and also provides a list of the important Hindu, Christian, and Muslim festivals.

Jainism

Federation of Jain Associations in North America
P.O. Box 700
Getzville, NY 14068
Phone: 716-636-5342
Website: http://www.jaina.org

This is the official website of the Federation of Jain Associations in North America.

Jain Center of Greater Boston
URL: http://www.jcgb.org

Of special interest at this site is the calendar at http://www.jcgb.org/jaincalendar.htm. The site also contains a listing of Jain sites of pilgrimage and a glossary of Jain terms, as well as a number of links to Jain-related sites.

Jain Festivals
URL: http://www.cs.colostate.edu/~malaiya/calendar.html

This page is a simple chart, listing the names of the Indian months, the corresponding Gregorian months, and any Jain festivals occurring in each month. There is also a good list of links for various calendars and astronomical time-keeping methods.

Jain Literature and Jain Logic Site
URL: AtmaDharma.com

This site provides original Jain texts with translations into various modern languages. Of special interest are the interactive Jain calendars at http://AtmaDharma.com/downloads/index.html#calendar.

Jainism: Principles, Sources, Images, History
URL: http://www.cs.colostate.edu/~malaiya/jainhlinks.html

This extensive and thorough page covers a wide range of topics relating to Jainism. Visitors will find hundreds of links to texts, and information subjects such as vegetarianism, pilgrimages, and yoga. "Jainism Through the Eyes of Others" is a unique sub-category that links to various sites with controversial or confused views on Jainism.

Sikhism

All About Sikhs
URL: http://allaboutsikhs.com

This site provides a plethora of information on the Sikh faith, including an overview of Sikh history, a description of the Sikh fairs, festivals, and ceremonies, and a number of Sikh scriptures in English translation. Of special interest is the calendar information at http://allaboutsikhs.com/way/sikhdates.htm, which includes a listing of the Sikh months and festival dates, organized by both date and guru, as well as a listing of the solar and lunisolar festivals.

Sikh Coalition
URL: http://www.sikhcoalition.org

"Nanakshahi: The Sikh Calendar" can be found at http://www.sikhcoalition.org/SikhismCalendar.asp. This site also contains a number of essays on Sikh history, the Sikh articles of faith, and Sikh theology.

Sikhism Home Page
URL: http://www.sikhs.org

This is an informative site developed by Sandeep Singh Brar. A brief overview of the Nanakshahi Calendar, which was adopted in 1999, is given at http://www.sikhs.org/dates.htm

Buddhism

Buddhist Information and Education Network
URL: http://www.buddhanet.net

This site offers a wealth of information on Buddhist history and culture. Of special interest is the listing of festivals and special days at http://www.buddhanet.net/festival.htm.

DharmaNet International
1612 Putnam Way
Petaluma CA 94954
Website: http://www.dharmanet.org

This site includes a "Buddhist Meditation Retreats and Events Calendar" at http://www.dharmanet.org/calendar.html where a compiled listing of Buddhist teachings, retreats, and other events is included. The list is arranged by months, is international in scope, and inclusive of all Buddhist traditions.

Taoism, Confucianism, and Chinese Folk Religions

Chinese Festivals and Holidays
URL: http://www.c-c-c.org/chineseculture/festival/festival.html

This is a listing of the major holidays celebrated in China, Taiwan, and overseas Chinese communities, along with their corresponding Gregorian dates.

Chinese Folk Religions
URL: http://www.csupomona.edu/~plin/folkreligion/chinesefolkrel.html

This site provides an overview of Chinese folk religions as well as a calendar of Chinese festivals.

Chinese New Year
URL: http://www.indiana.edu/~chasso/newyear.html

This website offers a comprehensive discussion of the Chinese calendar and the origins, traditions, and dating of the Chinese New Year. It also includes a Chinese calendar converter.

Holidays and Festivals in Taiwan

URL: http://www.gio.gov.tw/info/festival_c/index_e.htm

This site provides a description of the commemorative holidays and traditional festivals celebrated in Taiwan.

Taoism Information Page

URL: http://www.clas.ufl.edu/users/gthursby/taoism

This page provides links to many sites related to Taoism, including introductions to Taoism and translations of classical texts.

Shinto

Annual Calendar in Japan

URL: http://www.jinjapan.org/kidsweb/calendar/calendar.html

This site describes Japan's holidays, annual events, and school activities.

Focus on Japan: Descriptions of Japanese Holidays

URL: http://www.asij.ac.jp/elementary/japan/jp_holi.html

This site provides detailed descriptions of the major Japanese holidays.

Embassy of Japan, Spotlight

URL: http://www.dk.emb-japan.go.jp/spotlight/default.htm

This website features a collection of essays on different aspects of Japanese culture and society. Among them are a number of essays on Japanese holidays and festivals.

Shinto: Basic Information

URL: http://www.japan-guide.com/e/e2056.html

This page provides an overview of the Shinto religion, including a discussion of important festivals and shrines.

Native American Religions

American Indian Heritage Foundation

P.O. Box 6330
Falls Church, VA 22040
Website: http://www.indians.org

This is the official website of the American Indian Heritage Foundation. The "Resource Library" portion of the site offers cultural information and links to other sources.

Cherokee Nation: Traditional Stories

URL: http://www.cherokee.org/Culture/LiteratureCat.asp?Cat=Stories

This site features a number of traditional Cherokee stories.

Index of Native American Nations on the Internet

URL: http://www.hanksville.org/NAresources/indices/NAnations.html

This website provides links to the websites of many Native American nations.

Powwows and Festivals

URL: http://www.nativeculture.com/lisamitten/powwows.html

This site contains links to sites that maintain listings of upcoming powwows and provide information on powwow dancing and customs. Also of interest are the links to the websites of individual Native American nations.

Six Nations: What Is the Annual Cycle of Thanksgiving?

URL: http://sixnations.buffnet.net/Culture/?article=thanksgiving

This page includes a description of the Haudenosaunee (Iroquois) cycle of thanksgiving.

Paganism

Circle Sanctuary; Pagan Holidays

URL: http://www.circlesanctuary.org/pholidays

This site offers brief descriptions of a number of pagan holidays.

Covenant of the Goddess

P.O. Box 1226
Berkeley, CA 94701
Website: http://www.cog.org

This website provides a general overview of the Wiccan religion, including a brief discussion of its holidays.

Mystic's Wheel of the Year

URL: http://www.wheeloftheyear.com

This page features a multifaith calendar incorporating the holidays of a multitude of faiths worldwide and reflecting eco-egalitarian spirituality.

Pagan Federation

BM Box 7097
London WC1N 3XX England
Website: http://www.paganfed.demon.co.uk

This site offers a brief overview of the most common branches of paganism, including Wicca, shamanism, and druidry. Of special interest is the wheel of the year section, which describes the pagan holidays, and the section on seasonal festivals.

Stardancer's Wheel of the Year

URL: http://www.mindspring.com/~stardancer/index.htm

This website includes a description of each of the major pagan holidays, as well as a full moon almanac and a calendar of the major meteor showers of the year.

Western African Religions and Their New World Expressions

Church of the Lukumi Babalu Aye

URL: http://www.church-of-the-lukumi.org

Of special interest on this web page is the discussion of Lukumi celebrations at http://www.church-of-the-lukumi.org/celebrations.htm and articles on many aspects of the Lukumi religion at http://www.church-of-the-lukumi.org/newjournal.htm.

Egbe Isokan Yoruba

P.O. Box 90832
Washington, DC 20090
Phone: 202-270-6382
Fax: 301-499-5386
Website: http://www.yoruba.org

This site provides information about the Yoruba culture in Africa and America. Of special interest is the "Yoruba in the Diaspora" section, which describes a number of the Yoruba holidays.

OrishaNet

URL: http://www.seanet.com/~efunmoyiwa

This website provides information on the Santeria or La Regla Lucumi religion of the Yoruba peoples.

Palo and Lukumi Organization

P.O. Box 1053
Lancaster, CA 93584
Phone: 661-264-1697
Website: http://www.palo.org

This site is devoted to the Cuban Palo, Lukumi, and Santeria belief systems.

Ancient Wisdom, Metaphysical, Other Faith Communities

Eckankar, Religion of the Light and Sound of God

P.O. Box 27300
Minneapolis, MN 55427
Phone: (952) 380-2222
Website: http://www.eckankar.org

This site provides a basic overview of the Eckankar religion. A booklet providing an explanatory overview, "About Eckankar: An Overview of Eckankar and Its Teachings" is available online at http://www.eckankar.org/abouteckankar.pdf.

The Summit Lighthouse/Church Universal and Triumphant Home Page

P.O. Box 5000
Gardiner, MT 59030-5000
Toll-Free: 800-245-5445 (in the U.S.)
Phone: 406-848-9500
Website: http://www.tsl.org

This is the official website of the Summit Lighthouse, source for teachings of the ascended masters.

World Pantheism Movement

32158 Sailview Lane
Westlake Village, CA 91361
Phone: 877-829-5500
Website: http://www.pantheism.net

Of special interest at this site are the links to a pantheist calendar and a pantheist almanac, which provides dates of equinoxes, solstices, and meteor showers, and its discussion of seasonal celebration.

Universal Pantheist Society

P.O. Box 3499
Visalia, CA 93278
Website: http://www.pantheist.net

This is the official website of the Universal Pantheist Society.

Rosicrucian Order, AMORC

1342 Naglee Avenue
San Jose, CA 95191
Phone: 408-947-3600
Fax: 408-947-3677
Website: http://www.rosicrucian.org

This is the official website of the Rosicrucian Order, AMORC.

National Spiritualist Association of Churches

P.O. Box 217
Lily Dale, NY 14752
Phone: 716-595-2000
Fax: 716-595-2020
Website: http://www.nsac.org

This is the official website of the National Spiritualist Association of Churches. It provides a brief overview of the history, principles, and objects of the spiritualist movement.

Fraternitas Rosae Crucis

P.O. Box 220
Quakertown, PA 18951
Toll-Free: 800-779-3796
Phone: 215-536-7048
Website: http://www.soul.org

This is the official website of the Fraternitas Rosae Crucis, or the Rosicrucian Fraternity.

Ramtha's School of Enlightenment

P.O. Box 1210
Yelm, WA 98597
Phone: 360-458-5201 ext. 10
Website: http://www.ramtha.com

This website is devoted to spreading the teachings of Ramtha and is the official website of Ramtha's School of Enlightenment.

Scientology

URL: http://www.scientology.org

This official website of the Church of Scientology includes basic information about Scientology and lists current worldwide activities.

Other Miscellaneous Sources

Adherents.com

URL: http://www.adherents.com

This site provides statistics on number of adherents and religious geography for over 4,200 religions, churches, denominations, tribes, cultures, and so on.

Beliefnet

URL: http://www.beliefnet.com

This website provides essays on a variety of religious topics.

Hartford Institute for Religion Research

Phone: 800-509-9543
Fax: 860-509-9551
Website: http://hirr.hartsem.edu

This site provides social scientific research information on religion. Especially noteworthy is the extensive list of links to official denomination home pages at http://hirr.hartsem.edu/org/faith_denominations_homepages.html.

Religious Movements Homepage

URL: http://religiousmovements.lib.virginia.edu

This site is dedicated to the study of religious movements on the Web and in the world. Especially noteworthy are the profiles of religious movements and discussion of cults and sects.

Virtual Religion Index

URL: http://www.rci.rutgers.edu/~religion/vri/

This website analyzes and highlights the important content of religion-related websites to speed research on religion. It is broken down by subject and by individual religion and includes links to hundreds of sites.

APPENDIX B

Bibliography and Additional Reading

In addition to presenting information about sources of information used in this book, this bibliography also serves a starting point for further research into religions, calendars, and holidays. Materials are presented in a topical arrangement. General works and information about Greek and Roman Mythology are listed first followed by references about calendars and timekeeping systems. Individual religions are then listed to parallel this book's Table of Contents.

General

Appiah, Kwame Anthony and Henry Louis Gates, Jr. *The Dictionary of Global Culture*. New York: Knopf, 1997.

Bowker, J.W. *The Cambridge Illustrated History of Religions*. New York: Cambridge University Press, 2002.

Bradley, David G. *A Guide to the World's Religions*. Englewood Cliffs, NJ: Prentice-Hall, 1963.

Campbell, Joseph. *The Masks of God, Vol. 3: Occidental Mythology.* New York: Viking, 1964.

Campbell, Joseph, ed. *The Mysteries: Papers from the Eranos Yearbooks.* Translated by Ralph Manheim & R. F. C. Hull. Princeton, NJ: Princeton University Press, 1955.

Clark, Peter B. Ed., *The World's Great Religions: Understanding the Living Faiths*. Pleasantville, NY: Readers Digest Association, Inc., 1993.

Earhart, H. Byron (ed.) *Religious Traditions of the World*. New York: Harper Collins, 1993.

Ellwood, Robert S., Jr. *Religious and Spiritual Groups in Modern America*. Engleweed Cliffs, N.J.: Prentice-Hall, Inc., 1973.

Enroth, Ronald, et al. *A Guide to Cults and New Religions*. Downers Grove, IL: Inter-Varsity Press, 1983.

Green, Marian. *A Calendar of Festivals*. Rockport, MA: Element, 1991.

Green, Marian. *A Harvest of Festivals*. London: Longman, 1980.

Gregory, Ruth W. *Anniversaries and Holidays*. 4th ed. Chicago: American Library Assn, 1983.

Hammond, N. G. L., and H. H. Scullard. *The Oxford Classical Dictionary*. 2d ed. Oxford, Eng.: The Clarendon Press, 1970.

Harper, Howard V. *Days and Customs of All Faiths*. New York: Fleet Publishing, 1957.

Hutchison, Ruth, and Ruth Adams. *Every Day's a Holiday*. New York: Harper & Row, 1951.

Ickis, Marguerite. *The Book of Festivals and Holidays the World Over*. New York: Dodd, Mead, 1970.

Ickis, Margureite. *The Book of Religious Holidays and Celebrations*. New York: Dodd, Mead, 1966.

Kightly, Charles. *The Customs and Ceremonies of Britain: An Encyclopaedia of Living Traditions*. London: Thames & Hudson, 1986.

Langley, Myrtle. *Religions*. Elgin, IL: David C. Cook, 1981.

Mathers, S. L. MacGregor, ed. and trans. *The Greater Key of Solomon*. Chicago: De Laurence, Scott, 1914.

Melton, J.G. *Encyclopedia of American Religions, 6th Edition*. Detroit: Gale Research, 1998.

Mossman, Jennifer, ed. *Holidays and Anniversaries of the World*. Detroit, MI: Gale Research, 1985.

National Geographic Society. *Great Religions of the World*. Washington, DC: National Geographic Society, 1971.

Oxtoby, Willard G. ed. *World Religions: Eastern Traditions*. New York: Oxford University Press, 1996.

Parrinder, Geoffrey ed. *World Religions: From Ancient History to the Present*. New York, NY: Facts on File, 1983.

Pike, Royston. *Round the Year with the World's Religions*. New York: Henry Schuman, Inc., 1950. Republished by Omnigraphics, Detroit, 1993.

Queen, E.L.; Prothero, S.R.; Shatluck, G.H. *The Encyclopedia of American Religious History*. New York: Facts on File, Inc., 1996.

Religions of the World Interactive CD-ROM. Distributed by Mentorom Multimedia, Ontario, Canada. Copyright 1994 Interactive Learning Productions, a division of International Thomson Publishing.

Shemanski, Frances. *A Guide to World Fairs and Festivals*. Westport, Conn.: Greenwood Press, 1985.

Smart, Ninian. *The Religious Experience of Mankind*. New York: Charles Scribner's Sons, 1969.

Spangler, David. *Festivals in the New Age*. Moray, Scotland: Findhorn Foundation, 1975.

Spicer, Dorothy Gladys. *The Book of Festivals*. Detroit, MI: Gale Research, 1969.

Three Festivals of Spring (The). Ojai, CA: MGNA Publications, 1971.

Van Straalin, Alice. *The Book of Holidays Around the World*. New York: E.P. Dutton, 1986.

Wasserman, Paul, Esther Herman, and Elizabeth Root, eds. *Festivals Sourcebook*. Detroit, MI: Gale Research, 1977.

Wilkinson, P. *Illustrated Dictionary of Religions*. New York : DK Publishing, 1999.

Mythology (Greek and Roman)

Brand, John, and Henry Ellis. *Observations on the Popular Antiquities of Great Britain*. 3 vols. London: Bohn, 1853.

Burkert, Walter. *Homo Necans: The Anthropology of Ancient Greek Sacrifician Ritual and Myth*. Berkeley: University of California Press, 1983.

Clinton, Kevin. "The Sacred Officials of the Eleusinian Mysteries." *Transactions*, n.s. Vol. 63, pt. 3. Philadelphia, 1974.

Cook, Arthur Bernard. *Zeus: A Study of Ancient Religion*. 3 vols. Cambridge, Eng.: Cambridge University Press, 1914-1940.

Farnell, Lewis R. *The Cults of the Greek States*. 5 vols. London: Oxford University Press, 1896-1909.

Ferguson, John. *The Religions of the Roman Empire*. Ithaca, N.Y.: Cornell University Press, 1970.

Fontenrose, Joseph. *Python: A Study of Delphic Myth and Its Origin*. Berkeley: University of California Press, 1959.

Fowler, W. Warde. *The Roman Festivals of the Period of the Republic: An Introduction to the Study of the Religion of the Romans*. London: Macmillan, 1899.

Graves, Robert. *The Greek Myths*. 2 vols. New York: Penguin, 1955.

Harrison, Jane Ellen. *Prolegomena to the Study of Greek Religion*. 1903. Reprint. Princeton: Princeton Univer. Press, 1991.

Jung, Carl G., and C. Kerényi. *Essays on a Science of Mythology: The Myth of the Divine Child and the Mysteries of Eleusis*. Translated by R. F. C. Hull, 1949. 2d ed. Reprint. Princeton, NJ: Princeton University Press, 1963.

Kerényi, C. *Eleusis: Archetypal Image of Mother and Daughter*. Trans. by Ralph Manheim. 1960. Reprint. New York: Pantheon, Bollingen Series 65:4, 1967.

Mylonas, George E. *Eleusis and the Eleusinian Mysteries*. Princeton, NJ: Princeton University Press, 1961.

Neugebauer, Otto, and H. B. van Hoesen. *Greek Horoscopes*. Philadelphia: American Philosophical Society, 1959.

Nilsson, Martin P. *Greek Folk Religion*. New York: Columbia University Press, 1940.

Ogilvie, R. M. *The Romans and Their Gods in the Age of Augustus*. New York: W.W. Norton & Company, Inc., 1969.

Pollard, John. *Seers, Shrines, and Sirens: The Greek Religious Revolution in the Sixth Century B.C.* New York: A. S. Barnes, 1965.

Rose, H. J. *A Handbook of Greek Mythology*. 6th ed. London, England: Methuen & Co. Ltd., 1958.

Rose, H. J. *Religion in Greece*. New York: Harper, 1946.

Rose, H. J. *Religion in Greece and Rome*. New York: Harper, 1948.

Stapleton, Michael. *The Illustrated Dictionary of Greek and Roman Mythology*. London: The Hamlyn Publishing Group Ltd., 1978.

Thomson, George. *Studies in Ancient Greek Society*. Vol. I. 3d ed. London: Lawrence & Wishart, 1961. Vol. II, London: Lawrence & Wishart, 1955.

Wolverton, Robert E. *An Outline of Classical Mythology*. Totowa, N. J.: Littlefield, Adams & Co., 1975.

Zuntz, Günther. *Persephone: Three Essays on Religion and Thought in Magna Graecia*. London: Oxford University Press, 1971.

Chapters 1–4: Calendars

Andrewes, W.J.H. "A Chronicle of Timekeeping," *Scientific American*, Vol. 278, No. 3, September 2002, pp. 76-85.

Arcana Workshops. *The Full Moon Story*. Beverly Hills, CA: Arcana Workshops, 1967.

Asimov, Isaac. *The Clock We Live On*. Revised ed. New York: Abelard-Schumann, 1965.

Aveni, Anthony F. *Empires of Time: Calendars, Clocks, and Cultures*. New York: Kodansha International, 1989,

Bedini, S.A. *The Trial of Time = Shih-chien ti Tsu-chi: Time Measurement with Incense in East Asia*. New York: Cambridge University Press, 1994.

Colson, F.H. *The Week*. Cambridge, Eng.: Cambridge University Press, 1926.

Dale, R. *Timekeeping*, The British Library, 1992.

Doggett, L.E. "Calendars," in *Explanatory Supplement to the Astronomical Almanac*, ed. P.K. Seidelmann. Sausalito, CA: University Science Books, 1992.

Duncan, D.E. *Calendar: Humanity's Epic Struggle to Determine a True and Accurate Year*.

Ezzell, C. "Clocking Cultures," *Scientific American*, Vol. 278, No. 3, September 2002, pp. 75-75.

Howse, D. *Greenwich Time and the Longitude*. Philip Wilson, 1997.

Jastrow, M. *The Religion of Babylonia and Assyria*. New York: Ginn, 1898.

Jespersen, J. and Fitz-Randolph, J. *From Sundials to Atomic Clocks*, New York: Dover Publications, 1982.

Labrador, D. "From Instantaneous to Eternal," *Scientific American*, Vol. 278, No. 3, September 2002, pp. 56-57.

Moore, P. and Hunt, G. *The Atlas of the Solar System*. New York: Crescent Books, 1990.

Nilsson, Martin P. *Primitive Time-Reckoning: A Study in the Origins and First Development of the Art of Counting Time Among the Primitive and Early Culture Peoples*. Lund, Norway: Gleerup, 1920.

Old Farmer's Almanac (The). 1997 ed. Dublin, NH: Yankee Publishing, 1996.

O'Neil, W. M. *Time and the Calendars*. Sydney, Australia: Sydney University Press, 1975.

Parise, Frank, ed. *The Book of Calendars*. New York: Facts on File, 1982.

Renfrew, Colin. "Carbon-14 and the Prehistory of Europe." *Scientific American*, Oct. 1971:63-72.

Renfrew, Colin. "The Origins of Indo-European Languages." *Scientific American*, Oct. 1989:106-114.

Ward, F.A.B. *Handbook of the Collection Illustrating Time Measurement, Fourth Edition*. London: Her Majesty's Stationary Office (HMSO), 1961.

Welch, K.E. *The History of Clocks and Watches*. New York: Drake Publishers, 1972.

Whitrow, G.J. *Time in History*. Oxford University Press, 1989.

Wilson, P. W. *The Romance of the Calendar*. New York: Norton, 1937.

Wright, Lawrence. *Clockwork Man: The Story of Time, Its Origins, Its Uses, Its Tyranny*. New York: Horizon, 1968.

Zerubavel, Eviatar. *The Seven-Day Circle: The History and Meaning of the Week*. New York: Macmillan Free Press, 1985.

Individual Religions

Chapter 5: Judaism

Bamberger, Bernard J. *The Bible: A Modern Jewish Approach*. New York: B'nai B'rith Hillel Foundations, 1955.

Bloch, Abraham P. *The Biblical and Historical Background of the Jewish Holy Days*. New York: Ktav, 1978.

Diamant, Anita and Howard Cooper. *Living a Jewish Life*. New York: Harper Collins, 1991.

Eisenberg, Azriel Louis. *The Story of the Jewish Calendar*. London and New York: Abelard-Schuman, 1958.

Gaster, Theodore H. *Festivals of the Jewish Year: A Modern Interpretation and Guide*. New York: William Sloane, 1953.

Gaster, Theodore H. *Thespis: Ritual, Myth, and Drama in the Ancient Near East*. 2d ed. New York: Doubleday, 1961.

Goodman, Philip. *The Rosh Hashanah Anthology*. Philadelphia: The Jewish Publication Society of America, 1973.

Pfeiffer, Robert H. *Introduction to the Old Testament*. 2d ed. New York: Harper, 1948.

Rosenau, William. *Jewish Ceremonial Institutions and Customs*. 4th ed. New York: Bloch, 1929.

Strassfield, Michael. *The Jewish Holidays: A Guide and Commentary*. New York: Harper and Row, 1985.

Telushkin, J. *Jewish Literacy*. New York: William Morrow, 1991.

Tillem, Ivan L. *The Jewish Directory and Almanac*. Vol. I. New York: Pacific Press, 1984.

Trepp, Leo. *The Complete Book of Jewish Observance*. New York: Behrman House and Summit Books, 1980.

Chapter 6: Zoroastrianism

Boyce, M. *A Persian Stronghold of Zoroastrianism*. Oxford. UK: Clarendon Press, 1977.

Boyce, M. *Zoroastrians, Their Religious Beliefs and Practices*. New York: Routledge, repr. 2001.

Mehr, Farhang. *The Zoroastrian Tradition*, Rockport, MA: Element Books, 1991.

Nigosian, S.A. *The Zoroastrian Faith: Tradition and Modern Research*. Buffalo: McGill-Queen's University Press, 1993.

Pangborn, Cyrus R. *Zoroastrianism: A Beleaguered Faith*. New York: Advent Books, 1983.

Chapter 7: Christianity: Roman Catholic and Protestant Expressions

Allen, Richard. *The Life Experience and Gospel Labors of the Rt. Rev. Richard Allen*. Nashville: Abingdon Press, 1960.

Attwater, Donald. *The Penguin Dictionary of Saints*. New York: Penguin, 1965.

Barrett, Michael. *Footprints of the Ancient Scottish Church*. N.p., 1914.

Bede. *A History of the English Church and People*. Translated by Leo Sherley-Price. Baltimore, MD: Penguin, 1955.

Book of Common Prayer. New York: The Church Hymnal Corporation and The Seabury Press, 1979.

Butler, Alban. *The Lives of the Fathers, Martyrs, and Other Principal Saints*. 12 vols. 1846. Reprint (12 vols. in 4). New York: Sadlier, 1857.

Cowie, L. W., and John S. Gummer. *The Christian Calendar: A Complete Guide to the Seasons of the Christian Year*. Springfield, MA: Merriam-Webster, 1974.

De Bles, Arthur. *How to Distinguish the Saints in Art by Their Costumes, Symbols, and Attributes*. New York: Art Culture Publications, 1925.

Deems, Edward Mark. *Holy-days and Holidays*. 1902. Reprint. Detroit, MI: Gale Research Co. , 1968.

Delehaye, Hippolyte. *The Legends of the Saints*. Translated by D. Attwater. New York: Fordham University Press, 1962.

Delaney, John J. *Dictionary of Saints*. New York: Doubleday, 1980.

Drake, Maurice, and Wilfred Drake. *Saints and Their Emblems*. 1916. Reprint. Detroit: Gale Research, 1971.

Dowden, J. *The Church Year and Calendar*. Cambridge, 1910.

Engelbert, Omer. *The Lives of the Saints*. Translated by Christopher Fremantle and Anne Fremantle. David McKay, 1951.

Kenneth, Br., C.G.A. *A Pocket Calendar of Saints and People to Remember*. Oxford, Eng.: A. R. Mowbray, 1981.

Fotheringham, D. R. *The Date of Easter and Other Christian Festivals*. London, 1928.

National Conference of Catholic Bishops. *Holy Days in the United States: History, Theology, Celebration*. Washington, D.C.: United States Catholic Conference, 1984.

Roeder, Helen. *Saints and Their Attributes, with a Guide to Localities and Patronage*. London: Longmans, Green, 1955.

Weiser, Francis X. *Handbook of Christian Feasts and Customs: The Year of the Lord in Liturgy and Folklore*. New York: Harcourt, Brace, 1952.

Weiser, Francis X. *The Holyday Book*. New York: Harcourt, Brace, 1956.

Chapter 8: Christianity: Orthodox Expressions

Bulgakov, S. *The Orthodox Church*. Crestwood, NY: St. Vladimir's Seminary Press, 1988.

Davis, L. D. *The First Seven Ecumenical Councils (325-787)*. Delaware: Michael Glazier, 1987.

Dunlop, O., trans. *The Living God: A Catechism for the Christian Faith*. Crestwood, NY: St. Vladimir's Seminary Press, 1989.

Hussey, J. M. *The Orthodox Church in the Byzantine Empire*. Oxford: Clarendon Press, 1986.

Lossky, V. *The Mystical Theology of the Eastern Church*. London: James Clark, 1957.

Meyendorff, J. *Byzantine Theology*. Crestwood, NY: St. Vladimir's Seminary Press, 1983.

Papadakis, A. *Crisis in Byzantium: The Filioque Controversy in the Patriarchate of Gregory II of Cyprus (1283-1289)*. New York: Fordham University Press, 1983.

Parry, K., et al. *The Blackwell Dictionary of Eastern Christianity*. Malden, MA: Blackwell, 2001.

Pelikan, J. *The Christian Tradition*, vol. 2: *The Spirit of Eastern Christendom (600-1700)*. Chicago: University of Chicago Press, 1977.

Runciman, S. *The Great Church in Captivity*. Cambridge: Cambridge University Press, 1985.

Schmemann, A. *Historical Road of Eastern Orthodoxy*. Crestwood, NY: St. Vladimir's Seminary Press, 1977.

Schulz, H. J. *The Byzantine Liturgy: Symbolic Structure and Faith Expression*. New York: Pueblo, 1986.

Taft, R. E. *The Byzantine Rite: A Short History*. Collegeville, MN: Liturgical Press, 1992.

Ware, K. T. *The Orthodox Church*. Harmondworth: Penguin, 1993.

Wybrew, H. *The Orthodox Liturgy: The Development of the Eucharistic Liturgy in the Byzantine Rite*. London: SPCK, 1989.

Chapter 9: Christianity: Non-Trinitarian and Non-Traditional Expressions

Bushman, R.L. *Joseph Smith and the Beginnings of Mormonism*. Urbana, IL: University of Illinois Press, 1984.

Christian Science Publishing Society. *A Century of Christian Science Healing*. Boston: Christian Science Publishing Society, 1966.

Church, F.F. and Buehrens, J.A. *A Chosen Faith: An Introduction to Unitarian Universalism*. Boston: Beacon Press, 1998.

Eddy, M.B. *Science and Health with Key to the Scriptures*. Boston: Christian Science Board of Directors, repr. 1994.

Ludlow, D.H. *Encyclopedia of Mormonism*. New York: Macmillan, 1992.

Mickler, M.L. *A History of the Unification Church in America*. New York: Garland, 1993.

Robinson, D. *The Unitarians and the Universalists*. Westport (CT): Greenwood Press, 1985.

Wright, C. *The Beginnings of Unitarianism in America*. Boston: Starr King Press, 1955.

Chapter 10: Islam

Ali, A.Y. *The Meaning of the Holy Qur'an*, 10th ed. Beltsville, MD: Amana Publications, rev. 2001.

Armstrong, K. *Islam: A Short History*. New York: Modern Library, 2000.

Esposito, J.L. The Oxford History of Islam, New York: Oxford University Press, 1999.

Farah, C.E. *Islam: Beliefs and Observances*, Woodbury, NY: Barrons, 1968.

Gibb, H.A.R, and Kramers, J.H. *Shorter Encyclopedia of Islam*. Ithaca, NY: Cornell University Press, 1953.

Hughes, Thomas Patrick. *A Dictionary of Islam*. London, Allen, 1885.

Rahman, Fazlur. *Islam*. Chicago: University of Chicago Press, 1979.

Smith, J.I. *Islam in America*. New York: Columbia University Press, 1999.

Wilson, J.C. *Introducing Islam*. New York: Friendship, 1958.

Chapter 11: Bahá'í

Bahá'í Publishing Trust. *Bahá'í Meetings: The Nineteen Day Feast; Extracts from the Writings of Bahá'u'lláh, 'Abdu'l-Bahá, and Shoghi Effendi.* Wilmette, IL: Bahá'í Publishing Trust, 1976.

Bahá'í World Centre. *The Bahá'í World: An International Record*. Haifa: Bahá'í World Centre. Published biennially.

Esslemont, John E. *Bahá'u'lláh and the New Era*. Wilmette, IL: Bahá'í Publishing Trust, 1950, 1970, 1980.

Gaver, Jessyca Russell. *The Bahá'í Faith*. New York: Award Books, 1967.

Hatcher, W.S. and Martin, J.D.. *The Bahá'í Faith: The Emerging Global Religion*. Rev. ed. Wilmette, IL: Bahá'í Publishing Trust, 1998.

Momen, W., ed. *A Basic Bahá'í Dictionary*. Oxford: George Ronald, 1996.

National Spiritual Assembly of the Bahá'ís of the United States. *The Bahá'í World: A Biennial International Record* XII (1950-1954) Wilmette, IL: Bahá'í Publishing Trust, 1956.

Perkins, Mary, and Philip Hainsworth. *The Bahá'í Faith*. London: Ward Lock Educational, 1980.

Smith, P. *A Concise Encyclopedia of the Bahá'í Faith*. Oxford: Oneworld, 2000.

Chapter 12: Hinduism

Berry, Thomas. *Religions of India*. New York: Bruce, 1971.

Fasts and Festivals of India. New Delhi: Diamond, n.d.

Flood, Gavin D. *An Introduction to Hinduism*. New York: Cambridge University Press, 1996.

Hopikins, J. T. *The Hindu Religious Tradition*. Encino, CA: Dickenson, 1971.

O'Flaherty, Wendy Doniger. *Hindu Myths*. Middlesex, England: Penguin Books, 1975.

Pitt, Malcolm. *Introducing Hinduism*. New York: Friendship, 1965.

Stutley, M. and J. Stutley. *Harper's Dictionary of Hinduism*. New York: Harper, 1977.

Stutley, Margaret. *Hinduism*. Wellingborough, Northamptonshire: The Aquarian Press, 1985.

Zaehner, R.C. *Hinduism*. New York: Oxford University Press, 1962.

Chapter 13: Jainism

Dundas, P. *The Jains*. New York: Routledge, 1992.

Jaini, J.M.A. *Outlines of Jainism*. Cambridge: Cambridge University Press, 1940. Republished by Hyperion Press, Inc., Westport, CT, 1982.

Chapter 14: Skihism

Arora, Ranjit. *Sikhism*. New York: Bookwright Press, 1987.

Cole, W. Owen, and Piara Singh Sambhi. *The Sikhs: Their Religious Beliefs and Practices*. London: Routledge & Kegan Paul, 1978.

McLeod, W. H. *The Sikhs: History, Religion, and Society*. New York: Columbia University Press, 1989.

Sikh Missionary Center. *Sikh Religion*. Detroit, MI: Sikh Missionary Center, 1990.

Chapter 15: Buddhism

Ch'en, Kenneth Kuan Sheng. *Buddhism: The Light of Asia*. Woodbury, NY: Barron's Educational Series, 1968.

Domoulin, Heinrich, ed. *Buddhism in the Modern World*. New York: Macmillain, 1976.

Donath, Dorothy C. *Buddhism for the West: Theravada, Mahayana, Vajrayana*. New York, NY: Julian Press, 1971.

Humphreys, Christmas. *Zen Buddhism*. New York: Macmillan, 1948?.

Jumsai, M. L. Manich. *Understanding Thai Buddhism*. 2d ed. Bangkok, Thailand: Chalermnit Press, 1973.

Lopez, D.S. *The Story of Buddhism: A Concise Guide to Its History and Teachings*. San Francisco, CA: Harper SanFrancisco, 2001.

Reat, N. R. *Buddhism: A History*. Berkeley, CA: Asian Humanities Press, 1994.

Waddell, L. A. *The Buddhism of Tibet or Lamaism*. 2d ed. Cambridge, Eng.: Heffer, 1939.

Zen Lotus Society. *Handbook of the Zen Lotus Society*. Toronto: Zen Lotus Society, 1986.

Chapter 16: Taoism, Confucianism, and Chinese Folk Religions

Creel, Henlee Glessner. *Confucious and the Chinese Way*. New York: Harper, 1960.

Fischer-Schreiber, I.; Schuhmacher, S.; and Woerner, G. *The Encyclopedia of Eastern Philosophy and Religion*. Boston: Shambhala, 1989.

Gerth, Hans H., ed. *The Religions of China: Confucianism and Taoism*. Glencoe, IL: Free Press, 1951.

Hartz, P. *Taoism*. New York: Facts on File, 1993.

Liu, Wu-chi. *Confucious: His Life and Time*. Westport, CT: Greenwood, 1972.

Rice, E. *Eastern Definitions: A Short Encyclopedia of Religions of the Orient*. New York: Doubleday, 1978.

Wong, Eva. *The Shambhala Guide to Taoism*. Boston, MA: Shambhala, 1997.

Chapter 17: Shinto

Bauer, Helen and Sherwin Carlquist. *Japanese Festivals*. Garden City, NY: Doubleday, 1965.

Hori, Ichiro. *Folk Religion in Japan: Continuity and Change*. Chicago: University of Chicago Press, 1968.

Kitagawa, J.M. *On Understanding Japanese Religion*. Princeton: Princeton University Press, 1987.

Littleton, C.S. *Shinto: Origins, Rituals, Festivals, Spirits, and Sacred Places*. New York: Oxford University Press, 2002.

Ono, S. *Shinto: The Kami Way*. Rutland, VT: Bridgeway, 1962.

Picken, S.D.B. *Shinto: Japan's Spiritual Roots*, New York: Kodansha International Ltd., 1980.

Ross, F. H. *Shinto: The Way of Japan*. Boston: Beacon, 1965.

Chapter 18: Native American Religions

Amsden, Charles. *The Prehistoric Southwest from Basketmaker to Pueblo*, Los Angeles: Southwest Museum, 1949.

Brandon, W. and Josephy, A.M. *The American Heritage Book of Indians*. New York: American Heritage Publishing Co. 1961.

Caso, Alfonso. *The Aztecs: People of the Sun*. Lowell Dunham tr. Norman, OK: University of Oklahoma Press, 1958.

Cordell, L.S. *Ancient Pueblo Peoples*. Washington: Smithsonian Books, 1994.

Crown, Patricia L., and Judge, W. James. *Chaco and Hohokam: Prehistoric Regional Systems in the American Southwest*. Santa Fe, NM: School of American Research Press, 1991.

Dale, E.E. *The Indians of the Southwest: A Century of Development under the United States*. Norman, OK: University of Oklahoma Press, 1949.

Danziger, Edumnd Jefferson, Jr. *The Chippewas of Lake Superior*. Norman, OK: University of Oklahoma Press, 1979. repr 1990.

Dozier, E.P. *The Pueblo Indians of North America*. New York: Holt, Rinehart and Winston, 1970.

Fergusson, Erna. *Dancing Gods: Indian Ceremonials of New Mexico and Arizona*. Albuquerque, NM: University of New Mexico, 1931; repr 1991.

Fewkes, Jesse Walter. *Hopi Snake Ceremonies*. Albuquerque, NM: 1986, 4th ed 1991.

Fewkes, Jesse Walter. *Tusayan Katchinas and Hopi Altars*. Albuquerque, NM: Avanyu Publishing, 1990.

Gill, Sam D. *Native American Religions*. Belmont, Ca: Wadsworth Publishing, 1982.

Hoxie, F.E. *Encyclopedia of North American Indians*. Boston: Houghton Mifflin Company, 1996.

Hultkrantz, Ake. *The Religions of the American Indians*. Trans. Monica Setterwall. Los Angeles, CA: University of California Press, 1979.

Indian Pueblo Cultural Center, "Welcome to the 19 Pueblos Information Pages," and linked information, http://www.indianpueblo.org; accessed September 2003.

Johnston, Charles M. *The Valley of the Six Nations: A Collection of Documents on the Indian Lands of the Grand River*. Toronto: Champlain Society for the Government of Ontario/University of Toronto, 1964.

Kroeber, A.L.; Kniffen, F.B.; Macgregor, G.; McKennan, R. Mekeel, S. and Mook, M. *Walapai Ethnography*. Menasha, WI: American Anthropological Association, 1935.

Lake, H. and Parker, A.C. *The Code of Handsome Lake, The Seneca Prophet*. Albany: University of the State of New York, 1913.

Navajo Nation Washington Office. "Navajo Nation Profile," www.nnwo.org/nnprofileprintable.htm; accessed September 2003.

Page, Jake and Page, Suzanne, "Inside the Sacred Hopi Homeland," *National Geographic*, vol. 162, November 1982, p. 606 (24).

Ruland-Thorne, Kate, and Caillou, Aliza. *Yavapai: The People of the Red Rocks, the People of the Sun*. Sedona, AZ: Thorne Enterprises Publications, 1993.

Swanton, J.R. *The Indian Tribes of North America*. Washington: U.S. Government Printing Office, 1952.

U.S. Census Bureau. "American Indian/Alaska Native Heritage Month: November 2002," *Facts for Features*. CB02-FF.17, October 21, 2002.

Waldman, C. *Atlas of the North American Indian, Revised Edition*. New York: Facts On File, 2000.

Waters, Frank. *Masked Gods: Navaho and Pueblo Ceremonialism*. Athens, OH: Swallow Press, 1950.

Waters, Frank. *Book of the Hopi*. New York: Ballantine, 1963.

Chapter 19: Paganism

Adler, Margot. *Drawing Down the Moon: Witches, Pagans, Druids, and Other Goddess-Worshippers in America Today*. 2d ed. NY: Viking Press, 1979. Boston: Beacon Press, 1987.

Berger, H.A. *A Community of Witches: Contemporary Neo-Paganism and Witchcraft in the United States*. Columbia, SC: University of South Carolina Press, 1999.

Buckland, Raymond. *The Tree: The Complete Book of Saxon Witchcraft*. York Beach, ME: Samuel Weiser, 1974.

Burland, C. A. *Echoes of Magic: A Study of Seasonal Festivals Through the Ages*. London: Peter Davies, 1972.

Campanelli, Pauline. *Wheel of the Year: Living the Magical Life*. St. Paul, MN: Llewellyn Publications, 1989.

Crowley, Aleister. *Magick in Theory and Practice*. NY: Dover Publications, 1976.

Farrar, Stewart, and Janet Farrar. *Eight Sabbats for Witches*. London: Robert Hale, 1981.

Farrar, Stewart, and Janet Farrar. *The Witches' Way: Principles, Rituals, amd Beliefs of Modern Witchcraft*. London: Robert Hale, 1984.

Ferguson, Diana. *The Magickal Year: A Pagan Perspective on the Natural Year*. New York: Quality Paperback Book Club, 1996.

Fitch, Ed, and Janine Renee. *Magical Rites from the Crystal Well*. St. Paul, MN: Llewellyn, 1984.

Frazer, Sir James G. *The Golden Bough*. 3d ed. 13 vols. London: Macmillan, 1912.

Gardner, Gerald B. *Witchcraft Today*. London: Jarrolds, 1954.

Graves, Robert. *The White Goddess: A Historical Grammar of Poetic Myth*. 3d ed. London: Faber & Faber, 1948.

Glass-Koentop, Pattalee. *Year of Moons, Season of Trees*. St. Paul, MN: Llewellyn Publications, 1991.

Harvey, Graham and Charlotte Hardman. *Paganism Today*. San Fransicso: Thorsons (an imprint of Harper Collins), 1995.

Hawkins, Gerald S. *Stonehenge Decoded*. NY: Doubleday, 1965.

Higginbotham, J. and Higginbotham, R. *Paganism: An Introduction to Earth-Centered Religions*. St. Paul, MN: Llewellyn Publications, 2002.

Hoyle, Sir Fred. *Stonehenge*. San Francisco: W. H. Freeman, 1976.

Hutton, R. *The Triumph of the Moon: A History of Modern Pagan Witchcraft*. New York: Oxford University Press, 1999.

Matthews, Caitlín. *The Celtic Book of Days: A Guide to Celtic Spirituality and Wisdom*. Rochester, VT: Destiny Books, 1995.

Murray, Margaret A. *The God of the Witches*. London: Oxford University Press, 1931.

Murray, Margaret A. *The Witch-Cult in Western Europe*. London: Oxford University Press, 1962.

Pennick, Nigel. *The Pagan Book of Days*. Rochester, VT: Destiny Books, 1992.

Price, Nancy. *Pagan's Progress: High Days and Holy Days*. London: Museum Press, 1954.

Rees, Aylwin, and Brinsley Rees. *Celtic Heritage: Ancient Tradition in Ireland and Wales*. London: Thames & Hudson, 1961.

Regardie, Israel. *The Golden Dawn: An Account of the Teachings, Rites, and Ceremonies of the Order of the Golden Dawn*. 2d ed. Minneapolis, MN: Hazel Hills, 1969.

Ross, Anne. *Pagan Celtic Britain: Studies in Iconography and Tradition*. New York: Columbia University Press, 1967.

Starhawk. *The Spiral Dance: A Rebirth of the Ancient Religion of the Great Goddess*. 2d ed. San Francisco, CA: Harper & Row, 1989.

Valiente, Doreen. *The Rebirth of Witchcraft*. London: Robert Hale, 1989.

Chapter 20: Western African Religions and Their New World Expressions

Anderson, David A. *The Origin of Life on Earth: An African Creation Myth*. Mt. Airy, MD: Sights Productions, 1991.

Barashango, Ishakamusa. *Afrikan People and European Holidays: A Mental Genocide, Book I*. Washington, D.C.: IV Dynasty Publishing, 1980.

Church of Lukumi Babalu Aye v. City of Hialeah, 508 U.S. 520 (1993).

Huxley, F. *The Invisibles, Voodoo Gods in Haiti*. New York: McGraw Hill, 1969.

Johnson, S. *The History of the Yorubas: From the Earliest Times to the Beginning of the British Protectorate*. Lagos, Nigeria: CSS Ltd., repr. 2001.

Mason, M.A. *Living Santería: Rituals and Experiences in an Afro-Cuban Religion*. Washington: Smithsonian Institution Press, 2002.

Murphy, Joseph M. *Santeria: African Spirits in America*. Boston, MA: Beacon Press, 1988; repr 1993.

Murphy, Joseph M. *Working the Spirit: Ceremonies of the African Diaspora*. Boston, MA: Beacon Press, 1994.

Smith, R.S. *Kingdoms of the Yoruba, Third Edition*. Madison, WI: University of Wisconsin Press, 1988

Chapter 21: Ancient Wisdom, Metaphysical, Other Faith Communities

Dawson, L.L. *Comprehending Cults: The Sociology of New Religious Movements*. Toronto and New York: Oxford University Press, 1998.

Harrison, P. *The Elements of Pantheism: Understanding the Divinity in Nature and the Universe*. Shaftesbury: Element, 1999.

Hubbard, L. Ron. *What Is Scientology?* Los Angeles, CA: Church of Scientology of California, 1978.

Jenkins, P. *Mystics and Messiahs: Cults and New Religions in American History*. New York: Oxford University Press, 2000.

Klemp, Harold. *A Modern Prophet Answers Your Key Questions about Life*. Minneapolis, MN: Eckankar, 1998.

Klemp, Harold. *The Art of Spiritual Dreaming*. Minneapolis, MN: Eckankar, 1999.

Lewis, J.R., *The Encyclopedia of Cults, Sects, and New Religions*. Amherst: Prometheus Books, 1998.

Melton, J.G. *Biographical Dictionary of American Cult and Sect Leaders*. New York and London: Garland Publishing Inc., 1986.

Ryan, Charles J. *H. P. Blavatsky and the Theosophical Movement*. Pasadena, CA: Theosophical University Press, 1974.

Illustrations

Illustrations on pages 61, 63, 149, 164, 171, 192, 194, 199, 212, 244, 251, 253, and 283 are by Alison DeKleine. © 2004 Omnigraphics, Inc.

Illustrations on pages 7, 8, 127, and 131 are by Melanie Manos. © 2004 Omnigraphics, Inc.

Illustrations on pages 48, 93, 120, 200, 226, 228, 242, and 262 are by Mary Ann Stavros-Lanning. © 2004 Omnigraphics, Inc.

The photograph on page 111 depicts "The Lady of Kazan" from a Russian cathedral, Library of Congress, Prints and Photographs Division, Frank and Frances Carpenter collection LC-USZ62-132527.

The illustration on page 141 is from a photograph taken by Abdullah Frères, Library of Congress, Prints and Photographs Division, Abdul Hamid II Collection, LC-USZ62-81550.

The photograph on page 153 depicts the terraces approaching the Shrine of the Báb, Mount Carmel. © 2003 Bahá'í World News Service. Reprinted by permission.

The photograph of a sand mandala on page 214 is © Melitta Tchiacovsky. Reprinted by permission.

The artwork on page 269 depicting the Holly King is by Joanna Powell Colbert, www.jpc-artworks.com. Reprinted by permission.

The photograph on page 284 of an egungun masquerade costume, provided by the Museum of African Art, New York, NY, was taken by Jerry L. Thompson. Reprinted by permission.

Additional Illustrations

Brewster, H. Pomeroy. *Saints and Festivals of the Christian Church*. New York: F.A. Stokes, 1904. Republished by Omnigraphics, Detroit, 1990.

Chambers, Robert. *The Book of Days, Vol 1*. London: W. & R. Chambers, 1862-1864. Republished by Omnigraphics, Detroit, 1990.

Cole, Herbert. *Heraldry and Floral Forms as Used in Decoration*. Drawings by the author. New York: Dutton, 1922. Republished by Omnigraphics, Detroit, 1992.

Edidin, Ben M. *Jewish Holidays and Festivals*. Illustrations by Kyra Markham. New York: Hebrew Pub. Co., 1940. Republished by Omnigraphics, Detroit, 1992.

Pike, Royston. *Round the Year with the World's Religions*. Drawings by E. C. Mansell. New York: Henry Schuman, 1950. Republished by Omnigraphics, Detroit, 1993.

Five-Year Chronological List of Holidays

Symbols and Abbreviations

Sn	Sunday
M	Monday
Tu	Tuesday
W	Wednesday
Th	Thursday
F	Friday
St	Saturday
GMT	Greenwich Mean Time; given for phases of the moon and other astronomical events
~	an approximate date for a celebration to be determined by divination, established by consensus, or set by other means using methods that cannot be accurately predicted

Regarding Zoroastrian Dates

F	According to the Fasli Calendar
S	According to the Shahanshahi Calendar
Q	According to the Qadimi Calendar

Regarding Christian Holidays

Christian	The holiday is observed by more than one Christian group.
Christian-RC	Roman Catholic
Christian-Pr	Protestant
Christian-J	Date observed by Christian groups following the Julian calendar
Christian-O	Orthodox Christian

Notes

Although care has been taken regarding the dates shown, they are not guaranteed. In some cases, dates can be inferred, but they are subject to change. For example, Islamic months begin with the sighting of the first crescent of the new moon. Although the astronomical new moon can be calculated accurately, methods used to estimate when the first crescent will be sighted vary and discrepancies are not uncommon. Hindu holidays are shown based on a lunar calendar beginning with the first day of the waxing moon. Because different calendars are used in different regions and among the different sects of Hinduism, all dates for Hindu holidays should be considered approximate. In other cases, precise dates are difficult to predict because the means by which they are set are not fully disclosed to the uninitiated or are determined by divination.

2004

January 1, 2004 (Th)
Feast of the Circumcision (Christian-RC); St. Basil's Day (Christian-O); God's Day (Unification); World Peace Day and the Universal Hour of Peace (Unitarian); Oshogatsu begins (Buddhist); Ganjitsu begins (Shinto); Annual Forecast (Santeria/Lukumi)

January 2, 2004 (F)
The Twelfth Night (Pagan)

January 4, 2004 (Sn)
perihelion 18:00 GMT
Universal Week of Prayer begins (Christian)

January 5, 2004 (M)
Epiphany Eve (Christian); Guru Gobind Singh's Birthday (Sikh)

January 6, 2004 (Tu)
Epiphany (Christian); Old Christmas Day (Christian-J); Feast of Epiphany (Christian-O); St. Distaff's Day (Pagan)

January 7, 2004 (W)
full moon 15:40 GMT
4th Feast of Dae (Zoroastrian-F); ~Bounding Bush (Cherokee)

January 11, 2004 (Sn)
Feast of the Holy Family (Christian-RC); Baptism of the Lord (Christian)

January 12, 2004 (M)
Plough Monday (Christian)

January 13, 2004 (Tu)
Paitishahem (Zoroastrian-Q); Death of George Fox (Christian-Quaker); ~Maghi (Sikh)

January 14, 2004 (W)
~Makar Sankranti (Hindu)

January 15, 2004 (Th)
last quarter 04:46 GMT
Rukmini Ashtami (Hindu); ~White Dog Feast (Iroquois)

January 16, 2004 (F)
Feast of Vohuman (Zoroastrian-F)

January 18, 2004 (Sn)
Feast of Mithra (Zoroastrian-Q); Blessing of Animals (Christian-RC); World Religion Day (Bahá'í)

January 19, 2004 (M)
Birthday of Martin Luther King, Jr. (Christian); Nineteen-Day Feast, 1st of Sultán (Bahá'í); Swarupa Dwadashi (Hindu)

January 20, 2004 (Tu)
~World Religions Day (Unitarian); ~Kwakiutl Winter Ceremonial

January 21, 2004 (W)
new moon 21:05 GMT
Feast of Shahrewar (Zoroastrian-S); Nirvana of Risabha (Jain)

January 22, 2004 (Th)
~Pongal (Hindu); ~Thaipusam (Hindu); Lunar New Year (Chinese Folk)

January 24, 2004
Alacitas (Aymara)

January 25, 2004 (Sn)
Conversion of St. Paul (Christian)

January 26, 2004 (M)
Vasant Pañcami (Hindu)

January 27, 2004 (Tu)
Up-Helly-Aa (Pagan)

January 29, 2004 (Th)
first quarter 06:03 GMT
Bhishma Ashtami (Hindu)

January 30, 2004 (F)
Three Hierarchs (Christian-O); Id al-Adha begins (Islamic); Making Happiness Festival (Chinese Folk)

February 1, 2004 (Sn)
Triodion begins (Christian-O); ~True Parents' Birthday (Unification); Al-'id al-Kabir (Islamic); 'Id al-Adha begins (Islamic); ~Losar (Buddhist); Imbolg (Pagan); Homstrom (Pagan)

February 2, 2004 (M)
Mihragan (Zoroastrian-Q); Presentation of Jesus (Christian); Presentation of Christ in the Temple (Christian-O); Gaelic Fire Festival (Pagan); Honoring Orisa Oya (Santeria/Lukumi)

February 3, 2004 (Tu)
Setsubun (Shinto); ~Midwinter Dream Festival (Iroquois)

February 4, 2004 (W)
~Monlam Chenmo begins (Buddhist)

February 5, 2004 (Th)
Arrival of Roger Williams in the New World (Christian-Baptist); Lantern Festival (Chinese Folk)

February 6, 2004 (F)
full moon 08:47 GMT
Magha Purnima (Hindu); Minakshi Float Festival (Hindu); Chinese New Year (Buddhist)

February 7, 2004 (St)
Tu Bishvat (Jewish); Nineteen-Day Feast, 1st of Mulk (Bahá'í)

February 8, 2004 (Sn)
Meatfare Sunday (Christian-O); Star Festival (Chinese Folk); Hari-Kuyo (Shinto)

February 10, 2004 (Tu)
Sakata Chauth (Hindu)

February 11, 2004 (W)
Birthday of Richard Allen (Christian African Methodist Episcopal)

February 12, 2004 (Th)
Ayathrem (Zoroastrian-Q); Paitishahem (Zoroastrian-S)

February 13, 2004 (F)
last quarter 13:40 GMT

February 14, 2004 (St)
First Saturday of Souls (Christian-O); Lupercalia begins (Pagan)

February 15, 2004 (Sn)
Race Relations Sunday (Christian); Cheesefare Sunday (Christian-O); Ramtha's Appearance (Ramtha's School of Enlightenment)

February 17, 2004 (Tu)
Feast of Mithra (Zoroastrian-S)

February 18, 2004 (W)
Feast of Spendarmad (Zoroastrian-F); Vartanantz Day (Christian-Armenian)

February 20, 2004 (F)
new moon 09:18 GMT
Mauni Amavasya (Hindu)

February 21, 2004 (St)
Second Saturday of Souls (Christian-O); ~Monkey God Festival (Taoist); Powamu Bean Dance begins (Hopi)

February 22, 2004 (Sn)
Fasching (Christian); Awwal Muharram (Islamic)

February 23, 2004 (M)
Rose Monday (Christian); Clean Monday (Christian-O); Great Lent begins (Christian-O)

February 24, 2004 (Tu)
Mardi Gras (Christian-RC); Carnival ends (Christian-RC); St. Matthias's Day (Christian)

February 25, 2004 (W)
Ash Wednesday (Christian); Lent begins (Christian)

February 26, 2004 (Th)
Aban Parab (Zoroastrian-Q); Ayyám-i-Há begins (Bahá'í)

February 27, 2004 (F)
World Day of Prayer (Christian)

February 28, 2004 (St)
first quarter 03:24 GMT
St. Theodore (Christian-O)

February 29, 2004 (Sn)
Quadragesima (Christian); Sunday of Orthodoxy (Christian-O)

March 1, 2004 (M)
Parents Day (Unification); Omizutori Matsuri begins (Buddhist)

March 2, 2004 (Tu)
Ashura (Islamic); Yevmi Ashurer (Islamic); Husayn Day (Islamic); Nineteen-Day Feast, 1st of 'Alá' (Bahá'í); The Fast begins (Bahá'í); Amalaka Ekadashi (Hindu)

March 3, 2004 (W)
Mihragan (Zoroastrian-S); Hina Matsuri (Shinto)

March 5, 2004 (F)
Holi (Hindu)

March 6, 2004 (St)
full moon 23:14 GMT
Ta'anit Esther (Jewish); Dol Purnima (Hindu)

March 7, 2004 (Sn)
Purim (Jewish); Sunday of St. Gregory Palamas (Christian-O)

March 11, 2004 (Th)
Muktad (Zoroastrian-F)

March 12, 2004 (F)
~Maple Dance (Iroquois)

March 13, 2004 (St)
last quarter 21:01 GMT
Ayathrem (Zoroastrian-S); Birthday of L. Ron Hubbard (Scientology)

March 14, 2004 (Sn)
Sunday of the Holy Cross (Christian-O); Scriptural New Year (Sikh); Hola Mohalla (Sikh)

March 17, 2004 (W)
St. Patrick's Day (Christian)

March 19, 2004 (F)
~Gangaur begins (Hindu)

March 20, 2004 (St)
new moon 22:41 GMT; spring equinox 06:49 GMT
Mahashivarati (Hindu); Vasanta Navaratra begins (Hindu); Spring Higan (Buddhist); First New Moon of Spring (Cherokee); ~Thunder Dance (Iroquois); Ostara (Pagan); ~Ibu Afo Festival (Yoruba); Spring Equinox (Pantheism)

March 21, 2004 (Sn)
Frawardin 1 (Zoroastrian-F); Nawruz (Zoroastrian-F); Mothering Sunday (Christian); Sunday of St. John Climacos (Christian-O); Festival of Naw-Rúz (Bahá'í); Nineteen-Day Feast, 1st of Bahá (Bahá'í); Gudi Parva (Hindu); Ugadi Parva (Hindu); ~Iduna and Summer Finding (Pagan)

March 22, 2004 (M)
~Mandi Safar (Islamic); Honoring Orisaoko (Santeria/Lukumi)

March 23, 2004 (Tu)
Liturgical New Year (Jewish)

March 24, 2004 (W)
Qing Ming Festival (Chinese Folk); ~Eagle Dance (Navajo and Others)

March 25, 2004 (Th)
Annunciation of the Lord (Christian); Feast of the Annunciation (Christian-O)

March 26, 2004 (F)
Hordad Sal (Zoroastrian-F); Adar Parab (Zoroastrian-Q); ~Bobo Masquerade (Yoruba)

March 27, 2004 (St)
Sabbath of Rabbi Isaac Mayer Wise (Jewish); Aban Parab (Zoroastrian-S)

March 28, 2004 (Sn)
first quarter 23:48 GMT
Sunday of St. Mary of Egypt (Christian-O); Caitra Parb (Hindu); Sitala Ashtami (Hindu); Ashokashtami (Hindu)

March 29, 2004 (M)
Ramanavami (Hindu)

April 1, 2004 (Th)
Miriam's Yahrzeit (Jewish); All Fool's Day (Pagan)

April 2, 2004 (F)
Birth of Mahavira (Jain); ~Planting Dances (Iroquois)

April 3, 2004 (St)
Lazarus Saturday (Christian-O)

April 4, 2004 (Sn)
Palm Sunday (Christian); Palm Sunday (Christian-O); Shah Abdul Latif Death Commemoration begins (Islamic-Sufi)

April 5, 2004 (M)
full moon 11:03 GMT
Fast of the First-born (Jewish); The Lord's Evening Meal (Jehovah's Witnesses); Passover (United Church of God); ~Panguni Uttiram (Hindu); ~Caitra Purnima (Hindu); Hanuman Jayanti (Hindu); Magha Puja (Buddhist); Rara Festival (Voodoo)

April 6, 2004 (Tu)
Passover (Jewish); Founding of the Church of Jesus Christ of Latter-Day Saints (Mormon); Festival of Unleavened Bread begins (United Church of God)

April 7, 2004 (W)
Sefirah (Jewish)

April 8, 2004 (Th)
Feast of Frawardignan (Zoroastrian-F); Maundy Thursday (Christian); Paschal Thursday (Christian-O); Data Ganj Baksh Death Festival begins (Islamic-Sufi)

April 9, 2004 (F)
Good Friday (Christian); Holy Friday (Christian-O); Nineteen-Day Feast, 1st of Jalál (Bahá'í)

April 10, 2004 (St)
Holy Saturday (Christian); Salvation Army Founder's Day (Christian-Salvation Army); Holy Saturday (Christian-O)

April 11, 2004 (Sn)
Easter (Christian); Easter (Christian-O); Foundation Day (Ramtha's School of Enlightenment)

April 12, 2004 (M)
last quarter 03:46 GMT
Bright Week begins (Christian-O); Matsu Festival (Taoist; Buddhist; Chinese Folk)

April 13, 2004 (Tu)
Maimona (Jewish); Songkran begins (Buddhist)

April 14, 2004 (W)
Baisakhi (Sikh); Guru Nanak's Day (Sikh)

April 17, 2004 (St)
1st Feast of Dae (Zoroastrian-Q)

April 18, 2004 (Sn)
Yom ha-Shoah (Jewish); Quasimodo (Christian); St. Thomas's Day (Christian-O)

April 19, 2004 (M)
new moon 13:21 GMT

April 20, 2004 (Tu)
Vaisakhi (Hindu); ~Pooram begins (Hindu); ~Chongmyo Taeje (Confucian)

April 21, 2004 (W)
Festival of Ridván begins (Bahá'í); ~Earth Day (Pagan)

April 22, 2004 (Th)
Feast of Ardwahist (Zoroastrian-F); ~Earth Day (Unitarian); Akshya Tritiya (Hindu); Parasurama Jayanti (Hindu); Chandan Yatra begins (Hindu); Aksaya Tratiya (Jain)

April 23, 2004 (F)
St. George's Day (Christian-O)

April 24, 2004 (St)
2nd Feast of Dae (Zoroastrian-Q); Sankaracarya Jayanti (Hindu)

April 25, 2004 (Sn)
Yom ha-Zikkaron (Jewish); Adar Parab (Zoroastrian-S); St. Mark's Day (Christian)

April 26, 2004 (M)
Yom ha-Atzma'ut (Jewish)

April 27, 2004 (Tu)
first quarter 17:32 GMT
Zarthastno Diso (Zoroastrian-Q); Tam Kung Festival (Taoist); Birthday of the Third Prince (Taoist)

April 28, 2004 (W)
Nineteen-Day Feast, 1st of Jamál (Bahá'í); Janaki Navami (Hindu)

April 30, 2004 (F)
Maidyozarem (Zoroastrian-F); St. James the Son of Zebedee (Christian-O); Walpurgis Night (Pagan)

May 1, 2004 (St)
3rd Feast of Dae (Zoroastrian-Q); Saint Philip and Saint James's Day (Christian); ~Day of All Things (Unification); Beltane (Pagan)

May 2, 2004 (Sn)
Maidyarem (Zoroastrian-Q); Family Week begins (Christian); Mawlid al-Nabi (Islamic)

May 3, 2004 (M)
Narsimha Jayanti (Hindu)

May 4, 2004 (Tu)
full moon 11:03 GMT
Vesak (Buddhist)

May 5, 2004 (W)
Children's Day (Shinto)

May 6, 2004 (Th)
National Day of Prayer (Unitarian)

May 8, 2004 (St)
Death of Helena Petrovna Blavatsky (Theosophy)

May 9, 2004 (Sn)
Lag ba-Omer (Jewish); 4th Feast of Dae (Zoroastrian-Q); May 9 Day (Scientology)

May 11, 2004 (Tu)
last quarter 11:04 GMT
Sts. Cyril and Methodios (Christian-O)

May 15, 2004 (St)
Aaronic Priesthood Commemoration (Mormon); Aoi Matsuri (Shinto); Sanja Matsuri (Shinto); ~Ibeji Ceremony (Yoruba)

May 17, 2004 (M)
Yom Yerushalayim (Jewish); 1st Feast of Dae (Zoroastrian-S); Rogation Days (Christian); Nineteen-Day Feast, 1st of 'Azamat (Bahá'í)

May 18, 2004 (Tu)
Feast of Vohuman (Zoroastrian-Q)

May 19, 2004 (W)
new moon 04:52 GMT
Mata Tirtha Snan (Hindu)

May 20, 2004 (Th)
Ascension Day (Christian); Ascension (Christian-O)

May 21, 2004 (F)
Sts. Constantine and Helen (Christian-O)

May 23, 2004 (Sn)
Aldersgate Experience (Christian-Methodist); Declaration of the Báb (Bahá'í)

May 24, 2004 (M)
2nd Feast of Dae (Zoroastrian-S)

May 25, 2004 (Tu)
Feast of Hordad (Zoroastrian-F); Sithinakha (Hindu)

May 26, 2004 (W)
Shavuot (Jewish); Pentecost (United Church of God)

May 27, 2004 (Th)
first quarter 07:57 GMT
Zarthastno Diso (Zoroastrian-S); Jyestha Ashtami (Hindu)

May 29, 2004 (St)
Fourth Saturday of Souls (Christian-O); Ascension of Bahá'-u'lláh (Bahá'í); Ganga Dussehra (Hindu); Ute Bear Dance (Ute)

May 30, 2004 (Sn)
Pentecost (Christian); Pentecost (Christian-O); Nirjala Ekadashi (Hindu)

May 31, 2004 (M)
3rd Feast of Dae (Zoroastrian-S); Feast of the Visitation (Christian-RC); Holy Spirit Day (Christian-O)

June 1, 2004 (Tu)
Maidyarem (Zoroastrian-S); Birthday of Brigham Young (Mormon); ~Egungun Festival (Yoruba)

June 3, 2004 (Th)
full moon 04:20 GMT
Snan Yatra (Hindu); Buddha Jayanti (Hindu); Poson (Buddhist); Sanghamitta Day (Buddhist)

June 4, 2004 (F)
Caturmas begins (Jain)

June 5, 2004 (St)
Nineteen-Day Feast, 1st of Núr (Bahá'í)

June 6, 2004 (Sn)
Trinity Sunday (Christian); All Saints' Day (Christian-O); Honoring Oshosi (Santeria/Lukumi)

June 8, 2004 (Tu)
4th Feast of Dae (Zoroastrian-S)

June 9, 2004 (W)
last quarter 20:02 GMT

June 10, 2004 (Th)
Corpus Christi (Christian-RC)

June 11, 2004 (F)
Sacred Heart of Jesus (Christian-RC); St. Barnabas's Day (Christian)

June 13, 2004 (Sn)
Immaculate Heart of Mary (Christian-RC); Children's Day (Christian); Race Unity Day (Bahá'í); Honoring Elegbara/Esu (Santeria/Lukumi)

June 14, 2004 (M)
Rice Planting Festivals (Shinto)

June 15, 2004 (Tu)
Magna Carta Day (Christian-Anglican); ~Strawberry Festival (Iroquois); ~Rosicrucian Thanksgiving Ritual (Rosicrucianism)

June 16, 2004 (W)
Vata Savitri (Hindu); Martyrdom Anniversary of Guru Arjan (Sikh)

June 17, 2004 (Th)
new moon 20:27 GMT

Feast of Vohuman (Zoroastrian-S); Lily Festival (Shinto)

June 19, 2004 (St)

Ratha Yatra (Hindu)

June 20, 2004 (Sn)

Feast of Spendarmad (Zoroastrian-Q); New Church Day (Swedenborgian); Midsummer Eve (Pagan)

June 21, 2004 (M)
summer solstice 00:57 GMT

Celebration of Unifying Principles (Unitarian); Sun Dance (Navajo and Others); Litha (Pagan); Summer Solstice (Pantheism)

June 24, 2004 (Th)

Nativity of St. John the Baptist (Christian); Birth of St. John the Baptist (Christian-O); Nineteen-Day Feast, 1st of Rahmat (Bahá'í); St. John's Day (Voodoo)

June 25, 2004 (F)
first quarter 19:08 GMT

~Eje (Yoruba)

June 27, 2004 (Sn)

~Footwashing Day (Christian-Pr); Martyrdom of Joseph and Hyrum Smith (Mormon)

June 28, 2004 (M)

Hari-Shayani Ekadashi (Hindu)

June 29, 2004 (Tu)

Maidyoshahem (Zoroastrian-F); St. Peter's Day (Christian); St. Peter and St. Paul (Christian-O)

June 30, 2004 (W)

Birthday of Lu Pan (Taoist); ~Green Corn Ceremony (Cherokee); Honoring Ogun (Santeria/Lukumi)

July 1, 2004 (Th)

Tiragan (Zoroastrian-F); Most Precious Blood (Christian-RC); ~Hemis Festival (Buddhist)

July 2, 2004 (F)
full moon 11:09 GMT

Guru Purnima (Hindu)

July 3, 2004 (St)

Seminole Green Corn Dance begins; Dog Days begin (Pagan)

July 5, 2004 (M)
aphelion 11:00 GMT

July 6, 2004 (Tu)

Fast of the Seventeenth of Tammuz (Jewish); Three Weeks of Mourning (Jewish); Birthday of the Dalai Lama (Buddhist)

July 7, 2004 (W)

Airing the Classics (Buddhist); Esala Perahera (Buddhist)

July 9, 2004 (F)
last quarter 07:34 GMT

Martyrdom of the Báb (Bahá'í)

July 10, 2004 (St)

~Pilgrimage of Saut D'Eau (Voodoo)

July 11, 2004 (Sn)

Muktad (Zoroastrian-Q)

July 13, 2004 (Tu)

Nineteen-Day Feast, 1st of Kalimát (Bahá'í); Obon Festival begins in some regions (Buddhist)

July 15, 2004 (Th)

St. Vladimir (Christian-O)

July 17, 2004 (St)
new moon 11:24 GMT

Hill Cumorah Pageant begins (Mormon); Gion Matsuri (Shinto)

July 18, 2004 (Sn)

~Sravani Mela (Hindu)

July 20, 2004 (Tu)

Feast of Spendarmad (Zoroastrian-S); Hariyali Teej (Hindu)

July 21, 2004 (W)

Frawardin 1 (Zoroastrian-Q); Nawruz (Zoroastrian-Q)

July 22, 2004 (Th)

Nag Pañcami (Hindu)

July 23, 2004 (F)

Birthday of Guru Har Krishan (Sikh); ~Waso begins (Buddhist)

July 24, 2004 (St)

Pioneer Day (Mormon); Tulsidas Jayanti (Hindu)

July 25, 2004 (Sn)
first quarter 03:37 GMT

Feast of Amurdad (Zoroastrian-F); St. James's Day (Christian); Reek Sunday (Christian-RC)

July 26, 2004 (M)

Hordad Sal (Zoroastrian-Q); Niman Dance (Hopi)

July 27, 2004 (Tu)

Tisha be-Av (Jewish)

July 28, 2004 (W)

Volunteers of America Founder's Day (Christian-Volunteers of America); Putrada Ekadashi (Hindu)

July 31, 2004 (St)
full moon 18:05 GMT

Narieli Purnima (Hindu); Raksa Bandhana (Hindu); Jhulan Latra (Hindu); Festival of Hungry Ghosts (Taoist; Buddhist; Chinese Folk); Lammas Eve (Pagan)

August 1, 2004 (Sn)
Nineteen-Day Feast, 1st of Kamál (Bahá'í); Lammas (Pagan); ~Anniversary of the Founding of Summit Lighthouse (Church of the Universal and Triumphant)

August 2, 2004 (M)
Marya (Buddhist)

August 6, 2004 (F)
Feast of the Transfiguration (Christian); Feast of the Transfiguration (Christian-O)

August 7, 2004 (St)
last quarter 22:01 GMT

August 8, 2004 (Sn)
Feast of Frawardignan (Zoroastrian-Q)

August 10, 2004 (Tu)
Muktad (Zoroastrian-S); ~Ripe Fruits Ceremony (Cherokee)

August 11, 2004 (W)
Kamada Ekadashi (Hindu)

August 12, 2004 (Th)
~New Corn Dance (Iroquois)

August 13, 2004 (F)
Obon Festival begins in some regions (Buddhist)

August 14, 2004 (St)
Ghanta Karna (Hindu)

August 15, 2004 (Sn)
Assumption of the Blessed Virgin (Christian-RC); Feast of the Dormition of the Theotokos (Christian-O); Floating Lantern Ceremony (Buddhist); ~Carnea (Pagan); ~Perseid Meteor Shower (Pantheism)

August 16, 2004 (M)
new moon 01:24 GMT

~Snake-Antelope Dance, Flute Ceremony, or Snake Dance (Navajo)

August 17, 2004 (Tu)
~Tirupati Festival (Hindu); ~Gokarna Aunsi (Hindu); ~Onam (Hindu); ~Monkey God Festival (Taoist); Odin's Ordeal begins (Pagan)

August 19, 2004 (Th)
Haritalika Teej (Hindu)

August 20, 2004 (F)
Frawardin 1 (Zoroastrian-S); Nawruz (Zoroastrian-S); Nineteen-Day Feast, 1st of Asmá' (Bahá'í); Ganesa Caturthi (Hindu)

August 21, 2004 (St)
Feast of Shahrewar (Zoroastrian-F); Rishi Pañcami (Hindu)

August 22, 2004 (Sn)
Feast of Ardwahist (Zoroastrian-Q); Queenship of Mary (Christian-RC)

August 23, 2004 (M)
first quarter 10:12 GMT

August 24, 2004 (Tu)
St. Bartholomew's Day (Christian); ~Creek Green Corn Ceremony

August 25, 2004 (W)
Hordad Sal (Zoroastrian-S); ~Gelede (Yoruba)

August 28, 2004 (St)
African Methodist Quarterly Meeting Day (Christian-African Methodist)

August 29, 2004 (Sn)
Martyrdom of St. John the Baptist (Christian); Christ the King (Christian-Pr)

August 30, 2004 (M)
full moon 02:22 GMT

Maidyozarem (Zoroastrian-Q); Anant Chaturdashi (Hindu)

August 31, 2004 (Tu)
Mid-Autumn Festival (Chinese Folk)

September 1, 2004 (W)
Church New Year (Christian-O); Installation of Sri Guru Granth Sahib (Sikh)

September 2, 2004 (Th)
San Estevan (Christian-RC); Shinbyu (Buddhist)

September 4, 2004 (St)
Partyshana Parva (Jain)

September 5, 2004 (Sn)
Halashashti (Hindu); Dasa Laksana Parvan begins (Jain)

September 6, 2004 (M)
last quarter 15:11 GMT

September 7, 2004 (Tu)
Feast of Frawardignan (Zoroastrian-S); Janmashtami (Hindu); Radha Ashtami (Hindu); Honoring Yemaya/Yemonja (Santeria/Lukumi)

September 8, 2004 (W)
Nativity of the Blessed Virgin Mary (Christian); Feast of the Nativity of the Theotokos (Christian-O); Nineteen-Day Feast, 1st of 'Izzat (Bahá'í)

September 11, 2004 (St)

Coptic New Year (Christian-Egyptian); Sante Fe Fiesta (Christian-RC); ~Indra Jatra (Hindu)

September 12, 2004 (Sn)

Paitishahem (Zoroastrian-F); Laylat al-Miraj (Islamic); Honoring Oshun (Santeria/Lukumi); Auditors' Day (Scientology)

September 13, 2004 (M)

Anata-Chaturdashi (Jain)

September 14, 2004 (Tu)
new moon 14:29 GMT

Triumph of the Holy Cross (Christian); Elevation of the Holy Cross (Christian-O)

September 15, 2004 (W)

Mary as Our Lady of Sorrows (Christian-RC); ~Laksmi Puja (Hindu); ~Durga Puja (Hindu); Festival of the Nine Imperial Gods begins (Taoist; Buddhist); ~Memorial Ceremony (Rosicrucianism)

September 16, 2004 (Th)

Civil New Year (Jewish); Rosh Hashanah (Jewish); Feast of Trumpets (United Church of God)

September 17, 2004 (F)

Ten Days of Teshuva (Jewish); Feast of Mithra (Zoroastrian-F); Founder's Day (Eckankar)

September 18, 2004 (St)

Fast of Gedaliah (Jewish)

September 21, 2004 (Tu)
first quarter 15:54 GMT

Feast of Ardwahist (Zoroastrian-S); St. Matthew's Day (Christian)

September 22, 2004 (W)
fall equinox 16:30 GMT

~Vatsa begins (Buddhist); Autumnal Higan (Buddhist); Mabon (Pagan); Winter Finding (Pagan); Autumn Equinox (Pantheism)

September 24, 2004 (F)

Feast of Hordad (Zoroastrian-Q); Dussehra (Hindu); ~Confucius's Birthday (Confucian); ~Lakon (Hopi and Navajo); Honoring Obatala (Santeria/Lukumi)

September 25, 2004 (St)

Yom Kippur (Jewish); Day of Atonement (United Church of God)

September 26, 2004 (Sn)

~A Good Crop Dance (Navajo)

September 27, 2004 (M)

Nineteen-Day Feast, 1st of Mashíyyat (Bahá'í); Honoring Orisa Ibeji (Santeria/Lukumi); Cosmas and Damian Day (Candomblé)

September 28, 2004 (Tu)
full moon 13:09 GMT

Sharad Purnima (Hindu); Kojagara (Hindu); Valmiki Jayanti (Hindu)

September 29, 2004 (W)

Maidyozarem (Zoroastrian-Q); Michaelmas (Christian); ~Pitra Visarjana Amavasya (Hindu); Ksamavani (Jain); Honoring Orisa Erinle (Santeria/Lukumi)

September 30, 2004 (Th)

Sukkot (Jewish); St. Gregory the Illuminator (Christian-O); Feast of Tabernacles begins (United Church of God); Shab-Barat (Islamic)

October 1, 2004 (F)

~Children's Day (Unification)

October 2, 2004 (St)

Mihragan (Zoroastrian-F); Guardian Angels Day (Christian-RC); Shiprock Navajo Nation Fair (Navajo)

October 3, 2004 (Sn)

~Rally Day (Christian-Pr)

October 4, 2004 (M)

Honoring Orisa Orunmila (Santeria/Lukumi)

October 5, 2004 (Tu)

Bodhidharma Day (Buddhist)

October 6, 2004 (W)
last quarter 10:12 GMT

Hoshana Rabbah (Jewish); St. Thomas's Day (Christian-O)

October 7, 2004 (Th)

Shemini Atzeret (Jewish); Mary as Our Lady of the Rosary (Christian-RC); Last Great Day (United Church of God); Founding of the International Association of Scientologists (Scientology)

October 8, 2004 (F)

Simhat Torah (Jewish)

October 9, 2004 (St)

Birthday of Guru Ram Das (Sikh)

October 12, 2004 (Tu)

Ayathrem (Zoroastrian-F)

October 14, 2004 (Th)
new moon 02:48 GMT

Sending the Winter Dress (Chinese Folk); Great New Moon Ceremony (Cherokee)

October 15, 2004 (F)

~Kartika Snan (Hindu); ~Skanda Shashti (Hindu); Govardhan Puja (Hindu); ~Divali (Sikh)

October 16, 2004 (St)
Ramadan begins (Islamic); Nineteen-Day Feast, 1st of 'Ilm (Bahá'í); Bhaiya Duj (Hindu)

October 18, 2004 (M)
St. Luke's Day (Christian)

October 20, 2004 (W)
first quarter 21:59 GMT
Birth of the Báb (Bahá'í); Surya Shashti (Hindu); Ebisu Festival (Shinto)

October 22, 2004 (F)
Spiritual New Year (Eckankar)

October 23, 2004 (St)
St. James the Brother of the Lord (Christian-O); Atohuna (Cherokee)

October 24, 2004 (Sn)
Feast of Hordad (Zoroastrian-S)

October 25, 2004 (M)
Devathani Ekadashi (Hindu)

October 26, 2004 (Tu)
Aban Parab (Zoroastrian-F); St. Demetrios (Christian-O)

October 28, 2004 (Th)
full moon 03:07 GMT
St. Simon and St. Jude's Day (Christian); Kartika Purnima (Hindu); Puskar Mela (Hindu)

October 29, 2004 (F)
Maidyoshahem (Zoroastrian-Q)

October 31, 2004 (Sn)
Tiragan (Zoroastrian-Q); Reformation Day (Christian-Pr); Oidhche Shamhna (Pagan)

November 1, 2004 (M)
All Saints' Day (Christian); Karwachauth (Hindu); Samhain (Pagan)

November 2, 2004 (Tu)
All Souls' Day (Christian)

November 4, 2004 (Th)
Nineteen-Day Feast, 1st of Qudrat (Bahá'í); ~Tihar (Hindu)

November 5, 2004 (F)
last quarter 05:53 GMT
Guy Fawkes's Night (Pagan)

November 8, 2004 (M)
Saints, Doctors, Missionaries, and Martyrs Day (Christian-Anglican); St. Michael and All Angels (Christian-O)

November 9, 2004 (Tu)
Dedication of St. John Lateran (Christian-RC)

November 10, 2004 (W)
Birthday of Martin Luther (Christian-Lutheran); Dhan Teras (Hindu)

November 11, 2004 (Th)
Laylat al-Qadr (Islamic); Narak Chaturdashi (Hindu); Wuwuchim (Hopi); Old Halloween (Pagan)

November 12, 2004 (F)
new moon 14:27 GMT
Birth of Bahá'u'lláh (Bahá'í); Dewali (Hindu); Diwali (Jain)

November 13, 2004 (St)
Lantern's Festival (Islamic)

November 14, 2004 (Sn)
St. Philip (Christian-O); Id al-Fitr begins (Islamic)

November 15, 2004 (M)
Advent begins (Christian-O); Shichi-Go-San (Shinto)

November 16, 2004 (Tu)
St. Matthew (Christian-O)

November 17, 2004 (W)
Jnan Panchami (Jain)

November 19, 2004 (F)
first quarter 05:50 GMT
Tazaungdaing (Buddhist)

November 21, 2004 (Sn)
Presentation of the Blessed Virgin Mary (Christian-RC); Christ the King (Christian-RC); Feast of the Presentation of the Theotokos (Christian-O); ~Fast for a World Harvest (Unitarian)

November 23, 2004 (Tu)
Nineteen-Day Feast, 1st of Qawl (Bahá'í); Gita Jayanti (Hindu); Vaikuntha Ekadashi (Hindu)

November 24, 2004 (W)
Adar Parab (Zoroastrian-F); Feast of Amurdad (Zoroastrian-Q); Martyrdom Anniversary of Guru Teg Bahadur (Sikh)

November 25, 2004 (Th)
Thanksgiving (Christian); St. Catherine (Christian-O); Thanksgiving (Christian Science)

November 26, 2004 (F)
full moon 20:07 GMT
Day of the Covenant (Bahá'í); Dattatreya Jayanti (Hindu)

November 28, 2004 (Sn)
Maidyoshahem (Zoroastrian-S); Advent begins (Christian); Bible Sunday (Christian-Pr); Ascension of 'Abdu'l-Bahá (Bahá'í)

November 30, 2004 (Tu)

Tiragan (Zoroastrian-S); St. Andrew's Day (Christian)

December 1, 2004 (W)

Mother Seton Day (Christian-RC); ~Festival of Lights (Buddhist); ~ Shalako Ceremonial (Pueblo)

December 4, 2004 (St)

St. Barbara and St. John of Damascus (Christian-O); Bhairava Ashtami (Hindu); Honoring Orisa Shango (Santeria/Lukumi)

December 5, 2004 (Sn)
last quarter 00:53 GMT

December 6, 2004 (M)

St. Nicholas's Day (Christian); St. Nicholas's Day (Christian-O)

December 7, 2004 (Tu)

Vaikuntha Ekadashi (Hindu); Vaitarani (Hindu)

December 8, 2004 (W)

Hanukkah (Jewish); Immaculate Conception of Mary (Christian-RC); Rohatsu (Buddhist)

December 9, 2004 (Th)

Holy Theotokos (Christian-O)

December 10, 2004 (F)

~Human Rights Day (Unitarian); ~Geminid Meteor Shower (Pantheism)

December 12, 2004 (Sn)
new moon 01:29 GMT

Feast of the Forebearers of Christ (Christian-O); Nineteen-Day Feast, 1st of Masá'il (Bahá'í); ~Ta Chiu (Taoist)

December 13, 2004 (M)

Saint Lucy's Day (Christian)

December 14, 2004 (Tu)

~Lohri (Sikh)

December 16, 2004 (Th)

1st Feast of Dae (Zoroastrian-F); Posadas (Christian)

December 17, 2004 (F)

Honoring Babalu Aye (Santeria/Lukumi)

December 18, 2004 (St)
first quarter 16:40 GMT

December 20, 2004 (M)

The Mother Night (Pagan)

December 21, 2004 (Tu)
winter solstice 12:42 GMT

Feast of Shahrewar (Zoroastrian-Q); St. Thomas's Day (Christian); Winter Solstice (Chinese Folk); Soyal (Hopi); Guatemalan Winter Solstice (Mayan); Yule (Pagan); Winter Solstice (Pantheism)

December 22, 2004 (W)

Asarah be-Tevet (Jewish); New Year for Trees (Pagan); The Day that Is Not a Day (Pagan)

December 23, 2004 (Th)

2nd Feast of Dae (Zoroastrian-F)

December 24, 2004 (F)

Feast of Amurdad (Zoroastrian-S); Christmas Eve (Christian)

December 25, 2004 (St)

Christmas Day (Christian); Feast of the Nativity of Our Lord (Christian-O); ~Saturnalia (Pagan)

December 26, 2004 (Sn)
full moon 15:06 GMT

Zarthastno Diso (Zoroastrian-F); St. Stephen's Day (Christian); Synaxis of the Holy Theotokos (Christian-O)

December 27, 2004 (M)

St. John the Evangelist's Day (Christian); St. Stephen's Day (Christian-O)

December 28, 2004 (Tu)

Holy Innocents' Day (Christian)

December 29, 2004 (W)

Holy Innocents' Day (Christian-O)

December 30, 2004 (Th)

3rd Feast of Dae (Zoroastrian-F)

December 31, 2004 (F)

Maidyarem (Zoroastrian-F); Nineteen-Day Feast, 1st of Sharaf (Bahá'í); Omisoka (Shinto); Hogmany (Pagan)

2005

January 1, 2005 (St)

Feast of the Circumcision (Christian-RC); St. Basil's Day (Christian-O); God's Day (Unification); World Peace Day and the Universal Hour of Peace (Unitarian); Oshogatsu begins (Buddhist); Ganjitsu begins (Shinto); Annual Forecast (Santeria/Lukumi)

January 2, 2005 (Sn)
perihelion 01:00 GMT

Universal Week of Prayer begins (Christian); Kitchen God Festival (Taoist; Chinese Folk); The Twelfth Night (Pagan)

January 3, 2005 (M)
last quarter 17:46 GMT

Rukmini Ashtami (Hindu)

January 5, 2005 (W)

Epiphany Eve (Christian); Birth of Parsvanath (Jain); Guru Gobind Singh's Birthday (Sikh)

January 6, 2005 (Th)
Epiphany (Christian); Old Christmas Day (Christian-J); Feast of Epiphany (Christian-O); St. Distaff's Day (Pagan)

January 7, 2005 (F)
4th Feast of Dae (Zoroastrian-F); Swarupa Dwadashi (Hindu); ~Bounding Bush (Cherokee)

January 9, 2005 (Sn)
Feast of the Holy Family (Christian-RC); Baptism of the Lord (Christian)

January 10, 2005 (M)
new moon 12:03 GMT
Plough Monday (Christian)

January 11, 2005 (Tu)
~Pongal (Hindu); ~Thaipusam (Hindu)

January 12, 2005 (W)
Paitishahem (Zoroastrian-Q)

January 13, 2005 (Th)
Death of George Fox (Christian-Quaker); ~Maghi (Sikh)

January 15, 2005 (St)
first quarter 06:57 GMT
Vasant Pañcami (Hindu); ~White Dog Feast (Iroquois)

January 16, 2005 (Sn)
Feast of Vohuman (Zoroastrian-F); Blessing of Animals (Christian-RC); World Religion Day (Bahá'í)

January 17, 2005 (M)
Feast of Mithra (Zoroastrian-Q); Birthday of Martin Luther King, Jr. (Christian)

January 18, 2005 (Tu)
Bhishma Ashtami (Hindu)

January 19, 2005 (W)
Pilgrimage to Mecca (Hajj) begins (Islamic); Nineteen-Day Feast, 1st of Sultán (Bahá'í)

January 20, 2005 (Th)
Feast of Shahrewar (Zoroastrian-S); ~World Religions Day (Unitarian); ~Kwakiutl Winter Ceremonial

January 21, 2005 (F)
Al-'id al-Kabir; 'Id al-Adha begins (Islamic)

January 24, 2005 (M)
Conversion of St. Paul (Christian); Alacitas (Aymara)

January 25, 2005 (Tu)
full moon 10:32 GMT
Tu Bishvat (Jewish); Magha Purnima (Hindu); Minakshi Float Festival (Hindu); Chinese New Year (Buddhist); Up-Helly-Aa (Pagan)

January 29, 2005 (St)
Sakata Chauth (Hindu)

January 30, 2005 (Sn)
Three Hierarchs (Christian-O)

February 1, 2005 (Tu)
Mihragan (Zoroastrian-Q); ~True Parents' Birthday (Unification); ~Losar (Buddhist); Imbolg (Pagan)

February 2, 2005 (W)
last quarter 07:27 GMT
Presentation of Jesus (Christian); Presentation of Christ in the Temple (Christian-O); Gaelic Fire Festival (Pagan); Honoring Orisa Oya (Santeria/Lukumi)

February 3, 2005 (Th)
Vartanantz Day (Christian-Armenian); Setsubun (Shinto); ~Midwinter Dream Festival (Iroquois)

February 4, 2005 (F)
~Monlam Chenmo begins (Buddhist)

February 5, 2005 (St)
Arrival of Roger Williams in the New World (Christian-Baptist)

February 6, 2005 (Sn)
Fasching (Christian); Homstrom (Pagan)

February 7, 2005 (M)
Rose Monday (Christian); Nineteen-Day Feast, 1st of Mulk (Bahá'í)

February 8, 2005 (Tu)
new moon 22:28 GMT
Mardi Gras (Christian-RC); Carnival ends (Christian-RC); Mauni Amavasya (Hindu); Nirvana of Risabha (Jain); Hari-Kuyo (Shinto)

February 9, 2005 (W)
Ash Wednesday (Christian); Lent begins (Christian); Lunar New Year (Chinese Folk); Powamu Bean Dance begins (Hopi)

February 10, 2005 (Th)
Awwal Muharram (Islamic)

February 11, 2005 (F)
Paitishahem (Zoroastrian-S); Ayathrem (Zoroastrian-Q); World Day of Prayer (Christian); Birthday of Richard Allen (Christian-African Methodist Episcopal)

February 13, 2005 (Sn)
Quadragesima (Christian); Race Relations Sunday (Christian)

February 14, 2005 (M)
Lupercalia begins (Pagan)

February 16, 2005 (W)
first quarter 00:16 GMT

Feast of Mithra (Zoroastrian-S)

February 17, 2005 (Th)

Making Happiness Festival (Chinese Folk)

February 18, 2005 (F)

Feast of Spendarmad (Zoroastrian-F)

February 19, 2005 (St)

Ashura (Islamic); Yevmi Ashurer (Islamic); Husayn Day (Islamic); Amalaka Ekadashi (Hindu)

February 20, 2005 (Sn)

Triodion begins (Christian-O); Ramtha's Appearance (Ramtha's School of Enlightenment)

February 22, 2005 (Tu)

Holi (Hindu)

February 23, 2005 (W)

Lantern Festival (Chinese Folk)

February 24, 2005 (Th)
full moon 04:54 GMT

St. Matthias's Day (Christian); Dol Purnima (Hindu)

February 25, 2005 (F)

Aban Parab (Zoroastrian-Q)

February 26, 2005 (St)

Ayyám-i-Há begins (Bahá'í); Star Festival (Chinese Folk)

February 27, 2005 (Sn)

Meatfare Sunday (Christian-O)

March 1, 2005 (Tu)

Parents Day (Unification); Omizutori Matsuri begins (Buddhist)

March 2, 2005 (W)

Nineteen-Day Feast, 1st of 'Alá' (Bahá'í); The Fast begins (Bahá'í)

March 3, 2005 (Th)
last quarter 17:36 GMT

Mihragan (Zoroastrian-S); Hina Matsuri (Shinto)

March 5, 2005 (St)

First Saturday of Souls (Christian-O)

March 6, 2005 (Sn)

Mothering Sunday (Christian); Cheesefare Sunday (Christian-O)

March 8, 2005 (Tu)

~Gangaur begins (Hindu)

March 10, 2005 (Th)
new moon 09:10 GMT

Mahashivarati (Hindu); Vasanta Navaratra begins (Hindu); ~Monkey God Festival (Taoist); First New Moon of Spring (Cherokee)

March 11, 2005 (F)

Muktad (Zoroastrian-F); Gudi Parva (Hindu); Ugadi Parva (Hindu)

March 12, 2005 (St)

Second Saturday of Souls (Christian-O); ~Mandi Safar (Islamic); ~Maple Dance (Iroquois)

March 13, 2005 (Sn)

Ayathrem (Zoroastrian-S); Birthday of L. Ron Hubbard (Scientology)

March 14, 2005 (M)

Clean Monday (Christian-O); Great Lent begins (Christian-O); Scriptural New Year (Sikh); Hola Mohalla (Sikh)

March 17, 2005 (Th)
first quarter 19:19 GMT

St. Patrick's Day (Christian); Caitra Parb (Hindu)

March 18, 2005 (F)

Sitala Ashtami (Hindu); Ashokashtami (Hindu)

March 19, 2005 (St)

St. Theodore (Christian-O); Ramanavami (Hindu)

March 20, 2005 (Sn)
spring equinox 12:33 GMT

Palm Sunday (Christian); Sunday of Orthodoxy (Christian-O); Spring Higan (Buddhist); ~Thunder Dance (Iroquois); Ostara (Pagan); ~Ibu Afo Festival (Yoruba); Spring Equinox (Pantheism)

March 21, 2005 (M)

Frawardin 1 (Zoroastrian-F); Nawruz (Zoroastrian-F); Festival of Naw-Rúz (Bahá'í); Nineteen-Day Feast, 1st of Bahá (Bahá'í); ~Iduna and Summer Finding (Pagan); Rara Festival (Voodoo)

March 22, 2005 (Tu)

Honoring Orisaoko (Santeria/Lukumi)

March 23, 2005 (W)

Birth of Mahavira (Jain)

March 24, 2005 (Th)

Ta'anit Esther (Jewish); Maundy Thursday (Christian); ~Eagle Dance (Navajo and Others)

March 25, 2005 (F)
full moon 20:58 GMT

Purim (Jewish); Good Friday (Christian); Feast of the Annunciation (Christian-O); Shah Abdul Latif Death Commemoration begins (Islamic-Sufi); ~Panguni Uttiram (Hindu); ~Caitra Purnima (Hindu); Hanuman Jayanti (Hindu); Magha Puja (Buddhist)

March 26, 2005 (St)

Sabbath of Rabbi Isaac Mayer Wise (Jewish); Hordad Sal (Zoroastrian-F); Adar Parab (Zoroastrian-Q); Holy Saturday (Christian); ~Bobo Masquerade (Yoruba)

March 27, 2005 (Sn)

Aban Parab (Zoroastrian-S); Easter (Christian); Sunday of St. Gregory Palamas (Christian-O); Foundation Day (Ramtha's School of Enlightenment)

March 29, 2005 (Tu)

Data Ganj Baksh Death Festival begins (Islamic-Sufi)

April 1, 2005 (F)

Annunciation of the Lord (Christian); All Fool's Day (Pagan)

April 2, 2005 (St)
last quarter 00:50 GMT

~Planting Dances (Iroquois)

April 3, 2005 (Sn)

Quasimodo Sunday (Christian); Sunday of the Holy Cross (Christian-O)

April 6, 2005 (W)

Founding of the Church of Jesus Christ of Latter-Day Saints (Mormon)

April 8, 2005 (F)
new moon 20:32 GMT

Feast of Frawardignan (Zoroastrian-F)

April 9, 2005 (St)

Nineteen-Day Feast, 1st of Jalál (Bahá'í)

April 10, 2005 (Sn)

Liturgical New Year (Jewish); Salvation Army Founder's Day (Christian-Salvation Army); Sunday of St. John Climacos (Christian-O)

April 11, 2005 (M)

Aksaya Tratiya (Jain)

April 12, 2005 (Tu)

Qing Ming Festival (Chinese Folk)

April 13, 2005 (W)

Songkran begins (Buddhist)

April 14, 2005 (Th)

Baisakhi (Sikh); Guru Nanak's Day (Sikh)

April 16, 2005 (St)
first quarter 14:37 GMT

April 17, 2005 (Sn)

1st Feast of Dae (Zoroastrian-Q); Sunday of St. Mary of Egypt (Christian-O)

April 19, 2005 (Tu)

Miriam's Yahrzeit (Jewish)

April 21, 2005 (Th)

Mawlid al-Nabi (Islamic); Festival of Ridván begins (Bahá'í); ~Earth Day (Pagan)

April 22, 2005 (F)

Feast of Ardwahist (Zoroastrian-F); ~Earth Day (Unitarian)

April 23, 2005 (St)

Fast of the First-born (Jewish); Lazarus Saturday (Christian-O); St. George's Day (Christian-O); The Lord's Evening Meal (Jehovah's Witnesses); Passover (United Church of God)

April 24, 2005 (Sn)
full moon 10:06 GMT

Passover (Jewish); 2nd Feast of Dae (Zoroastrian-Q); Palm Sunday (Christian-O); Festival of Unleavened Bread begins (United Church of God); Vesak (Buddhist)

April 25, 2005 (M)

Sefirah (Jewish); Adar Parab (Zoroastrian-S); St. Mark's Day (Christian)

April 27, 2005 (W)

Zarthastno Diso (Zoroastrian-Q)

April 28, 2005 (Th)

Paschal Thursday (Christian-O); Nineteen-Day Feast, 1st of Jamál (Bahá'í)

April 29, 2005 (F)

Holy Friday (Christian-O)

April 30, 2005 (St)

Maidyozarem (Zoroastrian-F); Holy Saturday (Christian-O); St. James the Son of Zebedee (Christian-O); Walpurgis Night (Pagan)

May 1, 2005 (Sn)
last quarter 06:24 GMT

Maimona (Jewish); 3rd Feast of Dae (Zoroastrian-Q); Saint Philip and Saint James's Day (Christian); Family Week begins (Christian); Rogation Sunday (Christian); Easter (Christian-O); ~Day of All Things (Unification); Matsu Festival (Taoist; Buddhist; Chinese Folk); Beltane (Pagan)

May 2, 2005 (M)

Maidyarem (Zoroastrian-Q); Rogation Days (Christian); Bright Week begins (Christian-O)

May 4, 2005 (W)

Ascension Day (Christian)

May 5, 2005 (Th)

National Day of Prayer (Unitarian); Children's Day (Shinto)

May 6, 2005 (F)

Yom ha-Shoah (Jewish)

May 8, 2005 (Sn)
new moon 08:45 GMT

St. Thomas's Day (Christian-O); ~Chongmyo Taeje (Confucian); Death of Helena Petrovna Blavatsky (Theosophy)

May 9, 2005 (M)

4th Feast of Dae (Zoroastrian-Q); Vaisakhi (Hindu) ~Pooram begins (Hindu); May 9 Day (Scientology)

May 11, 2005 (W)

Sts. Cyril and Methodios (Christian-O); Akshya Tritiya (Hindu); Parasurama Jayanti (Hindu); Chandan Yatra begins (Hindu)

May 13, 2005 (F)

Yom ha-Zikkaron (Jewish); Sankaracarya Jayanti (Hindu)

May 14, 2005 (St)

Yom ha-Atzma'ut (Jewish); Sanja Matsuri (Shinto)

May 15, 2005 (Sn)

Pentecost (Christian); Aaronic Priesthood Commemoration (Mormon); Tam Kung Festival (Taoist); Birthday of the Third Prince (Taoist); Aoi Matsuri (Shinto); ~Ibeji Ceremony (Yoruba)

May 16, 2005 (M)
first quarter 08:56 GMT

May 17, 2005 (Tu)

1st Feast of Dae (Zoroastrian-S); Nineteen-Day Feast, 1st of 'Azamat (Bahá'í); Janaki Navami (Hindu)

May 18, 2005 (W)

Feast of Vohuman (Zoroastrian-Q)

May 21, 2005 (St)

Sts. Constantine and Helen (Christian-O)

May 22, 2005 (Sn)

Trinity Sunday (Christian); Aldersgate Experience (Christian-Methodist); Narsimha Jayanti (Hindu)

May 23, 2005 (M)
full moon 20:18 GMT

Declaration of the Báb (Bahá'í); Poson (Buddhist); Sanghamitta Day (Buddhist)

May 24, 2005 (Tu)

2nd Feast of Dae (Zoroastrian-S)

May 25, 2005 (W)

Feast of Hordad (Zoroastrian-F)

May 26, 2005 (Th)

Corpus Christi (Christian-RC)

May 27, 2005 (F)

Lag ba-Omer (Jewish); Zarthastno Diso (Zoroastrian-S); Sacred Heart of Jesus (Christian-RC)

May 28, 2005 (St)

Ute Bear Dance (Ute)

May 29, 2005 (Sn)

Ascension of Bahá'u'lláh (Bahá'í)

May 30, 2005 (M)
last quarter 06:24 GMT

May 31, 2005 (Tu)

3rd Feast of Dae (Zoroastrian-S); Feast of the Visitation (Christian-RC)

June 1, 2005 (W)

Maidyarem (Zoroastrian-S); Birthday of Brigham Young (Mormon); ~Egungun Festival (Yoruba)

June 4, 2005 (St)

Yom Yerushalayim (Jewish); Immaculate Heart of Mary (Christian-RC)

June 5, 2005 (Sn)

Nineteen-Day Feast, 1st of Núr (Bahá'í)

June 6, 2005 (M)
new moon 21:55 GMT

Mata Tirtha Snan (Hindu); Honoring Oshosi (Santeria/Lukumi)

June 8, 2005 (W)

4th Feast of Dae (Zoroastrian-S)

June 9, 2005 (Th)

Ascension (Christian-O)

June 11, 2005 (St)

Children's Day (Christian); St. Barnabas's Day (Christian)

June 12, 2005 (Sn)

Race Unity Day (Bahá'í); Sithinakha (Hindu)

June 13, 2005 (M)

Shavuot (Jewish); Pentecost (United Church of God); Honoring Elegbara/Esu (Santeria/Lukumi)

June 14, 2005 (Tu)

Jyestha Ashtami (Hindu); Rice Planting Festivals (Shinto)

June 15, 2005 (W)
first quarter 01:22 GMT

Magna Carta Day (Christian-Anglican); ~Strawberry Festival (Iroquois); ~Rosicrucian Thanksgiving Ritual (Rosicrucianism)

June 16, 2005 (Th)

Ganga Dussehra (Hindu); Martyrdom Anniversary of Guru Arjan (Sikh)

June 17, 2005 (F)

Feast of Vohuman (Zoroastrian-S); Nirjala Ekadashi (Hindu); Lily Festival (Shinto)

June 18, 2005 (St)

Fourth Saturday of Souls (Christian-O)

June 19, 2005 (Sn)

Pentecost (Christian-O); New Church Day (Swedenborgian)

June 20, 2005 (M)

Feast of Spendarmad (Zoroastrian-Q); Holy Spirit Day (Christian-O); Midsummer Eve (Pagan)

June 21, 2005 (Tu)
summer solstice 06:46 GMT

Celebration of Unifying Principles (Unitarian); Sun Dance (Navajo and Others); Litha (Pagan); Summer Solstice (Pantheism)

June 22, 2005 (W)
full moon 04:14 GMT

Snan Yatra (Hindu); Buddha Jayanti (Hindu); Caturmas begins (Jain)

June 24, 2005 (F)

Nativity of St. John the Baptist (Christian); Birth of St. John the Baptist (Christian-O); Nineteen-Day Feast, 1st of Rahmat (Bahá'í); St. John's Day (Voodoo)

June 25, 2005 (St)

~Eje (Yoruba)

June 26, 2005 (Sn)

~Footwashing Day (Christian-Pr); All Saints' Day (Christian-O)

June 27, 2005 (M)

Martyrdom of Joseph and Hyrum Smith (Mormon); Airing the Classics (Buddhist); Esala Perahera (Buddhist)

June 28, 2005 (Tu)
last quarter 18:23 GMT

June 29, 2005 (W)

Maidyoshahem (Zoroastrian-F); St. Peter's Day (Christian); St. Peter and St. Paul (Christian-O)

June 30, 2005 (Th)

~Green Corn Ceremony (Cherokee); Honoring Ogun (Santeria/Lukumi)

July 1, 2005 (F)

Tiragan (Zoroastrian-F); Most Precious Blood (Christian-RC); ~Hemis Festival (Buddhist)

July 3, 2005 (Sn)

Seminole Green Corn Dance begins; Dog Days begin (Pagan)

July 5, 2005 (Tu)
aphelion 05:00 GMT

Vata Savitri (Hindu)

July 6, 2005 (W)
new moon 12:02 GMT

Birthday of the Dalai Lama (Buddhist)

July 8, 2005 (F)

Ratha Yatra (Hindu)

July 9, 2005 (St)

Martyrdom of the Báb (Bahá'í)

July 10, 2005 (Sn)

~Pilgrimage of Saut D'Eau (Voodoo)

July 11, 2005 (M)

Muktad (Zoroastrian-Q)

July 13, 2005 (W)

Nineteen-Day Feast, 1st of Kalimát (Bahá'í); Obon Festival begins in some regions (Buddhist)

July 14, 2005 (Th)
first quarter 15:20 GMT

July 15, 2005 (F)

St. Vladimir (Christian-O)

July 16, 2005 (St)

Hill Cumorah Pageant begins (Mormon)

July 17, 2005 (Sn)

Hari-Shayani Ekadashi (Hindu); Gion Matsuri (Shinto)

July 19, 2005 (Tu)

Birthday of Lu Pan (Taoist)

July 20, 2005 (W)

Feast of Spendarmad (Zoroastrian-S)

July 21, 2005 (Th)
full moon 11:00 GMT

Frawardin 1 (Zoroastrian-Q); Nawruz (Zoroastrian-Q); Guru Purnima (Hindu)

July 23, 2005 (St)

Birthday of Guru Har Krishan (Sikh); ~Waso begins (Buddhist); Marya (Buddhist)

July 24, 2005 (Sn)

Fast of the Seventeenth of Tammuz (Jewish); Three Weeks of Mourning (Jewish); Pioneer Day (Mormon)

July 25, 2005 (M)

Feast of Amurdad (Zoroastrian-F); St. James's Day (Christian)

July 26, 2005 (Tu)

Hordad Sal (Zoroastrian-Q); Niman Dance (Hopi)

July 28, 2005 (Th)
last quarter 03:19 GMT

Volunteers of America Founder's Day (Christian-Volunteers of America)

July 31, 2005 (Sn)

Reek Sunday (Christian-RC); Lammas Eve (Pagan)

August 1, 2005 (M)

Nineteen-Day Feast, 1st of Kamál (Bahá'í); Lammas (Pagan); ~Anniversary of the Founding of Summit Lighthouse (Church of the Universal and Triumphant)

August 5, 2005 (F)
new moon 03:05 GMT

August 6, 2005 (St)

Feast of the Transfiguration (Christian); Feast of the Transfiguration (Christian-O); ~Sravani Mela (Hindu)

August 8, 2005 (M)

Feast of Frawardignan (Zoroastrian-Q); Hariyali Teej (Hindu)

August 10, 2005 (W)

Muktad (Zoroastrian-S); Nag Pañcami (Hindu); ~Ripe Fruits Ceremony (Cherokee)

August 12, 2005 (F)

Tulsidas Jayanti (Hindu); ~New Corn Dance (Iroquois)

August 13, 2005 (St)
first quarter 02:38 GMT

Obon Festival begins in some regions (Buddhist)

August 14, 2005 (Sn)

Tisha be-Av (Jewish); Auditors' Day (Scientology)

August 15, 2005 (M)

Assumption of the Blessed Virgin (Christian-RC); Feast of the Dormition of the Theotokos (Christian-O); Floating Lantern Ceremony (Buddhist); ~Carnea (Pagan); ~Perseid Meteor Shower (Pantheism)

August 16, 2005 (Tu)

Putrada Ekadashi (Hindu); ~Snake-Antelope Dance, Flute Ceremony, or Snake Dance (Navajo)

August 17, 2005 (W)

Odin's Ordeal begins (Pagan)

August 19, 2005 (F)
full moon 17:53 GMT

Narieli Purnima (Hindu); Raksa Bandhana (Hindu); Jhulan Latra (Hindu); Festival of Hungry Ghosts (Taoist; Buddhist; Chinese Folk)

August 20, 2005 (St)

Frawardin 1 (Zoroastrian-S); Nawruz (Zoroastrian-S); Nineteen-Day Feast, 1st of Asmá' (Bahá'í)

August 21, 2005 (Sn)

Feast of Shahrewar (Zoroastrian-F)

August 22, 2005 (M)

Feast of Ardwahist (Zoroastrian-Q); Queenship of Mary (Christian-RC)

August 24, 2005 (W)

St. Bartholomew's Day (Christian); Partyshana Parva (Jain); ~Creek Green Corn Ceremony

August 25, 2005 (Th)

Hordad Sal (Zoroastrian-S); Dasa Laksana Parvan begins (Jain); ~Gelede (Yoruba)

August 26, 2005 (F)
last quarter 15:18 GMT

August 27, 2005 (St)

African Methodist Quarterly Meeting Day (Christian-African Methodist Episcopal)

August 29, 2005 (M)

Martyrdom of St. John the Baptist (Christian)

August 30, 2005 (Tu)

Maidyozarem (Zoroastrian-Q); Kamada Ekadashi (Hindu)

August 31, 2005 (W)

Feast of Christ the King (Christian-Pr)

September 1, 2005 (Th)

Church New Year (Christian-O); Installation of Sri Guru Granth Sahib (Sikh)

September 2, 2005 (F)

San Estevan (Christian-RC); Laylat al-Miraj (Islamic); Ghanta Karna (Hindu); Anata-Chaturdashi (Jain); Shinbyu (Buddhist)

September 3, 2005 (St)
new moon 18:45 GMT
~Monkey God Festival (Taoist)

September 4, 2005 (Sn)

~Tirupati Festival (Hindu); ~Gokarna Aunsi (Hindu); ~Onam (Hindu)

September 6, 2005 (Tu)

Haritalika Teej (Hindu)

September 7, 2005 (W)

Feast of Frawardignan (Zoroastrian-S); Ganesa Caturthi (Hindu); Honoring Yemaya/Yemonja (Santeria/Lukumi)

September 8, 2005 (Th)

Nativity of the Blessed Virgin Mary (Christian-RC); Feast of the Nativity of the Theotokos (Christian-O); Nineteen-Day Feast, 1st of 'Izzat (Bahá'í); Rishi Pañcami (Hindu)

September 10, 2005 (St)

Sante Fe Fiesta (Christian-RC)

September 11, 2005 (Sn)
first quarter 11:37 GMT

Coptic New Year (Christian-Egyptian)

September 12, 2005 (M)

Paitishahem (Zoroastrian-F); Honoring Oshun (Santeria/Lukumi)

September 14, 2005 (W)

Triumph of the Holy Cross (Christian); Elevation of the Holy Cross (Christian-O)

September 15, 2005 (Th)

Mary as Our Lady of Sorrows (Christian-RC); ~Memorial Ceremony (Rosicrucianism)

September 17, 2005 (St)

Feast of Mithra (Zoroastrian-F); Anant Chaturdashi (Hindu); Mid-Autumn Festival (Chinese Folk); Founder's Day (Eckankar)

September 18, 2005 (Sn)
full moon 02:01 GMT

September 19, 2005 (M)

Shab-Barat (Islamic); Ksamavani (Jain)

September 21, 2005 (W)

Feast of Ardwahist (Zoroastrian-S); St. Matthew's Day (Christian)

September 22, 2005 (Th)
fall eqiunox 22:23 GMT

~Vatsa begins (Buddhist); Autumnal Higan (Buddhist); Mabon (Pagan); Winter Finding (Pagan); Autumn Equinox (Pantheism)

September 24, 2005 (St)

Feast of Hordad (Zoroastrian-Q); Halashashti (Hindu); ~Lakon (Hopi and Navajo); Honoring Obatala (Santeria/Lukumi)

September 25, 2005 (Sn)
last quarter 06:41 GMT

September 26, 2005 (M)

Janmashtami (Hindu); Radha Ashtami (Hindu); ~A Good Crop Dance (Navajo)

September 27, 2005 (Tu)

Nineteen-Day Feast, 1st of Mashíyyat (Bahá'í); Honoring Orisa Ibeji (Santeria/Lukumi); Cosmas and Damian Day (Candomblé)

September 29, 2005 (Th)

Maidyozarem (Zoroastrian-Q); Michaelmas (Christian); ~Indra Jatra (Hindu); Honoring Orisa Erinle (Santeria/Lukumi)

September 30, 2005 (F)

St. Gregory the Illuminator (Christian-O)

October 1, 2005 (St)

~Children's Day (Unification); Shiprock Navajo Nation Fair (Navajo)

October 2, 2005 (Sn)

Mihragan (Zoroastrian-F); Guardian Angels Day (Christian-RC); ~ Rally Day (Christian-Pr)

October 3, 2005 (M)
new moon 10:28 GMT

Festival of the Nine Imperial Gods begins (Taoist; Buddhist); Great New Moon Ceremony (Cherokee)

October 4, 2005 (Tu)

Civil New Year (Jewish); Rosh Hashanah (Jewish); Feast of Trumpets (United Church of God); ~Laksmi Puja (Hindu); ~Durga Puja (Hindu); Honoring Orisa Orunmila (Santeria/Lukumi)

October 5, 2005 (W)

Ten Days of Teshuva (Jewish); Ramadan begins (Islamic); Bodhidharma Day (Buddhist)

October 6, 2005 (Th)

Fast of Gedaliah (Jewish); St. Thomas's Day (Christian-O)

October 7, 2005 (F)

Mary as Our Lady of the Rosary (Christian-RC); Founding of the International Association of Scientologists (Scientology)

October 9, 2005 (Sn)

Birthday of Guru Ram Das (Sikh)

October 10, 2005 (M)
first quarter 19:01 GMT

October 12, 2005 (W)

Ayathrem (Zoroastrian-F); ~Confucius's Birthday (Confucian); Atohuna (Cherokee)

October 13, 2005 (Th)

Yom Kippur (Jewish); Day of Atonement (United Church of God); Dussehra (Hindu)

October 15, 2005 (St)

~Divali (Sikh)

October 16, 2005 (Sn)

Nineteen-Day Feast, 1st of 'Ilm (Bahá'í)

October 17, 2005 (M)
full moon 12:14 GMT

Sharad Purnima (Hindu); Kojagara (Hindu); Valmiki Jayanti (Hindu)

October 18, 2005 (Tu)

Sukkot (Jewish); St. Luke's Day (Christian); Feast of Tabernacles begins (United Church of God); ~Pitra Visarjana Amavasya (Hindu)

October 20, 2005 (Th)

Birth of the Báb (Bahá'í); Ebisu Festival (Shinto)

October 22, 2005 (St)

Spiritual New Year (Eckankar)

October 23, 2005 (Sn)

St. James the Brother of the Lord (Christian-O)

October 24, 2005 (M)

Hoshana Rabbah (Jewish); Feast of Hordad (Zoroastrian-S)

October 25, 2005 (Tu)
last quarter 01:17 GMT

Shemini Atzeret (Jewish); Last Great Day (United Church of God)

October 26, 2005 (W)

Simhat Torah (Jewish); Aban Parab (Zoroastrian-F); St. Demetrios (Christian-O)

October 28, 2005 (F)

St. Simon and St. Jude's Day (Christian)

October 29, 2005 (St)

Maidyoshahem (Zoroastrian-Q)

October 31, 2005 (M)

Tiragan (Zoroastrian-Q); Reformation Day (Christian-Pr); Laylat al-Qadr (Islamic); Oidhche Shamhna (Pagan)

November 1, 2005 (Tu)

All Saints' Day (Christian); Diwali (Jain); Wuwuchim (Hopi); Samhain (Pagan)

November 2, 2005 (W)
new moon 01:24 GMT

All Souls' Day (Christian)

November 3, 2005 (Th)

Lantern's Festival (Islamic); ~Kartika Snan (Hindu); ~Skanda Shashti (Hindu); Govardhan Puja (Hindu); Sending the Winter Dress (Chinese Folk)

November 4, 2005 (F)

Id al-Fitr begins (Islamic); Nineteen-Day Feast, 1st of Qudrat (Bahá'í); Bhaiya Duj (Hindu)

November 5, 2005 (St)

Guy Fawkes's Night (Pagan)

November 7, 2005 (M)

Jnan Panchami (Jain)

November 8, 2005 (Tu)

Saints, Doctors, Missionaries, and Martyrs Day (Christian-Anglican); St. Michael and All Angels (Christian-O); Surya Shashti (Hindu)

November 9, 2005 (W)
first quarter 01:57 GMT

Dedication of St. John Lateran (Christian-RC)

November 10, 2005 (Th)

Birthday of Martin Luther (Christian-Lutheran)

November 11, 2005 (F)

Old Halloween (Pagan)

November 12, 2005 (St)

Birth of Bahá'u'lláh (Bahá'í)

November 13, 2005 (Sn)

Devathani Ekadashi (Hindu)

November 14, 2005 (M)

St. Philip (Christian-O)

November 15, 2005 (Tu)

Advent begins (Christian-O); Shichi-Go-San (Shinto)

November 16, 2005 (W)
full moon 00:57 GMT

St. Matthew (Christian-O); Kartika Purnima (Hindu); Puskar Mela (Hindu)

November 19, 2005 (St)

Tazaungdaing (Buddhist)

November 20, 2005 (Sn)

Feast of Christ the King (Christian-RC); Karwachauth (Hindu)

November 21, 2005 (M)

Presentation of the Blessed Virgin Mary (Christian-RC); Feast of the Presentation of the Theotokos (Christian-O); ~Fast for a World Harvest (Unitarian)

November 23, 2005 (W)
last quarter 22:11 GMT

Nineteen-Day Feast, 1st of Qawl (Bahá'í); ~Tihar (Hindu)

November 24, 2005 (Th)

Adar Parab (Zoroastrian-F); Feast of Amurdad (Zoroastrian-Q); Thanksgiving (Christian); Thanksgiving (Christian Science); Martyrdom Anniversary of Guru Teg Bahadur (Sikh)

November 25, 2005 (F)
St. Catherine (Christian-O)

November 26, 2005 (St)
Day of the Covenant (Bahá'í)

November 27, 2005 (Sn)
Advent begins (Christian); Bible Sunday (Christian-Pr)

November 28, 2005 (M)
Maidyoshahem (Zoroastrian-S); Ascension of 'Abdu'l-Bahá (Bahá'í)

November 29, 2005 (Tu)
Dhan Teras (Hindu)

November 30, 2005 (W)
Tiragan (Zoroastrian-S); St. Andrew's Day (Christian); Narak Chaturdashi (Hindu)

December 1, 2005 (Th)
new moon 15:01 GMT

Mother Seton Day (Christian-RC); Dewali (Hindu); ~Festival of Lights (Buddhist); ~ Shalako Ceremonial (Pueblo)

December 2, 2005 (F)
~Ta Chiu (Taoist)

December 4, 2005 (Sn)
St. Barbara and St. John of Damascus (Christian-O); Honoring Orisa Shango (Santeria/Lukumi)

December 6, 2005 (Tu)
St. Nicholas's Day (Christian); St. Nicholas's Day (Christian-O)

December 8, 2005 (Th)
first quarter 09:36 GMT

Feast of the Immaculate Conception of Mary (Christian-RC); Rohatsu (Buddhist)

December 9, 2005 (F)
Holy Theotokos (Christian-O)

December 10, 2005 (St)
~Human Rights Day (Unitarian); ~Geminid Meteor Shower (Pantheism)

December 11, 2005 (Sn)
Feast of the Forebearers of Christ (Christian-O)

December 12, 2005 (M)
Nineteen-Day Feast, 1st of Masá'il (Bahá'í); Gita Jayanti (Hindu); Vaikuntha Ekadashi (Hindu)

December 13, 2005 (Tu)
Saint Lucy's Day (Christian)

December 14, 2005 (W)
~Lohri (Sikh)

December 15, 2005 (Th)
full moon 16:15 GMT

Dattatreya Jayanti (Hindu)

December 16, 2005 (F)
1st Feast of Dae (Zoroastrian-F); Posadas (Christian)

December 17, 2005 (St)
Honoring Babalu Aye (Santeria/Lukumi)

December 20, 2005 (Tu)
The Mother Night (Pagan)

December 21, 2005 (W)
winter solstice 18:35 GMT

Feast of Shahrewar (Zoroastrian-Q); St. Thomas's Day (Christian); Soyal (Hopi); Guatemalan Winter Solstice (Mayan; Yule (Pagan); Winter Solstice (Pantheism)

December 22, 2005 (Th)
Winter Solstice (Chinese Folk); New Year for Trees (Pagan); The Day that Is Not a Day (Pagan)

December 23, 2005 (F)
last quarter 19:36 GMT

2nd Feast of Dae (Zoroastrian-F); Bhairava Ashtami (Hindu)

December 24, 2005 (St)
Feast of Amurdad (Zoroastrian-S); Christmas Eve (Christian); Kitchen God Festival (Taoist; Chinese Folk)

December 25, 2005 (Sn)
Christmas Day (Christian); Feast of the Nativity of Our Lord (Christian-O); Birth of Parsvanath (Jain); ~Saturnalia (Pagan)

December 26, 2005 (M)
Hanukkah (Jewish); Zarthastno Diso (Zoroastrian-F); St. Stephen's Day (Christian); Synaxis of the Holy Theotokos (Christian-O); Vaikuntha Ekadashi (Hindu); Vaitarani (Hindu)

December 27, 2005 (Tu)
St. John the Evangelist's Day (Christian); St. Stephen's Day (Christian-O)

December 28, 2005 (W)
Holy Innocents' Day (Christian)

December 29, 2005 (Th)
Holy Innocents' Day (Christian-O)

December 30, 2005 (F)
3rd Feast of Dae (Zoroastrian-F)

December 31, 2005 (St)
new moon 03:12 GMT

Maidyarem (Zoroastrian-F); Nineteen-Day Feast, 1st of Sharaf (Bahá'í); Omisoka (Shinto); Hogmany (Pagan)

2006

January 1, 2006 (Sn)

Feast of the Circumcision (Christian-RC); Universal Week of Prayer begins (Christian); St. Basil's Day (Christian-O); God's Day (Unification); World Peace Day and the Universal Hour of Peace (Unitarian); Oshogatsu begins (Buddhist); Ganjitsu begins (Shinto); Annual Forecast (Santeria/Lukumi)

January 2, 2006 (M)

The Twelfth Night (Pagan)

January 4, 2006 (W)

perihelion 15+B755:00 GMT

January 5, 2006 (Th)

Epiphany Eve (Christian); Guru Gobind Singh's Birthday (Sikh)

January 6, 2006 (F)

first quarter 18:56 GMT

Epiphany (Christian); Old Christmas Day (Christian-J); Feast of Epiphany (Christian-O); St. Distaff's Day (Pagan)

January 7, 2006 (St)

4th Feast of Dae (Zoroastrian-F); ~Bounding Bush (Cherokee)

January 8, 2006 (Sn)

Feast of the Baptism of the Lord (Christian); Feast of the Holy Family (Christian-RC); Pilgrimage to Mecca (Hajj) begins (Islamic)

January 9, 2006 (M)

Plough Monday (Christian)

January 10, 2006 (Tu)

Asarah be-Tevet (Jewish); Al-'id al-Kabir; 'Id al-Adha begins (Islamic)

January 12, 2006 (Th)

Paitishahem (Zoroastrian-Q)

January 13, 2006 (F)

Death of George Fox (Christian-Quaker); ~Maghi (Sikh)

January 14, 2006 (St)

full moon 09:48 GMT

~Makar Sankranti (Hindu)

January 15, 2006 (Sn)

World Religion Day (Bahá'í); ~White Dog Feast (Iroquois)

January 16, 2006 (M)

Feast of Vohuman (Zoroastrian-F); Birthday of Martin Luther King, Jr. (Christian)

January 17, 2006 (Tu)

Feast of Mithra (Zoroastrian-Q); Blessing of Animals (Christian-RC)

January 19, 2006 (Th)

Nineteen-Day Feast, 1st of Sultán (Bahá'í)

January 20, 2006 (F)

Feast of Shahrewar (Zoroastrian-S); ~World Religions Day (Unitarian); ~Kwakiutl Winter Ceremonial

January 22, 2006 (Sn)

last quarter 15:14 GMT

Rukmini Ashtami (Hindu)

January 24, 2006 (Tu)

Alacitas (Aymara)

January 25, 2006 (W)

Conversion of St. Paul (Christian)

January 26, 2006 (Th)

Swarupa Dwadashi (Hindu)

January 28, 2006 (St)

Nirvana of Risabha (Jain)

January 29, 2006 (Sn)

new moon 14:15 GMT

Lunar New Year (Chinese Folk)

January 30, 2006 (M)

Three Hierarchs (Christian-O); ~Pongal (Hindu); ~Thaipusam (Hindu)

January 31, 2006 (Tu)

Awwal Muharram (Islamic); Up-Helly-Aa (Pagan)

February 1, 2006 (W)

Mihragan (Zoroastrian-Q); ~True Parents' Birthday (Unification); ~Losar (Buddhist); Imbolg (Pagan)

February 2, 2006 (Th)

Presentation of Jesus (Christian); Presentation of Christ in the Temple (Christian-O); Gaelic Fire Festival (Pagan); Honoring Orisa Oya (Santeria/Lukumi)

February 3, 2006 (F)

Vasant Pañcami (Hindu); Setsubun (Shinto); ~Midwinter Dream Festival (Iroquois)

February 4, 2006 (St)

~Monlam Chenmo begins (Buddhist)

February 5, 2006 (Sn)

first quarter 6:29 GMT

Arrival of Roger Williams in the New World (Christian-Baptist); Making Happiness Festival (Chinese Folk); Homstrom (Pagan)

February 6, 2006 (M)

Bhishma Ashtami (Hindu)

February 7, 2006 (Tu)

Nineteen-Day Feast, 1st of Mulk (Bahá'í)

February 8, 2006 (W)

Hari-Kuyo (Shinto)

February 9, 2006 (Th)

Ashura (Islamic); Yevmi Ashurer (Islamic); Husayn Day (Islamic)

February 11, 2006 (St)

Paitishahem (Zoroastrian-S); Ayathrem (Zoroastrian-Q); Birthday of Richard Allen (Christian-African Methodist Episcopal)

February 12, 2006 (Sn)

Race Relations Sunday (Christian); Triodion begins (Christian-O); Lantern Festival (Chinese Folk)

February 13, 2006 (M)
full moon 04:44 GMT

Tu Bishvat (Jewish); Magha Purnima (Hindu); Minakshi Float Festival (Hindu); Chinese New Year (Buddhist)

February 14, 2006 (Tu)

Lupercalia begins (Pagan)

February 15, 2006 (W)

Star Festival (Chinese Folk)

February 16, 2006 (Th)

Feast of Mithra (Zoroastrian-S)

February 17, 2006 (F)

Sakata Chauth (Hindu)

February 18, 2006 (St)

Feast of Spendarmad (Zoroastrian-F)

February 19, 2006 (Sn)

Meatfare Sunday (Christian-O); Ramtha's Appearance (Ramtha's School of Enlightenment)

February 21, 2006 (Tu)
last quarter 07:17 GMT

February 23, 2006 (Th)

Vartanantz Day (Christian-Armenian)

February 24, 2006 (F)

St. Matthias's Day (Christian)

February 25, 2006 (St)

Aban Parab (Zoroastrian-Q); First Saturday of Souls (Christian-O)

February 26, 2006 (Sn)

Fasching (Christian); Cheesefare Sunday (Christian-O); Ayyám-i-Há begins (Bahá'í)

February 27, 2006 (M)

Rose Monday (Christian)

February 28, 2006 (Tu)
new moon 00:31 GMT

Mardi Gras (Christian-RC); Carnival ends (Christian-RC); Mauni Amavasya (Hindu); ~Monkey God Festival (Taoist)

March 1, 2006 (W)

Ash Wednesday (Christian); Lent begins (Christian); Parents Day (Unification); ~Mandi Safar (Islamic); Omizutori Matsuri begins (Buddhist); Powamu Bean Dance begins (Hopi)

March 2, 2006 (Th)

Nineteen-Day Feast, 1st of 'Alá' (Bahá'í); The Fast begins (Bahá'í)

March 3, 2006 (F)

Mihragan (Zoroastrian-S); World Day of Prayer (Christian); Hina Matsuri (Shinto)

March 4, 2006 (St)

Second Saturday of Souls (Christian-O)

March 5, 2006 (Sn)

Quadragesima (Christian)

March 6, 2006 (M)
first quarter 20:16 GMT

Clean Monday (Christian-O); Great Lent begins (Christian-O)

March 11, 2006 (St)

Muktad (Zoroastrian-F); St. Theodore (Christian-O); Amalaka Ekadashi (Hindu)

March 12, 2006 (Sn)

Sunday of Orthodoxy (Christian-O); ~Maple Dance (Iroquois)

March 13, 2006 (M)

Ta'anit Esther (Jewish); Ayathrem (Zoroastrian-S); Birth of Mahavira (Jain); Birthday of L. Ron Hubbard (Scientology)

March 14, 2006 (Tu)
full moon 23:35 GMT

Purim (Jewish); Shah Abdul Latif Death Commemoration begins (Islamic-Sufi); Holi (Hindu); Dol Purnima (Hindu); Scriptural New Year (Sikh); Hola Mohalla (Sikh)

March 17, 2006 (F)

St. Patrick's Day (Christian)

March 18, 2006 (St)

Data Ganj Baksh Death Festival begins (Islamic-Sufi)

March 19, 2006 (Sn)

Sunday of St. Gregory Palamas (Christian-O)

March 20, 2006 (M)
spring equinox 18:26 GMT

Spring Higan (Buddhist); ~Thunder Dance (Iroquois); Ostara (Pagan); ~Ibu Afo Festival (Yoruba); Spring Equinox (Pantheism)

March 21, 2006 (Tu)

Frawardin 1 (Zoroastrian-F); Nawruz (Zoroastrian-F); Festival of Naw-Rúz (Bahá'í); Nineteen-Day Feast, 1st of Bahá (Bahá'í); ~Iduna and Summer Finding (Pagan)

March 22, 2006 (W)
last quarter 19:10 GMT

Honoring Orisaoko (Santeria/Lukumi)

March 24, 2006 (F)

~Eagle Dance (Navajo and Others)

March 25, 2006 (St)

Sabbath of Rabbi Isaac Mayer Wise (Jewish); Annunciation of the Lord (Christian); Feast of the Annunciation (Christian-O)

March 26, 2006 (Sn)

Hordad Sal (Zoroastrian-F); Adar Parab (Zoroastrian-Q); Mothering Sunday (Christian-RC); Sunday of the Holy Cross (Christian-O); ~Bobo Masquerade (Yoruba)

March 27, 2006 (M)

Aban Parab (Zoroastrian-S)

March 28, 2006 (Tu)

Mahashivarati (Hindu); Vasanta Navaratra begins (Hindu); ~Gangaur begins (Hindu)

March 29, 2006 (W)
new moon 10:15 GMT

Gudi Parva (Hindu); Ugadi Parva (Hindu); First New Moon of Spring (Cherokee)

March 30, 2006 (Th)

Liturgical New Year (Jewish)

April 1, 2006 (St)

Aksaya Tratiya (Jain); Qing Ming Festival (Chinese Folk); All Fool's Day (Pagan)

April 2, 2006 (Sn)

Sunday of St. John Climacos (Christian-O); ~Planting Dances (Iroquois)

April 5, 2006 (W)
first quarter 12:01 GMT

Caitra Parb (Hindu); Sitala Ashtami (Hindu); Ashokashtami (Hindu)

April 6, 2006 (Th)

Founding of the Church of Jesus Christ of Latter-Day Saints (Mormon); Ramanavami (Hindu)

April 8, 2006 (St)

Miriam's Yahrzeit (Jewish); Feast of Frawardignan (Zoroastrian-F)

April 9, 2006 (Sn)

Palm Sunday (Christian); Sunday of St. Mary of Egypt (Christian-O); Nineteen-Day Feast, 1st of Jalál (Bahá'í)

April 10, 2006 (M)

Salvation Army Founder's Day (Christian-Salvation Army); Rara Festival (Voodoo)

April 11, 2006 (Tu)

Mawlid al-Nabi (Islamic)

April 12, 2006 (W)

Fast of the First-born (Jewish); The Lord's Evening Meal (Jehovah's Witnesses); Passover (United Church of God)

April 13, 2006 (Th)
full moon 16:40 GMT

Passover (Jewish); Maundy Thursday (Christian); Festival of Unleavened Bread begins (United Church of God); ~Panguni Uttiram (Hindu); ~Caitra Purnima (Hindu); Hanuman Jayanti (Hindu); Songkran begins (Buddhist); Magha Puja (Buddhist)

April 14, 2006 (F)

Sefirah (Jewish); Good Friday (Christian); Baisakhi (Sikh); Guru Nanak's Day (Sikh)

April 15, 2006 (St)

Holy Saturday (Christian); Lazarus Saturday (Christian-O)

April 16, 2006 (Sn)

Easter (Christian); Palm Sunday (Christian-O); Foundation Day (Ramtha's School of Enlightenment)

April 17, 2006 (M)

1st Feast of Dae (Zoroastrian-Q)

April 20, 2006 (Th)

Maimona (Jewish); Paschal Thursday (Christian-O)

April 21, 2006 (F)
last quarter 03:28 GMT

Holy Friday (Christian-O); Festival of Ridván begins (Bahá'í); Matsu Festival (Taoist; Buddhist; Chinese Folk); ~Earth Day (Pagan)

April 22, 2006 (St)

Feast of Ardwahist (Zoroastrian-F); Holy Saturday (Christian-O); ~Earth Day (Unitarian)

April 23, 2006 (Sn)

Quasimodo Sunday (Christian); Easter (Christian-O); St. George's Day (Christian-O)

April 24, 2006 (M)

2nd Feast of Dae (Zoroastrian-Q); Bright Week begins (Christian-O)

April 25, 2006 (Tu)
Yom ha-Shoah (Jewish); Adar Parab (Zoroastrian-S); St. Mark's Day (Christian)

April 27, 2006 (Th)
new moon 19:44 GMT
Zarthastno Diso (Zoroastrian-Q)

April 28, 2006 (F)
Nineteen-Day Feast, 1st of Jamál (Bahá'í); Vaisakhi (Hindu) ~Pooram begins (Hindu); ~Chongmyo Taeje (Confucian)

April 30, 2006 (Sn)
Maidyozarem (Zoroastrian-F); St. Thomas's Day (Christian-O); St. James the Son of Zebedee (Christian-O); Akshya Tritiya (Hindu); Parasurama Jayanti (Hindu); Chandan Yatra begins (Hindu); Walpurgis Night (Pagan)

May 1, 2006 (M)
3rd Feast of Dae (Zoroastrian-Q); Saint Philip and Saint James's Day (Christian); ~Day of All Things (Unification); Beltane (Pagan)

May 2, 2006 (Tu)
Yom ha-Zikkaron (Jewish); Maidyarem (Zoroastrian-Q); Sankaracarya Jayanti (Hindu)

May 3, 2006 (W)
Yom ha-Atzma'ut (Jewish)

May 4, 2006 (Th)
National Day of Prayer (Unitarian)

May 5, 2006 (F)
first quarter 05:13 GMT
Tam Kung Festival (Taoist); Birthday of the Third Prince (Taoist); Children's Day (Shinto)

May 6, 2006 (St)
Janaki Navami (Hindu)

May 7, 2006 (Sn)
Family Week begins (Christian)

May 8, 2006 (M)
Death of Helena Petrovna Blavatsky (Theosophy)

May 9, 2006 (Tu)
4th Feast of Dae (Zoroastrian-Q); May 9 Day (Scientology)

May 11, 2006 (Th)
Sts. Cyril and Methodios (Christian-O); Narsimha Jayanti (Hindu)

May 13, 2006 (St)
full moon 06:51 GMT
Vesak (Buddhist); Sanja Matsuri (Shinto)

May 15, 2006 (M)
Aaronic Priesthood Commemoration (Mormon); Aoi Matsuri (Shinto); ~Ibeji Ceremony (Yoruba)

May 16, 2006 (Tu)
Lag ba-Omer (Jewish)

May 17, 2006 (W)
1st Feast of Dae (Zoroastrian-S); Nineteen-Day Feast, 1st of 'Azamat (Bahá'í)

May 18, 2006 (Th)
Feast of Vohuman (Zoroastrian-Q)

May 20, 2006 (St)
last quarter 09:21 GMT

May 21, 2006 (Sn)
Rogation Sunday (Christian); Aldersgate Experience (Christian-Methodist); Sts. Constantine and Helen (Christian-O)

May 22, 2006 (M)
Rogation Days (Christian)

May 23, 2006 (Tu)
Declaration of the Báb (Bahá'í)

May 24, 2006 (W)
Yom Yerushalayim (Jewish); 2nd Feast of Dae (Zoroastrian-S)

May 25, 2006 (Th)
Feast of Hordad (Zoroastrian-F); Ascension Day (Christian)

May 27, 2006 (St)
new moon 05:26 GMT
Zarthastno Diso (Zoroastrian-S); Mata Tirtha Snan (Hindu); Ute Bear Dance (Ute)

May 29, 2006 (M)
Ascension of Bahá'u'lláh (Bahá'í)

May 31, 2006 (W)
3rd Feast of Dae (Zoroastrian-S); Feast of the Visitation (Christian-RC)

June 1, 2006 (Th)
Maidyarem (Zoroastrian-S); Ascension (Christian-O); Birthday of Brigham Young (Mormon); ~Egungun Festival (Yoruba)

June 2, 2006 (F)
Shavuot (Jewish); Pentecost (United Church of God); Sithinakha (Hindu)

June 3, 2006 (St)
first quarter 23:06 GMT

June 4, 2006 (Sn)
Pentecost (Christian); Jyestha Ashtami (Hindu)

June 5, 2006 (M)
Nineteen-Day Feast, 1st of Núr (Bahá'í)

June 6, 2006 (Tu)

Ganga Dussehra (Hindu); Honoring Oshosi (Santeria/Lukumi)

June 7, 2006 (W)

Nirjala Ekadashi (Hindu)

June 8, 2006 (Th)

4th Feast of Dae (Zoroastrian-S)

June 10, 2006 (St)

Fourth Saturday of Souls (Christian-O)

June 11, 2006 (Sn)

full moon 18:03 GMT

Trinity Sunday (Christian); Children's Day (Christian); St. Barnabas's Day (Christian); Pentecost (Christian-O); Race Unity Day (Bahá'í); Snan Yatra (Hindu); Buddha Jayanti (Hindu); Poson (Buddhist); Sanghamitta Day (Buddhist)

June 12, 2006 (M)

Holy Spirit Day (Christian-O); Caturmas begins (Jain)

June 13, 2006 (Tu)

Honoring Elegbara/Esu (Santeria/Lukumi)

June 14, 2006 (W)

Rice Planting Festivals (Shinto)

June 15, 2006 (Th)

Corpus Christi (Christian-RC); Magna Carta Day (Christian-Anglican); ~Strawberry Festival (Iroquois); ~Rosicrucian Thanksgiving Ritual (Rosicrucianism)

June 16, 2006 (F)

Feast of the Sacred Heart of Jesus (Christian-RC); Martyrdom Anniversary of Guru Arjan (Sikh)

June 17, 2006 (St)

Feast of Vohuman (Zoroastrian-S); Lily Festival (Shinto)

June 18, 2006 (Sn)

last quarter 14:08 GMT

All Saints' Day (Christian-O); New Church Day (Swedenborgian)

June 20, 2006 (Tu)

Feast of Spendarmad (Zoroastrian-Q); Midsummer Eve (Pagan)

June 21, 2006 (W)

summer solstice 12:26 GMT

Celebration of Unifying Principles (Unitarian); Sun Dance (Navajo and Others); Litha (Pagan); Summer Solstice (Pantheism)

June 24, 2006 (St)

Feast of the Immaculate Heart of Mary (Christian-RC); Nativity of St. John the Baptist (Christian); Birth of St. John the Baptist (Christian-O); Nineteen-Day Feast, 1st of Rahmat (Bahá'í); Vata Savitri (Hindu); St. John's Day (Voodoo)

June 25, 2006 (Sn)

new moon 16:05 GMT

~Footwashing Day (Christian-Pr); ~Eje (Yoruba)

June 27, 2006 (Tu)

Martyrdom of Joseph and Hyrum Smith (Mormon); Ratha Yatra (Hindu)

June 29, 2006 (Th)

Maidyoshahem (Zoroastrian-F); St. Peter's Day (Christian); St. Peter and St. Paul (Christian-O)

June 30, 2006 (F)

~Green Corn Ceremony (Cherokee); Honoring Ogun (Santeria/Lukumi)

July 1, 2006 (St)

Tiragan (Zoroastrian-F); Most Precious Blood (Christian-RC); ~Hemis Festival (Buddhist)

July 3, 2006 (M)

first quarter 16:37 GMT

aphelion 23+B1281:00 GMT

Seminole Green Corn Dance begins; Dog Days begin (Pagan)

July 6, 2006 (Th)

Hari-Shayani Ekadashi (Hindu); Birthday of the Dalai Lama (Buddhist)

July 7, 2006 (F)

Birthday of Lu Pan (Taoist)

July 9, 2006 (Sn)

Martyrdom of the Báb (Bahá'í)

July 10, 2006 (M)

~Pilgrimage of Saut D'Eau (Voodoo)

July 11, 2006 (Tu)

full moon 03:02 GMT

Muktad (Zoroastrian-Q); Guru Purnima (Hindu)

July 13, 2006 (Th)

Fast of the Seventeenth of Tammuz (Jewish); Three Weeks of Mourning (Jewish); Nineteen-Day Feast, 1st of Kalimát (Bahá'í); Obon Festival begins in some regions (Buddhist)

July 15, 2006 (St)

St. Vladimir (Christian-O); Hill Cumorah Pageant begins (Mormon)

July 16, 2006 (Sn)

Airing the Classics (Buddhist); Esala Perahera (Buddhist)

July 17, 2006 (M)

last quarter 19:13 GMT

Gion Matsuri (Shinto)

July 20, 2006 (Th)

Feast of Spendarmad (Zoroastrian-S)

July 21, 2006 (F)

Frawardin 1 (Zoroastrian-Q); Nawruz (Zoroastrian-Q)

July 23, 2006 (Sn)

Birthday of Guru Har Krishan (Sikh); ~Waso begins (Buddhist)

July 24, 2006 (M)

Pioneer Day (Mormon)

July 25, 2006 (Tu)

new moon 04:31 GMT

Feast of Amurdad (Zoroastrian-F); St. James's Day (Christian)

July 26, 2006 (W)

Hordad Sal (Zoroastrian-Q); ~Sravani Mela (Hindu); Niman Dance (Hopi)

July 28, 2006 (F)

Volunteers of America Founder's Day (Christian-Volunteers of America); Hariyali Teej (Hindu)

July 30, 2006 (Sn)

Reek Sunday (Christian-RC); Nag Pañcami (Hindu)

July 31, 2006 (M)

Lammas Eve (Pagan)

August 1, 2006 (Tu)

Nineteen-Day Feast, 1st of Kamál (Bahá'í); Tulsidas Jayanti (Hindu); Lammas (Pagan); ~Anniversary of the Founding of Summit Lighthouse (Church of the Universal and Triumphant)

August 2, 2006 (W)

first quarter 08:46 GMT

August 3, 2006 (Th)

Tisha be-Av (Jewish)

August 5, 2006 (St)

Putrada Ekadashi (Hindu)

August 6, 2006 (Sn)

Feast of the Transfiguration (Christian); Feast of the Transfiguration (Christian-O)

August 8, 2006 (Tu)

Feast of Frawardignan (Zoroastrian-Q); Festival of Hungry Ghosts (Taoist; Buddhist; Chinese Folk)

August 9, 2006 (W)

full moon 10:54 GMT

Narieli Purnima (Hindu); Raksa Bandhana (Hindu); Jhulan Latra (Hindu)

August 10, 2006 (Th)

Muktad (Zoroastrian-S); ~Ripe Fruits Ceremony (Cherokee)

August 11, 2006 (F)

Marya (Buddhist)

August 12, 2006 (St)

~New Corn Dance (Iroquois)

August 13, 2006 (Sn)

Obon Festival begins in some regions (Buddhist)

August 14, 2006 (M)

Partyshana Parva (Jain)

August 15, 2006 (Tu)

Assumption of the Blessed Virgin (Christian-RC); Feast of the Dormition of the Theotokos (Christian-O); Dasa Laksana Parvan (Jain); Floating Lantern Ceremony (Buddhist); ~Carnea (Pagan); ~Perseid Meteor Shower (Pantheism)

August 16, 2006 (W)

last quarter 01:51 GMT

~Snake-Antelope Dance, Flute Ceremony, or Snake Dance (Navajo)

August 17, 2006 (Th)

Odin's Ordeal begins (Pagan)

August 20, 2006 (Sn)

Frawardin 1 (Zoroastrian-S); Nawruz (Zoroastrian-S); Nineteen-Day Feast, 1st of Asmá' (Bahá'í); Kamada Ekadashi (Hindu)

August 21, 2006 (M)

Feast of Shahrewar (Zoroastrian-F)

August 22, 2006 (Tu)

Feast of Ardwahist (Zoroastrian-Q); Queenship of Mary (Christian-RC)

August 23, 2006 (W)

new moon 19:10 GMT

Ghanta Karna (Hindu); Anata-Chaturdashi (Jain)

August 24, 2006 (Th)

St. Bartholomew's Day (Christian); ~Tirupati Festival (Hindu); ~Gokarna Aunsi (Hindu); ~Onam (Hindu); ~Monkey God Festival (Taoist); ~Creek Green Corn Ceremony

August 25, 2006 (F)

Hordad Sal (Zoroastrian-S); ~Gelede (Yoruba)

August 26, 2006 (St)

African Methodist Quarterly Meeting Day (Christian-African Methodist); Haritalika Teej (Hindu)

August 27, 2006 (Sn)

Feast of Christ the King (Christian-Pr); Ganesa Caturthi (Hindu)

August 28, 2006 (M)

Rishi Pañcami (Hindu)

August 29, 2006 (Tu)

Martyrdom of St. John the Baptist (Christian)

August 30, 2006 (W)

Maidyozarem (Zoroastrian-Q)

August 31, 2006 (Th)

first quarter 22:56 GMT

September 1, 2006 (F)

Church New Year (Christian-O); Installation of Sri Guru Granth Sahib (Sikh)

September 2, 2006 (St)

San Estevan (Christian-RC); Shinbyu (Buddhist)

September 6, 2006 (W)

Anant Chaturdashi (Hindu)

September 7, 2006 (Th)

full moon 18:42 GMT

Feast of Frawardignan (Zoroastrian-S); Mid-Autumn Festival (Chinese Folk); Honoring Yemaya/Yemonja (Santeria/Lukumi)

September 8, 2006 (F)

Nativity of the Blessed Virgin Mary (Christian-RC); Feast of the Nativity of the Theotokos (Christian-O); Shab-Barat (Islamic); Nineteen-Day Feast, 1st of 'Izzat (Bahá'í); Ksamavani (Jain)

September 9, 2006 (St)

Sante Fe Fiesta (Christian-RC)

September 10, 2006 (Sn)

Auditors' Day (Scientology)

September 11, 2006 (M)

Coptic New Year (Christian-Egyptian)

September 12, 2006 (Tu)

Paitishahem (Zoroastrian-F); Honoring Oshun (Santeria/Lukumi)

September 13, 2006 (W)

Halashashti (Hindu)

September 14, 2006 (Th)

last quarter 11:15 GMT

Triumph of the Holy Cross (Christian); Elevation of the Holy Cross (Christian-O)

September 15, 2006 (F)

Mary as Our Lady of Sorrows; Janmashtami (Hindu); Radha Ashtami (Hindu); ~Memorial Ceremony (Rosicrucianism)

September 17, 2006 (Sn)

Feast of Mithra (Zoroastrian-F); Founder's Day (Eckankar)

September 18, 2006 (M)

~Indra Jatra (Hindu)

September 21, 2006 (Th)

Feast of Ardwahist (Zoroastrian-S); St. Matthew's Day (Christian)

September 22, 2006 (F)

new moon 11:45 GMT

~Vatsa begins (Buddhist); Festival of the Nine Imperial Gods begins (Taoist; Buddhist)

September 23, 2006 (St)

fall equinox 04:03 GMT

Civil New Year (Jewish); Rosh Hashanah (Jewish); Feast of Trumpets (United Church of God); ~Laksmi Puja (Hindu); ~Durga Puja (Hindu); Autumnal Higan (Buddhist); Mabon (Pagan); Winter Finding (Pagan); Autumn Equinox (Pantheism)

September 24, 2006 (Sn)

Ten Days of Teshuva (Jewish); Feast of Hordad (Zoroastrian-Q); Ramadan begins (Islamic); ~Lakon (Hopi and Navajo); Honoring Obatala (Santeria/Lukumi)

September 25, 2006 (M)

Fast of Gedaliah (Jewish)

September 26, 2006 (Tu)

~A Good Crop Dance (Navajo)

September 27, 2006 (W)

Nineteen-Day Feast, 1st of Mashíyyat (Bahá'í); Honoring Orisa Ibeji (Santeria/Lukumi); Cosmas and Damian Day (Candomblé)

September 29, 2006 (F)

Maidyozarem (Zoroastrian-Q); Michaelmas (Christian); Honoring Orisa Erinle (Santeria/Lukumi)

September 30, 2006 (St)

first quarter 11:04 GMT

St. Gregory the Illuminator (Christian-O)

October 1, 2006 (Sn)

~Rally Day (Christian-Pr); ~Children's Day (Unification); Confucius's Birthday (Confucian)

October 2, 2006 (M)

Yom Kippur (Jewish); Mihragan (Zoroastrian-F); Guardian Angels Day (Christian-RC); Day of Atonement (United Church of God); Dussehra (Hindu)

October 4, 2006 (W)

Honoring Orisa Orunmila (Santeria/Lukumi)

October 5, 2006 (Th)
Bodhidharma Day (Buddhist)

October 6, 2006 (F)
St. Thomas's Day (Christian-O)

October 7, 2006 (St)
full moon 03:13 GMT
Sukkot (Jewish); Mary as Our Lady of the Rosary (Christian-RC); Feast of Tabernacles begins (United Church of God); Sharad Purnima (Hindu); Kojagara (Hindu); (Hindu) Valmiki Jayanti (Hindu); Shiprock Navajo Nation Fair (Navajo); Founding of the International Association of Scientologists (Scientology)

October 8, 2006 (Sn)
~Pitra Visarjana Amavasya (Hindu)

October 9, 2006 (M)
Birthday of Guru Ram Das (Sikh)

October 12, 2006 (Th)
Ayathrem (Zoroastrian-F)

October 13, 2006 (F)
Hoshana Rabbah (Jewish)

October 14, 2006 (St)
last quarter 00:26 GMT
Shemini Atzeret (Jewish); Last Great Day (United Church of God)

October 15, 2006 (Sn)
Simhat Torah (Jewish); ~Divali (Sikh)

October 16, 2006 (M)
Nineteen-Day Feast, 1st of 'Ilm (Bahá'í)

October 18, 2006 (W)
St. Luke's Day (Christian)

October 20, 2006 (F)
Laylat al-Qadr (Islamic); Birth of the Báb (Bahá'í); Ebisu Festival (Shinto)

October 22, 2006 (Sn)
new moon 05:14 GMT
Diwali (Jain); Sending the Winter Dress (Chinese Folk); Great New Moon Ceremony (Cherokee); Spiritual New Year (Eckankar)

October 23, 2006 (M)
St. James the Brother of the Lord (Christian-O); Lantern's Festival (Islamic); ~Kartika Snan (Hindu); ~Skanda Shashti (Hindu); Govardhan Puja (Hindu)

October 24, 2006 (Tu)
Feast of Hordad (Zoroastrian-S); Id al-Fitr begins (Islamic); Bhaiya Duj (Hindu)

October 26, 2006 (Th)
Aban Parab (Zoroastrian-F); St. Demetrios (Christian-O)

October 27, 2006 (F)
Jnan Panchami (Jain)

October 28, 2006 (St)
St. Simon and St. Jude's Day (Christian); Surya Shashti (Hindu)

October 29, 2006 (Sn)
first quarter 21:25 GMT
Maidyoshahem (Zoroastrian-Q)

October 31, 2006 (Tu)
Tiragan (Zoroastrian-Q); Reformation Day (Christian-Pr); Atohuna (Cherokee); Oidhche Shamhna (Pagan)

November 1, 2006 (W)
All Saints' Day (Christian); Samhain (Pagan)

November 2, 2006 (Th)
All Souls' Day (Christian); Devathani Ekadashi (Hindu)

November 4, 2006 (St)
Nineteen-Day Feast, 1st of Qudrat (Bahá'í)

November 5, 2006 (Sn)
full moon 12:58 GMT
Kartika Purnima (Hindu); Puskar Mela (Hindu); Guy Fawkes's Night (Pagan)

November 8, 2006 (W)
Saints, Doctors, Missionaries, and Martyrs Day (Christian-Anglican); St. Michael and All Angels (Christian-O)

November 9, 2006 (Th)
Dedication of St. John Lateran (Christian-RC); Karwachauth (Hindu)

November 10, 2006 (F)
Birthday of Martin Luther (Christian-Lutheran)

November 11, 2006 (St)
Old Halloween (Pagan)

November 12, 2006 (Sn)
last quarter 17:45 GMT
Birth of Bahá'u'lláh (Bahá'í); ~Tihar (Hindu)

November 14, 2006 (Tu)
St. Philip (Christian-O)

November 15, 2006 (W)
Advent begins (Christian-O); Shichi-Go-San (Shinto)

November 16, 2006 (Th)
St. Matthew (Christian-O)

November 18, 2006 (St)

Dhan Teras (Hindu)

November 19, 2006 (Sn)

Narak Chaturdashi (Hindu); Tazaungdaing (Buddhist); Wuwuchim (Hopi)

November 20, 2006 (M)
new moon 22:18 GMT

Dewali (Hindu)

November 21, 2006 (Tu)

Presentation of the Blessed Virgin Mary (Christian-RC); Feast of the Presentation of the Theotokos (Christian-O); ~Fast for a World Harvest (Unitarian)

November 23, 2006 (Th)

Thanksgiving (Christian); Thanksgiving (Christian Science); Nineteen-Day Feast, 1st of Qawl (Bahá'í)

November 24, 2006 (F)

Adar Parab (Zoroastrian-F); Feast of Amurdad (Zoroastrian-Q); Martyrdom Anniversary of Guru Teg Bahadur (Sikh)

November 25, 2006 (St)

St. Catherine (Christian-O)

November 26, 2006 (Sn)

Bible Sunday (Christian-Pr); Feast of Christ the King (Christian-RC); Day of the Covenant (Bahá'í)

November 28, 2006 (Tu)
first quarter 06:29 GMT

Maidyoshahem (Zoroastrian-S); Ascension of 'Abdu'l-Bahá (Bahá'í)

November 30, 2006 (Th)

Tiragan (Zoroastrian-S); St. Andrew's Day (Christian)

December 1, 2006 (F)

Mother Seton Day (Christian-RC); Gita Jayanti (Hindu); Vaikuntha Ekadashi (Hindu); ~Festival of Lights (Buddhist); ~ Shalako Ceremonial (Pueblo)

December 3, 2006 (Sn)

Advent begins (Christian)

December 4, 2006 (M)

St. Barbara and St. John of Damascus (Christian-O); Honoring Orisa Shango (Santeria/Lukumi)

December 5, 2006 (Tu)
full moon 00:25 GMT

Dattatreya Jayanti (Hindu)

December 6, 2006 (W)

St. Nicholas's Day (Christian); St. Nicholas's Day (Christian-O)

December 8, 2006 (F)

Immaculate Conception of Mary (Christian-RC); Rohatsu (Buddhist)

December 9, 2006 (St)

Holy Theotokos (Christian-O)

December 10, 2006 (Sn)

~Human Rights Day (Unitarian); ~Geminid Meteor Shower (Pantheism)

December 12, 2006 (Tu)
last quarter 14:32 GMT

Nineteen-Day Feast, 1st of Masá'il (Bahá'í)

December 13, 2006 (W)

Saint Lucy's Day (Christian); Bhairava Ashtami (Hindu)

December 14, 2006 (Th)

~Lohri (Sikh)

December 15, 2006 (F)

Birth of Parsvanath (Jain)

December 16, 2006 (St)

Hanukkah (Jewish); 1st Feast of Dae (Zoroastrian-F); Posadas (Christian); Vaikuntha Ekadashi (Hindu); Vaitarani (Hindu)

December 17, 2006 (Sn)

Feast of the Forebearers of Christ (Christian-O); Honoring Babalu Aye (Santeria/Lukumi)

December 20, 2006 (W)
new moon 14:01 GMT

~Ta Chiu (Taoist)

December 21, 2006 (Th)

Feast of Shahrewar (Zoroastrian-Q); St. Thomas's Day (Christian); The Mother Night (Pagan)

December 22, 2006 (F)
winter solstice 00:22 GMT

Winter Solstice (Chinese Folk); Soyal (Hopi); Guatemalan Winter Solstice (Mayan); Yule (Pagan); Winter Solstice (Pantheism)

December 23, 2006 (St)

2nd Feast of Dae (Zoroastrian-F); New Year for Trees (Pagan); The Day that Is Not a Day (Pagan)

December 24, 2006 (Sn)

Feast of Amurdad (Zoroastrian-S); Christmas Eve (Christian)

December 25, 2006 (M)

Christmas Day (Christian); Feast of the Nativity of Our Lord (Christian-O); ~Saturnalia (Pagan)

December 26, 2006 (Tu)

Zarthastno Diso (Zoroastrian-F); St. Stephen's Day (Christian); Synaxis of the Holy Theotokos (Christian-O)

December 27, 2006 (W)
first quarter 14:48 GMT

St. John the Evangelist's Day (Christian); St. Stephen's Day(Christian-O)

December 28, 2006 (Th)

Holy Innocents' Day (Christian)

December 29, 2006 (F)

Holy Innocents' Day (Christian-O); Pilgrimage to Mecca (Hajj) begins (Islamic)

December 30, 2006 (St)

Asarah be-Tevet (Jewish); 3rd Feast of Dae (Zoroastrian-F)

December 31, 2006 (Sn)

Maidyarem (Zoroastrian-F); Al-'id al-Kabir; 'Id al-Adha begins (Islamic); Nineteen-Day Feast, 1st of Sharaf (Bahá'í); Omisoka (Shinto); Hogmany (Pagan)

2007

January 1, 2007 (M)

Feast of the Circumcision (Christian-RC); St. Basil's Day (Christian-O); God's Day (Unification); World Peace Day and the Universal Hour of Peace (Unitarian); Oshogatsu begins (Buddhist); Ganjitsu begins (Shinto); Annual Forecast (Santeria/Lukumi)

January 3, 2007 (W)
full moon 13:57 GMT
perihelion 20:00 GMT

The Twelfth Night (Pagan)

January 5, 2007 (F)

Epiphany Eve (Christian); Guru Gobind Singh's Birthday (Sikh)

January 6, 2007 (St)

Epiphany (Christian); Old Christmas Day (Christian-J); Feast of Epiphany (Christian-O); St. Distaff's Day (Pagan)

January 7, 2007 (Sn)

4th Feast of Dae (Zoroastrian-F); Feast of the Holy Family (Christian-RC); Baptism of the Lord (Christian); Universal Week of Prayer begins (Christian); ~Bounding Bush (Cherokee)

January 8, 2007 (M)

Plough Monday (Christian)

January 11, 2007 (Th)
last quarter 12:45 GMT

Rukmini Ashtami (Hindu); Kitchen God Festival (Taoist; Chinese Folk)

January 12, 2007 (F)

Paitishahem (Zoroastrian-Q)

January 13, 2007 (St)

Death of George Fox (Christian-Quaker); ~Maghi (Sikh)

January 14, 2007 (Sn)

~Makar Sankranti (Hindu)

January 15, 2007 (M)

Birthday of Martin Luther King, Jr. (Christian); Swarupa Dwadashi (Hindu); ~White Dog Feast (Iroquois)

January 16, 2007 (Tu)

Feast of Vohuman (Zoroastrian-F)

January 17, 2007 (W)

Feast of Mithra (Zoroastrian-Q); Nirvana of Risabha (Jain)

January 19, 2007 (F)
new moon 04:01 GMT

Nineteen-Day Feast, 1st of Sultán (Bahá'í)

January 20, 2007 (St)

Feast of Shahrewar (Zoroastrian-S); ~World Religions Day (Unitarian); Awwal Muharram (Islamic); ~Pongal (Hindu); ~Thaipusam (Hindu); ~Kwakiutl Winter Ceremonial

January 21, 2007 (Sn)

Blessing of Animals (Christian-RC); World Religion Day (Bahá'í)

January 24, 2007 (W)

Vasant Pañcami (Hindu); Alacitas (Aymara)

January 25, 2007 (Th)
first quarter 23:01 GMT

Conversion of St. Paul (Christian)

January 27, 2007 (St)

Bhishma Ashtami (Hindu)

January 28, 2007 (Sn)

Triodion begins (Christian-O)

January 29, 2007 (M)

Ashura (Islamic); Yevmi Ashurer (Islamic); Husayn Day (Islamic)

January 30, 2007 (Tu)

Three Hierarchs (Christian-O); Up-Helly-Aa (Pagan)

February 1, 2007 (Th)

Mihragan (Zoroastrian-Q); ~True Parents' Birthday (Unification); ~Losar (Buddhist); Imbolg (Pagan)

February 2, 2007 (F)

Presentation of Jesus (Christian); Presentation of Christ in the Temple (Christian-O); Gaelic Fire Festival (Pagan); Honoring Orisa Oya (Santeria/Lukumi)

February 3, 2007 (St)
full moon 05:45 GMT

Tu Bishvat (Jewish); Magha Purnima (Hindu); Minakshi Float Festival (Hindu); Chinese New Year (Buddhist); Setsubun (Shinto); ~Midwinter Dream Festival (Iroquois)

February 4, 2007 (Sn)

Meatfare Sunday (Christian-O); ~Monlam Chenmo begins (Buddhist); Homstrom (Pagan)

February 5, 2007 (M)

Arrival of Roger Williams in the New World (Christian-Baptist)

February 7, 2007 (W)

Nineteen-Day Feast, 1st of Mulk (Bahá'í); Sakata Chauth (Hindu)

February 8, 2007 (Th)

Hari-Kuyo (Shinto)

February 10, 2007 (St)
last quarter 09:51 GMT

First Saturday of Souls (Christian-O)

February 11, 2007 (Sn)

Paitishahem (Zoroastrian-S); Ayathrem (Zoroastrian-Q); Race Relations Sunday (Christian); Birthday of Richard Allen (Christian-AFRICAN METHODIST EPISCOPAL); Cheesefare Sunday

February 14, 2007 (W)

Lupercalia begins (Pagan)

February 15, 2007 (Th)

Vartanantz Day (Christian-Armenian)

February 16, 2007 (F)

Feast of Mithra (Zoroastrian-S)

February 17, 2007 (St)
new moon 16:14 GMT

Second Saturday of Souls (Christian-O); Mauni Amavasya (Hindu); Powamu Bean Dance begins (Hopi)

February 18, 2007 (Sn)

Feast of Spendarmad (Zoroastrian-F); Fasching (Christian); Lunar New Year (Chinese Folk); Ramtha's Appearance (Ramtha's School of Enlightenment)

February 19, 2007 (M)

Rose Monday (Christian); Clean Monday (Christian-O); Great Lent begins (Christian-O); ~Mandi Safar (Islamic)

February 20, 2007 (Tu)

Mardi Gras (Christian-RC); Carnival ends (Christian-RC)

February 21, 2007 (W)

Ash Wednesday (Christian); Lent begins (Christian)

February 23, 2007 (F)

World Day of Prayer (Christian)

February 24, 2007 (St)
first quarter 07:56 GMT

St. Matthias's Day (Christian); St. Theodore (Christian-O)

February 25, 2007 (Sn)

Aban Parab (Zoroastrian-Q); Quadragesima (Christian); Sunday of Orthodoxy (Christian-O)

February 26, 2007 (M)

Ayyám-i-Há begins (Bahá'í); Making Happiness Festival (Chinese Folk)

February 28, 2007 (W)

Amalaka Ekadashi (Hindu)

March 1, 2007 (Th)

Parents Day (Unification); Omizutori Matsuri begins (Buddhist)

March 2, 2007 (F)

Nineteen-Day Feast, 1st of 'Alá' (Bahá'í); The Fast begins (Bahá'í)

March 3, 2007 (St)
full moon 23:17 GMT

Ta'anit Esther (Jewish); Mihragan (Zoroastrian-S); Holi (Hindu); Dol Purnima (Hindu); Hina Matsuri (Shinto)

March 4, 2007 (Sn)

Purim (Jewish); Sunday of St. Gregory Palamas (Christian-O); Shah Abdul Latif Death Commemoration begins (Islamic-Sufi); Lantern Festival (Chinese Folk)

March 7, 2007 (W)

Star Festival (Chinese Folk)

March 8, 2007 (Th)

Data Ganj Baksh Death Festival begins (Islamic-Sufi)

March 11, 2007 (Sn)

Muktad (Zoroastrian-F); Sunday of the Holy Cross (Christian-O)

March 12, 2007 (M)
last quarter 03:54 GMT

~Maple Dance (Iroquois)

March 13, 2007 (Tu)

Ayathrem (Zoroastrian-S); Birthday of L. Ron Hubbard (Scientology)

March 14, 2007 (W)

Scriptural New Year (Sikh); Hola Mohalla (Sikh)

March 17, 2007 (St)

St. Patrick's Day (Christian); Mahashivarati (Hindu); ~Gangaur begins (Hindu)

March 18, 2007 (Sn)

Mothering Sunday (Christian); Sunday of St. John Climacos (Christian-O)

March 19, 2007 (M)
new moon 02:43 GMT

Vasanta Navaratra begins (Hindu); ~Monkey God Festival (Taoist); First New Moon of Spring (Cherokee)

March 20, 2007 (Tu)

Liturgical New Year (Jewish); Gudi Parva (Hindu); Ugadi Parva (Hindu); ~Thunder Dance (Iroquois); ~Ibu Afo Festival (Yoruba)

March 21, 2007 (W)
spring equinox 00:07 GMT

Frawardin 1 (Zoroastrian-F); Nawruz (Zoroastrian-F); Festival of Naw-Rúz (Bahá'í); Nineteen-Day Feast, 1st of Bahá (Bahá'í); Spring Higan (Buddhist); Ostara (Pagan); ~Iduna and Summer Finding (Pagan); Spring Equinox (Pantheism)

March 22, 2007 (Th)

Honoring Orisaoko (Santeria/Lukumi)

March 24, 2007 (St)

~Eagle Dance (Navajo and Others)

March 25, 2007 (Sn)
first quarter 18:16 GMT

Annunciation of the Lord (Christian); Sunday of St. Mary of Egypt (Christian-O); Feast of the Annunciation (Christian-O)

March 26, 2007 (M)

Hordad Sal (Zoroastrian-F); Adar Parab (Zoroastrian-Q); ~Bobo Masquerade (Yoruba)

March 27, 2007 (Tu)

Aban Parab (Zoroastrian-S); Caitra Parb (Hindu); Sitala Ashtami (Hindu); Ashokashtami (Hindu)

March 28, 2007 (W)

Ramanavami (Hindu)

March 29, 2007 (Th)

Miriam's Yahrzeit (Jewish)

March 31, 2007 (St)

Sabbath of Rabbi Isaac Mayer Wise (Jewish); Lazarus Saturday (Christian-O); Mawlid al-Nabi (Islamic)

April 1, 2007 (Sn)

Palm Sunday (Christian); Palm Sunday (Christian-O); Birth of Mahavira (Jain); All Fool's Day (Pagan)

April 2, 2007 (M)

Fast of the First-born (Jewish); The Lord's Evening Meal (Jehovah's Witnesses); Passover (United Church of God); ~Planting Dances (Iroquois); Rara Festival (Voodoo)

April 3, 2007 (Tu)
full moon 17:15 GMT

Passover (Jewish); Festival of Unleavened Bread begins (United Church of God); ~Panguni Uttiram (Hindu); ~Caitra Purnima (Hindu); Hanuman Jayanti (Hindu); Magha Puja (Buddhist)

April 4, 2007 (W)

Sefirah (Jewish)

April 5, 2007 (Th)

Maundy Thursday (Christian); Paschal Thursday (Christian-O)

April 6, 2007 (F)

Good Friday (Christian); Holy Friday (Christian-O); Founding of the Church of Jesus Christ of Latter-Day Saints (Mormon)

April 7, 2007 (St)

Holy Saturday (Christian); Holy Saturday (Christian-O)

April 8, 2007 (Sn)

Feast of Frawardignan (Zoroastrian-F); Easter (Christian); Easter (Christian-O); Foundation Day (Ramtha's School of Enlightenment)

April 9, 2007 (M)

Bright Week begins (Christian-O); Nineteen-Day Feast, 1st of Jalál (Bahá'í)

April 10, 2007 (Tu)
last quarter 18:04 GMT

Maimona (Jewish); Salvation Army Founder's Day (Christian-Salvation Army)

April 13, 2007 (F)

Songkran begins (Buddhist)

April 14, 2007 (St)

Baisakhi (Sikh); Guru Nanak's Day (Sikh)

April 15, 2007 (Sn)

Yom ha-Shoah (Jewish); Quasimodo Sunday (Christian); St. Thomas's Day (Christian-O)

April 17, 2007 (Tu)
new moon 11:36 GMT

1st Feast of Dae (Zoroastrian-Q)

April 18, 2007 (W)

Vaisakhi (Hindu); ~Pooram begins (Hindu)

April 20, 2007 (F)

Akshya Tritiya (Hindu); Parasurama Jayanti (Hindu); Chandan Yatra begins (Hindu); Aksaya Tratiya (Jain); Qing Ming Festival (Chinese Folk)

April 21, 2007 (St)

Festival of Ridván begins (Bahá'í); ~Earth Day (Pagan)

April 22, 2007 (Sn)
Yom ha-Zikkaron (Jewish); Feast of Ardwahist (Zoroastrian-F); ~Earth Day (Unitarian); Sankaracarya Jayanti (Hindu)

April 23, 2007 (M)
Yom ha-Atzma'ut (Jewish); St. George's Day (Christian-O)

April 24, 2007 (Tu)
first quarter 06:35 GMT
2nd Feast of Dae (Zoroastrian-Q)

April 25, 2007 (W)
Adar Parab (Zoroastrian-S); St. Mark's Day (Christian)

April 26, 2007 (Th)
Janaki Navami (Hindu)

April 27, 2007 (F)
Zarthastno Diso (Zoroastrian-Q)

April 28, 2007 (St)
Nineteen-Day Feast, 1st of Jamál (Bahá'í)

April 30, 2007 (M)
Maidyozarem (Zoroastrian-F); St. James the Son of Zebedee (Christian-O); Walpurgis Night (Pagan)

May 1, 2007 (Tu)
3rd Feast of Dae (Zoroastrian-Q); Saint Philip and Saint James's Day (Christian); ~Day of All Things (Unification); Narsimha Jayanti (Hindu); Beltane (Pagan)

May 2, 2007 (W)
full moon 10:09 GMT
Maidyarem (Zoroastrian-Q); Vesak (Buddhist)

May 3, 2007 (Th)
National Day of Prayer (Unitarian)

May 5, 2007 (St)
Children's Day (Shinto)

May 6, 2007 (Sn)
Lag ba-Omer (Jewish); Family Week begins (Christian)

May 8, 2007 (Tu)
Death of Helena Petrovna Blavatsky (Theosophy)

May 9, 2007 (W)
4th Feast of Dae (Zoroastrian-Q); Matsu Festival (Taoist; Buddhist; Chinese Folk); May 9 Day (Scientology)

May 10, 2007 (Th)
last quarter 04:27 GMT

May 11, 2007 (F)
Sts. Cyril and Methodios (Christian-O)

May 12, 2007 (St)
Sanja Matsuri (Shinto)

May 13, 2007 (Sn)
Rogation Sunday (Christian)

May 14, 2007 (M)
Yom Yerushalayim (Jewish); Rogation Days (Christian)

May 15, 2007 (Tu)
Aaronic Priesthood Commemoration (Mormon); Aoi Matsuri (Shinto); ~Ibeji Ceremony (Yoruba)

May 16, 2007 (W)
new moon 19:27 GMT

May 17, 2007 (Th)
1st Feast of Dae (Zoroastrian-S); Ascension Day (Christian); Ascension (Christian-O); Nineteen-Day Feast, 1st of 'Azamat (Bahá'í); Mata Tirtha Snan (Hindu); ~Chongmyo Taeje (Confucian)

May 18, 2007 (F)
Feast of Vohuman (Zoroastrian-Q)

May 21, 2007 (M)
Sts. Constantine and Helen (Christian-O)

May 23, 2007 (W)
first quarter 21:02 GMT
Shavuot (Jewish); Pentecost (United Church of God); Declaration of the Báb (Bahá'í); Sithinakha (Hindu)

May 24, 2007 (Th)
2nd Feast of Dae (Zoroastrian-S); Tam Kung Festival (Taoist); Birthday of the Third Prince (Taoist)

May 25, 2007 (F)
Feast of Hordad (Zoroastrian-F); Jyestha Ashtami (Hindu)

May 26, 2007 (St)
Fourth Saturday of Souls (Christian-O); Ute Bear Dance (Ute)

May 27, 2007 (Sn)
Zarthastno Diso (Zoroastrian-S); Pentecost (Christian); Aldersgate Experience (Christian-Methodist); Pentecost (Christian-O); Ganga Dussehra (Hindu)

May 28, 2007 (M)
Holy Spirit Day (Christian-O); Nirjala Ekadashi (Hindu)

May 29, 2007 (Tu)
Ascension of Bahá'u'lláh (Bahá'í)

May 31, 2007 (Th)
3rd Feast of Dae (Zoroastrian-S); Feast of the Visitation (Christian-RC)

June 1, 2007 (F)
full moon 01:04 GMT
Maidyarem (Zoroastrian-S); Birthday of Brigham Young (Mormon); Snan Yatra (Hindu); Buddha Jayanti (Hindu); Poson (Buddhist); Sanghamitta Day (Buddhist); ~Egungun Festival (Yoruba)

June 2, 2007 (St)
Caturmas begins (Jain)

June 3, 2007 (Sn)
Trinity Sunday (Christian); All Saints' Day (Christian-O)

June 5, 2007 (Tu)
Nineteen-Day Feast, 1st of Núr (Bahá'í)

June 6, 2007 (W)
Honoring Oshosi (Santeria/Lukumi)

June 7, 2007 (Th)
Corpus Christi (Christian-RC)

June 8, 2007 (F)
last quarter 11:43 GMT
4th Feast of Dae (Zoroastrian-S); Sacred Heart of Jesus (Christian-RC)

June 9, 2007 (St)
Children's Day (Christian)

June 10, 2007 (Sn)
Race Unity Day (Bahá'í)

June 11, 2007 (M)
St. Barnabas's Day (Christian)

June 13, 2007 (W)
Honoring Elegbara/Esu (Santeria/Lukumi)

June 14, 2007 (Th)
Vata Savitri (Hindu); Rice Planting Festivals (Shinto)

June 15, 2007 (F)
new moon 03:13 GMT
Magna Carta Day (Christian-Anglican); ~Strawberry Festival (Iroquois); ~Rosicrucian Thanksgiving Ritual (Rosicrucianism)

June 16, 2007 (St)
Immaculate Heart of Mary (Christian-RC); Martyrdom Anniversary of Guru Arjan (Sikh)

June 17, 2007 (Sn)
Feast of Vohuman (Zoroastrian-S); New Church Day (Swedenborgian); Ratha Yatra (Hindu); Lily Festival (Shinto)

June 20, 2007 (W)
Feast of Spendarmad (Zoroastrian-Q); Midsummer Eve (Pagan)

June 21, 2007 (Th)
summer solstice 18:06 GMT
Celebration of Unifying Principles (Unitarian); Sun Dance (Navajo and Others); Litha (Pagan); Summer Solstice (Pantheism)

June 22, 2007 (F)
first quarter 13:15 GMT

June 24, 2007 (Sn)
Nativity of St. John the Baptist (Christian); ~Footwashing Day (Christian-Pr); Birth of St. John the Baptist (Christian-O); Nineteen-Day Feast, 1st of Rahmat (Bahá'í); St. John's Day (Voodoo)

June 25, 2007 (M)
~Eje (Yoruba)

June 26, 2007 (Tu)
Hari-Shayani Ekadashi (Hindu)

June 27, 2007 (W)
Martyrdom of Joseph and Hyrum Smith (Mormon)

June 29, 2007 (F)
Maidyoshahem (Zoroastrian-F); St. Peter's Day (Christian); St. Peter and St. Paul (Christian-O)

June 30, 2007 (St)
full moon 13:49 GMT
Guru Purnima (Hindu); ~Green Corn Ceremony (Cherokee); Honoring Ogun (Santeria/Lukumi)

July 1, 2007 (Sn)
Tiragan (Zoroastrian-F); Most Precious Blood (Christian-RC); ~Hemis Festival (Buddhist)

July 3, 2007 (Tu)
Fast of the Seventeenth of Tammuz (Jewish); Three Weeks of Mourning (Jewish); Seminole Green Corn Dance begins; Dog Days begin (Pagan)

July 5, 2007 (Th)
Airing the Classics (Buddhist); Esala Perahera (Buddhist)

July 6, 2007 (F)
Birthday of the Dalai Lama (Buddhist)

July 7, 2007 (St)
last quarter 16:54 GMT
aphelion 00:00 GMT

July 9, 2007 (M)
Martyrdom of the Báb (Bahá'í)

July 10, 2007 (Tu)
~Pilgrimage of Saut D'Eau (Voodoo)

July 11, 2007 (W)
Muktad (Zoroastrian-Q)

July 13, 2007 (F)
Nineteen-Day Feast, 1st of Kalimát (Bahá'í); Obon Festival begins in some regions (Buddhist)

July 14, 2007 (St)
new moon 12:04 GMT

Hill Cumorah Pageant begins (Mormon)

July 15, 2007 (Sn)

St. Vladimir (Christian-O); ~Sravani Mela (Hindu)

July 17, 2007 (Tu)

Hariyali Teej (Hindu); Gion Matsuri (Shinto)

July 19, 2007 (Th)

Nag Pañcami (Hindu)

July 20, 2007 (F)

Feast of Spendarmad (Zoroastrian-S)

July 21, 2007 (St)

Frawardin 1 (Zoroastrian-Q); Nawruz (Zoroastrian-Q); Tulsidas Jayanti (Hindu)

July 22, 2007 (Sn)
first quarter 06:29 GMT

July 23, 2007 (M)

Birthday of Guru Har Krishan (Sikh); ~Waso begins (Buddhist)

July 24, 2007 (Tu)

Tisha be-Av (Jewish); Pioneer Day (Mormon)

July 25, 2007 (W)

Feast of Amurdad (Zoroastrian-F); St. James's Day (Christian); Putrada Ekadashi (Hindu)

July 26, 2007 (Th)

Hordad Sal (Zoroastrian-Q); Birthday of Lu Pan (Taoist); Niman Dance (Hopi)

July 28, 2007 (St)

Volunteers of America Founder's Day (Christian-Volunteers of America)

July 29, 2007 (Sn)

Reek Sunday (Christian-RC)

July 30, 2007 (M)
full moon 00:48 GMT

Narieli Purnima (Hindu); Raksa Bandhana (Hindu); Jhulan Latra (Hindu)

July 31, 2007 (Tu)

Lammas Eve (Pagan)

August 1, 2007 (W)

Nineteen-Day Feast, 1st of Kamál (Bahá'í); Marya (Buddhist); Lammas (Pagan); ~Anniversary of the Founding of Summit Lighthouse (Church of the Universal and Triumphant)

August 5, 2007 (Sn)
last quarter 21:20 GMT

August 6, 2007 (M)

Feast of the Transfiguration (Christian); Feast of the Transfiguration (Christian-O)

August 8, 2007 (W)

Feast of Frawardignan (Zoroastrian-Q)

August 10, 2007 (F)

Muktad (Zoroastrian-S); Kamada Ekadashi (Hindu); ~Ripe Fruits Ceremony (Cherokee)

August 11, 2007 (St)

Laylat al-Miraj (Islamic)

August 12, 2007 (Sn)
new moon 23:02 GMT

Ghanta Karna (Hindu); ~New Corn Dance (Iroquois)

August 13, 2007 (M)

~Tirupati Festival (Hindu); ~Gokarna Aunsi (Hindu); ~Onam (Hindu); Obon Festival begins in some regions (Buddhist)

August 15, 2007 (W)

Assumption of the Blessed Virgin (Christian-RC); Feast of the Dormition of the Theotokos (Christian-O); Haritalika Teej (Hindu); Floating Lantern Ceremony (Buddhist); ~Carnea (Pagan); ~Perseid Meteor Shower (Pantheism)

August 16, 2007 (Th)

Ganesa Caturthi (Hindu); ~Snake-Antelope Dance, Flute Ceremony, or Snake Dance (Navajo)

August 17, 2007 (F)

Rishi Pañcami (Hindu); Odin's Ordeal begins (Pagan)

August 20, 2007 (M)
first quarter 23:54 GMT

Frawardin 1 (Zoroastrian-S); Nawruz (Zoroastrian-S); Nineteen-Day Feast, 1st of Asmá' (Bahá'í)

August 21, 2007 (Tu)

Feast of Shahrewar (Zoroastrian-F)

August 22, 2007 (W)

Feast of Ardwahist (Zoroastrian-Q); Queenship of Mary (Christian-RC); ~Creek Green Corn Ceremony

August 24, 2007 (F)

St. Bartholomew's Day (Christian)

August 25, 2007 (St)

Hordad Sal (Zoroastrian-S); African Methodist Quarterly Meeting Day (Christian-African Methodist); ~Gelede (Yoruba)

August 26, 2007 (Sn)

Feast of Christ the King (Christian-Pr); Anant Chaturdashi (Hindu)

August 27, 2007 (M)

Festival of Hungry Ghosts (Taoist; Buddhist; Chinese Folk)

August 28, 2007 (Tu)
full moon 10:35 GMT

August 29, 2007 (W)

Martyrdom of St. John the Baptist (Christian); Shab-Barat (Islamic)

August 30, 2007 (Th)

Maidyozarem (Zoroastrian-Q)

September 1, 2007 (St)

Church New Year (Christian-O); Installation of Sri Guru Granth Sahib (Sikh)

September 2, 2007 (Sn)

San Estevan (Christian-RC); Partyshana Parva (Jain); Shinbyu (Buddhist)

September 3, 2007 (M)

Halashashti (Hindu); Dasa Laksana Parvan (Jain)

September 4, 2007 (Tu)
last quarter 02:32 GMT

September 5, 2007 (W)

Janmashtami (Hindu); Radha Ashtami (Hindu)

September 7, 2007 (F)

Feast of Frawardignan (Zoroastrian-S); Honoring Yemaya/Yemonja (Santeria/Lukumi)

September 8, 2007 (St)

Nativity of the Blessed Virgin Mary (Christian); Sante Fe Fiesta (Christian-RC); Feast of the Nativity of the Theotokos (Christian-O); Nineteen-Day Feast, 1st of 'Izzat (Bahá'í); ~Indra Jatra (Hindu)

September 9, 2007 (Sn)

Auditors' Day (Scientology)

September 11, 2007 (Tu)
new moon 12:44 GMT

Coptic New Year (Christian-Egyptian); Anata-Chaturdashi (Jain); ~Monkey God Festival (Taoist)

September 12, 2007 (W)

Paitishahem (Zoroastrian-F); ~Laksmi Puja (Hindu); ~Durga Puja (Hindu); Honoring Oshun (Santeria/Lukumi)

September 13, 2007 (Th)

Civil New Year (Jewish); Rosh Hashanah (Jewish); Feast of Trumpets (United Church of God); Ramadan begins (Islamic)

September 14, 2007 (F)

Ten Days of Teshuva (Jewish); Triumph of the Holy Cross (Christian); Elevation of the Holy Cross (Christian-O)

September 15, 2007 (St)

Fast of Gedaliah (Jewish); Mary as Our Lady of Sorrows (Christian-RC); ~Memorial Ceremony (Rosicrucianism)

September 17, 2007 (M)

Feast of Mithra (Zoroastrian-F); Founder's Day (Eckankar)

September 19, 2007 (W)
first quarter 16:48 GMT

September 21, 2007 (F)

Feast of Ardwahist (Zoroastrian-S); St. Matthew's Day (Christian); Dussehra (Hindu)

September 22, 2007 (St)

Yom Kippur (Jewish); Day of Atonement (United Church of God); ~Vatsa begins (Buddhist)

September 23, 2007 (Sn)
fall equinox 09:51 GMT

Autumnal Higan (Buddhist); Mabon (Pagan); Winter Finding (Pagan); Autumn Equinox (Pantheism)

September 24, 2007 (M)

Feast of Hordad (Zoroastrian-Q); Honoring Obatala (Santeria/Lukumi)

September 25, 2007 (Tu)

Mid-Autumn Festival (Chinese Folk); ~Lakon (Hopi and Navajo)

September 26, 2007 (W)
full moon 19:45 GMT

Sharad Purnima (Hindu); Kojagara (Hindu); Valmiki Jayanti (Hindu); ~A Good Crop Dance (Navajo)

September 27, 2007 (Th)

Sukkot (Jewish); Feast of Tabernacles begins (United Church of God); Nineteen-Day Feast, 1st of Mashíyyat (Bahá'í); ~Pitra Visarjana Amavasya (Hindu); Ksamavani (Jain); Honoring Orisa Ibeji (Santeria/Lukumi); Cosmas and Damian Day (Candomblé)

September 29, 2007 (St)

Maidyozarem (Zoroastrian-Q); Michaelmas (Christian); Honoring Orisa Erinle (Santeria/Lukumi)

September 30, 2007 (Sn)

~ Rally Day (Christian-Pr); St. Gregory the Illuminator (Christian-O)

October 1, 2007 (M)

~Children's Day (Unification)

October 2, 2007 (Tu)

Mihragan (Zoroastrian-F); Guardian Angels Day (Christian-RC)

October 3, 2007 (W)
last quarter 10:06 GMT

Hoshana Rabbah (Jewish)

October 4, 2007 (Th)

Shemini Atzeret (Jewish); Last Great Day (United Church of God); Honoring Orisa Orunmila (Santeria/Lukumi)

October 5, 2007 (F)

Simhat Torah (Jewish); Bodhidharma Day (Buddhist)

October 6, 2007 (St)

St. Thomas's Day (Christian-O); Shiprock Navajo Nation Fair (Navajo)

October 7, 2007 (Sn)

Mary as Our Lady of the Rosary (Christian-RC); Founding of the International Association of Scientologists (Scientology)

October 9, 2007 (Tu)

Laylat al-Qadr (Islamic); Birthday of Guru Ram Das (Sikh)

October 11, 2007 (Th)
new moon 05:01 GMT

Festival of the Nine Imperial Gods begins (Taoist; Buddhist); Great New Moon Ceremony (Cherokee)

October 12, 2007 (F)

Ayathrem (Zoroastrian-F); Lantern's Festival (Islamic); ~Kartika Snan (Hindu); ~Skanda Shashti (Hindu); Govardhan Puja (Hindu)

October 13, 2007 (St)

Id al-Fitr begins (Islamic); Bhaiya Duj (Hindu)

October 15, 2007 (M)

~Divali (Sikh)

October 16, 2007 (Tu)

Nineteen-Day Feast, 1st of 'Ilm (Bahá'í)

October 17, 2007 (W)

Surya Shashti (Hindu)

October 18, 2007 (Th)

St. Luke's Day (Christian)

October 19, 2007 (F)
first quarter 08:33 GMT

October 20, 2007 (St)

Birth of the Báb (Bahá'í); Confucius's Birthday (Confucian); Ebisu Festival (Shinto); Atohuna (Cherokee)

October 22, 2007 (M)

Devathani Ekadashi (Hindu); Spiritual New Year (Eckankar)

October 23, 2007 (Tu)

St. James the Brother of the Lord (Christian-O)

October 24, 2007 (W)

Feast of Hordad (Zoroastrian-S)

October 26, 2007 (F)
full moon 04:52 GMT

Aban Parab (Zoroastrian-F); St. Demetrios (Christian-O); Kartika Purnima (Hindu); Puskar Mela (Hindu)

October 28, 2007 (Sn)

St. Simon and St. Jude's Day (Christian)

October 29, 2007 (M)

Maidyoshahem (Zoroastrian-Q)

October 30, 2007 (Tu)

Karwachauth (Hindu)

October 31, 2007 (W)

Tiragan (Zoroastrian-Q); Reformation Day (Christian-Pr); Oidhche Shamhna (Pagan)

November 1, 2007 (Th)
last quarter 21:18 GMT

All Saints' Day (Christian); ~Tihar (Hindu); Samhain (Pagan)

November 2, 2007 (F)

All Souls' Day (Christian)

November 4, 2007 (Sn)

Nineteen-Day Feast, 1st of Qudrat (Bahá'í)

November 5, 2007 (M)

Guy Fawkes's Night (Pagan)

November 7, 2007 (W)

Dhan Teras (Hindu)

November 8, 2007 (Th)

Saints, Doctors, Missionaries, and Martyrs Day (Christian-Anglican); St. Michael and All Angels (Christian-O); Narak Chaturdashi (Hindu); Wuwuchim (Hopi)

November 9, 2007 (F)
new moon 23:03 GMT

Dedication of St. John Lateran (Christian-RC); Dewali (Hindu); Diwali (Jain)

November 10, 2007 (St)

Birthday of Martin Luther (Christian-Lutheran); Sending the Winter Dress (Chinese Folk)

November 11, 2007 (Sn)

Old Halloween (Pagan)

November 12, 2007 (M)

Birth of Bahá'u'lláh (Bahá'í)

November 14, 2007 (W)

St. Philip (Christian-O); Jnan Panchami (Jain)

November 15, 2007 (Th)
Advent begins (Christian-O); Shichi-Go-San (Shinto)

November 16, 2007 (F)
St. Matthew (Christian-O)

November 17, 2007 (St)

first quarter 22:33 GMT
November 19, 2007 (M)
Tazaungdaing (Buddhist)

November 20, 2007 (Tu)
Gita Jayanti (Hindu); Vaikuntha Ekadashi (Hindu)

November 21, 2007 (W)
Presentation of the Blessed Virgin Mary (Christian-RC); Feast of the Presentation of the Theotokos (Christian-O); ~Fast for a World Harvest (Unitarian)

November 22, 2007 (Th)
Thanksgiving (Christian); Thanksgiving (Christian Science)

November 23, 2007 (F)
Nineteen-Day Feast, 1st of Qawl (Bahá'í)

November 24, 2007 (St)
full moon 14:30 GMT

Adar Parab (Zoroastrian-F); Feast of Amurdad (Zoroastrian-Q); Dattatreya Jayanti (Hindu); Martyrdom Anniversary of Guru Teg Bahadur (Sikh)

November 25, 2007 (Sn)
Bible Sunday (Christian-Pr); Feast of Christ the King (Christian-RC); St. Catherine (Christian-O)

November 26, 2007 (M)
Day of the Covenant (Bahá'í)

November 28, 2007 (W)
Maidyoshahem (Zoroastrian-S); Ascension of 'Abdu'l-Bahá (Bahá'í)

November 30, 2007 (F)
Tiragan (Zoroastrian-S); St. Andrew's Day (Christian)

December 1, 2007 (St)
last quarter 12:44 GMT

Mother Seton Day (Christian-RC); ~Festival of Lights (Buddhist); ~ Shalako Ceremonial (Pueblo)

December 2, 2007 (Sn)
Advent begins (Christian); Bhairava Ashtami (Hindu)

December 4, 2007 (Tu)
St. Barbara and St. John of Damascus (Christian-O); Honoring Orisa Shango (Santeria/Lukumi)

December 5, 2007 (W)
Hanukkah (Jewish); Vaikuntha Ekadashi (Hindu); Vaitarani (Hindu)

December 6, 2007 (Th)
St. Nicholas's Day (Christian); St. Nicholas's Day (Christian-O)

December 8, 2007 (St)
Immaculate Conception of Mary (Christian-RC); Rohatsu (Buddhist)

December 9, 2007 (Sn)
new moon 17:40 GMT
Holy Theotokos (Christian-O)

December 10, 2007 (M)
Tevet (Jewish); ~Human Rights Day (Unitarian); Ta Chiu (Taoist); ~Geminid Meteor Shower (Pantheism)

December 12, 2007 (W)
Nineteen-Day Feast, 1st of Masá'il (Bahá'í)

December 13, 2007 (Th)
Saint Lucy's Day (Christian)

December 14, 2007 (F)
~Lohri (Sikh)

December 16, 2007 (Sn)
1st Feast of Dae (Zoroastrian-F); Posadas (Christian); Feast of the Forebearers of Christ (Christian-O)

December 17, 2007 (M)
first quarter 10:17 GMT
Honoring Babalu Aye (Santeria/Lukumi)

December 18, 2007 (Tu)
Pilgrimage to Mecca (Hajj) begins (Islamic)

December 19, 2007 (W)
Asarah be-Tevet (Jewish)

December 20, 2007 (Th)
Al-'id al-Kabir; 'Id al-Adha begins (Islamic)

December 21, 2007 (F)
Feast of Shahrewar (Zoroastrian-Q); St. Thomas's Day (Christian); The Mother Night (Pagan)

December 22, 2007 (St)
winter solstice 06:08 GMT

Winter Solstice (Chinese Folk); Soyal (Hopi); Guatemalan Winter Solstice (Mayan); Yule (Pagan); Winter Solstice (Pantheism)

December 23, 2007 (Sn)
2nd Feast of Dae (Zoroastrian-F); New Year for Trees (Pagan); The Day that Is Not a Day (Pagan)

December 24, 2007 (M)
full moon 01:16 GMT

Feast of Amurdad (Zoroastrian-S); Christmas Eve (Christian)

December 25, 2007 (Tu)

Christmas Day (Christian); Feast of the Nativity of Our Lord (Christian-O); ~Saturnalia (Pagan)

December 26, 2007 (W)

Zarthastno Diso (Zoroastrian-F); St. Stephen's Day (Christian); Synaxis of the Holy Theotokos (Christian-O)

December 27, 2007 (Th)

St. John the Evangelist's Day (Christian); St. Stephen's Day (Christian-O)

December 28, 2007 (F)

Holy Innocents' Day (Christian)

December 29, 2007 (St)

Holy Innocents' Day (Christian-O)

December 30, 2007 (Sn)

3rd Feast of Dae (Zoroastrian-F)

December 31, 2007 (M)
last quarter 07:51 GMT

Maidyarem (Zoroastrian-F); Nineteen-Day Feast, 1st of Sharaf (Bahá'í); Omisoka (Shinto); Hogmany (Pagan)

2008

January 1, 2008 (Tu)

Feast of the Circumcision (Christian-RC); St. Basil's Day (Christian-O); God's Day (Unification); World Peace Day and the Universal Hour of Peace (Unitarian); Rukmini Ashtami (Hindu); Oshogatsu begins (Buddhist); Kitchen God Festival (Taoist; Chinese Folk); Ganjitsu begins (Shinto); Annual Forecast (Santeria/Lukumi)

January 3, 2008 (Th)
perihelion 00:00 GMT

Birth of Parsvanath (Jain); The Twelfth Night (Pagan)

January 5, 2008 (St)

Epiphany Eve (Christian); Swarupa Dwadashi (Hindu); Guru Gobind Singh's Birthday (Sikh)

January 6, 2008 (Sn)

Epiphany (Christian); Old Christmas Day (Christian-J); Universal Week of Prayer begins; Feast of Epiphany (Christian-O); St. Distaff's Day (Pagan)

January 7, 2008 (M)

4th Feast of Dae (Zoroastrian-F); Plough Monday (Christian); ~Bounding Bush (Cherokee)

January 8, 2008 (Tu)
new moon 11:37 GMT

January 9, 2008 (W)

~Pongal (Hindu); ~Thaipusam (Hindu)

January 10, 2008 (Th)

Awwal Muharram (Islamic)

January 12, 2008 (St)

Paitishahem (Zoroastrian-Q)

January 13, 2008 (Sn)

Feast of the Holy Family (Christian-RC); Feast of the Baptism of the Lord (Christian); Death of George Fox (Christian-Quaker); Vasant Pañcami (Hindu); ~Maghi (Sikh)

January 14, 2008 (M)

~Makar Sankranti (Hindu)

January 15, 2008 (Tu)
first quarter 19:46 GMT

~White Dog Feast (Iroquois)

January 16, 2008 (W)

Feast of Vohuman (Zoroastrian-F); Bhishma Ashtami (Hindu)

January 17, 2008 (Th)

Feast of Mithra (Zoroastrian-Q)

January 19, 2008 (St)

Ashura (Islamic); Yevmi Ashurer (Islamic); Husayn Day (Islamic); Nineteen-Day Feast, 1st of Sultán (Bahá'í)

January 20, 2008 (Sn)

Feast of Shahrewar (Zoroastrian-S); Blessing of Animals (Christian-RC); ~World Religions Day (Unitarian); World Religion Day (Bahá'í); ~Kwakiutl Winter Ceremonial

January 21, 2008 (M)

Birthday of Martin Luther King, Jr. (Christian)

January 22, 2008 (Tu)
full moon 13:35 GMT

Tu Bishvat (Jewish); Magha Purnima (Hindu); Minakshi Float Festival (Hindu); Chinese New Year (Buddhist)

January 24, 2008 (Th)

Alacitas (Aymara)

January 25, 2008 (F)

Conversion of St. Paul (Christian)

January 26, 2008 (St)

Sakata Chauth (Hindu)

January 29, 2008 (Tu)

Up-Helly-Aa (Pagan)

January 30, 2008 (W)
last quarter 05:03 GMT

Three Hierarchs (Christian-O)

January 31, 2008 (Th)

Vartanantz Day (Christian-Armenian)

February 1, 2008 (F)

Mihragan (Zoroastrian-Q); ~True Parents' Birthday (Unification); ~Losar (Buddhist); Imbolg (Pagan)

February 2, 2008 (St)

Presentation of Jesus (Christian); Presentation of Christ in the Temple (Christian-O); Gaelic Fire Festival (Pagan); Honoring Orisa Oya (Santeria/Lukumi)

February 3, 2008 (Sn)

Fasching (Christian); Setsubun (Shinto); ~Midwinter Dream Festival (Iroquois); Homstrom (Pagan)

February 4, 2008 (M)

Rose Monday (Christian); ~Monlam Chenmo begins (Buddhist)

February 5, 2008 (Tu)

Mardi Gras (Christian-RC); Carnival ends (Christian-RC); Arrival of Roger Williams in the New World (Christian-Baptist); Nirvana of Risabha (Jain)

February 6, 2008 (W)

Ash Wednesday (Christian); Lent begins (Christian); Mauni Amavasya (Hindu)

February 7, 2008 (Th)
new moon 03:44 GMT

Nineteen-Day Feast, 1st of Mulk (Bahá'í); Lunar New Year (Chinese Folk)

February 8, 2008 (F)

World Day of Prayer (Christian); Hari-Kuyo (Shinto); Powamu Bean Dance begins (Hopi)

February 9, 2008 (St)

~Mandi Safar (Islamic)

February 10, 2008 (Sn)

Quadragesima (Christian); Race Relations Sunday (Christian)

February 11, 2008 (M)

Paitishahem (Zoroastrian-S); Ayathrem (Zoroastrian-Q); Birthday of Richard Allen (Christian-African Methodist Episcopal)

February 14, 2008 (Th)
first quarter 03:33 GMT

Lupercalia begins (Pagan)

February 15, 2008 (F)

Making Happiness Festival (Chinese Folk)

February 16, 2008 (St)

Feast of Mithra (Zoroastrian-S)

February 17, 2008 (Sn)

Triodion begins (Christian-O); Ramtha's Appearance (Ramtha's School of Enlightenment)

February 18, 2008 (M)

Feast of Spendarmad (Zoroastrian-F); Amalaka Ekadashi (Hindu)

February 21, 2008 (Th)
full moon 03:30 GMT

Holi (Hindu); Dol Purnima (Hindu); Lantern Festival (Chinese Folk)

February 22, 2008 (F)

Shah Abdul Latif Death Commemoration begins (Islamic-Sufi)

February 24, 2008 (Sn)

St. Matthias's Day (Christian); Meatfare Sunday (Christian-O); Star Festival (Chinese Folk)

February 25, 2008 (M)

Aban Parab (Zoroastrian-Q)

February 26, 2008 (Tu)

Data Ganj Baksh Death Festival begins (Islamic-Sufi); Ayyám-i-Há begins (Bahá'í)

February 29, 2008 (F)
last quarter 02:18 GMT

March 1, 2008 (St)

First Saturday of Souls (Christian-O); Parents Day (Unification); Omizutori Matsuri begins (Buddhist)

March 2, 2008 (Sn)

Mihragan (Zoroastrian-S); Mothering Sunday (Christian); Cheesefare Sunday (Christian-O); Nineteen-Day Feast, 1st of 'Alá' (Bahá'í); The Fast begins (Bahá'í)

March 3, 2008 (M)

Hina Matsuri (Shinto)

March 6, 2008 (Th)

Mahashivarati (Hindu); ~Gangaur begins (Hindu)

March 7, 2008 (F)
new moon 17:14 GMT

Vasanta Navaratra begins (Hindu); First New Moon of Spring (Cherokee)

March 8, 2008 (St)

Second Saturday of Souls (Christian-O); Gudi Parva (Hindu); Ugadi Parva (Hindu); ~Monkey God Festival (Taoist)

March 10, 2008 (M)

Muktad (Zoroastrian-F); Clean Monday (Christian-O); Great Lent begins (Christian-O)

March 12, 2008 (W)

Ayathrem (Zoroastrian-S); ~Maple Dance (Iroquois)

March 13, 2008 (Th)

Caitra Parb (Hindu); Birthday of L. Ron Hubbard (Scientology)

March 14, 2008 (F)

first quarter 10:46 GMT

Scriptural New Year (Sikh); Hola Mohalla (Sikh)

March 15, 2008 (St)

St. Theodore (Christian-O); Sitala Ashtami (Hindu); Ashokashtami (Hindu)

March 16, 2008 (Sn)

Palm Sunday (Christian); Sunday of Orthodoxy (Christian-O); Ramanavami (Hindu)

March 17, 2008 (M)

St. Patrick's Day (Christian); Rara Festival (Voodoo)

March 20, 2008 (Th)

spring equinox 05:48 GMT

Ta'anit Esther (Jewish); Maundy Thursday (Christian); Mawlid al-Nabi (Islamic); Birth of Mahavira (Jain); Spring Higan (Buddhist); ~Thunder Dance (Iroquois); Ostara (Pagan); ~Ibu Afo Festival (Yoruba); Spring Equinox (Pantheism)

March 21, 2008 (F)

full moon 18:40 GMT

Purim (Jewish); Frawardin 1 (Zoroastrian-F); Nawruz (Zoroastrian-F); Good Friday (Christian); Festival of Naw-Rúz (Bahá'í); Nineteen-Day Feast, 1st of Bahá (Bahá'í); ~Panguni Uttiram (Hindu); ~Caitra Purnima (Hindu); Hanuman Jayanti (Hindu); Magha Puja (Buddhist); ~Iduna and Summer Finding (Pagan)

March 22, 2008 (St)

Holy Saturday (Christian); Honoring Orisaoko (Santeria/Lukumi)

March 23, 2008 (Sn)

Easter (Christian); Sunday of St. Gregory Palamas (Christian-O); Foundation Day (Ramtha's School of Enlightenment)

March 24, 2008 (M)

~Eagle Dance (Navajo and Others)

March 25, 2008 (Tu)

Adar Parab (Zoroastrian-Q); Annunciation of the Lord (Christian); Feast of the Annunciation (Christian-O)

March 26, 2008 (W)

Hordad Sal (Zoroastrian-F); Aban Parab (Zoroastrian-S); ~Bobo Masquerade (Yoruba)

March 29, 2008 (St)

last quarter 21:47 GMT

Sabbath of Rabbi Isaac Mayer Wise (Jewish)

March 30, 2008 (Sn)

Quasimodo Sunday (Christian); Sunday of the Holy Cross (Christian-O)

April 1, 2008 (Tu)

All Fool's Day (Pagan)

April 2, 2008 (W)

~Planting Dances (Iroquois)

April 6, 2008 (Sn)

new moon 03:55 GMT

Liturgical New Year (Jewish); Sunday of St. John Climacos (Christian-O); Founding of the Church of Jesus Christ of Latter-Day Saints (Mormon)

April 8, 2008 (Tu)

Feast of Frawardignan (Zoroastrian-F)

April 9, 2008 (W)

Nineteen-Day Feast, 1st of Jalál (Bahá'í); Aksaya Tratiya (Jain); Qing Ming Festival (Chinese Folk)

April 10, 2008 (Th)

Salvation Army Founder's Day (Christian-Salvation Army)

April 12, 2008 (St)

first quarter 18:32 GMT

April 13, 2008 (Sn)

Sunday of St. Mary of Egypt (Christian-O); Songkran begins (Buddhist)

April 14, 2008 (M)

Baisakhi (Sikh); Guru Nanak's Day (Sikh)

April 15, 2008 (Tu)

Miriam's Yahrzeit (Jewish)

April 16, 2008 (W)

1st Feast of Dae (Zoroastrian-Q)

April 19, 2008 (St)

Fast of the First-born (Jewish); Lazarus Saturday (Christian-O); The Lord's Evening Meal (Jehovah's Witnesses); Passover (United Church of God)

April 20, 2008 (Sn)

full moon 10:25 GMT

Passover (Jewish); Palm Sunday (Christian-O); Festival of Unleavened Bread begins (United Church of God); Vesak (Buddhist)

April 21, 2008 (M)

Sefirah (Jewish); Festival of Ridván begins (Bahá'í); ~Earth Day (Pagan)

April 22, 2008 (Tu)

Feast of Ardwahist (Zoroastrian-F); ~Earth Day (Unitarian)

April 23, 2008 (W)
2nd Feast of Dae (Zoroastrian-Q); St. George's Day (Christian-O)

April 24, 2008 (Th)
Adar Parab (Zoroastrian-S); Paschal Thursday (Christian-O)

April 25, 2008 (F)
St. Mark's Day (Christian); Holy Friday (Christian-O)

April 26, 2008 (St)
Zarthastno Diso (Zoroastrian-Q); Holy Saturday (Christian-O)

April 27, 2008 (Sn)
Maimona (Jewish); Rogation Sunday (Christian); Easter (Christian-O)

April 28, 2008 (M)
last quarter 14:12 GMT
Rogation Days (Christian); Bright Week begins (Christian-O); Nineteen-Day Feast, 1st of Jamál (Bahá'í); Matsu Festival (Taoist; Buddhist; Chinese Folk)

April 30, 2008 (W)
Maidyozarem (Zoroastrian-F); 3rd Feast of Dae (Zoroastrian-Q); St. James the Son of Zebedee (Christian-O); Walpurgis Night (Pagan)

May 1, 2008 (Th)
Maidyarem (Zoroastrian-Q); Ascension Day (Christian); Saint Philip and Saint James's Day (Christian); ~Day of All Things (Unification); National Day of Prayer (Unitarian); Beltane (Pagan)

May 2, 2008 (F)
Yom ha-Shoah (Jewish)

May 4, 2008 (Sn)
Family Week begins (Christian); St. Thomas's Day (Christian-O)

May 5, 2008 (M)
new moon 12:18 GMT
~Chongmyo Taeje (Confucian); Children's Day (Shinto)

May 6, 2008 (Tu)
Vaisakhi (Hindu); ~Pooram begins (Hindu)

May 8, 2008 (Th)
4th Feast of Dae (Zoroastrian-Q); Akshya Tritiya (Hindu); Parasurama Jayanti (Hindu); Chandan Yatra begins (Hindu); Death of Helena Petrovna Blavatsky (Theosophy)

May 9, 2008 (F)
Yom ha-Zikkaron (Jewish); May 9 Day (Scientology)

May 10, 2008 (St)
Yom ha-Atzma'ut (Jewish); Sankaracarya Jayanti (Hindu)

May 11, 2008 (Sn)
Pentecost (Christian); Sts. Cyril and Methodios (Christian-O)

May 12, 2008 (M)
first quarter 03:47 GMT
Tam Kung Festival (Taoist); Birthday of the Third Prince (Taoist)

May 14, 2008 (W)
Janaki Navami (Hindu)

May 15, 2008 (Th)
Corpus Christi (Christian-RC); Aaronic Priesthood Commemoration (Mormon); Aoi Matsuri (Shinto); ~Ibeji Ceremony (Yoruba)

May 16, 2008 (F)
1st Feast of Dae (Zoroastrian-S); Sacred Heart of Jesus (Christian-RC)

May 17, 2008 (St)
Feast of Vohuman (Zoroastrian-Q); Nineteen-Day Feast, 1st of 'Azamat (Bahá'í); Sanja Matsuri (Shinto)

May 18, 2008 (Sn)
Trinity Sunday (Christian)

May 19, 2008 (M)
Narsimha Jayanti (Hindu)

May 20, 2008 (Tu)
full moon 02:11 GMT
Poson (Buddhist); Sanghamitta Day (Buddhist)

May 21, 2008 (W)
Sts. Constantine and Helen (Christian-O)

May 23, 2008 (F)
Lag ba-Omer (Jewish); 2nd Feast of Dae (Zoroastrian-S); Declaration of the Báb (Bahá'í)

May 24, 2008 (St)
Ute Bear Dance (Ute)

May 25, 2008 (Sn)
Feast of Hordad (Zoroastrian-F); Aldersgate Experience (Christian-Methodist)

May 26, 2008 (M)
Zarthastno Diso (Zoroastrian-S)

May 28, 2008 (W)
last quarter 02:57 GMT

May 29, 2008 (Th)
Ascension of Bahá'u'lláh (Bahá'í)

May 30, 2008 (F)
3rd Feast of Dae (Zoroastrian-S)

May 31, 2008 (St)
Yom Yerushalayim (Jewish); Maidyarem (Zoroastrian-S); Immaculate Heart of Mary (Christian-RC); Feast of the Visitation (Christian-RC)

June 1, 2008 (Sn)
Birthday of Brigham Young (Mormon); ~Egungun Festival (Yoruba)

June 3, 2008 (Tu)
new moon 19:23 GMT
Mata Tirtha Snan (Hindu)

June 5, 2008 (Th)
Ascension (Christian-O); Nineteen-Day Feast, 1st of Núr (Bahá'í)

June 6, 2008 (F)
Honoring Oshosi (Santeria/Lukumi)

June 7, 2008 (St)
4th Feast of Dae (Zoroastrian-S)

June 8, 2008 (Sn)
Children's Day (Christian); Race Unity Day (Bahá'í)

June 9, 2008 (M)
Shavuot (Jewish); Pentecost (United Church of God); Sithinakha (Hindu)

June 10, 2008 (Tu)
first quarter 15:04 GMT

June 11, 2008 (W)
St. Barnabas's Day (Christian); Jyestha Ashtami (Hindu)

June 13, 2008 (F)
Ganga Dussehra (Hindu); Honoring Elegbara/Esu (Santeria/Lukumi)

June 14, 2008 (St)
Fourth Saturday of Souls (Christian-O); Nirjala Ekadashi (Hindu); Rice Planting Festivals (Shinto)

June 15, 2008 (Sn)
Magna Carta Day (Christian-Anglican); Pentecost (Christian-O); ~Strawberry Festival (Iroquois); ~Rosicrucian Thanksgiving Ritual (Rosicrucianism)

June 16, 2008 (M)
Feast of Vohuman (Zoroastrian-S); Holy Spirit Day (Christian-O); Martyrdom Anniversary of Guru Arjan (Sikh)

June 17, 2008 (Tu)
Lily Festival (Shinto)

June 18, 2008 (W)
full moon 17:30 GMT
Snan Yatra (Hindu); Buddha Jayanti (Hindu)

June 19, 2008 (Th)
Feast of Spendarmad (Zoroastrian-Q); Caturmas begins (Jain); Midsummer Eve (Pagan)

June 20, 2008 (F)
summer solstice 23:59 GMT
Sun Dance (Navajo and Others); Litha (Pagan); Summer Solstice (Pantheism)

June 21, 2008 (St)
Celebration of Unifying Principles (Unitarian)

June 22, 2008 (Sn)
~Footwashing Day (Christian-Pr); All Saints' Day (Christian-O); New Church Day (Swedenborgian)

June 23, 2008 (M)
Airing the Classics (Buddhist); Esala Perahera (Buddhist)

June 24, 2008 (Tu)
Nativity of St. John the Baptist (Christian); Birth of St. John the Baptist (Christian-O); Nineteen-Day Feast, 1st of Rahmat (Bahá'í); St. John's Day (Voodoo)

June 25, 2008 (W)
~Eje (Yoruba)

June 26, 2008 (Th)
last quarter 12:10 GMT

June 27, 2008 (F)
Martyrdom of Joseph and Hyrum Smith (Mormon)

June 29, 2008 (Sn)
Maidyoshahem (Zoroastrian-F); St. Peter's Day (Christian); St. Peter and St. Paul (Christian-O)

June 30, 2008 (M)
~Green Corn Ceremony (Cherokee); Honoring Ogun (Santeria/Lukumi)

July 1, 2008 (Tu)
Tiragan (Zoroastrian-F); Most Precious Blood (Christian-RC); Vata Savitri (Hindu); ~Hemis Festival (Buddhist)

July 3, 2008 (Th)
new moon 02:19 GMT
Seminole Green Corn Dance begins; Dog Days begin (Pagan)

July 4, 2008 (F)
aphelion 08:00 GMT

July 5, 2008 (St)
Ratha Yatra (Hindu)

July 6, 2008 (Sn)
Birthday of the Dalai Lama (Buddhist)

July 9, 2008 (W)
Martyrdom of the Báb (Bahá'í)

July 10, 2008 (Th)
first quarter 04:35 GMT
Muktad (Zoroastrian-Q); ~Pilgrimage of Saut D'Eau (Voodoo)

July 13, 2008 (Sn)
Nineteen-Day Feast, 1st of Kalimát (Bahá'í); Obon Festival begins in some regions (Buddhist)

July 14, 2008 (M)
Hari-Shayani Ekadashi (Hindu)

July 15, 2008 (Tu)
St. Vladimir (Christian-O); Birthday of Lu Pan (Taoist)

July 17, 2008 (Th)
Gion Matsuri (Shinto)

July 18, 2008 (F)
full moon 07:59 GMT
Guru Purnima (Hindu)

July 19, 2008 (St)
Feast of Spendarmad (Zoroastrian-S); Hill Cumorah Pageant begins (Mormon)

July 20, 2008 (Sn)
Fast of the Seventeenth of Tammuz (Jewish); Three Weeks of Mourning (Jewish); Frawardin 1 (Zoroastrian-Q); Nawruz (Zoroastrian-Q); Marya (Buddhist)

July 23, 2008 (W)
Birthday of Guru Har Krishan (Sikh); ~Waso begins (Buddhist)

July 24, 2008 (Th)
Pioneer Day (Mormon)

July 25, 2008 (F)
last quarter 18:42 GMT
Feast of Amurdad (Zoroastrian-F); Hordad Sal (Zoroastrian-Q); St. James's Day (Christian)

July 26, 2008 (St)
Niman Dance (Hopi)

July 27, 2008 (Sn)
Reek Sunday (Christian-RC)

July 28, 2008 (M)
Volunteers of America Founder's Day (Christian-Volunteers of America)

July 31, 2008 (Th)
Laylat al-Miraj (Islamic); Lammas Eve (Pagan)

August 1, 2008 (F)
new moon 10:13 GMT
Nineteen-Day Feast, 1st of Kamál (Bahá'í); Lammas (Pagan)

August 2, 2008 (St)
~Sravani Mela (Hindu)

August 4, 2008 (M)
Hariyali Teej (Hindu)

August 6, 2008 (W)
Feast of the Transfiguration (Christian); Feast of the Transfiguration (Christian-O); Nag Pañcami (Hindu)

August 7, 2008 (Th)
Feast of Frawardignan (Zoroastrian-Q)

August 8, 2008 (F)
first quarter 20:20 GMT
Tulsidas Jayanti (Hindu)

August 9, 2008 (St)
Muktad (Zoroastrian-S)

August 10, 2008 (Sn)
Tisha be-Av (Jewish); ~Ripe Fruits Ceremony (Cherokee)

August 12, 2008 (Tu)
Putrada Ekadashi (Hindu); ~New Corn Dance (Iroquois)

August 13, 2008 (W)
Obon Festival begins in some regions (Buddhist)

August 15, 2008 (F)
Assumption of the Blessed Virgin (Christian-RC); Feast of the Dormition of the Theotokos (Christian-O); Floating Lantern Ceremony (Buddhist); Festival of Hungry Ghosts (Taoist; Buddhist; Chinese Folk); ~Carnea (Pagan); ~Perseid Meteor Shower (Pantheism)

August 16, 2008 (St)
full moon 21:16 GMT
Narieli Purnima (Hindu); Raksa Bandhana (Hindu); Jhulan Latra (Hindu); ~Snake-Antelope Dance, Flute Ceremony, or Snake Dance (Navajo)

August 17, 2008 (Sn)
Shab-Barat (Islamic); Odin's Ordeal begins (Pagan)

August 19, 2008 (Tu)
Frawardin 1 (Zoroastrian-S); Nawruz (Zoroastrian-S)

August 20, 2008 (W)
Nineteen-Day Feast, 1st of Asmá' (Bahá'í)

August 21, 2008 (Th)
Feast of Shahrewar (Zoroastrian-F); Feast of Ardwahist (Zoroastrian-Q); Partyshana Parva (Jain)

August 22, 2008 (F)
Queenship of Mary (Christian-RC); Dasa Laksana Parvan (Jain)

August 23, 2008 (St)
last quarter 23:50 GMT

August 24, 2008 (Sn)
Hordad Sal (Zoroastrian-S); St. Bartholomew's Day (Christian); ~Creek Green Corn Ceremony

August 25, 2008 (M)

~Gelede (Yoruba)

August 27, 2008 (W)

Kamada Ekadashi (Hindu)

August 29, 2008 (F)

Maidyozarem (Zoroastrian-Q); Martyrdom of St. John the Baptist (Christian)

August 30, 2008 (St)

new moon 19:58 GMT

African Methodist Quarterly Meeting Day (Christian-African Methodist); Ghanta Karna (Hindu); Anata-Chaturdashi (Jain)

August 31, 2008 (Sn)

Feast of Christ the King (Christian-Pr); ~Tirupati Festival (Hindu); ~Gokarna Aunsi (Hindu); ~Onam (Hindu); ~Monkey God Festival (Taoist)

September 1, 2008 (M)

Church New Year (Christian-O); Ramadan begins (Islamic); Installation of Sri Guru Granth Sahib (Sikh)

September 2, 2008 (Tu)

San Estevan (Christian-RC); Haritalika Teej (Hindu); Shinbyu (Buddhist)

September 3, 2008 (W)

Ganesa Caturthi (Hindu)

September 4, 2008 (Th)

Rishi Pañcami (Hindu)

September 6, 2008 (St)

Feast of Frawardignan (Zoroastrian-S); Sante Fe Fiesta (Christian-RC)

September 7, 2008 (Sn)

first quarter 14:04 GMT

Honoring Yemaya/Yemonja (Santeria/Lukumi)

September 8, 2008 (M)

Nativity of the Blessed Virgin Mary (Christian); Feast of the Nativity of the Theotokos (Christian-O); Nineteen-Day Feast, 1st of 'Izzat (Bahá'í)

September 11, 2008 (Th)

Coptic New Year (Christian-Egyptian)

September 12, 2008 (F)

Paitishahem (Zoroastrian-F); Honoring Oshun (Santeria/Lukumi)

September 13, 2008 (St)

Anant Chaturdashi (Hindu)

September 14, 2008 (Sn)

Triumph of the Holy Cross (Christian); Elevation of the Holy Cross (Christian-O); Auditors' Day (Scientology)

September 15, 2008 (M)

full moon 09:13 GMT

Mary as Our Lady of Sorrows (Christian-RC); Mid-Autumn Festival (Chinese Folk); ~Memorial Ceremony (Rosicrucianism)

September 16, 2008 (Tu)

Ksamavani (Jain)

September 17, 2008 (W)

Feast of Mithra (Zoroastrian-F); Founder's Day (Eckankar)

September 20, 2008 (St)

Feast of Ardwahist (Zoroastrian-S)

September 21, 2008 (Sn)

St. Matthew's Day (Christian); Halashashti (Hindu)

September 22, 2008 (M)

last quarter 05:04 GMT

fall equinox 15:44 GMT

~Vatsa begins (Buddhist); Autumnal Higan (Buddhist); Mabon (Pagan); Winter Finding (Pagan); Autumn Equinox (Pantheism)

September 23, 2008 (Tu)

Feast of Hordad (Zoroastrian-Q); Janmashtami (Hindu); Radha Ashtami (Hindu)

September 24, 2008 (W)

~Lakon (Hopi and Navajo); Honoring Obatala (Santeria/Lukumi)

September 26, 2008 (F)

~Indra Jatra (Hindu); ~A Good Crop Dance (Navajo)

September 27, 2008 (St)

Laylat al-Qadr (Islamic); Nineteen-Day Feast, 1st of Mashíyyat (Bahá'í); Honoring Orisa Ibeji (Santeria/Lukumi); Cosmas and Damian Day (Candomblé)

September 28, 2008 (Sn)

Maidyozarem (Zoroastrian-Q); ~ Rally Day (Christian-Pr)

September 29, 2008 (M)

new moon 08:12 GMT

Michaelmas (Christian); Festival of the Nine Imperial Gods begins (Taoist; Buddhist); Honoring Orisa Erinle (Santeria/Lukumi)

September 30, 2008 (Tu)

Civil New Year (Jewish); Rosh Hashanah (Jewish); St. Gregory the Illuminator (Christian-O); Feast of Trumpets (United Church of God); Lantern's Festival (Islamic); ~Laksmi Puja (Hindu); ~Durga Puja (Hindu)

October 1, 2008 (W)

Ten Days of Teshuva (Jewish); ~Children's Day (Unification); Id al-Fitr begins (Islamic)

October 2, 2008 (Th)
Fast of Gedaliah (Jewish); Mihragan (Zoroastrian-F); Guardian Angels Day (Christian-RC)

October 4, 2008 (St)
Shiprock Navajo Nation Fair (Navajo); Honoring Orisa Orunmila (Santeria/Lukumi)

October 5, 2008 (Sn)
Bodhidharma Day (Buddhist)

October 6, 2008 (M)
St. Thomas's Day (Christian-O)

October 7, 2008 (Tu)
first quarter 09:04 GMT
Mary as Our Lady of the Rosary (Christian-RC); Founding of the International Association of Scientologists (Scientology)

October 8, 2008 (W)
~Confucius's Birthday (Confucian)

October 9, 2008 (Th)
Yom Kippur (Jewish); Day of Atonement (United Church of God); Dussehra (Hindu); Birthday of Guru Ram Das (Sikh)

October 12, 2008 (Sn)
Ayathrem (Zoroastrian-F)

October 14, 2008 (Tu)
full moon 20:02 GMT
Sukkot (Jewish); Feast of Tabernacles begins (United Church of God); Sharad Purnima (Hindu); Kojagara (Hindu); Valmiki Jayanti (Hindu)

October 15, 2008 (W)
~Pitra Visarjana Amavasya (Hindu); ~Divali (Sikh)

October 16, 2008 (Th)
Nineteen-Day Feast, 1st of 'Ilm (Bahá'í)

October 18, 2008 (St)
St. Luke's Day (Christian)

October 20, 2008 (M)
Hoshana Rabbah (Jewish); Birth of the Báb (Bahá'í); Ebisu Festival (Shinto)

October 21, 2008 (Tu)
last quarter 11:55 GMT
Shemini Atzeret (Jewish); Last Great Day (United Church of God)

October 22, 2008 (W)
Simhat Torah (Jewish); Spiritual New Year (Eckankar)

October 23, 2008 (Th)
Feast of Hordad (Zoroastrian-S); St. James the Brother of the Lord (Christian-O)

October 26, 2008 (Sn)
Aban Parab (Zoroastrian-F)

October 28, 2008 (Tu)
new moon 23:14 GMT
Maidyoshahem (Zoroastrian-Q); St. Simon and St. Jude's Day (Christian); Diwali (Jain); Great New Moon Ceremony (Cherokee)

October 29, 2008 (W)
~Kartika Snan (Hindu); ~Skanda Shashti (Hindu); Govardhan Puja (Hindu); Sending the Winter Dress (Chinese Folk)

October 30, 2008 (Th)
Tiragan (Zoroastrian-Q); Bhaiya Duj (Hindu)

October 31, 2008 (F)
Reformation Day (Christian-Pr); Oidhche Shamhna (Pagan)

November 1, 2008 (St)
All Saints' Day (Christian); Samhain (Pagan)

November 2, 2008 (Sn)
All Souls' Day (Christian); Jnan Panchami (Jain)

November 3, 2008 (M)
Surya Shashti (Hindu)

November 4, 2008 (Tu)
Nineteen-Day Feast, 1st of Qudrat (Bahá'í)

November 5, 2008 (W)
Guy Fawkes's Night (Pagan)

November 6, 2008 (Th)
first quarter 04:03 GMT
Atohuna (Cherokee)

November 8, 2008 (St)
Saints, Doctors, Missionaries, and Martyrs Day (Christian-Anglican); St. Michael and All Angels (Christian-O); Devathani Ekadashi (Hindu)

November 9, 2008 (Sn)
Dedication of St. John Lateran (Christian-RC)

November 10, 2008 (M)
Birthday of Martin Luther (Christian-Lutheran)

November 11, 2008 (Tu)
Old Halloween (Pagan)

November 12, 2008 (W)
Birth of Bahá'u'lláh (Bahá'í)

November 13, 2008 (Th)
full moon 06:17 GMT
Kartika Purnima (Hindu); Puskar Mela (Hindu)

November 14, 2008 (F)
St. Philip (Christian-O)

November 15, 2008 (St)
Advent begins (Christian-O); Shichi-Go-San (Shinto)

November 16, 2008 (Sn)
St. Matthew (Christian-O)

November 17, 2008 (M)
Karwachauth (Hindu)

November 19, 2008 (W)
last quarter 21:31 GMT
Tazaungdaing (Buddhist)

November 20, 2008 (Th)
~Tihar (Hindu)

November 21, 2008 (F)
Presentation of the Blessed Virgin Mary (Christian-RC);
Feast of the Presentation of the Theotokos (Christian-O);
~Fast for a World Harvest (Unitarian)

November 23, 2008 (Sn)
Feast of Amurdad (Zoroastrian-Q); Feast of Christ the
King (Christian-RC); Nineteen-Day Feast, 1st of Qawl
(Bahá'í)

November 24, 2008 (M)
Adar Parab (Zoroastrian-F); Martyrdom Anniversary of
Guru Teg Bahadur (Sikh)

November 25, 2008 (Tu)
St. Catherine (Christian-O); Dhan Teras (Hindu)

November 26, 2008 (W)
Day of the Covenant (Bahá'í); Narak Chaturdashi (Hindu);
Wuwuchim (Hopi)

November 27, 2008 (Th)
new moon 16:55 GMT
Maidyoshahem (Zoroastrian-S); Thanksgiving (Christian);
Thanksgiving (Christian Science); Dewali (Hindu)

November 28, 2008 (F)
Ascension of 'Abdu'l-Bahá (Bahá'í); ~Ta Chiu (Taoist)

November 29, 2008 (St)
Tiragan (Zoroastrian-S); Pilgrimage to Mecca (Hajj) begins
(Islamic)

November 30, 2008 (Sn)
Advent begins (Christian); St. Andrew's Day (Christian);
Bible Sunday (Christian-Pr)

December 1, 2008 (M)
Mother Seton Day (Christian-RC); Al-'id al-Kabir (Islamic);
'Id al-Adha begins (Islamic); ~Festival of Lights (Buddhist);
~ Shalako Ceremonial (Pueblo)

December 4, 2008 (Th)
St. Barbara and St. John of Damascus (Christian-O); Honoring
Orisa Shango (Santeria/Lukumi)

December 5, 2008 (F)
first quarter 21:26 GMT

December 6, 2008 (St)
St. Nicholas's Day (Christian); St. Nicholas's Day
(Christian-O)

December 8, 2008 (M)
Immaculate Conception of Mary (Christian-RC); Gita
Jayanti (Hindu); Vaikuntha Ekadashi (Hindu); Rohatsu
(Buddhist)

December 9, 2008 (Tu)
Holy Theotokos (Christian-O)

December 10, 2008 (W)
~Human Rights Day (Unitarian); ~Geminid Meteor Shower
(Pantheism)

December 12, 2008 (F)
full moon 16:37 GMT
Nineteen-Day Feast, 1st of Masá'il (Bahá'í); Dattatreya
Jayanti (Hindu)

December 13, 2008 (St)
Saint Lucy's Day (Christian)

December 14, 2008 (Sn)
Feast of the Forebearers of Christ (Christian-O); ~Lohri (Sikh)

December 16, 2008 (Tu)
1st Feast of Dae (Zoroastrian-F); Posadas (Christian)

December 17, 2008 (W)
Honoring Babalu Aye (Santeria/Lukumi)

December 19, 2008 (F)
last quarter 10:29 GMT

December 20, 2008 (St)
Feast of Shahrewar (Zoroastrian-Q); Bhairava Ashtami
(Hindu); Kitchen God Festival (Taoist; Chinese Folk); The
Mother Night (Pagan)

December 21, 2008 (Sn)
winter solstice 12:04 GMT
St. Thomas's Day (Christian); Winter Solstice (Chinese
Folk); Soyal (Hopi); Guatemalan Winter Solstice (Mayan);
Yule (Pagan); Winter Solstice (Pantheism)

December 22, 2008 (M)

Hanukkah (Jewish); Birth of Parsvanath (Jain); New Year for Trees (Pagan); The Day that Is Not a Day (Pagan)

December 23, 2008 (Tu)

2nd Feast of Dae (Zoroastrian-F); Feast of Amurdad (Zoroastrian-S); Vaikuntha Ekadashi (Hindu); Vaitarani (Hindu)

December 24, 2008 (W)

Christmas Eve (Christian)

December 25, 2008 (Th)

Christmas Day (Christian); Feast of the Nativity of Our Lord (Christian-O); ~Saturnalia (Pagan)

December 26, 2008 (F)

Zarthastno Diso (Zoroastrian-F); St. Stephen's Day (Christian); Synaxis of the Holy Theotokos (Christian-O)

December 27, 2008 (St)
new moon 12:22 GMT

St. John the Evangelist's Day (Christian); St. Stephen's Day (Christian-O)

December 28, 2008 (Sn)

Holy Innocents' Day (Christian)

December 29, 2008 (M)

Holy Innocents' Day (Christian-O); Awwal Muharram (Islamic)

December 30, 2008 (Tu)

3rd Feast of Dae (Zoroastrian-F)

December 31, 2008 (W)

Maidyarem (Zoroastrian-F); Nineteen-Day Feast, 1st of Sharaf (Bahá'í); Omisoka (Shinto); Hogmany (Pagan)

Holiday Index

This index provides an alphabetical listing of all the holiday entries in the main text. Initial articles (a, an, the) have been omitted. Names of holidays beginning with phrases such as "Feast of," "Festival of," "Day of," "Anniversary of," and "Birth of" have been inverted (for example: Epiphany, Feast of). Personal names have been inverted (for example: Fox, George, Death of). Names of holidays beginning with titles of religious significance, such as Saint, Guru, or Orisa, are alphabetized according to the title (for example: Saint Andrew's Day and Guru Har Krishan, Birthday of). Holidays shown in **bold** are primary entries in the text. Holidays shown in regular type are alternate names and variant spellings.

A

Calendar Index

This index is divided into two parts. The first section contains references to all the calendars discussed in the text. The second section contains an alphabetical listing of all the month names from the various calendars and provides page ranges for the holidays that fall within each month.

Calendar Descriptions

Months

Aban

Adar

Master Index

Page number in *italics* refer to information in tables or captions.

A

B

L

M

N

Q

R

S

Z

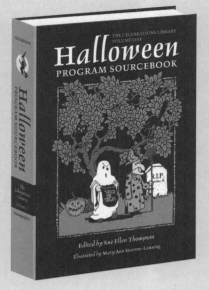

Encyclopedia of Christmas & New Year's Celebrations

Over 240 Alphabetically Arranged Entries Covering Christmas, New Year's, and Related Days of Observance, Including Folk and Religious Customs, History, Legends, and Symbols from Around the World. Supplemented by a Bibliography and Lists of Christmas Web Sites and Associations, as well as an Index

NEW EDITION! *2nd edition. By Tanya Gulevich. Library binding. 6 x 9. 1,004 pages. Illustrated. Appendices. Index. 2003. 0-7808-0625-5. $68.*

The *Encyclopedia of Christmas & New Year's Celebrations* offers teachers, students, parents, and librarians more than 1,000 pages of information about this joyous holiday season. The first edition was named an Outstanding Reference Source by the American Library Association. The second edition expands this popular title with new entries on American Christmas traditions, Christmas in other countries, New Year's celebrations, and updates on previous entries.

This handy reference contains more than 240 entries ranging in length from about 100 words to well over 2,500 words. Each entry includes a list of books for further reading, and many entries list web sites that contain information on the topic.

"Librarians everywhere can breathe a sigh of relief—the encyclopedia to answer all of those Christmas questions is finally here." —*School Library Journal*

Encyclopedia of Easter, Carnival & Lent

A Guide to This Season's Joyous Celebration and Solemn Worship, Including Folk Customs, Religious Observances, History, Legends, Folklore, Symbols, and Related Days from Europe, the Americas, and Around the World. Supplemented by a Bibliography, List of Web Sites, and Index

By Tanya Gulevich. Library binding. 6 x 9. 729 pages. Illustrated. Index. 2001. 0-7808-0432-5. $56.

This encyclopedia provides teachers, students, parents, and librarians with a convenient source of information on virtually every aspect of Easter and related holidays. The book also covers customs and observances associated with Lent as well as the Carnival celebrations that traditionally precede it. More than 150 alphabetically arranged entries on Easter, Carnival, and Lent cover folk customs and religious observances from around the world, the biblical figures associated with them, and their history, myths, legends, and symbols. Each entry includes a list of books for further reading, and many entries list web sites that contain further information.

"A good source for information on how these holidays are celebrated in different regions. [Selected as a Top 40 Young Adult Reference Title of 2002.]"
—*Pennsylvania School Library Association, May 2003*

Halloween Program Sourcebook

Edited by Sue Ellen Thompson. Library binding. 6 x 9. 336 pages. Illustrations. Indexes. 1999. 0-7808-0388-4. $48.

Students, teachers, librarians, and others will use this book to discover new ways to celebrate this holiday's rich tradition. It collects a wide range of material about Halloween that can be read aloud or performed as part of a Halloween program, including:

- Stories and legends
- Tales of strange happenings
- Poems
- Plays
- Activities
- Recipes

Special attention has been given to material that can be used in developing a program or celebration for school, church, family, community, and other groups.

"Sure to be a welcome addition to public library reference collections and school media centers." —*Libres*